New Jersey: A Guide to the State

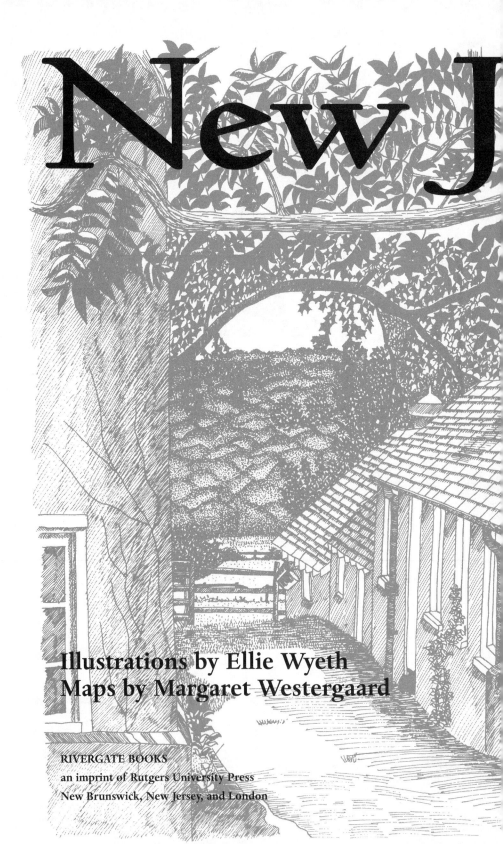

New J

Illustrations by Ellie Wyeth
Maps by Margaret Westergaard

RIVERGATE BOOKS
an imprint of Rutgers University Press
New Brunswick, New Jersey, and London

ersey

A Guide to the State
Third Edition

Barbara Westergaard

LIBRARY OF CONGRESS CATALOGING-IN-PUBLICATION DATA

Westergaard, Barbara, 1930–
    New Jersey, a guide to the state / Barbara Westergaard ; illustrations
by Ellie Wyeth ; maps by Margaret Westergaard. — 3rd ed.
      p.   cm.
    Includes indexes.
    ISBN 978-0-8135-3685-9 (pbk : alk. paper)
    1. New Jersey—Guidebooks.   2. Automobile travel—New Jersey—
Guidebooks.   I. Title.
    F132.3.W47   1998   97-23594
    917.4904'43—DC21   CIP

A British Cataloging-in-Publication record for this book is available from the
British Library.

Manufactured in the United States of America

DESIGNED BY: Judith Martin Waterman

This is a very good
Land to fall with,
and a pleasant
Land to see.

—JUET'S JOURNAL, 1609

To my family

Contents

Note to the Third Edition

I have left unchanged the introduction to the first edition of this guide. Although some of the examples used there may be out of date, the main thrust still holds: New Jersey is a state of striking physical and social contrasts. Generic housing developments continue to eat up land, but the largest piece of open space between Boston and Washington is still in New Jersey, and it occupies almost one-quarter of the state. We may be the country's most densely populated state, but agriculture is still a major contributor to the economy. The turnpike may no longer go straight through an oil refinery, but New Jersey is still a leader in pharmaceuticals, a major exporter, and home to many foreign firms. And tourism remains our second largest industry, in 2003 supporting more than 400,000 jobs and contributing more than $30 billion to the economy.

Some of the changes have been for the better, some not. We now have a highly successful science museum in Liberty State Park, an agriculture museum in New Brunswick, an aquarium in Camden, and a performing arts center in Newark. Despite the loss of open space, the bank of permanently protected land has grown. But with the reduction in state budgets, state historic sites have had to cut back—some have even lost their curators or been forced to share them with other facilities—and state parks have lost staff (not to mention their trash baskets). Many small museums have had a hard time finding the volunteers they need and have had to give up regular hours. I cannot urge too strongly the need to call ahead, even if regular hours are listed.

I have also left unchanged the basic structure of this guide. Except for the turnpike tour, entries are arranged alphabetically by town. If you can't find the town you're interested in, look in the index under towns, for it may be part of another town's entry. If you don't know the location of a museum or park, check in the index under museums or parks. At the top of each entry is the town name, the county it's in, its population in the 2000 census, and the roads that lead you there (*I* indicates an interstate, *US* a federal, *NJ* a state, and *C* a county road). If no census figures are available for an unincorporated community, the township it is part of is listed instead. The dot on the little state map tells you what part of the state the entry is in, and an asterisk tells you that a building or district is listed in the national register of historic places. The street (not mailing) address of sites you might want to visit is given, with a telephone number you can call for information and an indication of whether there is an admission charge. Dates are inclusive: January–March means January through March. For more practical details, please check the introduction.

A major change since the last edition is the prevalence of websites. Perhaps a majority of the organizations and sites mentioned here have their own. Although some are excellent resources for information about a destination, the addresses are not included here. Web addresses are apparently less stable than telephone numbers, so that many would be out of date by the time readers wanted to use them. And it has been my experience that a search engine will usually give you the site you're looking for as quickly as (sometimes more quickly than) typing in the address.

Once again I would like to stress that this guide is meant to get you started, not to be all inclusive. I'd like to apologize in advance to those who feel I have neglected their communities and to ask my readers to let me know about the places you think I should have mentioned.

As with the first edition, listing by name all the people who have contributed to this revision would consume much too much paper. Let me again single out the staff at the Turnpike Authority, in particular Tom Suszka, and then repeat what I said in the first two editions: to all those who helped me, to those who accompanied me on my trips around New Jersey, to the members of historical societies, the curators of museums, the park superintendents and rangers, the officials of federal, state, county, and municipal agencies, the librarians, I offer my heartfelt thanks.

Introduction

You will find in this guide information on several hundred of New Jersey's towns and parks. The guide is meant to serve both those who are contemplating a trip to New Jersey and are wondering what they can expect to find there, and those who are already in New Jersey and wondering what there is to look at. It's meant, in other words, to serve not just tourists but those who live in or commute to or through the state, and it's meant to serve the many newcomers—victims of corporate relocation, New York City rents, or economic and political hardship in other parts of the world. The word "guide" is chosen advisedly: this book is meant to get you started on your explorations, not to describe everything you will discover.

New Jersey is a state of unusual diversity, particularly in relation to its size (with c. 7,500 sq. miles, it's the fourth smallest state in the nation). Consider for a moment some of the contrasts it presents. New Jersey is one of the nation's leading industrial states. Its chemical industry, the state's largest, is second only to that of Texas (and actually employs more people), and New Jersey is the country's leading producer of pharmaceuticals, detergents, and toiletries. Yet almost two-thirds of the state's land is in farms and woodlands, and the gross average income per farm is the highest in the nation. It is one of the country's leading producers of blueberries, cranberries, peaches, eggplant, and nursery stock. It is the country's most densely populated state, yet within it is the largest wilderness area east of the Mississippi. It has more helipads than any other state, yet it also has the third largest state-park system. A leader in the high-tech industries (10 percent of the revenue from programming goes to New Jersey; 11 percent of its research budget is spent in the state), New Jersey is one of only four states where you can see 200 species of birds in one day, and the site of the largest annual gathering of migratory shorebirds. It has the third highest number of corporate headquarters, but is also the ninth state in wine production.

The contrasts extend to the landscape as well. The southern tip of Cape May (which is below where the Mason-Dixon Line would have been if it had continued due east) is only 144 miles from the Appalachian mountain ridges of the northwestern corner of the state. The flat and sandy lands of the southern portion of the state (actually, the coastal plain occupies over half the state's area) give way to the rolling hills of the central section, which in turn give way to the mountains of the north (the Kittatinny to the west, the Highlands to the east). In terms of feet above sea level, the mountains may not be high, but for a variety of reasons, including the lack of east-west passes in the Highlands, when you are in them, they look and feel high. This variety in terrain has produced a similar variety in ecosystems, and for that reason you can see an unusual diversity of plants and animals in New Jersey, with many species reaching their southern or northern limit in the state.

The natural contrast between north and south has been reinforced by the state's history. Early in its development (in 1676) the colony was divided in two, and East Jersey (roughly the same as today's northern New Jersey) and West Jersey (today's southern New Jersey) were owned by separate groups. The settlers in the two areas were different as well: largely Quakers in the south, a mixture of New Englanders, Scots, Dutch, and others in the north. Southern New Jersey was oriented toward Philadelphia, northern New Jersey toward New York. The appearance of many communities still reflects the differences in the way these groups built. The Dutch stone houses of northern New Jersey are perhaps the best known example, but you will also find in central and northern New Jersey many villages that are similar to New England villages, with white frame houses clustered fairly close together. In the southern Quaker towns, on the other hand, the streets are wider, and the color and texture of red brick often dominate your first impression of a town.

And consider the contrast between the past and the future: a state rich in 18th-century historical associations is the site of the laboratory that is developing what may become the world's principal source of energy in the 21st century. New Jersey was not just one of the 13 original colonies, but an important battleground in the Revolution, and on two occasions the capital of the country was here. The United States's first national historical park is in New Jersey. But New Jersey's leadership in the high-tech world is not new: you can visit sites and museums associated with the inventors of the telephone, the telegraph, motion pictures, the electric light, patent leather, submarines, revolvers, streptomycin, commercial blueberries.

Yet, in part because of its long-term division between the Philadelphia– and New York–oriented areas (Benjamin Franklin spoke of New Jersey as a barrel tapped at both ends), the state has had difficulty establishing an identity, and its negative image as an amalgam of oil refineries and toxic waste dumps has been tenacious. It's not as if no one has discovered New Jersey: tourism is in fact the state's second largest industry, generating some $11 billion a year in revenues, three-quarters of it from the shore. In terms of drawing tourists it is the fifth most popular state. Nevertheless, the New Jersey jokes continue, and the state's poor reputation—derived, many believe, from the fact that much of the world forms its impression of the state from driving through it on the turnpike—is becoming increasingly annoying to many New Jersey residents. At its northern end the turnpike goes right through one of the world's largest oil refineries, but to judge the rest of the state from this portion is clearly unfair. It's also unfair to the turnpike, which as eastern interstate highways go, is a pleasure to ride on: it's one of the safest, and even when the road is crowded, the traffic usually moves. And it's even unfair to the oil refineries, which can be breathtaking to look at, particularly at night. Since presumably every user of this book will have occasion to use the turnpike, the book closes with a tour of the turnpike.

Now, a few words on how to use the guide: Except for the turnpike tour, the entries are arranged alphabetically by town. This means that if you are interested in a particular park, say, but don't know which town it's in, you should look in the index under parks and find the town you need. Similarly, if you don't find an entry for a town you're interested in, check the index under towns to see if the town you're looking for is part of a larger entry. If you're thinking of planning a trip around a visit to a museum, check the index for museums.

Each entry begins with the name of the town, followed by the county it's in and the major roads that lead to or go through the town. *I* followed by a number is an interstate, *US* a federal highway, *NJ* a state road, and *C* a county road. The dot on the state map at the beginning of each entry is meant to help you find that town on a larger map. The numbers in the entry headings are the population figures from the 1980 census. When no census figures are available for the community in question, the township it is part of appears in brackets. To avoid confusion, I have sometimes indicated whether the figures refer to the borough or the township, or what the census calls a census-designated place (CDP). For the fast-growing areas—and there are many in the state—the 1980 census figures may be far too low. An asterisk tells you that something is listed in the state and national register of historic places.

When a building or other place open to the public is listed, it is generally followed by its actual (not mailing) address and telephone number in parentheses. Times of opening come at the end of the description. (The months or days on either side of a dash are inclusive; that is, October–March means October through March.) Admission charges are noted; exact amounts are not.

Although every attempt has been made to secure accurate and up-to-date information, it is always advisable to call ahead, particularly for smaller museums and historic houses. Hours change, and in many cases the curators have no substitutes to take over when they cannot be on the job. Do not be surprised if you reach the past president of the local historical society, who is no longer involved in the museum you want to visit. He or she will be glad to help you find the current curator. Even the state parks can change their hours as their budgets change. Definitions of summer and winter also vary. For the state parks and many seaside resorts summer usually means Memorial Day to Labor Day, but it is always best to call ahead. Since some admission charges can be high while others are nominal, you might want to check on those too.

Parking fees are usually in effect in the state parks during the summer. For both state and county parks, it's a good idea to call about regulations if you want to camp, boat, fish, horseback ride, or hold group picnics. Also, when an entry says that an area is open to hunting or fishing, please remember that this means open to hunting or fishing with the proper license. For information about hunting and fishing regulations call 609-292-2965 or the number listed for the particular area.

Each entry should contain enough information to allow you to find your way to the place you're looking for, but you may want to call ahead for more detailed directions. The state gives away an excellent road map (available at state tourist centers and some state parks, by calling 609-292-2470, or by writing NJ Department of Commerce and Economic Development, Division of Travel and Tourism, CN 826, Trenton, NJ 08625). If, however, you're going to do any real exploring, you should arm yourself with a county map. These are particularly helpful now that most counties are posting numbered signs for most of their routes. (But be warned: some counties mark the roads they maintain with an abundance of signs; others may leave you feeling neglected.)

The state's Division of Travel and Tourism also publishes booklets and brochures useful to those who want to explore the state. There are many specialized guides available, including ones for antiques lovers, bird-watchers, canoeists, history buffs, naturalists, and shopping enthusiasts. Tourist centers and chambers of commerce at the major tourist areas have literature you may find useful. There are also wonderful books not specifically intended for tourists on various parts of the state—John McPhee's *The Pine Barrens* and Charles Funnell's *By the Beautiful Sea* simply being among the best known—and most public libraries have large New Jersey collections. Many bookstores have New Jersey material, and the book sections in the larger state park visitor centers, in the Audubon sanctuaries, and in many historical museums are often good sources of local literature.

The preparation of this book has converted me and my husband into fervent, even proselytizing, patriots. I hope some of this fervor, much of which rubbed off on many who worked with me, will spread to those who use this guide.

I would have liked to thank here by name all the people all over the state who helped me with this guide, but as they number in the hundreds, I am afraid this is not possible. Some of my friends will recognize my unabashed exploitation of their ideas, which I trust they will take as an expression of gratitude. I would also like to single out the authorities at the New Jersey Turnpike, particularly Gordon Hector and Jack Seymour, for their unfailing cooperation and to thank Susan B. Scheuermann for letting me look at the turnpike material put together by the State Council of the Junior Leagues of New Jersey. And to all those who helped me, to those who accompanied me on my trips around New Jersey, to the members of historical societies, the curators of museums, the park superintendents and rangers, the officials of federal, state, county, and municipal agencies, the librarians, I offer my heartfelt thanks.

New Jersey, North to South

New Jersey, Alphabetically

Cities, Towns, and Villages

Absecon Atlantic 7,638

US 9, 30, NJ 157, C 585

Although many visitors to the shore may think of Absecon (pronounced *Ab-see'-con*) as simply the entrance to Atlantic City, the town long predates Atlantic City (it was a stagecoach stop before the Revolution) and in a sense was essential to its development. In 1820, Dr. Jonathan Pitney, the man who more or less invented Atlantic City (*see* Atlantic City), moved to Absecon. His house* (57 N. Shore Rd.; 609-569-1799), formerly known as the Reed house, dates from 1799. Enlarged by Pitney in 1848, it is now a bed and breakfast; tours by appointment. Other older houses can be seen on the quiet streets away from the busy commercial highways.

Pitney was also involved in both the Methodist and Presbyterian congregations. Near his home is the brick United Methodist Church (50 W. Church St.), first built in 1823 and rebuilt in 1856. (Methodism had taken hold in Absecon when Francis Asbury visited in 1796–97.) The Presbyterian Church building (New Jersey Ave.) dates from 1867. (The first Presbyterian churchmen to preach in Absecon were also distinguished: John Brainerd in the 1750s, Philip Vickers Fithian in the 1770s.)

Absecon Wildlife Management Area contains about 3,600 acres of salt marsh in Reeds and Absecon bays. This is an excellent area for bird-watching, fishing, boating, and waterfowl hunting. The town has a public boat ramp (Faunce Landing Rd., off US 9), and you can fish from the northern part of the old Brigantine Bridge.

The heated seat used by the National Football League to warm benches in late-season games was invented by a plumber from Pleasantville, a short distance south of Absecon.

Allentown Monmouth 1,882

C 524, 526, 539

First settled by Quakers, Scotch, and Dutch (and known as Allens Town from the gristmill Nathan Allen built in 1706 near the site of the present mill), Allentown was an active milltown by the mid-18th century. The village, officially recognized as a village center by the state planning commission, retains many attractive 18th- and 19th-century buildings, both in its historic district*

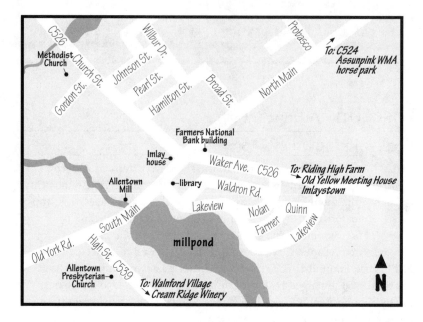

The map shows: Methodist Church, C526, Church St., Gordon St., Johnson St., Wilbur Dr., Pearl St., Hamilton St., Broad St., North Main, Probasco, To: C524 Assunpink WMA horse park, Farmers National Bank building, Imlay house, Waker Ave., C526, To: Riding High Farm, Old Yellow Meeting House, Imlaystown, Allentown Mill, library, Waldron Rd., Lakeview, Nolan, Quinn, South Main, Farmer, Lakeview, millpond, Old York Rd., High St., C539, Allentown Presbyterian Church, To: Walnford Village, Cream Ridge Winery, N

(approximately 24 blocks centered around the mill and N. and S. Main sts., containing over 200 buildings and homes built before 1860) and along the county roads that radiate out from the center.

Small as it is, Allentown can claim at least two prominent citizens: Molly Pitcher, the Revolutionary War heroine who carried water to the soldiers during the Battle of Monmouth (*see* Freehold), and Dr. William A. Newell, founder of the United States Life-Saving Service. In 1848 Newell worked out the principle of throwing a line (Joseph Francis of Toms River improved the system by developing a closed lifeboat). Newell became a congressman in 1848 and again in 1865; he was governor of the state in 1856 and 1858. After serving as governor of the Washington Territory (1880–84), he returned to Allentown and once more took up his medical practice, living until 1901. His house is at the corner of Main and High streets. Allentown can also claim one of the first temperance organizations in the United States: the Allentown Sober Society, started in 1805.

The Allentown Mill* (42 S. Main St.), built in the mid-19th century on the site of earlier mills, now houses several shops and artists' studios. The John Imlay house (28 S. Main St.) was built c. 1790. Some of its imported French wallpaper is in the Metropolitan Museum of Art and at Winterthur. The Allentown Presbyterian Church (20 High St.) was founded in the 18th century; this lovely building dates from the early 19th century. The Methodist Church (23 Church St.) dates from 1810 (enlarged 1830, rebuilt 1936), and the former Baptist Church (1879) serves as the town library (16 S. Main; 609-259-7565). The local historical society maintains a display case devoted to local history in the foyer of the library. Open Monday and Wednesday, 10–5, Tuesday and Thursday, 10–9, Friday, 2–5, Saturday, 10–3.

The early-20th-century Farmers National Bank building* (9 N. Main St.), severely damaged in a fire in 2003, is being restored.

The nation's tenth-largest wholesaler of seedlings, Kube Pak, is located just south of Allentown (194 C 526; 609-259-3114). In 18 acres of greenhouses, some 130 million seedlings (resulting in 450,000 flats) are raised each spring. Tours by appointment.

Two miles east of Allentown, also on 526, is Riding High Farm (609-259-3884), which focuses on the disabled. Group and individual lessons are offered year-round to riders of varying ages and disabilities. Call for more information. The Horse Park at Stone Tavern, the state equestrian facility, is five miles east of Allentown, off 524, in the Assunpink Wildlife Management Area (*see* Roosevelt).

Three miles south of Allentown, in Crosswicks Creek Park (C 539 east to Walns Mill Rd., right, or south, on Walns Mill), is Historic Walnford* (78 Walnford Rd.; 609-259-6275). Established in 1734 by an Allentown merchant, Walnford was purchased in 1771 by Richard Waln and once included a gristmill, sawmill, dye house, cooper's shop, blacksmith shop, and family mansion. Now part of a 1,000-acre county park, Walnford Village consists of an 18th-century homestead surrounded by a gristmill (built in 1872 and in use until 1917), carriage house, icehouse, and other farm buildings. The mill, one of the finest of its type, has been restored, and demonstrations are given weekends, April–November. There are interpretive exhibits in the other buildings. The park is open daily, 8–4:30. Group tours by appointment.

Also south of Allentown on C 539 (at the point where Polhemustown and Holmes Mill rds. join) is the Cream Ridge Winery (609-259-9797), a family-run winery that opened in 1988. Special events are held throughout the year. Open Monday–Saturday, 11–6, Sunday, 11–5; group tours by appointment (fee charged).

East of Allentown (take C 526, which becomes Red Valley Rd., to Yellow Meeting House Rd.) is the Yellow Meeting House* (609-259-7100), sometimes referred to as the Upper Freehold Baptist Meeting. Built c. 1737, the church is said to be the oldest Baptist church in the state, the third oldest in the country. A garden has been planted around the church, and historical signs have been put up. Tours by appointment. On your way to the meetinghouse note the Imlaystown Historic District* (Imlaystown–Davis Station and Red Valley rds.), with its well-preserved 18th- and 19th-century buildings.

Alpine   Bergen 2,183

US 9W, C 502

The small, wealthy community of Alpine (in 2000 per capita income was the seventh highest in the state, the median house value was over $1 million, and the median household income over $130,000) is perched on top of the Palisades, which at this point rise abruptly 530 feet above the Hudson River. Volcanically formed, the Palisades, which Verrazano came upon in 1524, are a national natural landmark. Threatened with destruction by quarrying in the late 19th century, they were saved by a federation of women's clubs, and the Palisades Interstate Park* was established in 1900.

The park headquarters are at exit 2 of the Palisades Interstate Parkway* in an interesting stone building with wonderful views of the river. The Blackledge-Kearney house* (Closter Dock Rd.; 201-768-1360), a fieldstone and frame 18th–early-20th-century building known as Cornwallis's Headquarters, was once believed to have been used by the British major general Cornwallis during the retreat of the American forces in November 1776, after Cornwallis's surprise attack at Fort Lee. Although doubt has been cast on this theory, the theory saved the house from being razed in the 1920s and makes it a rare monument to an enemy general. Open May–October, weekends and holidays, 12–5; other times by appointment.

You can hike along the river and on the cliffs, and crabbing and fishing are both allowed. In the northern section of the park, at State Line Lookout, you will find some 7½ miles of ski trails (for information on skiing, call 201-768-1360). Special events, such as nature walks and history hikes, are held throughout the year; for schedules call 201-768-0379. The park commission planted wildflowers along the parkway, hoping to cut down on maintenance costs. The result was so attractive that the plantings are now cited as another reason for using the parkway.

THE PALISADES

At various times such celebrities as Joe Piscopo, Eddie Murphy, and Stevie Wonder have lived in Alpine, a town that used to do without house numbers and still does without mail delivery (house numbers have been assigned because of the 911 emergency service, but many people choose not to use or post them). After the Civil War millionaires built lavish estates along the Palisades, most of which were destroyed with the establishment of the park and the building of the parkway. Edwin Armstrong, the developer of FM radio, lived in one of these mansions and sent from his radio tower (still visible from exit 2 of the Palisades Pkwy) the first static-free FM broadcasts. (In 1954 Armstrong killed himself, though not, as legend sometimes has it, by jumping from the tower.) The tower itself is still in use, serving a variety of contemporary communication purposes, among them acting as a backup for New York City television stations. A small Armstrong museum (US 9W; 201-930-0533), containing, among other things, some of Armstrong's old equipment, is open by appointment.

To the west of Alpine, in Demarest, is the Old Church Cultural Center (561 Piermont Rd.; 201-767-7160). Housed in what was once the Demarest Baptist Church (1875), the center sponsors a variety of art shows and offers classes in fine arts and crafts for children and adults. Exhibits in the gallery change each month; among the regular shows are an invitational pottery exhibit, a New Jersey–artist small-works show, and a faculty show. An annual international program, Voices of the World, focuses on a different culture each year. Open Monday–Thursday, 9–5:30 and 7–10, Friday, 9–5, Saturday, 9:30–12:30. There are still 18th-century houses to be seen on County Road. Also in Demarest is the Demarest Nature Center (between Columbus Rd. and C 35), 55 acres where you can hike daily from a half-hour before dawn to a half-hour after sunset. The center also sponsors a variety of programs and special events; for more information consult their website.

Asbury Park Monmouth 16,930

NJ 33, 66, 71

The seaside resort of Asbury Park, named after the Methodist bishop Francis Asbury, was developed in 1870 by James A. Bradley, a New York brush manufacturer who had been visiting the camp meeting of Ocean Grove. Like Ocean Grove, Asbury Park was intended as a temperance resort, but in other respects it catered to more worldly tastes. ("Stimulated by the fiery influence of ice-cream and ginger-pop, its permanent and floating population may plunge into the vortex of social dissipation afforded by pool, billiards, bowling, smoking, and dancing" was Gustav Kobbé's description in 1889.) The first trolleys in New Jersey ran in Asbury Park in 1877, and Bud Abbott of Abbott and Costello was born here. Stephen Crane, author of *The Red Badge of Courage*, born in Newark to an old New Jersey family, was raised here and as a young man worked as a journalist out of Asbury Park. His house (508 Fourth Ave.; 732-775-5682), built in the 1870s, is probably the oldest house still standing in Asbury Park. It is now a museum and is open once a month for readings and for various special events, but plans call for eventually establishing regular hours. Tours by appointment.

One of the country's worst marine disasters occurred off the Asbury Park beach when the *Morro Castle*, a cruise ship, burned under mysterious circumstances in 1934. Many rock-and-roll musicians developed their reputations in Asbury Park, including, of course, Bruce Springsteen; the Stone Pony he made famous reopened in the early 1990s. And the Amerada Hess Company grew out of a two-truck oil delivery company in Asbury Park.

Asbury Park suffered a decline in the 1970s and '80s, but many people are working on bringing it back to something like its early glory. Some of that early splendor can still be seen in the wide streets, the Convention Hall* (Ocean Ave.; 1928), the Paramount Theatre* (300 Ocean Ave.; 1920), and the former Berkeley-Carteret Hotel (Ocean Ave; 1925). The Paramount, built as a vaudeville house, converted to a movie theater, and converted back to a performance space, has been restored and now serves as a venue for jazz, light rock, and classical concerts, dance, opera, and multicultural events. Convention Hall is being restored, but is still open for concerts, trade shows, gym shows, carnivals, and the like. For information on programs in both places, call 732-775-3533. Each July the town holds a jazz festival (2004 was the 68th annual festival); town festivals also take place at Easter and at many other times. Call 732-775-2100 for information. The boardwalk may have fewer concessions, but the beach is still the beach (for information on beach fees, call 732-775-0900).

At 618 Bangs Ave. is Marimba Productions, an internationally recognized manufacturer of marimbas (as well as xylophones, glockenspiels, and mallets). The company sponsors summer workshops and occasional contests, festivals, and public concerts. Tours of the factory may be arranged by appointment (732-774-0011).

Atlantic City Atlantic 40,517

US 30, 40, 322, ATLANTIC CITY EXPRESSWAY

Because of the board game Monopoly, the names of Atlantic City's streets—Boardwalk, Park Place, Indiana Avenue—are as familiar to most Americans as those in their own town. That the game depends on buying and selling and developing real estate is peculiarly appropriate, for Atlantic City itself was the creation of a speculative real estate venture. In 1850 today's resort was simply Absecon Island, an eight-mile stretch of sand with but a handful of inhabitants. For many years Jonathan Pitney, a doctor and congressman who lived nearby on the mainland (*see* Absecon), had mulled over the possibilities of building a railroad to the shore and developing the island. Atlantic City does have certain natural advantages as a resort: its particular configuration moderates the waves, and the position of the Gulf Stream moderates the climate; nearby Philadelphia supplied a ready clientele. The rest was the work of the developers. The railroad was built in 1852, and an engineer named Richard B. Osborne formulated a plan for the new city as grandiose as its name: streets parallel to the ocean were named after seas and oceans (Baltic, Mediterranean, etc.), and streets at right angles were named for the states.

In 1870 Atlantic City built its first boardwalk, probably the first boardwalk anywhere. It was the joint idea of a hotel man and a railroad conductor who, in one version of the tale, didn't like sand in their hallways and corridors or, in another, saw in the walkway the potential for increasing business. The original boardwalk was eight feet wide and made of wood laid directly on the sand. Today, wood planking is laid on a steel and concrete foundation. Hotels, stores that catered to a wide variety of tastes, restaurants, and the kind of attractions one finds at carnivals were built along the boardwalk, and several entrepreneurs built piers that jutted out into the ocean and featured similar attractions. For those tired of walking there were tramcars and pushchairs; the pushchairs, now known as rolling chairs, remain today in a modified form.

Another of Atlantic City's trademarks—saltwater taffy—was also invented in the 1870s. And yet another—the Miss America Pageant—resulted, like the city itself, from a deliberate promotion. Begun in 1921, the pageant was held each fall from 1935 to 2004. (The first Miss America, Annie Laurie, died in 1985.)

The word "airport" was apparently coined in Atlantic City, when the editor of the *Atlantic City Press* used it in referring to Bader Field. Opened c. 1918 (and sold to the city in 1922), it may have been the country's, perhaps the world's, first official airport. Ironically, airplanes were one of the major factors in Atlantic City's later decline, as lower airfares made it possible for people to vacation farther afield. And the country's first Ferris wheel was built in Atlantic City in 1891, the brainchild of William Somers, not George Ferris.

To a large extent the resort flourished because of day-trippers, but gradually, as more and larger hotels were built, it became known as a center for conventions. After World War II, Atlantic City entered a long period of decline, broken only (and only partially) in the 1970s with the advent of state-authorized casino gambling. After 1978, when the first casino opened, there was an upsurge of speculative activity reminiscent of the 1890–1912 boom. Unfortunately, it has not solved the city's problems. Casino operations are approaching a $4 billion a year business; the casinos employ some 50,000 people and pay over three-quarters of the municipal budget; some 32 million people visit Atlantic City each year (compared to 2 million before the casinos), which makes Atlantic City one of the top tourist destinations in the United States. But the upward trend is threatened by increased competition in nearby states, the unemployment rate, though down, is still twice the state average, and until all the planned construction projects are actually completed, visitors will continue to approach the glitter of the casinos across what still has some of the character of a bombed-out wasteland—the city has been likened to a collection of "pleasure palaces in the midst of a war zone."

The casinos have, however, changed the appearance of the boardwalk. The wicker rolling chairs and the benches (a few facing the ocean, most facing the crowd) are still there, as are the candy stores selling fudge and salt water taffy. Many of the piers are gone; the Million Dollar Pier was converted to Ocean One, a ship-shaped shopping mall, which is now being converted to the Pier at Caesars, a multistory, high-end shopping center. Most of the elegant hotels (including those listed in the national register of historic places) and the seedier of the shops are gone. The beautiful beach is still there, but even in its heyday Atlantic City was rather urban for a seaside resort. Unlike Las Vegas, Atlantic City permits no slot machines in public places other than the casinos (this still allows you over 43,000 opportunities to use a slot machine), and only hotels with 500 rooms can apply for casino status. The idea was to raise the tone of the resort and encourage people to stay longer, but neither goal has been achieved entirely, although over the years hotel occupancy has picked up.

Many visitors to Atlantic City are still day-trippers, despite the efforts of the casinos to encourage longer stays (one-quarter of the country's population lives within a few hours' drive of the casinos). Most arrive by car, but a significant portion arrives by bus (the casinos have been credited with changing public attitudes toward motor coaches and leading to a boom in the bus business). Parking can be a problem, but jitney buses run on Pacific Ave. 24 hours a day to get you from casino to casino. Rail service to Atlantic City was reinstituted in 1989, though the service requires a good-sized subsidy, and a minor-league baseball team now plays in a new stadium at Bader Field.

To protect their customers, the casinos may use cards or dice for only 24 hours, after which they must be destroyed or have holes drilled in them. Over 2 million decks of cards and 160,000 pairs of dice are destroyed or given to charitable organizations each year; some mutilated remains are made into key rings and sold as souvenirs.

For those who like gambling or glitz or observing either of them (the paintings of Hieronymus Bosch may come to mind), Atlantic City is an exciting place. Other options include strolling on the boardwalk and watching the people or shopping. The beach is patrolled by lifeguards in the summer months, and you can visit the Absecon Lighthouse* (Pacific and Rhode Island aves.; 609-449-1360), another project inspired by Dr. Pitney. Built in the 1850s, the lighthouse, like the Barnegat Lighthouse, was designed by George Gordon Meade, later the Union commander at Gettysburg. Decommissioned in 1933, the lighthouse tower was restored in the 1990s, and a replica of the lightkeeper's house was constructed to serve as a visitor center and museum, only to be lost in a fire. Rebuilt again, the lightkeeper's house also houses the lighthouse offices. In the museum are pictures and artifacts relating to local history and the role of the lighthouse. Long-range plans include reconstructing the lifesaving station and possibly restoring the oil house and using it for a display on Fresnel lenses. Open daily, 10–5, July and August; 11–4, Thursday–Monday, September–June; closed major holidays. Groups by appointment. Admission charge.

In the same area of the city, known as Gardner's Basin, is the Ocean Life Center (800 N. New Hampshire Ave; 609-348-2880). Opened in 1999, the center features close to 30,000 gallons of water exhibits, including a large aquarium with fish from the New Jersey coast and a touch tank where visitors can handle, among others, crabs, mussels, and sea urchins. There are also interactive exhibits and several computer stations, and visitors can learn about sailing, for example, by seeing how a model boat acts in a wind tunnel or match pictures of deep-sea animals with recordings of their sounds. Open daily, 10–5. Admission charge.

Boardwalk Hall,* a national historic landmark formerly known as Convention Hall (Boardwalk between Mississippi and Florida aves.; 609-348-7000), which once had the world's largest unobstructed room and still has what is said to be the world's largest pipe organ, has been restored to all its late-1920s glory. The hall, apparently the nation's top-grossing mid-sized hall, now serves as a venue for a variety of events, from musical and sporting events to ice shows, circuses, and professional bull riders.

What is now called Convention Hall (1 Miss America Way; 609-449-2000) opened in 1997. This large building (500,000 square feet on 31 acres) with its dramatic lobby serves as a venue for conventions, trade shows, meetings, and conferences, ranging from a classic car show to college fairs, from meetings of the New Jersey State League of Municipalities to an international DJ expo and an imprinted-sportswear show.

The Atlantic City Art Center on the Garden Pier (Boardwalk and New Jersey Ave.; 609-347-5837) has three galleries with exhibits that change every month or two and feature works by contemporary artists and artisans, both local and national. Across the pier is the Atlantic City Historical Museum (609-347-5839). Its permanent exhibit features artifacts and memorabilia from the city's past. Its photography gallery has changing exhibits that concentrate on different aspects of Atlantic City's history. Both the art center and the museum are open daily except major holidays, 10–4. Also on the boardwalk is Ripley's Believe It or Not! Museum (Boardwalk and New York Ave.; 609-347-2001). Part of a chain, the museum features a variety of what have been described as wacky, far-out exhibits. Open Sunday–Friday, 10–7, Saturday, 10–10. Admission charge.

There are still abundant opportunities to fish and boat in the area. The Senator Frank S. Farley Marina (600 Huron Ave.; 609-441-8482) is one of five state marinas.

In the mid-1990s development frenzy picked up again (some say because the state loosened its oversight of gambling), and Atlantic City is likely to continue to change. In addition to the new convention center (and the city's first new shopping center in over 20 years), more casinos, non-casino hotels, and restaurants are being built.

Annual events include a dog show in December, an antique car show in February, an arts festival in April, a professional fine arts show in June, and a crafts show in September.

Atlantic Highlands Monmouth 4,705

NJ 36

Formerly known as Portland Poynt, Atlantic Highlands was first settled in 1671. Developed as a Methodist camp meeting in 1881, it was incorporated as a borough six years later and today is more of a residential and less of a tourist community than some of its neighbors along Sandy Hook and Raritan bays. You will find a downtown movie theater on First Ave., and the Hofbrauhaus on Scenic Dr. is said to feature the oldest Oktoberfest in the state.

The Mt. Mitchill Scenic Overlook (Ocean Blvd.; 732-842-4000) is part of the Monmouth County park system; the mountain itself, at 250 feet, is the highest natural point along the mid-Atlantic seacoast and the first spot seen by ships coming in from the east. (The Fresh Kills landfill on Staten Island is the highest man-made point.) If you can ignore the high-rise building that adjoins the park, you will be rewarded with a spectacular view of Sandy Hook and New York City from the overlook. There are coin-operated telescopes, a playground, and picnic facilities at the park, and a 9/11 memorial is expected to be in place in the park by September 2005.

Many fine views can also be had on the drive along Ocean Blvd. (also known as Scenic Dr.) from the center of town to the overlook. Closer to the bay, on Bayside Dr., is Henry Hudson's Spout, a spring frequented by Native Americans, by 19th-century packet steamers, and, according to tradition, by Hudson's crews as well.

The Adolph Strauss house (27 Prospect Cir.; 732-291-1861) is a 20-room Victorian mansion built in the 1890s, operated as a house museum by the Atlantic Highlands Historical Society. The house is furnished with period pieces, and a variety of artifacts and memorabilia, most related to the history of the town, is on display. There are steamship memorabilia, a Lenape exhibit, and material on the Shakespearean troupe that used to rehearse its winter program in Atlantic Highlands in the summer. Each year there is a new thematic exhibit, dealing, for example, with subjects like fancy place settings or the vocabulary of fans or the Roaring Twenties (this last inspired by the town's connection to rum-running; there are caves at the beach where liquor was stored, and a tunnel to the beach was found in one of the houses). Open Sunday, 1–4, except during the coldest months. The society also sponsors an annual house tour.

Within the borough is the Lenape Woods Nature Preserve (732-291-1444), 50 acres that include the headwaters of the Many Mind Creek (named for the creek's tendency to change direction). Rescued from its use as an illegal dump and the possibility of future development, the preserve has several miles of trails and an abundance of wildlife. Although the preserve is now in three sections, there are plans to connect them. For now you can enter the eastern section at E. Highland Ave. and Ocean Blvd., the western at Sears and E. Washington Ave., but until the connection is made, there is no public access to the small third section.

If you head west and north from Atlantic Highlands along NJ 36, passing through the villages of Leonardo and Belford, you will come to Port Monmouth (turn right off NJ 36 on East Rd. to Main St. to the Port Monmouth Rd.). Here in the county's Bayshore Waterfront Park you will find the Wilson-Seabrook House* (119 Port Monmouth Rd.; 732-842-4000), said to be the first house built on the New Jersey shoreline. Formerly referred to as the Shoal Harbor Museum or the Spy House, it was built in 1663 by Thomas Whitlock, and remained in the hands of his descendants until the early 1900s. It was called the Spy House because of various tales about its having been converted to an inn by the time of the Revolution, and serving as a clearinghouse for information collected by Americans spying from a nearby hill. In one version 39 raids were supposed to have been made possible by information relayed to the house. An effort is being made to find out the extent to which these stories accurately represent actual events. In the meantime, plans call for using the house for programs and classes, and some cultural artifacts will be on display.

Barnegat Ocean 15,270

US 9, C 554

Located on an inlet of Barnegat Bay, Barnegat (from the Dutch *Berende-gat,* meaning "inlet with breakers") was regularly visited by Native Americans during the summer months. The spot was observed by Hudson in 1609 (Juet noted in the log that "this is a very good Land to fall with, and a pleasant Land to see"). The village was first settled around 1720, and during the Revolution was the site of an important saltworks. The community has always lived from the water, from the whalers and pirates of colonial days to the shipbuilders and fishermen, both commercial and sport, of more recent times. Although the village of Barnegat has preserved some of its past, the surrounding township is multiplying rapidly, and some of the waterfront growth is causing concern about pollution of the bay. (The township's population in 2000 was almost ten times that of 1970.)

The Barnegat Historical Society Heritage Village (E. Bay Ave.; 609-698-0038) consists of seven buildings moved to the site to save them from destruction. They include the Lippincott-Falkenburg house, a typical bay house, probably from the 18th century, with handmade nails and squared-off tree trunks used for structural members; the Edwards house, traced to 1813 but probably older; a barbershop; the necessary; a corncrib; and a butcher shop (the storage shed was once a motel cabin). Open Memorial Day–Labor Day, Saturday, 1–4. Also on E. Bay is the Friends Meeting House, built in 1767; the cemetery has some gravestones that predate the meetinghouse.

On the northwest corner of the intersection of Main St. and Bay Ave. is the Cox Memorial Library (609-698-0080). The Cox house was built in the 1840s and remained in the Cox family until the last owners, publishers of a local newspaper, gave it to the town. The house is furnished as it might have been in the mid-19th century and contains many antiques, portraits, and items of historical interest that belonged to the Cox family. It is undergoing extensive restoration, but is opened to the public on special occasions and by appointment. When the restoration is complete, the town hopes to convert it into a museum with regular hours. Note also the Wright Memorial Presbyterian Church (S. Main St.), acquired by the congregation in 1876, but before that used as an opera house (a later opera house was converted to a movie theater); the United Methodist Church (E. Bay Ave. and Birdsall St.), built in the 1880s (its early-20th-century steeple replaces one blown off in a gale); and the former Tuckerton railroad station (Memorial Dr.), now a private house.

If you continue on E. Bay Ave. past the Heritage Center you will come to the bay and the town's public docks and beach.

North and west of Barnegat (you can take the Garden State Pkwy or US 9 north to C 532 and turn left) is Wells Mills County Park (Wells Mills Rd., C 532; 609-971-3085), the county's largest park. Its 900 acres encompass a variety of environments, and therefore a large variety of plants and animals. Records for this land go back to colonial days, and Atlantic white cedar was once harvested here—the first sawmill was built in the late 18th century—clay was mined, and sphagnum gathered. In the 1930s it was bought as a rustic retreat, and a cabin built then still overlooks the lake. You can fish or boat (electric motors only) on the lake, and there are trails, playgrounds, and a picnic area. Trail maps are available at the Wells Mills Nature Center, where you will also find an exhibit of plants and animals indigenous to the area and a third-floor observation deck. The center offers a variety of programs, including canoeing and kayak instruction, Pinelands walks, and weekend video and slide shows. The nature center is open daily, 10–4; the park daily, 8–sunset.

Barnegat Light   Ocean 764

C 607

This tiny seaside community at the northern tip of Long Beach Island can be reached only by crossing from the mainland on the Manahawkin Bay Bridge (NJ 72) or by boat. At the very tip of the island is Barnegat Lighthouse State Park (609-494-2016), 31 acres whose main attraction is the lighthouse* (affectionately referred to as Old Barney), built in the late 1850s after the earlier one (1834) fell into the sea in 1857. Designed by George Gordon Meade, the Union army commander at Gettysburg, and first lit in 1859, the lighthouse was decommissioned in 1927 when a lightship took over its duties. The lighthouse, 27 feet in diameter at the base and 15 feet above the walkway, is built of two concentric cones, which makes it flexible and permits it to sway in the wind. The hollow pipe in the center supports the cast-iron circular stairs and once enclosed the pendulum mechanism that turned the five-ton lens and lamp. There are splendid views for those willing to climb the 217 steps (but watch out for the sand falling from those climbing above you). A protective wall has been built to keep this lighthouse from following its predecessor into the ocean. The park also contains facilities for fishing, swimming, and picnicking.

The lens itself contained over 1,000 prisms, each of which could be individually adjusted, and the lamp was visible more than 30 miles out at sea. It can be seen today at the Barnegat Light Museum* (5th St. and Central Ave.; 609-494-8578), housed in a 1904 one-room schoolhouse. In addition to the lamp, the museum contains memorabilia from the school and the area, including old fishing equipment, school desks and diaries, and old photographs. Around the museum are the Edith Duff Gwinn Gardens, a seashore garden of plants, trees, and herbs that are able to grow on a barrier island. Open June and September, weekends, 2–5; July and August, daily, 2–5. Groups by appointment.

Saint Peter's at the Light (7th St. and Central Ave.), c. 1890, has 18th-century pews taken from the Wading River Methodist Church and an antique organ. Also on 7th Street is a former coast guard station that will eventually house the borough offices.

Barnegat Light was settled largely by Scandinavian fishermen, and some of their bayside huts, dating from the early 1900s, have been converted into shops and christened Viking Village (20th St. and Bayview Ave.).

South of Barnegat Light in Loveladies is the Long Beach Island Foundation of the Arts and Sciences (120 Long Beach Blvd.; 609-494-1241). The foundation offers classes for adults and children in art and nature and presents lectures, art exhibitions, children's theater, and concerts. It also offers nature walks through the 25-acre wetland preserve that is on the site. Open June–September, weekdays, 9–5, weekends, 10–4. Groups by appointment.

Basking Ridge Somerset [Bernards Township]

I 287 EXIT 26, C 525 SPUR, 527 SPUR

A colonial village, Basking Ridge sits on the western edge of the Great Swamp, the 6,700-acre remains of Glacial Lake Passaic. This was the home of William Alexander, a major general and quartermaster in the Continental army during the Revolution, who had not long before that established his claim to the earldom of Stirling (but no lands) in Scotland. All that remains of his 18th-century manor house are two small brick structures* intended as slaves' quarters (96 Lord Stirling Rd.), now a national historic site, but his memory has been honored in Lord Stirling Park, 900 acres devoted to an environmental education center, a riding stable, and natural areas.

The Environmental Education Center (190 Lord Stirling Rd.; 908-766-2489), a county facility adjacent to the Great Swamp National Wildlife Refuge, encompasses more than 430 acres of freshwater marsh, swamp, bog, streams, rivers, fields, and woods. There are more than eight miles of trails, with two miles of boardwalk. Two observation towers and two observation blinds allow a closer look at the abundant wildlife. There is also a quarter-mile barrier-free special-use trail. When it was built the center's education building was said to be the first interpretive center in the nation to rely almost entirely on solar energy (the system eventually became antiquated and was replaced by a more conventional one): solar heating and cooling had supplied some 60 percent of the total energy needs and a substantial portion of the hot water (representing a saving of roughly 6,000 gallons of fuel oil a winter). On display is a kind of three-dimensional time line dealing with the history and natural history of the Great Swamp, from glacial days through the jetport controversy (in the 1960s the Port Authority planned to build a major airport in the Great Swamp, but was thwarted by a massive citizens' campaign) to the present. Although European settlers arrived here in the mid-17th century, Native Americans were in this area 12,000 years ago, and some of the exhibit deals with them. Geology, the varied habitats found in Lord Stirling Park, and the ecology of the area are also included. The center offers many educational programs for children and adults (including, for example, owl walks and bat walks) and sponsors summer programs for children. There are several annual festivals, among them the wildlife art and carving show (now over 20 years old) in the spring and the Lord Stirling 1770s festival in the fall. Open daily, 9–4:30; closed most holidays. Trails open daily, sunrise to sunset. Groups by appointment only.

The riding stable (256 S. Maple Ave.; 908-766-5955) offers group and individual lessons and, in the summer, workshops. Experienced riders can rent horses during limited hours most days; trail riding can be arranged when the trails are open. The stable also hosts a variety of special events and shows. Call for exact times and dates.

To the east of Lord Stirling Park is the Great Swamp National Wildlife Refuge. Its eastern two-thirds is a wilderness area, with limited access to some 10 miles of trails. There is a wildlife observation center off Long Hill Rd., with a mile of trails, interpretive displays, and blinds. The western third is operated as a wildlife management area. The visitors' areas are open daily year-round, dawn to dusk; tours by appointment. (Morris County runs an environmental center on the eastern edge of the swamp, with one mile of trail and boardwalk and a half-mile barrier-free trail; see Chatham.)

Among the many well-kept buildings in town note the Presbyterian Church* (6 W. Oak St.), built in 1839 on the site of two earlier buildings; the oak tree may have been standing for 300 years before the earliest (pre-1731) church. St. Mark's (S. Finley Ave. and Lewis St.), with its vertical siding, was built in 1853; the municipal building (S. Finley Ave. and Collyer La.) was once a summer home on an estate owned by the Astors. The Brick Academy* (15 W. Oak St.; 908-221-1770), built in 1809, has served as a school and a municipal building; it is now the headquarters of the historical society. Inside are various artifacts connected with the history of the area, including, for example, displays relating to the academy when it functioned as a school and to Lord Stirling Manor. The society's changing exhibits also focus on local history, and the society sponsors walking tours and public lectures. Open Sunday, September–June, 2–4.

If you continue east on Lord Stirling Rd., which becomes White Bridge Rd., you will come to the Raptor Trust (1390 White Bridge Rd.;

908-647-2353), a 20-acre refuge devoted to caring for, and when possible releasing, orphaned and injured birds, particularly birds of prey. Some of the center's residents have been reproducing. The chicks are shielded from visitors and sent to Canada, where they learn to hunt so they can be released. Birds that cannot be rehabilitated are housed in cages that can be observed by the public; those that can be expected to live on their own are kept in secluded aviaries. The center engages in educational programs both at its education facility and in the schools (call for details). Open daily during daylight hours; groups by appointment. The Raptor Trust is actually in Millington, also the home of Garden State Fireworks, a family-run company founded in the early 1890s that is one of the largest in the country.

At 287 Childs Rd. (just west of 202), on a lovely site, is the Van Dorn Mill. Built in 1842, it is said to have replaced one that supplied George Washington during the Revolution. The building has been converted to office space, but the wheel is still there.

Bayonne   Hudson 61,842

NJ TNPK EXIT 14A, I 78, NJ 169, 440

Situated on the peninsula separating New York Bay from Newark Bay, the city of Bayonne (pronounced with a long *o*: *bay-own*) presents a remarkably solid appearance. Extensive neighborhoods of single- and two-family houses look well tended, no skyscrapers are apparent, the main streets are broad, and the stores seem to be selling things people need rather than reflecting trends. Bayonne, in fact, has the reputation of being a remarkably stable community, where people remain in the same neighborhoods for generations. First settled by the Dutch in 1646, Bayonne became a resort area in the 18th century and an industrial one in the 19th. Oil companies began their transformation of the waterfront in 1875, and the city became home to a variety of industries.

One of the world's largest military ports, the Military Ocean Terminal, was located on Bayonne's waterfront and was for a time Hudson County's largest employer. Extending into Upper New York Bay, the facility covered over 400 acres of land and 200 acres of water, and had its own apartment complex, movie theater, and restaurant. The complex closed in 1999 amid concern about what would become of the facility. It is now known as Peninsula at Bayonne Harbor, and in 2004 a cruise line began operating out of the port.

Bayonne is considered the birthplace (in 1913) of the manufactured diner: although the idea of modeling a restaurant on the lunch wagon apparently dates to the 1870s, a bar-and-grill owner named Jerry O'Mahoney is credited with being the first to build the structure we think of today as the original diner. Bayonne has also been the birthplace, or the home, of many entertainers, among them Frank Langella, Sandra Dee, and Mickey Rooney. And a Bayonne company was the first to use ball bearings in an electric motor (in 1903).

At the southeastern tip of the peninsula is Constable Hook, the first area in town to be settled; it is now an industrial enclave and occupied by oil refineries, tank farms, warehouses, and trucking terminals. Yet in other parts of the city industrial concerns sit cheek by jowl with well-kept residential neighborhoods. The city has had a rich ethnic mix with significant populations of Irish, Polish, English, Italian, and Jewish background. Some of this diversity is still reflected in the number and variety of religious buildings.

At the southern tip of the peninsula is Major Dennis P. Collins Park (named for one of Bayonne's two Medal of Honor recipients), where you can watch the river traffic on the Kill van Kull (the narrow waterway separating Staten Island from Bayonne) from the water's edge. You can also

BAYONNE BRIDGE

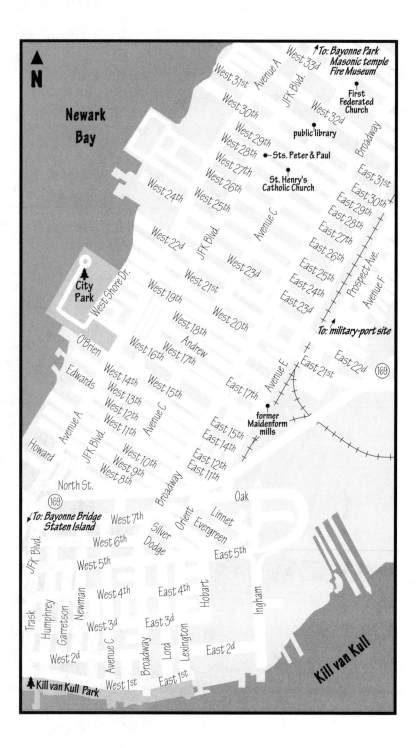

N

Newark
Bay

To: Bayonne Park
Masonic temple
Fire Museum

West 33d
West 31st
Avenue A
JFK Blvd.
West 30th
West 32d
First
Federated
Church
West 29th
public library
Broadway
West 28th
Sts. Peter & Paul
West 27th
West 26th
St. Henry's
Catholic Church
East 31st
West 24th
West 25th
East 30th
East 29th
East 28th
Avenue C
East 27th
West 22d
JFK Blvd.
East 26th
West 23d
East 25th
Prospect Ave.
Avenue F
West 21st
East 24th
City
Park
West Shore Dr.
West 19th
East 23d
To: military-port site
West 18th
West 20th
Andrew
O'Brien
West 16th
West 17th
East 22d
169
Edwards
West 14th
West 15th
Avenue E
East 21st
West 13th
East 17th
West 12th
Avenue C
West 11th
Avenue A
East 15th
former
Maidenform
mills
JFK Blvd.
West 10th
East 14th
Howard
West 9th
East 12th
West 8th
Broadway
East 11th
North St.
Oak
169
To: Bayonne Bridge
Staten Island
West 7th
Orient
Linnet
West 6th
Silver
Evergreen
JFK Blvd.
West 5th
Dodge
East 5th
Trask
Humphrey
Garretson
Newman
West 4th
East 4th
Hobart
Ingham
West 3d
East 3d
Lexington
Avenue C
Broadway
Lord
East 2d
West 2d
Kill van Kull
Kill van Kull Park
West 1st
East 1st

18   Bayonne

find facilities for skating and biking. The park forms one end of the Hudson River walkway, which traverses much of the water's edge in Bayonne.

Just west of the park is the Bayonne Bridge, which crosses the Kill van Kull to link Bayonne with Staten Island. Opened in 1931, the steel-arch structure carries four lanes of traffic (over seven million vehicles use the bridge each year) and is one of the world's longest steel-arch bridges, with an arch span of 1,675 feet.

Stephen R. Gregg–Bayonne County Park is another waterfront park, this one on Newark Bay. Its 97 acres provide an interesting combination of formal landscaping, natural and open areas, and sports facilities. Here you can find picnic grounds, playgrounds, and athletic fields. Much of the park's three-quarters of a mile of bay frontage is reclaimed land, from a project completed early in the 20th century.

At 10 West 47th St. is the Chief John T. Brennan Fire Museum* (201-858-6008). It contains old equipment (including one of the oldest hose units in the state), photographs, and other paraphernalia. The building itself dates from 1875. Open by appointment only. The urban park next door is locked on weekends.

Other buildings worth noting are the elegant public library, with its Neoclassic wing design (Ave. C and 31st St.); the somewhat Spanish Romanesque Masonic temple (Ave. C at the entrance to Bayonne Park); the First Federated Church (Ave. C between 33d and 34th), built in 1866; Saints Peter and Paul (28th St. between Kennedy Blvd. and Ave. C), a Russian Orthodox church with bronze minarets; Saint Henry's Catholic Church (Ave. C between 28th and 29th), an English Gothic church modeled on Durham cathedral and dedicated in 1915; the Victorian house on seven lots at Broadway and 3d, unlike other houses in Bayonne; and the red brick mid-19th-century mills used from the 1920s until the mid-1990s by Maidenform (17th St. and Ave. E). In the library (201-858-6970) exhibits, generally put up by local community groups, change roughly once a month. Concerts are given once a month, October–December and February–April, and a movie series takes place mid-June–August. Open Monday–Thursday, 9–9, Friday and Saturday, 9–5; mid-June–mid-September also closed Saturday.

Beach Haven Ocean 1,278

C 607

Beach Haven is located on Long Beach Island south of the Manahawkin Bay Bridge (NJ 72), the only land route to the island. The town has many Victorian seaside houses (Beach Haven's historic district* includes Atlantic, S. Atlantic, Beach, N. Beach, and Engleside aves. and Amber, Centre, Coral, Pearl, 2d, and 3d sts.). In the historic district, in the former Holy Innocents' Church (1882), is the Long Beach Island Historical Society museum (Engleside and

Beach aves.; 609-492-0700). Its exhibits, which change periodically, focus on the history of the area. You might see a display of Victorian furniture or clothing or an exhibit showing the type of fishing once practiced in the area. The museum also offers a variety of special programs, including a summer lecture series. Open daily, last week of June through first week of September, 2–4 and 7–9; also Tuesday and Friday, 10–12; open weekends last week of May, June, second and third weeks of September, 2–4. Groups by appointment. During July and August, the society sponsors walking tours that leave from the museum, Tuesday and Friday, 9:30.

The Chamber of Commerce (265 W. 9th St.) sponsors an annual chowder cook-off in the fall. For information on the cook-off and on beach fees, call 609-494-7211.

During July and August the Alliance for a Living Ocean (609-492-0222) runs three-hour eco-tours of the island that leave from Ship Bottom (north of Beach Haven at the Manahawkin Bay Bridge), on Wednesdays (one week the trip does the north half of the island, the next week it does the south half). The alliance also sponsors a variety of field trips and nature programs for children and adults during the summer.

At the southern tip of Long Beach Island is the Holgate Unit of the Edwin B. Forsythe National Wildlife Refuge (609-652-1665), 400 acres of barrier beach, dunes, and tidal salt marsh. The area is important to beach-nesting birds, including the endangered piping plover. You are welcome to walk along the beach, September–March; during the nesting season the area is closed to visitors.

Beemerville Sussex [Wantage Township]

C 519, 629, 649

A tiny crossroads community in rural Sussex County, Beemerville has long been the home of the Space family. Their farm today occupies over 425 acres, 100 of which are devoted to the Space Farms Zoo and Museum (C 519; 973-875-5800), which has been managed by three generations of Space family members (a fourth generation is learning the business). The zoo has more than 500 animals, representing more than 100 species, and is involved in programs to restore threatened and endangered species. At 12 feet and 2,000 pounds, Goliath, a long-term resident of the zoo who died in the early 1990s, was believed to be the largest Kodiak bear in the world.

When the zoo opened in 1927, the family also ran a general store that served the local farm community. During the Depression many of the customers brought in family mementos in lieu of cash, which Mr. and Mrs. Space hung on the wall until the items were redeemed. Out of this collection grew the museum, which in the late 1970s moved into buildings that used to house the Rutgers University cattle research facilities. (At those facilities Sir

Mutual Ormsby Jewel Alice in 1938 contributed semen for the country's first cooperative artificial breeding association.) The museum's eleven buildings contain a variety of old cars, tools, toys, firearms, sleighs, carriages, wagons, Native American artifacts, and the like. Open daily, May–October, 9–5, but you cannot enter after 4; groups by appointment. Admission charge.

While in Beemerville, note the windows of the First Presbyterian Church (1834).

Belvidere Warren 2,482

C 620, 623, 624

Located at the confluence of the Delaware and Pequest rivers, Belvidere was settled early in the 18th century and incorporated in 1845. The county seat, Belvidere has grown little over the last 70 years, one of the factors contributing to its special quality.

In the mid-18th century, there had been hopes that the power of the Pequest River could be harnessed and that Belvidere would become a flourishing industrial area. Robert Hoops, whose slaughterhouse supplied Washington's army when it was quartered in Morristown, had conceived the plan but was forced to sell his holdings along the river. The purchaser, Robert Morris (a signer of the Declaration of Independence and financier important to the Revolutionary cause), tied up the lands with a restrictive deed that took an act of the legislature to set aside; many believe Morris's deed permanently hobbled Belvidere's development. (The area is not without industry today; vitamins, for example, are produced in neighboring White Township.)

Belvidere's 19th-century historic district* encompasses Market, Race, Greenwich, and Mansfield sts. and the Pequest River, and includes some 200 buildings, but it is worth exploring outside this area as well. Included in the historic district is Belvidere's large green, another factor contributing to the town's appeal. On one side of the green is the red brick county courthouse (Second St. between Mansfield and Hardwick sts.), built in 1827 shortly after Warren County became independent of Sussex County; it has been modified, and the roof line was extended forward some 35 years ago. In the middle of each of the other three sides of the square is a church: the Presbyterian (1861) on Mansfield, the Methodist (1840s) on Hardwick, and the Episcopal (1900) on Third St. The green is known as Garrett Wall Park, named for a state governor who had donated the land for the courthouse, the square, and the churches, stipulating that the green was to remain undeveloped for the use of the county's residents forever. Some of the houses are open to the public during the town's Victorian Days (908-475-4124), held each year the first weekend after Labor Day.

Many of the county's offices are located in Belvidere's old houses; particularly beautiful is the stone Cummins house (1834; Second and

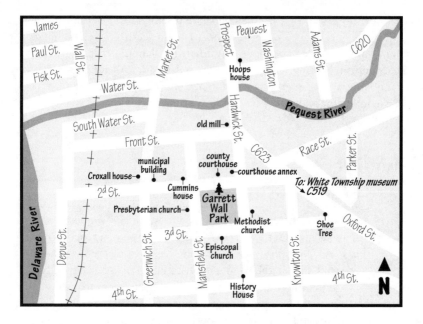

Mansfield sts.), now being used by the departments of education and mental health. Among many other attractive and interesting buildings note the county library and courthouse annex (1860s; Hardwick St.); the old mill (Hardwick St.); the Croxall house (1780; Greenwich St.), built by Robert Morris for his daughter; the tiny Robert Hoops stone house (c. 1700; Prospect St.), probably built as servants' quarters; the Queen Anne house at Second and Greenwich sts.; and the mid-19th-century brick house that serves as the municipal building (Second and Greenwich sts.). At Oxford and Third sts. note the Shoe Tree, a 300-year-old oak; it bears the legend "Barefoot folk sat under this tree to put on shoes before going to worship across the village green."

In an elegant 1850s house built of local brick the Warren County Historical and Genealogical Society runs History House (313 Mansfield St.; 908-475-4246), a museum specializing in the history of Warren County. The collection includes a wide variety of artifacts: from Native American objects found in the area to what may be an 18th-century child's high chair, from a dungeon door found when the courthouse was remodeled to handwoven linen sheets made from flax grown in the county. In the Victorian parlor is Eastlake furniture that belonged to the last family to live in the house. Special exhibits change roughly once a year. Open Sunday, 2–4, and by appointment.

Public access to the Delaware River for bank fishing is available just south of Water Street.

About four miles east of Belvidere, in Bridgeville, is the White Township museum, located on Titman Rd. behind the White Township School at the intersection of NJ 46 and C 519 (908-453-2379). The first story dates to the 1770s, the second to the 1830s, when the building was converted from a house to a store. It has been restored as a store with an apartment upstairs and one room devoted to artifacts relating particularly to local history. Open June–October, 2d and 4th Sunday of the month, 2–4; other times by appointment.

Berkeley Heights Union 13,407

C 512, 527, 531

Located in the Watchung Mountains and possibly named for Lord John Berkeley who, with Sir George Carteret, once owned all of New Jersey, Berkeley Heights was settled by the 18th century (but not so named until 1952). After a railroad spur reached it in the 1870s, Berkeley Heights became popular as a resort and vacation area. Now a residential suburb, the township experienced a dramatic increase in population after World War II.

In 1910 the community of Free Acres, one of the few attempts in the United States to put into practice the single-tax ideas of Henry George, was founded in Berkeley Heights. (Nineteenth-century philosophical anarchism was also an element in the thinking of Bolton Hall, Free Acres' founder, who saw in the colony a chance to support his principles and perhaps realize something on his investment in land at the same time.) The roughly 90-acre community, which lies in the southwestern corner of Berkeley Heights (along Emerson La., between Apple Tree Rd. and Beachwood La.), began as a summer retreat for poor New York City intellectuals and artists and gradually evolved into a year-round community. Although it has had to bend some of its original principles to accommodate the demands of the township of Berkeley Heights, within the colony itself land is still held not by individuals but by the association, and problems involved in maintaining the roads, water system, public grounds, swimming pool, and the like are still resolved in open meetings at the 18th-century community farmhouse. James Cagney and MacKinlay Kantor are among the many well-known former residents of Free Acres.

Centered around Cataract Hollow Rd. within the Watchung Reservation (*see* Mountainside) is Feltville* (908-527-4900), an 1840s mill village, known as the Deserted Village. Intended as a model mill town by its founder, the mill village went through several changes of ownership and in the 1880s was transformed into a resort community known as Glenside Park. Now owned by the county, it is being restored to reflect its appearance as Glenside between 1882 and 1916, although it is still easy to imagine what the mill village would have looked like. Montclair State University has done extensive archaeological investigation of the site through summer field schools; fifth graders worked at the village each year in a program that taught them about archaeology both in the classroom and in the context of a site under investigation. The church store has been restored, and there are hopes that it will eventually function as a small museum. The site is included in Union County's annual Four Centuries in a Weekend, when you are free to wander about, on foot, on your own.

The Littell-Lord Farmhouse Museum* (31 Horseshoe Rd.; 908-464-3947, 908-771-8875), run by the Historical Society of Berkeley Heights, is located in a farmhouse whose earliest part dates to the mid-18th century (additions were made in the 19th and 20th centuries). The house is furnished to show what life was like in the 18th and 19th centuries. The farm occupies 18 acres, and on the property are several outbuildings, including a mid-19th-century springhouse and a Carpenter Gothic house, known as Grandmother's House, that served for a short time as a school. A period farm garden has been recently planted, and there are plans to restore the spring. Open May–October, the 3d Sunday of the month, 2–4; groups and other times by appointment. Note also the Erie Lackawanna railroad station (Plainfield and Springfield aves.), c. 1888, an outstanding example of Stick style. Off Springfield Ave. is the Passaic River County Park, where you can fish, picnic, and walk on the nature trail.

At the Lucent Technologies facility, once the Bell Telephone Laboratories (600 Mountain Ave., at South St.; 908-582-3275; the entrance is actually in New Providence), the transistor was developed and the *Telstar* satellite, launched in 1962, was built. The oldest building here dates from the 1940s and marks one of the first instances of a research laboratory moving to the suburbs. Close to 4,000 people work in this seven-building facility. In the lobby is an exhibit dealing with the history of Bell Labs, including the development of the transistor, the laser, and talking movies; the actual computer that was first declared a chess master; and some of the lab's Nobel-prize winners; some of the exhibits are interactive (but not intended for very young children). At the facility is an apple tree said to have been grafted from the tree in Newton's orchard, and copper from the building's roof was used to repair the Statue of Liberty. Open daily, all day.

Directly northeast of Berkeley Heights is New Providence, once known as Turkey. In the Saltbox Museum (1350 Springfield Ave.; 908-665-1034), run by the local historical society, two rooms are furnished to show how a bedroom, eating area, and living room would have looked in a simple late-18th-century house. Also in the house are changing exhibits of period clothes and artifacts. Open the 1st and 3d Sunday of the month, 2–4. The society's archives, containing many photographs, maps, and other material related to New Providence, as well as genealogical records, can be found in the Mason Room of the New Providence Municipal Library (377 Elkwood Ave., 908-665-1034). Open Tuesday, 10–12, and Thursday, 10–12 and 2–5).

Bernardsville Somerset 7,345

I 287, US 202, C 525

Although Bernardsville's population doubled between the 1930s and the '80s, the borough has not experienced the explosive growth of some of its neighbors in the Somerset Hills. Not only has it not allowed corporations to build within its borders, it has also decided to build low-cost housing itself rather than let a developer build a large project that would also include some mandated low-cost housing. For many years the town was known for its large estates and wealthy population.

The town is also known as the home of the Gill St. Bernard's independent school, of Meryl Streep, and of Millicent Fenwick. Fenwick, who entered Congress at the age of 64 and served as the model for Lacey Davenport in the comic strip "Doonesbury," began her political career on the local school board. Near the train station is a statue of her, said to be the only statue in the state to honor a female politician.

The borough offices are housed in an early 19th-century building that at various times functioned as a gristmill, a sawmill, a cider mill, and a distillery. The commercial building at 2 Morristown Rd. is one of Bernardsville's few remaining 18th-century structures and one of Somerset County's oldest buildings. Built as a farmhouse, it served as a tavern during the Revolution, and according to local legend is visited by the ghost of the tavern keeper's daughter, who went mad when her fiancé was hanged as a spy.

Not all of Bernardsville's old estates remain in private hands. The Scherman-Hoffman Wildlife Sanctuary (11 Hardscrabble Rd.; 908-766-5787), for example, a New Jersey Audubon facility, occupies 276 acres of streams, lush floodplains, hardwood and second-growth forests, and open meadows that were once private. The facility is involved in a wide array of educational programs and field trips for both adults and children. The imposing 1930s Hoffman house has been enlarged and has become the Hoffman Center for Conservation and Environmental Education. The new wing contains offices and classrooms, with an observation deck on the top floor. The exhibit room features, among other exhibits, a collection of porcelain birds. There are three miles of hiking trails in the sanctuary, a haven for diverse plants and wildlife; material for self-guided walks is available at the Hoffman center. (When the center is closed, consult the map at the Scherman parking lot.) Hour-long guided nature walks take place on Friday and Saturday mornings at 8. The office is open Tuesday–Saturday, 9–5, Sunday 12–5; the trails are open daily, 9–5. Groups by appointment. The Hoffman house can be difficult to get to when there is snow on the ground.

If you continue on Hardscrabble Rd. past the Audubon facility toward Jockey Hollow Rd., you will come to a sign for the New Jersey Brigade Area. Here you will find the Cross Estate Gardens (973-539-2016), once part of another of Bernardsville's estates, now within Morristown National Historical Park (*see* Morristown) and administered by the National Park Service and the New Jersey Historical Garden Foundation. The gardens include a formal walled garden, a native plant area, shade gardens, and much else. Open dawn–dusk. If you drive the other direction on Hardscrabble Rd. until you get to Childs Rd., you will reach the Franklin Corners Historic District,* with its 18th- and 19th-century buildings.

In the northwest corner of the township is Little Brook Sanctuary (take C 659, Claremont Rd., north out of town to Post La.; left on Post La.; left on Mountain Top Rd.; right on Clark Rd.; right on Stevens La.), a 100-acre natural area of woods, rolling meadows, and mountain streams belonging to the county park system. The area attracts a wide variety of wildlife, and there are hiking trails.

At 18 Claremont Rd. is the CWJ Classic Automobile Museum (203-221-7883), where you can see a collection of Cadillacs and LaSalles, as well as changing exhibits. Open weekends, 1–5 (except major holidays), weekdays by appointment.

Bevans   Sussex [Sandyston Township]

C 521, 615, 640

A rural crossroads village in the Kittatinny Mountains, Bevans is within the Delaware Water Gap National Recreation Area, and the home of the Peters Valley Craft Center (take C 521 west off US 206 toward Layton and Dingmans Ferry; turn left, or south, on the first road, C 615; 973-948-5200), a crafts community founded in 1970 as an unintended result of the Tocks Island project. The federal government, proposing a massive dam at Tocks Island in the Delaware River, had already bought the houses and evicted the tenants of several communities along the river before the project was stopped. Bevans was one of those communities. At Peters Valley artists in several crafts— among them pottery, woodworking, metalworking and smithing, weaving, and photography—live and work in the community year-round and (except in winter) teach classes open to the public. Among the facilities at Peters Valley is a traditional Japanese wood-fired Anagama kiln, which is fired every other year. (To watch a firing, call the office for the schedule.) The 19th-century Peters Valley historic district* includes an old cemetery, a Dutch Reform church, a Greek Revival house, farmhouses, and slate-roofed barns; several of the buildings are open to the public. A large, juried outdoor craft show is held at the Sussex County Fairgrounds (*see* Branchville) the last weekend in September. Gallery and store (201-948-5202) open daily, mid-May–mid-September, 11–5, but it is advisable to check before coming. You are welcome to wander around the village; to arrange for studio tours, call the office.

Also in Bevans is the popular Flatbrook-Roy Wildlife Management Area, over 2,000 acres of fields and uplands. The area attracts a wide variety of songbirds and migrating waterfowl and is an excellent place for hiking, fishing, bird-watching, horseback riding (by permit), and cross-country skiing. Big and Little Flat Brooks, both noted trout streams, run through the area, and at the office (on C 521 between Layton and Flatbrookville) you can see the Flatbrook Valley Clubhouse. This fishermen's club, one of the many that used to line the streams, was formed in 1893; by 1911 it owned 12 miles of stream, which it stocked from its own pond; in 1943 it was sold to the state.

Blackwood Camden 4,692

NJ 42, 168, C 534

Settled in the early 18th century, Blackwood is the site of Camden County College (College Dr.), founded in 1967. The college's concerts, theater programs, and lectures are open to the public. Exhibits in the art gallery (Lincoln Hall) include an annual student show. Call 856-227-7200, ext. 4364, for details.

Blackwood's historic district* includes over 100 buildings, dating from roughly 1830 to 1930, along Black Horse Pike, Baptist La., Church and Elm sts., and Central and East Railroad aves. Older buildings are also to be seen on Good Intent and Asayla rds. (including a 17th-century house at 500–502 Good Intent Rd.).

North of Blackwood in Glendora, also part of Gloucester Township, is the Gabreil Daveis Tavern* (Floodgate Rd.; 856-228-4000). This brick and stone tavern dates to 1756; for a time the township meetings were held there (Gloucester Township was incorporated in 1695). Open Sunday, 1–4, April–November. In July and August, concerts are given Thursday evenings; the house is also open then. Groups and other times by appointment.

East of Blackwood and north of Pine Hill (which not so long ago boasted a ski resort), in Clementon, is the Clementon Amusement and Splash World Water parks (144 Berlin Rd.; 856-783-0263), a 100-year-old amusement park with water rides, a wooden roller coaster, a carousel that has been in place since 1915 (although the wooden horses have been removed and replaced by fiberglass ones), and a showboat on the lake. Open daily most of July and all of August. For the limited May, June, August, and September hours, it is best to call. Admission charged.

Heading south out of Clementon on US 30 will bring you to Atco and Amalthea Cellars Farm Winery (209 Vineyard Rd.; 856-768-8585). Open for tastings weekends, 11–5.

Continuing on US 30 you will come to Berlin, formerly known as Long-a-Coming. Here you will find the Berlin Hotel (1822), once the oldest commercial structure on the White Horse Pike. In 2001 it was moved to

Berlin, where it now serves as an adjunct to the library, a community center, and a home for the Long-a-Coming Historical Society's exhibits (856-767-4147). The building retains its original trim and most of its original hardwood floors. Tours by appointment.

The railroad went through Berlin from Camden to Atlantic City and was known as the Gamblers' Express. The station* (Washington Ave. at the railroad; 856-767-4147), the oldest in the state, dates to 1856 and is used for community meetings. Buried in the Berlin cemetery (40 Clementon Rd.; 856-767-0206), which dates to 1766 and was a land grant from King George III, are veterans from every war the country has fought in as well as the country's first Eagle Scout. The Berlin Historic District* includes Washington, E. Taunton, and Haines aves. and parts of S. White Horse Pike, Jackson Rd., and Jefferson Ave.

In Pine Hill the Isaac Tomlinson House (Blackwood-Tomlinson Rd.; 856-783-7400) is being restored as a 19th-century Federal-style house, with plans to open it as a museum.

Blairstown Warren 5,747

NJ 94, C 521

Situated on the Paulins Kill, Blairstown is the site of Blair Academy* (2 Park St.; 908-362-6121), founded in 1848 by John I. Blair, who made a fortune from the Lackawanna Railroad and other ventures. It opened as a coeducational independent school, became all male in 1915, and in the 1970s became coeducational again. Its 300-acre campus, atop a hill, is impressive. Exhibits in the Romano Gallery (908-362-6121, ext. 5692) in the school's new performing arts center change roughly every month. The shows feature a wide variety of media and styles and usually represent the work of a single artist, and there is usually one show devoted to the Pahaquarry landscape artists. Open Monday–Friday, 10–4, Saturday, 10–1:30. Music, dance, and theater performances are also open to the public; call or visit the school's website for a schedule.

The downtown has several buildings of charm, among them the old Blair Waterworks (1889), now apartments for the school. Next door in a former bank building (1891) is the Ridge and Valley Conservancy (16 Main St.; 908-362-7989). The conservancy is dedicated to land preservation and sponsors various special events, including nature hikes and lectures, and arranges exhibits on the history and natural resources of the area in a variety of venues. Call for information. The office is open Tuesday–Friday, 10–2.

The Paulinskill Trail, which covers 26 miles on a former railbed, goes through Blairstown near the center of town. Twenty percent of the known species of birds in New Jersey have been spotted on this trail, and it is also a good place to watch for other wildlife. The state may open an equestrian center in an old stable near the trail.

West of the center of Blairstown is Raccoon Ridge, known as a spot for seeing hawks and, on clear days, the Poconos, Catskills, and Shawangunks. You can get to Raccoon Ridge by picking up the Appalachian Trail (*see* below).

Also west of Blairstown is the Yards Creek Pumped Storage Electric Generating Station (908-362-6163; south from Blairstown on NJ 94 c. 4 mi., right on Walnut Valley Rd. to the gates of the station; register here). At the center are a picnic area and a visitor center. The center contains an exhibit on the history of the Delaware; a model of the station, which pumps water to the upper reservoir and sends it down to create electricity for peak times (*see* Rockaway); and a film explaining how the station works. Open weekdays, 8–3, weekends, 8–7.

Worthington State Forest (Old Mine Rd. just off the last New Jersey exit from I 80; 908-841-9575) is a 6,400-acre tract that was once part of the Worthington estate. In 1912 the Worthington family built a terra-cotta pipeline down Mount Kittatinny to tap water from Sunfish Pond, a glacial pond (and a national natural landmark) that sits at 1,380 feet on the top of the mountain, surrounded by hardwood forest. The Douglas Trail to the pond honors U.S. Supreme Court Justice William O. Douglas, who helped in the campaign to save Sunfish Pond from being converted into a reservoir. A popular section of the Appalachian Trail goes through the forest, and there are opportunities for fishing, cross-country skiing, hunting, and (from April through December) camping. Dunnfield Creek, which descends 1,000 feet from Mount Tammany to the Delaware, is one of the few streams in New Jersey to support native brook trout. The 1,000 acres surrounding it are particularly lovely in mid-June when the mountain laurel are blooming. Trail maps are available at the ranger's station, itself an old house belonging to the Van Campen family, early settlers in this area.

Farther north on the Old Mine Road (c. 7 mi. north of I 80) are the Pahaquarry copper mines. It was once thought by some that these mines were worked in the mid-17th century; it is certain they were worked for a brief time in the mid-19th century, and for the last time in the early 20th. The single bar of ingot produced in the last attempt is in the New Jersey State Museum in Trenton. Be prepared for rugged trails in this area.

The Old Mine Road extended 104 miles from the mines to what is now Kingston, New York (it used to be known as Esopus). Some controversy surrounds the dating of the Old Mine Road, long believed to be the first commercial road of any extent in the colonies. (Parts of the road are no longer maintained and can be rough on a car.)

North of Blairstown in the Delaware Water Gap is the Appalachian Mountain Club's Mohican Outdoor Center (50 Camp Rd.; 908-362-5670). The center, situated near the Appalachian Trail on the shore of Catfish Pond, offers a variety of weekend programs throughout the year, which run from

CPR workshops to ski instruction to guided hikes. Office open daily, 9–5. If you pick up the Appalachian Trail at the center, you can hike two miles south and get to the hawk watch at Raccoon Ridge. Within the Delaware Water Gap National Recreation Area (*see* Walpack) you can hike, bike, swim, canoe, rock climb, bird-watch, cross-country ski, snowshoe, and ice-skate.

Bloomfield Essex 47,683

GARDEN STATE PKWY EXIT 148, C 506, 509

Bloomfield in the 18th century was a suburb of Newark. In 1794 some of its residents decided to form their own church and two years after that named the church in honor of Joseph Bloomfield, a Revolutionary War general who was later (1801–12) to become governor of the state. The town, established in 1812, took its name from the church.

The sandstone church, finished in 1797 but altered several times in the 19th century, is known as the First Presbyterian Church on the Green (Broad St., opposite Park Ave.). According to legend, the deacon moved the surveyor's stakes in the middle of the night to make the church larger. The green itself, thought to be New Jersey's largest, was a Revolutionary War parade ground purchased by the town and converted to a park. The Bloomfield Green historic district* encompasses Montgomery, Spruce, State, Liberty, and Franklin sts. and Belleville Ave. and includes buildings from the 18th to the 20th century. On the green, note the parish house (at Church St.), a brick and sandstone Greek Revival building (1840) of considerable charm; the manse (Park Pl. south of Monroe Pl.), a clapboard building dating from 1800; and Bloomfield College, another Presbyterian institution.

Founded in Newark in 1868 as the German Theological Seminary, what is now Bloomfield College moved to Bloomfield in 1872, growing over the years and becoming known as Bloomfield Theological Seminary, Bloomfield College and Seminary, and finally, in the 1960s, Bloomfield College (973-748-9000). The college has continued its tradition of serving diverse ethnic groups and has developed a nationwide reputation for its multicultural emphasis and programs. Note, on the green, the yellow brick Seibert building, the college's first, built in 1808 to house the Bloomfield Academy. The Robert V. Van Fossan Theatre, formerly a Presbyterian church dating to 1892, became part of the college in 1966. The theater offers film festivals, poetry readings, jazz concerts, and professional theater. The Westminster Arts Center, which was built in 1902 and retains its 75 original stained-glass windows, is part of the same Richardsonian-style complex. Exhibits in its gallery feature works in a variety of media by professional artists; shows change every four to six weeks. The gallery is open Monday–Friday, 10–4; and by appointment.

South of the green is the 12 Miles West Theatre Company and Performing Arts Center (562 Bloomfield Ave.; 973-259-9187). Built in 1913 on the site of a steam paper mill as a vaudeville house, the former Levin Theater has seen many changes in its appearance and function. It is being restored and converted into a performing arts center, which will host a variety of theatrical and musical events and provide an educational program. The company's first productions in its new space took place in 2005.

On the second floor of the library (90 Broad St.; 973-743-3765) is the museum of the Bloomfield Historical Society. This small museum contains memorabilia from Bloomfield's earlier years, including some examples of items manufactured in town. (The Peloubet-Pelton Organ Company and the Thomas Oakes Woolen Mills were both located in Bloomfield; the museum's Peloubet melodeon is said to be the only remaining example in the country.) Open Wednesday, 2–4, year-round; Saturday 10–12, October–May, but it is advisable to call ahead; other times by appointment.

The Oakes estate,* a 31-room Colonial Revival mansion built in 1895, is the last surviving Oakes building in town. It now serves as the home of the Oakeside-Bloomfield Cultural Center (240 Belleville Ave.; 973-429-0960), which offers lessons in the fine arts studio and presents a program of lectures, exhibitions, and concerts. Call for a schedule. Tours of the building may be arranged by appointment.

There are two county parks in Bloomfield, both designed by the noted Olmsted firm. To the north is Brookdale Park (Bellevue Ave.; 973-268-3500; go north on Broad St., C 509, to the intersection with Watchung; part of this park is located in Montclair), 121 acres with a playground, playing fields, tennis courts (some with lights), fitness and interpretive trails, and a rose garden. To the south is Watsessing Park (Glenwood Ave.; 973-268-3500; take Broad St. south to the intersection with Bloomfield Ave., when Broad St. becomes Glenwood; the park is shared with East Orange). This 70-acre park includes playgrounds and playing fields, a network of paths, and a lawn-bowling green.

Boonton Morris 8,496

I 287, US 202, C 511

Situated on a ledge overlooking the Rockaway River, Boonton was a prosperous iron town during much of the 19th century. What may have been the first rolling and slitting mill in the country operated in the 18th century at nearby Old Boonton (since the early 20th century displaced by the Jersey City reservoir), but Boonton's real prosperity developed after the building of the Morris Canal in the 1830s. For forty years Boonton was Othmar Ammann's home, and the George Washington Bridge was designed in Boonton.

The distinctive look of Boonton's downtown results from the combination of its location on a steep hill with the fact that it was once one of the most important iron centers in the country and did not decline completely after the iron industry went elsewhere (the first plant to manufacture Bakelite was in Boonton). The 19th-century historic district* encompasses Main, Church, Birch, Cornelia, and Cedar streets. Note particularly the public library* (1849; 619 Main St.); the Miller-Kingsland house* (c. 1740, 1808; 445 Vreeland Ave.); the railroad station* (1904; Myrtle Ave.), now converted to commercial use; and the two octagon houses on Cornelia Street. Note also the pre–World War I brick factories along Myrtle Ave. east of the station. Boonton has also preserved attractive older residential districts.

The Darress Theater (615 Main St.; 973-334-9292), built just after World War I as a vaudeville house, has been restored, and the auditorium is used for live theater, concerts (the community boasts a resident Baroque orchestra), and films. Upstairs is an art gallery and space that is also used for concerts. The late-19th-century John Taylor house (210 Main St.; 973-402-8840) has also been restored and serves as a local history museum. On display are the Boonton Historical Society's permanent exhibits of local artifacts, as well as temporary exhibits that change roughly four times a year. The society sponsors walking tours and other special events. Open Saturday, 1–4; other times by appointment.

In the township offices (155 Powerville Rd.; 973-402-4002) you can see a bust of James Doolittle, remembered for his flying exploits in World War II. Doolittle flew the world's first instrument-only flight out of Boonton (the equipment was manufactured by the local Radio Frequency Laboratories). Open weekdays, 9–5.

Continuing north along Powerville Road will bring you to the Oscar A. Kincaid Home of History★ (591 Powerville Rd.; 973-334-9563), run by the Historical Society of Boonton Township. The farmhouse, also known as the Decker-Miller house, is named for its last owner and former mayor. The first section dates from 1785, the rest from 1837. The society is working on restoring the house and converting it into a museum and community center. Remarkable in the 19th-century section is the image of a face that was worked into the plaster when Decker refused to pay the plasterer; the face has never been plastered over. Also on the property is the oldest continuously operating farmstand in the state. The house is open during society programs and by appointment. The society has also restored a pier used to support a mule bridge for the Morris Canal (the bridge can be seen in the town seal).

At the New Jersey Firemen's Museum (565 Lathrop Ave.; 973-334-0024), located in a home for the state's retired paid and volunteer fire fighters (said to be the only one of its kind in the country), you can see old equipment, memorabilia, and photographs. Open daily, 8–4; groups by appointment.

North of Boonton, in Montville (take Myrtle Ave., which becomes Main Rd., and turn left at Taylortown Rd.), is the Montville Historical Society's museum (6 Taylortown Rd.; 973-334-3665). The museum was built in 1867 as a schoolhouse and later housed a temperance hall, a post office, and the town offices. In the museum are a large collection of pitchers, historic photographs and furniture, and material on and models of the Morris Canal. There were three inclined planes in Montville, more than in any other town, and a change bridge (immortalized in Change Bridge Rd.). Open Sunday, 1–4 and by appointment. Another historical society building is

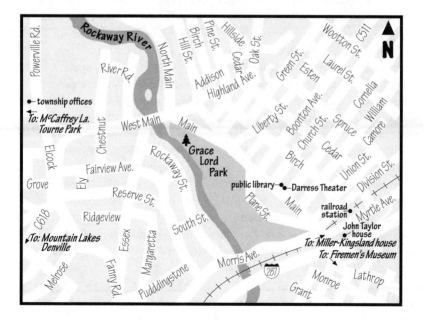

the 18th-century Doremus house (490 US 202, less than a half-mile from exit 47 off I 287; 973-334-3665). The earliest part of the house dates to 1762; additions were made in the late 1700s and early 1800s. Once the house is restored, it will function as a museum illustrating Dutch architecture and house construction.

A mile or two southwest of Boonton on C 618 is Mountain Lakes (population 3,847). The railroad station (Midvale Rd.) in this wealthy suburb, first built in 1912 and rebuilt in 1919 after a fire, is on land once owned by Hero Bull, a former slave; the cornerstone was laid by Belle de Rivera, a well-known suffragist. The station has been converted to a restaurant. Mountain Lakes was an early-20th-century planned community; its developer (who built the railroad station) dredged the swamps to create the lakes, and much of the land is parkland. Many of the bridges, walls, and chimneys were built of the colorful local stone, and if you drive in the area of Tower Hill, Sunset, and Lookout rds., you will see many Craftsman-style houses.

Just west of Mountain Lakes and Boonton is Tourne Park (Powerville and Old Denville rds.; 973-326-7600), 545 acres of county land with facilities for picnics (to reserve the picnic shelter call 973-326-7631), hiking (there is a glacial erratic to be seen, a wildflower trail with over 200 species of native plants, and a spectacular view from the top), off-road biking, horseback riding, cross-country skiing, and sledding. McCaffrey La., the main entrance to the park, was built in 1767 to haul iron to Old Boonton (cannonballs used by the Continental army during the Revolution were manufactured here).

Also west of Mountain Lakes (and south of Tourne Park), in Denville, is the Denville Historical Society Museum (Diamond Spring Rd.; 973-625-1165). Exhibits in the museum (a house built in 1834 and moved to its current site next to the library) usually change twice a year; past exhibits have ranged from World War II (Denville is not far from the Picatinny Arsenal; *see* Dover) to the history of Denville to the history of teapots. The society sponsors occasional lectures, a house tour in the fall, a holiday concert in December, and a flea market in the spring. Open Saturday, 10–4, and by appointment. The society also offers tours of the Second Union Schoolhouse in Union Hill, which dates to 1860, by appointment. Also on Diamond Spring Rd. is the New Jersey Foundation for the Blind's training and recreation center, established in 1942, which teaches the blind how to live independently.

South and east of the Denville museum is the Ayres-Knuth Farm* (25 Cooper Rd.; 973-625-9345), described as one of the most complete surviving examples of a 19th-century farm in the county. The early- to mid-19th-century farm buildings are being restored by the Ayres-Knuth Farm Foundation, which hopes to use the property as a focus for educational, historical, and environmental programs. Schoolchildren have been involved in archaeological investigations on the property, and the foundation hopes to bring more children in to share the archaeological experience. In the meantime it sponsors a popular annual fall festival with pony rides, other animals, a tractor show and tractor rides, and craft demonstrations; it also sponsors an annual Christmas-tree sale.

Bordentown Burlington 3,959

US 130, 206, C 528, 545

Situated on a bluff overlooking the Delaware River at the confluence of Crosswicks Creek and the Delaware, Bordentown was settled in 1682 by an English Quaker, Thomas Farnsworth, and was originally known as Farnsworth's Landing. It takes its current name from Joseph Borden, who arrived 35 years later, organized travel by stage and boat between New York and Philadelphia, and ended up owning most of the land in present-day Bordentown. A transportation center, Bordentown was for many years an important town, and the list of famous people connected with it is out of all proportion to its size. The historic district* (Farnsworth, Second, and Third aves.; Crosswicks, Prince, Walnut, Burlington, Park, and Spring sts.) takes up a large portion of the town, and despite the heavy loss of notable buildings through arson, an extraordinary amount of the past remains to be explored.

The first American to sculpt in wax, Patience Lovell Wright, grew up in Bordentown in the mid-1700s. After her husband's death, she supported herself doing what had begun as a hobby. In England during the Revolution, she served as a spy for the colonies. Her son Joseph, born in Bordentown, designed the first American coin. The Wright house is at 100 Farnsworth Avenue.

Francis Hopkinson, lawyer, poet, musician, political satirist, designer (he helped design the great seal of New Jersey and the American flag), composer (his "Ode to Music" is said to be the first piece written by someone born in America), member of the Continental Congress, and signer of the Declaration of Independence, married Ann Borden, the daughter of Joseph Borden, and lived at 101 Farnsworth Avenue. The mid-18th-century Hopkinson house* is a national historic landmark. Hopkinson's son Joseph wrote the words to "Hail, Columbia" and is buried in the Old Burial Ground (Church St. toward the river).

Thomas Paine, best known perhaps for the stirring pamphlets he wrote supporting the Revolutionary cause, lived at 2 W. Church Street. While in Bordentown he developed the single-span iron bridge and worked on other scientific projects. He lived longer in Bordentown than in any other place in North America, and this was the only place in this country in which he bought property. A monument honoring him, designed by Lawrence Holofcener, was unveiled in June 1997. At the foot of Prince St., not far from where Paine lived and worked, the site overlooks the property he owned and a bridge named in his honor. The Tom Paine Society sponsors walking tours the first Saturday of the month, April–November at 4. These leave from the corner of Farnsworth Ave. and Church (609-324-9909). A celebration of Paine's birthday takes place the last Saturday in January. The society's walking-tour brochures are available at local businesses and at Farnsworth House (135 Farnsworth Ave.).

Clara Barton, who was to found the Red Cross in 1881, opened one of the state's first free public schools in 1852. The schoolhouse stands at 142 Crosswicks Street. Tours by appointment (609-298-1740).

The former Friends Meeting House (302 Farnsworth Ave.; 609-298-1740) was built in 1740 on land donated by Joseph Borden. It now serves as the Bordentown Historical Society headquarters. The building has been restored to its mid-18th century appearance. It still has the original floor boards and many of the original benches; other benches from the same period come from a nearby meetinghouse. On the first floor are the society's history center and exhibition gallery. Exhibits change every few months. Open Saturday, 11–3 and by appointment. The historical society sponsors a variety of special events, including an annual garden tour in June and an annual holiday house tour (known as the holiday rout) in December.

The 18th-century Gilder house (Crosswicks St. opposite Union St.; 609-298-1740) was the birthplace of Richard Watson Gilder, editor of *Century Magazine*, and home to many of the other distinguished members of his family. Now the Gilder House Museum, it has been furnished with period pieces and artwork by the Bordentown Historical Society. An authentic early- to mid-18th-century kitchen is to be found downstairs, and upstairs are exhibits that change several times a year. The house has been closed for restoration, but is expected to reopen in late 2005. Gilder Field, behind the house, is a 15-acre municipal park with picnic facilities, which was built in the mid-1930s by the Works Progress Administration.

The John Bull, the country's first railroad engine, was shipped in parts from England and assembled in Bordentown, without instructions, by a man who had never seen one. A memorial to him is in the center of town (Farnsworth Ave. by the railroad tracks), and the River Line, the light rail line between Camden and Trenton, which began service in 2004, runs on the railbed used by the John Bull.

For some 18 years in the early part of the 19th century, Bordentown was the home of Joseph Bonaparte, former king of Naples and Spain and older brother of Napoleon. The only building from his day that remains on his estate at Point Breeze* (US 206 and Park St.), now occupied by a Catholic order, is the garden house, although some of the furnishings are preserved in the Gilder house, and Saint Mary's Roman Catholic Church (45 Crosswicks St.) has a Bonaparte chalice that is brought out on special occasions. The row houses at 47–53 Park St. were, however, once part of a girls' boarding school run by his nephew Prince Lucien Murat and Murat's wife, the former Caroline Frazer of Bordentown. At the end of Park St. the Bordentown Garden Club maintains a formal garden appropriate to Napoleon's time.

Since the buildings mentioned here represent only a fraction of what Bordentown has to offer, you might wish to buy a copy of the Bordentown walking tour, available at City Hall (324 Farnsworth Ave.) and at various stores throughout the historic district. In the tower of Old City Hall (11 Crosswicks St.), an 1888 building that once housed the police and fire departments and the courtroom, is a Seth Thomas clock dedicated to William F. Allen (1846–1915), the designer of standard time, who was born in Bordentown.

At the end of Farnsworth Ave. you can walk along the bluff; at the end of Prince St. you can go down to the river, where there is another small municipal park with picnic facilities. Some days you may notice the smell of cranberries from the Ocean Spray bottling plant (the company's largest), warehouse, and distribution center at the edge of town.

South of Bordentown City but within the township is the former Bordentown School (Burlington St.), founded in 1886 as the New Jersey Manual Training Center for Colored Youth* and for a time the only publicly funded secondary boarding school for African Americans in the northern United States. Established six years after Booker T. Washington's Tuskegee, the school moved to this location in 1902 and at one time had 30 buildings on over 400 acres. A leading educational facility for African Americans in the first half of the century, it was often referred to as the Tuskegee of the North. A memorial to the facility, which is used today by the State Juvenile Justice Commission, was erected in 2003.

Branchville Sussex 845

US 206, C 519

Unlike some other Sussex County communities, the tiny borough of Branchville, situated near some of the state's most beautiful scenery, grew less than 28 percent between 1930 and 1990 and actually decreased in population in 2000. At the Garris Center (Broad St.; 973-948-4631) the Culver Brook Restoration Foundation has several turn-of-the-20th-century buildings, including an ice cream parlor where historic pictures of the area are on display. In a former livery stable is a small (56-seat) theater, where the Little Lost Arts company mounts productions and offers educational programs for children. Also in the center is a blacksmith's shop; there are hopes that demonstrations and educational programs will be given there soon. Open by appointment.

About a mile west of Branchville is the Bear Swamp Wildlife Management Area (C 521, 630, and 633; 973-383-0918), 2,000 acres where you can hike, cross-country ski, mountain-bike, fish, bird-watch, and hunt. Continuing west, you will reach Stokes State Forest (US 206, C 519; 973-948-3820), one of six nearly contiguous undeveloped public areas in the western part of Sussex County. The state began purchasing land for this reserve in 1907, buying over 5,000 acres, some of it for a dollar an acre. The forest, which covers close to 16,000 acres now, is named in honor of Governor Edward Stokes, who donated the first 500 acres. Much of the original hardwood forest was burned to feed the iron industry and to clear land for farming, but between 1919 and 1942 the state and the Civilian Conservation Corps (CCC) planted more than 650,000 trees.

Located within Stokes at the site of one of the largest CCC camps in the country is the New Jersey School of Conservation (1 Wapalanne Rd.; 973-655-7614; 800-624-7780). Here the CCC built barracks, developed the forest's trail network, and created a lake by damming a stream. Since 1949 there has been an environmental program at the site, and today Montclair State University administers a residential environmental-education field center, which brings close to 10,000 students and teachers a year to the forest. Programs last from one to four days, with most students enrolled in the three-day, two-night programs. Participants study not just environmental issues, but the reasons they become issues, as well as techniques for achieving successful outcomes.

Within Stokes State Forest is a large variety of forest types, of plant and animal life, and of recreational possibilities. The extensive trail network allows many sorts of hiking, from a stroll to something more strenuous. Tillman's Ravine is a particularly picturesque 500-acre natural area with interesting rock formations and a hemlock forest that has not been cut in more than 100 years. Some of its hemlocks are 150 years old, and the density of the woods so cools the ravine that warblers nest there, unusual this far south. The Tinsley Trail has a geological area where the record of the last glacier can be read in the rock formations. From Sunrise Mountain there is a spectacular view out over the New Jersey Highlands and the Poconos, and hawks often appear at eye level. (This is a prime site for viewing hawks during the fall migration.) There are bubbling springs, and beavers are active in the streams. The Appalachian Trail goes through Stokes, and dog-sled racing began here in the winter of 1985–86. Camping and picnic facilities are available. Adjacent to Stokes are two wildlife management areas, Hainesville (*see* Montague) and Flatbrook-Roy (*see* Bevans).

About a mile east of Branchville on US 206 (turn left at Plains Rd. in Augusta) are the fairgrounds for the Sussex County Farm and Horse Show, founded in 1940 and now known as the New Jersey State Fair (37 Plains Rd.; 973-948-5500). This 10-day August event generally draws some 200,000 visitors. Although there is a midway, the fair's mission is to showcase agriculture, so the emphasis is on the agricultural exhibits and contests.

Also on Plains Rd. is the Frankford Plains Octagon Schoolhouse (99 Plains Rd.; 973-702-0334). Apparently the only wooden octagonal schoolhouse in New Jersey, it was built c. 1850 and used until 1924, when the county closed the one-room schools and regionalized the school system. The building, which deteriorated badly, has been restored, and some of the original elements remain. It is being used as a church office, but tours by appointment are possible.

If you continue south to C 565 (about a half-mile south of Plains Rd.), you will arrive at Skylands Park (94 Champion Pl.; 973-579-7500), once the home park for the minor-league New Jersey Cardinals. The park also features batting cages and a miniature golf course. Open 9–5 daily.

If you continue south to NJ 94 (when 206 intersects NJ 15, stay straight on NJ 15), and turn left (north) on 94, in about three miles you will come to the Old Monroe Schoolhouse* (973-663-0075), which dates back to at least 1819. This restored one-room building is a rare example of a hand-hewn-stone schoolhouse. The museum's educational program includes holding classes for visiting school groups in the schoolroom, using *McGuffey Readers*, slates, slate pencils, and the like. There are picnic facilities on the grounds. Open May–October, 1st Sunday of the month, 1–4; groups by appointment.

On your way to the Old Monroe Schoolhouse you will pass through Lafayette, settled in the late 18th century and said to be the first community in the United States to be named for the marquis de Lafayette, who fought on the side of the colonies in the Revolution. Note the mill complex just off NJ 15 (12 Morris Farm Rd.; 973-383-0065); the mill dates to the 1840s. Within the complex are a general store, a restored carriage house, and many shops, all in buildings of a certain age. Open Thursday–Monday, 10–5. The Lafayette Center Preservation Foundation (115 NJ 15; 973-383-5801) has taken over the former municipal building, an early-19th-century clapboard building that was once part of the mill complex. After it is restored, the foundation intends to use it for a local-history museum. The foundation sponsors an annual flea market in September and maintains the cemetery (NJ 15 south of the town hall), which contains some 18th-century headstones.

About a mile and a half south of Branchville (take 519 to C 655 and turn left) is the Homestead Complex, a group of county buildings built on the site of an old farm. In the 1830s the farmhouse, with a stone addition, became the county almshouse, and another addition was made when the building was converted to a convalescent home in the 1950s. It now houses a county nursing home.

Bridgeton Cumberland 22,771

NJ 49, 77, C 552

Bridgeton, which celebrated its 300th birthday in 1986, was first settled in 1686 when Richard Hancock built a sawmill at the head of the Cohansey River. The community grew considerably when the river was bridged in 1716 (at which point its name changed to Cohansey Bridge), becoming the county seat in 1749. In the mid-1760s it became known as Bridge Town and finally (because a bank printed the wrong name on its letterhead), in 1816, as Bridgeton. A raceway was dug in 1814, and the Cumberland Nail and Iron Company became Bridgeton's largest industry until it closed in the 1890s. More recently, Bridgeton was a center for food processing and glass manufacturing. Although these industries are no longer active in Bridgeton, other industries have moved in, and there are plans to revitalize the Cohansey as a low-cost shipping lane. Bridgeton is also faring well as a tourist center. Its symphony orchestra performs regularly at the performing arts centers in Vineland and Pomona.

When the Cumberland Nail Company folded, the city bought its property, an unusual move for 1903, and created the City of Bridgeton Park (856-455-3230). The park's 1,200 wooded acres (one-sixth of Bridgeton's area) contain a lake; an amphitheater; picnic, swimming, and boating areas (the raceway is used by canoeists); sports facilities; nature trails; and the Cohanzick Zoo (856-455-3230, ext. 242), said to be the oldest and largest municipal zoo in New Jersey. It is also a popular attraction, drawing as many as 100,000 visitors a year. Among other attractions is the zoo's unusual outdoor walk-through aviary. Summer weekends are known as Wild Weekends; zoo personnel are available throughout the park to interpret the exhibits and explain the habits of the various animals. The zoo is also involved in educational programs, both on- and off-site. Open daily (except Christmas Day), 9–5 during daylight savings time, 9–4 during standard time.

Added to the park in 1988 as part of the celebration of the 350th anniversary of the New Sweden colony in America is the New Sweden Farmstead Museum (856-455-9785). The farmstead is a faithful re-creation (built mostly by hand) of the 17th-century farmsteads the Swedish-Finnish settlers erected in what became southern New Jersey. The buildings, which include barns, a blacksmith shop, a bathhouse and smokehouse, and a stable, are furnished with artifacts dating to the 17th century. Open mid-May–Labor Day, Saturday 11–5, Sunday 12–5; groups and other times by appointment year-round. Admission charged.

Also in the park is the Nail House Museum (1 Mayor Aitken Dr.; 856-455-4100). This small museum, in what was formerly the office of the Cumberland Nail and Iron Works (1815), features memorabilia from the nail industry, pottery, glasswork, lanterns, and South Jersey's oldest public clock. Open Tuesday–Saturday, 10:30–3:30. Next to the museum is Dame Howell's School (c. 1830), an example of an early dame's school, which was moved to the park in the 1970s.

Bridgeton's historic district★ is New Jersey's largest: its 2,200 Colonial, Federal, and Victorian buildings make up one-third of the town's structures. Particularly noteworthy is Potter's Tavern★ (49–51 W. Broad St.; 856-451-8454), a small, pre-1767 clapboard tavern, which has been restored and furnished as an 18th-century tavern. Here New Jersey's first newspaper, the *Plain Dealer*, a wall sheet, was published weekly between Christmas Day 1775 and March 1776. Open by appointment.

The Old Broad Street Presbyterian Church★ (W. Broad and Lawrence sts.; 856-455-0809), built in the meetinghouse style out of bricks fired on the site on land donated by a Quaker, was begun in 1792. When the builders ran out of money, the state legislature authorized a lottery to provide the necessary funds. The church, open for services in August and the first week of September and for various special events, has two Atsion stoves with their original cast-iron flue pipes in place, made in New Jersey c. 1815, and the whale-oil lamps added as an amenity in the early 19th century, as well as the original collection poles, which are still used.

The George Woodruff Indian Museum (150 E. Commerce St.; 856-451-2620), in the Bridgeton Free Public Library, features artifacts relating to the Lenape, all collected within a 30-mile radius of the library. Open Monday–Friday, 1–4; guided tours Saturday, 11–2. The library's 1816 building originally housed the bank whose mistake on its letterhead led to Bridge Town becoming Bridgeton.

In the county courthouse (Broad and Fayette sts.) is Cumberland County's own liberty bell, cast in 1763 and rung to announce the Declaration of Independence. The town is also proud of its Hall of Fame (Burt Ave.; 856-451-7300), located in the 55-acre Bridgeton Recreation Area across from Alden Field. The museum features local (and other) sports heroes; in the collection, for example, is one of Jackie Robinson's bats. Open Tuesday–Saturday, 10–12, 1–3. Other noteworthy buildings include St. Andrew's Church (1864; 186 E. Commerce St.); the Buck house* (297 E. Commerce St.), built for Jeremiah Buck, a mill owner, in 1808; and the Giles house* (143 W. Broad St.), built in 1791 by one of George Washington's generals, perhaps visited by Lafayette, and now used for commercial purposes. What now serves as the administration building for the school system (Bank St.) was built as the city's first public school (1847).

Perhaps the best way to see Bridgeton is to start at the information center, housed in the former railroad station (early 1900s) at the junction of NJ 49 and 77 (856-455-3230, ext. 264). You can pick up a free walking-tour map and rent an audio cassette for your walk. Open weekdays, 9–4, year-round; weekends, 10–4, May–Labor Day; closed major holidays. Many special events take place along the riverfront promenade, particularly in summer.

Some three miles south of Bridgeton (take 553 or Clarks Pond Rd.) is Clarks Pond Wildlife Management Area, 78 acres with three ponds where you can fish. About four miles northwest of Clarks Pond is Dix Wildlife Management Area with about 2,600 acres. Some three-quarters is marshland, but the rest is divided between hardwood forests and farmland. This is a good spot to view fall foliage, and you can also fish, hike, and hunt.

A few miles north of Bridgeton (take NJ 77) you will come upon the community of Seabrook, once the heart of an agricultural enterprise that for a time was the largest in the state, renowned for its introduction of industrial methods to farming. C. F. Seabrook, referred to by one of his sons as the Henry Ford of agriculture, experimented with overhead irrigation, mechanization, time clocks for farm workers, and cold storage, and dominated the frozen-foods-for-household market—in the 1950s about 2 million packages of frozen vegetables were produced daily. Faced with a labor shortage in World War II, Seabrook brought interned Japanese Americans to live and work on the farm; after the war the farm offered housing and jobs to refugees from the displaced-persons camps in Europe; and many other ethnic groups were part of this community. The Seabrook Educational and Cultural Center, housed on the lower floor of the Upper Deerfield Township Municipal Building (NJ 77; 856-451-8393), tries to preserve something of Seabrook Farms' extraordinary past. The center collects oral histories as well as published materials, and has on display artifacts, photographs, and a large diorama of the village in its heyday. Open Monday–Thursday, 9–2. Each mid-July the Seabrook Buddhist temple (11 Northville Rd., C 711; 856-451-6367) sponsors the traditional Japanese Obon Festival, which draws visitors from all over the East Coast.

Bridgewater Somerset 42,940

I 287, US 22, 202, 206, NJ 28, C 525, 616, 620

Although for many, the name Bridgewater Township brings to mind the Somerville traffic circle or the Bridgewater Commons mall, this formerly agricultural area appears in some of the earliest records of land transactions in New Jersey. Washington's troops spent the winter of 1778–79 here at what is now called the Middlebrook Encampment* (Mountain Ave., C 527); Washington reported to the marquis de Lafayette that they were "in a more agreeable and fertile country than they were last winter at Valley Forge." By special act of Congress, the Betsy Ross flag is flown here 24 hours a day.

During the encampment the Van Veghten house* (Van Veghten Rd.; 908-218-1281), then a working farm, served as headquarters for Nathaniel Greene, Washington's quartermaster general. The earliest section of the house dates to 1720; it was renovated in the mid-19th century. Today it serves as the library for the Somerset County Historical Society. The society also holds an annual open house the 1st Sunday in December, at which time it displays items of historical interest from various local collections. Open Tuesday, 12–3, and the 2d Saturday of the month, 12–4, April–November. The Vosseller-Castner-Allen Tavern (664 Foothill Rd.), c. 1753, functioned as a store in the 18th century, a tavern and stagecoach stop in the 19th, and a farm and residence in the 20th and 21st.

The Van Horne house* (941 E. Main; 732-356-8856), built in the 1750s, serves as headquarters for the Heritage Trail Association, an organization created to "celebrate and preserve" the community's history. The association sponsors a variety of events, including walking and bus tours, an annual storytelling festival, and a celebration of the Battle of Bound Brook, and sells a booklet for self-driving tours. Temporarily in the Van Horne house are exhibits from the U.S. Bicycling Hall of Fame (*see* Somerville). Open by appointment.

West of the encampment is Washington Valley Park (take Vosseller Ave., a road that appears on a mid-18th-century map, to Miller La.; 908-766-2489), an undeveloped 700-acre preserve with a reservoir, woodlands, and fields. From the Miller La. parking area you can get to the Washington Park Hawk Watch Area (once known as Chimney Rock Overlook); during the spring and fall migrations this is an excellent place to view hawks (and other birds). Unimproved trails wind through the area, and you can also park farther west off Newman's Lane.

Farther west in the township is the Green Knoll golf course (587 Garretson Rd.; 908-722-1301) and tennis center (908-722-1303). Golf course and courts open daily; pro shop hours are more limited.

In the southwestern corner of the township is Duke Island Park (C 567, the Old York Rd.; 908-722-7779), one of the county's first parks. Its 300-plus acres are divided by the Raritan Water Power canal. The park includes playgrounds and playing fields; a trail along the water; bicycle trails; and facilities for family and group picnics, fishing, and ice-skating. Concerts are given in the amphitheater in the summer. At the visitor center you can pick up park brochures and maps.

North of Duke Island Park (take Milltown Rd. off C 567, crossing US 202) is North Branch Park (908-722-1200), another county facility with frontage on the river (part of the park is in Branchburg Township). The county fairgrounds are here—the county 4-H fair has been going for close to 60 years and draws over 60,000 people each summer. This is a popular spot for fishing, and there are picnic groves, a playground, and a softball field.

West of North Branch Park in Branchburg Township (take 202 south to Old York Rd., C 637; the house is just west of the intersection), the Branchburg Historical Society is restoring the Andrew Ten Eyck house* (671 Old York Rd.; 908-722-2124; 908-369-2927), built in 1790 by a Revolutionary War veteran and a stop on the Swift-Sure Stagecoach line. The house will eventually function as a museum; for now the library is open for research by appointment.

Also in Branchburg, the only town by that name in the country, is the Little Red Schoolhouse* (S. Branch Rd. opposite Studdiford Dr.), said to have been the last one-room schoolhouse operating in the state. It was built in 1873, closed in the 1950s, renovated in the '60s, and used for one year by the board of education before it was closed again in 1965. Its belfry, removed in the 1940s, has been restored and reinstalled by the historical society. The building is used for community functions.

If after leaving the Ten Eyck house you continue west on the Old York Road but stay straight when it turns south and remain on Dreahook Rd., you will come into Readington (Hunterdon County) and the Solberg Airport (Solberg Rd.; 908-534-4000). Named for and founded by the first man to fly from the United States to Norway, the airport hosts an extremely popular three-day balloon festival the last weekend in July, with as many as 125 balloons, some of them over 13 stories high (973-882-5464).

Brigantine Atlantic 12,594

NJ 87

Built on a barrier beach reachable by car only from Atlantic City, Brigantine started as a real estate speculation in the 1920s. A hotel and some 100 houses were built before the crash put an end to the development. Population growth took off after World War II; the opening of the Atlantic City casinos intensified that growth, and the population, half of which lives on the island year-round, has almost tripled since the 1960s. You can see some of the 1920s flavor in the former Brigantine Inn (1400 Ocean Ave.) or in the Byzantine-looking church (1927) on 8th St. S.

At 3625 Brigantine Blvd. is the Marine Mammal Stranding Center (609-266-0538), a rehabilitation center devoted to rescuing stranded or injured whales, dolphins, porpoises, and turtles and making it possible for them to return to the sea. Founded in the late 1970s and operated by the only person in New Jersey (and one of only 11 in the Northeast) licensed to work on marine animals, the center has a remarkable success rate with the animals it rescues (its release rate is close to 90%). It has also been successfully experimenting with solar panels (it has even sold power on occasion) and has installed a special wood and plastic deck. In the center's marine-life museum are fiberglass casts of various species, a perils-of-pollution exhibit, and, in summer, a tank containing local marine life. In the summer the museum is open Tuesday–Sunday, 10–4; in the winter the hours vary, but it is a good idea to call ahead, winter or summer—a mass stranding can empty the facility and close the museum. Groups by appointment.

Next door to the stranding center is the Brigantine Beach Historical Museum (3607 Brigantine Blvd; 609-266-9339). On display are photographs and memorabilia from the town's past, including material relating to the pirates who were once important in the area. Open Memorial Day–4 July and Labor Day–30 September, Saturday, 10–1, Sunday, 1–4; 5 July–Labor Day, Monday–Saturday, 10–1, Sunday, 1–4.

For beach information (Memorial Day–Labor Day), call 609-266-1122.

Burlington Burlington 9,736

"The identifying mark of BURLINGTON (20 alt., 10,844 pop.) is the single track of the Pennsylvania Railroad that runs through the center of the main street without benefit of curb or fence. In many other respects Burlington seems to have changed little from its eighteenth century character as capital of the Province of West New Jersey." These sentences were written over 65 years ago when the great WPA guide to New Jersey was published. Amazingly, both are still accurate. It is indeed startling to see the tracks in the middle of the city (and trains can tie up traffic, even if they no longer belong to the Pennsylvania Railroad), yet much of Burlington, with its wide streets and heavy use of red brick, has the particular aura of an 18th-century southern New Jersey town.

Settled in 1677 by Quakers from Yorkshire and London (who divided the area so that the Yorkshiremen lived east of High St. and the Londoners west of it), Burlington became the capital of the Province of West New Jersey in 1681, and when West and East Jersey were joined in 1702, shared the honor of being capital with Perth Amboy. A pottery joined the sawmill and gristmill in the 1680s, other industries followed, and by the 1740s Burlington's port ranked with those of New York, Philadelphia, and Boston. Although the port is no longer active and Burlington went through a period of stagnation common to many eastern cities, it now shows the positive effects of an active redevelopment program.

On W. Broad St. in the small brick Proprietors Office many old documents relating to early transactions in West Jersey are stored, including the original Concessions and Agreements, signed by the Proprietors in England in 1676. The Council of Proprietors has met in Burlington in mid-April each year since 1688, usually on the sidewalk at Broad and High. A plaque on the side of the bank marks the spot.

Burlington can claim a large number of firsts, among them the oldest educational trust in the country. Burlington Island (Matinicunck Island when the Swedes established a trading post on it in 1624) was given to the town in 1682 with the stipulation that the revenue be used for the schools. The country's first scheduled public transportation began here, when regular stagecoach service between Burlington and Perth Amboy was initiated in 1733 (there had, of course, been irregular stages between the two cities long before). Although its current sandstone building dates from 1864, the Library Company of Burlington (23 W. Union St.; 609-386-1273), chartered in 1757, is the oldest continuously operating library company in New Jersey (Trenton's was founded in 1750 but discontinued operation for many years). It was also the first library in the country to publish its own catalogue. Now a public library, it displays some of its collection of rare books and other artifacts.

You can also see its original 19th-century shelving. The second floor, recently restored, is used once a year for a public exhibition. Open Monday, Tuesday, Thursday, 2–8; Wednesday, 11–8; Saturday, 10–3 (closed Saturday, July and August).

Burlington can also claim many famous citizens. Captain James Lawrence of "Don't give up the ship" fame (his words as he was dying in a battle in the War of 1812; his men were unable to carry out his command) was born in 1781 at 459 High St.* (c. 1696; front portion added c. 1750). His house has become a historic-house museum, run by the Burlington County Historical Society (609-386-4773). On display here is material relating to Lawrence and the War of 1812, as well as a changing costume exhibit.

James Fenimore Cooper, the novelist, was born next door* (c. 1780; 457 High St.) in 1789. Although Cooper did not spend much time in Burlington (the family left for upstate New York shortly after his first birthday but returned occasionally when the father was serving in Congress in Philadelphia), his house is also a museum run by the historical society. Here you can see artifacts relating to Cooper, as well as some that belonged to Joseph Bonaparte (see Bordentown). The society also operates as a museum the Bard-How House* (c. 1743; 453 High St.), decorated to show how an 18th-century Quaker tradesman would have lived, and the Corson

BURLINGTON

Poley Center (454 Lawrence St., behind the Cooper House). The center contains the society's library and exhibition space; here you can see, for example, quilts, tall case clocks, and samplers, as well as exhibits highlighting what was crafted and manufactured in the area. All the society's museums are open Tuesday–Saturday, 1–5. The society arranges bus and walking tours year-round and has an audio cassette available (for tours call 609-386-3993).

The cast-iron plow was developed (in 1797) by a Burlington resident, Charles Newbold. In the 1830s, during the silkworm mania that afflicted much of New Jersey and other eastern states, Burlington planted what was probably more mulberry trees (over 300,000 of them) than any other city and in 1838 built a cocoonery. (A cold spring the next year killed thousands of trees, and the mania.) James H. Birch, known as the wagonmaker to the world, began business in Burlington in 1862 on Broad and Liberty streets. His 15-acre plant closed after World War I, but while he was in business, he manufactured some 200 models, shipping out 10,000 carriages in a good year, and even exporting jinrikishas to the Far East.

Ulysses S. Grant had a house here (c. 1813; 309 Wood St.) and may have been on his way to Burlington when he learned the news of Lincoln's assassination. His daughter went to St. Mary's Hall–Doane Academy (south side of Delaware St. at Ellis), an Episcopal girls' school founded in 1837. Now usually referred to simply as St. Mary's Hall, it has become a coeducational school. (Its Gothic Revival Chapel of the Holy Innocents, 1845–47, was designed by John Notman.) The Edward Shippen family of Philadelphia had a summer home along the Delaware (c. 1756; Talbot St. at the river). Peggy Shippen, who spent summers here and also visited her uncles in Oxford (*see* Oxford) but apparently didn't like New Jersey, married Benedict Arnold and seems to have had a good deal to do with his eventual betrayal of his country.

Burlington can also claim some interesting churches. Old St. Mary's Episcopal Church* (southwest corner of Wood and W. Broad sts.), a brick church dating to 1703, is one of the oldest church structures in the state. The new St. Mary's (1854) was built from a design of Richard Upjohn, the architect of Trinity Church in New York City. It still uses a silver communion service presented to the congregation by Queen Anne. The two churches and the cemetery between them form a national historic landmark. The Friends Meeting House (west side of High St., near Broad) was built in 1783 to replace one built a century earlier, which the congregation had outgrown. Now a religious retreat and teaching center, it still retains much of its original hardware and many of the original window-panes. The Native American king Ockanickon was buried behind the meetinghouse in 1681; a stone commemorating him is under an ancient sycamore tree.

On Wood St. is the Revell house (1685), probably the oldest house in the county. Benjamin Franklin told the story of a kindly woman in the Revell house who gave him gingerbread one day when he missed his ferry back to Philadelphia and of how he wandered about Burlington with the piece of gingerbread in his hand. At the annual Wood St. fair each fall, gingerbread is sold to commemorate the event. On the northeast corner of Broad and York sts. is another house with a connection to Franklin—the Collins-Jones House (c. 1750). Isaac Collins produced the state's first modern newspaper, the *New Jersey Gazette* (1777–86), printing it at the same shop Ben Franklin had earlier used to print the country's first currency.

The city maintains a promenade along the Delaware the length of the city. Another waterfront site to note (in addition to St. Mary's Hall and the Shippen house) is the Grubb estate (Grubb was a Civil War general and ambassador to Spain; the house dates to 1850).

Burlington's 18th- and 19th-century historic district* includes W. Delaware, Wood, and Broad sts., and there are many other buildings of interest not mentioned here. Elias Boudinot, for example, lived on Broad St. when he was superintendent of the mint in Philadelphia; in a 1730s building is a drugstore that's been there for over 100 years and may well be the oldest continuously operating drugstore in the state; at York and Penn sts. is the

Quaker School, which dates from 1792 and has been furnished to reflect a schoolroom of that period (tours by appointment; call 609-386-3993).

West of Burlington in Edgewater Park (take 130 west and turn right, or north, on C 630, or Cooper St.) is the Whitebriar farmhouse (1029 Cooper St.; 609-871-3859), part of which dates from 1739, the rest from 1886. Tours (for groups, by appointment only) vary with the season but can include demonstrations of colonial crafts. Admission charge. Also on the street is a house that was part of the Underground Railroad and one in which Woodrow Wilson lived. Also in Edgewater Park is the Red Dragon Canoe Club* (221 Edgewater Ave.; 609-387-9847), the oldest canoe club remaining on the Delaware. The club is housed in a pre–Civil War mansard-style building used as a summer home; the club has been there since the mid-1920s.

If you take 130 west and turn left, or south, on Charleston Rd. you reach the township of Willingboro. For five years (1958–63) Willingboro was known as Levittown, after the post–World War II builder who achieved international fame by building large subdivisions of similar, reasonably priced houses. Each September the town holds a jazz festival at Millcreek Park (Beverly-Rancocas Rd.; 609-871-5700).

Caldwell Essex 7,584

C 508, 527

Situated along the Watchung Mountains, Caldwell was named for the Reverend James Caldwell of "Give 'em Watts, boys" fame (*see* Springfield), who was involved in organizing the Presbyterian congregation in 1779 (the settlement was then known as Horse Neck). Grover Cleveland, the only president of the United States to be born in New Jersey and the only one to serve two nonconsecutive terms, is probably Caldwell's most famous native son. His birthplace* (207 Bloomfield Ave.; 973-226-0001), a clapboard house dating from 1832 that once served as the Presbyterian manse, has been operated as a memorial since 1913 (Cleveland died in 1908 and is buried in Princeton). The kitchen, rear parlor, and the room Cleveland was born in have been furnished to reflect the years of his childhood, 1834–53. The gallery in the front parlor contains artifacts related to his public life from the time he was 18 until he retired, and the gallery in the foyer contains artifacts from his private life. The house contains the largest collection of Cleveland artifacts in the country. Among the many personal belongings on display are his wooden cradle, the desk he used when he was a lawyer in Buffalo, his fishing gear, a chair he used in the White House, and a piece of his wedding cake. Visiting children will find 1830s costumes to try on and 1830s games to play with. Open Wednesday–Saturday, 10–12 and 1–4; Sunday, 1–4. Reservations recommended; group tours by appointment.

Caldwell College (Ryerson Ave.; 973-618-3000), founded in 1939 as a college for women, became coeducational in 1986 and in recent years has experienced one of the highest growth rates of any college in the state. Exhibits in the Visceglia Art Gallery change three to four times a year and feature national and regional artists representing a wide range of contemporary art, including design, new media, and photography. The gallery (973-618-3457) is open weekdays, 9–5. Concerts are also open to the public (call 973-618-3520 for information). While on campus note the stained-glass windows in the chapel and library; they were created by the former head of the art department.

Camden   Camden 79,904

I 76, 676, US 30, 130, NJ 70, C 537, 543, 551

When Camden was first settled, it functioned as a satellite of Philadelphia, and Philadelphia continued to dominate it until the coming of the Camden and Amboy Railroad in 1834. Camden was settled by Quakers, the first of whom was probably William Cooper who in 1681 built a house on Pyne Poynt. Cooper ran the ferry to Philadelphia, and as late as the mid-19th century, ferrying goods and people to Philadelphia was still the town's primary industry. The settlement was long known as Cooper's Ferry despite the fact that it had been renamed to honor the earl of Camden, friend of the colonies. (The name Camden was first used unofficially in 1773 as part of a real estate venture; it became official in 1828.) A few of the houses of William Cooper's descendants remain: Pomona Hall, for example (discussed below); the Benjamin Cooper house (1734; Erie and Point sts.), which served as headquarters for the commander of the British and Hessian outpost during the occupation of Philadelphia and has recently served as the offices of maritime-related companies; the ruins of the Joseph Cooper Jr. house* (c. 1695; Erie and 7th sts. in Pyne Poynt Park); and the Samuel Cooper house (1790; 1104 N. 22d St.).

Camden has been the seat of Camden County since the 1840s, although there was a long gap between the formation of the county in 1844 and the building of the first courthouse in 1853, caused by irregularities in the voting on where to place the county seat. Its courthouse (Market and 6th sts.), which houses both city and county offices, dates from 1931 and is one of the tallest in the state. The Benjamin Franklin Bridge, painted a grayish shade of blue and illuminated at night, was the longest suspension bridge in the world when it was opened by President Coolidge in 1926. In 1933, the country's first drive-in movie theater was built in Camden.

Camden became a large industrial city toward the end of the 19th century and reached its peak in the 1950s. During Camden's industrial heyday, a wide range of products was manufactured, the best known being pens, canned foods, phonograph records, and ships. The earliest of these was pens: the Esterbrook company began manufacturing steel pens in 1858; it later switched to fountain pens.

The Campbell Soup Company was set up in 1869 when Joseph Campbell and Abram A. Anderson began packing fancy peas and tomatoes, but the company's growth exploded when John T. Dorrance, who developed the idea of condensing soup, was hired as a chemist in 1897. Dorrance eventually became head of the company and died in the 1930s a very wealthy man. (One story has it that the inheritance tax on his estate was so large that even though it was the Great Depression, for a time the state did not need to worry about funds for relief.) The company's waterfront plant at Market and Front sts. was remarkable for its water towers: four soup cans with hats on. Although the company's headquarters remain in Camden, it no longer manufactures here and has recently threatened to move out completely. When the plant was demolished, one of the towers was rescued; there is hope it can be installed on the waterfront. In 1996 the company's remarkable public museum of tureens and other objects connected with serving and eating soup was also closed.

Eldridge R. Johnson was running a repair shop in Camden when, in 1894, a customer brought in a broken phonograph. Whether Johnson repaired the machine is not clear, but he did develop a way to improve it, moving from Thomas Alva Edison's cylinder to a plate. In 1901 Johnson formed the Victor Talking Machine Company, and in the early years of the 20th century, all the major performers traveled to Camden to record for Victor. In the 1920s he sold the company to what became part of RCA, and he too died a wealthy man. Johnson Park, the site of Cooper Library* (1916–18; Cooper and 2d sts.), now the Walt Whitman Cultural Arts Center (856-964-8300), was his personal gift to the city. The center features art exhibits in its Andrew Vitagliano gallery, theater programs (including a children's theater series), poetry readings, and concerts. Exhibits at the gallery change roughly every two months. Gallery open weekdays, 10–4.

The last of Camden's major industries was shipbuilding; at their peak the Camden yards had a tremendous capacity and built or refitted many of the warships used in both world wars. The industry's final moment of glory came with the launching of the nuclear-powered steamship *Savannah* in the mid-1950s. Although ships are no longer built in Camden, the port, which occupies over 250 acres at the most navigable part of the Delaware River, is the East Coast's largest exporter of scrap metal and largest importer of plywood. Over 2 million tons move through it annually.

Considered the state's most economically distressed big city (the population has been falling, unemployment has been a problem, and boarded-up buildings are not a rarity), Camden has recently been making a comeback. Adventure Aquarium (1 Riverview Dr.; 856-365-3300) has replaced the New Jersey State Aquarium, which opened in 1992 as one of the first steps in an ambitious plan to revitalize the waterfront. At first focusing

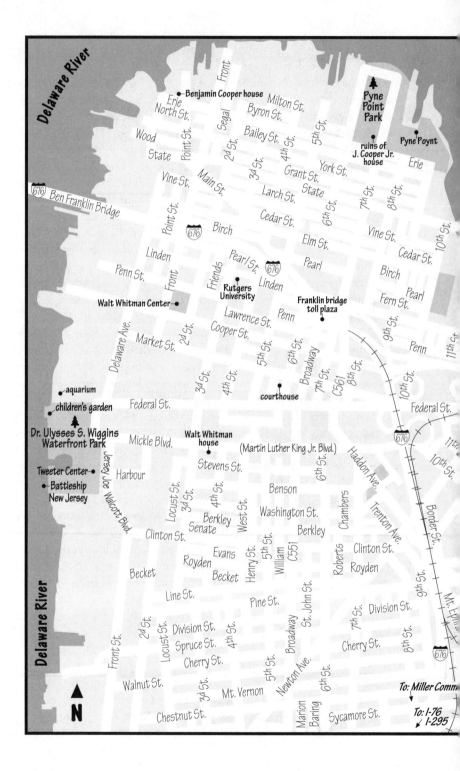

Delaware River

Front

Benjamin Cooper house
Milton St.

Erie
North St.

Byron St.

Segal

Bailey St.

Wood

Point St.

State

2d St.

4th St.

5th St.

Pyne
Point
Park

Pyne Poynt

ruins of
J. Cooper Jr.
house

Erie

York St.

Grant St.

State

7th St.

8th St.

Vine St.

Main St.

3d St.

Larch St.

6th St.

Vine St.

Cedar St.

676 Ben Franklin Bridge

Point St.

Cedar St.

676

Birch

Elm St.

10th St.

Linden

Pearl St.

676

Pearl

Birch

Penn St.

Front

Friends

Linden

Fern St.

Pearl

Rutgers
University

Walt Whitman Center

Franklin bridge
toll plaza

Penn

9th St.

Lawrence St.

Penn

11th St.

Delaware Ave.

Market St.

2d St.

Cooper St.

5th St.

6th St.

Broadway

10th St.

aquarium

3d St.

4th St.

7th St.

C561

8th St.

Federal St.

children's garden

Federal St.

courthouse

676

Dr. Ulysses S. Wiggins
Waterfront Park

Mickle Blvd.

Walt Whitman
house

(Martin Luther King Jr. Blvd.)

11th.

Tweeter Center

Harbour

Stevens St.

6th St.

Haddon Ave.

10th St.

Battleship
New Jersey

Jersey Joe Walcott Blvd.

Locust St.

3d St.

4th St.

West St.

Benson

Washington St.

Chambers

Border St.

Berkley

Berkley

Trenton Ave.

Senate

Clinton St.

5th St.

William

C551

Roberts

Clinton St.

Becket

Royden

Evans

Henry St.

Royden

Becket

9th St.

Line St.

St. John St.

Division St.

Pine St.

7th St.

Mt. Ephm.

2d St.

Locust St.

Division St.

4th St.

Broadway

Cherry St.

8th St.

Front St.

Spruce St.

5th St.

676

Cherry St.

6th St.

Walnut St.

3d St.

Mt. Vernon

Newton Ave.

To: Miller Comm

Marion

To: I-76

Chestnut St.

Baring

Sycamore St.

I-295

N

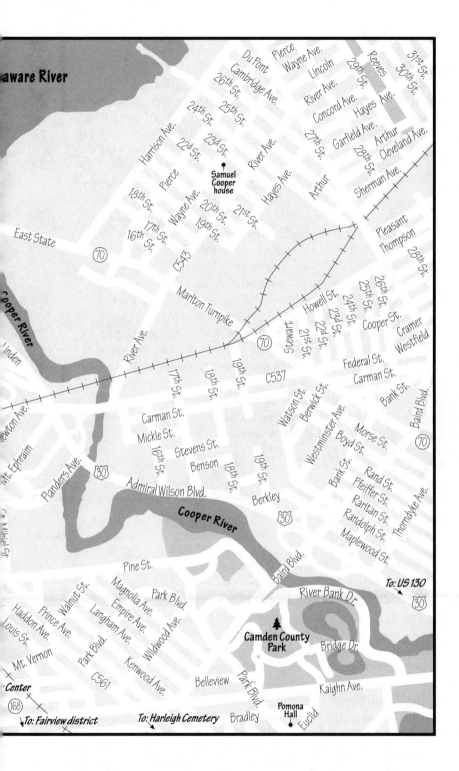

aware River

Du Pont
Pierce
Wayne Ave.
Cambridge Ave.
26th St.
Lincoln
River Ave.
Concord Ave.
Reeves
29th St.
31st St.
30th St.
Hayes Ave.
25th St.
24th St.
23d St.
22d St.
Harrison Ave.
Pierce
27th St.
Garfield Ave.
Arthur
28th St.
Cleveland Ave.
River Ave.
Hayes Ave.
Arthur
Sherman Ave.

Samuel
Cooper
house

18th St.
Wayne Ave.
20th St.
21st St.
17th St.
19th St.
16th St.
C543

East State

70

Pleasant
Thompson
28th St.

Marlton Turnpike

Howell St.
25th St.
24th St.
23d St.
22d St.
26th St.
Cooper St.
Cramer
Westfield

ooper River

inden

River Ave.

70

Stewart
21st St.

C537

Federal St.
Carman St.
Bank St.
Baird Blvd.

17th St.
18th St.
19th St.

Watson St.
Berwick St.
Westminster Ave.
Boyd St.
Morse St.
Bank St.
70

wton Ave.

Carman St.

Mickle St.

16th St.
Stevens St.
Benson
18th St.
19th St.
Berkley
30

Bank St.
Rand St.
Pfeiffer St.
Raritan St.
Randolph St.
Maplewood St.
Thorndyke Ave.

Mt. Ephraim

Flanders Ave.
30

Admiral Wilson Blvd.

Cooper River

Baird Blvd.

To: US 130
30

Pine St.

Walnut St.
Magnolia Ave.
Park Blvd.
Empire Ave.
Langham Ave.
Wildwood Ave.

River Bank Dr.

Prince Ave.
Haddon Ave.
Louis St.

Park Blvd.
Kenwood Ave.

Camden County
Park
Bridge Dr.

Mt. Vernon

Center
168

C561

Belleview

Park Blvd.
Kaighn Ave.

To: Fairview district

To: Harleigh Cemetery
Bradley

Pomona
Hall
Euclid

exclusively on local species, the aquarium was remodeled soon after it opened to include more interactive exhibits and more tropical species. It closed again in 2004. Adventure Aquarium features a West African river exhibit with crocodiles, hippos, and free-flying birds, and a 40-foot walk-through tunnel with sharks and stingrays. The now-smaller terrace still gives a spectacular view out over the Delaware, and you can take a ferry to Philadelphia (service was restored 40 years to the day from the last trip). Open daily; call for the hours. Groups by appointment. Admission charge.

South of the aquarium is the Tweeter Center at the Waterfront (1 Harbour Blvd.; 856-365-1300), which opened in 1995. This entertainment complex can seat 25,000 outdoors, but with almost one-third of its seats under a roof, it can also be closed in for the winter, providing venues for music and theater that range from approximately 1,500 to 7,000 seats. (It takes six people and a crane three working days to effect the conversion.) At the center you can attend concerts ranging from major pop stars to classical musicians, and theater, dance, magic, and family shows.

The Tweeter Center is also one of the venues for the South Jersey Performing Arts Center (856-342-6633), which uses the smallest configuration, known as the Walter Rand Theatre. SJPAC is also allied with Rutgers-Camden; the resulting CityArts on Stage, devoted to presenting the best performers "from around the world and around the corner," puts on some 16–20 main-stage performances a year, primarily at the Walter Rand and Rutgers' Gordon Theater, but also at various other venues throughout the community. SJPAC has an extensive education program for children, intended to introduce them to a wide variety of theater, classical music, jazz, puppetry, and dance.

The Campbell manufacturing plant has been replaced by the Lockheed Martin Camden Aerospace Center, an office and manufacturing facility that contains some 575,000 square feet. Other new buildings include a parking garage, and next to it a Delaware River Port Authority office building designed by Michael Graves.

Both the entertainment center and the aquarium are in Wiggins Park, which includes a marina (foot of Mickle St.; 856-795-7275; see below); open April–October. Next to the park is a four-acre interactive children's garden (856-365-8733), designed to complement the aquarium as an educational facility. Among its features are a butterfly garden, a dinosaur garden (which includes a dinosaur made from recycled automobile parts), a maze, and a storybook garden. Children can make rubbings of fossils and ride on a train and a carousel. Open daily, mid-April–mid-September, 9:30–5:30; weekdays, 9:30–4:30, weekends, 10–5, mid-September–mid-April. Admission charge; extra charge for train and carousel.

Also on the waterfront is the Battleship New Jersey Naval Museum and Veterans' Memorial* (856-877-6262). The country's most decorated battleship (and one of the largest), the USS *New Jersey* was decommissioned for the fourth and final time in 1991 and has been in Camden officially since 2000.

Built in 1943 across the river from its current location, the ship was decommissioned in 1948 and was reactivated and again decommissioned three more times. The sheer size of the ship is startling, but that size does not necessarily translate into space inside. You can tour the ship on your own or with a guide. Open for tours daily, 9–5, April–September, daily, 9–3, March, October, and November; and Friday–Monday, 9–3, January and February. For those who cannot handle the stairs, a video is available.

At the base of the Ben Franklin Bridge is Campbell's Field, Camden's new (2001) minor league stadium (501 N. Delaware; 856-963-2600), a partnership between the resident Atlantic League team and Rutgers University.

Camden's most famous resident was undoubtedly Walt Whitman, who came here to live with his brother, an inspector of pipes at a local foundry. By the time his brother moved to Burlington, Whitman had made enough money from *Leaves of Grass* to buy his own house at 328 Mickle Street. The house and the building next door are operated by the state as the Whitman House and Library (856-964-5383). (The Walt Whitman Neighborhood* is bounded by Mickle, 3d, and 4th sts.; if you continue on Mickle St. toward the river, you will come to the original section of the Dr. Ulysses S. Wiggins Waterfront Park, where you can get a wonderful view of the river and both the Camden and Philadelphia waterfronts. From here you can walk along the river to the Ben Franklin Bridge.) Whitman lived in the house, which dates from the 1840s and is now a national historic landmark, from 1884 until his death in 1892, and many of the items he lived with are there to see. The house was restored in the late 1990s so that it accurately reflects the way it looked when Whitman lived there. The library, established in 1984 and open by appointment only, contains the Colonel Richard Gimbel collection of rare and out-of-print editions of Whitman's works, as well as writings on Whitman. A visitor center is expected to open next door to the house by 2008. Open Wednesday–Friday, 9–12 and 1–6; Saturday, 10–12 and 1–6; Sunday, 1–6. Tours by appointment. Whitman is buried at Harleigh Cemetery (Haddon Ave.), where you can read on his headstone the epitaph he wrote for himself.

Another famous Camden resident was Peter McGuire, commonly credited with having thought up the idea of Labor Day. He moved to Camden in 1884, two years after he first suggested the holiday and two years before he became the first secretary of the American Federation of Labor. Labor Day was first celebrated in New Jersey in 1887.

Rutgers University–Camden (Cooper and 3d sts.), grew out of a small two-year college that was incorporated into Rutgers in 1950. The campus is a blend of converted Victorian and modern buildings. The Rutgers-Camden Center for the Arts (3d and Pearl sts.) includes the Stedman Art Gallery (609-225-6350), which features changing exhibits, and the Gordon Theater (856-225-2700), a venue for concerts and theater. Call for the exact schedules. Prospective students can arrange tours of the campus by calling 856-225-6104.

Pomona Hall* (1900 Park Blvd.; 856-964-3333), built in 1726 by Joseph Cooper Jr., with an addition by Marmaduke Cooper in 1788, is run as a house museum by the Camden County Historical Society. This lovely Georgian brick building is furnished primarily with objects from the 18th and 19th centuries. At the same site the historical society also operates another museum and a library. The museum's collections include early craft tools, American glass, fire-fighting equipment, toys, and memorabilia from the history of industrial Camden. In the collection, but not on display, is one of the original stained-glass windows, 14½ feet in diameter, showing Nipper, the "His Master's Voice" dog, that used to be in the tower of the Victor waterfront plant. The society engages in an active educational program. Pomona Hall and the museum are open Wednesday–Friday, 12:30–4:30, Sunday and the 1st and 3d Saturdays of the month, 12–5; groups and other times by appointment.

One of Camden's most successful revitalization projects has been a program that encourages children, with the aid of professional artists, to paint murals on buildings, thereby reducing the amount of graffiti. The Perkins School of the Arts (*see* Moorestown) is one of the groups involved in this project. For an example, see the South Jersey Legal Services building (745 Market Ave. at Haddon St.).

The Fairview district* (Hull and Olympia rds., Mt. Ephraim Ave., Crescent Blvd.) is a neighborhood of brick houses built in 1917 by the planner and architect Electus Litchfield.

Camden is now the southern terminus of New Jersey Transit's light-rail system, which goes north along the Delaware, making 20 stops between Camden and Trenton.

Cape May Cape May 4,034

GARDEN STATE PKWY EXIT 0, US 9

Calling itself the oldest seaside resort in the United States, Cape May City* is one of a handful of cities to be designated a national historic landmark. Situated at the southern tip of the state (Cape May would be below the Mason-Dixon Line if the line had continued due east from Pennsylvania), the city is a living museum of Victorian architecture. Over 600 Victorian buildings, most dating from the 1880s to c. 1910, are preserved in an area of less than two square miles.

Named for (and by) the Dutch explorer Captain Cornelius Mey, who pronounced the area as pleasant as his homeland and claimed it for the Netherlands in the 1620s, the peninsula was first settled early in the 1600s by whalers. Cape May began to become well known as a resort before the Revolution—an advertisement for a house appearing in the *Pennsylvania Gazette* in 1766 mentioned that the property would be "very convenient for taking in" tourists—but it was not until the early 19th century, with the introduction first of regular steamship connections between Philadelphia and Cape May (1819) and later of train service (1830s) that Cape May achieved its reputation as a fashionable and special place. It was so popular in the 1840s and '50s that ships from Philadelphia to Cape May ran daily and so fashionable that it liked to be known as the "playground of presidents." Abraham Lincoln stayed at the Mansion House in 1849 when he was still a congressman; Franklin Pierce visited in 1855, James Buchanan in 1858, Ulysses S. Grant in 1873, and Chester A. Arthur in 1893. In the summers of 1890 and 1891 President Benjamin Harrison's summer White House was at the Congress Hall Hotel, although he himself stayed in Cape May Point. Other noteworthy visitors included the bandmaster and composer John Philip Sousa, who wrote a "Congress Hall March"; Senator Henry Clay, who came in 1847; and Henry Ford, who in the early 1900s staged an automobile race on the beach against Louis Chevrolet (driving a Fiat) and Alexander Christy (driving a Winton). Ford in his Ford was ahead, but a wave broke over the car and the motor stalled. To pay his hotel bill he offered stock in his company, which was refused, and he finally sold his car to Dan Focer, who opened an agency in Cape May three years later, becoming the country's first Ford dealer.

Tourists at first stayed in private homes, but soon seaside hotels were built. For two seasons Cape May boasted the world's largest hotel—the Mount Vernon, with over 3,000 rooms. It burned in 1856, as did many of Cape May's buildings over the years. In fact, the city's present appearance is largely a result of the rebuilding that took place after a fire in 1878 destroyed most of the city's tourist accommodations. (Cape May's charm also reflects its decline in popularity: after Atlantic City's rise in the early 1900s, new building virtually ceased in Cape May.)

Although the beaches, despite serious problems with erosion, are an obvious attraction (for many beaches it is best to check on tides to make sure you can enjoy both sand and water) and fishing and boating are also popular, most people come to Cape May to spend time in the town. The best way to see the town is on foot or bicycle. The Mid-Atlantic Center for the Arts (609-884-5404, 800-275-4278) sponsors walking, trolley, and boat tours (the boat tours leave from 2d Ave. and Wilson Dr.). The tours are daily in season, less frequently the rest of the year; call for the detailed schedule; groups of over 20 can arrange in advance for individualized tours, and in the summer the center also features special tours for children aged 3–12. The center and the city both sponsor many special events: Victorian Week, spanning two weekends and featuring tours of many private homes, in October; a music festival in early summer; a Christmas candlelight tour; and many other fairs and tours throughout the year. Call for specific schedules.

To tour on your own, stop in at the Welcome Center (Lafayette St. near Ocean St., in the bus depot; 609-884-9562), or at the information booth at the head of the Washington St. pedestrian mall (Ocean St.); maps are available for self-guided walking tours. The information booth was formerly a guardhouse in Philadelphia's Fairmount Park. At both places you can pick up a variety of brochures and information on beach passes. (For information on passes, you can also call 609-884-9525.) The Welcome Center is open daily, 8:30–4:30; off season, the information booth's hours are irregular.

Not to be missed is the Emlen Physick house (1048 Washington St.), a 16-room Stick-style house designed by Frank Furness, which sits on over eight acres in the center of town. It was built in 1881 for Physick, a member of a prominent Philadelphia medical family (his grandfather is often referred to as the father of surgery). Now open as a house museum, the rooms are furnished with 19th- and early-20th-century pieces, much of it Physick's, and contain toys, clothes, and other Victorian artifacts. Of particular note are the Eastlake-style furniture, much of it designed by Furness, and the lincrusta wall coverings. Also on the property is the restored Carriage House, which contains an art gallery and a tearoom. Exhibits in the gallery usually change three times a year. In the winter the exhibit is often related to Cape May's African American heritage; in the spring and fall exhibits can range from Victorian clothing to the model T to Cape May during World War II.

Also on Washington St. (in the direction of the Information Center) is the Prickly Pear cottage, home of the Cape May County Art League (670

Washington St.; 609-884-8628). Founded in 1929 and said to be the oldest continuously operating county art league in the country, the league offers classes and lectures and sponsors a variety of special events. Exhibits in the gallery, which concentrate on members' work in a wide variety of media, change roughly once a month. Gallery open Wednesday and Friday, 1–4, Saturday, 1–7, Sunday, 11–5 in the winter. In the summer the gallery is open every day but Tuesday; call for the hours.

The Cape May Stage (Bank and Lafayette sts.; 609-884-1341) is an equity theater. Its home was built as a Presbyterian church in 1853, then became an Episcopal church, and then served as Cape May's Welcome Center for many years. The theater has an eight-month season and is involved in an outreach program with the local middle and high schools.

Almost any street has its rewards. Compared to some other Victorian seaside resorts, Cape May has an unusual variety of buildings. It also sports an unusual abundance of gingerbread and other decorative exuberance. Some of the most interesting private houses have been converted to bed-and-breakfast inns or hotels. The Abbey (Columbia Ave. and Gurney St.), for example, an 1869 Gothic Revival estate built by a Pennsylvania coal baron, has a 60-foot tower and elaborate stained-glass windows. The Mainstay Inn (635 Columbia Ave.) was a gentleman's gambling club. The Wilbraham Mansion (133 Myrtle Ave.) was an 1840s farmhouse expanded in 1900 by Philadelphia industrialists. Windward House (24 Jackson St.), an Edwardian Shingle-style house, has unusual stained and beveled glass; the glass is also striking in the Prince Edward (38 Jackson St.). The oldest hotel, the Chalfonte (Sewell and Howard sts.), was built in 1876 as a private home by Colonel Henry Sawyer, who was taken prisoner in the Civil War by the Confederates and exchanged for a son of Robert E. Lee. (The Congress Hall was first opened in 1816, but after the fire was not rebuilt until 1879 and did not operate as a hotel between the 1930s and 1990s.) Volunteers help maintain and restore the Chalfonte on working weekends in fall and spring. Space prohibits listing all the enjoyable buildings here, but the brochures available from the information centers will help identify them.

The Nature Center of Cape May (1600 Delaware Ave.; 609-898-8848) has exhibits focusing on the state's natural environment, particularly the marine environment, including a seasonal (spring, summer, and fall) aquarium and exhibits for children. The center runs a variety of workshops, field trips, and educational programs, many hands-on, including harbor tours with marine biologists, indoor and outdoor garden workshops, and butterfly workshops. Open January–March, Tuesday–Saturday, 10–1, April, May, October–December, Tuesday–Saturday, 10–3, June–September, daily 9–4. (The center is part of the New Jersey Audubon Society, which in 1997 opened a new research and education facility in Cape May Court House; *see* Cape May Court House.)

The Cape May Firemen's Museum (Franklin Ave. and Washington St.; 609-884-9512), constructed on the site of an earlier firehouse, features a 1928

LaFrance pumper and other memorabilia; exhibits are also devoted to Cape May's fire history. Open daily, May–October, 8–8; groups and other times by appointment.

The U.S. Coast Guard's only station for training recruits is located on 500 acres northeast of the center of town (609-884-6900), in an area used as a harbor by the Continental navy during the Revolution. The station is no longer open for public tours, but the Coast Guard's sunset parades (usually four each summer) are open to the public.

Northwest of town (take US 9 to Lincoln Rd. and Sandeman Blvd.) is the terminal for the Cape May–Lewes, Delaware, ferry (609-889-7200). The trip takes about 80 minutes, and the ferries run all winter, carrying over one million passengers and 375,000 vehicles each year. From mid-April through early December (although the schedule can be affected by the weather) you can also look for whales and dolphins on cruises run by the Cape May Whale Watch and Research Center (1286 Wilson Dr.; 609-898-0055).

North of the ferry slip is the state's southernmost winery, Cape May Winery and Vineyard (709 Townbank Rd.; 609-884-1169). The area is congenial to grapes, and the winery grows most of its own (all the grapes it uses are grown in the state). Open for tasting daily, May–October, 12–5, for tours Wednesday, 3–5; open Wednesday–Sunday, November–April, 12–5, for tours Saturday, November, December, March, and April, 3–5.

North of town is Historic Cold Spring Village (720 US 9, 609-898-2300), intended as a reconstruction of a 19th-century southern New Jersey village. The Cold Spring Grange (1897) serves as a restaurant; and buildings from other sites in the county have been moved here, among them the James Hathorne house (1722), the oldest building at the site; the Cape May Point jailhouse (c. 1850, actually a place for those who had drunk too much to get home safely); the Dennisville Inn (c. 1775); a blacksmith's shop (1865); and two railroad stations. Artisans, including a blacksmith, weaver, tinsmith, ropemaker, and potter, demonstrate their crafts and sell their products in the shops. The welcome center is housed in a late-19th-century building that was once a Junior Order of American Mechanics hall and later the municipal hall for Lower Township. In the center are orientation exhibits for Cape May County and the village. Special programs—antique and craft shows, fall festivals, concerts, colonial and Civil War encampments—take place on weekends. Open daily, Father's Day–Labor Day, 10–4:30; weekends, Memorial Day–Father's Day and September. Admission charge.

Also north of town (take Seashore Rd., C 626, to Tabernacle Rd., turn left, and turn left again on Shunpike Rd.) is Bennett Bogs Preserve, home to 250 species of plants, of which some are at their northern limits and many are rare or endangered. The preserve contains three vernal ponds; in normal-rain years these flood in winter and spring and dry out in summer and fall, displaying then an abundance of plant life. Managed jointly by the New Jersey Audubon Society and the Nature Conservancy, the preserve is open for walking (but be prepared for muddy conditions), except when the trails are flooded.

In North Cape May is another winery that grows its own grapes, Turdo Vineyards (3911 Bayshore Rd.; 609-898-3424). Open Friday–Sunday, 12–5, May–October; Saturday and Sunday, November–April, but it is always advisable to call first.

Cape May Court House Cape May 4.704

US 9

The seat of Cape May County, Cape May Court House, though still small, saw its population double between 1960 and 1980. Known as Middletown when the first courthouse was built in 1745, the city has kept its mid-19th-century white frame courthouse* for meetings, conducting county business elsewhere.

The Cape May County Historical and Genealogical Society Museum occupies the John Holmes House (504 US 9; 609-465-3535). The house dates to the 18th century, the earliest part to 1755. It contains 18th- and 19th-century period rooms and a wide variety of artifacts, from medical aids to military memorabilia to children's toys. In the barn are whaling implements, the lens from the Cape May Point lighthouse, and other maritime-related exhibits, as well as some horse-drawn vehicles. The society also sponsors a monthly program for children aged 12 and under and is involved in various outreach programs. Museum open 9–3, Tuesday–Saturday, Memorial Day–October; Saturday, November–May. Closed holidays; groups and other times by appointment. Admission charged. The office is open 8:30–4:30, Tuesday–Saturday, year-round. The library is open 10–4, Thursday–Saturday and by appointment.

East of US 9 is the Performing Arts Center of Middle Township (212 Bayberry Dr.; 609-463-1924). The center schedules a wide variety of musical, theatrical, and dance events. The Cape May County Art League sponsors exhibits in the lobby art gallery; these feature the work of local artists. Open weekdays, 9:30–1:30 and during performance intermissions.

Roughly two miles north of town on US 9 is the Cape May County Park (609-465-5271). Its 128 acres include a natural area with jogging, nature, and bicycle trails, picnic areas, and a wide variety of facilities for active sports. There is also a small accredited zoo with some 200 species of domestic and exotic animals. Zoo open daily, 10–3:45 in winter, 10–4:45 in summer; park open daily 9–dusk. Closed Christmas Day.

About four miles north of town on US 9 is Leaming's Run Gardens and Colonial Farm (1845 US 9 north, one mile north of Avalon Blvd.; 609-465-5871), said to be the largest annual garden in the country. There are 25 gardens on 30 acres, each garden with a different theme; paths lead you from one calculated effect to another. This is an unusually peaceful spot in the midst of a busy resort world. Also on the property is a small reproduction of a colonial farm and the only remaining colonial whaler's home (1706) in the county (the whaler's home is not open to the public). In August the gardens attract impressive numbers of ruby-throated hummingbirds. Open mid-May–mid-October, 9:30–5; groups by appointment. Admission charged.

Just beyond Leaming's Run is Beaver Swamp Wildlife Management Area, 2,900 acres of swamp, dense forest, creeks, and small ponds. Here you can hike, bird-watch, and hunt; this is also a good spot to see muskrats, beavers, and river otters.

Both north and south of Beaver Swamp are parcels of the Cape May National Wildlife Refuge (24 Kimbles Beach Rd.; 609-463-0994). The refuge, which now contains 11,000 acres and will eventually grow to over 21,000, is an important link on the Atlantic Flyway. It is home to a wide variety of birds, reptiles, mammals, amphibians, fish, and shellfish. The Two Mile Beach Unit (Ocean Dr. south of Wildwood Crest), formerly part of a Coast Guard Loran unit, has a trail along the beach. The rest of this unit is closed to the public during the shorebird breeding season, April–September. There is also a short trail near the headquarters building and a longer one at the end of Woodcock Lane. The refuge is open daily, dawn–dusk for wildlife observation and, in season, hunting. The office is open weekdays, 8–4.

About a half-mile north of Leaming's Run (in Clermont) is the Flyertown Toy Train Museum (US 9 just north of 83; 609-624-3173). The museum features a large layout and a collection of trains and train-related paraphernalia. Open weekends, 10–3:30.

West of Cape May Court House is Reeds Beach (take Hand Ave., C 658, to NJ 47, turn right, and turn left on Reeds Beach Rd.). Because horseshoe crabs breed at Reeds Beach, it is a famous spot for viewing migratory shorebirds, who stop here each spring exhausted from their flight from their winter grounds. They stock up on the horseshoe crab eggs, which give them the energy they need for the long journey to their breeding grounds. You will find interpretive signs and an observation platform here.

Also west of town is the New Jersey Audubon's Center for Research and Education (600 NJ 47; 609-861-0700), one of its newer facilities. Outside are a demonstration garden and an observation deck, inside a wildlife art gallery. The center, which also houses the society's research facility, concentrates on backyard habitats that will be attractive to birds and butterflies. Open daily, 9–4:30.

Cape May Point Cape May 241

Cape May Point was founded as Sea Grove in 1875 by a group of wealthy Philadelphia Presbyterians, including John Wanamaker of the department store family, later postmaster general under Benjamin Harrison (Harrison spent his summers at the point in the 1890s). Apparently their aim was to establish a beach community like the successful Methodist ones at Ocean Grove and Ocean City. (Visitors journeying to Cape May by boat used to dock here and travel overland the three miles to Cape May City.)

Still primarily a summer community, Cape May Point has some typical seaside resort architecture. Saint Peter's-by-the-Sea,* a gray wooden church with white gingerbread trim, was taken from the Philadelphia centennial exhibition in 1880 and moved to Cape May Point by train. The erosion problem at the point is extreme: this is the church's fourth location; the last one, two blocks away, is now in the ocean. With an artificial reef in place, a dune-replenishment program, and constant vigilance, the town is optimistic that it is at least not losing the battle.

Even before the community was founded, there was a lighthouse at the point. The current one* (Lighthouse Ave.; 609-884-5404, 800-275-4278), built in 1859, is the third, the land the previous two stood on now being underwater. It is still being used, and on a clear night you can see its light for 24 miles. Restored by the Mid-Atlantic Center for the Arts (*see* Cape May), the lighthouse offers a spectacular view from the top, and on the landings are exhibit panels dealing with the history of the area you can see from the window, the structure of the building, and the functioning of the light. Open most weekends, December–March, daily the rest of the year; the schedule can vary so it is best to call before visiting. Admission fee for climbing the lighthouse; the grounds and the Oil House (visitors' center) are open without charge.

This is prime territory for bird-watchers, one of the best spots in the country for observing migratory birds, particularly raptors (birds of prey). On the Atlantic Flyway, it is the last stop on the southern journey before the 18-mile flight over the open water of Delaware Bay. Birds congregate here, resting, eating, and waiting for good weather. At its Cape May Bird Observatory Northwood Center (701 E. Lake Dr.; 609-884-2736) the New Jersey Audubon Society has been studying migration at the point since 1975. The center sponsors birding weekends in spring and fall, weeklong workshops on shorebirds and raptors, and a variety of walks and educational programs. The observatory is open daily, 9–4:30 (hotline 609-898-2473). Lily Lake is across the street from the observatory; it is home to geese, ducks, and swans, and you can ice-skate here in the winter.

The Cape May Migratory Bird Refuge (Sunset Blvd. opposite

Cape May Point **65**

S. Bayshore Rd.; 609-861-0600) is a 220-acre reserve between Cape May and Cape May Point, owned by the Nature Conservancy. A well-marked trail goes through the meadow to the beach and back by another route. This was land that used to belong to South Cape May, a resort town destroyed in the 1950s by a storm. Open daily, dawn–dusk.

Cape May Point State Park (Lighthouse Ave.; 609-884-2159) consists of some 235 acres of sand dunes and freshwater marsh used during World War II as a coastal defense base. In 1942 bunkers were built here (and across the bay at Lewes, Delaware) 900 feet from the sea. Today you can still see the bunker, and its turrets are visible at low tide. The dunes were blown away by Hurricane Gloria in 1985 and have been replaced by a smaller system. The Army Corps of Engineers has recently embarked on a beach-replenishment project. At the visitor center (once a military building) you can pick up trail guides. The visitor center contains an aquarium filled with local marine life, and there are a few other exhibits of and relating to local wildlife. At the museum (another former military building) are live local fauna, as well as exhibits dealing with historic local wildlife, migration, and the seashore. The park has facilities for picnicking and fishing, observation decks for watching the birds, and over three miles of hiking and nature trails. There is also a half-mile trail for the handicapped, and two beach wheelchairs are available without charge. Park open daily, dawn–dusk; museum and visitor center open daily, 8–4:30.

At the end of Sunset Blvd. (C 606) is Sunset Beach, a good spot to find Cape May diamonds. These are pebbles of clear quartz smoothed and rounded by weathering, which, when polished, take the light like a precious stone. At Sunset Beach you can also see the remains of an experimental concrete ship, used in World War I. It was apparently being towed to be used as part of a wharf but broke loose in a storm and sank.

On Sunset Blvd. shortly before you reach Sunset Beach is a World War II concrete fire tower.* The Mid-Atlantic Center for the Arts (609-884-5404, 800-275-4278) has restored the tower, adding a spiral staircase inside. MAC is planning to open a museum at the base, which will concentrate on World War II as it related to the area and its people. The museum is expected to open in 2007.

North of Sunset Beach is Higbee Beach, a wildlife management area containing roughly 1,000 acres of beach front, dunes, marsh, woodlands, fields, and ponds. Higbee Beach is another good place to look for Cape May diamonds (in fact, it used to be called Diamond Beach) and for birds. The area is important as a nesting and resting station since Pond Creek Meadow is the last freshwater area before the flight across Delaware Bay. Seventeen endangered species of birds frequent the area, over 250 species are around at some time during the year, and millions of songbirds and over 50,000 raptors migrate through this area each year. Millions of monarch butterflies stop here each fall during their southwestern migration. It is also very popular with people, some tens of thousands from many countries visiting each year, and between Memorial Day and Labor Day the parking lots can fill up. Some of the visitors swim, sunbathe, picnic, hike the trails (a trail map and brochure can be picked up at the head of the trail), watch the spectacular sunsets, and, in (a restricted) season, hunt, but the main attraction is the birds.

Cassville   Ocean [Jackson Township]

C 528, 571

The crossroads community of Cassville* was important to the development of cranberry cultivation in the Pinelands. John Webb began growing cultivated berries in the 1840s and also developed the idea for the mechanical berry sorter; his success encouraged others to follow his example. Today, what is most noticeable about Cassville is its Russian settlement. If you drive into the village on C 571 from the north, you cannot miss the gilt onion domes of two Russian Orthodox churches. St. Vladimir, the one to the south, is modeled on an 11th-century Russian church; for tours, call 732-928-1337. The trees that 50 years ago surrounded all the houses (and made them look like Russian dachas) have been giving way over the years to American lawns, and you are less likely to see women in babushkas than you once were. Rova Farms, founded in 1934 under the auspices of a Russian mutual aid society, was a cooperative community on 1,400 acres with 3,000 shareholders (the Rova Farms district is listed in the state register of historic places). The children of the original members are evidently losing interest in the venture, but Rova Farms (732-928-0928) is still open for old-style Russian meals Tuesday, 7 A.M.–3 P.M., and weekends, 12–7; there is also a flea market on Tuesday, 7 A.M.–3 P.M.

Jackson Township itself (population 33,233) is a large township that has seen its population more than quintuple over the last 30 years. Ocean County as a whole is one of the fastest-growing counties in the state, and because of the striking number of retirement colonies has been dubbed the St. Petersburg of the North. Jackson Township has its share of retirement colonies, but it also has large tracts that remain undeveloped. One of these is the 660-acre state seedling nursery, now known as the Forest Resource Education Center, which was moved here from Washington Crossing State Park in 1982 and located on the site of the state's former quail farm (370 E. Veterans Hwy, C 527, 528, between the Meadowbrook and South Wind retirement communities c. 4 mi. south of I 195 exit 17; 732-928-2360). Forty-five of the acres are devoted to the seed orchards (some 300,000 seedlings are produced each year), and trees used in reforestation projects around the state are grown at the nursery. (If the turnpike authority, for example, destroys trees in a building project, the trees must be replaced somewhere else, and trees are available not just to government agencies but to private individuals with enough land.) Some of the woodlands have been turned into demonstration areas, and along some of the trails are learning stations with information kiosks. The center's resources also include an ABC arboretum, with one tree for each letter of the alphabet, to help teach tree identification. A wide variety of group educational programs can be arranged. You can also hike here, horseback ride, mountain-bike, and fish in the Toms River, which flows through the tract and is stocked with trout. The building, which includes forestry- and site-related exhibits, is open to the public weekdays, 7–4; groups and tours by appointment. The trails are open dawn-dusk.

Across C 527, 528 from the nursery is the Butterfly Bogs Wildlife Management Area (Bennetts Mill Rd.), 103 acres of pitch pine and scrub oak with three lakes suitable for fishing.

Farther west is Colliers Mills Wildlife Management Area (accessible from 528 and 571), more than 12,000 acres of both pitch pine and scrub oak uplands and white cedar swamp lowlands, with fields, wetlands, and six major impoundments. One of the most heavily hunted areas in the state, Colliers Mills offers opportunities for hikers and bird-watchers on its sandy roads. The Pine Barrens tree frog and bluebirds are some of the unusual animals to be seen here. Prospertown Lake Wildlife Management Area (access road off C 537 just north of Prospertown) consists of 130 acres with facilities for fishing and boating.

Between Butterfly Bogs and Colliers Mills is Patriots County Park (Bowman Rd.; 732-296-9090), more than 200 acres with open playing fields; softball and soccer fields; bocce, horseshoes, and shuffleboard courts; picnic facilities; and bicycle, hiking, and fitness trails.

CASSVILLE

North of Butterfly Bogs (take Butterfly Rd. to Frank Applegate Rd. and continue almost to C 638; 908-234-1225) is the Schulman tract, an 80-acre natural area preserved by the New Jersey Conservation Foundation. A trail through the area offers opportunities for hiking and bird-watching.

Behind the Jackson municipal building (95 W. Veterans Hwy) is a restored (and expanded) one-room schoolhouse now functioning as a museum (732-928-1200). One of the exhibits re-creates a classroom atmosphere from the 1920s, when the building was last used as a school, and the collection features local artifacts, including memorabilia related to cranberry and blueberry cultivation and to the Lakehurst Naval Air Engineering Station, site of the explosion of the dirigible *Hindenburg* in 1937 (*see* Lakehurst). Historic local photographs can also be seen in the area between the east and west wings of the municipal building. The museum is open Saturday, 2–4, and by appointment; the municipal building weekdays, 8:30–4:30.

Just north of Prospertown Lake is Six Flags Great Adventure (C 537; 732-928-1821), a 2,200-acre amusement park featuring "the tallest [over 450 feet], fastest [over 125 miles per hour] roller coaster on earth"; a water park, and a drive-through safari. Open daily, June–August; more limited schedule April, May, September, and October. Hours vary; call for the exact schedule. Admission charge.

Chatham   Morris   8,460 (borough)   10,086 (township)

NJ 24, 124

A colonial town that in the mid-19th century attracted commuters and in the late 19th century became, with Madison, a center for rose growing, Chatham has converted many of its older buildings to modern uses. This is particularly apparent on Main St., which, incidentally, follows the old Minisink Trail; in other parts of the Chatham historic district (listed in the state register of historic places), which also includes Parrot Mill and Tallmadge rds. and Summit, Hedges, Hillside, and University aves., the older buildings are sometimes less apparent. Pre-Revolutionary houses are to be seen on Watchung Ave. overlooking the Passaic River and on Kings Street.

South of the center of town (take Fairmount Ave., C 638, to Southern Blvd., C 647, and turn left) is the Great Swamp Outdoor Education Center (247 Southern Blvd.; 973-635-6629). Located at the eastern border of the Great Swamp National Wildlife Refuge, the center is run by the Morris County Park Commission. (Somerset County's Lord Stirling Environmental Education Center is located at the western edge of the refuge; *see* Basking Ridge.) At the education center are four trails, including a half-mile barrier-free trail. The center has an active educational program for children and adults, including weekend nature walks. In July and August (the buggy months) the center continues its programs at the Kay Outdoor Education Center (*see* Chester). Open daily, 9–4:30.

At the intersection of Fairmount Ave. and Southern Blvd. in a 19th-century former schoolhouse is the Historical Society of the Township of Chatham Museum (973-635-4911). On display is a wide variety of items dealing with the development of the township, from toys and clothing to maps and photographs to farm implements. There are a lot of pictures of fighters, because for about 50 years, beginning before World War I, Chatham was a major center for training professional boxers. A world champion had set up the center, and when he left to fight in World War I, the job was taken over by a woman.

Cherry Hill Camden 69,965

The township of Cherry Hill, which remained rural until the 1950s, has seen its population increase almost twelvefold since the 1940s. Known as Delaware Township until 1961, Cherry Hill is now largely a commuter town with many big hotels, housing developments, and shopping malls. The Cherry Hill Mall (NJ 38 at Haddonfield and Church rds.), in fact, was one of the country's first enclosed malls, and its skylit corridors, fountains, courts, plantings, and sculpture were frequently published as examples of good design.

The township attracted national attention when the Garden State Park racetrack was somehow built here in 1942. After a fire in 1977, the track reopened in 1985 as a state-of-the-art facility with a glassed-in paddock and a mahogany sculpture of a horse's head. For a while in the 1980s and '90s the site was used by the New Jersey State Fair; it now is home to housing and commercial development, though you should be able to see a reproduction of the old clock tower from the track at Haddonfield Rd. and NJ 70, and the streets have been named after horses.

Barclay Farmstead* (209 Barclay La., off NJ 70 east between the Kings Hwy, NJ 41, and I 295; 856-795-6225) is a living-history museum showing early farm life in the southern portion of New Jersey. The land first changed hands in 1684; after that, only three families held title to the property before it was purchased by the township in 1974. The present house, built by the second owner, Joseph Thorn, dates to 1816; in the 1820s it was bought by a member of the Cooper family, a descendant of the founder of Camden, as a summer retreat. (The Barclay Farm housing development is on land that belonged to the original Barclay Farmstead; within the development is a wooden covered bridge built in the 1950s, the first wooden covered bridge to be built in the state in over 90 years.)

The house is decorated as it would have appeared in the early 1800s when the Thorns lived in it. Also on the property, which is liberally supplied with interpretive signs, are an herb garden, a forge barn with an 1830s blacksmith's shop, a corncrib, and a Victorian springhouse. Some of the land is rented to members of the community who farm it. A footbridge leads over the pond and connects with a nature trail along the north branch of the Cooper River. The farmstead sponsors a variety of programs and special events, including a December open house, concerts, a pumpkin festival, a quilting program, a living-history day, and a spinning and weaving show. Open Tuesday–Friday, 12–4, and the first Sunday of the month, 1–4, year-round except for major holidays; group tours by appointment. Admission fee except for residents of Cherry Hill.

Although most of Cherry Hill's buildings are of relatively recent vintage, on Old Cuthbert Rd. is the Samuel Coles House* (1743), and at the intersection of Kings Highway and Church Rd., note the gatehouse at the Colestown Cemetery* (1858). Another historic building is the Croft Farm* (100 Borton Mill–Evans Mill Rd.). The oldest portion of the house dates to the mid-18th century; when an addition was made early in the 19th century, the orientation of the house was moved from the pond (where the mill was) to the road, reflecting the change in the area's economic engine. The house later served as a stop on the Underground Railroad and is now home to the Croft Arts Center (856-216-0669). During the week the center offers a wide variety of classes in the fine and performing arts. On weekends art exhibits, orchestra performances, and community festivals open to the public take place at the house. Call for the hours.

Located in a former industrial building in an area of similar buildings is the Garden State Discovery Museum (2040 Springdale Rd., Suite 100; 856-424-1233). Focusing on children from infancy to the age of ten, the museum features hands-on exhibits, many of them educational, and hosts a variety of special events. Open Tuesday–Sunday, 9:30–5:30; Saturday, 9:30–8:30 October–April, Monday, 9:30–5:30 July–August and Monday holidays. Admission charge.

Northwest of Cherry Hill is the borough of Merchantville, said to be the only town in the United States bearing that name. In Victorian days the town was a fashionable commuting suburb of Philadelphia. Note in particular the stick-style Centennial House* (17–19 E. Chestnut St.), Collins and Pancoast Hall* (1887, 1893; 4–8 S. Centre St.), the Cattell Tract Historic District* (parts of Chestnut, Walnut, Cedar, Gilmore, and Leslie aves.; Cove Rd.; and N. Centre St.), and the Oaks Historic District* (W. Maple Ave., Browning Rd., Volan St., and Oak Ter.). Walking-tour pamphlets are available at Borough Hall (1 W. Maple; 856-662-2474); while you are there take a look at the exhibit of photographs and art work showing Merchantville's historic structures. Open Monday–Friday, 9–5.

The Merchantville Historical Society's collection of photographs, postcards, artifacts, and period clothes relating to local history is at the Community Center (Somerset Ave. and Greenleigh Ct.; 856-662-4909). Open by appointment. The historical society also sponsors an annual house tour and programs featuring guest speakers.

Chester Morris 1,635 (borough) 7,282 (township)

US 206, NJ 24, C 510, 513

Chester, originally Black River, is a popular tourist town, which was settled early in the 18th century, primarily by immigrants from Long Island. By 1740 the community was known as an iron village, its mills supplying munitions to the Revolutionary army. The iron industry flourished in the second half of the 19th century, and many of the town's handsome buildings date from that

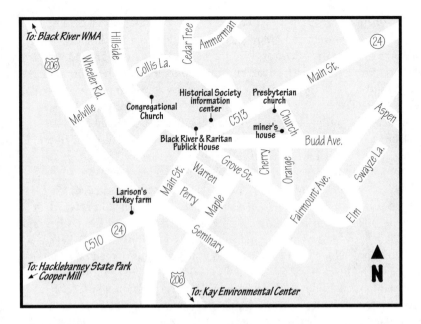

To: Black River WMA

206

Hillside

Wheeler Rd.

Melville

Cedar Tree

Collis La.

Ammerman

24

Main St.

Historical Society information center

Congregational Church

Presbyterian church

C513

Church

miner's house

Black River & Raritan Publick House

Budd Ave.

Aspen

Swayze La.

Main St.

Warren

Perry

Grove St.

Cherry

Orange

Maple

Fairmount Ave.

Elm

Larison's turkey farm

C510

24

Seminary

206

To: Hacklebarney State Park
Cooper Mill

To: Kay Environmental Center

N

prosperous period. By the 1890s the discovery of the Mesabi Range in Minnesota had ended local iron mining.

A walk along Main St., Hillside Rd., Budd Ave., and Grove St. will reveal many restored and converted buildings, often with plaques giving their builders' names and the dates they were built. At the northwest corner of Main St. and Hillside Rd. stands the Brick Hotel* (now known as the Publick House), whose brick portion dates from c. 1810. A stagecoach stop for many years, it was used for a while in the mid-19th century as a school. The Congregational Church* (Hillside Rd.) dates from 1856 (its organ was built in 1873), the Presbyterian (Main St.) from 1825. An example of a two-family miner's house can be found at 60 Budd Ave., an 18th-century house at 50 Budd. Many of the roads leading into the center of town are lined with attractive houses; at the intersection of US 206 and NJ 24 is Larison's Turkey Farm Inn, housed in an early-19th-century building that incorporates two 18th-century rooms from the first house on the site.

In the public library (250 West Main St.; 908-879-2761) are the offices of the Chester Historical Society. Here you can buy self-guided walking and driving tours of the town. The society also sponsors monthly events.

Two miles west of Chester on NJ 24 (formerly the Washington Turnpike, opened early in the 19th century) stands the Cooper Mill (908-879-5463), the last surviving building from a community known as Milltown or Milldale. It is a working mill with two sets of grinding stones and is run by the Morris County Park Commission. The current mill was built in 1826 by Nathan Cooper, but a flour mill had been on the site in the 1760s and a sawmill and gristmill in the 1780s. The wooden water wheels were replaced by metal ones in the 1850s, and the mill incorporated the latest in 19th-century technological improvements. It is set up now to operate like a typical gristmill of the 1880s. Open 10–5, weekends, May–October; Wednesday–Sunday, July and August; last tour at 3:45. Visitors can purchase organic stone-ground whole wheat, oat, rye, spelt, buckwheat, and corn flours made at the mill, though not all kinds are always available. Group tours by appointment (973-631-5343). At any time of year you can hike on the fairly undeveloped trails that start from the mill's parking area and go along the Black River. Trail maps are available, and it is important that you stay on the trails because not all the mines that were once worked in the area have been fenced off.

About three miles southwest of Chester is Hacklebarney State Park (take Hacklebarney State Park Rd. off 24 or Pottersville Rd. off 206; 908-879-5677 in summer, 908-638-6969 in winter). Established in 1924, when Adolphe E. Borie donated 32 acres to the state in memory of his mother and granddaughter, the park now contains 977 acres. Much of the park lies in a beautiful gorge along the Black River, and the footing is rugged on some of the trails. The Black River is stocked with trout, there are beautiful picnic sites, and in winter you can cross-country ski. The park also contains a playground and an area open for hunting in season. The office is open 8–8, Memorial Day–Labor Day, 8–4, the rest of the year; the park is open 8–dusk year-round.

Also off Pottersville Rd. (southwest of Chester but north of Hacklebarney) is the Elizabeth D. Kay Environmental Center (200 Pottersville Rd.; 908-879-7262), part of the county park system (the New Jersey chapter office for the Nature Conservancy is in the center). The conservancy, in cooperation with the county park system, sponsors a variety of educational programs, including nature talks, a butterfly program, and an annual woodcock walk (woodcocks nest in the area). At the center you can pick up trail maps for all the Morris County parks. Open weekdays, 9–4:30.

Also along the Black River, about two miles northeast of Chester, is the Black River Wildlife Management Area (North Rd. or C 513), some 3,000 acres open to hikers, bird-watchers, and hunters.

Clark Union 14,597

Named for Abraham Clark, a signer of the Declaration of Independence, what is now the township of Clark was settled late in the 17th century. The first mill was built on the Rahway River in the late 1700s, and for a time in the 19th century the American Felt Company was active in Clark. One of the first to buy land in the area was Dr. William Robinson, who arrived in 1686. His small red farmhouse, c. 1690, now known as Dr. Robinson's plantation* (593 Madison Hill Rd.; 732-388-3600, ext. 3025), has been restored. Thought by many to be the oldest house in New Jersey, it has been decorated to show what a 17th-century farmhouse would have looked like. Also on display are a collection of historical artifacts and an exhibit on early medical practice and the influence of Native American lore on medicine. Period craft demonstrations are given, and school tours can be arranged. Open April–December, 1st and 3d Sundays of the month, 2–4; groups by appointment other times. The house has been closed for restoration, but is expected to reopen in April 2006.

The Polish Cultural Foundation sponsors exhibits at its Skulski Art Gallery (177 Broadway; 732-382-7197). The shows, which change monthly, feature works in a variety of media by artists from a variety of ethnic backgrounds. Open September–July, Monday, 10–5, Tuesday–Friday, 11–9, Saturday, 11–2. The foundation also sponsors concerts, lectures, and educational activities.

The Oak Ridge golf course (Oak Ridge Rd.; 732-574-0139) is a county facility located on land that belonged to a later, unrelated, Robinson, and the clubhouse uses the former homestead* of that Robinson. Its kitchen wing is pre-Revolutionary; the central section dates to the early 19th century, the library wing to the Civil War. Directly adjacent, and also part of the county system, is the Ash Brook Reservation, 650 acres that have been described as a haven for golfers and bird-watchers. (The Ash Brook golf course is off Raritan Rd. in Scotch Plains: 908-756-0414; pitch and putt: 908-756-0550.)

Clinton Hunterdon 2,632

I 78, US 22, NJ 31, C 173, 513

Clinton, situated at the confluence of Spruce Run and the South Branch of the Raritan River, is remarkable for the beauty of its site. The entire town, which lies on the migratory route of many bird species, is a bird and wildlife sanctuary.

At the junction of the two rivers are two mills separated by a 200-foot waterfall. The red mill,* now part of the Red Mill Museum Village (56 Main St.; 908-735-4101), was built c. 1810 and has been used as a fulling mill, to make flour, and, from 1903 to 1920, to make talc and graphite. Described as the most photographed building in New Jersey, it even appeared on the cover of a national edition of a New York State map. The museum, which opened in 1963, displays a wide variety of artifacts dealing with daily life, focusing on the period the mill was in operation—farm tools, clothing, machinery, spinning wheels and looms, and furnishings. Also part of the Museum Village complex is the former Mulligan's Quarry.* where fertilizer and crushed stone were produced from the 1840s to 1964. From the grounds you can see the limestone cliffs; also on the grounds are the quarry office, the stone crusher, the kilns, the tenant house (which now contains a turn-of-the-20th-century general store and the interior of the old Lebanon post office), a schoolhouse dating from the 1860s, church sheds (used by

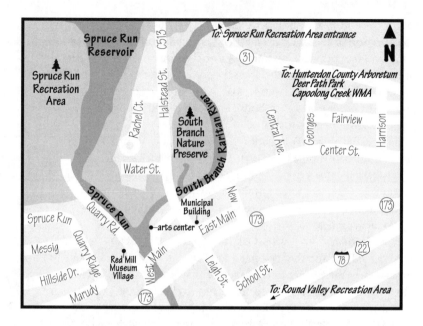

Map labels: Spruce Run Reservoir, Spruce Run Recreation Area, To: Spruce Run Recreation Area entrance, C513, Halstead St., Rachel Ct., South Branch Nature Preserve, Water St., South Branch Raritan River, Central Ave., Georges, Fairview, Harrison, Center St., To: Hunterdon County Arboretum / Deer Path Park / Capoolong Creek WMA, 31, N, Spruce Run, Quarry Rd., Spruce Run, Municipal Building, New, East Main, 173, 173, arts center, Messig, Quarry Ridge, Red Mill Museum Village, West Main, Leigh St., School St., 78, 22, Hillside Dr., Marudy, 173, To: Round Valley Recreation Area

parishioners to park their wagons during services) from two of Clinton's churches, and a log cabin built as a bicentennial project. Many educational programs and special events take place at the museum, including concerts and Revolutionary and Civil War encampments. The museum is open April–mid-October, Tuesday–Saturday, 10–4, Sunday 12–5; the office is open year-round; groups by appointment. Admission charged.

Across an 1870 iron bridge is the old stone mill,* an early-19th-century stone gristmill in use until the 1950s. Now the home of the Hunterdon Museum of Art (7 Lower Center St.; 908-735-8415), it has been restored to its 1836 appearance (the original gray fieldstone and red brick arches were stuccoed over in the late 19th century) and converted into a beautiful building containing galleries, studios, and a salesroom. The galleries feature changing exhibits, often focusing on New Jersey artists, and including an annual show for children in kindergarten through eighth grade. The museum also sponsors educational programs, a children's summer camp, and various special events. The galleries and shop are open Tuesday–Sunday, 11–5; the office, Tuesday–Friday, 9–5.

It is worth walking along Main, Center, and Water streets. The Clinton House dates from c. 1736, and there are many buildings from the Civil War period. (See, for example, the Municipal Building, c. 1865, on Leigh St. off Main.)

Three miles north of Clinton, on Van Syckels Rd. off NJ 31, is the entrance to Spruce Run Recreation Area (908-638-8572). This park, which includes New Jersey's third-largest reservoir (1,290 acres of surface and 15 miles of shoreline), offers abundant opportunities for swimming (between Memorial Day and Labor Day; on nice weekends it is advisable to get to the swimming area early), boating, fishing, and, in winter, ice-boating, ice-skating, and ice-fishing. The camping and picnicking areas are in particularly lovely spots. Call for details on facilities and regulations. Adjacent to the western end of the park is the Clinton Wildlife Management Area, a heavily used area of fields and woodland, which is open for fishing, hunting, and hiking. Camping area open April–October. Office open daily at 8; closing hours vary with the season. Parking fee in summer.

About eight miles east of Clinton (off US 22) is another, larger (3,600 acres) state park, Round Valley Recreation Area (1220 Lebanon-Stanton Rd., C 629; 908-236-6355), with a large (1 mi. by 3 mi.) reservoir surrounded by hilly, wooded land. This park, too, has abundant opportunities for swimming, boating, and fishing (particularly trout: 24-pound lake trout and 21-pound brown trout have been caught here), and there is a special area for scuba diving. There are wilderness campsites accessible only by foot or boat. In winter you can ice-boat, ice-skate, ice-fish, and cross-country ski. The hiking and bridle trails can be rugged, but they offer beautiful views, and there are gentler paths as well. Open year-round, but hours vary with the season. Parking fee for day-use area Memorial Day–Labor Day.

Adjacent to Round Valley is the Cushetunk Mountain Nature Preserve (Old Mountain Rd.; 908-782-1158), 380 acres of rugged, hilly land where you can hike and hunt. In recent years, bald eagles have been nesting here and in Round Valley, and in the spring certain areas may be closed to the public to protect the nesting sites.

Some six miles south of Clinton on NJ 31 is the Hunterdon County Arboretum, a 100-acre special-purpose park and the headquarters of the Hunterdon County park system (908-782-1158). Conceived as an educational and experimental resource, the facility contains a greenhouse and a variety of gardens, including an alphabet herb garden, a butterfly garden, and a children's interactive educational garden. Vegetables are being added to the arboretum's All-America Selection garden, which also serves to test seeds. There is an 1893 gazebo in the garden (thought to be the oldest in the state), another gazebo by the pond, and two miles of nature trails, including a boardwalk trail through a wetland study area.

Another three miles south on 31, turn left (east) on W. Woodchurch Rd. for Deer Path Park (908-782-1158). There are woods, meadows, a pond, and playing fields, with places to fish and picnic, and trails for hiking, riding, jogging, and cross-country skiing. The parks department presents its summer concerts here.

One of the few streams in New Jersey that can support trout naturally can be found about three miles south of Clinton. Take 513 to 617 and continue to the Capoolong Creek Wildlife Management Area, which runs along an old railroad right-of-way.

About six miles west of Clinton (take C 173 to Mine Rd.) is the Jugtown Mountain Nature Preserve (908-788-1157), one of Hunterdon County's newer preserves (also referred to as Hoffman Park). Although the name comes from the fact that bootleggers worked and hid their jugs in this area, mining of magnetite was a more important industry—in the 19th century some 16,000 tons of ore were mined each year—and you can still come across rock pits and ore dumps. Hiking, mountain-biking, horseback riding, and hunting are possible here.

Closter Bergen 8,393

C 502, 505

Known locally as the "hub of the Northern Valley," Closter (pronounced with a long *o*) was an early settlement—the first individual purchases found in the records date to 1701—and many of its Dutch stone houses remain (try Hickory La. and Piermont Rd.). The town also has a large stock of 19th- and early-20th-century buildings. The Closter Historical Society (201-768-2935) sponsors historic walking tours and a winter lecture series.

The Closter Nature Center (Ruckman Rd. southwest of Piermont Rd.; 201-768-1442) encompasses 137 acres of ponds, woods, and meadows. Operating since 1962, the center owes its existence to a concerned mayor and council who rescued these wetlands from developers. There are hiking trails here, and you can fish in the pond (trail maps are available at the log cabin). The center offers monthly lectures September–June and after-school and summer programs for children. Educational programs for groups during the rest of the year by appointment. Grounds open daily, dawn–dusk; log cabin usually open Monday–Saturday, 1–5 (if the naturalist is off doing a program in the schools, the cabin will be closed).

The Belskie Museum of Art and Science (280 High St.; 201-768-0286), opened in 1994, displays the work of Abram Belskie, sculptor, medal designer, and pioneer in the construction of three-dimensional medical models. Belskie was a long-term resident of Closter, which has had an active community of sculptors since the early years of the 20th century. The museum also offers changing exhibits of local, national, and international artists in a variety of media. The exhibits, which change monthly, have also included material from local historical societies. Open September–June, Monday and Wednesday, 7–9 P.M., weekends, 1–5.

Colts Neck Monmouth 12,331

NJ 34, C 537

One of Monmouth County's fastest-growing townships (the population has more than doubled in the last 30 years and has more than quintupled in the last 40 years), and one of the most expensive (a zoning law in the 1980s required 10-acre lots for most houses, and the housing market has the reputation of being one of the most expensive in the United States), Colts Neck has long been known for its horse farms. New Jersey apparently has more horses per square mile and more horses per capita than any other state, and the horse industry, although it has been declining in recent years, still brings to the state over $280 million a year in revenue. More Standardbreds are bred in New Jersey than in any other state, and Quarter horses and Thoroughbreds are also well represented in the 60-odd varieties to be found on 81,000 acres of horse facilities. Although some of Colts Neck's farms have been sold to developers, there are still enough left to make a drive along C 537 and the smaller roads off of it a treat to horse lovers, especially in the spring. There are also some older houses to be seen (try Bucks Mills Rd.) as well as the original Colts Neck Inn, built in the early 18th century by a member of the Laird family (*see* below).

Dorbrook Recreation Area (on both sides of C 537 between Laird and Hockhockson rds.; 732-542-1642) contains a playground, a horseshoe-pitching area, tennis courts, and places where you can cross-country ski. The house on the property has been converted into an activity center, at which a wide variety of programs and events takes place.

Also in this Scobeyville section of Colts Neck is the bottling facility of Laird & Company, makers of applejack. The distillery has moved to Virginia, but the company bottles some 2 million cases a year locally. Established in 1780, Laird is the oldest distillery in the country (George Washington is said to have written Laird requesting its recipe for "cyder spirits"). Before Prohibition there were over 350 cider distilleries in the country; Laird, run by the ninth and tenth generations of a family that began making apple brandy in Monmouth County in the 17th century, is the only remaining firm to make aged apple brandy.

The Montrose Schoolhouse (Cedar Dr. and Montrose Ave.; 732-462-1378), formerly run as a museum by the local historical society, has been closed for extensive renovation. The hope is that it can eventually be reopened as a museum.

On land that has been farmed since 1735 is Four JG's Orchards & Vineyards (127 Hillsdale Rd.; 732-827-9463). One house dates to the early 18th century, and two of the old barns are being used for the winery (the vintners are living in a Sears kit house). Call for the hours.

Cranbury Middlesex 3,227

C 535, 539

First settled in the late 17th century, the village of Cranbury* today presents a striking concentration of 19th-century architecture with a few 18th-century buildings as well. David Brainerd preached to the Native Americans here in the 1740s;

Brainerd Lake and the Brainerd Institute (an 1860s school at 96 N. Main St., now serving as an apartment building) are named for him. Cranbury's first inn was built in 1686, and the current one (S. Main St., north of Station Rd.) dates from 1780; Aaron Burr changed horses here in 1804 after his duel with Alexander Hamilton. (Another inn, this one c. 1850, used to be on Main St. but was moved to Maplewood and Scott aves. and has been converted to apartments.) Farther south on Main St. is the site of the Dr. Hezekiah Stites house, where George Washington, the marquis de Lafayette, and Hamilton were entertained en route to the Battle of Monmouth (*see* Freehold).

Both the United Methodist Church (1848; N. Main St.) and the First Presbyterian Church (1839, 1859, though some of the foundation of the 1788 church may still remain; S. Main St.) look like picture-book examples of traditional American church architecture. Note also the old schoolhouse* (1896; 23 N. Main St.; 609-395-0544), now used by the township for its offices.

The Cranbury Museum (4 Park Pl. E.; 609-655-2611) is in a 19th-century house (c. 1834, with additions 1850–62) that still has its wide pine floors and a fireplace with its crane. The dining room was the original house; the parlor is part of the addition. The museum, which has a permanent collection of Native American artifacts, early farm implements, tools, china, pottery, and glass, is furnished to give a sense of what a 19th-century small-town home would have been like; there are also special exhibits (past ones have included cut glass, quilts, and Victorian clothing) that change every three to four months. Open Sunday, 1–4, and by appointment.

In the Gristmiller's House (6 S. Main St.; 609-860-1889) is the Cranbury History Center, run by the Cranbury Historical and Preservation Society, which also runs the museum and sponsors a biennial house tour. The house dates to c. 1860, but a gristmill had been on the site since early in the 18th century. The society keeps all its historical records at the center, as well as its textile collection, its artifacts and memorabilia, and other holdings not currently on exhibit. Open Monday and Thursday, 10–1, and by appointment.

Although there is some industry in the township outside the village and Cranbury is facing development pressures, some 30 percent of the land surrounding the village has been preserved permanently for agricultural purposes—grain, soybeans, and spinach are major crops—and half the preserved farmland in Middlesex County lies within Cranbury's borders. In 2000 Cranbury was the county's least densely populated municipality.

Cranford Union 22,578

GARDEN STATE PKWY EXIT 137, C 509

The Minisink Trail once went across the area now occupied by this attractive town, which takes its name from Stephen Crane, one of the original associates who laid the town out in 1699 (and a forebear of the novelist). At one time there were 11 mills on the Rahway River, and during the Revolution, grain for George Washington's army was ground here and woolen blankets for the soldiers manufactured in the Williams-Droescher Mill* (347 Lincoln Ave. E.). This 18th-century structure, the only one of the original 11 to survive, has been converted to an office building. It is worth taking a look at this lovely corner. It is also worth looking at the brown shingle First Presbyterian Church (Springfield and N. Union aves.) and driving out N. Union to see some of the large houses.

The Crane-Phillips house (124 N. Union Ave.; 908-276-0082) is maintained by the Cranford Historical Society as a museum. The earliest records of the house are from the 1840s, but parts may be older, and other parts were added in the 1860s and 1960s. Furnished to reflect the late 19th century, the museum concentrates on Cranford history and has many early photographs, but it also has an extensive collection of Native American artifacts. Open September–June, Sunday, 2–4; groups and other times by appointment. The historical society also maintains a library nearby in the 19th-century Hanson House (38 Springfield Ave.; 908-276-0082). The society's costume collection here can be seen by appointment. Library and office open September–June, Tuesday and Thursday, 9–12, or by appointment.

Union County College's main campus is in Cranford (1033 Springfield Ave.; 908-709-7000). Exhibits at the Tomasulo Gallery in the Kenneth Campbell MacKay Library (908-709-7155) usually change every five to six weeks and feature works in a variety of media by established and emerging contemporary artists. The gallery has been closed for renovation and until its expected reopening in 2006 is hanging works in the Commons. Open September–June, Tuesday–Thursday and Saturday, 1–4; Tuesday–Thursday evening, 6–9. Plays at the school's theater are also open to the public; call for the schedule. Also on campus is the Sperry Observatory (908-276-7827). Every Friday evening (except the 3d Friday of the month), 7:30–10:30, the observatory is open to the public: a slide or video program is followed, weather permitting, by a viewing with the observatory's two telescopes, two of the largest on the East Coast. Programs for groups by appointment; youth groups are encouraged to sign up.

At Nomahegan Park (Springfield Ave.) you can fish, ice-skate, bicycle, and picnic. The park also has athletic fields, a two-mile fitness course, and a playground. Other points along the river where you can fish include McConnell Park (Eastman St.) and Sperry Park (Riverside Dr.).

Crosswicks Burlington [Chesterfield Township]

(c 660, 672, 677)

Crosswicks, settled in the late 1670s by English Quakers, is said to be the only community in the United States to bear that name. Although the land around Crosswicks is being developed, the village center, which makes up the Crosswicks historic district* and includes 18th- and 19th-century buildings on the Chesterfield-Crosswicks Rd. (C 677) and Front St., preserves a strong flavor of the past. (Chesterfield Township has won awards for its policies designed to protect the township's villages and farmland, so one can be optimistic about Crosswicks retaining its distinctive flavor.)

David Brainerd first preached to the Native Americans here in 1745; his attempts to teach them trades that would enable them to fare better in the colonial world were thwarted by his failing health. Crosswicks claims to be the home of Taylor's Pork Roll, named for John Taylor, a descendant of one of Crosswick's earliest settlers, who ground ham for the market in 1856.

The Crosswicks Friends' Meeting (just northeast of the intersection of Front and Church sts.; 609-298-4362), a large two-story brick building, dates from 1773. Built partly with bricks from an older structure, the building still has its original flooring and one of the few Atsion stoves (purchased in 1772 and made in Atsion of New Jersey bog iron) to be found in New Jersey. In the Revolutionary battle of 23 June 1778, Hessian troops used the meetinghouse as a barracks and hospital, and one of the cannonballs fired during that battle (by Continentals) is still to be seen in the north wall (secured with cement). After the Battle of Trenton, Continental troops occupied the building. Open Wednesday, 9–12, and by appointment.

The former Orthodox Meeting House, built in the 1850s (Ward Ave. across from Buttonwood St.; 609-298-0566), now houses the Chesterfield Township Historical Society Museum. Included in the collection are artifacts and memorabilia related to local people and history, from 18th-century furniture and pottery to a model of the older meetinghouse made by Crosswicks schoolchildren in 1934. The collection is rich in archival material on the day-to-day concerns of the people who have lived and worked in Crosswicks. Open May–October, last Sunday of the month, 2–4. The museum is also open a second Sunday during the summer; other times and groups by appointment.

The oldest house in the area, the Singleton-Latham-Large House* (c. 1700; Bordentown-Chesterfield Rd. near the turnpike), is being restored by the historical society, which hopes to turn it into a living-history farm museum.

Dover Morris 18,188

US 46

Dover was formerly an iron town and for a time the shipping center for New Jersey's iron industry. The iron industry was active in this area more or less steadily from the 18th century, and the Dover mines continued in operation until the late 1950s. Dover's Blackwell St. historic district* (including portions of

Blackwell, Dickerson, Sussex, Bergen, Essex, Morris, Warren, Prospect, and Dewey sts.), a mixture of 19th- and 20th-century buildings, is of interest; note, in particular, the Baker building* (16 W. Blackwell St.), dating from 1884, and the former Delaware, Lackawanna and Western Railroad station* (N. Dickerson St.), dating from 1901. The Old Stone Academy* (25–27 E. Dickerson St.), c. 1827, once housed the state's first coeducational boarding school. The Baker Theater* (41 W. Blackwell St. between Warren St. and Towpath Sq.; 973-537-8600), used by Woody Allen for scenes in *The Purple Rose of Cairo*, was built in 1905 as a vaudeville house. Among those who appeared at the theater were Houdini and George Burns. The theater was converted to a movie theater and also used for rock concerts; it has recently been restored for use as a multipurpose entertainment facility: a venue for plays and concerts and children's programming, as well as for corporate events. Every Sunday from mid-April to mid-December, Dover closes off a fair number of its downtown streets from 9 to 4 for a street-fair-style flea market (973-989-7870).

Dover has a large and relatively prosperous Hispanic community, which makes up some 60 percent of the town's population. The original Hispanic settlers were recruited as farmers by the federal government in the 1940s, and for a time a large fraction of the Hispanic population traced its lineage back to one town in Puerto Rico. Now the community represents a wide range of Hispanic cultures and backgrounds.

One mile north of town on NJ 15 (in part occupying the former village of Spicertown) is the U.S. Army Armament Research, Development and Engineering Center (ARDEC), also known as the Picatinny Arsenal. It was established in the late 19th century on land that held a Revolutionary graveyard and a 17th-century forge. Although there is no more manufacturing at the facility, it is still an impressive operation (6,500 acres, some 4,500 employees, 90 percent of them civilians); it is, in fact, the largest employer in the county.

West of Dover, in Mine Hill, is a well-preserved 19th-century miner's house, the Bridget Smith–Ida McConnell House* (124 Randolph Ave.; 973-659-9001). This two-family house, which was once one of many like it, has remained basically unaltered. Furnished to show what 19th-century working-class life was like in a Morris County mining town, the house also includes exhibits of artifacts (including items found in the archaeological investigations of the site), photographs, and documents relating to the history of the local area. Out back are gardens and a restored outhouse. The house is maintained by the Ferromonte Historical Society, which also sponsors various special events. Open June–October, 1st 3 Saturdays of the month, 1–4. Tours and other times by appointment.

Also in Mine Hill (and in Dover and Randolph townships) is Hedden County Park (Concord Rd., Reservoir Ave., and Ford St.; 973-326-7600), 380 acres with facilities for hiking, bicycling, boating, fishing, picnicking, and, in winter, cross-country skiing and ice-skating.

East Brunswick   Middlesex 46,756

NJ TNPK EXIT 9, NJ 18, C 527

In the southeastern corner of the rapidly growing township of East Brunswick (in 1960 the population was not quite 20,000), along the South River, is the historic district of Old Bridge* (Emerson, Squire, Oak, Maple, Kossman, Pine, Chestnut, and Main sts., Rutgers and River rds.). The district encompasses some 42 acres with about 80 structures, roughly one-fifth of them shops. The soil here led to the early development of the pottery and ceramics industry; potters are known to have been working in this area by the mid-18th century (the first settlers came toward the end of the 17th century). This is also an area of rich fossil finds; in the mid-1990s, 90-million-year-old insects and mushrooms were found in a large piece of amber, by far the oldest mushrooms yet discovered.

In what was formerly the Simpson Methodist Church (c. 1860) is the East Brunswick Museum (16 Maple St.; 732-257-1508). The museum's permanent collection features local history, a Victorian kitchen and parlor, a sewing room, farm equipment, and the Governor Hoffman room (with memorabilia and the thousands of elephants collected by Harold Hoffman, governor of the state from 1935 to 1938). There are also changing exhibits. Open weekends, 1:30–4; group tours other times by appointment.

In the western part of the township is the Discovery House (152 Tices La.; 732-254-3770), a hands-on museum for children, with games that illustrate scientific principles. The museum also sponsors summer science workshops. Open Tuesday–Sunday, 10–5. Admission charged.

At Dunhams Corner Rd. is the East Brunswick Community Park (732-390-6806), 102 acres with tennis and basketball courts and the Crystal Springs water park. Just west of Community Park (off Church La.) are the Tamarack Golf Course (732-821-8881) and Ireland Brook Park (732-745-3900), both county facilities. Ireland Brook Park, which will eventually be linked to the golf course and Davidson's Mill Pond Park (*see* South Brunswick), is as yet undeveloped; large portions of its 380 acres have been designated conservation areas, and some hiking trails will be developed. East of East Brunswick Park are the Middlesex County Fairgrounds (Cranbury Rd.); among the regular events taking place at the fairgrounds are the 4-H's haunted-house festival in October and its historic-car festival in the spring (732-745-3446).

East Rutherford Bergen 8,716

NJ TNPK EXIT 16W, NJ 3, 120

Much of East Rutherford's land is taken up by the Meadowlands Sports Complex (201-935-8500), a project begun by the New Jersey Sports and Exposition Authority in the 1970s. The concrete complex, which was erected in the midst of the marshlands of the Hackensack Meadowlands (*see* Lyndhurst), contains a racetrack, stadium, and indoor arena (formerly the Brendan Byrne Arena, now the Continental Airlines Arena), all protected against flooding by a system of dikes, lagoons, and pumps. Over 7 million visitors a year come to watch Thoroughbred and harness racing; professional football, soccer, basketball, and hockey; college sports; the circus; ice shows; and concerts. The complex supports programs designed to help compulsive gamblers. Unconfirmed rumors suggest that some of the manure hauled away from the racetrack finds its way to Pennsylvania's mushroom farmers. Admission charges. Groups can arrange for behind-the-scenes tours of the sports complex (201-460-4038), Monday–Saturday, 10 and 12:30, by appointment.

Scheduled to open before 2010 is a large private recreation, entertainment, and retail complex, which plans to include the first indoor ski slope in the country.

Eatontown Monmouth 14,008

NJ 35, 71, C 13, 537, 547

The borough of Eatontown is named for Thomas Eaton, an Englishman from Rhode Island who in 1670 built a mill at what is now Wampum Lake. A village thrived here in 1730, the township was incorporated in 1873, and the borough was formed in 1925, after two communities in the township—West Long Branch (in 1908) and Oceanport (in 1919)—broke off and went their own ways.

In the Read house, one of the oldest in town, is the Eatontown Historical Museum (75 Broad St.; 732-542-0832). The earliest part is believed to date from 1730, with additions in the 19th and early 20th centuries. The parlor, dining room (the original house), kitchen, and one upstairs bedroom are furnished with 19th-century pieces; the other two bedrooms are devoted to exhibits of artifacts and memorabilia relating to the history of Eatontown. Among the items on display are historic clothing, maps, ledgers, and photographs. Out back is a shed with farm implements, including a hand-carved shovel. Open last Sunday of the month, 12–3, for the annual December open house, and by appointment.

Other buildings to keep an eye out for in Eatontown include the St. James Memorial Episcopal Church★ (1866; 69 Broad St.); the community center (58 Broad St.), housed in the former Presbyterian church, a building that had once served the Little Church around the Corner in New York City and was brought to Eatontown by barge and reassembled there in the 1870s; and the oldest church in town, the African Methodist Episcopal Zion Church (1845; 271 South St.).

Just north of town on NJ 35 is the main entrance to Fort Monmouth, the headquarters for the army communications and electronics command and (in 2000) the largest employer in Monmouth County. Built during World War I on the 128-acre site of the old Monmouth Park racetrack, the camp, until 1925, was known as Camp Vail, after Alfred Vail, who helped Samuel Morse develop the telegraph (*see* Morristown). Many advances in communication technology were developed here—the first radio-equipped weather balloon to be sent into the upper atmosphere was launched at Fort Monmouth in 1928, and in 1946 radar signals from the base were bounced off the moon. In 2000 some 8,200 military employees worked at the 1,500-acre base. In Kaplan Hall (Building 275) is the Army Communications–Electronic Museum (732-532-1682), devoted to the development of communications and electronic equipment within the army and to the history of Fort Monmouth itself. Among its collections are memorabilia from the days when the base served as headquarters for the army's homing pigeons (Fort Monmouth was the U.S. Army's pigeon breeding and training center). Some exhibits change periodically, and there is also an outdoor exhibit that includes satellite dishes, mortar-locating radar sets, and a tank carrying equipment developed at the fort. Open by appointment only; it is advisable to call well in advance of your visit.

Edgewater Bergen 7,667

NJ 5, C 505

A long, narrow borough situated on the Hudson River, Edgewater was a popular resort for Manhattanites in the late 19th century, and a center of shad fishing from colonial times until the disappearance of the shad. (From about 300 commercial shad fishers in the 1930s, the number declined to about 100 in the '80s; today they are no longer to be seen on the New Jersey side of the Hudson.) Edgewater became an industrial city late in the 19th century, attracting, among major companies, Ford Motor Company, Alcoa, Jack Frost Sugar, Hess Oil, and Hills Brothers Coffee, but when trucking replaced the railroad, Edgewater's factories closed. The 25-acre Ford Motor Company assembly plant★ (309 River Rd.), built in 1929–31 to the design of Albert Kahn Associates, has been converted to condominiums (the assembly-line floor is now a parking area). Plans to convert the Alcoa

Edgewater Works* (700 River Rd.), which closed in 1964, to apartments were stalled for many years by problems with PCBs and other industrial contaminants—once the factory shell was demolished, the site had to be cleaned—and then once construction had started, a serious fire struck the site, but apartments now stand where the factory was. The Sugar Factory apartments (840 River Rd.) were once part of the Jack Frost Sugar Company's local complex. Upscale shopping centers as well as housing now line the waterfront, including the Mitsuwa Marketplace, said to be the largest Japanese shopping center on the East Coast.

At one time, more than 100 decommissioned and abandoned barges dotted the northern section of Edgewater's riverfront, many of them serving as clubhouses for various groups, including the Knickerbocker Canoe Club, the country's oldest (founded 1880). They are gone now, and only the Lehigh Valley Railroad's barge No. 79,* built in 1914, was saved; it was moved to Brooklyn where it functioned as a museum.

Docked near the former Alcoa plant is the *Binghampton** (725 River Rd.), a ferryboat built in 1904–5 in Newport News. The only double-ender ferryboat still floating in the Hudson, the *Binghampton* was in continuous service between Hoboken and New York City from 1905 to 1967 and carried some 125 million passengers. It is now used as a restaurant.

Edison Township Middlesex 97,687

US 1, NJ 27, C 501, 514

Edison is, of course, named for Thomas Alva Edison (*see* West Orange), who from 1876 to 1886 had a laboratory in the Menlo Park section of the township. During those 10 years Edison took out over 400 patents and worked on the incandescent lamp, a method of distributing electricity, the phonograph, the carbon telephone transmitter, the dynamo, the magnetic separator, and the electric traction railway. One of Edison's buildings together with much of the contents of the laboratory (not to mention four carloads of Middlesex County soil) were transported by Henry Ford to his Greenfield Village in Michigan (Ford was fined for importing New Jersey beetles into Michigan). On the exact spot of the laboratory was erected in 1937 the art deco Thomas A. Edison Memorial Tower* (Christie St. off NJ 27; 732-549-3299), a cement tower 131 feet high with an amber glass replica of an incandescent light at the top. A museum is also on the site, and on display are some of the machines Edison invented, patent models, original notebooks, other memorabilia, and an eternal light that commemorates the first practical incandescent bulb. Open Tuesday–Sunday, 10–4. Groups by appointment.

A large (32 square mi.) and rapidly growing township (the population has more than doubled since 1960 and increased by over 10% between 1990 and 2000), Edison has become home to a wide variety of ethnic groups.

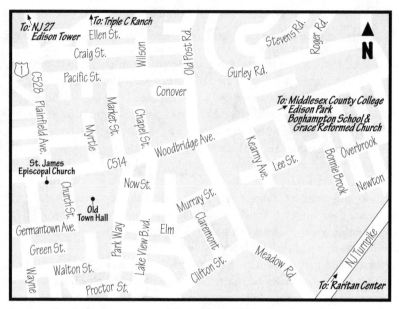

Seventy-five languages are spoken in the public schools, and the township boasts the largest Chinese and Taiwanese population, the second largest Filipino, and the second largest Asian population in the state. The annual Indian harvest festival draws some 100,000 people and is the largest festival of its type outside India.

Like many other New Jersey townships, Edison is made up of several older communities. In Piscatawaytown (in the western section of the township) the Episcopal congregation was established in the late 17th century. The present Saint James Episcopal Church (2136 Woodbridge Ave., C 514), a white frame building with a Doric portico, dates from the 1830s. The congregation's 1724 building was occupied by British troops during the American Revolution (British soldiers are buried in the churchyard; there are also some 17th-century headstones, including one that is probably the oldest marked grave in the county). A late-18th-century replacement was destroyed by a tornado in the 1830s, and the pulpit is supposed to have washed up on Staten Island. Many of the materials from the old church were used in constructing the church you see today. If you turn off onto Park Way (south off Woodbridge Ave.), you will see some older houses and the Edison Commons with the Old Town Hall.

At the eastern edge of the township, in Bonhampton (also spelled *Bonhamtown* and pronounced *bottom town*), note the late-18th-century Grace Reformed Church (Woodbridge Ave. and Grace St.) and the Bonhampton School (2825 Woodbridge Ave.), built in 1908 and now a commercial building.

The township has been home to many corporate headquarters, research facilities, and factories. Over 5 million cars were assembled in the Ford Motor Company's plant on US 1 between the late 1940s and 2004, when it closed; a Frigidaire plant on NJ 27 for a while turned out one of every three air conditioners and dehumidifiers sold in the United States; and a Mobil Company laboratory was the first in the nation to win a safety award from the Occupational Safety and Health Administration. The four-square-mile Raritan Center (NJ Tnpk exit 10), carved out of the old Raritan Arsenal, is the largest business park in the state, with 13 million square feet of office space and more than 100 buildings, including a convention center, retail outlets, restaurants, and a child-care center. (For the *New York Times*'s color printing plant and distribution facility, *see* the Turnpike Tour, 87 N.)

On the northwest side of US 1 is the 217-acre Roosevelt Park (732-745-3900), the county's oldest park. Plays and concerts are given in the summer, and there are hiking and biking trails, tennis courts, playing fields, fishing ponds, and places to ice-skate in the winter.

Also on the site of the Raritan Arsenal are Middlesex County College (Woodbridge Ave.; 732-548-6000) and Thomas A. Edison Park (Mill Rd.; 732-745-3900), formerly Raritan Arsenal Park. The college, founded in the 1960s, occupies 200 acres, and the campus presents an interesting juxtaposition of modern campus buildings with reused army buildings. When there are exhibits, the College Center and Presidential Galleries are open to the public weekdays, 9–5; events at the performing arts center are also open to the public. (For information on exhibits and events, call 732-906-2569.) The park consists of 161 acres on the flatlands to the north of the Raritan River estuary; it has running paths, a model-airplane field, tennis courts, and playing fields.

Within the 650 acres of wetlands known as the Dismal Swamp is the Triple C Ranch and Nature Center (206 Tyler Rd.; 732-287-5111), an environmental center established on the last remaining horse farm in the county. At the ranch, which is run by the Edison Wetlands Association, are various farm animals, and the surrounding area is home to over 150 species of birds and several species of amphibians and reptiles. There are walking trails at the ranch, guided tours are available by appointment, there are occasional special events. More extensive riding, hiking, and biking trails within Dismal Swamp, as well as a variety of public activities, are planned. Open May–October, Saturday, 12–4, Sunday, 1–4; groups and other times by appointment.

Egg Harbor City Atlantic 4,585

C 561 ALT., 563

Settled by Germans in the 1850s, Egg Harbor City (which is not the same as Egg Harbor Township, and is not on Egg Harbor) derives its name from a never-realized scheme to connect the town by canal to the Mullica River. After the discovery in 1858 that the land was extremely well suited to growing grapes, more Germans came to Egg Harbor City. (Note the street names in the area: Bremen, Frankfurt, Darmstadt, Heidelberg, Hamburg, among others.) Yet it was a Frenchman from Rheims, Louis Nicholas Renault, who established the best-known venture, the Renault Winery (72 N. Bremen Ave., three-quarters of a mile northeast of the intersection of Bremen and C 561 Alt., Moss Mill Rd.; 609-965-2111), listed on the state register of historic places. The oldest continuously operating winery in the United States (during Prohibition the winery produced its "medicinal" Renault tonic with an alcohol content of 22%), it was at one time the country's largest producer of champagne and may now be the country's only producer of blueberry champagne. Occasionally on a back road in South Jersey, you will come across one of the company's old 20-foot promotional champagne bottles, now a little dingy, standing in front of a liquor store. At the winery there is a small collection of wine and champagne glasses, including some medieval ones, and you can tour the facilities. Special events are regularly scheduled, including a grape stomping in the fall. The winery and glass museum are open for tours Monday–Friday, 11–4, Saturday, 11–8, Sunday, 12–4. Admission charge for tour. Closed New Year's Day, Easter, Thanksgiving, and Christmas. Recently added to the property are a restaurant, golf course, and conference center.

The Roundhouse Museum (533 London Ave.; 609-965-4677) is a museum of local history run by the Egg Harbor City Historical Society. The permanent exhibits include glass, German band instruments, many pictures of John Philip Sousa (who visited town around 1930), and boats; there are also changing exhibits. Open Wednesday, 1–3; the 2d, 4th, and 5th Saturdays of the month, 1–4; and by appointment.

Elizabeth   Union   120,568

NJ TNPK EXITS 13, 13A, US 1, 9, NJ 27, C 514

Elizabeth is Union County's oldest and largest community. Elizabeth, in fact, is one of the state's first permanent European settlements (going back to 1664), its oldest English-speaking settlement, and its first colonial capital (from the mid-1660s to 1686). For many years a busy industrial and commercial town, Elizabeth today serves as the county seat of New Jersey's youngest county (Union County was founded in 1857).

As in other industrial cities that lost much of their manufacturing base, Elizabeth's population declined for a time, but the loss was not as extreme as in some other urban areas, and many revitalization plans are in place. For over 100 years (1873–1982) Elizabeth was the home of the Singer Sewing Machine Company's oldest plant, which at its peak employed 10,000 people. Some of the former Singer buildings on the site* (Trumbull and First sts.) are being used by various smaller manufacturers; others have been incorporated into the Elizabethport Industrial Park. Near Port Elizabeth (not the same as Elizabethport), two large retailing centers have been developed on either side of North Avenue. The Jersey Central Railroad station* (Julian Pl.), built in the 1890s and closed in 1976, has been restored and is being converted to commercial uses; the area around the station will become a pedestrian plaza. The city's midtown historic district* includes Broad St. in the area bounded roughly by Rahway, Westfield, Union, and Jefferson avenues. Brochures for self-guided walking tours (in English or Spanish) are available from the Union County Office of Cultural and Heritage Affairs (633 Pearl St.; 908-558-2550).

The city's role as a transportation center goes back to the 18th century, when it was an important ferry link to New York City; regular steam service began in 1808 (the city is hoping to see service restored before too long).

PORT ELIZABETH

The railroad lines running along the water were important to the city's industrial development. In the late 1950s, the Port Authority of New York and New Jersey developed a new terminal at Port Elizabeth, which has since become a major containership port (almost 11 million long tons were handled there in 1993; *see* Turnpike Tour, 103 N,S). The Goethals Bridge, which crosses Arthur Kill to reach Staten Island, was opened in 1928 (it is named for the builder of the Panama Canal who was the Port Authority's first consulting engineer). The cantilevered structure, which carries over 14 million vehicles to Staten Island annually, is eligible for listing on the National Register. The Port Authority, however, is considering replacing the bridge and expects to finish a draft of its environmental-impact statement some time in 2006.

The list of Elizabeth's famous residents is long. James Caldwell, known as the fighting parson (*see* Springfield), became minister of one of the oldest English-speaking congregations in New Jersey, the First Presbyterian, in 1761. During the Revolution he often preached with loaded pistols on either side of the Bible and with armed sentries guarding the church, and he preached the Sunday after the British burned the parsonage. The church itself was burned in 1780, and the present building* (Broad St. and Caldwell Pl.) dates from 1784. Caldwell, killed by an American sentry in 1781 (*see* Westfield), is buried in the graveyard. In 1946 another fire destroyed most of the interior, and today's church has been rebuilt inside the 18th-century walls. (The restoration took the church back to its colonial interior, rather than reconstructing its 19th-century Gothic one.) The chandelier in the narthex was a gift from Louis XVI. Upstairs is a small museum of colonial artifacts. Tours can be arranged on request; call 908-353-1518.

Among Caldwell's famous parishioners at First Presbyterian were William Livingston, the state's popular first governor (he was reelected until his death in 1790; his house, Liberty Hall, at Morris and North aves., is a national historic landmark; *see* Union); Elias Boudinot, a lawyer and president of the Continental Congress (and as such the signer of the peace treaty with Great Britain), member of the U.S. Congress, initiator in Congress of the resolution leading to the establishment of Thanksgiving Day, and superintendent of the mint at Philadelphia; Jonathan Dayton, Continental army general, congressman, and developer of Dayton, Ohio; and Abraham Clark, one of New Jersey's five signers of the Declaration of Independence. Princeton University was founded in Elizabeth, in 1746 (it was known then as the College of New Jersey), by one of Caldwell's successors at First Presbyterian, Jonathan Dickinson.

Other prominent residents of Elizabeth include Lorenzo Da Ponte, librettist for Mozart's *The Marriage of Figaro, Don Giovanni,* and *Così fan tutte,* and Admiral William F. Halsey (his birthplace at 134 W. Jersey St. is no longer standing).

Boudinot's house, Boxwood Hall* (1073 E. Jersey St.; 908-282-7617), built c. 1750 by Samuel Woodruff, the mayor of Elizabeth, and purchased by Boudinot in 1772, is a national historic landmark. Boudinot gave a funeral oration over Caldwell's body from its steps; George Washington visited the house en route to his inauguration as the country's first president; Alexander Hamilton lived with the Boudinots while attending school in town. When Boudinot became superintendent of the mint, he sold the house to Jonathan Dayton; during the time Dayton lived there, the marquis de Lafayette was a guest (early in the 20th century, Lafayette's great-grandson visited Boxwood). Boxwood Hall, operated as a state historic-house museum, retains some of its original moldings and is furnished with period pieces. There are also changing exhibits related to local history. Open July–October, Monday–Saturday, 9–5; for the rest of the year, call for the hours (it is always a good idea to call ahead in case there are school groups in the house).

In the same block is the Belcher-Ogden House* (1046 E. Jersey St.; 908-289-8479). This historic-house museum is run by the Elizabethtown Historical Foundation. Dating from c. 1742, the house was owned for a time by Jonathan Belcher, royal governor first of Massachusetts and New Hampshire and then of New Jersey (from 1747 until his death in 1757), who was also active in promoting the College of New Jersey. The house was later occupied by Colonel Aaron Ogden, a senator from New Jersey in 1801–3 and the state's governor in 1812. Open by appointment.

Across the street is the Nathaniel Bonnell house (1045 E. Jersey St.), which dates from c. 1682 and is probably now the town's oldest house. It is currently being used for offices. The Elizabeth Playhouse (1110 E. Jersey St.), a community theater, is housed in the Italianate former Third Presbyterian Church (1855); apartments and offices are also in the building. The Ritz Theatre (1148 E. Jersey St.) dates to the turn of the 20th century; musical, dance, and theatrical events are presented here. Note also the art deco Altenberg Piano House (1150 E. Jersey St.).

St. John's Episcopal Church (61 Broad St.; 888-990-3008), founded in 1705, was once the largest Episcopal congregation in the state, but like many other inner-city churches, has a much smaller congregation today. Anna Seton's parents were married in St. John's, Winfield Scott was a member, the Kean family vault is in the churchyard, and Jonathan Dayton is buried under the church. The splendid Gothic building, dating from 1859, has five Tiffany windows; an Italian font is the church's only colonial possession. A large population from the Caribbean Islands migrated to Elizabeth after the French Revolution (Elizabeth at one time had the state's largest concentration of Haitians); note the fleurs-de-lis on the gravestone of a lady from Martinique (1799). Tours by appointment.

North of St. John's on Broad is the Hersh Tower (125 Broad St.). This striking 14-story art deco building, restored in the 1990s, was the tallest building in the county when it was built. South of St. John's is the public library (11 S. Broad St.), built in 1912 on the site of the Red Lion Inn.

Englewood Bergen 26,203

NJ 4, C 501, 505

Once known as a bedroom community for wealthy commuters, Englewood now has a large number of multifamily houses and low-income housing projects, as well as a large commercial center. John Travolta was born here, and the painter Richard Anuskiewicz lived here for many years. In 1951 Englewood was the site of the first customer-dialed long-distance telephone call in the United States, when Englewood's mayor called the mayor of Alameda, California. (Through windows of the telephone building at Bergen and Engle sts. you can even see some of the circuitry, not possible in later windowless telephone buildings.) Vince Lombardi coached at St. Cecilia's High School (Demarest St.; the former school is part of a large stone complex with some interesting buildings) before moving on to college and professional teams. Englewood was also the site of Helicon Hall, Upton Sinclair's ill-fated experiment in communal living. Built with the royalties from Sinclair's exposé of the meat-packing industry, *The Jungle* (1906), Helicon Hall burned after six months. The 20-room house built on its site was occupied for many years by Victor Wallace Farris, inventor of the paper milk carton and the paper clip.

Gloria Swanson was another Englewood resident. She lived in the 32-room Italianate villa of the Gloria Crest estate (N. Woodlawn Ave.), built in 1926 by a member of the Polish royal family (and named for his wife, not Swanson). To see some of the houses that gave Englewood its reputation, drive up the hill on N. Woodlawn Ave. (east off Palisade Ave.); as you start note on your left the Dwight-Englewood preparatory school (northeast corner of N. Woodlawn and Palisade; among its graduates are George Schultz and Brooke Shields). Gloria Crest is farther up the hill, on your right.

Also in Englewood is the Actors' Fund retirement home (155 W. Hudson Ave.), known as the Lillian Booth Actors' Home. The fund was started in the late 19th century; a home was opened early in the 20th. In 1928 the fund purchased a house in Englewood that Stanford White had designed; the grand piano in the sitting room was donated by Enrico Caruso. In 1959 the house was demolished and the current building erected (a nursing home was added later); the antique grand piano in the lounge was donated by Harold Prince.

The Bergen Performing Arts Center (30 N. Van Brunt St.; 201-227-1030) in downtown Englewood occupies a 1926 building, unprepossessing on the outside but reflecting on the inside its origin as a "movie vaudeville emporium." From September through May the center presents a wide variety of theater, musical events (popular, classical, jazz, opera), and dance. Art exhibits are hung in the Intermission Gallery from September through May; the shows, which often feature regional artists, change monthly. Gallery open during performances and by appointment; box office open year-round, Monday–Saturday, 11–6.

The Englewood public library (31 Engle St.; 201-568-2215), housed in a striking round building designed for it in the late 1960s, hosts a wide variety of public programs, including art exhibits, a summer film festival, poetry readings, and public affairs programming. The art exhibits change every month and concentrate on local artists. Open Monday–Thursday, 9–9, Friday and Saturday, 9–5, and Sunday 1–5; closed major holidays and Sunday in the summer.

Many of Englewood's older downtown buildings have been converted to new uses. The Renaissance Office Court (northeast corner of Bergen and Engle), for example, built in 1917, was once the well-known Englewood High School. It became a junior high and then a grade school before being converted to its present use. Note also the former Citizens National Bank building (71 E. Palisade) and the former railroad station, now a recording studio.

Even in this built-up area you can still see some early Dutch stone houses. Many are on Grand Ave.; the Red Cross, for example, is in the early-18th-century John G. Benson house* (60 Grand Ave.), and others are farther south on Grand (at 228,* 285,* 370,* and 488).

In the midst of this densely populated area is the Flat Rock Brook Center (443 Van Nostrand Ave., the eastern end of Van Nostrand; 201-567-1265), 150 acres of woodland, with wetlands, two ponds, a stream, meadows, and a stone quarry. One area is devoted to native plants, designed to provide habitat and serve as a model for home gardeners. There is a large greenhouse at the nature center and more than three miles of trails, a boardwalk at the quarry, and picnic facilities. You can pick up trail maps at the center or the picnic area. The center also offers a wide range of educational programs. Grounds open dawn to dusk; office Tuesday–Friday, 9–5, weekends 1–5; groups by appointment.

Englishtown Monmouth 1,764

US 9, C 522, 527

Englishtown is known today primarily because of its huge weekend flea market, but it also has historical interest because of its connections with the Battle of Monmouth. Washington and his men spent the night here before the battle, eating at the Village Inn* (Main and Water sts.; 732-446-9061). After the battle Washington and Lord Stirling drew up the charges that were used in General Charles Lee's court-martial. They may have done this in the dining room of the inn, and Lee is said to have sat in the dining room to write some of the letters that sealed his guilt. Whether or not these events took place at the inn, they definitely took place in Englishtown. Built in 1726 (the eastern portion was added in 1820), the inn was for a long time one of the oldest continuously operating taverns in the state. The building, which serves as the headquarters for the Battleground Historical Society, has been restored and is being furnished with period pieces. A variety of events is scheduled throughout the year, and tours can be arranged by appointment.

The flea market (90 Wilson Ave.; 732-446-9644), known as the Englishtown Auction Sales (it is actually in Manalapan Township), began in 1929 as a farmers' auction and is being run by the third generation of the same family. There hasn't been an auctioneer since 1980, but over 1,000 merchants and craftspeople set up on its 50 acres on weekends. Open Saturday, 7–4, Sunday, 9–4.

Ewing Township Mercer 35,707

I 95, NJ 29, 31

Ewing, which developed primarily as a suburb of Trenton, is home to what used to be known as Trenton State College (in 1996 the trustees decided, not without controversy, to change the college's name to the College of New Jersey, Princeton University's name for its first 150 years). The college moved to its 275-plus-acre Hillwood Lake campus over 75 years ago, when many of its red brick buildings were built. (There are also several buildings from the 21st century.) The College of New Jersey began as a normal school in the 1850s (it was then located in Trenton); it now has seven undergraduate schools, close to 6,000 undergraduate students, and a reputation for quality. Tours of the campus start from Paul Loser Hall, Monday–Thursday, 10 and 12, Friday and Saturday at 10; reservations should be made in advance (609-771-2131; 800-624-0967). The Holman Hall Art Gallery (609-771-2198) presents five or six exhibits a year; these are open to the public September–May, weekdays, 12–3, Thursday evening, 7–9, Sunday, 1–3. The music department (609-771-2775) puts on concerts of classical music almost every week, and theater productions, both student and professional, also take place in Kendall Hall (609-771-2775). Call for the schedules.

Also on the campus is the William Green house,* which dates to the 18th century. Greens born in the house served in the Revolutionary War, and Revolutionary soldiers may have been billeted there. The house is being restored and cared for by the college and the Friends of the William Green House. The aim is to preserve the historic character of the house and make it possible for it to serve as a college facility, perhaps for students or alumni.

In Ewing the state makes all the signs used on state-maintained roads (in the Department of Transportation Fernwood complex) and raises useful bugs. The Philip Alampi Beneficial Insect Rearing Laboratory (State Police Dr.; 609-530-4192) looks into ways that bugs can replace chemical pesticides for control of agricultural pests. The lab also raises in quantity beneficial bugs that cannot survive the winter. Tours can be arranged for specialized adult groups.

The state police, which celebrated its 75th anniversary in 1996 (the first superintendent was Col. H. Norman Schwarzkopf, father of the Gen. H. Norman Schwarzkopf made famous by the First Gulf War), have a museum and learning center in the West Trenton area of the township (River Rd. between I 95 and W. Upper Ferry Rd.; 609-882-2000, ext. 6401). The museum, built in the 1990s, incorporates a log cabin constructed in 1934 to house recruits. On display is material relating to the Lindbergh trial (*see* Flemington); the Lindbergh archives, which contain more than seven million items, can be seen by appointment. A Prohibition exhibit includes a complete 1920s still and a tin of whiskey confiscated from a bootlegger, and there are also exhibits of equipment, both old and new, used by the troopers. Many of the exhibits are hands-on or interactive. Open Monday–Saturday, 10–4; group tours by appointment. In this area is the Trenton bathhouse* (999 Lower Ferry Rd.), Louis Kahn's landmark buildings, built in the 1950s for the Jewish Community Center. They are in serious need of restoration, and the pavilions have been fenced off while the center works on restoration plans.

The Benjamin Temple house* (27 Federal City Rd. at Violet Cox Dr.; 609-883-2455) is a mid-18th-century house with a mid-19th-century addition, which was moved to its present location in the 1970s. The 27-acre Drake Farm Park in which it sits formed part of the tract that James Monroe suggested would be suitable for the country's capital (which, of course, is how Federal City Rd. got its name). Exhibits in the house feature artifacts related to local history as well as decorative arts, textiles, and the like. Open Wednesday 10–4; other times by appointment.

Paul Whiteman, the famous bandleader, is buried in the Ewing Church Cemetery (100 Scotch Rd.; 609-882-0273); open daily sunrise–sunset.

Fair Lawn   Bergen 31,637

NJ 4, 208, C 507

Fair Lawn, an old Dutch settlement, gained attention as the site of Radburn,* a world-famous experiment in postautomobile city planning. The concepts behind Radburn, which was built in 1929 by Clarence Stein and Henry Wright, have been widely influential in British and continental town planning. Organized in superblocks, Radburn segregated cars from people and had the fronts of the houses face common greens. Parking was close enough to a house to enable a shopper to carry groceries easily, but children could walk to school without ever crossing a street. The Depression interfered with completion of the original plan, and many post–World War II houses coexist with the 1929 buildings. It used to be possible to get a better sense of the original flavor by looking at the photographs in the lobby of the commercial building at Plaza Rd. and High Street, but in 2002 part of the building burned so it may be a while before the photographs reappear. The Radburn historic district* includes Fair Lawn, Berdan, and Prospect aves. and Plaza and Radburn roads. (For information, write or call the Radburn Association, 29-20 Fair Lawn Ave., 07410; 201-796-1300.)

Just west of Plaza Rd. on Pollitt Dr. is the Cadmus House* (201-796-7692), an early-19th-century Dutch stone house, moved to its present site (it weighed 50 tons). Once part of a farm that covered half of present-day Fair Lawn, the house has been converted to a museum. One room is furnished with Victorian pieces, another with old fire-fighting equipment, another with artifacts from a farmhouse destroyed to build a highway interchange. Two of the original 1915 rooms downstairs contain exhibits of local artifacts, memorabilia, and archaeological discoveries going back to the Native Americans. Open March–December, 3d Sunday of the month, 1–3, and by appointment; it is best to call ahead, though, as the opening times can change (in May, for example, the house is open on Memorial Day). Other early stone houses can be seen on River and Dunderhook roads.

West of Radburn near the Passaic River is the Garretson Forge and Farm Restoration* (4-02 River Rd.; 201-797-1775, 201-797-7545). The Garretson family left the Netherlands in 1660 and apparently bought this land early in the 18th century. Six generations lived on the farm until Mary Garretson died in 1950. The main section of the 18th-century house (1719) was made of dressed stone; the sandstone blocks were held together with mortar made of river mud mixed with straw and hogs' hair (the kitchen wing used undressed stone); the kitchen wing has a beehive oven. Also on the property, which was rescued from a developer, are a carriage shed, a butterfly garden, an herb garden, and gardens devoted to heirloom crops. Among the furnishings are a rope bed and a *kas* (a Dutch cupboard), and there are periodic displays of 19th- and 20th-century artifacts, early ironwork, and antique farming tools. Events on the property include outdoor cooking demonstrations and sheep-shearing, spring, fabric, and fall harvest festivals. Open Sunday, 1–4, September–November and March–June; groups and other times by appointment.

Oreos, once the country's most popular cookie (if all the Oreos eaten since 1912 were stacked on end, they would reach to the moon and back more than five times), are manufactured at the Fair Lawn Bakery (NJ 208 at McBride Ave.), as are animal crackers (50,000 animals a minute), Ritz crackers, and Fig Newtons.

One of the county's bicycle-pedestrian paths starts from Williams and Union streets.

Far Hills Somerset 859

US 202, C 512, 523

Situated on the east bank of the North Branch of the Raritan River, Far Hills is part of Somerset County's estate and hunt country. South off US 202 on Far Hills Rd. (C 512) is the Leonard J. Buck Garden (11 Layton Rd.; 908-234-2677). Now part of the county park system, the garden was once the private rock garden of a wealthy mining engineer. The rock formations on its 33 acres are covered with rare plants from Europe, Asia, and North America. In 1986 an extensive collection of ferns was added to the garden. The visitor center is in the former carriage house. The trails are open weekdays, 10–4; Saturday, 10–5; Sunday, 12–5. Closed weekends and major holidays, December–March. Guided group tours by appointment (fee charged for these tours). Just north of the garden is Moggy Hollow, a National Natural Historic Landmark. This is a narrow ravine walled off at one end by a ledge of basaltic rock that was once the spillway of the Glacial Lake Passaic. From the ledge, you can see terraces of glacial debris.

If you continue south on 512, crossing I 287 and Douglas Rd., you will come to the headquarters, museum, and library of the United States Golf Association (908-234-2300), located on the grounds of a 62-acre 1919 estate, whose main house was designed by John Russell Pope. The museum displays its permanent collection, which includes artifacts from ancient Scottish, Flemish, and Dutch games that were the ancestors of today's golf, chronologically. There is also a gallery that contains the museum's large collection of art related to the game of golf. Open daily, 10–5; closed New Year's Day, Easter, Thanksgiving, and Christmas.

On the west bank of the North Branch, directly across from the center of Far Hills, is Bedminster (population 7,086), another hunt-country village that attracted some attention as the site of the state's first Mount Laurel housing. The Hills housing development (US 202) is noticeable in a town that used to have five-acre zoning for single-family houses (it also was part of the reason the population almost tripled between 1980 and 1990). The Somerset Art Association (2020 Burnt Mills Rd.; 908-234-2345), housed in the old Pluckemin school (c. 1907), offers a wide range of classes for children and adults year-round. Its exhibits, lectures, and other programs are open to the public. Open Monday–Thursday, 9:30–4:30; Friday and Saturday, 9:30–1:30. The Pluckemin Village Historic District,* concentrated on US 206 and Burnt Mills Rd., contains many 18th- and 19th-century buildings.

At Fairview Farm Wildlife Preserve (2121 Larger Cross Rd.; 908-234-1852) the Upper Raritan Watershed Association maintains a natural area of 170 acres with five miles of trails. In addition to being a wildlife preserve, the facility has a bird and butterfly garden. The early 19th-century barns have been restored and are used for a variety of educational purposes. The association sponsors programs for children, including a summer camp. Information is available at the kiosk. Open daily during daylight hours.

Farmingdale Monmouth 1,587

C 35, 524, 547

A village with interesting 18th- and 19th-century buildings, Farmingdale was once known as Marsh's Bog and then as Upper Squankum. The historic district runs along Main St. from Asbury Ave. to the W. Main St.–N. Main St. fork.

About three miles south of Farmingdale (take Main St.) is Allaire State Park (C 524, 2 mi. west of Garden State Pkwy exit 98, 1 mi. east of I 195 exit 31; 732-938-2371). The park itself is lovely—with hiking, cross-country skiing, and nature trails (the red nature trail crosses an excellent example of a swamp forest); bridle paths; a nature center; and facilities for picnicking, canoeing, and camping—but what sets it off from other parks is Allaire Village.*

Allaire Village was once a flourishing part of New Jersey's bog-iron industry. A sawmill operated on this site in 1750, and an ironworks was here in 1813. In 1822 James Allaire, who operated a foundry in New York City and had cast the brass air chamber for Robert Fulton's steamboat the *Clermont* and the iron cylinder of the *Savannah*, the first steamship to cross the Atlantic, bought the property (then known as Howell Furnace or Howell Works). Presumably he saw it as a source of iron for his New York foundry. The community he built at Allaire (it took this name after his death in 1858) was not just self-sufficient, common enough in the 1830s, but contained a church and school as well. Stoves, pots, screws, some pipe, and hand irons were cast here before the works stopped operating in 1846. Allaire's son lived on in the village until 1901, apparently resisting any offers to make use of its facilities. Arthur Brisbane, a noted editor with the Hearst newspapers, bought the property in 1907, building himself a home across from the village. Starting in 1927 he leased the village to the Monmouth Council Boy Scouts for $1 a year, and they began the work of restoring the village. In 1941 Brisbane's widow deeded the village to the state.

Because so much of the village was left, restoration was relatively easy. Of particular note is the furnace stack, but all the buildings—the general store, the farmhouse, the blacksmith shop, the tenant's house, the enameling shop, and more—are of interest. The church (c. 1831), with its unusually placed steeple (at the rear, not the front), is still used for services in the summer. The village sponsors many special events: there are craft demonstrations, a re-creation of Saint Nicholas Day as it would have been in 1823, a farmers' market, a theater on the green, and the like (for information about special programs, call 732-938-2253). Children (and only children) may fish in the millpond, and the Pine Creek Railroad runs a steam train on a short loop through the park, weekends and holidays, April–October (diesel trains run weekdays in July and August). At the nature center (732-938-2003)

ALLAIRE VILLAGE

you will find displays relating to the natural history of the area. Nature
tours are given every afternoon the center is open (groups by appointment),
and lectures are often given on Sunday afternoon. The center is open
Memorial Day weekend–Labor Day, Wednesday–Sunday, 9–5. The village
is open May–Labor Day, Monday–Saturday, 10–5, Sunday, 12–5; September
and October, Saturday, 10–4, Sunday, 12–4. The railroad operates daily
July and August, weekends April–June and September and October, 12–5.
Admission charged for village and railroad. Brochures are available in the
visitor center.

   A fire-engine museum is planned for a site across from Allaire State
Park (north of 18th St.; 732-222-5783). The museum will have a large display
of equipment and artifacts going back to colonial times. A fire-fighters'

memorial will be at the entrance to the museum, but the hands-on interactive family-safety education center that is part of the project may well be built in an urban location. The target date for opening is 2008.

Two miles south of Farmingdale on Preventorium Rd. is the Howell Park Golf Course (732-938-4771), a county facility on 300 acres of gently rolling land bordering the Manasquan River. Near the entrance to the golf course on Southard Ave. is one of the parking lots for the Manasquan Linear Park, a greenway along the river. You can hike along the greenway and canoe and fish in the river. (The other two lots are on Jackson Mills Rd. and Casino Dr.)

To the west of the golf course is the Manasquan Reservoir (Windler Rd.; 732-919-0996). Swamplands were drained to form this reservoir, built to supply water for the growing population in the area. This 1,200-acre county park has facilities for boating (canoes, kayaks, rowboats, and sailboats; electric motors only), fishing, and ice-skating, and a five-mile trail around the reservoir. Boat tours are offered weekend afternoons, Memorial Day–September. Weekday tours can be arranged by appointment. The woods are attractive, but when the trail is on the perimeter of the park, the traffic noise can be intrusive. On the shore of the reservoir is the Manasquan Reservoir Environmental Center (Georgia Tavern Rd., Howell, 732-751-9453), a striking geothermally heated building that opened in 2002. The center features a large variety of exhibits, many interactive, and offers a wide range of educational programs for children from age three to high school seniors, as well as for adults. Open daily, 10–5, Friday until 8:30 P.M.; closed Christmas Day.

Between Allaire and Howell Park is the MacKenzie Museum and Library (C 547 between Herbertsville Rd. and I 195; 732-938-2212), run by the Howell Historical Society. This was a miller's house, started early in the 19th century and expanded in midcentury. Some of the rooms have been decorated to reflect a typical miller's house of the period, and there are period artifacts on display. There is also an outhouse out back and a barn that was originally a horse shed at the Old Tennent Church (*see* Freehold); farm implements are on display in the barn. There is also a library for genealogical research. Open Saturday, 9–12:30, and by appointment.

Continuing south on Preventorium Rd. from Howell Park to Old Tavern Rd. brings you to the Old Ardena Schoolhouse (732-938-2212), also run as a museum by the Howell Historical Society. The schoolhouse, in use from 1855 to 1938, is one room. It has the original blackboards, stove, clock, and tower bell. Open May–September, the last Sunday of the month, 1–4, and by appointment.

The fastest growing township in Monmouth County, Howell saw its population almost double between 1980 and 2000. It also has perhaps the largest Kalmyk community in the state. A special act of Congress brought several thousand Mongolians to this area in the 1950s, and at one time the town had three Buddhist temples.

Flemington Hunterdon 4,200

NJ 12, 31, C 523

Since 1785 the county seat of Hunterdon County, Flemington takes its name from Samuel Fleming, who bought land from William Penn and Daniel Coxe and in 1756 built the house now known as Fleming Castle. Flemington's first industries depended on agricultural products, but gradually poultry and cattle became more important than crops. The Flemington Auction Market, in fact, was considered the first successful cooperative egg and livestock market. (Its building has been converted to office space.) Known as an important center for flour milling, Flemington also had iron foundries, and the first of its well-known potteries dates to the early 19th century. The Flemington Cut Glass Company (156 Main St.; 908-782-3017; 800-990-8666) opened in 1908 (in 1920 it began selling seconds from the front of its factory, thus presaging today's factory outlets; *see* below). Bill Healy Crystal (Renaissance Plaza; 908-806-2100) is run by one of the country's twelve master glass cutters. Future plans call for making it possible to see demonstrations of glassblowing by appointment. Except for the cut glass, all these earlier industries are gone, but you can still see the Stangl company's old kilns at the Hill-Fulper-Stangl Museum, located at the Pfaltzgraff outlet (Mine St.; 732-846-1368). On display in the museum are examples of pottery made at the site between 1814 (when it opened as Hill Pottery) and 1978, when production ceased. Open by appointment.

Some 65 percent of Flemington's structures are listed in the state and national historic registers, and the historic district* includes Broad, Main, E. Main, N. Main, Spring, Court, Bonnell, Mine, William, Brown, Academy, Capner, and Church sts.; Park, Bloomfield, Emery, Maple, Grant, Dewey, Hopewell, Pennsylvania, New York, Central, and Lloyd aves.; and Chorister Place. The old county courthouse (northwest corner of Main and Court), with its Greek Revival details, dates to the late 1820s and uses some of the walls from the burned-out courthouse of 1791–93. This building received international attention in 1935 when the trial of Bruno Hauptmann for kidnapping and murdering the baby son of aviation hero Charles Lindbergh was held there. Memorabilia from the Lindbergh trial are on display in the lobby of the courthouse. In 1996 the county opened a new courthouse (Park Ave. and Capner St.). Plans for the future of the old courthouse are under discussion, but in the meantime the display remains in the lobby (call 908-788-1168 to make sure it is still there).

Across the street from the old courthouse is the Union Hotel (76 Main St.), rebuilt in 1862 after a fire. (There has been a hotel on this site since the early 19th century.) The hotel was altered again in 1877–78 to produce today's mansard-roofed extravaganza with its towers and deep front porch. Baron Renfrew, later England's George VII, is among the celebrities who have signed the Union Hotel's guest register, and during the Lindbergh trial the reporters all congregated here.

Also across the street from the old courthouse is the Doric House (114 Main St.; 908-782-1091), a Greek Revival structure built by Mahlon Fisher (responsible for many of Flemington's mid-19th-century houses). Formerly a residence, a restaurant, and a church school, it is now the home of the Hunterdon County Historical Society and contains a museum and a library. Among the items in the museum are Empire furniture, pier glass mirrors, a tall case clock made by a Flemington craftsman, and a collection of Fulper pottery. Open by appointment. Library open Thursday, 1–3, 7–9, and by appointment.

Fleming Castle (5 Bonnell St.; 908-735-4857, 908-237-1132), the town's oldest remaining house and now owned by the Daughters of the American Revolution, has served as an inn and a stage depot. Tours by appointment.

You may enjoy wandering about the downtown streets, for there are many interesting buildings. Note the Calvary Church (Broad St. and New York Ave.), built in the 1880s. Henry Beck, the well-known New Jersey popular historian, was rector here from 1949 to 1956. The county building at 3 Chorister Pl. was once used by the Flemington Children's Choir School, which trained children to sing in choirs from early in the 20th century until 1958. Memorabilia from the choir school can be seen upstairs by appointment weekdays, 8:30–4:30; call 908-788-1256.

In 1965 a development began that has changed Flemington considerably. What was described as a post–Revolutionary War version of colonial Williamsburg, known as Turntable Junction (Mine St.), was assembled on the site of a former railroad turntable and brickyard. It was followed by Liberty Village (Church St.), which featured weavers, candlemakers, glassblowers, and the like dressed in period costumes, giving public demonstrations of their craft. Although Turntable Junction and Liberty Village both still exist, they changed owners in the late 1970s, and they now no longer operate as late-18th-century reconstructions but as outlet areas. In fact, since 1980 or so, Flemington has become widely known as an upscale discount center, and on weekends the influx of shoppers can be impressive.

The Black River & Western Steam Railroad runs passenger trains between Flemington (Stangl Rd. and NJ 12; 908-782-9600) and Ringoes. (*See* Ringoes for details.)

One mile north of the Flemington circle is Northlandz (495 US 202; 908-782-4022), "home of the Great American Railway," a model railroad setup said to be the world's largest. With some eight miles of track and over 100 trains running through a variety of realistic and fanciful scenery, all made by hand, the exhibit has an idiosyncratic quality attributable to its being the creation of a single person. Also at Northlandz are a theater with a 2,000-pipe organ, changing art displays, and a doll collection. Open weekdays, 10:30–4, weekends, 10–6. Admission charge.

Some five miles north and east of the US 202–NJ 31–NJ 12 Flemington circle is Schaefer Farm (1051 C 523; 908-782-2705). The farm features a large barnyard petting zoo attractive to children and a farmstand made from an old wagon shed. Hayrides, including haunted hayrides, are offered in the fall. There is also a haunted corn maze (Mass Acre) and a haunted walk. Open early spring through Halloween, Monday–Saturday, 9–6, Sunday, 9–5. In October, there are evening events on Friday, Saturday, and Sunday (not recommended for children under ten), 7–10.

A little further along C 523 is the Readington River Buffalo Company (937 C 523; 908-806-0030), New Jersey's only bison farm. An annual buffalo watch takes place Memorial Day weekend, there are special events in August and October, and hayrides in October, but you are welcome to visit the farm when the store is open, weekends 9–4; other times and tours by appointment.

Continuing on C 523 in Readington Township you will reach one of the Readington Museums, the Eversole-Hall house (509 C 523; 908-236-2327). The timber-frame farmhouse basically dates to the 1830s, and the house has been furnished to reflect that era, but what is now the keeping room is probably pre-Revolutionary. Also on the property are a kitchen garden, a barn, a corncrib, a hand pump (still the only source of water to the house), a washhouse, and an outhouse. Open by appointment. Another of the

Readington Museums is the Cold Brook School (Potterstown Rd. near I 78; 908-236-2327), a one-room schoolhouse dating to 1828 and furnished as a school would have been in the 1830s. Open by appointment. A third Readington Museum, the Bouman-Stickney house (114 Dreahook Rd., near Stanton; 908-236-2327), is a stone Dutch bank house built in 1741. (Bouman was the original owner, Stickney was the actress Dorothy Stickney, whose husband, Howard Lindsay, bought it as a weekend retreat in the 1930s.) Documents relating to the early families in the area have helped make it possible to furnish the house as authentically as possible. Also on the property is a reconstructed New World Dutch barn, probably built before 1820, and moved from another location. Open the first Sunday of the month, 1–4, except for major holidays, and by appointment. On open Sundays, someone demonstrates a traditional craft. A self-guided nature trail goes through the surrounding 68 acres, and the trails are open year-round, dawn to dusk, for horseback riding and cross-country skiing.

Forked River Ocean 4,914

US 9

Located at the head of the Forked River, which empties into Barnegat Bay, the village of Forked (pronounced *For-ked*) River, like many of the nearby bay towns, was settled before the Revolution and lived off fishing and shipbuilding. Boating and fishing are still important, but the fishing tends to be sport fishing, and the boating tends to center around the Forked River state marina (311 S. Main St.; 609-693-5045).

Many of Forked River's older buildings are still standing, some being restored, others showing evidence of the various functions they have served over the years. The mid-19th-century Worden House at the corner of US 9 and Jones Rd. now serves as a meeting place for community groups; the late-19th-century Methodist Church (Main St.) stands next to the site of the Forked River House, built in 1820 and destroyed by an arson fire in the early 1990s. The building had been frequented by Captain Joshua Huddy during his patrols (Huddy was looking for loyalists; his capture and execution by the British caused a minor incident toward the end of the Revolution). The Captain's Inn (Lacey Rd.) dates to 1813 and at one time was a state-licensed gambling casino. North of the marina, off US 9, is the state's former game farm, which was run by the Corrections Department on an 18th-century estate; the land is now part of the Forsythe National Wildlife Refuge (*see* Oceanville).

Across from the site of the Forked River House is the Old Schoolhouse Museum (Main St.; 609-971-0467), run by the Lacey Township Historical Society. The building dates to 1860, and the collection features local tools and other artifacts relating to the history of Forked River. The society also sponsors an apple festival the last weekend in September. Open mid-June–Labor Day, Monday, Wednesday, Friday, 1–3, Saturday, 10–12; groups by appointment other times.

South of the center of town is the Jersey Central Power & Light's Oyster Creek Nuclear Generating Station (US 9; 609-971-2180), one of the oldest nuclear power plants in the country (it opened in 1969). Tours of the facility may be arranged by appointment.

North of Forked River (take 9 north about 5 mi. to C 618, Central Pkwy, turn left, and continue past the Garden State Pkwy) is Double Trouble State Park* (Double Trouble Rd.; 732-341-6662), 8,000 acres along the eastern edge of the Pinelands National Reserve. A sawmill was first built on this stretch of the Cedar Creek in the 1760s, and the name Double Trouble was in use by the 1800s. Cranberries were harvested here in the 1830s, and the state, having restored the sawmill and the packing house, is working to protect the cranberry workers' houses and other buildings. It is hoped that some day these buildings can be open to the public for tours, but in the meantime you can walk on the self-guided nature trail. It has been said that the Cedar Creek watershed is the most pristine in the state.

West of Forked River (take Lacey Rd. c. 6½ mi. from exit 74 of the Garden State Pkwy and turn right on Humane Way), within the Greenwood Forest and Pasadena Wildlife Management Area, is Popcorn Park Zoo (609-693-1900). The zoo started as a refuge for wildlife that could not exist on its own and now provides a home for both wild and exotic species that have been abandoned, neglected, or mistreated. A dog and cat shelter and an animal hospital are also on the property, and the Pinelands vegetation has not been landscaped away. Zoo open daily, 11–5, shelter open 12–6. Groups by appointment with two weeks' notice. Admission charged.

The rest of the Greenwood Forest and Pasadena Wildlife Management Area (609-292-2965) consists of over 27,000 acres of pitch pine, white oak, and white cedar scrub. This is a good place to see Pine Barrens frogs, and at Webb's Mill Bog Cedar Swamp (toward the northern end of the area, just off C 539), a boardwalk and trail give you a good vantage point from which to observe the local plants and animals.

Fort Lee Bergen 35,461

I 95, US 9W, 46, NJ 4, 5, 67, C 505

Known to many commuters simply as one end of the George Washington Bridge, Fort Lee sits on the cliffs of the Palisades overlooking the Hudson River. It takes its name from the fort George Washington located there during the Revolution to prevent the British from sailing up the Hudson. Washington was forced to abandon Fort Lee when Fort Washington across the river fell to the British.

From about 1903 to 1920, Fort Lee was the national center of the young motion-picture industry; the adventures of Pearl White were filmed here, and D. W. Griffith, Fatty Arbuckle, and Theda Bara, among others, began their film careers in Fort Lee. Altogether some 900 movies were shot in Fort Lee, and folk etymology has it that the word "cliffhanger" derives from the serials that were shot on the Palisades.

In 1931 the George Washington Bridge, considered by many one of the most beautiful suspension bridges in the world, was opened; a second level was added in 1962. A National Historic Civil Engineering Landmark, the bridge is a key link in the system of roads bypassing the metropolitan area. With 14 lanes and a center span of roughly 3,500 feet, the bridge connects with the New Jersey Turnpike and many other major roads. The only 14-lane suspension bridge in the world and the busiest bridge in the state, it is used by almost 106 million vehicles a year. The Hudson River Waterfront Walkway that will eventually extend uninterrupted along the Hudson to the Bayonne Bridge starts at the George Washington Bridge.

Since the building of the bridge, Fort Lee's population has increased significantly. In 1962, Horizon Houses, a group of award-winning high-rise apartments, created the first silhouette on the Palisades skyline. There are many more such buildings now. The bridge has also caused the borough some financial concerns: apparently one-quarter of the land in Fort Lee is taken up by the bridge or belongs to the Port Authority, and to deal with the traffic the bridge generates, the town has a much larger police force than most towns its size.

One-quarter mile east of the original Fort Lee, in Fort Lee Historic Park (Hudson Terrace; 201-461-1776), are reconstructed Revolutionary gun batteries, soldiers' huts, and campsites. At the visitor center exhibits and films explain the British assault. The park, which is run by the Palisades Interstate Park Commission, also sponsors educational programs for school groups and an annual Revolutionary reenactment. Picnic facilities are available at the north end of the park. Grounds open daily, sunrise to sunset; visitor center open Wednesday–Sunday, 10–5. School groups by appointment.

The art gallery at the public library (320 Main St.; 201-592-3615) highlights the work of local artists, but others from the metropolitan area are also shown. Exhibits change once a month. Open Monday–Thursday, 9:30–9; Friday and Saturday, 9:30–5; Sunday (except in July and August), 1–5.

Highlighting local history is the Fort Lee Museum at Judge Moore House (1588 Palisade Ave.; 201-592-3580). The museum, run by the Fort Lee Historical Society, occupies a 1920s house built of Palisades bluestone and contains the society's archives and exhibits. Exhibits focus on items related to Fort Lee and change every few months. Open weekends 12–4; groups and other times by appointment. The museum is part of Monument Park (Palisade ave. and Angioletti Place), a small area that was used by Washington's army. Summer concerts are given in the park, which contains a Revolutionary War monument. Open 8 A.M.–10 P.M. during daylight savings time, 8 A.M.–7 P.M. the rest of the year.

About two miles west of Fort Lee (in the communities of Leonia, Palisades Park, Ridgefield Park, and Teaneck) is Overpeck County Park (Fort Lee Rd., Cedar La., Roosevelt St.; 201-944-3249, 201-944-7474, 201-807-0201), over 800 acres with a golf course (201-837-3020), tennis courts, playing fields, hiking and bicycle paths, picnic areas, a year-round horseback riding center (201-242-1920), and a wildlife refuge. You can also fish from the lakeshore.

Franklin Sussex 5,160

NJ 23, C 517

Franklin was once the leading zinc-mining town in the United States. In the early 19th century, Samuel Fowler, a physician and member of Congress, who was largely responsible for the settlement of Franklin, found zinc ore on his land. Having perfected a process for making zinc-based paint in the 1830s, he tried to persuade New York City to ban the use of lead-based paints. He also helped persuade Congress, when it passed a weights-and-measures law in 1836, to stipulate that the brass used in the weights must contain New Jersey red oxide zinc. Fowler did not profit from these developments, however, for by the time an inexpensive method of extracting zinc from the ore was developed (in 1848), he had died. The New Jersey Zinc Company, which operated the mine on what had been his property, continued to work it for over 100 years, until it was depleted in 1954.

The Franklin area is rich in minerals (over 300 have been found here). Many of them are fluorescent, and some are not found anyplace else. On the site of the old zinc mine is the Franklin Mineral Museum (Evans St. between Main St. and Buckwheat Rd.; 973-827-3481). Here you can see exhibits of the minerals found at Franklin, in various stages of refinement; an exhibit of fluorescent minerals that lets you see how they glow under ultraviolet light; and, in the old enginehouse, a replica of a mine, built entirely from materials used in Franklin zinc mines. This is a popular goal of school trips in spring and fall. The museum also administers the slag heap, known as the Buckwheat Dump, where collectors can look for their own rocks. Picnic sites are available. Each fall the museum sponsors a mineral show. Open weekdays, 10–4, Saturday, 10–5, Sunday, 11–5, April–November, weekends only, March; groups by appointment. Admission charged.

In the same mineral-rich area, about two miles south of Franklin (take 517), is the Sterling Hill Mining Museum (30 Plant St.; 973-209-7212). Located in Ogdensburg on the site of the Sterling Hill Mine,* the last operating zinc mine and the last operating underground mine in the state, the museum emphasizes the history of mining and the history of the area. You can take the only underground mine tour in the state, which includes two underground fluorescent displays. Open 10–5, daily, March–November, with tours at 1; other times by appointment. On the same property in an early-20th-century ore mill is the Thomas S. Warren Museum of Fluorescence, which contains displays of a large variety of types of fluorescence. The Warren Museum is included in the mining museum tour; for special arrangements call 973-209-7212.

Also in Ogdensburg is the Old Schoolhouse and Firehouse Museum (6 Passaic Ave.; 973-827-3444). The building, which dates to 1910, was put up as an addition to a 19th-century school building. In 1930, the older part of the school was demolished, and this building was moved and turned into the borough's first firehouse. Exhibits include old fire equipment, memorabilia relating to the school and to the Sterling Mine, material on Thomas Edison's nearby iron mine (a few of the houses from Edison's mining town are now in Ogdensburg), and other artifacts and documents relating to Ogdensburg's past. Open by appointment.

Franklin Lakes Bergen 10,422

I 287, US 202, NJ 208, C 502

This rapidly growing suburbanized area still has a large number of early Dutch stone houses (drive along Franklin, Pulis, Woodside, Circle, Summit, Mabel Ann, and Ewing aves., Franklin Lake Rd., and Vee Dr.). On Ewing Ave. about one mile south of NJ 208 is the New Jersey Audubon Society's Lorrimer Sanctuary and Nature Center (790 Ewing Ave.; 201-891-2185). In the sanctuary are self-guided nature trails, a butterfly and hummingbird garden, and two picnic areas. Part of the visitors' center dates to the late 18th century. In the building are both permanent and changing exhibits, some of them hands-on, and the society offers many educational programs and tours. Open Wednesday–Friday, 9–5; Saturday, 10–5; Sunday, 1–5. High Mountain just south of the sanctuary is a good spot for viewing hawks.

The Gallery at the Presbyterian Church at Franklin Lakes (730 Franklin Lake Rd. between Ewing Ave. and Mountain Lake Rd.; 201-891-0511) offers exhibits of professional artists hung in several spaces in the church; exhibits tend to change every 4–6 weeks. Open weekdays, September–May, 10–4, and by appointment.

The Saddle Ridge horseback riding center (Shadow Ridge Rd. off Pulis Ave.; 201-847-9999), operated for the county park system, offers lessons daily, as well as trail rides, after-school programs, and a summer camp. The area, a former Nike missile site high on Campgaw Mountain, adjoins the Campgaw Reservation (*see* Mahwah).

Freehold Monmouth 19,976 (borough) 31,537 (township)

US 9, NJ 33, 79, C 522, 537

The seat of Monmouth County, Freehold was settled in 1715 by a group of Scottish immigrants who had traveled inland from Matawan. The center of a rich agricultural area, Freehold Township was also the scene of one of the major battles of the American Revolution, the Battle of Monmouth (28 June 1778). Although this was not a clear-cut victory for the Continental army, it did establish the fact that the newly trained troops could hold their own in conventional open-field fighting. It also created a folk heroine, Molly Pitcher; bringing water to the troops throughout the hot day (102°F), she, according to tradition, took over her husband's position at his cannon when he was wounded. (It is likely the water was actually intended for the cannons, not the soldiers.) And because Major General Charles Lee unexpectedly ordered a retreat (Washington arrived in time to countermand the order and rally the troops, giving vent to what was for him an unusual display of temper), considerable controversy surrounds the battle.

At Monument Park in the center of town, near the spot where the fighting first broke out, a 100-foot tower commemorates the battle. On the top of the monument, which was dedicated in 1884, is a statue of Columbia, and, near the base, there are five bas-relief plaques, one of which shows Molly Pitcher at work during the battle. At 70 Court St. (732-462-1466) near the monument, in a Georgian-style building built especially for the purpose in 1931, are the headquarters and library of the Monmouth County Historical Association (founded in 1898). The museum has exceptional collections of furniture, clothing, paintings, and decorative arts, much of which was made in New Jersey or owned by New Jersey residents. Changing exhibits from the collection also include folk art and military objects, and the museum owns Emanuel Leutze's painting of the Battle of Monmouth (Leutze's familiar painting of Washington crossing the Delaware hangs in the Metropolitan Museum in New York City). Open Tuesday–Saturday, 10–4. Admission fee.

The association also runs several historic houses, including, in Freehold, the early-18th-century Covenhoven House* (150 W. Main St.; 732-462-1466), a national historic landmark, which was used by Sir Henry Clinton (the British general) as his headquarters the day before the Battle of Monmouth. Using an inventory from 1790, the association has furnished the house to illustrate how a successful farmer lived in the last years of the 18th century. Open May–September, Thursday–Saturday, 1–4. Closed 4 July. Groups by appointment other times. Admission fee.

The courthouse dates from the 1950s and replaces four earlier buildings. Saint Peter's Episcopal Church (33 Throckmorton St.; 732-462-9264) is a mid-18th-century church that was used as an army storehouse and a hospital during the Battle of Monmouth. Near it (51–53 Throckmorton) is the volunteer fire department's first building (1874)—now used for shops and offices. Note also the American Hotel (1824) at 20 E. Main St. (732-462-0819). Main St. on summer evenings presents an unusually lively scene.

Monmouth Battlefield,* the main battleground for the Battle of Monmouth, remains practically as it was in June 1778. A national historic landmark, it lies northwest of the village and forms part of Monmouth Battlefield State Park (347 Freehold-Englishtown Rd.; C 522, the extension of Throckmorton St., just west of US 9; 732-462-9616). The visitor center (off NJ 33) has exhibits explaining the battle and other interpretive displays. The park's 1,800 acres include a variety of habitats and some 25 miles of trails (many of them unmarked). You can pick up descriptive brochures at the visitor center. About one-quarter of the park is cultivated by local farmers to whom the state leases land. One farmer, whose family has been in the area since the Revolution, grows wheat, corn, and soybeans; another has a pick-your-own orchard and pumpkin fields. Visitor center open daily, summer (Memorial Day weekend–Labor Day), 9–5; winter, 9–4. Park open daily summer, 8–8, winter, 8–4:30.

On park property is Craig House (turn west off US 9, at Schibanoff Rd., north of the intersection with C 522; 732-462-9616). This house, which was built in 1710 and has chunks of local bog iron in its foundation, belonged to

John Craig, paymaster for the local militia, and may have been used as a British hospital during the Battle of Monmouth. It has been restored to its 18th-century appearance. Open Sunday, April–mid-November, 12:30–4:30.

At the northwestern corner of the park (Craig and Tennent rds.) is the Old Tennent Presbyterian Church.* The congregation was founded in the 1690s, and the current church, which still has the original 17th-century weather vane, was built in 1751. In its cemetery, listed on the state register of historic places, are buried many who fell in the Battle of Monmouth. The church sponsors an annual drive-through Christmas pageant the first weekend in December (732-446-6299).

At the intersection of US 9 and NJ 33 is the Freehold Raceway (732-462-3800). The oldest pari-mutuel harness track in the country, it was established in the 1850s by the Monmouth County Agricultural Society on a site that may have seen racing in the 1830s (the track has not run continuously). Live races August–May.

Several county parks are in the area. The East Freehold Park (Kozloski Rd.; take Center St. east c. 2 mi. from the center of town; 732-842-4000) is an 81-acre showground, the site of the county fair held each July and attended by over 100,000 visitors, and the Monmouth County Horse Show, held in mid-August and over 100 years old.

Durand Park (east on C 537 c. 3 mi.; turn left, or north, on Randolph Rd.; 732-294-2000) is a county reservation currently being leased to Freehold Township. In the park is a prize-winning memorial garden. South of Durand across C 537 (on Burlington Rd.) is the Baysholm Conservation Area (732-842-4000), 70 acres that are undeveloped and used for nature observation.

Some six miles southwest of the center of Freehold (within Freehold Township) are Turkey Swamp Park (Georgia Rd.; turn west off US 9; 732-462-7286) and Turkey Swamp Wildlife Management Area. Within the park's 1,500 acres are areas devoted to family and group camping; there are also open recreation areas, hiking and nature trails, picnic areas, and a 17-acre lake available for paddleboating, canoeing, fishing, and skating. Camping March–November. Registration for group use. The wildlife area (west of the park) consists of some 3,500 acres of noncontiguous parcels that include upland woodlands, lowlands, swampy areas, and fields. It is used for birding, hiking, archery (access to the archery area is through Turkey Swamp Park), and hunting.

Today's West Freehold, centered on the intersection of C 537, Wemrock Rd., and Stillwell's Corner Rd., has several surviving older buildings, sometimes referred to as West Freehold Historic Village. The Oakley Farm Museum* (Wemrock Rd. and Oakley Dr.; 732-577-9766) is in a 17th-century farmhouse that apparently came through the Revolution unscathed because it belonged to a loyalist family. The house was also reputed to have been a stop on the Underground Railroad. Among the items on display are the contents of the village's original blacksmith shop. Moore's Inn, formerly Mount's Tavern, also dates to the 17th century. One of its original rooms remains. A mid-19th-century one-room schoolhouse (on Wemrock Rd. ½ mile from the museum) also survives. Spring and fall festivals with crafters take place at the museum. Open by appointment.

Frenchtown   Hunterdon   1,488

NJ 12, 29, C 513, 610, 619

Located on the Delaware River between Milford and Stockton, Frenchtown began as a ferry town in the mid-18th century; its strategic importance was considered sufficient to exempt the ferry operator from service in the Revolutionary War. In the 1790s the land was bought by a French-speaking Swiss aristocrat, Paul Henri Mallet-Prevost, wanted by the French for having saved his countrymen in the French Revolution. The town came to be called French's Town, then Frenchtown, after Mallet-Prevost.

Thomas Lowrey, from whom Mallet-Prevost bought the land, had already erected a gristmill and sawmill, both of which continued to operate into the 20th century, grinding corn into feed for the area's poultry industry. (One hatchery in Frenchtown was producing between 5 and 6 million chicks annually in the 1880s; by the 1930s production was up to some 15 million chicks a year.) Today many of Frenchtown's renovated and restored buildings house artists, antiques dealers, and restaurants.

Mallet-Prevost experimented with growing grapes on his land, and the Delaware grape is the result of crossing some of his vines with native American grapes. In a return to local viticulture, one of the state's first farm wineries opened on the site of one of the chicken hatcheries. (In 1982 licensing arrangements for wineries were relaxed to allow the establishment of wineries that used New Jersey grapes; the requirement was further relaxed to allow farm wineries to purchase up to 49 percent of their grapes outside the state for the first five years.) In the early 1990s another winery opened in the area, but neither is active today.

The Oak Summit School (190 Oak Summit Rd.; take Ridge Rd. to 519, turn left, or north, and continue to the first right; 908-996-4633) is a one-room schoolhouse built c. 1849. Closed in 1953, the school has been restored and looks as it did in the 1920s and '30s, outhouses and all; inside are slate blackboards, old textbooks, and a wood-burning stove. Tours by appointment. On the same corner is the Oak Summit Cemetery (five Revolutionary and four Civil War veterans are buried there) and a stone church built in the 1830s.

Going south on 519 from the Oak Summit School, you will soon reach the Kingwood Township Municipal Building (C 519 and Oak Grove Rd; 908-996-4276). Prehistoric artifacts unearthed in the township are on display here weekdays, 9–3. Continuing south on 519 to Fairview Rd. brings you to the Old Fairview School (12 Fairview Rd.; 908-996-4851). A one-room schoolhouse converted to a community center, it houses the Kingwood Historical Society archives as well as memorabilia and artifacts. Exhibits change from time to time. Tours by appointment.

Glassboro   Gloucester   19,068

US 322, NJ 47, C 536, 553

Glassboro was founded in 1775 by a family of German glassblowers, the widow Stanger and her seven sons, who had worked at the Casper Wistar works in Salem County. Although the town derived its name from its glass factories, cheaper production methods elsewhere have forced all the works to shut down. The Stangers did not themselves prosper from their glassworks, but the works survived, reaching their peak of production in the 1840s, when they were under the control of Thomas and Samuel Whitney. The Stangers, were, however, highly influential and took the style of South Jersey glass they developed to other glass factories throughout the East. You will find many examples of their work in museums that collect decorative arts. In the 1840s the Whitney Glassworks produced an enormously popular bottle, shaped like a log cabin and supposedly modeled on William Henry Harrison's house, which was filled by a Philadelphia liquor distiller named E. C. Booz, leading to the spread of the word "booze" in this country (the use of the word to mean "drink," however, can be dated at least as far back as 1732).

In 1849 the Whitney brothers built themselves a mansion* (Whitney Ave.) on a 55-acre estate called Holly Bush. Of native Jersey sandstone, the mansion may have been designed by John Notman. Now the administration building for Rowan University, it became internationally famous in June 1967 when it served as the site of a three-day summit meeting between President Lyndon B. Johnson and Soviet premier Aleksei Kosygin. A second presidential visit to Glassboro occurred in June 1986, when President Ronald Reagan delivered the high school graduation address. Most of the campus buildings are new, but the university grew out of a state teachers' college founded in 1923. Formerly known as Glassboro State College, it changed its name in the early 1990s when Henry and Betty Rowan, the owners of a Rancocas firm that is the country's largest manufacturer of industrial furnaces, gave the institution $100 million, at the time the largest single gift ever given to a public college. Productions by the School of Fine and Performing Arts are open to the public; for information and schedules call 856-256-4545. At the Westby Art Gallery (856-256-4521) exhibits focus on contemporary art, and every other year there is a faculty show. Exhibits change roughly every six weeks, but there is not always an exhibit during vacation periods. Open weekdays, 10–4.

Another 1840s building of native sandstone with Gothic Revival details, St. Thomas' Episcopal Church* (Main and Focer sts.), is also tentatively

Rowan University
N
Campus
Pomona
Baldwin
Carpenter St.
Delsea Dr.
Focer Dr.
C536
West St.
302
Whitney-Capie house
Focer St.
St. Thomas' Episcopal Church
47
MacClelland Ave.
Holly Bush
Eben Pl.
Franklin House
Over Rd.
Whitney Ave.
New St.
Eben Pl.
Wright
Victoria St.
New St.
High St.
Holly St.
302
Cedar Ave.
Lake St.
Poplar St.
Main St.
Academy
State St.
To: Glassboro WMA
Oakwood Ave.
Franklin St.
Ellis St.
Church
Heritage Glass Museum
Center
Liberty

attributed to Notman. It supersedes a frame church that may have been located at Main and Broadway, where many members of the Stanger family are buried.

At the corner of High and Center sts., on land that was once the site of the Whitney Glassworks, is the Heritage Glass Museum (856-881-7468). Housed in a 1926 bank building (when the bank closed in 1931, two of its directors faced embezzlement charges), the museum preserves and exhibits historic bottles, glass, and related items. Open Saturday, 11–2 and the 3d Sunday of the month, 12–4.

Another building of interest is the Whitney-Capie house (29 West St.), a Victorian house built by a member of the Whitney family during the Civil War; enclosed in one of its clapboard wings is an earlier brick house that stood on the site. At the corner of Main and West is a new building that replaced a late-18th-century inn, which in turn had replaced a tavern built by Solomon Stanger in the early 1770s.

South of the city (access lies off NJ 47) is the Glassboro Wildlife Management Area, one of the earliest such areas (it was started in 1935). The 2,300 acres of woodlands and fields are open to hikers, photographers, bird-watchers, and hunters. East of the wildlife management area is Scotland Run Park (Clayton-Williamstown Rd., C 610, and Fries Mill Rd., C 655; 856-881-0845), a county facility of over 900 acres. You can boat and fish on Wilson Lake, and on the other side of C 610 from the lake is a nature center, which sponsors a variety of programs, including bird walks, nature hikes, and camps for children. Behind the center is a nature trail; you can pick up maps in the center. There are other trails in the park, but because of the wetlands, not all the area is accessible. Also in the park are an

arboretum, a playground, and a picnic grove. The nature center is open
Tuesday–Thursday, 8:30–1; groups, tours, and scout camping by appointment.

Glen Gardner Hunterdon 1,902

NJ 31

Situated on the Spruce Run and once known as Sodom (Sodom
La. still appears on maps), Glen Gardner was an iron-mining
town in the 19th century, and although the population doubled
between 1980 and 1990, much of the part of the town lying east
of NJ 31 preserves the look of another era, with the houses and
balconies right up against the street. Of architectural interest are the
Masonic Temple (converted to commercial purposes) and, coming into town
on School St., the iron bridge* (1870). If you climb Mt. Kipp on Sanatorium
Rd., you will come to a state-run psychiatric center, formerly a tuberculosis
sanatorium. The road runs through a game refuge and pine forests with
wonderful views; some of the buildings at the center have the look of a
European spa or Adirondack sanatorium.

Some two miles east of Glen Gardner is Voorhees State Park (251 C 513,
off 31; 908-638-6969), whose 630 wooded acres are particularly lovely in fall.
The land, once the farm of Foster M. Voorhees, a governor of New Jersey
from 1898 to 1902, was willed to the state in 1927. It was also the site of a
Civilian Conservation Corps camp in the 1930s, and one barn, the pavilion,
and much of the infrastructure dates from the work of the CCC. There are
picnic sites here, as well as hiking trails and facilities for camping and fishing;
in winter you can cross-country ski. Stop by at the office for maps of the
park. The office is open 8–8, Memorial Day–Labor Day, 8–4, the rest of the
year; the park is open 8–dusk year-round.

Also within the park is the New Jersey Astronomical Association's Paul
H. Robinson Observatory (Observatory Rd.; 908-638-8500). The public is
welcome for talks, tours, and viewing through the telescope Saturday,
8:30–10:30 P.M., Sunday, 2–5, Memorial Day–October; the 4th Saturday of the
month, November and February–April. Saturday nights are devoted to
watching the night sky; on Sunday afternoons, filtered telescopes are used to
observe the sun. Additional hours may be scheduled for special events like
meteor showers or eclipses. Groups by appointment, usually on Friday.

West of Voorhees is the Ken Lockwood Gorge Wildlife Management
Area (Raritan River Rd.; 609-984-0547), 400 particularly beautiful acres of
mixed hardwood forest with varied understory and ground cover bisected by
the South Branch of the Raritan River. It is highly recommended for hikers,
bird-watchers, and photographers.

South of Voorhees in High Bridge is the High Bridge Historical Society's
Solitude House Museum (7 River Rd.; 908-638-3200). The house dates to the
early 18th century and is connected with the iron industry which flourished

in 18th-century High Bridge. One room of the museum is devoted to that industry; two other rooms feature changing exhibits, including artifacts found on the property (such as a penny dated 1695). The museum is building up a collection of oral histories and also sponsors various special events. Open May–November, 2d and 4th Sunday, 2–4. Groups and other times by appointment.

Northwest of Glen Gardner in New Hampton (57 Musconetcong River Rd.; take 31 north c. 2 mi. to Musconetcong River Rd. and turn right) is the Township of Lebanon Museum (908-537-6464). Built as a one-room schoolhouse in 1825, the building was enlarged in the 1870s. A 19th-century schoolroom has been re-created on the first floor; on the second are a gallery and a lecture hall. Permanent exhibits include a Lenape collection and farm tools. Other exhibits, which change roughly every two months, have featured such collections as poison bottles, clothespin dolls, and Stangl pottery; there are also art shows, quilt shows, regular lecture series, and craft classes. School groups frequently come to experience a day in a 19th-century one-room school. Open Tuesday and Thursday, 9:30–5; Saturday, 1–5; groups by appointment.

Green Brook Somerset 5,654

US 22, C 529

According to tradition George Washington in 1777 stood at the site that is now Washington Rock State Park (C 529; 201-915-3401), watched the British troops on the plain below, and was able to plan a strategy that cut off their retreat. At this 50-acre park are an overview, woods to walk in, and facilities for picnicking.

North of Green Brook, in Watchung, is the Watchung Arts Center (18 Stirling Rd.; 908-753-0190). Housed in a former school building dating to 1860, the center sponsors jazz, folk, and classical concerts, art shows, and theater, and offers classes for children and adults as well as a children's summer art camp. Shows in the center's two art galleries change every month. Open Monday, Thursday–Saturday, 1–4.

Southeast of Watchung in the borough of North Plainfield is the Fleetwood Museum of Art and Photographica (614 Greenbrook Ave. at Clinton Ave.; 908-756-7810). Housed in the early-19th-century Vermeule mansion, the museum features a large collection of antique and classic cameras as well as more modern specialized cameras. Open Saturday, 10–4; groups and other times by appointment. The North Plainfield Exempt Firemen's Museum (300 Somerset St.; 908-757-5720) contains antique fire equipment, including horse- and hand-drawn pieces and a silver hose cart from New York City. Open 1st Sunday of the month, May–November, plus one Sunday in mid-April, 11–3; groups and other times by appointment. The Washington Park historic district,* most of which dates from 1868 to 1917, contains a variety of Victorian architecture and landscaping. The district includes Rockview Terrace, Park Pl., and Linden, Mercer, Myrtle, Orchard, Rockview, Sycamore, Washington, and Willow avenues. The high school, which celebrated its 100th birthday in 1995, is said to be the oldest in Somerset County.

Greenwich Cumberland 847

C 602, 623

Situated on the Cohansey River in the tidewater country of southern New Jersey, Greenwich (pronounced *Green-witch* by many oldtimers) reached its apogee before the Revolution. For a time it was the largest town in Cumberland County, and for some 10 or 11 months in 1748, it served as the county seat. It is now one of New Jersey's most Brigadoon-like communities. The town was laid out by John Fenwick, the English Quaker who founded Salem. He envisioned a main street two miles long and 100 feet wide, and by 1684 (the year after his death) Quakers, Presbyterians, and Baptists had begun buying 16-acre lots. Today the Greate St. is indeed 100 feet wide and tree lined, and the Greenwich Historic District,* with its 17th-, 18th-, and 19th-century buildings, extends along the Greate St. from the Cohansey River north to Othello.

So prosperous was the shipping at Greenwich that in 1687 the village was named the official port of entry for all ships traveling on the Delaware River, and in 1695 it was chosen as a market town. Market fairs were held twice yearly in Greenwich until the mid-1760s. It was a blow to Greenwich when Bridgeton was chosen as the county seat in late 1748, and by 1800 road travel had become so much easier that Greenwich's position as a transportation center declined. The town's remarkable 18th-century appearance was discovered after World War II, but although it now attracts many tourists, it has not become a tourist town.

In 1774, when the colonists were boycotting tea as a protest against import duties, a British captain unloaded his cargo of tea in Greenwich, believing it would be safer in the basement of a loyalist merchant there than in Philadelphia, its ultimate destination. The plan was to smuggle it overland to Philadelphia. Ten days later a group of Greenwich men dressed as Native Americans entered the merchant's shop at night, took the tea, and burned it in a giant bonfire in town. Although seven of them were brought to trial, they were never convicted. Like the participants in the Boston Tea Party, these "Native Americans" were among the most responsible citizens in town. The sheriff who selected the jury (he later became one of New Jersey's first two senators) was the brother of one of the tea burners and the nephew of the foreman. It is claimed that the ringleader was the Reverend Philip Vickers Fithian, a recent Princeton graduate, whose journals were used in the Williamsburg, Virginia, restoration. Other participants included the Reverend Andrew Hunter, who founded Woodbury Academy, and two future governors of the state, Richard Howell and Joseph Bloomfield. In 1908 the state erected a monument commemorating the event.

On the northeast side of the Great St., just west of the intersection with Bridgeton-Greenwich Rd., is the Gibbon house (856-455-4055), headquarters of the Cumberland County Historical Society. Built in 1730 by Nicholas Gibbon, a shipowner and merchant, the house is operated as a museum. On display are the famous Ware chairs (made just north of Greenwich, in Roadstown), children's toys, 19th-century clothing, Canton china, and mementos of Reverend Fithian. Behind the Gibbon house is the Swedish granary, a c. 1650 cabin built of notched cedar logs (moved to the site from a nearby township) that is an extremely rare example of this early type of building. Also behind the Gibbon house is the Red Barn Museum, housing 19th-century tools, implements, and artifacts used by farmers, shipbuilders, and homemakers. Open April–mid-December, Tuesday–Saturday, 12–4, Sunday, 1–4. Tours by appointment. Admission fee for nonmembers. The Warren Lummis Library is across the street from the Gibbon house (856-455-8580). It serves as the society's library; a former bank building, its vault has proved extremely convenient for climate-controlled storage of delicate items. The library is open year-round Wednesday, 10–4:30, Friday–Sunday, 1:30–4:30. With two weeks' notice, the historical society will arrange tours of Greenwich (call 856-455-4055). Children's programs can be arranged by appointment on Tuesday–Friday in April, May, September, and October (call 856-455-4055). The society also sponsors many special events, including an annual craft show, farm day, and antiques show.

Also across the street from the Gibbon house, in the former lecture room built by the congregation of the Greenwich Presbyterian Church in 1852, is the John DuBois Maritime Museum (856-455-4055), named for a Mauricetown shipyard owner who donated most of the artifacts. Among the items on display are models of some of the boats that sailed out of Greenwich, shipbuilding tools, and a pole boat. Open weekends, 1–4, April–mid-December; tours by appointment.

Just south of the Gibbon house is the Cumberland County Prehistorical Museum (1461 Bridgeton Rd.; 856-455-8141), which contains a large collection of fossils and Native American artifacts. Open Wednesday, Saturday, and Sunday, 12–4, April–mid-December; groups and special tours by appointment.

Among the many other buildings of interest are the Richard Wood house (1785, 1795; northwest corner of Greate and Bacon's Neck rds.) and, on the southwest corner, the Wood store—this late-18th-century store is reputed to be one of the oldest in the country—and across from these the Old Stone Tavern (c. 1730), built of fieldstone from Pennsylvania and Maine that had been carried as ballast; the Friends Meetinghouse (1770s; northeast side of Greate St., toward the river); the old schoolhouse (1810; southwest side of Greate St., just southeast of Sheppard's Mill Rd.), possibly the oldest in the county; and the First Presbyterian Church (1835; north on the Greate St., toward Othello), whose grounds were once planted with seeds from Boston Commons elms.

A wooden observation deck, known as Caviar Tower, once stood at the end of Bayside Rd. (take Bacon's Neck Rd. to Tindall Island Rd., turn right, then left), giving you spectacular views out over the bay. It was destroyed by vandals, the second to be lost at that spot, but there are plans to replace it with something more durable. This area was once full of sturgeon, hence the tower's name.

Griggstown   Somerset [Franklin Township]

ACROSS MILLSTONE RIVER FROM C 533

Named for the Griggs brothers, who migrated to the area from Long Island in the early 18th century, this idyllic village sits on the eastern side of the Delaware and Raritan Canal* and the Millstone River, connected by a causeway to River Rd. (C 533).

Benjamin Griggs built the first gristmill on the Millstone River before 1733; George Washington marched his troops through the Millstone River valley after the Battle of Princeton; and John Honeyman, a Continental spy who is given a large part of the credit for the successful surprise attack at Trenton, lived in Griggstown. Honeyman's house still stands on Canal Rd. across from Bunker Hill Rd., and there are many other 18th- and 19th-century houses along Canal Rd. in the Griggstown Historic District.* The Griggstown Reformed Church (1261 Canal Rd.) was dedicated in 1843; its bell dates from 1858 and its stained-glass windows from the 1870s. Behind the church is a one-room schoolhouse moved to this location. Built in the mid-19th century, it closed in 1932 and has been maintained by the Griggstown Historical Society. Open by appointment (908-359-3589). Note also the lock tender's station and the barracks on the causeway. Although they are usually referred to as mule-drivers' barracks, there is some question as to whether the canal's mule-drivers actually ever used them. The barracks used to house a museum but was severly damaged by floods.

Across the road on a farm dating back to the 1840s (1079 Canal Rd.; 908-359-9387) you will see llamas and alpacas. Also on the farm is a farm-fiber studio. Open by appointment.

In the 1920s Griggstown became a summer resort for Norwegians living in Brooklyn. Their subdivision, which included Lincoln, Washington, and Leif Erikkson rds., was followed by another subdivision, Sunset Hill, in which other Scandinavians also participated. After World War II, these summer homes became a year-round settlement, and a large portion of today's population is of Norwegian descent. Until the mid-1980s Griggstown boasted a Scandinavian delicatessen with a considerable reputation.

Griggstown is adjacent to the Delaware and Raritan Canal State Park (see

GRIGGSTOWN

Kingston). This is a particularly lovely stretch of park suitable for walking, fishing, canoeing, and riding. To the north, the next bridge across the canal is at Blackwells Mills. The Blackwells Mills Canal House (732-873-2133), maintained by the Blackwells Mills Canal House Association, is open once a month for special programs, ranging from crafts demonstrations to an ice-cream social.

Hackensack Bergen 37,049

I 80, NJ 4, 17, C 503

Situated on the Hackensack River and once a busy ocean port, Hackensack was first settled by Dutch traders in the 17th century. The seat of Bergen County, it was until 1921 officially known as New Barbadoes (two of its early landholders came from Barbados). During the Revolution, the Hackensack green was used as a campground for both Continental and British regiments. The courthouse complex* (Main and Essex sts.; 201-527-2700) includes buildings dating from 1910 to 1933. The courthouse is Neoclassic, but the former jail (designed by the same architect, now used for offices) has medieval turreting. The Administrative Building dates from the 1930s. The public buildings are open weekdays, 8:30–4:30; limited tours by appointment.

Also on the green is the First Reformed Church* (42 Court St.), built in 1791 and altered in the mid-19th century. The congregation, organized in 1686, had its first building by 1696, and stones from this and the next church (built in 1728) are worked into the present building. Many revolutionary soldiers are buried in the graveyard, as is General Enoch Poor (a monument to him is just east of the green). George Washington and the marquis de Lafayette attended Poor's funeral. On the northwest corner of Church St. and Washington Pl. is the Bank House, built in the 1830s for the first bank in Bergen County. Traffic makes it hard to appreciate the green unless you leave your car. Farther west on Essex St. (entrance on Prospect Ave.) is the Hackensack University Medical Center, founded in 1888 and in 2004 the largest employer in Bergen County and the largest provider of patient services in the state. For a look at an earlier Hackensack, drive by the John Hopper house* (1812; 231 Polifly Ave.), which stayed in the same family until 1937; it is now a restaurant.

A big treat in Hackensack is the New Jersey Naval Museum (78 River St.; 201-342-3268). There you can visit the USS Ling,* a diesel-electric-powered World War II submarine commissioned in 1945. After one patrol run, the Ling was decommissioned (in 1946), and from 1962 to 1971 it was used as a training vessel at the Brooklyn Navy Yard. Since 1973 the Ling has been berthed at the Hackensack River. Renovated, it is open for tours. Inside the museum are exhibits dealing with the science and history of submarines; models, including a five-foot handmade model of a British World War I cruiser; a two-man German submarine; and submarine-related memorabilia. Among the outside exhibits are missiles, German and Japanese submarines, a suicide torpedo, and an experimental fiberglass sail. Open weekends, 10–4; groups and other times by appointment. The Ling can also be reserved weekdays for birthday parties.

Much of Hackensack's downtown has a 1920s or 1930s flavor. Note the stone Johnson Free Public Library (274 Main St.), built in 1901 and enlarged in 1915 and 1967; the Oritani Field Club (1887; 18 E. Camden); and the group of 1930s Sears, Roebuck stores (436 Main St.), a prototype of post–World War II shopping centers.

The Hackensack River county park (NJ 4 and Hackensack Ave.; 201-336-7275) consists of 30 acres along the river behind the Riverside Square Mall. Trails go through a tidal marsh and forested wetlands, and there are overlooks, bird blinds, and interpretive signs. Parking on lower level of mall parking deck.

Recitals sponsored by the Center for Modern Dance Education (84 Euclid Ave.; 201-342-2989), a school founded in the early 1960s, are open to the public. Call for the schedule.

Maywood Station* (269 Maywood Ave.; 201-845-3323), an 1872 railroad station in the neighboring borough of Maywood, has been restored and functions as a museum. On display are railroad artifacts, including some found in the station, as well as items relating to the town, and exhibits on the role of the railroads in local development. Open one weekend day every other month and for a visit by Santa in December. Call for details of the schedule. The local historical society also has a small display of changing exhibits on local history at the library (459 Maywood Ave.; 201-845-8830). Call for the hours.

Hackettstown Warren 10,403

US 46, NJ 57, 182, C 517

Situated in the Musconetcong Valley between Schooley's and Scott's mountains, Hackettstown is reputed to be the only town in the United States with this name. According to one legend, the town was named for Judge Samuel Hackett, who served free drinks to the local citizenry. But there are records that refer to the town of Hackettstown dating to 1767, and Judge Hackett wasn't born until 1757. In any case Hackettstown grew as the center for the surrounding agricultural area, as a service town for those vacationing on Schooley's Mountain (see Long Valley), and as a center for carriage manufacturing. One of the oldest nudist establishments in the United States (founded in the early 1930s) is to be found in Hackettstown, as is M&M Mars, which has been making M&Ms for over 60 years.

In the mid-19th century, the Newark Methodist Conference located its Centenary Collegiate Institute, now Centenary College (400 Jefferson St.; 908-852-1400), in Hackettstown. Because of a fire, the campus was rebuilt; many of the imposing buildings you see today date from the late 19th century. Note particularly the parlors and chapel in Seay Hall. The Centenary Performing Arts Guild (908-979-0900) sponsors programs of theater (including productions of the Centenary Stage Company, a professional equity group), music, and dance, as well as a young performers' workshop. For specific schedules, call the box office (908-979-0900). At the Ferry Gallery you can see the work of student artists.

Hackettstown's old commercial district is well preserved; note particularly the handsome buildings on Main, High, and Washington sts. and on Grand Avenue. The state trout hatcheries, once located here, used to attract many visitors; although the Hackettstown Hatchery is still operating, the trout hatchery open to the public is in Pequest (see Oxford). At 106 Church St., in a 1915 house, is the Hackettstown Historical Society museum (908-852-8797), with a collection focusing on local and state history and extensive genealogical materials. Exhibits in the display case in the main room change roughly every three months. Open Wednesday, Friday, and Sunday, 2–4. Groups and other times by appointment.

In the northeastern corner of Hackettstown is the Stephens section of Allamuchy Mountain State Park (C 604; 908-852-3790); Allamuchy Mountain Park itself is just north on 604. The two areas combined contain over 9,000 acres. The smaller Stephens section (800-plus acres) has picnic facilities, playgrounds, campsites, and hiking trails. In season you can also fish, cross-country ski, and sled. The Allamuchy section has a natural area with untouched, undeveloped hardwood forest, old fields in various stages of succession, northern marshlands, and Deer Park and Allamuchy ponds. There are extensive trails where you can hike, jog, ride horses and mountain bikes, and cross-country ski. Both ponds are rich in bass and pickerel, and at Saxton Falls, upstream from the Stephens section, you can see the remains of one of the Morris Canal locks.

About two miles south of Hackettstown, on Grand Ave., is the state's Rockport Pheasant Farm (908-852-3461), where more than three million pheasants have been raised since the 1960s. Children, particularly, might enjoy looking at the deer and the unusual birds to be seen in pens here. A hiking loop goes around the breeder yards. Also on the property is a memorial to those who died in a train wreck at Rockport in 1925. Open daily, 7:30–dusk. Group orientations by appointment. Across the road from the pens is one of the few remaining segments of the Morris Canal (the *port* in the name Rockport dates to canal days). You can take a short walk along the towpath in this beautiful spot.

Haddonfield Camden 11,659

C 551, 561, 573

Haddonfield is perhaps the only colonial town to be directly founded by a woman. Elizabeth Haddon, a Quaker, who had come to the colonies to develop a large tract bought by her father in 1698, built a house on Cooper's Creek in 1701. In 1702, she married John Estaugh, a Quaker missionary (to whom, it is said, she had proposed), and in 1713 they moved to the site of Haddonfield. They had no children, and the name died out. Even their house is gone; the so-called Elizabeth Haddon house now on the site (201 Wood La.) was built in the 1840s, theirs having burned some 100 years before. Their story, though, has been immortalized by Longfellow in *Tales of a Wayside Inn*.

The town's location on the main road from Burlington to Salem (the Kings Highway, laid out in 1686 and still the main street) gave it a place in Revolutionary history. The Indian King Tavern House Museum* (233 Kings Hwy; 856-429-6792) served as a tavern, an inn, a temporary statehouse, and a stop on the Underground Railroad. In it the Continental Congress, the New Jersey legislature, and the Council of Safety all met. Both the great seal of New Jersey and a law substituting the word "state" for "colony" in all official papers were adopted in legislative sessions here. Among those who stopped at the inn were Light-Horse Harry Lee, Mad Anthony Wayne, and Lord Cornwallis, and the future Dolley Madison was the innkeeper's niece.

Built as a home in 1750 by a wealthy Philadelphia merchant, the inn was bought by the state in 1903, the first such historic structure to be managed by the state. It is being furnished with authentic reproductions to show what an 18th-century tavern would have been like. There are several open houses during the year, including celebrations of the Fourth of July, the adoption of the state seal, and the law changing "colony" to "state." Open Wednesday–Saturday, 10–12 and 1–4; Sunday 1–4; groups by appointment. It is strongly recommended that all visitors call ahead to schedule their tour.

Although Haddonfield is today primarily a suburb of Philadelphia, and a prosperous one at that, it has the feel of a town that had its own identity before it became a suburb. Over 450 Colonial, Federal, Victorian, and in other ways significant structures are included in its historic district,* which covers almost half the borough's total area. In 1858, on a farm near

Haddonfield, the first major dinosaur discovery in North America was made. The dinosaur is now in Philadelphia, but there is a reproduction of it in the State Museum in Trenton, and the place in which it was discovered (end of Maple Ave.) is a national historic landmark. A plaque marks the spot.

The Haddonfield Historical Society has its headquarters in Greenfield Hall* (343 Kings Highway E.; 856-429-7375); Lafayette and General Howe are both supposed to have stayed here. Most of the building dates from 1841, though the oldest part was built in 1747. Four rooms on the first floor are furnished to reflect four distinct architectural periods from colonial times through Victorian. The society's collection includes New Jersey glass, pottery, dolls, and toys, and Elizabeth Haddon's Queen Anne table and mirror. The basement is filled with tools and household implements. Open Wednesday–Friday and Sunday, 1–4; groups by appointment. On the same property is the Samuel Mickle House,* often called the hip-roof house (though it actually has a gambrel roof), and a saddler's shop (dated variously 1710 and 1742), which houses the society's library. Open Tuesday and Thursday, 9:30–11:30 A.M.; 1st Sunday of the month, 1–3. The museum and library are closed in August.

There are many other interesting buildings in town, many of them with identifying plaques. In addition to Kings Highway, you may want to walk or drive along Tanner, Lake, Grove, Chestnut, Centre, Potter, Clement, Mechanics, and Warwick sts. and Washington, Colonial, Friends, Lincoln, W. Park, E. Park, E. Atlantic, and W. Cottage avenues.

The Friends Meetinghouse (Friends Ave.) dates from 1851, and the cemetery wall was built of bricks from the old meetinghouse. Dolley Madison may have worshipped here. In the cemetery is a plaque honoring Elizabeth Haddon as a woman remarkable for "resolution, prudence, and charity." There is a little park around the lake below the meetinghouse.

During the period the Friends were split into two factions, this meetinghouse was used by the Orthodox group. The Hicksite building also dates to 1851 and can be found at Ellis and Haddon sts., entirely incorporated into a supermarket building.

At the corner of Kings Highway and Haddon Ave. is Haddon Fire Company No. 1 (856-429-4308), formed in 1764 and the second oldest volunteer fire company in continuous operation in the United States (the oldest is in Mount Holly). There is a small museum at the firehouse, organized to suggest what a firehouse would have looked like 200 years ago. In the museum are two old pumpers, one dating from 1818 (it can be seen spraying water on Independence Hall in the movie *Cinerama*), the other from 1873. The collection also includes the fire company's original banner, a window from the company's original building (this building dates to 1952), helmets and uniforms, and a marvelous collection of old metal toy fire equipment. The museum is open weekdays, 9–5; groups by appointment (the tour also includes the more modern equipment).

The so-called Elizabeth Haddon house at 201 Wood La. (between Merion Ave. and Hawthorne St.) dates from 1844 and is built of local bricks taken from an earlier house on the site. A two-story brick still, built in 1713 and used by Elizabeth Haddon to produce medicinal whiskey, still stands, possibly the oldest building in Haddonfield.

Among the large houses on the Kings Highway heading north is the splendid Queen Anne–style building of the Bancroft School (at Hopkins La.), a private school specializing in children with mental and physical disabilities. Closer in town note also the former Third Methodist Church* (301 Kings Highway E.), now the Haddon Fortnightly clubhouse, and the John Roberts house (344 Kings Highway E.).

Directly south of Haddonfield (take Warwick Rd., C 669) is Tavistock, which, with its 2000 population of 24, is New Jersey's third smallest municipality. Basically a country club and a few houses, Tavistock managed to incorporate itself as a borough in the 1920s after the members of a country club in Haddonfield, dissatisfied because the club could not sell liquor on Sundays, moved their activities to a new site.

Directly south of Tavistock is the borough of Lawnside. Established as an African American community in 1840, and formerly known as Free Haven, Lawnside remains primarily African American today. The Peter Mott house* (26 Kings Ct., off Moore Ave.; 609-546-8850), built in 1845, was an important stop on the Underground Railroad. Threatened by a housing development, which now surrounds it, the house was saved from destruction in part by the efforts of Clarence H. Still, a descendant of William Still, the Philadelphia businessman often referred to as the father of the Underground Railroad. Restored, the house now serves as a museum of African American history. Furnished with period furniture, including a 19th-century washstand of a kind that might actually have been used there, the house also has some of William Still's more urban furniture and personal items. Open Saturday, 12–3. Groups and other times by appointment.

In the Haddon Heights Public Library (608 Station Ave.; 609-547-7132) is a "corner museum" run by the Haddon Heights Historical Society (Haddon Heights is southwest of Haddonfield; you can pick up Station Ave. in Haddonfield off Chews Landing Rd., C 573). On display are various artifacts connected with the history of Haddon Heights, including the wooden turbine from a 1740 fulling mill. The library also has a good collection of photographs of Haddon Heights from about 1890 to 1930. Open by appointment. The library is in the Station Ave. historic district,* an area of commercial buildings dating from c. 1890–1925. The nearby White Horse Pike Historic District,* with buildings from the same era, also includes parts of Station Ave. as well as White Horse Pike, Garden, Green, and High sts., and E. Atlantic and 4th avenues. You can also find a few pre-Revolutionary houses scattered about town on Sycamore St., New Jersey and N. Park aves., and Sylvan Dr., but the town has primarily the look of a well-preserved turn-of-the-20th-century railroad town.

Haledon Passaic 8,252

C 504, 509

An excellent example of a streetcar suburb, Haledon developed as a satellite of industrial Paterson after trolley lines from the city were laid in the 1870s. What had been a small rural village became not only a working- and upper-middle-class suburb but a late-Victorian resort as well.

Haledon is the site of the American Labor Museum* (83 Norwood St.; 973-595-7953), one of the few museums in the country devoted to presenting post–Industrial Revolution history from the point of view of the worker. The museum is located in the house* (1908, 1913), now a national historic landmark, of Pietro and Maria Botto, immigrants from northern Italy who came to work in the Paterson silk mills in the 1890s and built their house in 1908. The house is important to American labor history because it served as headquarters for the famous Paterson silk strike. For seven months in 1913, some 24,000 workers in Paterson, known then as Silk City, stayed off their jobs in a drive for improved working conditions, an eight-hour day, and a minimum wage. Legal harassment made it impossible for the workers to meet in Paterson; the mayor of Haledon offered them a refuge in his city, and the Bottos offered their house as a meeting place. Every Sunday some 20,000 workers would gather on the front lawn and listen to speeches by members of the I.W.W. (International Workers of the World, known as the Wobblies, who were coordinating the strike), including Elizabeth Gurley Flynn, the journalist John Reed, and the writer Upton Sinclair.

Four rooms of the museum are furnished to reflect the living conditions of immigrants in 1913, other rooms have been converted to galleries, and the Old World gardens, including the grape arbor and bocce court, have been restored. There is a permanent exhibit on the silk strike, and the upstairs rooms feature exhibits that change roughly three times a year. The museum's extraordinary collection of photographs and other documents from the peak years of immigration vividly re-create an important period of American history. The museum sponsors a variety of special programs and educational projects as well as an annual Labor Day parade, which starts at the museum and ends at the Great Falls in Paterson (see Paterson) with a Great Falls festival. Open Wednesday–Saturday, 1–4; groups and other times by appointment. Closed major holidays except Labor Day.

Just north of Norwood St., off Belmont Ave., is the Kossuth Street School* (47 Kossuth St.), built at the turn of the 20th century. Note also the converted ribbon mill from the same era (510 Belmont Ave.), now housing borough offices.

Hamilton Township Mercer 87,109

I 295, US 206, NJ 33, C 533

Though often thought of as a suburb of Trenton, Hamilton Township is actually New Jersey's eighth most populous municipality. Much of this growth has been recent, and although parts of the township were settled long ago (some so long ago that Hamilton has been called the richest archaeological site east of the Mississippi; see below), this large (40 sq. mi.) township is a city without a center. (Occasionally, though, you may come across reminders of an early crossroads village.)

Celebrating the Native American settlements of Hamilton is the Civil War and Native American Museum (2002 Kuser Rd.; 609-275-0143). Two rooms of the joint museum are dedicated to the memory of the Lenape Indians, who frequented the area between the Delaware River and Gropps Lake; on display are artifacts that until recently were readily found by anyone walking through that area. The Civil War portion, said to be the largest museum in the state dedicated to that war, includes memorabilia as well as changing exhibits dealing with New Jersey residents involved in the war. The museum is housed in a building that once was used to dry vegetables on the Abbott Farm (*see* below). Jim Thorpe lived there for a year as a migrant worker, and reports of his ghost surface from time to time. Open weekends, 12–5.

The museum is located in Veterans Park (between Kuser and Klockner rds., east of I 295; 609-890-3684) behind the 1730s Abbott House* (2200 Kuser Rd.; 609-585-1686), where New Jersey tried to sequester the state treasury during the Revolution. Restored and furnished as a house museum by the Historical Society of Hamilton Township, the house retains some of its original hinges and buttermilk paint. Open weekends, 12–5; groups by appointment. In the 300-acre park are formal gardens, two greenhouses where the flowers used by the township are grown, meadows, woodlands, and a stream and lake where you can fish. There are also athletic fields and what is reputed to be the largest tennis complex in the country. Open daily, dawn–dusk.

West of Veterans Park is the Kuser Farm Mansion and Park (390 Newkirk Ave. or Kuser Ave; 609-890-3630). The mansion was built as a summer home in 1892 and became the Kusers' winter home in the 1920s. The family pioneered in several businesses (Fred Kuser helped finance the forerunner of 20th Century–Fox and was involved with the Roebling family in producing the Mercer car) and sports (tennis and flying), and the furnishings in the lavishly built house reflect their interests. A brochure is available for a self-guided tour of the grounds. A Victorian Christmas is celebrated in December, and the Jersey Valley Model Railroad Club, which houses its displays in the basement, has an annual open house one weekend in early December. Open Thursday–Sunday, May–November, weekends, February–April, 11–3 (last tour, 2:30); groups by appointment.

Closer to the river is John A. Roebling Park (just south of S. Broad St.; access from Sewell or Wescott aves.; 609-989-6530), 250 acres of freshwater marsh and a lake. The park is beloved of bird-watchers, and you can fish in the lake. There is also a small picnic area, and there are walking paths through the woods and among the shrubs near the picnic area. The oldest house in Mercer County, the Isaac Watson house* (151 Wescott Ave.; 609-882-2062), built in 1708, is the state headquarters for the D.A.R. and can be seen by appointment.

Roebling Park falls within the boundaries of the 1,250-acre Hamilton-Trenton marsh, the northernmost and largest freshwater tidal marsh on the Delaware River, boundaries that are almost the same as those of the Abbott Farm National Historic district,* a national historic landmark. The Abbott district is the largest Middle Woodland site east of the Mississippi, and much older artifacts (as far back as 6000 B.C.) have been found as well. The marsh also contains an extraordinary diversity of species: some 850 varieties of plants, some 235 varieties of birds. Guided tours of the area are given by the Friends for the Marsh and the D&R Greenway Land Trust (609-924-4646).

Sayen House and Gardens (155 Hughes Dr.; 609-587-7356), is a 30-acre township property noteworthy for its naturalized plantings of close to 500 rhododendrons, more than 1,000 azaleas, and some 250,000 flowering bulbs. Narrow trails wind through the property, making this spot an oasis in one of the more built-up parts of the township. The house is open for the azalea festival on Mother's Day. Gardens open dawn–dusk.

On the old New Jersey State Fairgrounds is Grounds for Sculpture (18 Fairgrounds Rd.; 609-586-0616), a 35-acre sculpture park. The elaborate landscaping and gardens highlight the outdoor exhibits. There are two 10,000-square-foot indoor spaces—the museum and the domestic arts building—both exhibit halls from the fair. Shows change three times a year, alternating one-person and group shows. Open April–October, Tuesday–Sunday, 10–8; November–March, Tuesday–Sunday, 10–6. Admission charge; groups by appointment.

The Grafton Mansion (Edgebrook Rd.; 609-890-3636) is an 1860s mansion acquired by the township when a developer built one of the largest malls in the country and was required to move and restore the house. Plans call for using the mansion for historical exhibits, as a venue for local talent, and for township events.

Hammonton   Atlantic   12,604

US 30, 206, NJ 54, C 542, 559, 561

Named for John Hammond Coffin, the son of an early-19th-century glass manufacturer, Hammonton was developed in the late 1850s by Charles K. Landis (*see* Vineland). Landis encouraged New Englanders and Italians to settle in Hammonton, and the Italian Carnival held on North 3d Street in mid-July has been a major ethnic and religious festival for over 100 years. Fruit growing is important in the area around Hammonton, and the town serves as a center for the blueberry industry (*see* Pemberton). The world's largest cultivated-blueberry plantation is here: 50 employees work on its 1,300 acres of berries year-round, 2,000 in season. New Jersey in fact leads all other states in the production of blueberries for consumption fresh (Michigan is first in total production; *see* Pemberton).

The Hammonton Historical Society's museum is located behind the town hall on Vine Street. On exhibit are photographs and artifacts connected to local history, particularly from the Victorian era. Open by appointment only (call 609-561-0295). In the old Hammonton railroad station (1904), the Chamber of Commerce runs a visitor center (10 S. Egg Harbor Rd.; 609-561-9080). Stop here for maps and guides to the area. Open weekdays, 8:30–4. Also in Hammonton is the Tomasello Winery (225 White Horse Pike; 800-666-9463), a large 70-year-old family-run winery. Open Monday–Saturday, 9–8, Sunday, 11–6; groups by appointment. A smaller and younger winery, DiMatteo Vineyards (779 11th St.; 609-561-8106), is set in the midst of blueberry and peach farms, and is another of the state's wineries that grows its own grapes. Open weekends, 12–5. Some Jerseyites who live north of Hammonton may be interested to know that US 206 begins here.

Hammonton lies just south of Wharton State Forest (609-561-0024; 609-268-0444), New Jersey's largest state forest (over 115,000 acres) and the largest tract of public land in the Pinelands (or, for that matter, in the state park system). The Pinelands are a unique New Jersey treasure: 2,000 square miles unlike those anywhere else, the largest wilderness east of the Mississippi in the nation's most densely populated state. Because of the Pinelands' particular geological and human history, they contain an unusual variety of rare plants and animals—the Pinelands represent the southern limit for many northern species and the northern limit for many southern species. Beneath the ground lies an enormous reservoir (17 trillion gallons) of pure water. The land is generally sandy, and much of it is forested with pine and oak, particularly pitch pine, which is better able than other species to withstand the frequent fires. There are cedar swamps and bogs here; there are forests of pygmy pine; and the rivers are often the color of tea. Seen from a car, the Pinelands often look featureless—mile after mile of sand and scrubby trees—but once you leave the paved roads to walk or canoe, you will be struck by the mysterious quiet and beauty. (It is important when hiking, though, to pay close attention to landmarks until you know the area well—it is easy to get lost.) Although much of the Pinelands seems devoid of people, there once was considerable industrial activity here: the iron found in the bogs was processed (cannons, cannonballs, firebacks, and water pipes were manufactured here); there were paper mills and glassworks; and sphagnum moss (used by nursery owners to protect plants) and salt hay were gathered. Today, cultivation of cranberries and blueberries is the major economic activity, but what is perhaps most unusual about the Pinelands economy is that so many of those who live in the region have chosen not to enter the economic mainstream, supporting themselves by seasonal work related to the Pinelands' natural resources. Although the various grandiose schemes to develop the Pinelands as a resort area came to naught, large segments are now being used for retirement communities. Remains of old forges and villages are still apparent, varying from those noticeable only to a trained eye to the completely restored iron village of Batsto* (see below). The fact that sand quickly obliterates traces of the past has suggested that the Pinelands might be serving as a criminal burial ground.

Batsto is now a historic museum village. That it still exists we probably owe to Joseph Wharton, a Philadelphia industrialist, who purchased large tracts of land in this area in the 1870s, including the village, which he partially restored. The first furnace in this area was erected in the 1760s; the last was dismantled in 1858. In between, munitions were manufactured for the Revolution and the War of 1812, and for a short time the furnace was used by a glassworks. Among the many schemes Wharton was involved in was one to export the Pinelands' pure water to Philadelphia, but he failed to stir up much interest, and in any case the New Jersey legislature eventually forbade the exportation of water. He also experimented with growing and processing sugar beets. His large holdings remained intact after his death in 1909 and were sold to the State of New Jersey in the 1950s. The ironmaster's mansion has been restored, as have the gristmill, the sawmill, the general store, many of the workers' houses, and various outbuildings; crafts demonstrations are given in some of the houses during the summer. The Wharton park headquarters are here, as are a nature center and nature trails; there is also a picnic area. The Batsto grounds are open year-round, the buildings Memorial Day–Labor Day, 10–4; call 609-561-0024 about winter hours, which vary. Closed New Year's Day, Thanksgiving, and Christmas.

Within the forest are many miles of hiking trails (including a stretch of the Batona Trail), as well as trails for horses and mountain bikes. The lakes and rivers provide opportunities to swim, fish, and boat. Canoeing the Pinelands rivers, among them the Mullica, Batsto, Wading, and Oswego, is very popular. The Oswego River goes by the former paper-manufacturing town of Harrisville; there are ruins to explore here. Campsites range from the primitive to screened cabins; some are accessible only by foot or canoe. All require permits. The forest also has picnic areas, and in the winter you can ice-skate and fish. For information and maps, stop at the park headquarters in Batsto or at the ranger's station at Atsion* (US 206; 609-268-0444), also a former iron town. Both are open daily (except New Year's Day, Thanksgiving, and Christmas), 9–4; May–September, Friday and Saturday evenings, for campers only, until 9. At the Wharton Forest Nature Center (609-567-4559) you will find a few exhibits related to the natural history of the area; guided nature tours can be arranged. Open Memorial Day–Labor Day.

A short distance east of Wharton State Forest is Penn State Forest (east off C 563; 609-296-1114), 3,300 acres with hiking trails and bridle paths, a picnic area, and Lake Oswego, where you can fish and boat.

To the east of the northern end of Wharton is the village of Chatsworth (C 532, C 563), often referred to as the capital of the Pinelands. Each October the village hosts a two-day cranberry festival, which is attended by as many as 100,000 people; the proceeds go toward the restoration of the mid-19th-century White Horse Inn.* New Jersey is the country's fourth most important grower of cranberries (behind Wisconsin, Massachusetts, and Oregon), which in 2003 contributed over $15 million to the state's economy. Many field guides are available to help you explore the Pinelands (*see also* Pemberton, Tuckerton, Vineland, Woodbine).

West of Hammonton is the Winslow Wildlife Management Area (access from US 322 and Piney Hollow, New Brooklyn–Blue Anchor, Malaga, and Folsom rds.), over 7,300 acres of woodland bisected by the Egg Harbor River (and the Atlantic City Expressway). These woods are open for hiking, bird-watching, hunting, and fishing.

Hancock's Bridge Salem [Lower Alloways Creek Township]

C 658

Hancock's Bridge is a tiny hamlet now, but the drawbridge over Lower Alloways Creek was considered so important during the Revolution that the militia was stationed there to guard it. In the early morning of 21 March 1778, 300 British troops under Colonel Charles Mawhood massacred some 30 militiamen asleep in Judge William Hancock's house* (Main St.; 856-935-4373). This was the only time during the Revolution that a massacre occurred in a house; the building is now a historic-house museum run by the state. Built in 1734 of brick in a Flemish-bond pattern, it is notable for the design on one side: the date and the initials of Judge Hancock and his wife, Sarah, are worked into the brick, with a zigzag pattern below. Everyone who owned the Hancock house before the state bought it in the 1930s was related by marriage or blood to the Hancock who built the bridge. The house has been and a kitchen garden planted, and many special events take place at ˌse. Also on the property is a Swedish cedar plank house (1640–45) ˌ to the site from the Tyler tract just south of Salem. The planks are of ˌp cedar, shaped with an adze and dovetailed at the corners. Open Wednesday-Saturday, 10–12, 1–4, Sunday, 1–4, but it is advisable to call ahead as the house may be closed for special programs.

About a half-mile west of the Hancock house, on Poplar St., are the John Maddox Denn house (1725) and the Ware-Shourds house* (1730), both of which served as hospitals after the massacre. South on Main St. a short way is the Lower Alloways Creek Friends Meeting House.* It still has the original glass in many of its windows and early-19th-century cast-iron stoves made of New Jersey bog iron.

Buried in the local cemetery is Cornelia Hancock, who, as a very young woman, served as a nurse in the Civil War. Much beloved of the troops, she was the first woman to reach the battlefield at Gettysburg.

For an unsettling contrast, continue from Hancock's Bridge south and west on Alloway Creek Neck Rd., following the signs to the Salem Generating Station, an atomic energy installation. The distant sight of the reactor tower rising out of the tideland marshes would probably be striking in any context, but following so close on an 18th-century hamlet, it is eerie.

South of Hancock's Bridge (off Alloway Creek Neck and Canton rds.) is the Mad Horse Creek Wildlife Management Area, over 9,300 acres, mostly tidal marsh. The area, which is rich in waterfowl and frequented by migratory birds including snow geese, hawks, and eagles, is open for bird-watching, hiking, fishing, and hunting.

South and east of Hancock's Bridge, in the village of Canton (take Hancock's Bridge–Harmersville Rd., 658, to Harmersville–Canton Rd., 623; turn right to Smick Rd., 652, and turn left), is the Lower Alloways Creek Historical Museum (736 Smick Rd.; 856-935-1549). This is a reconstructed log house (one interior wall is original) probably built in the late 18th century and known to have been on the spot since the 1870s. Exhibits in the museum feature displays relating to local crafts and occupations. Also on the property are several other buildings, two of which house a large collection of tools and equipment relating to fishing and farming. Open April–June and September–November, 3d Sunday of the month, 1–4.

Harrison   Hudson   14,424

I 280, C 508

The population density of this small (just over 1 sq. mi.) industrial town is relieved by West Hudson Park (Davis Ave.; 201-915-1388), a 43-acre county park whose rustic trails are designed to make the rolling land seem rural. In addition to playgrounds and athletic fields, the park contains wooded groves, grassy lawns, a lake, and wading pools, and the abundance of hardwood trees makes the fall colors noteworthy. Although most of the industries for which it was once known (vacuum tubes, elevators, steel, industrial pumps) have left, Harrison has kept as its motto "The Beehive of Industry," a designation bestowed on it before World War I by William Howard Taft. A 275-acre redevelopment project is expected to reinvigorate the town and bring amenities like riverwalks and possibly river taxis to the waterfront. When Harrison mayor Frank Rogers retired in 1995, he had been in office longer (since 1947) than any other mayor in the country. Another record may have been set when a casting call for *The Sopranos* television series attracted more than 13,000 auditioners.

Helmetta Middlesex 1,825

c 615

In the center of Helmetta is a large brick complex, until 1993 the oldest snuff factory operating in the United States. The present C. W. Helme Snuff Mill district* (Main St., Helmetta Pond, and the area between it and Manalapan Brook) dates from the 1880s, but the operation descends directly from a factory built in 1812. This complex, set directly along the tracks of the old Camden and Amboy Railroad, dominates the western end of the town.

East of the factory, on Main St., note St. George's Church (1894) and the municipal building (1909), once a public school. Note also the plantings along the railbed. The Helmetta Historical Society holds an annual museum day each spring, exhibiting its collection of papers, artifacts, and photographs, as well as collections on loan from others, in Holy Trinity Church (100 Main St.). It also sponsors a fall walking tour and a few other special events. For information call 732-521-0386.

The undeveloped 1,500-acre Jamesburg County Park (Helmetta Blvd. and Old Stage Rd.; 732-745-3900) is an island of Pinelands vegetation in a densely populated area. The park is being maintained as a conservation area, but nobody knows what will happen to the Pinelands species without the genetic variety of a larger population. You can fish and boat at Helmetta Pond, and hike along the trails and fire roads; two endangered species live in the area, and the birding is considered excellent. Tours can be a arranged by calling the Middlesex County Citizens' Conservation Council (732-846-1825).

Highland Lakes Sussex 5,051

c 638

This community, centered on Highland Lake, abuts Wawayanda State Park (973-853-4462), 14,000 acres of wilderness, mountains, lakes, and streams. Here you can picnic, fish, swim, hike, and, in season, cross-country ski, sled, snowshoe, and hunt. The 40 miles of bicycle and hiking trails include an 11-mile section of the Appalachian Trail. In the park are some natural curiosities, among them the oldest rock to be seen in the Middle Atlantic states and northern white cedar rarely seen elsewhere in the state (here it is at the extreme southern limit of its habitat). The park is known for its display of rhododendron bloom in late June and early July, and for the quality of the fishing in Wawayanda Lake. Three natural areas—Wawayanda Hemlock Ravine, Wawayanda Swamp, and Bearfort Mountain—occupy over 3,500 acres of the park. Open 5 A.M.–9 P.M.

Included in Wawayanda is High Breeze Farm* (Barrett Rd.; 973-853-4462), described as a "high-mountain subsistence farm" that remained in the same family from the mid-19th century to the 1980s. The farm is no longer being worked, although a local farmer grazes his cattle on the land. On the property is a Federal farmhouse, dating to 1815, and 14 outbuildings. Little was changed over the years (the house was minimally electrified in 1948), and the Barretts continued to farm with traditional methods. The state is working to stabilize the buildings, and the hope remains that it might be possible some day to use the property to show what 19th- and 20th-century subsistence farming was really like.

East of Wawayanda is the 2,000-acre Abram S. Hewitt State Forest (C 513; 973-853-4462), with hiking trails and some spectacular views; cross-country skiing is also possible in season. East of Hewitt is the Wanaque Wildlife Management Area, some 2,200 acres just to the east of Greenwood Lake and including Green Turtle Pond. The area is open for fishing, hiking, and hunting.

Directly south of Highland Lakes is Newark's 35,000-acre Pequannock Watershed (accessible from NJ 23 and C 515 and 638), much of it open for recreation. The necessary permits for hiking, fishing (in the Echo Lake, Clinton, Canistear, and Oak Ridge reservoirs), horseback riding, and hunting can be obtained from the Newark Watershed Conservation and Development Corporation (40 Clinton St., Newark 07102; 973-622-4521, or, within the reserve, 223 Echo Lake Rd., Newfoundland 07435; 973-697-2850).

Highlands   Monmouth   5,097

Highlands takes its name from the bluffs that rise 200 feet above the Atlantic Ocean, said to be the first land sighted by ships sailing from the east. On the promontory between the Navesink River and Sandy Hook Bay is the Twin Lights Historic Site* (Hillside Ave.; 732-872-1814), a twin-towered lighthouse decommissioned in 1949. The first twin towers of the Navesink Light Station were built in 1828, although a light was probably operating at this point in the mid-18th century; the present brownstone and brick buildings date from 1862. This was the first lighthouse in the United States to be equipped with Fresnel lenses (1841), and the first to be electrically powered (1898). When electrified, it was the strongest maritime light in the country, visible 22 miles out to sea. At Twin Lights, Marconi demonstrated that wireless telegraphy was commercially feasible: in 1899 he wired the results of the America's Cup yacht race from a ship 15 miles offshore to a receiving mast erected at Twin Lights. Twin Lights is now a museum; the exhibits focus on maritime history as it relates to Twin Lights, with an emphasis on lighthouses and lifesaving. In the former generator building of this popular site (more than 100,000 visitors a year) is a display of the South Tower Fresnel lens with the equipment used to generate electricity. Also on the property is the lifesaving station from Sandy Hook, built in 1849 (the U.S. Life-Saving Service resulted from the initiative of a New Jersey congressman, William A. Newell; *see* Allentown). There is an overlook in front of the museum as well as in the towers, and on a clear day you have a wonderful view of Sandy Hook, the bay, the ocean, and the New York City skyline. Picnic sites available. Memorial Day–Labor Day, open daily, 10–5; the rest of the year, Wednesday–Sunday, 10–5. Group tours by appointment. Grounds open daily 9–sunset.

Beautiful views can also be had by driving along Scenic Dr. (Ocean Blvd.) and from the Mt. Mitchill overlook (*see* Atlantic Highlands). For information on beach fees, call 732-872-1959.

Off Navesink Rd. is Hartshorne Woods Park (732-872-0036), a 741-acre county facility with woods that once belonged to Richard Hartshorne, who acquired the land (as part of a much larger parcel) from the Proprietors of New Jersey in the mid-17th century. The woods have remained undisturbed, and many of the trees are very old. Multi-use trails for hikers, bikers, riders, and cross-country skiers wind through this undeveloped area. Part of the park was once an army missile center, and in that part there are almost two miles of paved trails and a pier from which you can fish.

Between Navesink Rd. and Hartshorne is the former Water Witch Club Casino,* part of a late-19th-century summer community frequented by business and professional people from New York City. The Shingle-style clubhouse, originally a casino, survives, as do many of the original houses, now winterized. The Water Witch Club Historic District* is roughly defined by Water Witch and Serpentine drs., Sea View Terrace, Windlass Path, and NJ 36; you will find many interesting early-20th-century houses along these roads.

About three miles west of Highlands is Huber Woods Park (take Navesink Ave. west to Locust or Monmouth Ave.; from either of these turn on Browns Dock Rd.; 732-872-2670), with over 250 acres of county woods, primarily oaks, beech, and tulip trees, which once formed part of the Huber family's estate. The Huber house, a 1920s Tudor, now serves as an environmental center, with programs aimed at children and exhibits that

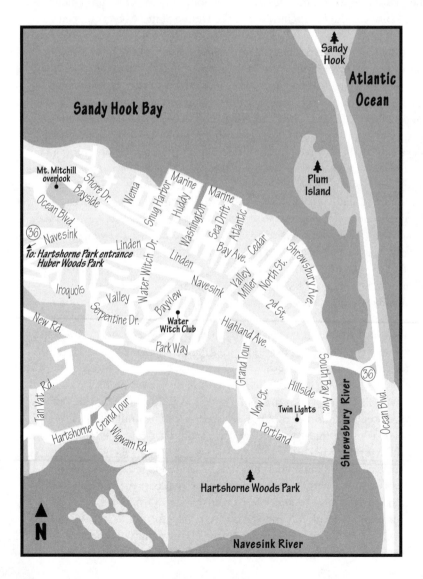

include an active beehive, a weather station, and a bird-viewing area (the plantings were chosen to attract birds, which can be watched through glasses from inside). There are also natural-history exhibits, which change every two years or so. Open daily, 10–4. Bridle paths and hiking and cross-country ski trails go through the woods. Groups and guided tours by appointment.

To the north of Highlands is Sandy Hook, a six-mile-long sandspit extending into the Atlantic Ocean and Lower New York Bay (to get there take NJ 36 east across the Shrewsbury River and turn left). On this spit are long stretches of open beach, salt- and freshwater marshes, back-dune forests, and a spectacular holly forest (the largest stand of holly on the East Coast), as well as the Sandy Hook unit of the Gateway National Recreation Area, Fort Hancock, and the oldest original operating lighthouse in the United States. The lighthouse,* a national historic landmark, was first lit on 11 June 1764. It was built by a group of New York merchants who were appalled at the losses suffered by ships coming into New York harbor (until 1907 the Sandy Hook Channel was the only entrance for large ships) and sponsored two lotteries to raise funds for its construction. The first use of a steam-powered fog signal took place at Sandy Hook in 1868. When the lighthouse, a 103-foot octagonal tower, was built, it stood some 500 feet from the water; it is now a mile and a half away. Tours of the lighthouse are available weekends, April–December, 12–4.

Because of its strategic position, Sandy Hook has always been of military interest. The British and Continental troops fought over it during the Revolution, and the federal government began building a fort there before the Civil War. Fort Hancock,* a national historic landmark, dates from the 1890s, and for many years Sandy Hook was a proving ground. (It was also a Nike missile site, which the army left looking like a dump.) You can still see the massive concrete batteries of the seacoast guns used to fire on ships at sea. A Coast Guard unit at the point operates a loran monitoring station for the northeast chain of command. One of the first U.S. Life-Saving Service boat stations was built at Sandy Hook in 1849 (it can be seen at Twin Lights).

The Fort Hancock buildings,* one of which was designed by Robert E. Lee, have an air of deserted elegance. In the 1899 guardhouse and jail is a museum that concentrates on the history of the armaments used at the fort. Open daily, July and August, weekends only the rest of the year, 1–5; weekends only the rest of the year. The history house, once an officer's house, is also a museum; it concentrates on World War II and what it was like to live at the fort. Usually open weekends, 1–5. Tours of the Battery Potter, housing for a gun that rose up like the Radio City orchestra to fire and then sank back out of sight, are arranged by the visitor center; call for the schedule.

Some Fort Hancock buildings are being used for various environmental and educational programs. In the James J. Howard Marine Sciences

Laboratory building, completed in the mid-1990s, research is conducted by the National Marine Fisheries Service and others (in 1985, 20-years-worth of research was destroyed when the Marine Fisheries building—the old Fort Hancock hospital—burned in what was probably an arson fire). The 300-seat theater has been restored and is used year-round by the local high school; various schemes to restore more of the old buildings are afoot. Ferry service to other New Jersey cities and to New York City runs weekends in the summer; it is hoped that the schedule can be expanded.

Sandy Hook is heavily used for recreational purposes in the summer (some 2–2.5 million visitors a year), but although well over half the visitors come to use the beaches, the area is also beloved of bird-watchers and other naturalists. At the Spermaceti Cove visitor center,* housed in an 1894 lifesaving station, are displays relating to the area. Brochures and other material to help you tour Sandy Hook on your own are available. A wide range of tours and special events is offered at Sandy Hook, some dealing with the natural aspects of the spit, others with Fort Hancock or the Coast Guard facility. Many of them start from the visitor center; to find out what is available and whether reservations are required, call 732-872-5970. Visitor center open daily, 10–5. A self-guided nature tour, the Old Dune Trail, starts at the center. Notice the prickly pears, the state's only native cactus (often seen with the leaves trimmed by rabbits), and the holly forest with 150-year-old trees that are 50 to 70 feet tall. A 5½-mile multi-use trail starts at the parking lot. Parking fee Memorial Day weekend–Labor Day.

In 2001 New Jersey Audubon opened the Sandy Hook Bird Observatory in one of the Fort Hancock buildings (20 Hartshorne Dr.; 732-872-2500). Sandy Hook is one of the best year-round birding sites in the state and is also on both the spring and fall migration routes. At the observatory, which features a bird and butterfly garden, you can pick up maps of the hot spots on Sandy Hook. Among the activities offered at the observatory are morning bird and butterfly walks, classes for schoolchildren, birding and natural-history workshops, and an annual Sandy Hook migration watch in the spring. Open Tuesday–Saturday, 10–5, Sunday, 10–3; groups and tours by appointment.

Hightstown   Mercer 5,216

NJ 33, C 539, 571

Settled in the 1720s by John and Mary Hight, Hightstown owed its period of greatest prosperity to the railroads. After the Camden and Amboy arrived in 1831, Hightstown became the transportation hub for the surrounding agricultural country, shipping produce to New York and Philadelphia. Growth stopped when the railroad was rerouted farther north to connect with Trenton, but not before the well-off farmers had built the splendid Victorian

The map shows:
Lincoln, Hutchinson, Park Ave., Reed, William, Shapiro, Ely house, Monmouth St. (33), Grant Ave., Academy, Purdy, Bank St., To: Twin Rivers, C571, Stockton St., North Main, Broad St., 2ᵈ Ave., Rogers, Church St., Maxwell Ave., Manlove Ave., 1ˢᵗ Ave., Center St., Outcalt, Railroad Ave., Cole, Franklin, Clinton St., Morrison Ave., Main St., Summit, Dey, West Ward, East Ward, Farr, Samuel Sloan house, Mercer St., South St., C571, C539, Peddie School, Ward, Davison, Grape Run, Taylor, To: Meadow Lakes ↓ Etra Lake Park, Peddie Lake, N, (33)

homes that today distinguish Hightstown. The last passenger train went through in 1939, but considerable railroading interest was generated when, some 30 years later, stone sleepers that had supported the tracks on which the John Bull, the country's first steam locomotive, had come into Hightstown were discovered. Some of those sleepers line Railroad Ave.; others are to be found behind the Ely house (*see* below).

Peddie Lake, in the center of town, is popular for fishing. For a few years there was no fishing—construction of the New Jersey Turnpike and Twin Rivers had filled the lake with silt, and it had to be dredged and stocked before it could once again be fished.

The Peddie School (S. Main St. between E. Ward St. and Etra Rd., C 571), a preparatory school founded in 1864, has a handsome campus; note particularly the white octagonal house. The recipient of the largest gift ever given by an individual to an independent school in the United States, Peddie has an active cultural program that is open to the public. Exhibits at the Mariboe Art Gallery (609-490-7550) change roughly every two months and feature works by faculty and area artists; there is also an annual small-works show. Open Monday–Friday, 9–12 and 1:15–3; closed August. At the William Mount-Burke Theatre (609-490-7550) professional music, dance, and theater performances are presented, as are student productions, lecture series, a summer theater season, and summer arts programs for children.

Across the street from the campus are some splendid houses, among them the Samuel Sloan house★ (1856; 238 S. Main). A characteristic feature of Hightstown architecture is the grillwork on many of the houses; this is particularly in evidence on Stockton St. (C 571) near the intersection with Main Street.

The Ely house (164 N. Main St.; 609-371-9580) is the headquarters and museum of the Hightstown–East Windsor Historical Society. The house, which dates from the 1840s, features Native American artifacts, a candlestick holder and other objects belonging to John and Mary Hight, relics from the John Bull locomotive, and period furnishings. Behind the house, in the Camden and Amboy's old freight station (1869), is the society's Grace Hutchinson West Educational Center. The society sponsors an annual Christmas tea and, every other fall, a historic-house tour; Ely house and the station are open then and on other special occasions. The society will arrange tours of the town by appointment. Call for details.

Just east of town on C 571, on the site of a former estate, is Meadow Lakes, a 103-acre community for 400 senior citizens with a completely staffed medical facility. Farther east on 571 is Etra Lake Park, a 160-acre East Windsor Township facility with a two-mile fitness trail, picnic tables, soccer and baseball fields, a shuffleboard court, a pavilion, and an environmental center. Concerts are held in the park during the summer, and you can fish in the lake. The environmental center focuses on programs for school-age children; for information call the township recreation department (609-443-4000, ext. 214).

A mile or two east of Hightstown, on NJ 33, is Twin Rivers, New Jersey's first planned-unit development. At one time nearly half the population of East Windsor Township lived on its 700-plus acres. The community has its own schools and shopping center and a mix of apartments, single-family houses, and townhouses, and has attracted the scrutiny of countless researchers, from sociologists and anthropologists to specialists in energy conservation.

South of East Windsor in Eilers Corner is the Silver Decoy Winery (610 Windsor-Perrineville Rd., ¼ mi. from C 539; 609-448-0008). Founded in 2001, the winery grows a large variety of grapes. Open Saturday 10–5, Sunday, 12–5; tours of the vineyard and winery by appointment.

Hillside Union 21,747

I 78, GARDEN STATE PKWY EXIT 142, US 22, C 509

Part of Union Township until 1913, Hillside has for over 50 years been the home of baseball's Phil Rizzuto. Lionel trains were once manufactured here, and today the Atlas Company produces HO-gauge track (enough, it is said, to have wrapped around the world several times), as well as other HO, N, and O locomotives, rolling stock, and accessories.

On the site of a tract purchased by John Woodruff in 1666, the Hillside Historical Society maintains the Woodruff House* (111–113 Conant St.; 908-353-8828) as a "museum of three centuries." The earliest part of the house, which remained in the Woodruff family until 1978, dates to 1735, the central section to 1790. In the central section the furnishings are generally mid-19th century, but the house also contains 18th-century items and an 1890s kitchen, and there is a smokehouse in the attic. In front of the house is the Eaton Store, a 1900–1930 store, which the museum has restored to reflect a general or neighborhood store of the early 20th century. Other buildings include a barn in which farm artifacts are displayed and a 1913 garage recently converted into an archival center. Attached to the barn is a room with a Rizzuto exhibit, containing pictures, plaques, and other memorabilia. Also on the property is a memorial garden. Open the 3d Sunday of the month, 2–4, and during Union County's Four Centuries in a Weekend; groups and other times by appointment.

East of the Woodruff House is Evergreen Cemetery* (1137 N. Broad St.; 908-352-7940; the cemetery extends into Newark and Elizabeth), one of only two in New Jersey to be on the national register (the other is Mount Pleasant in Newark). Started in 1853, Evergreen spreads out over 115 acres. Influenced in its design by the rural cemetery movement, it is beautifully landscaped, and some of the trees are believed to be over 350 years old. The writers Stephen Crane and Mary Mapes Dodge are buried here; there is also a section of Gypsy graves. You can pick up a guide to the cemetery at the office, which is open weekdays, 8:30–4, Saturday, 9–12.

Hoboken   Hudson 38,577

(HUDSON RIVER BETWEEN HOLLAND AND LINCOLN TUNNELS)

 The country's first brewery was established in Hoboken, a community first settled by Dutch from New Amsterdam, in 1642. But beer is no longer brewed in Hoboken, and the city's current character was shaped more by the Stevens family than by the earlier settlers. Colonel John Stevens, a Revolutionary War officer and a famous inventor, in 1784 purchased an estate known as Hobuck Island, which had been confiscated from its Tory owner, and auctioned off lots in what he referred to as the New City of Hoboken. Stevens has been called the father of American railroading, and he and his sons can take credit for many of the events that happened first in Hoboken. Stevens inaugurated the world's first regular steam ferry service (in 1811). He was responsible for the first successful American run of a locomotive (the tracks were near Newark and Washington sts.) and the invention of the T rail and the ironclad ship. His son John Cox Stevens founded the first yacht club in the United States (in 1844); it was located near 12th Street. John Cox Stevens also originated the first America's Cup race. His brother Edwin made possible the founding (in 1870) of Stevens Institute of Technology, one of the first colleges in the country to offer a degree in mechanical engineering (and, many years later, one of the first to require freshmen to have personal computers). Together the brothers built New Jersey's first railroad.

Other Hoboken firsts include the first organized game of what has become modern baseball. Controversy still surrounds this claim, but in 1846, a uniformed team (only one of the teams wore uniforms) played with stipulated rules on the cricket pitch known as the Elysian Fields. What remains of the Elysian Fields can be seen at 10th St. and Hudson, and a commemorative plaque is to be found at 11th and Washington streets. The first international cricket match in which the United States took part was played in 1859 (the United States was badly beaten). And in 1984 Hoboken was the first city in New Jersey to declare itself a nuclear-free zone.

In the early years of the 19th century Hoboken was a popular resort. Visitors came by ferry from New York to frequent the beer gardens, taverns, and boardinghouses and to enjoy the river walks. (Sybil's Cave by the river

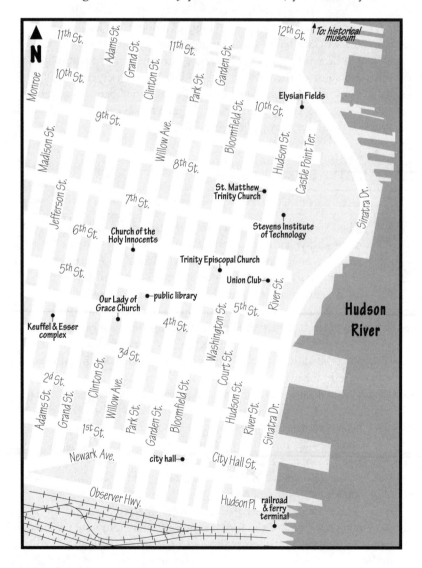

was a popular meeting place for lovers until a New York sales clerk was murdered there; newspaper accounts of her death are said to have inspired Edgar Allan Poe's "The Mystery of Marie Roget.") Washington Irving and Martin Van Buren were among those who visited John Jacob Astor at his villa at 2d and Washington streets.

By the mid-19th century Hoboken was an active manufacturing center, but of the many industrial firms once in Hoboken, none remains. The last— the Maxwell House coffee plant, whose aroma often permeated the town— closed in 1992. The old Keuffel and Esser complex* (3d St., Jefferson, and Grand), part of which dates to the 1880s, has been converted to apartments. Keuffel and Esser, which produced a variety of precision instruments, was the first company in the country to manufacture slide rules, and during World War II it raised spiders in Hoboken to supply webs for telescope cross hairs.

At the beginning of the 20th century Hoboken was an important shipping center, and during World War I it was a major port of embarkation for American troops (40% of the American soldiers who were sent to Europe apparently passed through Hoboken). There were taverns along River St., and like many other port cities, Hoboken had a reputation as a wide-open town, even during Prohibition. *On the Waterfront* was filmed in Hoboken, and in the 1950s the Port Authority spent considerable sums to refurbish piers, but with the rise in container shipping, Hoboken's port inevitably declined. After many years of wrangling over how much development the town wanted, ground was finally broken in 1996 on a mixed-use development, which includes 10 acres of open space on two piers, at the former port.

The trans-Hudson train tubes were opened in 1904, and the Erie Lackawanna's railroad and ferry terminal* (Hudson Pl. at the river), which also served as a warehouse, was built in 1907. This wonderful building with its striking copper roof, Tiffany ceiling, and period fixtures, is said to have been the first American building with platform train sheds. In 1930, one of the early electric trains left from this terminal, with Thomas Alva Edison at the controls. Ferry service continued until 1966; it started up again in 1989 using a temporary dock, and when the restoration of the terminal is complete—this is a long-term project—the ferries will return to their slips at the terminal. Close to 20,000 commuters use this striking terminal every day, making it the second-busiest passenger terminal in the state. A festival celebrating it and the city is held most years on a Saturday in September.

For a time Hoboken was a wealthy suburb. In the late 1920s it was considered bohemian. At one point there were 20 legitimate theaters in operation, and Christopher Morley, who ran a highly successful theater season in Hoboken, called it "the last seacoast of Bohemia."

The Stevens Institute of Technology demolished John Stevens's mid-19th-century house in 1959, but the view from the building that replaced it makes clear why he built his house on that spot. The gatehouse (1853) from the Stevens estate remains, as does the institute's first building (5th and

Hudson), designed by Richard Upjohn. At the northern end of the 55-acre campus, the fraternities occupy what were once the homes of wealthy commuters. At the college's Davidson Laboratory, named for a Stevens Institute faculty member who towed model ships in the swimming pool to learn how they worked, scientists have worked on the design of America's Cup yachts and nuclear submarines. From time to time they build an artificial beach in the lab to study wave erosion at the New Jersey shore. Volunteers from the school help inflate the balloons for the Macy's Thanksgiving Day Parade, which can turn into a party for the children in town the day before the parade. In 1985 Stevens Institute made national nonscientific news when it awarded an honorary degree to Hoboken native son Frank Sinatra, to the displeasure of many students and members of the faculty. (Other well-known figures connected to the town include Alexander Calder, Dorothea Lange, Alfred Stieglitz, and Daniel Pinkwater.)

In Stevens's Upjohn building is the Center for the Performing Arts at DeBaun Auditorium (201-216-8937). A wide range of theater, dance, and music programs and workshops for children and adults is offered at the theater. Exhibits of contemporary art, which change monthly during the school year, are hung in the elegant hallway. Open when there are performances in the auditorium.

Although the charms of Hoboken have been discovered by New York commuters—one often hears Hoboken referred to as Manhattan West—and many old-timers worry about overgentrification (signs saying "Speculators, keep out" used to appear with some frequency), the wide main street (Washington) still has an old-time, small-town air. There are no tall buildings on it (tall buildings are, however, gradually appearing, particularly at the northern edge of town and the waterfront), and although the boutiques and coffeehouses have arrived, you can still find shoe repair shops and dry cleaners.

Almost every street in Hoboken has interesting buildings, from rows of brownstones to mid-19th-century churches to late-19th-century firehouses to early-20th-century public buildings and hotels. There are also a large number of restaurants for the size of the town. The southern Hoboken historic district includes parts of Bloomfield, Hudson, Newark, River, Washington, 1st, 2d, 3d, and 4th sts. and Observer Highway, but you should also take in Willow Ave., Court, Garden, Jefferson, Park, Clinton, and Grand sts., and the rest of the numbered streets. Particularly interesting are the city hall* (Washington and 1st); the Church of the Holy Innocents (Willow and 6th); the Trinity Episcopal Church (Washington and 6th), another Upjohn design; the public library (Park and 5th); and Our Lady of Grace Roman Catholic Church (Willow and 4th), featured in On the Waterfront. The strong German influence on Hoboken (the 1880 census called it "the most German city" in the country) is apparent along Hudson St.: at St. Matthew Trinity Church (8th St.), the words "gerichtet 1877" can be seen; the Union Club (6th St.), now condominiums, was the Deutsche Club until World War I.

Within the southern historic district is the Hoboken Exempt Firemen's Association museum (213 Bloomfield St.; 201-420-2397). The museum's collection includes memorabilia going back to 1850 as well as hundreds of photographs of all kinds of fires and a 1932 hose wagon that children can play on. Usually open Saturday, but it is advisable to call first. Groups by appointment (201-420-2007).

In the Shipyard Development (so called because the buildings formerly housed shipyards) in a restored 19th-century machine shop are the new quarters of the Hoboken Historical Museum (201-656-2240). Exhibits, which change twice a year, feature memorabilia relating to the history of the city. The museum organizes special events, including an annual house tour in the fall and garden tour in the spring, and is involved in educational and community programs. Open Tuesday–Thursday, 2–9, Friday, 1–4, weekends, 12–5; groups and other times by appointment.

Ho-Ho-Kus Bergen 4,060

GARDEN STATE PKWY EXIT 1685, NJ 17, C 502

Ho-Ho-Kus, an early Dutch settlement, has a Lenape name, which you will see both with and without the hyphens. Some of the older buildings remain: along E. Saddle River Rd., for example, are three 18th-century stone houses (at 745,* 825,* and 933*). At 335 N. Franklin Turnpike is the Hermitage* (201-445-8311), a national historic landmark building operated as a house museum. Also known as the Colonel Marc Prevost house, it has associations with George Washington, Aaron Burr (he married Theodosia Prevost), and the marquis de Lafayette. The nucleus of the house was built in the early 18th century, but in the mid-19th century it was expanded and altered to become the Gothic Revival house you see today. From 1807 until 1970, when it was willed to the state, it was occupied by only one family, the Rosencrantzes. When the state acquired it, the house was in bad condition. The decision was made to restore it to its late-19th-century appearance, and by 2004, only a few rooms remained uninterpreted. The John Rosencrantz house (1892), a family house moved to the property from down the street on what was once part of the estate's original 100 acres, contains the Hermitage offices and two parlors that serve as exhibition spaces. Displays change three to four times a year. In 1999 a large wing was added, and the Rosencrantz house is now known as the Hermitage Education and Conference Center. The museum has a large collection of clothing, furniture, decorative objects, and other artifacts, dating from the mid-18th-century through the 20th. The museum offers a wide range of lectures, other educational programs, and clothing and textile exhibits; it also takes programs into the schools and sponsors a crafts boutique four weeks before Thanksgiving. The Hermitage is open for tours Wednesday–Sunday, 1–4 (the last tour begins at 3:15), with other times and groups by appointment; the office is open daily, 9–5. Closed legal holidays and the Friday after Thanksgiving.

Holmdel Monmouth 15,781

GARDEN STATE PKWY EXIT 114, C 520

One of the oldest settlements in Monmouth County, the township of Holmdel was named for the Holmes family, Baptists who came to this area in the mid-1660s to escape religious persecution in Massachusetts. The first Baptist sermon in New Jersey was preached here in the late 1660s. The township has been growing rapidly, its population increasing over sevenfold over the last 40 years. (In the village note the 19th-century Dutch Reformed church* at 41 Main St.)

About two miles north of Holmdel village is Holmdel Park (take NJ 34 or Holmdel Rd. north to Longstreet Rd; turn right on Longstreet; 732-946-2669). Within this 573-acre county park is the mid-18th-century Longstreet Farm* (732-946-3758), which is being run by the county parks system as an 1890s working farm. Many of the furnishings in the house, the first part of which dates to the 1700s, were the Longstreet family's original belongings and reflect several periods. You can watch as the park workers go about the regular activities of a working farm, and there are self-guided tours. Many special events, such as sheep and wool days, harvest festivals, and Halloween and Christmas celebrations, are scheduled. The park is open daily except Christmas; 9–5, Memorial Day–Labor Day, 10–5, Labor Day–Memorial Day. Farmhouse open weekends, March–December, 12–3:30. Groups and other times by appointment.

Also within the park is the 20-acre Holmdel Arboretum, with specimen trees, bushes, and plants suitable for growing in Monmouth County. In the park there are mature stands of American beech, hickory, and white, red, and chestnut oaks; over five miles of trails (because the terrain is rolling, not all the walks are easy); a fitness trail; tennis courts; an activity center for scheduled programs (732-842-4000); picnic areas (group areas by appointment); playgrounds, shuffleboard courts; and, in winter, opportunities for cross-country skiing, sledding, and skating. This is a popular park (up to 1 million visitors a year), and in spring and fall access to the parking lots is sometimes cut off for an hour or so because they are full. Guided nature walks by appointment.

On the edge of the park is the Holmes-Hendrickson house* (Longstreet and Robert rds.; 732-462-1466), a mid-18th-century house run as a museum by the Monmouth County Historical Association. Unusually well preserved when the association acquired it, the house contains excellent examples of mid-18th-century furnishings and working tools of 18th-century farm life.

Open May–September, Thursday–Saturday, 1–4. Groups and other times by appointment.

Southeast of the park are the Bell Laboratories (now part of Lucent Technologies) where the *Telstar* satellite was developed. There is still some activity in the Saarinen-designed building where in 1962 the first telecast from a satellite was received and in 1964 traces of cosmic energy presumed to have originated in the big bang with which the universe began were recorded for the first time. The 20-foot horn antenna* used in this work is now a national historic landmark.

South of the laboratories, in the former St. Catherine's Church, are the headquarters of the Holmdel Historical Society (64 Stillwell Rd.; 732-946-4881). Inside are exhibits of historical artifacts, many of local interest. The society also runs the Dr. Robert W. Cooke office (intersection of McCampbell and Middletown rds.), an 1820s medical building, which is used for meetings and historical programs. Both buildings are open by appointment.

North of Holmdel Park is Telegraph Hill Park (Garden State Pkwy exit 116; 732-888-2034; 732-888-5000). The park is home to the former Garden State Arts Center, now the PNC Bank Arts Center (732-442-9200), owned and formerly run by the New Jersey Highway Authority (the legislation establishing the Garden State Parkway required that recreation be provided along the route). Seating some 17,500 people, this open shell is the scene of concerts, primarily popular music, in the summer. The plaza is also used for special events, including several ethnic celebrations known as heritage festivals. The park provides limited opportunities for picnicking and hiking and a nice view from Telegraph Hill. To the east of the arts center is Phillips Park, which includes a former Nike missile site. Trails open daily, 9–dusk.

On a slope overlooking the parkway is the state's Vietnam War Memorial, dedicated in 1995. A Vietnam Era Educational Center (800-648-8387), "devoted soley to gaining an understanding of the conflict in Southeast Asia and the surrounding political strife in America," is said to be the first of its kind in the country. The center includes a library, a meeting room, and an exhibit area with a time line, eyewitness accounts, and an oral-history theater. Open Tuesday–Friday, 10–6; weekends, 10–5, but it is probably advisable to call first. Groups by appointment.

Hopatcong Sussex 15,888

C 602, 607, 631

The borough of Hopatcong lies on the western shore of Lake Hopatcong, the largest lake entirely within New Jersey. Reports of monsters in the lake can be found as far back as the 17th century, although until the mid-18th century there were actually two smaller lakes on the site. In the 1750s ironmakers constructed a dam, raising the water level and making the two lakes into one; in the 1830s, construction of the Morris Canal, which ran from Newark to Phillipsburg and used the lake as a water source, raised the level again. The lake was also an important source of ice, with several icehouses located on its shores.

Situated over 900 feet above sea level, with some 50 miles of shoreline and clear water, the lake became a popular summer resort. Before World War I it was known as a haven for burlesque performers—Bert Lahr, for example, was a regular visitor. With the arrival of excursion trains in 1882, hotels were built on the lake; there were 3 in 1882 and 40 by 1900. Most are gone, victims of the Depression, the automobile, and World War II, but the Windlass, formerly Allan's Pavilion, dates from the 1880s and still has some of its original docks. The Lake Hopatcong Yacht Club,* founded in 1905, is said to be the second-oldest inland yacht club in the country. Its building, which dates from 1910, remains almost unaltered (it has no air conditioning). The amusement park on Bertrand Island, which closed in the early 1980s, boasted the first roller coaster in northern New Jersey. Between 1960 and 1980, as summer cottages were winterized and new developments built, Hopatcong saw its year-round population increase by over 350 percent (in 1990 it was over 23 times what it had been before World War II), and there is some concern about traffic congestion and speeding on the lake, as well as the need to control eutrophication.

At the southwestern end of the lake is the popular Hopatcong State Park (973-398-7010), over 100 acres with facilities for picnicking, swimming, and fishing (a small-boat launch is also available, though not on weekends in high season). The lake is considered one of the best spots in the state for ice-fishing, and it is also favored by other winter sports fans. Lake Musconetcong, four miles west of Lake Hopatcong, is also part of the park and was also created as a water source for the Morris Canal. It too is a popular spot for boating and fishing. Toward the southern end of the park you can see some reminders of the Morris Canal, including the dam, gatehouse, and one of the water turbines that lifted canalboats up the inclined planes. In the former lock tender's house (next to the park administration building) the Lake Hopatcong Historical Society runs a small museum (973-398-2616). Permanent exhibits deal with the history of the area—from the Lenape who lived here, to the transformation caused by the canal, to the railroads, to the lake's glory days as a resort, to Bertrand Island Amusement Park. Open Sunday, 12–4, March–May and October–December and in the evening for special programs, but the hours can change, so it is best to call ahead; groups and other times by appointment. The park is open daylight hours throughout the year; in the summer an admission fee is charged.

Hope Warren 1,891

C 519, 521

Although the nearness of I 80 may one day change Hope's appearance radically, the town today presents a striking concentration of 18th- and early-19th-century buildings, many of them of local bluestone, with little intrusion from later periods. Settled by Moravians from Pennsylvania in 1769, it may represent one of the country's first planned communities. The Moravians bought 1,000 acres from Samuel Green, who had been their host when they passed through the area on missionary trips up the Delaware. Green had become interested in their church (he had even tried to give them the land). The town plan was devised in 1774, and in 1775 the community's name was changed from the original Greenland to Hope. The community began to decline in the 1790s, and in 1807 the inhabitants were ordered by the mother church to sell it; the last Moravian service in Hope took place in April 1808.

The first building to be erected (c. 1769–70) was the gristmill (north side of High St., east of the bridge). It has burned twice but still retains its original walls. Flour was produced here for George Washington's troops when they were quartered at Jockey Hollow, and the mill continued to operate well into the 20th century. At the rear of the mill is the original millrace, cut through solid slate to a depth of 22 feet. The stone bridge that crosses Beaver Brook, although not built by the Moravians, dates to 1807. The little building by the bridge was once the tollhouse. It is now a local museum (908-459-4884), which is open Sunday, 1–3, May–October. Groups other times by appointment.

When the museum is not open, you can pick up a leaflet that describes a walking tour of the town at many of the local stores. Rye whiskey and beer were made at the distillery (1773), and services were held at the Gemeinhaus, or community house (1781), on the southwest corner of High St. and C 519-521. Now a bank, the building has also been a tavern and a hotel, and in 1824 it served as Warren County's first courthouse. The Moravian cemetery (off High St.) dates to 1773; the graves are arranged according to the date of death, and the numbers on the slabs correspond to a chrono-logical list of burials in the Moravian Archives in Pennsylvania. The earliest residence in town (1775) is across from the distillery; the farm manager lived in the house and stored the farm produce in the barn. This farm has been in continuous use since Moravian days. At the northeast corner of Union St. and Moravian Alley is the American House Hotel (c. 1799–1803), originally a schoolhouse. It has recently been restored and is being used for offices. There are several other 18th-century houses and stores in the center of Hope (the historic district* encompasses Union, High, Hickory, and Walnut sts., C 519, 521, Beaver Brook, and the millrace) and on the outskirts as well—for example, the Israel Swayze house and outkitchen, dating from

1759, on C 519 a little over a mile south of town, and what is often called the Moravian Farmhouse on the west side of the Hope-Blairstown Rd., three-quarters of a mile north of town. In addition, both St. John's United Methodist Church and St. Luke's Episcopal Church (High St. south of the intersection with Hickory St.) are worth a glance; both date to 1832. Walking tours of the town (908-459-9177) leave at 9:30 from the Inn at Millrace Pond (313 Johnsonburg Rd. [C 519 north]) the first two Saturdays of the month, June–October; groups by appointment.

Roughly 5½ miles south of Hope, on the west side of C 519, is the Four Sisters Winery (908-475-3671). A 250-acre farm winery, Four Sisters sponsors a variety of special events, including grape stomping and murder-mystery nights. Regularly scheduled tours are given on weekends and by appointment other times. Open daily, 9–6, April–December; closed Wednesday, January–March.

Northeast of Hope is Jenny Jump State Forest (take C 519 northeast to Shiloh Rd. and turn right; 908-459-4366), 4,200 acres with facilities for picnicking, camping, fishing, boating, cross-country skiing, ice-fishing, and hunting, a playground, a lookout point, hiking trails, and an astronomy center. The center is open during the camping season (April–October), with programs on Saturday night, 8–10. Jenny Jump is a good place to look at fall foliage.

A mile or two southeast of Hope (take 519 east to C 611 and turn right) is the Land of Make Believe (Great Meadows Rd.; 908-459-5100), a 50-year-old commercial theme park for children. Open daily, 3d Saturday in June through Labor Day, weekends only, Memorial Day weekend through the 2d weekend in June and the weekend after Labor Day, 10–6. Admission charge.

Farther south on 611 is Hemknoll Farm (908-459-5778), one of the largest display gardens of hybrid daylilies in the East. The farm grows over 865 varieties, and although the period of peak display can vary with the weather, July and August are always safe. Visitors are welcome, but you must make an appointment first.

Hopewell Mercer 2,035 (borough) 16,105 (township)

C 518, 569

An attractive small town in the midst of a rapidly growing township, Hopewell was settled in the 17th century. One of its first residents was a son of Richard and Penelope Stout (*see* Middletown). On the north side of the main street, in a handsome Mansard-roofed 19th-century house (with a 20th-century addition), is the Hopewell Museum (28 E. Broad St.; 609-466-0103). Its collection is made up almost entirely of items donated over the last 80 years by Hopewell residents, and rotating exhibits focus on local life from colonial times to the present. One room is devoted to a notable collection of

Native American artifacts. Open Monday, Wednesday, and Saturday, 2–5; groups by appointment. Open for research Monday and Wednesday by appointment only. A little farther west is the Old School Baptist Church (north side of W. Broad St.), a brick and stucco structure first built c. 1747 and rebuilt c. 1825. John Hart, one of the signers of the Declaration of Independence, is buried in the cemetery.

Across the street (19 W. Broad St.) is a pre-1756 (but much altered) clapboard building that housed the first Baptist school of higher education in the state, founded in 1756 by the Reverend Isaac Eaton, the pastor of the Baptist church in Hopewell. Eaton's first pupil was James Manning, the founder of Brown University. Other buildings of interest include two Second Empire–style structures: the railroad station* (Railroad Pl.), built in 1876 and restored in the 1990s, now containing offices upstairs and used for community meetings downstairs, and the Valley Inn (E. Broad St.).

Northeast of the railroad station (Railroad Pl. becomes Somerset Pl.) is the Princeton Doll and Toy Museum (8 Somerset Pl.; 609-333-8600). Also a shop, the museum has a wide range of historic dolls and toys. Open Monday, Friday, and Saturday, 10–5; groups and tours by appointment. Programs on doll history are offered on Thursday. Admission charge.

Highfields* (Van Dyke Rd.), in the township, was the home of Charles and Anne Lindbergh when their young son was kidnapped (*see* Flemington). It now belongs to the state, which uses it as a facility for troubled youths.

Close to the eastern edge of the township is Mercer County's first winery (take Pleasant Valley Rd., which becomes the Pennington-Harbourton Rd. east to Burd Rd., turn left on Burd and right on Yard), Hopewell Valley Vineyards (46 Yard Rd.; 609-737-4465), run by a descendant of Italian winemakers. There are lovely views from the winery and historic Hopewell photographs on display inside (and on the labels). Open Thursday–Sunday, 12–5, or by appointment.

There are many lovely places to walk in and about the township. The Cedar Ridge Trail (Van Dyke Rd. north of C 518) and the McBurney Woods Preserve (Mountain Rd. east of Runyons Mill Rd. in East Amwell) are both preservation projects of the D&R Greenway Land Trust (formerly the Delaware & Raritan Greenway; 609-924-4646). Cedar Ridge is a modest trail through an area that was a lake; bordering Stony Brook, the trail takes you through varied vegetation and wildlife. The McBurney Woods Preserve consists of 178 acres in the Sourland Mountains and forms part of a chain of woods unbroken for 60 miles. A two-mile trail takes you through mature forest and along a field of wildflowers. If you continue east on Mountain Rd. and turn right on Rileyville Rd. (C 607) you will come to the Sourland Mountain Reservation (908-782-1158), a Hunterdon County preserve of some 200-plus hilly, wooded acres. The reservation is rich in forest birds and a good place to look for early spring wildflowers. Most of the woods are wet, but there are also some interesting rock formations to be seen. Open for hiking, biking, cross-country skiing, and hunting.

At the western end of Hopewell Township is the Bald Pate Mountain Preserve (NJ 29 between Fiddler's Creek and Pleasant Valley rds.; 609-989-6530), also known as Kuser Mountain, 1,100 acres of county land that was threatened by traprock mining and development in the 1990s. You can hike and bike on the trails, and plans call for a more elaborate system of trails that would allow for skiers and riders. The greenhouse on the property will become a botanical growth and study area and the mansion will become a visitor center. This is prime birding territory.

Jamesburg Middlesex 5,025

C 522

Jamesburg's first settlers, Scots fleeing religious persecution, arrived in the late 17th century, and its first mill dates to 1734, but the town's period of greatest prosperity began 100 years later when the railroad came through. Jamesburg eventually had two railroad lines and three depots and became the commercial and social center for the township and the surrounding agricultural area. This prosperity continued until after World War II.

Much of the town's growth can be attributed to James Buckelew, whose great-grandfather had arrived in the area around 1715. In 1832 Buckelew purchased Lakeview* (203 Buckelew Ave.; 732-521-2040), originally a small 17th-century farmhouse overlooking the millpond (now Lake Manalapan), and enlarged it into a 23-room mansion with a colonnaded porch overlooking the lake.

Buckelew farmed some 4,000 acres (and was the first in the area to use marl on his land), supplied 700 mules for the Delaware and Raritan Canal,* established the Freehold and Jamesburg Agricultural Railroad, and helped establish the First National Bank. Because an African American child was excluded from the existing school, Buckelew built another school, open to all, which, at the dedication ceremony was referred to as the James B. School; James B. eventually became Jamesburg. When President-elect Lincoln was in Trenton on his way to his inauguration, he rode in Buckelew's coach from the Clinton St. station to the capitol. The house, also known as Buckelew's Mansion, is now open as a house museum, and Lincoln's coach is one of the items on display. Among those who helped restore the mansion were students from the New Jersey Training School for Boys, a school built in 1867 as the New Jersey State Reform School on a large farm owned by Buckelew, which may have been the site of a mid-18th-century French and Indian War stockade.

The museum has some period furnishings, items relating to local history, and a high school memento room. In one room the Jamesburg Historical Railroad Society has set up a model of Jamesburg at its industrial prime, 1900–1930, which includes all three of the town's turn-of-the-century railroad stations. Out back are a blacksmith's shop and a smokehouse, and the museum has a large collection of old farm implements and tools and anvils used by blacksmiths. In the front yard are some track from the Camden and Amboy Railroad and several anchoring stones. Open the 2d and 4th Sundays of the month, 1–3; groups, other times, and guided tours by appointment.

The Fourteenth Regiment New Jersey Volunteers also has its headquarters in Lakeview, and on the annual Buckelew Day in August does a Civil War reenactment. The Buckelew birthday celebration also includes crafts demonstrations. In February there's a Presidents Day celebration, and in December a town holiday festival.

Although Jamesburg is one of Middlesex County's more densely populated communities (more than 5,000 people in less than one square mile), it abuts a county park that is larger than the borough (675 acres). Thompson Park (732-745-3900) includes the 30-acre Lake Manalapan, where you can fish, boat, and skate; there are also athletic fields, hiking trails, picnic areas, tennis courts, playgrounds, and a small zoo. Part of the park has been designated a bird sanctuary. Several horse and dog shows, as well as Sunday-afternoon concerts in the gazebo, take place in the summer.

Just west of Jamesburg is the Forsgate Country Club (Forsgate Dr.); each hole on the east course is modeled on a famous hole from a British course. South of the club is Rossmoor (Rossmoor Dr.), a retirement community built around a golf course. The land was once an early-20th-century estate and dairy farm; the clubhouse was formerly a residence.

East of Jamesburg, in Monroe Township (take Buckelew Rd., C 522, to Hoffman–Mounts Mill Rd., turn left and turn left again on Spotswood-Englishtown Rd., C 613; there are plenty of signs), is the Displayworld Stone Museum (476 Spotswood-Englishtown Rd., C 613; 732-521-2232). Part of a landscaping business, this picturesque (there are five waterfalls and a lake) and idiosyncratic collection of stones, dinosaur bones, fossils, and two tons of fluorescent rock, also contains exhibits on the past and present techniques of masonry. Open April–Thanksgiving, Monday–Saturday, 8–5, Sunday, 10–4:30; Thanksgiving–Christmas, weekdays 8–5.

Jefferson Township Morris 19,717

NJ 15, C 699

Located in Jefferson Township, the northwesternmost township of Morris County, is the Mahlon Dickerson Reservation (Weldon Rd.; 973-326-7631). Dickerson, a Morris County native, served as governor of the state, as U.S. senator, and as secretary of the navy under presidents Jackson and Van Buren. With 3,200 acres this is the largest park in the county, and its trails reach 1,395 feet above sea level, the highest point in the county. You can fish and skate on Saffin Pond, and there are over 20 miles of trails, on which you can hike, ride, bike, and cross-country ski. From Headley Overlook (1,300 feet above sea level), you can see the surrounding area, including the northern end of Lake Hopatcong. There are also facilities for camping and picnicking, a trailer park, and a ball field. For the camping and trailer facilities, call 973-663-0020.

Jersey City Hudson 240,055

NJ TNPK EXITS 14A, B, C, US 1, 9, NJ 440

Jersey City, the state's second most populous city, has been the state's first in other ways: the site of the state's first permanent settlement (1660), the first place to be occupied by the enemy in the Revolution (1776). It was one of the first to declare itself a nuclear-free zone, and it can boast a variety of other, perhaps less significant, firsts: the first automobile tunnel under a river has one end in Jersey City; the first woman elected to the House of Representatives in the eastern United States and the first native-born American to fly a balloon in the continental United States came from Jersey City; the first professional heavyweight fight to produce $1 million in gate receipts and the first mass production of a modern wood-and-graphite pencil took place in Jersey City. Jersey City has the largest concentration of visual artists in the state (a studio tour takes place each October) and was voted the leading walking city in the state (and one of the 12 best in the country).

Although there were sporadic settlements in the early years of the 17th century, disputes with the local Native Americans caused the early residents to leave, and it was not until 1660 that a permanent settlement, known as Bergen (or Bergan), was formed. You can still trace the outline of the original town square—the area bounded by Newkirk, Van Reypen, and Vroom sts. and Tuers Ave., surrounding Bergen Square, south of Journal Square. Alexander Hamilton saw the potential for developing Jersey City as a transportation center and formed an association similar to the one he had established for Paterson. His plans never materialized: he was killed in 1804. Until 1834, New York asserted its right to control the Hudson to the low-water mark on the west bank, thus preventing Jersey City from developing its own waterfront; and the railroads came to own the association's waterfront land.

The city nevertheless developed as a transportation and manufacturing center, and some sense of its former prosperity can be seen in the abundance of extravagant architecture; there are any number of architecturally exuberant churches and public buildings to be seen in Jersey City. Like many of the state's other cities, Jersey City suffered an economic decline, but in the 1970s New Yorkers and others rediscovered it as a desirable place to live; many of the city's brownstones and row houses have been rehabilitated and many of the commercial buildings converted into condominiums; the process continues today. At the same time, developers have been working on ambitious plans for the waterfront. Although not all the grand schemes of the '80s have come to pass, the waterfront has totally changed. Like other rediscovered cities, Jersey City has become involved in the "cargo versus quiche" controversy, the commercial equivalent to the displacement of longtime residents in the gentrification of a neighborhood: many of the few shipping-related businesses that have managed to survive along the waterfront are being forced to relocate by the more glamorous developments.

There are many different neighborhoods to explore, and within many neighborhoods there are great contrasts between buildings in different states of renovation. The Paulus Hook historic district* is a 19th-century area that includes portions of York, Grand, Sussex, Morris, Essex, Greene, Washington, Warren, Henderson, and Van Vorst streets. It is bounded on the east by the Colgate Center, formerly the site of the Colgate factory. Colgate began manufacturing in Jersey City in 1847, and its unusual clock tower was long a landmark along the river; the clock now rises from ground level and is still visible from the river. Within Colgate Center is the state's tallest building (30 Hudson St.).

To the west of the Paulus Hook area is the Van Vorst Park historic district,* with both 19th- and 20th-century structures; it includes Jersey Ave. and Varick, Barrow, Grove, Wayne, Mercer, Montgomery, York, Bright, and Grand streets. The Hamilton Park historic district* includes a 19th-century residential square and 19th- and 20th-century buildings around Hamilton Park, Jersey Ave., and 6–10th streets. Just east of Hamilton Square is Manila Ave., once Grove St. but renamed in honor of Jersey City's large Filipino population.

Journal Square in the heart of the city boasts many striking buildings. Loew's Jersey Theater* (54 Journal Sq.; 201-798-6055), an art deco theater with a terra cotta facade and an ornate Spanish Baroque interior, was built in the late 1920s. It was one of the first theaters to be engineered expressly for the new talking pictures. Threatened with demolition in the late 1980s, it was rescued by a group of concerned citizens who wanted to renovate it and reopen it as a "combination of the Beacon Theater, Carnegie Hall, and Radio City." Although the renovation is not complete and the work continues, the Friends of the Loew's have been able to put on a monthly program of classic films and an increasing number of live events. Tours by appointment. The Stanley Theater (2932 J. F. Kennedy Blvd.) is another art deco building, also listed on the state register of historic buildings. Built in 1928, it now belongs to the Jehovah's Witnesses (some of the classical statues have been removed); open for tours weekdays, 8:30–5. Potential visitors should ring the doorbell (groups larger than 30 should write the Watchtower Society, 25 Columbia Heights, Brooklyn, NY 11201, to set up an appointment). At 26 Journal Square is the Labor Bank Building, a 15-story office building with a marble lobby, molded ceiling designs, and ornamental frieze. Just north of Journal Square (Newark Ave. between Kennedy and Tonnelle) is an Indian enclave.

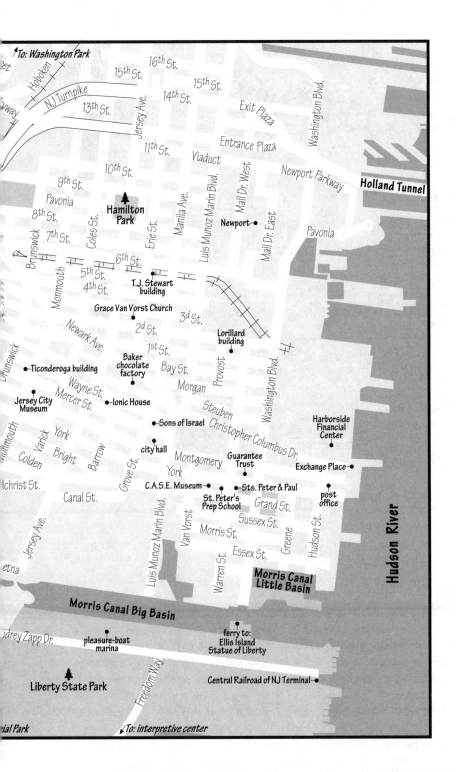

To: Washington Park

Hoboken

NJ Turnpike

16th St.
15th St.
15th St.
14th St.
13th St.
Jersey Ave.

Washington Blvd.

Exit Plaza

Entrance Plaza

11th St.

Viaduct

Newport Parkway

Holland Tunnel

10th St.

9th St.

Pavonia

8th St.

7th St.

Coles St.

Brunswick

Monmouth

Hamilton Park

Erie St.

Manila Ave.

Luis Munoz Marin Blvd.

Mall Dr. West

Mall Dr. East

Newport

Pavonia

6th St.

5th St.

4th St.

T.J. Stewart building

Grace Van Vorst Church

3d St.

2d St.

Newark Ave.

1st St.

Baker chocolate factory

Bay St.

Morgan

Lorillard building

Provost

Ticonderoga building

Wayne St.

Mercer St.

Ionic House

Steuben

Christopher Columbus Dr.

Washington Blvd.

Harborside Financial Center

Jersey City Museum

York

Varick

Bright

Barrow

Sons of Israel

city hall

Grove St.

Montgomery

York

Guarantee Trust

Exchange Place

Colden

C.A.S.E. Museum

Sts. Peter & Paul

post office

Ichrist St.

Canal St.

Luis Munoz Marin Blvd.

St. Peter's Prep School

Van Vorst

Grand St.

Sussex St.

Greene

Hudson St.

Jersey Ave.

Morris St.

Essex St.

etna

Warren St.

Morris Canal Little Basin

Hudson River

Morris Canal Big Basin

udrey Zapp Dr.

pleasure-boat marina

ferry to:
Ellis Island
Statue of Liberty

Freedom Way

Liberty State Park

Central Railroad of NJ Terminal

ial Park

To: interpretive center

The William J. Brennan Court House* (Newark Ave. at Central), a large Beaux Arts building completed in 1910, dominates a city block. Inside are murals painted by Howard Pyle, F. D. Millet, Kenyon Cox, Charles Turner, and Edwin Howland Blashfield. Closed in 1966, the courthouse was rescued and restored; it now houses civil courts and the offices of the county executive. Open for self-guided tours weekdays, 9–4. The city hall (1896; Montgomery and Grove sts.), the post office building (Montgomery and Washington sts.), and the main library (1899; 472 Jersey Ave. at Montgomery) all testify to the size and former wealth of Jersey City. The Old Bergen Church* (the west side of Bergen Ave. at Highland Ave.) belongs to what is said to be the oldest organized congregation west of the Hudson (it received its charter in 1660). The present building, which dates from 1841 and was built with stones taken from earlier buildings, seems unusually sedate in the context of Jersey City's architectural exuberance—for example, directly across Bergen Ave. is the fanciful brickwork of St. Aedans.

Housed since 2001 in a remodeled late-1920s former U.S. Postal Service garage in the Van Vorst district is the Jersey City Museum (350 Montgomery St.; 201-413-0303). The museum mounts ten to twelve major exhibits a year, featuring the works of new and emerging artists, as well as material relating to local history; an exhibit of works by students in the city's public schools is an annual event. The museum sponsors jazz and other concerts, theater programs, lectures, movie screenings, and a variety of other events and programs. Open Wednesday and Friday, 11–5, Thursday, 11–8, weekends 12–5; tours by appointment.

The Afro-American Historical and Cultural Museum (1841 J. F. Kennedy Blvd.; 201-547-5262) has a wide range of exhibits. The history of African Americans in New Jersey, particularly in relation to civil rights and the development of black churches, is one thread; also on display are musical instruments and dolls from the West Indies and Africa; a reconstructed 1930s kitchen; African artwork, including masks and sculpture; and busts of major black figures. Open Monday–Saturday, 10–5.

The C.A.S.E. Museum of Russian Contemporary Art in Exile (80 Grand St.; 201-332-5200) is housed in a brownstone once used by the city (across the street from the Ukrainian National Center, also an interesting building, now condominiums). Run by the Committee for the Absorption of Soviet Emigrees, the museum features paintings by artists from former Eastern Bloc countries living both here and in Europe. Open by appointment.

At New Jersey City University (2039 Kennedy Blvd.; 201-200-2000), art exhibits can be seen at the Courtney Gallery and the visual arts building. These feature contemporary works as well as annual student, faculty, and alumni shows. Open weekdays, 11–4; weekends and other times by appointment (201-200-3246). The university has been involved with running the Black Maria Film and Video Festival for many years; for information call 201-200-2043. Music, dance, and theater programs are also open to the public (201-200-2017), as are an annual lecture series (201-200-2000) and a variety of programs for children.

The former Jersey City Medical Center* (Baldwin Ave. and Montgomery St.) is a large art deco complex built in the 1920s. The city removed some exterior ornamental grillwork, but the interiors, with their marble, terrazzo, and bronze elevators, remain. Murdoch Hall (114 Clifton Pl.), now a county office building, may be one of the most striking in the complex. Note also 79 Clifton Pl.; this house was a stop on the Underground Railroad.

Here are some other buildings you might want to look out for: near the Paulus Hook and Van Vorst districts are St. Peter's Preparatory School, which is over 100 years old; the New Jersey Guarantee Trust Company (Montgomery St.), a splendid late-19th-century extravaganza with the relief of a dog guarding the entrance, now converted to condominiums; Sts. Peter and Paul (near Grand St.); the Congregation of the Sons of Israel (Grove

St.), with its lions; the 1888 building at 133 Grand St., with its decorative red tiles (the T. J. Stewart building at 88–92 Erie St. also dates from 1888 and has tiles produced by the Perth Amboy Terra Cotta Company); the Ionic House* (1835–40; 83 Wayne St.); the Grace Van Vorst Church* (1850–53; 268 2d St.); and the Salem Community Center (northwest corner of Clinton and Crescent aves.), formerly the home of the Jersey City Athletic Club (1886). On J. F. Kennedy Blvd. you will find the First Baptist Church (at Fairmount), a small stone castle; Temple Bethel (at Harrison); and St. Peter's College (at Montgomery), from which Will Durant received a bachelor's and a master's degree. The former Lorillard snuff factory (111 1st St.), opened in 1870, was converted to artists' studios (the city has become something of a mecca for area artists), but is in danger of being destroyed; the Dixon Ticonderoga Company administrative office building (167 Wayne St.), a Romanesque Revival building from the 1890s, is now a condominium; Pohlmann's Hall* (154 Ogden Ave.), the Joseph Dixon Crucible Company complex, and the former Baker Chocolate factory (Barrow St.), have also been converted to housing. The Lembeck and Betz Eagle Brewing Company district* (9th, 10th, and Grove and Henderson sts.) is where "the beer that made Milwaukee jealous" was once brewed. You may also find your eye caught by many of the firehouses; in any case, this list only skims the surface of Jersey City's interesting buildings.

Liberty State Park (Morris Pesin Dr.; take exit 14B from the northern extension of the New Jersey Tnpk; Henderson St. and Johnston and Jersey aves. out of Jersey City; 201-915-3403) consists of over 1,100 acres with 2½ miles of shoreline, land that in the early 1970s was an industrial wasteland. Opened in 1976, the park is a tribute to the perseverance of Morris Pesin. A Jersey City native who had fought to save the trees along the J. F. Kennedy Blvd. and to save the county courthouse from demolition, Pesin was appalled by how long it took to travel to the Statue of Liberty (which, like Ellis Island, is much closer to Jersey City than to New York City), and spearheaded the drive to create Liberty State Park. At the northern end of the park is the Central Railroad of New Jersey Terminal* (1889; 201-915-3440), a national landmark French château with Neo-Romanesque details. Historically important because of its connection to Ellis Island (for some 8 million immigrants this was the first U.S. soil they set foot on), it now contains exhibits on the history of the area. In July and August there are concerts in the terminal on Sunday afternoon and Tuesday evening; it is also used for special events. Group tours of the historic areas of the park can be arranged throughout the year by calling 201-915-3411. Also at this site are a shed for 20 trains (1913–14) and a ferry slip. During the summer (Memorial Day–Labor Day) ferries run from here to Liberty and Ellis islands every half to three-quarters of an hour, 9:15–4:30; the rest of the year the schedule is reduced (call 201-435-9499). The Morris Canal* basin (Jersey City formed one end of the Morris Canal) still exists at the northern end of the park; a 200-slip pleasure-boat marina (201-985-8000) has been constructed here.

An interpretive program, revolving around the park's salt marsh and mud flats, was instituted in 1985; the interpretive center (Freedom Way; 201-915-3409) is toward the southern end of the park just north of the Liberty Park Natural Area. Within the center are displays dealing with the natural history and environment of the area. The 60 acres of the natural area are predominantly salt marsh, one of the few remaining salt marshes along New York Bay. Since the Clean Water Act of 1972, the area has seen the gradual return of the wildlife driven away by the pollution of the river. The intertidal area serves as a natural nursery for fish; this is also a good place to see canvasback ducks. The interpretive center offers educational programs, and group tours may be arranged by calling 201-915-3409. There is a brochure for a self-guided tour of the nature walk. The interpretive center is open 9–4 daily July and August, Monday–Saturday the rest of the year, but it is always good to call ahead, as budget changes can affect staffing.

At the southern end of the park are picnic tables, a swimming pool, tennis courts, a boat launch, a display of the flags of all the states, and the Liberation Monument (designed by sculptor Natan Rappaport). The park is open 6 A.M.–10 P.M. daily; the visitor center (Morris Pesin Dr.) is open 6 A.M.–6 P.M. in summer (Memorial Day–Labor Day) and 8–4 the rest of the year.

At the northwestern corner of the park, on the spot where Henry Hudson landed the *Half Moon* in 1609, is Liberty Science Center (251 Phillip St.; 201-200-1000), a four-story museum filled with interactive exhibits. Three of the floors are thematically organized: the lower floor is the invention floor, the second the health floor, and the third the environment floor. Live demonstrations take place daily, and traveling exhibits change frequently. The museum also includes two theaters, one of them the country's largest domed IMAX theater. There is something here to interest people of almost any age, and the museum can be noisy when it is full (it attracts some 700,000 visitors a year). Views from the terrace are spectacular. Open September–February, Tuesday–Sunday, 9:30–5:30; March–August, daily, 9:30–5:30; closed Thanksgiving and Christmas days. Admission charge. The museum is expected to close in 2005 for a major expansion and to reopen in 2007; during that period there will be some exhibits from the museum in the Central Railroad of New Jersey Terminal.

Lincoln Park is Hudson County's oldest and largest. (It is also one of the most popular: an estimated 25,000 people use it each summer weekend.) The principal entrance, on Kennedy Blvd. at Belmont Ave., is a formal plaza with a statue of Lincoln, designed by James Earle Fraser, who designed the buffalo nickel. The plaza is the highest point in the park and offers good views to the west. It is particularly lovely in spring when the bulbs and flowering shrubs are·in bloom. Note also the Saint Aloysius complex north of the entrance and the fountain at the circle that ends the formal entrance (the fountain, requiring 365 tons of concrete, is said to be the world's largest concrete monument; it was finished in 1911). The plaza is particularly popular with mothers of young children. In the less formal parts of the park are athletic fields, a playground, a lake for sailing model boats, a driving range, and places to walk and drive. There are plans to develop the underused 100-odd acres between US 1 and the Hackensack River. Jersey City also shares Washington Park (North St. and Central Ave.) with Union City. This smaller park contains tennis courts and other athletic facilities, a children's playground, and an outdoor swimming pool.

Jersey City has continued to be important as a transportation center: the Holland Tunnel,* a national civil and mechanical engineering landmark, starts (or ends) here. Opened in 1927, the tunnel was taken over by the Port Authority of New York and New Jersey in 1931. It is named for its first chief engineer, Clifford M. Holland, who developed its giant ventilating system (the air is completely changed every 90 seconds) and more or less lived in the tunnel, dying in 1924 at the age of 41. When the ceiling was replaced in the mid-'80s, over 4 million blue and white tiles (weighing more than 1,200 tons) were needed. Over 16.5 million cars go eastbound through the tunnel each year. Jersey City is also a stop on the PATH trains, which are used by more than 70 million passengers each year, and weekday ferry service to New York City has been restored at Colgate pier near Exchange Plaza.

Harborside Financial Center (north of Exchange Pl.) is an office complex with a mix of companies. Converted railroad warehouses dating from the late 1920s, these buildings were designed with ground floors strong enough to hold railroad cars and upper floors heavy enough to hold trucks; when the center first opened, its sales pitch was directed toward companies specializing in finance and trade, as the buildings were especially suited to mainframe computers.

North of Harborside on what were once Erie Railroad yards is Newport, a large complex containing housing, office buildings, and the county's first mall. Another large building was put up by the Lefrak Organization (Samuel Lefrak built more apartment units in New York City than any other private developer).

To the west of Newport is the Harismus Cove Historic District* (Jersey Ave.; Bay, Cole, Erie, and 1–5th sts.; and Manila Ave.). This is one of the oldest communities in Jersey City, but most of the 400-plus buildings in the district are late-19th-century three-story brick Italianate row houses.

On the Hudson River side of the city a condominium complex, Society Hill (Society Hill Dr.), occupies the site of Roosevelt Stadium. Here, a year before he joined the Brooklyn Dodgers, Jackie Robinson, then with the Montreal Royals, became the first African American to play on a previously all-white team.

Within Liberty Industrial Park (just north of Morris Pesin Dr. in Liberty State Park) is the site of the Black Tom explosion, possibly the only successful act of sabotage in the United States in World War I. The Germans blew up an ammunition train, resulting in an explosion that was felt as far away as Connecticut and Maryland.

Kearny   Hudson   40,513

NJ 17

An industrial town with a large Scots population—Robert Burns's birthday is still celebrated here each year—Kearny (pronounced *car-knee*) was settled in the 17th century. It is named for Philip Kearny, a one-armed American general who fought in five wars, including the Civil War, and was the first American to receive the Legion d'honneur. A statue of Kearny, a replica of the Borglum statue in Military Park in Newark, stands on Midland Ave. just west of Kearny Ave. in front of the main post office.

Kearny Marsh, owned by the Meadowlands Commission (*see* Lyndhurst), is the only freshwater marsh in the Meadowlands. Its 380 acres contain one of the largest breeding populations of American bitterns and pied-billed grebes, both endangered species, in New Jersey. It is also one of the few nesting sites in New Jersey for the ruddy duck, and is home to several other birds on the state's threatened or endangered list. One European species of ladybug was reputed to be so abundant here that it was captured for use by gardeners in less-fortunate areas.

The Kearny Museum (318 Kearny Ave.; 201-997-6911), housed on the second floor of the town's Carnegie library, features displays relating to local history, including Kearny memorabilia, period clothes, and household items. Open mid-September–mid-June, Wednesday 2–4 and 6–8, Thursday, 2–4, Saturday, 10–12; other times by appointment.

Keyport   Monmouth   7,568

NJ 35, 36

Situated on an inlet of Raritan Bay, Keyport was once known for its oyster and shipbuilding industries. Oysters were being planted in nearby creeks as far back as the early 18th century, and the *River Queen*, built at the Terry shipyards where Terry Park now stands, was active in the Civil War. Some shipbuilding continues, and there are signs that the oyster industry may have turned the corner, but recreational fishing and boating are more important now. Along American Legion Dr. there are lovely views of the waterfront (which in 1889 Gustav Kobbé described as "a very animated scene"), a fishing dock, a bulkhead used for fishing and crabbing, and a launching ramp. Fred and Adele Astaire made their debut in Keyport, P. T. Barnum had a house here (still to be seen on Main St.), and the old opera house, which once attracted leading singers, still stands.

At the corner of American Legion Dr. and Broad St. is the Steamboat Dock Museum (732-264-1734, 732-264-7822, 732-264-6119), devoted to Keyport history. Located in a building once used by the Keansburg Steamboat Company as a machine shop and winter quarters for the crew, the museum features a variety of exhibits. Among them are a working printing exhibit; artifacts (including a partially refurbished wing section) from the Aeromarine Corporation, one of the country's first aircraft factories, once located in Keyport; 19th-century clothing; exhibits on the oyster and shipbuilding industries; and many other items related to Keyport's early history. In addition there is a special exhibit each season. Open mid-May–September, Sunday, 1–4, Monday, 10–12; groups and other times by appointment. While in Keyport note also St. Mary's Church (E. Front St.), built in the late 1870s.

In a sea captain's house from the 1860s is Masters Octave (80 W. Front St.; 732-264-2445), an art gallery with informal exhibits. Open Saturday and holidays, 1–4, or by appointment.

Kingston Middlesex 1,292

NJ 27, C 522

Settled early in the 18th century, Kingston was a stop on the stage route between New York and Philadelphia. George Washington paused in Kingston after the Battle of Princeton, making the decision not to go on to New Brunswick and continue the battle but to retire to winter quarters instead. The Kingston Village Historic District* includes portions of NJ 27, Laurel and Euclid aves., Church, Union, and Academy sts., Shaw Dr., Sycamore Pl., and Kingston–Rocky Hill, Heathcote Brook, and Raymond rds.; the buildings date from the 1730s to the 1930s. Many of the houses lining the attractive main street (Lincoln Highway, NJ 27) date from the 19th century. Cook Natural Area (Heathcote Rd.; 732-873-3050), 26 acres of forest and ponds, is a good place to hike.

The Kingston Mill historic district* includes the area where 27 crosses the Millstone River and the Delaware and Raritan Canal.* The present mill (which is actually in Princeton Township) was built in 1888 (and continued in operation until 1942), but there has been a mill on this site since 1755. The stone bridge dates to 1798. The dam, which backs up the river to form Lake Carnegie, was created in 1911, financed by a gift from Andrew Carnegie. It is used for Princeton University and national crew races and by local sailors and sailboarders.

At this point there is access to the Delaware and Raritan Canal State Park (732-873-3050), a 67-mile linear park that follows the Delaware and Raritan main canal and feeder line through central New Jersey and is part of the East Coast Greenway. Opened in 1834, the canal went from Bordentown to Trenton to New Brunswick, the feeder from Raven Rock to Trenton, thereby facilitating traffic between Philadelphia and New York. One of the world's busiest waterways, the canal in its best year (1871) carried more tonnage, much of it coal, than the much longer Erie Canal ever did. Profits began to fall toward the end of the century, and the canal was officially closed in the 1930s. Some parts have been filled in (one mile under US 1 in Trenton and another mile under NJ 18 in New Brunswick), but unlike the Morris Canal, most of the Delaware and Raritan Canal still exists. It provides water for several communities in central New Jersey, and its towpath is much beloved of boaters, hikers, joggers, bicycle and horseback riders, bird-watchers, cross-country skiers, and those who like to fish. In fact, you can walk, ride a horse or bicycle, and canoe from the US 1 crossing in Lawrence Township all the way to New Brunswick; you can canoe from the west end of Trenton to Bull's Island and walk or ride a bicycle from the Battle Monument in Trenton to north of Frenchtown (part of this walk is on an old railroad right-of-way). The trail system has been designated a National Recreation Trail. You are welcome to picnic informally along the path, but more formal picnic areas with tables or fireplaces can be found at Bull's Island (across from Raven Rock, about 4 mi. upriver of Stockton), Lambertville, Titusville (at Washington Crossing State Park), Trenton (in Cadwalader Park), Princeton (Basin Park off Alexander St.), Griggstown, and Blackwells Mills (about 3 mi. north of Griggstown). Many of the historic buildings along the canal, which include lock-tenders' houses and a mule-drivers' barracks, have been or are being restored (*see* Griggstown, Lawrenceville, Stockton). For most of its length the park is narrow (its total area is only five square miles), but at Bull's Island it widens out, and you can camp on the island. Future plans for the park include instituting a canal boat ride.

At the Hasty Acres Farm (121 Laurel Ave.; 609-921-8389), the Heads Up Special Riders program gives lessons to handicapped riders once a week, weather permitting. You are welcome to observe a lesson if you call first.

Kinnelon Morris 9,365

c 618

In Kinnelon, a rapidly growing borough in the northern section of Morris County (just south of NJ 23), is Silas Condict Park (Kinnelon Rd.; 973-326-7600), a 265-acre county park with scenic overlooks, hiking trails, picnic sites, a playing field, and a seven-acre lake. Silas Condict was a Morris County farmer and surveyor who was a member of the Continental Congress. Elected to the New Jersey Assembly eight times, he served as its speaker in 1792–94 and 1797. The park has facilities for fishing and boating, and in the winter you can skate and cross-country ski. The casino at the lake, a 1920s stone building restored in the 1990s and available for private functions, once housed a large still and hidden storerooms where, it is said, up to 16,000 gallons of illegal liquor could be kept.

Also in Kinnelon is Pyramid Mountain Natural Historic Area (Boonton Ave.; 973-334-3130). This extraordinary geological area, once threatened with development, includes land on Pyramid, Stony Brook, Turkey, and Rock Pear mountains. These 2,000 acres contain a rich diversity of flora and fauna—some 400 plant species, more than 100 bird species, 20 mammals. The extraordinary glacial rock formations, which include Tripod Rock, a large boulder somehow perched on three smaller boulders, and Bear Rock, one of the largest glacial erratics in the state, were once sacred to the Lenape. There are breathtaking views, and the many miles of hiking trails are beautiful, though some can be rugged. You can pick up trail maps at the visitor center, which has an exhibit of local and historical artifacts and photographs. The center offers programs for schools and scout groups, and sponsors a wide variety of public events for children and adults, from walks and talks to workshops on building bat boxes. Open Wednesday–Sunday, 10–4:30.

Lakehurst Ocean 2,522

NJ 37, 70, C 547

Lakehurst has the misfortune of being best known to the rest of the world as the site of the naval station where the dirigible *Hindenburg* burned in 1937. The station specialized in lighter-than-air ships, which had many advantages over today's airplanes, but the *Hindenburg* disaster put an end to serious consideration of dirigibles. At the Naval Air Engineering Station (732-818-7520), the Navy Lakehurst Historical Society maintains a visitor center with displays connected with the station's past and present. The center is in Hangar No. 1 (c. 1921),* now a national historic landmark. The society offers tours the 2d and 4th Saturday of the month. These include the hangar and the field where the *Hindenburg* crashed; a small monument is on the site. To arrange a tour, you must call two weeks in advance.

Lakehurst was settled in the 18th century; its iron forge supplied cannonballs to the Continental army. In the mid-19th century it became an industrial center, with a rope factory, railroad shops, and a roundhouse; in the late 19th and early 20th centuries it was known as a winter resort. The rope factory burned, and most of the railroad buildings and the Pine Tree Inn, a large resort building, were demolished in the 1940s, but some of the older buildings remain.

At the former St. John's Roman Catholic Church,* the oldest Catholic church in the county (c. 1874), which was built by Irish railway workers, is the historical society's museum (300 Center St.; 732-657-8864). Displays include memorabilia relating to the railroad, the fire department, and airships (including charred remains of the *Hindenburg*). Open Wednesday and Sunday, 12–3; groups and other times by appointment.

Lakewood Ocean 60,352

One of the first areas in the United States to be developed as a winter health resort, Lakewood reaped from its fresh pine air and proximity to New York and Philadelphia a long reign as a leading resort. Described in the 1880s as "a little winter paradise created by good taste and sound judgment backed by the necessary capital," its golden period lasted from the 1880s to the 1930s, and for most of those years the socially prominent flocked to the hotels and estates of this former mill and iron town situated on the northern edges of the Pinelands.

The abundant forests had drawn sawmills in the late 18th century. The discovery that the soil was rich in iron led to the establishment in the early 19th century of ironworks, first by Jesse Richards, whose family was involved in the Batsto ironworks (*see* Hammonton), and then in 1832 by Joseph W. Brick. First called Three Partners Mill, then Washington's Furnace, then Bergen Iron Works, on Brick's death the town was renamed Bricksburg in his honor.

The discovery in the 1860s of hard coal close to iron deposits in Pennsylvania put an end to the Pinelands' iron industry, but by then Lakewood had begun to build hotels. When in 1879 two New York stockbrokers bought 19,000 acres of land, Lakewood's career as a resort took off. In 1880 the town's name was changed from Bricksburg to Lakewood, but Brick's family is still memorialized in the names of the two lakes: Carasaljo (for Brick's three daughters, Caroline, Sally, and Josephine) and Manetta (for his wife).

Many of the hotels were large and lavish, akin to Old World alpine hotels. The Lakewood, for example, covered 14 acres and was used by the federal government as a hospital during World War I. (It was also for a time the winter headquarters of Tammany Hall.) The Laurel House, built in 1880, counted among its guests the Goulds, the Rockefellers, the Vanderbilts, the Astors, the Claflins; Rudyard Kipling and Oliver Wendell Holmes were frequent visitors. Emma Calvé and Mark Twain spent time in Lakewood; Grover Cleveland built a cottage in town; the Goulds, Rockefellers, and Claflins, among others, built large estates. By the end of World War I, Lakewood had over 100 hotels.

The Depression, the automobile, and inexpensive airline travel combined to end Lakewood's golden years. World War II brought some prosperity, for the town served as a center for nearby military camps. There was a considerable migration of people from the city, and an influx of refugees from Eastern and Central Europe (including Kalmuks, who built a Buddhist temple in nearby Howell Township). The refugees built up an egg-and-poultry business; for many years Lakewood was a leading egg center.

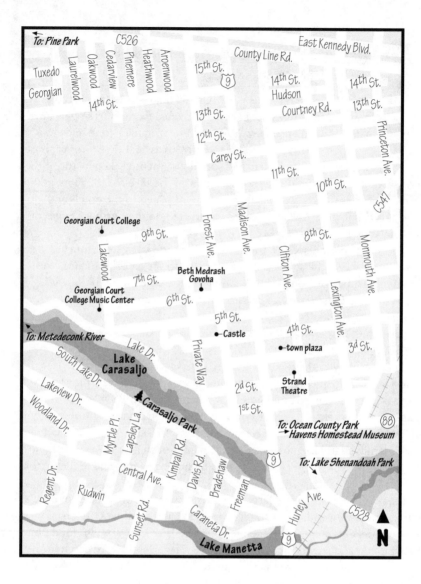

The egg-and-poultry business has also declined, and many of Lakewood's citizens are now commuters. The town fathers have been successful in attracting light industry, and the town is home to several educational establishments, among them Georgian Court College (*see* below) and the internationally known Beth Medrash Govoha of America (Forest Ave.), a yeshiva founded in 1943 by Rabbi Aaron Kotler, who, with a few students, had arrived in Lakewood the year before as a refugee from Poland. After World War II there was a boom in building: housing developments, particularly retirement communities, sprang up, perhaps attracted by some of the same features that brought vacationers, and now a significant portion of Lakewood's citizens are retired. The Orthodox Jewish population has also increased dramatically—by some estimates it now makes up 40 percent of the population.

The grand old hotels are gone—some burned, others were replaced by motels—but it is still possible to get some idea of what Lakewood must once have been like. One way is to drive around Lake Carasaljo. The area occupied by the Laurel in the Pines (S. Lake Dr.), for example, is now occupied by condominiums, but the scale of the hotel is apparent from that of the condos. Note also the Georgian Court University Music Center (Sixth St. and Lakewood Ave.) and the Castle (Forest Ave.), once a house, which has been converted to apartments. The Strand Theatre* (400 Clifton Ave.; 732-367-7789), a national historic landmark, is an active performance space. The building dates from the early 1920s and the heyday of art deco theaters. Pearl Bailey was at its reopening in 1983. Its renovation and the new town plaza at Clifton Ave. and Third St. are part of a program to improve the downtown area and restore it to a late-19th-century appearance.

The best way to recapture Lakewood's past, though, is to visit Georgian Court University* (Lakewood Ave. and Ninth St.). The school is run by the Sisters of Mercy, who, having outgrown their quarters in Plainfield, in 1924 purchased the estate of George Jay Gould (a son of Jay Gould). The sisters have added buildings, and in 1950 they sold some 30 acres along the road, but what they have managed to preserve is remarkable. Reservations are necessary to tour the college; for an appointment, call 732-987-2760. Allow at least an hour.

Four of the estate's original buildings remain: the mansion, the stable, the casino, and the small building now used as the chaplain's house. (In addition, Hamilton House, the administration building, which is off the campus proper, occupies a house Gould built for his son.) Started in 1898, the entire estate—grounds and buildings alike—was designed by Bruce Price, the architect of Tuxedo Park and Château Frontenac. The mansion, built with an extraordinary attention to detail, is an imposing reflection of the styles and characters of several types of European country houses. The casino was the Goulds' recreation building and boasted an indoor polo field, a swimming pool, a bowling alley, and squash and tennis courts. The polo field has been converted to a gymnasium that is also used as an auditorium, but the students still bowl in the 1899 bowling alley and swim in the 1899 pool, with its marble diving platform. The stable area has been converted into a dining room and offices.

Included on the grounds are an Italian garden, a sunken garden, and a lovely Japanese tea garden. The statuary and the fountains are noteworthy; unfortunately the fountains can only be turned on for special occasions.

Other old estates have been preserved in parks. Ocean County Park* (Ocean Ave., NJ 88, at the east end of town; 732-506-9090) was formerly the John D. Rockefeller estate. Most of the buildings are gone, but included in its 323 acres are magnificent stands of trees planted by the Rockefellers. The park has facilities for hiking, swimming, tennis, fishing, cross-country skiing, skating, games, and picnics.

Pine Park, a municipal park at the west end of town (500 Country Club Dr.; take County Line Rd., C 526; 732-367-6737), is on the site of the Claflin estate, once the Newman School. The park has playing fields and picnic sites, but only one of the buildings remains. Lake Shenandoah Park (Ocean Ave., NJ 88; 732-506-9090) consists of 100 acres with fishing, bike trails, and a picnic area. Fishing is also possible in the Metedeconk River (in Carasaljo Park) and in both Lake Manetta and Lake Carasaljo.

East of Lakewood (take NJ 88 to NJ 70 and turn left on Herbertsville Rd.; continue until you cross Sawmill Creek) is the Havens Homestead Museum (521 Herbertsville Rd.; 732-785-2500). The oldest part of this building dates to the 1820s. It has been restored by the Brick Township Historical Society and is furnished to reflect life in the area in the mid-19th century. Also on the property is the late-19th-century Lizzie Herbert house, which serves as a gift shop. The society offers a variety of special events and programs, including quilting, weaving, and knitting workshops. Open mid-April–October, Saturday 10–12, Sunday 12–2; closed major holidays. In 2002 Brick was named the second-safest town in the country.

Lambertville Hunterdon 3,868

NJ 29, 179, C 518

One of Hunterdon County's oldest communities and its only city (Flemington, the county seat, which in 2000 was a little larger, is a borough), Lambertville has seen its fortunes wax and wane. Once a thriving industrial town, it has become a magnet for artists, restaurateurs, and those interested in historic renovation.

Situated on the banks of the Delaware River directly across from New Hope, Pennsylvania, Lambertville prospered because of its location. It began as a ferry town; the arrival of the Delaware and Raritan Canal* in the 1830s and the Belvidere and Delaware Railroad in the 1850s helped turn it into a flourishing regional industrial and commercial center. Settled in 1705 by John Holcombe, who managed to make sure that the main road from Philadelphia to New York City passed through his land, the town took the name Coryell's Ferry after Emmanuel Coryell established his ferry service. In 1814 the name was changed to Lambertville when U.S. Senator John Lambert set his nephew up as postmaster. That same year saw the ferry replaced by a wooden bridge; its masonry piers still support today's bridge, built in 1904. (Under that bridge nests a large colony of cliff swallows, an endangered species. When the nests had to be removed so that the bridge could be repaired, artificial nests were supplied for the birds.)

George Washington twice (July 1777 and June 1778) made his

headquarters in Coryell's Ferry, staying both times at the mid-18th-century Richard Holcombe house (NJ 29, north of the center). At least two other presidents have visited Lambertville: Andrew Johnson and Ulysses S. Grant were both guests at the Lambertville House* (32 Bridge St.), built by Senator Lambert in 1812, and still serving as an inn.

With ready waterpower at Wells Falls, gristmills, paper mills, cotton mills, and lumber mills were established. Other industrial enterprises included a railroad machine shop, rubber plants, ironworks, and a sausage factory. The population peaked (at 5,100) in the early years of the 20th century, and there has been little new construction since then (in 1985 a new hotel was built along the river). Now the older buildings are being renovated and used for new purposes: the sausage factory houses restaurants and art

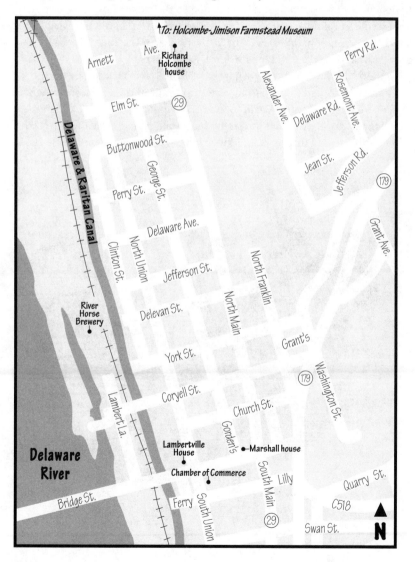

galleries; the Pennsylvania Railroad station has been restored and converted to a restaurant; old warehouse buildings serve as artists' studios; a private home, which had been converted to a church, has been converted to an art gallery; former mansions have become bed-and-breakfasts. In the factory where Trenton oyster crackers were once made, the River Horse Brewery (80 Lambert La.; 609-397-7776) brews, kegs, and bottles beer. Open for tours Monday–Friday, 12–5.

Another part of Lambertville's past that is reviving is the shad industry. In 1896 some 19 million pounds of shad were caught in the Delaware River and Bay; by the 1960s none were to be found in the river. Although only one commercial shad fisherman remains in business in the nontidal parts of the Delaware (established in the 1880s, this family business is now run by the fifth generation), enough fish have returned to the cleaned-up Delaware that Lambertville in 1981 decided to celebrate the rebirth of an old industry and held its first annual shad festival. The event now attracts some 35,000–40,000 visitors. Look for the festival in late April, early May.

Lambertville was the home of James Wilson Marshall, who set off the 1849 Gold Rush, called by some the largest migration in U.S. history, when he discovered gold at Sutter's Mill in California in 1848. His house* (62 Bridge St.; 609-397-0770), built in 1816 by his father, is operated as a museum by the Lambertville Historical Society. Exhibits change every two to three years. Open weekends May–October, 1–4; guided tours 1st Sunday of the month May–October at 2. The society also sponsors a juried art show each winter.

Lambertville's historic district* includes the area around NJ 29 (Main St.) and NJ 179. One remnant of Lambertville's importance as a transportation center now serves recreational purposes: there is access to the Delaware and Raritan Canal at Lambertville. Brochures for a self-guided walking tour are available at the Chamber of Commerce (239 N. Union St.; 609-397-0055) and at various businesses around town.

North of town on NJ 29 is the Holcombe-Jimison Farmstead Museum (609-397-2752, 609-397-1810), dedicated to depicting Hunterdon County rural life in the past. The oldest recorded house in the county (1711) is on the property. In the bank barn, which probably also dates from the early 18th century, is a large collection of agricultural tools and equipment (both hand- and machine-made), items used for spinning and weaving, and items used in the kitchen. On display on the top floor of the barn is a large collection of objects, including plows, stoves, and corn shellers, made at Hiram Deats's foundry. Deats was a wealthy late-18th-century Hunterdon County foundryman who had forges at Stockton and Pittstown. Also on the property are a woodworking shop (in the carriage house), a printing shop, a country doctor's office, and a general store and post office. A blacksmith

LAMBERTVILLE

sometimes works on the property, and plans call for opening the 1711 house in the near future. Open May–October, Wednesday, 9–12, Sunday, 1–4; groups and other times by appointment. Admission charged.

Laurel Springs Camden 1,970

US 30

This small, densely populated borough is perhaps best known because it is where Walt Whitman spent his summers between 1876 and 1881. (He is said to have called Laurel Lake "the prettiest lake in either America or Europe.") Indeed, according to one legend, the borough was formed (in 1893) because some of its citizens decided that their connection to Whitman was a marketable commodity. The Whitman-Stafford Farmhouse (315 Maple Ave.; 609-784-1105), an 18th- and 19th-century farmhouse where Whitman stayed, has been restored and is furnished with pieces from Whitman's time. Exhibits include New Jersey glass, local photographs, tools, and old toys, and the South Jersey Organic Gardeners' Club maintains an attractive herb garden. In July and August concerts are given regularly on Wednesday evening, and a special event is scheduled each March. Open by appointment.

Lawrenceville Mercer 4,081

US 206, C 546

First settled in 1660 in an area that had been a Native American camp and known until 1816 as Maidenhead, Lawrenceville is perhaps familiar today primarily because it is the home of the Lawrenceville School, one of the country's best-known independent preparatory schools. Much of the school and the town directly across from it on Main St., once the Kings Highway and now part of US 206, form Lawrence Township's historic district,* a national historic district. (The school itself has been designated a national historic landmark.) For two miles along both sides of 206, from the southwest corner of Franklin Corner Rd. (C 546) to just north of Carter Rd., are well-preserved structures from the 18th and 19th centuries. One of the oldest houses, Old Brick (1706), is on the east side of the road in the school's golf course. Wayside (the school side of Main St. opposite Phillips Ave.) is perhaps some 30–40 years older and was once a tavern. The Presbyterian Church (Main St. north of Gordon St.) dates to 1764, although it was enlarged and altered in the mid-19th century. The 1815 Richard Montgomery Green house (2549 Main St.) was built from stones from the nearby Cherry Grove quarry. Lord Cornwallis was quartered in Lawrenceville in 1776 (and apparently recorded in his journal later that "one night in Maidenhead was more than enough"). On 2 January 1777, Colonel Edward Hand stalled Cornwallis at Lawrence Rd. (US 206) near Darrah La., thereby preventing Cornwallis from reaching Trenton before dark and thus giving George Washington his chance to escape to Princeton. This event is reenacted every January.

In 1810 the Reverend Isaac Van Arsdale Brown of the Presbyterian Church founded the Academy of Maidenhead; Brown was also a leader in the move to change the town's name, "for reasons of delicacy," from Maidenhead to Lawrenceville in honor of the 1812 naval hero, Captain James Lawrence, of "Don't give up the ship" fame (*see* Burlington). Brown was a victim of the silkworm craze (*also see* Burlington), and although his house on Main St. was torn down in the 1940s to make room for the post office, some of the mulberry trees he planted remain. Much of the present appearance of the school dates from the 1880s, when a legacy from one of the original graduates made it possible to convert the academy into a boarding school (the trustees looked to the best schools of England for inspiration). Frederick Law Olmsted drew up the overall plan (which included planting more than 300 species of trees and shrubs), and the circle, with its nine Richardsonian buildings, dates from that expansion. Thornton Wilder taught at the school in the 1920s and wrote *The Bridge of San Luis Rey* during his years there. In 1987, the school became coeducational.

The township, which celebrated its tricentennial in 1997, is expanding rapidly, attracting corporate headquarters and research facilities. Long established in the area is the world-famous Educational Testing Service (entrances on Rosedale and Carter rds.; 609-921-9000), best known for its standardized college-admission tests and said to be the largest private testing organization in the world. (Although ETS has a Princeton address, its campus actually lies within Lawrence Township.) There are art exhibits in Lounge B of Conant Hall (open weekdays, 8:30–4:30) and in the Brodsky Gallery at the Henry T. Chauncy Conference Center (open daily, 9–9, but it is advisable to call ahead). Shows change every six to eight weeks.

Southwest of ETS (take Rosedale Rd. to Carter Rd., turn left, and take the first right) is Terhune Orchards (330 Cold Soil Rd.; 609-924-2310), the first farm in Lawrence Township to enter the state and county farmland preservation programs. The friendly farm animals make this a favorite spot for families with children, and there is a mile-long farm trail that wanders through a meadow and along a pond. Terhune's sponsors three special events: a kite day in May, an apple festival in September, and a Halloween party in October. Open daily, 9–6, though weekend hours may be shortened in the depths of the winter.

Among the more striking headquarters buildings are those of Lenox (US 206 south of the village) and Bristol-Myers Squibb (US 206, c. 2 mi. north of the village; 609-252-6275). At Bristol-Myers Squibb there is an art gallery with exhibits that change periodically. There is also a permanent exhibit on the history of the company. Open weekdays, 9–5; weekends and holidays, 1–5. Like many other corporations with ponds on their lawns, Bristol-Myers Squibb has been plagued by a superfluity of resident Canada geese (New Jersey is home to some 90,000 resident Canada geese, and the number continues to climb). The company's attempt to scare off the geese by establishing live swans on the property apparently failed; they now use a dog service to keep the geese in check.

Another art gallery open to the public is in the Bart Luedeke Center at Rider University (US 206; 609-895-5588; 609-895-5168); exhibits here feature work in a wide variety of media by professional artists from the United States and abroad, and usually change four or five times a year. The gallery is also used for lectures and occasionally for concerts. Usually open Tuesday–Thursday, 11–7 and Sunday, 12–4, but it is advisable to call first. Rider University developed out of Trenton Business College, founded in Trenton in 1865. Its present campus dates from 1965.

If you continue about a half-mile south of Rider on US 206, and turn left on Eggerts Crossing Road, you will come to the New Jersey National Guard Militia Museum annex (351 Eggerts Crossing Rd.; 609-530-6802). Like the parent museum (*see* Manasquan), the annex features artifacts and photographs from the beginning of the national guard to the present, and includes uniforms, weaponry, vehicles, and models. Open by appointment although there are plans to establish regular hours.

On Lawrence Station Rd. (take 546 east from Lawrenceville past US 1 and I 295) is the 50-acre John Dempster fire service training center for Mercer County's 24 volunteer fire departments (609-799-3245). Most responsible for the center's surreal look is the concrete tower built to resemble a high-rise apartment building. At the center firefighters can also gain experience with chemical fires, simulated airplane crashes, and house fires. The center recently installed a propane system to make its simulations more environmentally friendly, and the water used in the exercises is recycled. Visits by appointment (ask to speak to the director).

The Port Mercer Canal house* (Quaker Bridge Rd. at Quaker and Province Line rds.; 609-895-1728), operated as a house museum by the Lawrence Historical Society, dates to the 1830s (the kitchen was added later in the 19th century). The building was the first bridgetender's house along the Delaware and Raritan Canal* to be completely restored. Also on the property is a pre–Civil War outhouse, moved from Dutch Neck in the 1990s. Open the 1st Saturday of the month in spring and fall and for special occasions. Tours by appointment.

The Brearley House* (Meadow Rd. off the Princeton Pike; 609-895-1728), was built in 1761 from bricks brought from England; in the cellar an 18-by-12-inch oak timber supports the first floor. Once the home of John Brearley, it was lived in by members of his family until the late 19th century. Now owned by the township, the house was restored in 2000. Eighth graders in the Lawrence Township schools participate in a hands-on archaeological demonstration workshop for three days each spring and fall. A display case in the house contains artifacts uncovered by their work. The Lawrence Historical Society arranges a variety of special events at the house, including an annual wassail party, an annual New Year's Eve bonfire, and an annual history lecture, and offers tours the first Saturday of the month, 10–12. Group tours by appointment.

Lincroft Monmouth 6,255

GARDEN STATE PKWY EXIT 109, C 520

The village of Lincroft dates to the late 17th century. From 1901 to 1932 it was the site of Harry Payne Whitney's racing stable, where the first filly to win the Kentucky Derby was foaled and trained. The Brookdale Breeding and Stock Farm, where Whitney kept his horses, dated to the late 1880s; in the 1890s it became the property of William Payne Thompson, who built a mansion on the farm and founded the Monmouth Park Jockey Club. After 1932 the facilities (which included an indoor track) were leased by independent trainers. When Geraldine Livingston Thompson, Thompson's daughter-in-law, died, the 700-acre estate was put to a variety of uses. On this land you will now find Thompson Park, Brookdale Community College, the Lincroft Elementary School, and the Monmouth Museum and Cultural Center.

The Thompson mansion (1893), now in Thompson Park (C 520, Newman Springs Rd.; 732-842-4000), houses a visitor center. The mansion has undergone a thorough renovation, and the park system hopes to reopen in 2005. The new exhibit will feature the history of the Thompsons and of horse racing on the property. There is summer theater in a former barn, fishing on the lake (electric motors only), a creative arts center for programs offered by the park, craft studios, tennis courts, picnic facilities, hiking trails, and a popular off-leash dog area.

The Monmouth Museum (Newman Springs Rd.; 732-747-2266) is located on the Brookdale Community College campus (use parking lot 1). The small museum contains an attractive gallery, with shows that change four or five times a year and may feature the arts, culture, science, or local history; the Wonder Wing, for children up to age 6, has a permanent exhibit containing large objects, like a pirate ship and a tree house; the Becker Children's Wing, for older children, features large hands-on exhibits that change roughly every two years. Past Becker Wing exhibits have included the Oregon trail and the change in culture from the Lenape to the urban age. Open Tuesday–Saturday, 10–4:30; Sunday, 1–5. On school days the children's wing is open to the public 2–4:30, the Wonder Wing from 12 or 1 to 4:30, but it is best to call first. Tours by appointment. Admission charge for nonmembers.

The college's performing arts center is in the same part of the campus (use parking lot 2); dance, music, theater, and children's series are presented there. Box office (732-224-2411) open weekdays, 10–4. Shows at the college's Center for the Visual Arts Gallery (732-224-2520; parking lots 1 and 2) change roughly every six weeks during the academic year and usually include a faculty and a student show.

Phalanx Rd., which cuts through the campus, takes its name from the North American Phalanx, a mid-19th-century Fourier-inspired experiment in communal living. The community, built on over 600 acres, was founded in 1843 and lasted until 1855. Its last remaining building burned in the 1970s. Albert Brisbane, the father of Hearst writer and editor Arthur Brisbane and one of the prime movers in the colony, interested Horace Greeley (the journalist and political leader, perhaps best remembered for having told a young clergyman, "Go west, young man, go west") in the project, and Greeley wrote a regular column about it in the *New York Tribune*. Alexander Woolcott, the man of letters and model for Sheridan Whiteside in *The Man Who Came to Dinner*, was born in the Phalanx.

Little Silver Monmouth 6,170

C 520

Settled in the late 1660s, Little Silver was apparently named for Silverton, the Rhode Island estate of a Mr. Parker, the father of two of the town's founders (Silverton itself may have been named after the town of Little Silver in England). Descendants of these Parkers lived at the 17th- and 18th-century Parker Homestead (235 Rumson Rd.; 732-842-2400), listed in the state register of historic places, until 1995. The last Parker deeded the house and several acres to the borough. Also on the property are three barns, a greenhouse, and a pond. The borough would like to use the property as a museum and educational facility and is working on a plan to open it to the public as a small working farm, to be known as the Parker Homestead 1665. For now you can try out the nature walk.

In the late 1800s a steamboat dock was built, adding vacationers to the farmers, fishermen, and nurserymen who until then made up most of Little Silver's population. The Post Office Museum (480 Prospect Ave.; 732-842-2400) is located in Little Silver's first post office building (1875), and the original post office has been re-created in the front of the museum. There are other exhibits of historical interest, and the museum is used for lectures and other community activities. Open by appointment and in conjunction with town events, like parades or Sunday evening concerts in the summer. Other buildings of interest in town include the Embury United Methodist Church (1869; 25 Church St.), St. John's Episcopal Church* (1876; Point Rd.), and the railroad station* (1890; Sycamore and Branch aves.).

Livingston   Essex 27,391

Livingston is named for William Livingston, New Jersey's first governor after the Revolution. Settled early in the 18th century, the village for a time supported a considerable shoe industry, supplying many of what shoes the Revolutionary Army did wear (these shoes, incidentally, fit either foot). One of Livingston's remaining 18th-century houses, the Force Homestead* (366 S. Livingston Ave.; 973-535-4378), is maintained as a museum by the Livingston Historical Society. The house dates from 1745, with later-18th-century additions, and contains, among other attractions, a buttery, a museum room, and an authentically furnished lower kitchen. Among the Victorian pieces on display is a clothes rack that belonged to General George McClellan, Civil War general, governor of New Jersey (1878–81), and inventor of the notorious McClellan army saddle. Also on the property is a barn museum containing old tools and farm implements and the Condit family cookhouse, which was moved from the Ira Condit farm where the Livingston Mall now stands and is probably one of the oldest buildings in Livingston. Open September–December and April–June, 2d Sunday, 2–4. Tours by appointment (call Helen Shumsky at 973-992-3017).

Livingston is also home to Newark Academy (91 S. Orange Ave.), the state's second-oldest independent day school (founded in 1774), which moved to Livingston in the 1960s. New Jersey architects Bernard and Howard Grad and former U.S. treasury secretary William Simon are among its graduates.

Livingston is the hometown of former governor Thomas Kean, a descendant of Governor Livingston. On the family estate you will now find a housing development.

On the site of a former regional missile command center in the heart of the Watchung Mountains is Riker Hill Art Park (take Eisenhower to Beaufort and watch for signs; 973-268-3500, ext. 254), named for a family that lived in the area before the Revolution. (This was also once the site of the smallest dinosaur tracks ever found.) The county rents space in the former barracks to working artists, some of whom also give lessons. Their work is shown to the public in annual spring and fall open houses.

The state's oldest hospital, Saint Barnabas Medical Center (94 Old Short Hills Rd.), is also one of its largest (645 beds and 3,200 employees in 2004). Saint Barnabas was founded in Newark in 1865; its burn center, the only one in New Jersey that is state certified, is one of the largest of its kind in North America. The hospital is part of the Saint Barnabas Health Care System, which includes several hospitals, nursing homes, assisted-living systems, and geriatric centers, and is the second largest private employer in the state.

Long Branch Monmouth 31,340

NJ 36, 71, C 537

Although Long Branch, one of the largest cities on the shore, is enjoying a rebirth, it is hard to realize, looking at it today, that from roughly the 1860s to World War I it was one of the most glamorous resorts in the country. It was also one of the earliest—a boarding house for summer visitors opened in 1788. At first the resort's clientele came from Philadelphia, then, particularly after the Civil War, from New York as well. Mrs. Lincoln visited in 1861, but it was President Grant's first visit in 1869 that gave Long Branch its cachet. Grant was to visit every summer he was president, and many summers after that. A racetrack opened in 1870, gambling casinos soon thereafter, and during the 1880s and '90s Long Branch's reputation as a fashionable place was at its height. (It was described at the time as "not a place whither a circumspect parent would take his family for a quiet summer by the sea," and "an object-lesson in certain extreme phases of American life.") A partial list of the people who frequented Long Branch includes such members of society as the Astors, Fiskes, Goulds, Biddles, and Drexels; high-liver Diamond Jim Brady; General Winfield Scott; actors Edwin Booth, Lillie Langtry, and Lillian Russell; painter Winslow Homer; and writers Bret Harte and Robert Louis Stevenson.

Grant was not the only president associated with Long Branch. James Garfield was a frequent visitor, and after the attempt on his life he was taken here (a half-mile railroad spur from the main line to a borrowed cottage was built overnight so that his journey could be more comfortable) in the vain hope that the sea air would help him recover. Chester A. Arthur, Rutherford Hayes, Benjamin Harrison, William McKinley, and Woodrow Wilson also spent some time in Long Branch.

Although much of Long Branch's former elegance is no longer to be seen, you can still see the church at which these seven presidents worshipped. Built in 1879 as St. James Episcopal Church, it is now known as the Church of the Presidents* (1260 Ocean Ave.; 732-280-3522) and is a museum run by the Long Branch Historical Society. The collection focuses on Long Branch's relation to the national scene. Also on the grounds is a teahouse built from the wood used in the spur laid to transport Garfield to Long Branch. The church is currently closed for major renovation and stabilization and is expected to reopen in 2009.

A return to the city's theatrical past is also underway. An industrial building on Broadway has been converted into theater space by the New Jersey Repertory Company (179 Broadway; 732-229-3166), a professional theater devoted exclusively to new plays. Plans call for converting another industrial building on Broadway into more theater space and welcoming more companies.

Seven Presidents Oceanfront Park (Ocean and Joline aves.; 732-229-0924, 732-842-4000), a 38-acre county park, has facilities for swimming, fishing, boating, and picnicking. Long Branch is working to transform itself into a year-round community, and high-rise hotels and condominiums have replaced some of the summer cottages. A stretch of the wooden boardwalk has been replaced by a cement promenade, but you can still walk on "boardwalk" from Brighton Ave. in West End to Sea View Ave. in Long Branch, and along part of the way is an exercise walk with fitness stations.

Long Branch once boasted the longest pier in New Jersey, from which visitors could fish all day long the year-round. The pier, built in 1902, burned in the '80s, but there are hopes that it will eventually be rebuilt. For city beach information, call 732-571-6545; for county information, 732-571-6545.

Long Valley Morris 1,818

NJ 24, C 510, 513, 517

Settled by Dutch and Germans at the turn of the 18th century, Long Valley was known as German Valley until the United States entered World War I and anti-German sentiment inspired the change of name. The German Valley historic district* includes portions of Fairview, E. Maple, and W. Maple aves., and Fairmount, E. Mill, and W. Mill roads. The mid-18th-century Long Valley Inn (1 W. Mill Rd., C 513) was identified by the WPA guide in the 1930s as serving liquor "longer than any other tavern in the State N. of Trenton." The 18th-century stone barn behind the inn has been converted to a brew pub. On Fairview Ave. note the remains of the Old Stone Union Church, built in 1774 to replace an earlier log church and abandoned in 1832 by the two congregations (Dutch Reformed and Lutheran) that used it. Many of the tombstones in the cemetery are inscribed in German; the oldest goes back to 1765. Next door to the church walls, in an 1830s schoolhouse, is the Washington Township Historical Society museum (908-876-9696). In one section of this local-history museum is a replica of an old schoolroom; other exhibits change every two to three months. Open Sunday, 2–4, except on holiday weekends; other times by appointment.

At 12 East Mill Rd. you will find the Obadiah LaTourette Grist and Saw Mill (908-876-5986). Built in 1750, the mill was powered by two waterwheels until 1870, when it was converted to turbine power. It continued as an active mill until World War II. The Washington Township Land Trust now owns the building and 11 acres of waterfront property. It is working to restore the mill, which was in such bad condition that it had been condemned by the township, and hopes to convert it to a valuable educational and environmental resource. Open most Saturdays, 10–2; tours by appointment (908-986-4476).

At 18 Schooley's Mountain Rd. is the Myhelan Cultural Arts Alliance (908-876-5959). Among the alliance's programs is an annual Indie Film Festival. The gallery is open Tuesday–Friday, 10–5, Saturday 10–2.

Southwest of Long Valley, on C 513, is Middle Valley, settled early in the 18th century. Its historic district* includes some 40 buildings from the mid-18th to the 20th century on Beacon Hill, Middle Valley, and W. Mill roads.

Northwest of Long Valley (take 24 west and turn north on Springtown Rd.) is Schooley's Mountain Park (973-326-7600), a 797-acre county park. Schooley's Mountain was a popular and fashionable health resort in the 19th century (General Grant was a visitor): not only is the mountain 1,000 feet above sea level, but there are springs there, known to the Native Americans for the supposed healing qualities of the water, and famous among the colonists at least since the 1770s. The back roads around Schooley's Mountain are worth exploring: the scenery is lovely, occasionally you will see reminders of the elegant resort of the past, and old buildings line many of the roads. The Schooley's Mountain Historic District* includes Schooley's Mountain, Pleasant Grove, and Flocktown rds. and Heath Lane. The park itself has facilities for hiking, riding, picnicking, boating, fishing, softball, and many winter activities.

Lyndhurst Bergen 19,383

NJ TNPK EXIT 16W, NJ 3, 17, C 507

Situated on the eastern bank of the Passaic River, Lyndhurst is bounded on the east by the Hackensack Meadowlands, some 19,000 acres of salt- and freshwater marshes, tidal pools, and uplands that were once thought of as wasteland, suitable only for dumping garbage. (Many travelers on the New Jersey Turnpike have been aware of the dumps as the only hills in an otherwise almost flat landscape.) These now-protected wetlands are recovering from past abuse, and some 8,400 acres of them, including the Saw Mill Creek Wildlife Management Area, make up the Richard W. DeKorte Park. All the dumps are now closed, and part of the county landfill has been landscaped and integrated into the park. This is not a simple task because the decaying garbage generates heat, which makes it hard for plants to establish themselves unless moisture is increased. If too much moisture is added, though, there is a risk of pollutants leaching into the marsh.

Already in place is the Meadowlands Environmental Center (2 DeKorte Park Plaza; 201-460-8300), a museum and nature center that focuses on environmental problems, which the New Jersey Sports and Exposition Authority, as part of its proposal to build the Meadowlands Sports Complex (see East Rutherford), agreed to help build, finance, and maintain. Since 2003 operation of the center has been in the hands of Ramapo College. The road to the center first passes corporate warehouses and offices, and as you get close to the center, you will still see an occasional dump truck, but the mountains of garbage and the steady stream of dump trucks still visible in the mid-'80s are no longer apparent.

In working to reclaim the landfills without causing adverse environmental effects, the Meadowlands Commission has been pursuing a variety of approaches that may serve as models for others. In some cases methane collection wells are placed in the dumps, and the methane gas is sold to local utility companies. The center has also been able to establish a garden of local plants, and as water quality improves, fish that have not been seen in the area for many years are reappearing. The commission's research unit pursues an active environmental research program and monitors progress (the closed landfills must be monitored for 30 years).

The center, which provides programs for some 10,000 students and handles perhaps 40,000 general visitors a year, sits on stilts out over the Kingsland Creek marsh. A variety of trails is available, some around the marshes and some in upland areas, some of them handicapped accessible. The area attracts many birds, particularly in May, late August, and early September, and there are observation decks on the trails (trail maps are available at the center). The boardwalk used on the marsh trail is made of an environmentally friendly (and springy) synthetic material. The Lyndhurst

HACKENSACK MEADOWLANDS

Nature Reserve, two and a half acres devoted to serving as an educational example, has been designed to show how natural succession works; it also contains bird blinds and wildlife observation areas. Meadows Path, which goes along the road, will eventually link the entire area, from Little Ferry in the north to Kearny in the south. For now, you can see corporate workers in shirtsleeves and ties walking toward or away from the center during their lunch breaks.

Exhibits in the museum, many of which are interactive, focus on the history of the Meadowlands area and the nature of urban salt marshes. Open weekdays, 9–5; weekends, 10–3; groups by appointment.

The remaining section of the county landfill will become part of the Meadowlands Golf Redevelopment Project, which will remediate and redevelop some incompletely secured landfills. The 785-acre project includes two golf courses, office and retail space, housing, and 685 acres of open space. It is expected to be completed by 2011.

Lyndhurst's downtown has some interesting buildings, among them the town hall (Valley Brook Ave.), the library (Valley Brook Ave.), and the railroad station (Stuyvesant Ave.). The Little Red Schoolhouse Museum* (400 Riverside Ave.; 201-804-2513), dating from the 1890s, functions as the Lyndhurst Historical Society museum. Focusing on local history, it contains a c. 1912 schoolroom, artifacts and local memorabilia, and changing exhibits. Open 2d and 4th Sundays of the month, 2–4; groups and other times by appointment.

One block north of the museum, at 316 Riverside Ave., is the 18th-century stone Jacob van Winkle house*; in 1804 van Winkle donated the property for the first schoolhouse on the Little Red Schoolhouse Museum site. Just south of the schoolhouse, at 410 Riverside Ave., is the mid-19th-century Jeremiah Yeareance house,* where teachers at the school often boarded. Across Riverside Ave. is a section of Riverside County Park (201-336-7275), with tennis courts, picnic groves, playing fields, a fitness area, and a pedestrian and bicycling path.

Madison Morris 16,530

NJ 124

A colonial town (Mad Anthony Wayne had his headquarters here when the Revolutionary Army was quartered in the Loantaka Valley), Madison became a spot favored by wealthy commuters in the 19th century. For many years it was known as the rose capital of the country, a huge industry having developed out of what had begun as a hobby of the rich. By the turn of the 20th century, 50,000 roses were shipped from Madison to New York City alone, and at the height of production 25 million roses a year were being grown under 1 million square feet of glass. Advances in refrigeration ended

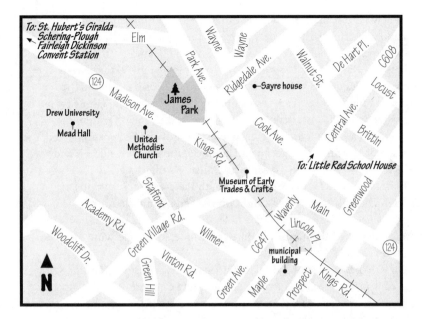

To: St. Hubert's Giralda
Schering-Plough
Fairleigh Dickinson
Convent Station

Elm

Wayne

Wayne

Ridgedale Ave.

Walnut St.

De Hart Pl.

C60B

Park Ave.

Locust

(124)

Madison Ave.

James Park

●Sayre house

Central Ave.

Brittin

Drew University

Mead Hall

United Methodist Church

Kings Rd.

Cook Ave.

To: Little Red School House

Stafford

Museum of Early Trades & Crafts

Greenwood

Academy Rd.

Green Village Rd.

Wilmer

Waverly

Main

Lincoln Pl.

(124)

Woodcliff Dr.

Green Hill

Vinton Rd.

Green Ave.

C647

Maple

Prospect

Kings Rd.

municipal building

N

Madison's rose industry; although there were still 17 rose growers in New Jersey in the 1960s, the last left the state in the late '90s, and most roses today are flown in from South America.

The Museum of Early Trades & Crafts* (Main St. and Green Village Rd.; 973-377-2982) is housed in the former public library, a gift of Willis James, a Wall Street commuter. The small stone Gothic building, built in 1900, has an imported-tile roof, leaded handblown-glass windows, forged bronze chandeliers, stenciled walls and ceilings, and many other remarkable details. The museum was created in 1970 and is devoted to encouraging better understanding of the state's heritage by preserving and exhibiting artifacts showing how people have lived and worked since New Jersey was first settled. The permanent exhibits feature early and mid-19th-century tools used by farmers, by distillers, by coopers, by blacksmiths, and by cabinet-makers. Other exhibits change roughly twice a year. The museum is popular with schools—some 6,000–7,000 children go through on school tours each year. Open Tuesday–Saturday, 10–4; Sundays, 12–5. Closed major holidays. Admission charge.

At 36 Madison Ave. (NJ 24) is Mead Hall,* also known as the Gibbons Mansion. This 1830s building forms part of the Drew University campus. Founded in 1866 as a Methodist seminary on land donated by Daniel Drew, a stock-market speculator, Drew has since become a liberal arts college with a graduate school as well. On its wooded 186 acres are two other remnants from the Gibbons estate, a red-brick dormitory, whose walls once enclosed the stable, and Embury Hall, the former granary. The library is the official depository for the United Methodist Archives. The Korn Gallery (in the Dorothy Young Center for the Arts; 973-408-3796) mounts six shows a year. Two are student shows; the others tend to emphasize works by metropolitan-area artists, but ethnographic and photography shows are also featured. Open Tuesday–Friday, 12:30–4, and by appointment. The Shakespeare Theatre of New Jersey (973-408-5600), a professional repertory company in residence at Drew in a theater rebuilt for its needs, is the longest-running Shakespeare festival on the East Coast. The company puts on several productions a year (including one in the Greek theater at St. Elizabeth; *see* below), and engages in a large number of educational and outreach programs, for children and adults (some 100,000 children and adults a year take in some aspect of the theater's offerings).

Farther west in Madison is the Florham Park–Madison campus of Fairleigh Dickinson University. Built on 180 acres from the 1,000-acre Twombly estate, Fairleigh Dickinson has as its main building a 100-room mansion designed by Stanford White and modeled on one wing of Hampton Court.

Directly northwest of Fairleigh Dickinson's campus, in Convent Station, is the campus of the College of St. Elizabeth (2 Convent Rd.; 973-290-4442), the oldest four-year college for women in the state (men have been enrolled in the continuing education program, known as the weekend college though classes also meet during the week, since the 1970s). Convent Station's name dates to the 1870s, when the Sisters of Charity financed the establishment of a train station to serve their Academy of St. Elizabeth, a school they had founded 10 years earlier. In the 1890s the nuns gave the town the road to the station (the station building dates to 1913). The order's motherhouse is also here; the college itself dates to 1899. Although some of the handsome Victorian buildings have been demolished, the main building remains, and this is still an extraordinary campus. The Shakespeare garden is a particular treat. Located next to the conservatory (Seton Dr. and Midway), where many winter plants are grown, the garden is planted with the flowers grouped according to the play in which they are mentioned. The Greek theater, modeled on the one at the bottom of the Acropolis, was built in the 1930s as a way to employ out-of-work laborers.

There are many other buildings of interest in Madison, including several in Queen Anne style on NJ 124 as you come into town from the east. Note also the United Methodist Church (1730; 120 Madison Ave.); the Daniel Sayre house* (c. 1740–45; 31 Ridgedale Ave.), possibly Wayne's headquarters; and the elaborate municipal building (Maple Ave.), donated in 1935 by Geraldine R. Dodge. Madison has worked to preserve the classic small-town look of its shopping streets; its Commercial Historic District,* roughly centered on Main St. and Waverly Pl., includes some 60 buildings dating from about 1870 to 1936 on Green Ave., Central, Lincoln, and Waverly pls., Green Village and Kings rds., and Main Street.

Giralda Farms, Mrs. Dodge's former estate, has been subdivided and now contains corporate offices and, in a former cow barn, St. Hubert's Animal Welfare Center. St Hubert's, which hopes to expand its quarters in the near future, is an animal shelter actively engaged in placement, rehabilitation, and educational efforts.

North of Madison (take Central Ave., C 608, to Ridgedale Ave.), in Florham Park, is the Little Red Schoolhouse Museum* (Ridgedale Ave. and Columbia Tnpk, C 510; 973-418-5304). Originally a one-room schoolhouse (the basement is a later addition), the mid-19th-century red-brick Gothic building is now a museum of local history, with changing exhibits relating to local history and the agricultural past. Among the objects in the collection are the old school desks, the old post office, and a broom-making machine. Open September–December and April–June, 1st Sunday of the month, 2–4; groups and other times by appointment.

Mahwah Bergen 24,062

I 287, US 202, NJ 17

Located along the northern border of the state, the township of Mahwah includes within its boundaries both extensive undeveloped areas and many corporate complexes. (The superhighways that go through town can make it difficult to get from one part to another.) For over 25 years Ford Motor Company had an assembly plant here (near NJ 17), which closed in 1980 after turning out close to 6 million cars and trucks. Its 172-acre site is now home to a hotel, offices, and corporate headquarters. In fact, most manufacturing in Mahwah has been replaced by housing and corporate headquarters, and the town's population has nearly doubled since the Ford closing threw 5,000 people out of work.

Bergen County runs two large reservations in the township, the 3,100-acre Ramapo Valley County Reservation (US 202; 201-327-3500) and the 1,350-acre Campgaw Mountain County Reservation (Campgaw Rd.; 201-327-3500). Both are wildlife reservations, and both are open year-round for hiking and camping (permits are necessary for camping and fishing), with marked and rough trails. Fishing is available in a mountain pond in Ramapo Valley; Campgaw has a ski area (201-327-7800). For information on trail maps and guided tours, call 201-891-5571. Adjacent to Campgaw is Darlington County Park (Darlington Ave.; 201-327-3500), which has two lakes for swimming and a third for fishing. Open daily, Memorial Day weekend–Labor Day for swimming (admission is charged); open limited hours, April–Memorial Day and Labor Day–October. There is also a county golf course (201-327-8770).

The Mahwah Museum Society runs two local-history museums, a town museum and a railroad museum. The town museum (201 Trenton Tnpk.; 201-512-0099) has permanent and changing exhibits. The permanent exhibit concentrates on the general history of Mahwah, the changing exhibits may deal with specific aspects of local history. Open Sunday, 2–5. The train museum, located in the town's first railroad station (1871 Old Station La.;

201-512-0099), which dates from 1871 (the new station dates from the early 1900s), concentrates on the Erie Railroad and includes a caboose, a working model from 1918, a scale model, and other railroad memorabilia. Open June–October, Sunday, 2–5; groups by appointment.

There are many 18th- and 19th-century Dutch stone houses to be seen in Mahwah, particularly along Ramapo Valley Rd. (US 202). George Washington is believed to have stayed in one of these houses, and Joyce Kilmer lived for a time on the southwest corner of Airmount and Armour rds., commuting to his job at the *New York Times*. For many years Mahwah has been home to Les Paul, who developed the electric guitar when patrons of a barbecue stand where he was performing complained they couldn't hear his acoustic instrument; he was also responsible for the development of overdubbing. In 1996 he was inducted into the New Jersey Inventors Hall of Fame.

At Ramapo College of New Jersey (505 Ramapo Valley Rd.; 201-684-7500) are several galleries with exhibits open to the public. Two are in the Berrie Center for Performing and Visual Arts (201-684-7202), one in the Selden Rodman Gallery of Popular Arts (201-684-7147), and one, which specializes in regional artists and student works, in the Potter Library (201-684-7575). The galleries are generally open midweek afternoons, but the hours vary so it is best to call ahead. The college was founded in the late 1960s. Its campus, formerly the Stephen Birch estate, lies on 300 wooded acres in the foothills of the Ramapo Mountains. The college's original building, the late-19th-century Havemeyer mansion, has been augmented by award-winning contemporary buildings.

At the Bergen County's Law and Public Safety Institution (281 Campgaw Rd.; 201-785-6008) is a state-of-the-art training facility for firefighters (and police); some 11,000 students are trained here each year. The simulations—which include residential buildings, retail stores, hotel hallways and guest rooms, movie theaters, elevators, and a commercial kitchen—are set up so that firefighters can learn to battle blazes in the cluttered situations and poor visibility they are likely to encounter in real fires. Tours for groups can be arranged by appointment (the tours include safety instruction); each year the facility provides tours for about 3,000 children and 1,000 adults.

Southeast of Mahwah, in Upper Saddle River, is the Hopper-Goetschius house* (245 Lake St.; 201-327-2236), run as a house museum by the Upper Saddle River Historical Society. On the property are a Dutch sandstone house, built c. 1739 and lived in by only two families, a Dutch barn (moved from another property), an outkitchen, and a privy. Furnishings in the house are those of the original families and date from the 18th to the early 20th century. Changing exhibits display items of local historical interest. Open Sunday, June–August, 2–4, and by appointment. The New North Reformed Low Dutch Church* (E. Saddle River Rd. at Old Stone Church Rd.) dates from c. 1789, and there are 18th-century houses to be seen at 54 Pleasant Ave.,* 72 Hopper Farm Rd.,* and 349 W. Saddle River Rd.*

Manahawkin Ocean 2,004

The last town before the bridge to Long Beach Island, Manahawkin (whose name means "land good for growing corn") was formerly the site of a Native American village. It was here that William A. Newell, living with his uncle on Main St. for a time, developed the idea that led him to found the United States Life-Saving Service (*see* Allentown).

In the Stafford Township Heritage Park (Bay Ave., just west of Main St.; 609-597-5947), you will find the township historical society's Old Stone Store Museum and the old Railroad Station. The Old Stone Store building dates to the mid-18th century; the stones were added in 1838; when the building was rebuilt in 1979, the 1838 stones were reused. The museum has exhibits that focus on local history as it ties into national history. On display at the station, which dates from 1872, are model trains and memorabilia from the old Tuckerton Railroad line, which used to run through Manahawkin. The Old Baptist Church★ (N. Main St.; 609-597-5947), started in 1758 and enlarged in the 19th century, has exhibits in the lobby, which generally change seasonally. The building serves as a venue for concerts and lectures as well as private events. A widely varied mix of concerts is presented Monday evenings, June–August. Cavalry Cottage (100 Stafford Ave.), dating to 1740, is being restored by the historical society and will serve as a research center and library and as the repository for the society's archives. The society sponsors student tours and a variety of annual events, including a Founders Day festival in June and a Heritage Weekend in September, which features Revolutionary War reenactors and has attracted as many as 6,000 visitors. Open Sunday, 1–4, year-round; Wednesday and Friday, 10–4, July and August; and by appointment. At Manahawkin Lake are the A. Paul King County Park (732-506-9090) and township open space. At the park are picnic tables and a beach area.

East of town (take Stafford Ave. off Main St.) is the Manahawkin Wildlife Management Area (609-292-2965), one of the oldest in the state. Begun in 1933, it now contains over 1,000 acres of woodlands, fields, and salt marsh and is a good place for fishing, crabbing, and bird-watching (raptors are common in the winter).

North of the area is the Barnegat division of the Edwin B. Forsythe Wildlife Management Area (609-698-1387). Here you will find an observation platform and boardwalk (Bay Shore Dr. between Ridgeway and Edison Aves.).

Manasquan Monmouth 6,310

A seaside community near the outlet of the Manasquan River at the southern end of Monmouth County, Manasquan retains in its downtown much of the flavor of another era. Native Americans frequented this area, and the name is said to mean "enclosed area with a house in it," referring to the practice of leaving the women behind when the men went hunting. The settlement began to grow early in the 19th century. In 1888, before embarking for the South Seas, Robert Louis Stevenson stayed here for six weeks and wrote part of *The Master of Ballantrae*. Note the Holy Trinity Lutheran Church (Main St.), built in 1848.

The town has the reputation for being a family resort in the summer. This characteristic is recognized in the historical society's Big Sea Day, a local festival that remembers the early-19th-century custom of families from all around gathering for one day at the Manasquan beach. Held the second Saturday in August, the event ends with fireworks on the beach. For information on beach fees, call 732-223-0544.

Thirty-five acres on the north shore of the Manasquan Inlet (across from Point Pleasant Beach) that once belonged to the American Timber Company, and whose ownership was contested some fifteen years ago by the Board of Proprietors of Eastern New Jersey, now form the Fisherman's Cove Conservation Area. The land is open for passive recreation.

In the Bailey-Reed house (105 South St.; 732-223-6770) is the Squan Village Historical Society museum. The original one-room house probably dates to the 18th century; some nine rooms have been added over the years. The house has been decorated to reflect different periods: the kitchen, which is in the original room, reflects the 18th century, the parlor and the upstairs bedroom the mid 19th, and the dining room the early 20th. The exhibits concentrate on various aspects of the local history and economy; in one room the exhibits change every three months. The research room contains papers relating to the area. Outside is an early-19th-century carriage house built from material salvaged from a local shipwreck and an 1860s four-seater outhouse. Open the second Sunday of the month, 1–4; open for research Monday and Thursday, 1:30–4; groups and other times by appointment.

North of Manasquan in Sea Girt is the National Guard Militia Museum (at the National Guard training center near the intersection of NJ 70 and Sea Girt Ave.; 732-974-5966). Located on land that was once a farm belonging to Commodore Richard Stockton's estate, in a 1930s building that served as the morgue for the victims of the sinking of the *Morro Castle* (*see* Asbury Park), the museum highlights the history of the guard from 1609 to the present. Of particular interest is the Civil War–era submarine known as the Intelligent Whale, but the museum also has an extensive collection of photographs and a wide variety of artifacts. Exhibits change from time to time. Open Tuesday, Thursday, Saturday, and Sunday, 10–3, mid-April–October; 1st weekend of the month, November–March.

The Sea Girt lighthouse (Beacon Blvd. and Ocean Ave.; 732-974-0514), a brick Victorian structure, was the first in the country to use a radio fog signal (which worked in tandem with those from the Ambrose and Fire Island lightships) and the last to be constructed with living quarters in the same structure as the light. Built in 1896, it was decommissioned in 1945. The tower is equipped with a fourth-order Fresnel lens, similar to the one actually used in the lighthouse. You can tour both the living quarters and the tower; the keeper's office is furnished with period furniture, and on display are historic photographs, maps, memorabilia, and paintings relating to lighthouses and to the *Morro Castle*. Open Sunday, 2–4, Memorial Day–mid-November; groups and other times by appointment.

About three miles northwest of Manasquan is the Manasquan River Wildlife Management Area (go south from Manasquan to NJ 35, west on 35 to NJ 34, west on 34 to Ramshorn Dr.), 744 acres open for hiking, fishing, and hunting.

A few miles south of Manasquan in Point Pleasant (Ocean County) is the New Jersey Museum of Boating (732-859-4767). Housed in one of the local boat works, the museum has exhibits on the history of boatbuilding in the area and on lifesaving, as well as a collection of small boats and artifacts, including some from the *Morro Castle*. Open daily, 10–4. Also in Point Pleasant is the Point Pleasant Historical Society's museum (416 N. Jersey Ave.; 732-892-3091), housed in the municipal complex. The museum focuses on photographs and memorabilia relating to local history. Open the 2d Thursday of the month, 1–4, and by appointment.

Margate City Atlantic 8,193

c 563

A shore community south of Atlantic City (and Ventnor City), Margate City is known today as the home of Lucy,* the Margate elephant (9200 Atlantic Ave.; 609-823-6473). Built in 1881 by a real estate developer as a gimmick to attract potential customers, Lucy is now a national historic landmark. She appears frequently in tourist promotions and is visited by some 50,000 people every summer. Six stories tall and weighing 90 tons, Lucy was built of wood and covered with a tin skin; she cost about $33,000. Lucy's builder constructed two other elephants, one of which, the Colossus, was 18 stories tall. It burned in 1897. Sold in 1887, Lucy continued her career as a tourist attraction, even serving for a while as a hotel. She began to decline after World War II and was nearly destroyed in the 1960s. Rescued by a citizens committee in the 1970s, she has been relocated; she has also been given a new steel frame, and her exterior has been restored. Also relocated was a Camden and Atlantic Railroad depot from 1881, which forms part of the building that houses the ticket office and gift shop. Plans for Lucy include restoring the train station and adding an accessible interpretive center on the ocean side of the gift shop. Band concerts are given in the summer, and there is a fine view from her howdah. Open for visits daily, mid-June–Labor Day, Monday–Saturday, 10–8, Sunday, 10–5; weekends, April–mid-June, and September–December, 10–5. Group tours by appointment throughout the year. Lucy is also open on some holidays; call or check the website for details. Admission charged.

Behind city hall is the Margate City Historical Society museum (7 S. Washington Ave.; 609-823-6546). The collection includes antique fire-fighting equipment, artifacts from the police department, old photographs, advertisements, and genealogical records. Open Saturday, 11–1, April–December; other times by appointment (609-822-5658).

Despite the rash of new construction, there are still some splendid houses to be seen in Margate. The Marven Gardens historic district* lies between Ventnor, Fredericksburg, Winchester, and Brunswick avenues. For information on beach fees, call 609-822-0424 or 609-822-2508.

Matawan Monmouth 8,910

GARDEN STATE PKWY EXIT 117, NJ 34

Matawan, originally settled by Scots and known variously as New Aberdeen and Middletown Point, has seen its population quadruple over the last 60 years. It was the home of Major John Burrowes, who organized the first New Jersey company of militia. His scallop-shingled house,* built in 1723, has become the Burrowes Mansion Museum (94 Main St.; 732-566-5605, 732-765-8157). Having also served as a hotel and a restaurant, the house is now operated as a local-history museum by the Matawan Historical Society. Furnished with period furniture, it contains a permanent exhibit of locally made pottery and tile, as well as exhibits relating to the history of the local brickmakers and a pharmacy exhibit. There are also changing exhibits and a special December musicale. Open March–December, 1st and 3d Sunday of the month, 2–4. Tours by appointment.

West of Matawan is Cheesequake State Park (Garden State Pkwy exit 120; 732-566-2161), close to 1,300 acres of rolling land, 380 acres of which are a natural area. The park exhibits a wide diversity of plant communities, including Pinelands vegetation typical of the southern part of the state, deciduous forests typical of the northern part, a cedar swamp, white pine stand, freshwater swamp, and flood plain. This is a good place for bird-watchers, and the park is home to the largest number of nesting ospreys in the area. The extensive trail system goes into the marsh to an abandoned landing on the Cheesequake River, where once bricks made from local clay, salt hay harvested from the marsh, and agricultural products from nearby farms were loaded for transportation elsewhere. The park also has facilities for swimming, camping, fishing (the lake is stocked with trout), sledding, and cross-country skiing, as well as a trail open to mountain bikes. The interpretive center (732-566-3208) offers a mix of weekly programs and environmental education programs for school groups and youth organizations. In the center are various exhibits relating to the natural and cultural history of the area, as well as aquariums containing a variety of reptiles, turtles, and fish. The park can be crowded in the summer. The interpretive center is open 8–4 daily in summer (Memorial Day–Labor Day), Wednesday–Sunday, in winter; the park daily, 8–a half-hour before dusk. Parking fee in summer.

Also west of Matawan, in Old Bridge Township (take Old Bridge Rd., C 516), is the Thomas Warne Historical Museum and Library (C 516, between Morganville and John Partridge rds.; 732-566-2108). This was a one-room schoolhouse, built in 1885, which still has its original wainscoting and slate blackboards. The collection includes artifacts from the area, as well as documents, photographs, and research files. Open Tuesday, 7–9 P.M., Wednesday, 9:30–12, and the first Sunday of the month, 1–4; groups and guided tours by appointment.

Mauricetown Cumberland [Commercial Township]

c 670, 676, 744

Although the first settlers arrived in what is now Mauricetown (pronounced *Morristown* locally) in the early 18th century, the town was not really developed until the early 1800s. It thrived as a fishing port during the 19th century, when fleets of boats worked the Delaware River, and in the mid-1800s attracted captains of three-masted schooners, who built houses in town. Mauricetown is an unusually well-preserved entity, with most of the houses dating from 1815 to 1870 (but note the Caesar Hoskins house at the foot of 2d St., which dates at least to 1714 and possibly to 1680). Today most of the residents commute to nearby jobs, although there is a sand works outside town. There are plaques on many of the houses giving their dates and often identifying them as captains' houses. The Greek Revival Mauricetown Academy (High St.), a two-room elementary school from 1860, was used as a school for over 100 years. The Elizabeth Compton house (Front St.; 856-785-0457, 856-785-1137), built in 1862, is being restored by the Mauricetown Historical Society as a house museum and library. The rooms, which include a river room and a children's room, are furnished appropriately to the age of the house. In the Victorian bedroom are various artifacts of local interest, and another room contains tools used in local trades. Open 1st and 3d

Sundays, 1–3; groups and other times by appointment. The Methodist Church (Noble and 2d sts.) dates from 1880; its tall spire once served as a navigational aid. At the foot of High St., where the 1888 drawbridge used to be, is Riverside Park; you can sit here and watch the river go by. One of the benches is placed on the remaining fragment of the bridge. The Maurice River, together with its tributaries the Manumuskin and Menantico rivers and Muskee Creek, is part of the Wild and Scenic River project, unusual in that almost all the land along the river is privately owned.

The historical society sponsors an annual house tour, usually in December, and various other special events. The fire company sponsors three antique shows each year (the first weekends in March, June, and December), as well as a seafood festival in October that draws some 2,500 people. Statewide oyster-shucking contests have been among the events taking place at the seafood festival, and if you continue on to Bivalve (take High St. west to C 649 and turn left; at Port Norris, turn right on Main St. and left on C 631), you will come to the heart of New Jersey's oyster industry, now devastated by a parasite that has drastically reduced yields. Before the parasite hit Delaware Bay in the late 1950s, 2 million bushels of oysters a year were harvested, but the industry's biggest crop today is quahog clams. The Rutgers Shellfish Research Laboratory in Bivalve is actively engaged in research that it hopes will find a way to overcome the parasite.

In the meantime you can visit a restored Delaware Bay oyster schooner, the *A. J. Meerwald,** New Jersey's official tall ship, which often docks in Bivalve. Built in 1928, the *Meerwald*, after a career as an oyster schooner, a fireboat, an oyster dredger, and a surf clammer, was retired in the 1960s. It was raised and restored by the Delaware Bay Schooner Project (since 2002 known as the Bayshore Discovery Project; 2800 High St.; 856-785-2060), which uses the boat in many ways, all geared toward raising people's awareness of the history, culture, and environment of Delaware Bay. The project sponsors hands-on educational sails and workshops, dockside tours (when the sailing schedule permits), public sails, and various land-based programs. Call to find out where the boat is docked and to arrange a tour. The Delaware Bay Museum (2800 High St.; 856-785-2060) is located in former shipping sheds (1904) on the Bivalve waterfront and contains artifacts and photographs related to the history of the bay area. When the restoration of the shipping sheds is complete, the project will take up work on the *Cashier*, an oyster boat that dates to 1849 and holds the New Jersey oyster license No. 1. Office open weekdays, 9–5; museum open April–October, Thursday–Saturday, 12–3.

The schooner project is one of the sponsors and the host of Bay Days (609-785-2060), a two-day June event that includes an oyster-shucking contest, a blue-crab race, river tours, family games revolving around fish and shellfish, traditional crafts, local seafood, educational displays, folk music, and Saturday evening fireworks.

At the mouth of the Maurice River is the East Point Lighthouse (C 616; 856-327-3714). Built in 1849, the lighthouse is the second oldest still standing in New Jersey (Sandy Hook is older) and the only remaining one on the Jersey side of Delaware Bay. The light was extinguished on 7 December 1941 but reinstalled in 1980, and the Maurice River Historical Society has been working on restoring the building. Long-range plans call for setting up a museum in the lighthouse. Open the third Sunday of the month, 1–4, and on special occasions like Bay Days and the New Jersey Lighthouse Challenge weekend; tours and groups by appointment.

In this area is the Heislerville Wildlife Management Area, 6,700 acres of diked and tidal marshes, impoundments, and uplands. To the east of East Point are Thompsons Beach and Moores Beach, where horseshoe crabs spawn and attract migrating shorebirds. The impoundments also attract wintering snow geese. This is prime territory for bird-watchers, but you can also fish and hunt.

Mays Landing Atlantic 2,321

US 40, NJ 50, C 552, 559

Located at the head of Great Egg Harbor River, Mays Landing has been the county seat since Atlantic County was formed in 1837. The original red brick courthouse (1838) remains the center of the greatly expanded county buildings. The smallest county seat in the state, Mays Landing was founded in 1760 by George May, a trader from Philadelphia. It is an attractive spot, with large trees and a common. Note the Presbyterian Church* (1841) at the corner of Main St. and Cape May Avenue. The Mays Landing Historic District* includes over 250 buildings along E. and W. Main St. and the intersecting streets. Along the river in the heart of town is Gaskill Park (609-625-8219), a 10-acre county facility where you can fish, boat, and picnic. (At the time of the Revolution, the park served as a deep water port.) In the summer the gazebo is used for concerts.

In the Little Red Schoolhouse, built in 1904, is the Hamilton Township Historical Society museum (49 Mill St.; 609-909-0272). Exhibits, which may feature the history of different areas of the township or different eras, change roughly four times a year, and the museum also has materials on older families from the area. Open Thursday, 6:30–9 P.M., Saturday, 10–4.

Northeast of the center of town (on US 322) is the main campus of Atlantic Cape Community College (5100 Black Horse Pike; 609-343-4900). Shows at the campus art gallery change monthly except in the summer; there is a faculty show, a student show, a community show, and a high-school show, as well as shows focusing on black history and women's history. For hours, call 609-343-5040. From September through May the college sponsors occasional open houses and tours; call the admissions office for the schedule.

During those same months the college's Academy of Culinary Arts runs a restaurant that is open to the public by reservation Monday–Friday for lunch and dinner (609-343-4940). The college's active performing arts program includes contemporary folk concerts, student theater productions, and authors' lectures; these events, which take place at the Walter Edge Theater, are open to the public (call 609-343-5040 for the schedule). There is also a folk series at the restaurant.

North of the center of town is Lake Lenape Park, 2,000 acres that are open for hiking, boating, fishing, and camping (call 609-645-5960 for information). The park also includes Lake Lenape, the end point in a 12-mile canoe trip through the Pinelands along the Great Egg Harbor River that begins in Penny Pot County Park in Folsom (spur 561 and US 322), where you can also fish and picnic. A shorter version starts at Weymouth County Park (US 322 and C 559), in the early 1850s a flourishing community and the site of the Weymouth iron forge (1802–62) and paper mills (1866–97). Some foundations remain, and you can find interpretive signs here as well as picnic tables and grills.

Three miles south of Mays Landing, on NJ 50, is Estell Manor Park (609-645-5960, 609-625-1897), a county facility with 1,700 acres located primarily on the site of the World War I Bethlehem Loading Company plant. Built in 1918, the plant ceased operations in 1919. All the usable steel and iron was removed, and all that remains now are concrete foundations and railbeds (the nature trail goes along the railbed; occasionally chunks of coal, slag, and cinders can be seen, although the forest has almost reclaimed the site). Also in the park are the remains of the Estellville Glassworks, which dates from the 1820s and is remarkable for being built of local sandstone. The works operated until the late 1870s; window glass was the principal product. The Estellville Glassworks Industrial Historic District* includes Estell Manor Park, Stevens Creek, Maple Ave., Walkers Forge Rd., and NJ 50.

Located in Estell Manor Park is the Warren E. Fox Nature Center (109 Boulevard, NJ 50; 609-825-1897), Atlantic County's headquarters for environmental education. Inside the building, which is constructed with a passive solar envelope design, is a collection of indigenous live animals, as well as exhibits focusing on the history and the plant and animal life of the Pinelands. The park also has facilities for fishing, boating, picnicking, camping, hiking, biking, and cross-country skiing, as well as a fitness trail and a nature trail (a brochure describing the nature trail is available at the center). Many special programs are offered for school groups and the general public, including orienteering and environmental education programs. Guided nature and history tours are available by appointment to groups of 10 or more. The park is open daily, 7:30–dusk; the nature center daily, 8–4.

Among New Jersey cities, Estell Manor is second in area only to Vineland. Over the years the city has supported a wide variety of trades, from shipbuilding to glassmaking to piracy, and it is known for having had the state's first female mayor. The 1913 Risley schoolhouse (Cape May and Cumberland aves.; 609-476-1100), built on the site of an 1897 school that burned in 1911, has been restored and serves as a meeting place for community groups, an electronic museum of local history, and a local-history library.

Two miles west of Mays Landing is Balić Winery (6623 US 40; 609-625-2166), established in 1966 on land that has been used for growing grapes since early in the 20th century. Open Monday–Saturday, 9–8, Sunday, 11–7.

Medford Burlington [Medford Township]

NJ 70, C 541

The village of Medford is a tiny dot at the edge of what used to be Pinelands in the midst of an extremely fast growing township. (The population of Medford Township, 22,253 in 2000, more than quadrupled between 1960 and 1990, more than doubled between 1970 and 1990.) This was Native American territory before the first settlers began arriving, possibly late in the 17th century, more definitely early in the 18th, and the excavations for the many housing developments keep turning up artifacts. C 541, in fact, follows an old Native American path to the sea (NJ 70 follows an old Camden and Atlantic Railway route).

The first real community probably didn't develop until the mid-18th century (the oldest gravestone reads "M. S. 1759"), and from the 1760s to the 1780s Medford profited from the nearby Etna and Taunton bog-iron furnaces. The first machine to manufacture cut nails was built in Medford by Mark Reeve, who arrived in town in 1800; however, he did not patent his invention. According to tradition, he was so impressed with Medford, Massachusetts, that he urged changing his adopted town's name from Upper Evesham to Medford. His former factory, now a private home, can be seen on Jennings Rd. off NJ 70.

When the railroad arrived in 1869, Medford was a prosperous village with sawmills, a gristmill, and a glass factory. The area was an important cranberry-growing region, and the many lakes that have made it into something of a resort area resulted from damming the streams and draining cranberry bogs.

A famous native son was James Still, known as the Doctor of the Pines. Born in 1812 to freed slaves from Maryland, he managed to educate himself and, surmounting incredible obstacles, built up a practice, based mainly on herbal remedies, that enabled him to die (in 1882) the largest property holder in the area. His son became the second African American to graduate from Harvard Medical School (in 1871). A modern housing development sits where his house once sat, but his office,* with its double fireplaces in the

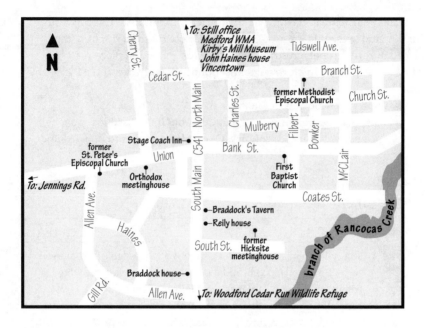

basement for boiling syrups, is still standing (Church Rd., just east of 541, north of the village).

Many of the village's buildings date from the 19th century (and some from the 18th). The Jersey Devil (Main and Union sts.), which houses shops and a cafe, was originally the Stage Coach Inn and was built in 1810. Braddock's Tavern (Main St.) is on the site of the old Medford House, which had pillars cast at Batsto. The Quakers still use the Orthodox meetinghouse (1814; Union St.); the Hicksite meetinghouse (1842; off Main St. at South St.) now belongs to a Catholic charity. The former Saint Peter's Episcopal Church (Union St.), a 19th-century Gothic structure, served for a time as a doctor's office and is now a private home. The former Methodist Episcopal Church (1854; 1896; Branch and Filbert sts.) is being used by another group; the First Baptist Church (Bank St.) dates from 1893. Note also the Reily house (53 S. Main St.) and the Braddock insurance office (70 S. Main). The Medford Historical Society (609-654-7767) sponsors house tours the first Saturday in December as well as a quilt show the first weekend in June and an apple festival the second Saturday in October.

The Kirby's Mill Museum* (Church and Fostertown rds.; take 541 north out of the village to Church, C 616; 609-654-7767) is in an old gristmill (the foundations date to 1788, and a sawmill was on the site before that) that operated with waterpower until 1961 and with combined waterpower and electricity for a short period more. The historical society has restored the mill and returned it to working condition. A restored blacksmith's shop is also on the property. In the museum are the mill's old stones and wheels, farm tools, woodworking equipment, a printshop, a period kitchen, and a collection of period clothes and costumes. Both the quilt show and the apple festival are held at the mill, as is a juried art show the first weekend in August. Open June–August, Sunday, 1–4; other times by appointment. On Monday, Wednesday, and Friday, 10–4 and Saturday in the morning there are often workmen on the site; you're welcome to stop by then.

Close by the mill is the oldest house in the county still on its original foundations (the Revell house was moved; *see* Burlington). The earliest part of the John Haines house* (26 Fostertown Rd.) was built c. 1690; the Flemish-bond brick section dates to 1720; alterations and additions were made in 1810 and c. 1850. The house remained in the Haines family until early in the 20th century; today it is once again lived in by a descendant of the original builder.

About three miles north of the village at the South Jersey Regional Airport (take Main St., C 541, north to Fostertown Rd., C 636, turn left and take the first left at Stacy Haines Rd., C 612) is the Air Victory Museum (68 Stacy Haines Rd.; 609-267-4488). Here you will find displays of historic and modern aircraft and engines, as well as a large collection of artifacts, including a wind tunnel built under the supervision of the Wright Brothers. The museum's uniform collection includes examples from every American service as well as some from six foreign countries. In the winter of 2005 the museum began a family-oriented educational program. Call for details. Open Wednesday–Sunday, 10–4, March–November. December–February, Sunday hours depend on the weather; call for information. Groups by appointment. Closed Thanksgiving Day, Christmas Day, and New Year's Day. Admission charge.

If you continue east from Kirby's Mill on C 616 about three miles, you will come to Vincentown. In this small village are many interesting buildings: the Vincentown-Tabernacle Telephone Museum (17 Mill St.) was severely damaged in the 2004 floods, but the expectation was that it would be reopened in 2005. The museum is housed in a c. 1898 building and has an exhibit showing what the telephone company was like in the early 20th century. The collection includes old switchboards, numerous old telephones, and other artifacts. A one-room schoolhouse (Race St. at the millpond), c. 1860, is furnished as an 1860s schoolroom, and visiting schoolchildren are treated to lessons using the materials and methods of the 19th century. Behind the Old Vincentown Town Hall, 1876 (Plum St.), is a two-cell lockup, 1891. The telephone museum, lockup, and schoolhouse are open by appointment (609-859-9237). You can pick up walking-tour pamphlets of Vincentown at the Sally Stretch Keen Memorial Library (94 Main St.; 609-859-3598), in a 1920s building, with a children's library next door in the old firehouse.

About two miles north of the village (take 541 to Brace Rd. and turn left, or west) is the Medford Wildlife Management Area, 200 acres of fields and hedgerows open for hiking, bird-watching, and hunting.

Seven miles southwest of the village (6 Sawmill Rd.; 856-983-3329) is the Woodford Cedar Run Wildlife Refuge. The refuge's 180 acres of pinelands support a rehabilitation center for wounded animals and, across Cedar Lake, an education center. A one-mile trail circles the lake (for those who don't want to walk, a bridge connects the two centers), and there are two other trails that go through the wetlands and uplands. At the wildlife compound you can observe a large variety of native species, and each month one of the species is featured. The center offers many programs for school and scout groups (some 13,500 schoolchildren participate each year) and senior citizens. On the weekends, programs (which might involve guided hikes or crafts or guided van trips) are open to the public. Open Monday–Saturday, 10–4, Sunday, 1–4. Admission charge.

Some five to eight miles southeast of the village, in Shamong, is Valenzano Winery (1320 Old Indian Mills Rd.; 609-268-6731). What started in the early 1990s as a 3-acre hobby has become a 30-acre winery that grows its own grapes and operates out of a converted early-20th-century farmhouse. Open Thursday and Friday, 11–6, Saturday and Sunday, 11–4, other times by appointment. Between Thanksgiving and Christmas the hours are extended, but it is always best to call ahead.

Mendham Morris 5,097 (borough) 5,400 (township)

NJ 24, C 510, 525

A region of rich soil and abundant waterpower, the Mendham area was first settled in the early 18th century. At least three stories have grown up to explain its name: it derived from a Native American word, from a town in England, or from a clergyman who, when apprised of the settlers' bad habits, said, "Don't worry, I'll mend 'em." Although like much of Morris County it grew considerably between 1960 and 1980 (the borough and the township each doubled its population over those 20 years), a lot remains from the 18th and 19th centuries. The Mendham Historic District,* with buildings dating from the 18th to the 20th century, includes Bridge, Halstead, E. and W. Main, New, Orchard, and Prospect sts.; Talmadge and Hampton rds.; and Mountain and Hillcrest avenues. The Black Horse Inn (Main St.) has been in continuous operation since 1742, and on the other side of the street another 18th-century hotel, the Phoenix House* (Main St. and Hilltop Rd.), now contains borough offices. On Hilltop Rd. is the First Presbyterian Church (1860), the third church built by a congregation that goes back to the 1730s. When the church celebrated its 150th anniversary in 1888, it is supposed to have coined the word "sesquicentennial," used later by Princeton University to celebrate its 150th anniversary (the *OED,* however, does cite an example from 1880).

A Morris County linear park, Patriots' Path, starts here (and ends in Hanover Township). You can enter at Ironia or Pitney rds. and Mountain Ave.

About one mile west of Mendham is the historic district of Ralston* (NJ 24 and Roxiticus Rd.; the community was formerly known as Rocksitious or Roxiticus). At this corner are the general store and manor house, both dating from the 1780s. The general store continued in business until 1893. It then served as the Ralston post office until 1941 (at which point it was reputed to be the oldest building in the United States to house a post office). The store is now operated as a small museum and contains household and other items of historical interest. Open Sundays and holidays, June–October, 2–5. Groups by appointment (973-543-6878).

Another mile or so southwest off 24 is Mount Paul Memorial Park (East Fox Chase Rd.; 973-326-7600), an undeveloped county park of 251 acres where you are welcome to hike. East of Mount Paul off Pleasant Valley Rd. is the Schiff Reservation (the former Mortimer Schiff estate), a 300-acre natural area open for hiking.

Also west of the center of town is the Levi Lewis Memorial Museum (159 Mountainside Rd.; 973-543-4724), commemorating a family that came to the area in the 1730s. Lewis ran a sawmill, a forge, iron mines, and a tanyard. The museum contains items related to Lewis's life, including the tools needed to run a forge and various farm implements. Open by appointment only.

About midway between Mendham and Chester on the south side of NJ 24 is the Nesbitt Cider Mill, built in 1848 as a gristmill and converted to a cider mill in 1908. The excellent condition of the cider-making equipment has raised hopes that it can be brought back to working condition.

About three miles east of the town center (take 24 east to Tempe Wick Rd., C 646, and turn right) is the Jockey Hollow Girl Scout Camp (Leddell Rd.; 973-927-7722). Dating to 1929, the camp is on some 200 acres, with woods and the headwaters of the Passaic River. Individuals are welcome to hike on the property except when camp is in session (mid-June–August; call for the exact schedule) or during one of the camp's construction projects. Hiking is also possible at the nearby Mendham Township Buck Hill (or Dos Passos) Park (north of Tempe Wick Rd., west of Corey La.); at the Dismal-Harmony Natural Area (Woodland and Mt. Pleasant rds.), a 150-acre township preserve about three miles east of the town center (take 24 east to Cherry La. and turn left, or north; Cherry La. turns into Woodland Rd.); and at Buttermilk Falls (take Mountain Ave. north out of town until it becomes Calais Rd.; continue to Combs Hollow Rd.).

Metuchen Middlesex 12,840

NJ 27, C 501, 531

Settled in the late 17th century by Dutch and English colonists, Metuchen became a commuters' town in the 1830s. It remained rather an exclusive community until the rapid growth of neighboring Edison Township after World War II. Because it attracted many literary and intellectual figures, Metuchen gained the nickname "Brainy Borough." Its older buildings are generally well preserved. Note in particular the Franklin Meeting House (291 Middlesex Ave.), built in 1805, used as a school from 1807 to 1872, and since then serving a variety of civic purposes; and the railroad station (off Main St.), dating from 1888. St. Luke's Episcopal Church (Middlesex and Oak aves.), a charming frame building with vertical siding and Gothic Revival details, dates from 1868 and was designed by Richard Upjohn. Joyce Kilmer was married in St. Luke's, and Mark Twain, William Dean Howells, Helen Keller, and Ogden Nash have been among its visitors. Continuing the Brainy Borough tradition, the writer and critic John Ciardi lived his adult life here. The pianist Robert Taub is a Metuchen native.

In the center of town is the Forum Theatre (314 Main St.; 732-548-4670), built as a vaudeville house in 1928 and later converted to a movie house. It is now used by the Forum Theatre Group, which puts on four to five plays and musicals each year, as well as a nine-production children's series.

Twelve acres of the 650-acre Dismal Swamp are located in the northwestern corner of the borough (Liberty St. off Central Ave.). The area, which supports some 165 species of birds, several species of mammals, amphibians, and reptiles, and possibly the endangered bog turtle, has been designated "priority wetlands" by the federal government. The borough has developed some eight miles of in-town walking paths both to reduce traffic congestion and to improve the inhabitants' health. The Middlesex County Greenway also goes through Metuchen on the old right of way of the Lehigh Valley freight line, and you can find walking paths in Centennial Park (Grove Ave. to Wakefield Ave.), where you can also bird-watch from the highest point in town (169 feet).

Middletown Monmouth 66,327

NJ 35

The village of Middletown, set in the middle of a rapidly growing and densely populated township, is one of the state's oldest continuously settled communities. Dutch settlers were among the first, followed in the 1660s by Baptists seeking freedom from the religious intolerance they had experienced on Long Island. Among the early settlers were Richard and Penelope Stout. He was one of the founders of the Middletown Baptist Church and a recipient of the Monmouth Patent; she was a Dutch immigrant who early in the 17th century had been attacked by Native Americans, who left her for dead. Nursed to health by other Native Americans, she found her way to New York (then New Amsterdam), where she met and married Stout. Eventually they settled in Middletown and had 10 children; at her death at 90, she reputedly had 492 descendants.

The Kings Highway historic district* (the intersection of Kings Hwy with NJ 35) is an 18th- and 19th-century neighborhood, and it is even possible to find a 17th-century structure or two by wandering about the village. (The Kings Highway was supposedly built wide so that horses could be raced along it, and there is a record of a race being run as early as 1699.) The best known of the older buildings is Marlpit Hall (137 Kings Hwy; 732-462-1466), built in the mid-18th century (and not, as previously thought, in the late-17th and early-18th centuries). The house was bought by Edward Taylor in 1771 and remained in the Taylor family until 1936, when it became the property of the Monmouth County Historical Association. The house retains most of its original paneling, hardware, and doors, one of which has bull's-eye panes. The dining room is particularly gracious. Marlpit Hall was restored in the late 1990s; part of the house has been furnished to reflect the life of a loyalist family before the Revolution, part to elucidate early-20th-century sensibilities on historic preservation and restoration. Open May–September, Thursday–Saturday, 1–4. Closed 4 July. Groups by appointment other times. Admission fee.

The Taylor-Butler House (127 Kings Hwy; 732-462-1466), on the adjoining property, is a Victorian Italianate mansion that was built in the 1850s by a member of the same Taylor family. It too belongs to the Monmouth County Historical Association, which rents it out for weddings and parties.

Middletown's Baptist Church was the first in the state. The congregation was organized in 1668; the present building (69 Kings Hwy) dates from 1832. Christ Episcopal Church* (92 Kings Hwy at Church St.) was organized in 1702; this building dates from 1835. Part of the church's funds derive from money left to it by William Leeds, a convert who had been a member of Captain Kidd's pirate crew. Note the octagon house (1885) on Church St. and the blacksmith's shop (1825).

On Leonardville Rd., between Chamone and Bellvue aves. (in the Leonardo section of the township), is the MacLeod-Rice House at Croydon Hall (732-291-2835), once the home of Melvin A. Rice, a gentleman dairy farmer who served as a roving ambassador for Woodrow Wilson. The turn-of-the-20th-century building, which may actually incorporate an older small farmhouse, for many years housed a private school and is now the Middletown Township Historical Society's local-history museum. The museum room was once the ballroom. Open Sunday, May–3d week in November, 1–4; groups and other times by appointment.

South of the Kings Highway on Red Hill Rd. (or c. 1½ miles east of Garden State Pkwy exit 114) are two county parks. Deep Cut Gardens (732-671-6050) consists of 54 acres of greenhouses and gardens that have been planned to serve as "a living catalogue of cultivated and native plant material." Among the park's features are a butterfly and hummingbird garden and walk, a lily pond, a home-compost demonstration area, and a horticultural library. The park sponsors educational programs and has a reference library devoted to horticultural materials (the second largest horticultural library in the state), classrooms, and a shop that features rare horticultural items. The park is near the highest point in the county, and on a clear day you can see the ocean from the library.

Directly across Red Hill Rd. is the entrance to Tatum Park (732-671-6050), 365 acres of rolling hills, open fields, and woods. There are multiple-use trails, open play areas, and two activity centers for public cultural programs. The Red Hill center was a radio-wave generation center for the U.S. Army, the Holland center was the Tatum mansion (classes are held in the former ballroom). Both buildings are open only to program participants.

South of the village on Oak Hill Rd. (east off NJ 35) is Poricy Park Nature Center (732-842-5966). On the property are an 18th-century farmhouse and barn listed in the state historic register, a 250-acre nature preserve, a 65-million-year-old fossil bed, a 20-acre pond, and 4 miles of trails that wander through fields, forests, and marshlands. Educational programs concentrate on the environment and colonial history. The environmental programs are run out of the nature center, the historical programs out of the farmhouse. The historical programs are hands-on and family oriented; past programs, for example, have dealt with sheepshearing, spinning, and weaving. Nature center open weekdays, 9–4; Sunday, 12:30–3:30; groups by appointment. Farmhouse open last Sunday of the month, 1–2:30, but it is advisable to call ahead.

Also south of the village on the Middletown-Lincroft Rd. is the Sunnyside Recreation Area (732-842-4000). There is a short trail suitable for hiking, skating, bicycling, and riding. The county has an equestrian facility here that specializes in therapeutic riding.

For over 30 years, the Visiting Nurse Association of Central New Jersey (732-224-6791) has been sponsoring a December holiday house tour, concentrating on houses in the Middletown-Rumson-Locust area, which includes some of the most affluent parts of the county. Not all the houses are historic, but in past years buildings on the tour have included restorations of 19th-century mills and farmhouses, converted turn-of-the-20th-century riverside luxury cottages, and converted garages from large estates.

Milford Hunterdon 1,195

C 519, 627

Like many other Delaware River towns, Milford began as a ferry landing. Although there was a sawmill here in the mid-18th century, real development came toward the end of the century with the establishment of three mills and the ferry. The town was known first as Burnt Mills (after fire destroyed an early mill), then Burnt Mills Ferry, then Mill-ford Ferry. Milford lost its ferry in 1842 when the first bridge was built. Today's bridge, dating from 1933, was built on the concrete and rubble abutments from the original wooden bridge.

Today Milford is a lovely river town with many old buildings, antique shops, inns, and restaurants. It has attracted artists, among them Clarence Holbrook Carter and Wanda Gág, the children's book writer and illustrator. Many of the old buildings have been converted to other uses: the railroad station, for example, has shops and a restaurant; other old houses have been converted to restaurants or bed-and-breakfasts. The Riegel Paper Company, which began operations up the river in a converted gristmill in Finesville in 1862, had one of its largest plants in Milford; before it closed in 2003 it made up over 15 percent of the borough's tax base. Plans call for a mixed-use redevelopment of the site, and there is some hope that a few of the old brick buildings can be incorporated in the plans.

The last two miles of 627 heading into Milford are particularly beautiful, though this is not the route to take if you are in a hurry. The road, in many places only wide enough for one car, goes right along the Conrail tracks and the Delaware River.

The Volendam Windmill Museum (231 Adamic Hill Rd.; 908-995-4365) can be reached off 627 about 3½ miles northwest of Milford. (Take Crabapple Hill Rd. to Alfalfa Hill Rd. and watch for signs. You can also take Mt. Joy Rd., farther north on 627, to Adamic Hill Rd., or approach from 519 and go west on Anderson Rd., jog left when it ends, and turn right on Adamic Hill Rd.) The roads climb through lovely woods that have become increasingly developed. The windmill, which stands near a splendid 18th-century house, is a replica of a Dutch or Danish wind-driven grain mill. Structural problems made it necessary to close the mill, but until it is repaired, you are welcome to park and walk around it.

Continuing north on 627 will bring you to Finesville. Situated on the Musconetcong River, considered one of the state's finest trout streams, this attractive village has many lovely stone buildings. The church dates from

FINESVILLE

1879. The Alba Vineyard (C 627, slightly over 2 mi. south of Warren Glen and north of the bridge at Riegelsville; 908-995-7800) grows grapes on the slopes of the Musconetcong Valley above an early-19th century cut-limestone dairy barn (now the winery) and outbuildings. Open for tours, tasting, and picnics, Wednesday–Friday and Sunday, 12–5; Saturday, 11–6; groups by appointment.

About two miles north of Finesville (take 627 north to Warren Glen and turn south on 519 to the intersection with Dennis Rd.) is the Musconetcong Gorge Nature Preserve (908-788-1158), part of the Hunterdon County park system. This is a rugged area of over 400 acres, with steeply wooded terrain overlooking the Musconetcong River. There are many small streams and a variety of plant and wildlife, and you can hike, fish, and hunt.

Millburn Essex 19,765

NJ 24, 124, C 527

Settled early in the 18th century, Millburn became a wealthy commuter town in the 19th. Within the township is Short Hills, established in 1877, which for many typifies the affluent suburb. The Short Hills Park historic district* encompasses 19th- and 20th-century buildings in the area roughly between Hobart Ave. and Parsonage Hill Road. At the eastern edge is the Wyoming historic district, listed in the state register of historic places, also with 19th- and 20th-century buildings, roughly bounded by Sagamore Rd. and Wyoming Avenue. Walking-tour brochures are available at the Millburn public library (200 Glen Ave.; 973-376-1006). Open Monday–Thursday, 9:30 A.M.–8:45 P.M.; Friday and Saturday, 9:30–5:15; Sunday, 1–4:45; closed Saturday in August.

At the westbound waiting room of the Short Hills railroad station (1 Station Plaza near Hobart Ave.; 973-564-9519) is a museum run by the Millburn–Short Hills Historical Society. The station, built in 1907 of brick with glazed clay tile roofing and mahogany detailing, and restored in the 1990s, contains the town archives as well as artifacts and photographs relating to local history. Periodic special exhibits focus on subjects like local schools or veterans or the impact of electricity on the area, and the society also uses the building for educational programs. Open Tuesday, 5:30–7:30, Wednesday, 3:30–5:30, and the first Sunday of the month, 2–4; groups and other times by appointment. It is advisable to call before visiting.

Just west of the station is the Cora Hartshorn Arboretum and Bird Sanctuary (324 Forest Dr. S.; 973-376-3587), over 16 acres of natural woodlands with 3 miles of trails. The arboretum was founded in 1923 by Cora Hartshorn, the daughter of the founder of Short Hills (and inventor of the spring-loaded window shade), on land given her by her father. Stone House, built with traprock and oak from Hartshorn property, houses a small museum with changing nature exhibits and a small collection of live animals; there is also a library. The grounds and trails are open daily, dawn–dusk. The museum is open weekdays, 9–4:30; Saturday, 10–12, September–July; weekdays, 9–12, August; if, however, a class is using the museum, it is not open to the public, so it is best to call ahead; tours by appointment. Closed during school vacations and state holidays.

Part of the South Mountain Reservation is in Millburn. This 2,000-acre park has many miles of trails, many lookout points, picnic areas, and a wildlife preserve (*see also* West Orange). At the entrance to the reservation is the Paper Mill Playhouse (Brookside Dr.; 973-376-4343). The theater takes its name from its original house, a converted 18th-century mill that had continued to produce paper until after World War I. After a fire in 1980 destroyed all but a few fragments of the mill, the theater built a new house on the site (and incorporated some of the fragments). The company puts on six shows a year, specializing in musicals; it also hangs art exhibits that change with each production. Each year there are shows from the New Jersey Watercolor Society, from the Millburn–Short Hills Art Center, and of miniature art; other shows have included prints, soft sculpture, and oriental rugs. Open Friday, 12–3, and one hour before performance through intermission; closed non-performance weeks (for information on the exhibits, call 973-379-3636, ext. 2272).

Just west of South Mountain Reservation is Greenwood Gardens (274 Old Short Hills Rd. between the reservation and Old Short Hills Park; 973-258-4026). Formerly an elaborate private garden, the 22 acres were neglected for some 30 years. The gardens are being restored by a nonprofit conservancy, and until they are stabilized, tours are by appointment only.

Millstone Somerset 410

C 419, 533

Tiny in area as well as population (it occupies 0.6 sq. mi.), this picture-book village and former agricultural center situated on the Millstone River and the Delaware and Raritan Canal* was once called Somerset Courthouse because for almost 50 years in the mid-18th century it was important enough to be the county seat. (After the British burned the courthouse in 1779, the seat was moved to Somerville.) Millstone's 19th-century historic district* includes Ann, S. River, West, and Main sts., Alley Way, and Amwell Road. Set back from the road in the midst of these 19th-century houses, but not visible from it, is one of Frank Lloyd Wright's Usonian houses.

In what was once a blacksmith shop is the Old Millstone Forge Association's blacksmith museum (C 533; 732-873-2803). The building probably dates to the mid-to-late 18th century (although there may have been some kind of blacksmith shop on the site much earlier), and the collection of old blacksmiths' tools, both hand- and machine-made, includes some late-17th-century Dutch pieces. There are also wheelwrights' tools on display. Demonstrations are given. Open Sunday, 1–4, April–June and the 3d Sunday in September through the last Sunday in November; groups by appointment.

The Millstone Dutch Reformed Church (Main St. and Amwell Rd.) dates from 1828. Troops came through Millstone during the Revolution, and George Washington stopped at the John van Duren house (1754; W. River Rd., 1 mi. south of Amwell Rd.) after the Battle of Princeton; he may also have made it his headquarters on other occasions.

Across the water is East Millstone, even smaller but also picturesque. Its 18th- and 19th-century historic district* includes the area along Amwell Rd. and the canal. Just beyond the bridge is the Franklin Inn (2371 Amwell Rd.; 732-873-5244 when open, 732-297-5548 when closed). Built as the van Lieuw homestead in 1734, it served as Cornwallis's headquarters for a week. Enlarged in the 1830s to serve as an inn and take advantage of the newly built canal, it was also an important stagecoach stop. Long-range plans call for restoring the building to serve as an example of 19th-century inns. For now it houses a bookstore, all of whose income goes toward restoration of the inn. Bookstore open weekends, 1–4, Wednesday, 12–3. Note also, closer to the canal, the locktender's house.

About a mile east of the village, on the south side of Amwell Rd., is the Hutcheson Memorial Forest, formerly Mettler's Woods, a national natural landmark. This virgin forest is one of the oldest undisturbed stands of oak-hickory forest remaining in the United States. It has apparently never been cut over and has not burned since the early 18th century. The original 145-acre tract (it is now over 500 acres) was bought by the United Brotherhood of Carpenters and Joiners of America and given to Rutgers University, which uses it as a laboratory for ecological and biological research. The woods have been described as a living museum of the eastern United States as it was 200 years ago, and "the most intensively studied primeval woods on the continent." Open for guided tours by appointment only (write Director, Hutcheson Memorial Forest, Department of Biological Sciences, Rutgers University, Piscataway 08903). For information on reservations, call 732-932-9631.

On the north side of Amwell Rd. is Somerset County's 467-acre Colonial Park (Mettlers Rd., with access from Amwell Rd. and Elizabeth Ave.; 732-873-2695). In the western section are a 5½-acre arboretum and the Rudolf van der Goot Rose Garden, with over 3,000 plants and a sensory garden at one end. The western boundary of the park includes frontage on the canal and the river. Park facilities include a canoe-launching ramp and a paddle-boat area, as well as family and group picnic sites, playgrounds, fishing ponds, open playing fields, a bicycle path, a nature trail, hiking and bridle trails, and tennis courts (732-873-8716). The Spooky Brook Golf Course (Elizabeth Ave.; 732-873-2242) is at the eastern end of the park. Both open daily, dawn–dusk.

North and east of Colonial Park in the town of South Bound Brook (take Elizabeth Ave., C 621, to New Brunswick Rd., turn right, and then left on Davidson Ave.) is the Ukrainian Orthodox Memorial Church Museum (135 Davidson Ave.; 732-356-0090). The museum is part of a large complex that forms the administrative center of the Ukrainian Orthodox Church and includes, in addition to the church and museum, a cultural center, a store, a library, and a cemetery. In the 18th century this was the Henry Fisher farm. At least one of the remaining houses dates to the 18th century, and the cemetery, which serves as a burial place for Ukrainians from a wide area, is attached to the old Fisher family cemetery. Much of the material in the museum is church related, and the collection is strong in folk art. Among the items on view are paintings, books, textiles, decorated Easter eggs (*pysanky*), pottery, and a striking collection of embroidery. The museum expected to start expanding in late 2004, and while the larger space is under construction, a small part of the collection can be seen at the cultural center. Call for an appointment. The museum hopes to reopen by 2006; at this point regular hours will be reinstituted. The Revolutionary War affected South Bound Brook, too, for Baron von Steuben (*see* River Edge) was on duty here in the winter of 1778–79.

Also in South Bound Brook is the Staats–Von Steuben House* (17 Von Steuben La.; 732-469-5836). This is a large farmhouse whose earliest section may date to the late 17th century; later portions were added in 1740, 1800, and 1825. The original Dutch doors remain. Baron von Steuben spent the winter of the second Middlebrook encampment here; George Washington was among his guests. The house is open for several special events, such as a colonial weekend in the spring or a canal day in the fall; tours by appointment.

If you continue east on Amwell Rd. from East Millstone and turn right on S. Middlebush Rd., you will come to three of the houses preserved by the Meadows Foundation (1289 Easton Ave.; 732-828-7418). Hageman farm (209 S. Middlebush Rd.; 732-937-5708) is just south of Bennetts Lane. The house was started in the mid-18th century, but the main portion of today's house and the barns were built in the 19th. The Wyckoff-Garretson (215 S. Middlebush Rd.; 732-846-3345) and the Van Liew–Suydam houses (280 S. Middlebush Rd.; 732-738-5262) are south of the farm; the Van Liew is set back from the road. Both date to the 18th century, and the earliest portion of the Wyckoff house is probably the oldest structure in Franklin Township. Taking Amwell Rd. east until Demott La. and Demott to the end brings you to the Van Wickle house* (1722), headquarters for the foundation, which is also involved with the Blackwells Mills Canal House (*see* Griggstown). All the properties managed by the foundation are open the 2d Sunday of the month, 1–3, and for special occasions; the foundation also sponsors colonial and other period historic reenactments, and tours can be arranged by appointment.

Milltown Middlesex 7,000

OFF US 1

Known in the early 19th century as Bergen's Mill after Jacob I. Bergen, who built a gristmill on Lawrence Brook, Milltown for a time was the center of the nation's rubber industry (at the end of the 19th century the industry shifted to Trenton and in the 20th century to the Midwest). In 1843 the Meyer Rubber Company built a plant* on Bergen's mill site (Main St. at Mill Pond); the plant was later run by the India Rubber Company and the International Rubber Company before the Michelin Tire Company bought and expanded it in 1907. At peak production the Michelin plant employed as many as 3,000 people. The company stopped producing rubber in Milltown in the 1930s, and parts of the large complex have been converted to other uses.

The Milltown Museum (116 S. Main St.; 732-828-0249) occupies two mid-19th-century farmhouses, one of which may be the second-oldest house in town. The rooms are furnished with period furniture; the exhibits include the town's original post office, a schoolroom, a general store, a sewing room, a doll collection, and memorabilia and photographs relating to local history. There are also changing exhibits. Open 1st Sunday of the month, March–June and September–December, 1–3; groups and other times by appointment.

Next door to the museum and behind the red, fish-scale shingled firehouse is the Eureka Fire Museum (732-828-0221, 732-846-7134). In a converted 1899 barn the museum has a large collection of early fire-fighting equipment, with rotating exhibits of old apparatus, extinguishers, helmets, hand-pulled hoses, and the like. The museum's restored 1921 American LaFrance pumper is a favorite at local parades and car shows. Guided tours by appointment.

A walk along Main St. will reveal many mid- and late-19th-century buildings. Some, like the hardware store at Main and W. Church St. or the funeral home at 170 Main, have been converted from homes to other uses. On Washington Ave. the old Russell Playing Card factory* has been converted to condominiums.

Millville Cumberland 26,847

NJ 47, 49, C 555

Situated at the head of the tidewater of the Maurice River, Millville was settled as a shipping center around 1720. Word of vast sand deposits led to the establishment, in 1739, of Millville's first successful glassworks. Over the years glassmaking became Millville's major industry; it remains that today, followed by aircraft repair.

Wheaton Industries, once the largest family-owned glassworks in the world, descends from a firm founded in 1888 by Dr. T. C. Wheaton, who arrived in Millville in the 1880s intending to establish both a medical practice and a pharmaceutical business. The need for pharmaceutical bottles led him to buy into a recently established glassworks. Although Wheaton Industries was sold in the mid-1990s, it still employs 2,500 people in Millville alone.

In Millville's first bank,* built in 1857 (E. Main and 2d sts.; 856-825-7000, ext. 275), is the museum of the Millville Historical Society. The collection contains period furniture and a variety of artifacts and old records, including a display of Millville glass and a ship's bell alleged to have come from Spain on Columbus's last voyage. Next door is the Baracha Dunn house (1798), recently restored by the society. Both buildings are open Wednesday and Sunday, 1–4; groups by appointment.

At 126–130 N. High St. is the Levoy Theatre* (856-327-9870), which opened in 1908 as a vaudeville house. It became a movie theater, but was closed in the 1970s. After several threats of demolition, it was rescued by the Levoy Theatre Preservation Society and is now being restored to function as a community arts center and museum. The lobby is open for tours the third Friday of the month. The society hopes to open the theater in 2008, in time for its 100th anniversary.

Wheaton Village (1501 Glasstown Rd., off Coombs and Valley rds. between NJ 55 and Wheaton Ave; 856-825-6800; 800-998-4552) is a re-creation of an 1880s South Jersey town. Founded in 1970 by Frank H. Wheaton Jr., T. C. Wheaton's grandson, it centers on the Wheaton Museum of American Glass and a replica of his grandfather's first factory. The museum contains one of the world's largest collections of American glass, with the style of the rooms designed to reflect the era of the glass on display. The museum has rescued chandeliers from the Roxy Theater in New York City and the Traymore Hotel in Atlantic City. Bottles, decorative glass, paperweights, and lighting devices are some of the items on display.

The glass factory has been re-created following early photographs and partial blueprints (but with modern precautions against the fires that plagued 19th-century glassworks). You can watch the glassblowers while they work; at certain times of the day they give a set talk explaining what they are doing. Ask at the gatehouse for the day's demonstration schedule. You can also arrange in advance to blow your own paperweights.

The Down Jersey Folklife Center opened in the village in the summer of 1995. Devoted to preserving the folk traditions of southern New Jersey, the center contains a small museum and sponsors a variety of programs featuring folk traditions from boatbuilding to origami. Also in the village are a Crafts and Trades Row, where potters, a decoy carver, and a lampworker demonstrate their crafts; a miniature railroad; a playground; and various old buildings, shops, and restaurants. The village sponsors a large variety of special events, many focusing on antiques, collectibles, and cars. Open 10–5, Tuesday–Sunday, April–December; Friday–Sunday, January–March (the last glass demonstration is at 3:30); the Crafts and Trades Row is not open in the winter except for special occasions; closed New Year's Day, Easter, Thanksgiving, and Christmas. Admission charge (except for the stores and restaurants). Group tours by appointment.

The Riverfront Renaissance Center for the Arts (22 N. High; 856-327-4500) is a visual arts center, part of Millville's Arts District, established to revitalize the town. The center has two galleries, with exhibits that change monthly (shows open on the third Friday of the month, and the center hosts a reception to celebrate the opening). The center offers classes in a variety of media for children and adults, provides studio space, and sponsors a lecture series. Open Tuesday–Thursday, 11–5; Friday, 11–8, Saturday, 11–7; Sunday, 11–4.

Millville was once known as Holly City because it was home to the largest American-holly farm in the United States (the English-holly farms in Oregon are bigger). The farm grew out of the aversion the president of the New Jersey Silica Sand Company had to sending liquor as a Christmas gift to his customers and employees. In 1926 he began sending boughs of holly, and in 1939, after frost had killed the native trees, he planted 2,800 trees. The farm passed through various hands and various modes of operation (at one time a holly-motif museum was open to the public); plans for its future have varied from preserving the entire tract as open space to letting a developer build houses and a golf course on 400 acres, leaving 900 for a holly preserve and open space.

At the Millville Municipal Airport (southwest of town off Cedar St., C 610) is the Millville Army Airfield Museum (856-327-2347). Said to be the first airfield constructed for defense in World War II, it retains many of its original buildings. Plaques identify the functions once served by the look-alike, bare-bones buildings. Open Tuesday–Sunday, 10–4; Monday and tours by appointment.

Several wildlife management areas lie close to Millville. Northwest of the center of town is Union Lake, the largest freshwater lake in southern Jersey. Created in the 1860s (by damming the Maurice River), the lake has long had a reputation as a good place to fish (in 1978 a 27-pound striped bass was caught here), and you can hike in the surrounding area. At the head of the lake is Union House, which dates at least to the early 18th century. The first known record of the house is on a 1709 deed. Roughly 40 years later William Penn's sons added the main structure you see today. The house is furnished with period pieces. Tours can be arranged through the Millville Historical Society (call 856-825-7000, ext. 275); donation requested.

South of Millville, on C 555, is the Edward G. Bevan Wildlife Management Area (formerly the Millville Wildlife Management Area). One of the oldest such areas in the state (it was started in 1932), it contains over 13,000 acres of woodlands and fields and is a good place for hiking, fishing, and hunting. You can also fish in the Menantico Ponds Wildlife Management Area, just east of Millville off NJ 49. The access road, just after the Menantico Creek crossing, is suitable for walking. Some seven miles east of

Millville, on NJ 49, is the Peaslee Wildlife Management Area (609-984-0547). Its 25,000 acres make it one of the largest such areas in the state. It consists of pine-oak woodlands and lowlands, and it is bordered on the east by the upper reaches of the Tuckahoe River. It has a field-trial course and is open for hiking, fishing, and hunting.

Montague Sussex 3,412

US 206, C 521, 650

A stagecoach stop on the Hoboken-Buffalo route in the 18th century, Montague is now within the Delaware Water Gap Recreation Area (*see* Bevans, Walpack). The Foster-Armstrong house* (320 River Rd., C 521; 973-293-3106) dates from the 1790s (with a post–1812 addition) and served as a hotel for many years. According to local legend, rafters taking logs down the Delaware to the Trenton sawmills used to stay here. It is now run by the Montague Association for the Restoration of Community History (MARCH), and on display in the house are local artifacts and photographs, as well as quilts, military items, and Victorian clothing. Also run by MARCH is the Neldon-Roberts Stonehouse (501 US 206; 973-293-3106), which was probably built in the early 1800s and was used as a schoolhouse before it became a private residence. It contains a 19th-century schoolroom; paintings showing the history of the area; an exhibit on quilting, spinning, and weaving; and changing exhibits and craft demonstrations. On the grounds is a colonial herb garden. A holiday event takes place in late November or early December, and both sites are open Sunday during the summer, for special events, and by appointment. It is advisable to call first.

A few miles north of the MARCH houses is the Westfall Winery (141 Clove Rd., C 653; 973-293-3428), which occupies part of a 300-plus-acre farm dating back to the 18th century (Elias Boudinot was the lawyer for the original land transaction). The farm, with its handsome peg-and-beam barns and stately white house, sits in an idyllic setting with splendid views of the Highlands. Open April–December, Thursday–Sunday, 12–5, and by appointment.

South of Montague (off US 206) is the Hainesville Wildlife Management Area (609-984-0547), 600 acres of fields, hedgerows, and woodlands, with a 30-acre pond. You can fish here and in the Little Flat Brook.

East of Montague and surrounded by Stokes State Forest and High Point State Park (take Deckertown Rd., C 650) is Mashipacong Bogs, 1,000 acres formerly owned by Doris Duke (*see* Somerville), now a Nature Conservancy preserve (973-300-0311). Part of the land, described as a black-spruce swamp and possibly the state's southernmost glacial bog, is leased to a camp for inner-city youth; the rest is undeveloped. A short loop trail goes into the preserve roughly a quarter of a mile before the intersection of Deckertown and Grigger roads. Hikers are asked to stay on the trail.

Montclair   Essex 38,977

Although Montclair was first settled in the 1660s, today's community took shape in the 1860s, when Montclair broke away from Bloomfield in a dispute over the routing of a railroad line. Frank and Lillian Gilbreth, the efficiency experts about whom *Cheaper by the Dozen* was written, raised their large family (12 children) on Eagle Rock Way; a junior high school is named after the painter George Inness, who lived in Montclair for a time; the noted golf course designer Robert Trent Jones was a longtime Montclair resident, as was Yogi Berra.

Like many of the early suburbs, Montclair suffered a period of population decline, but the community engaged in a vigorous program to revitalize its downtown. The Montclair railroad station* (Lackawanna Plaza), for example, designed in 1913 by William H. Botsford, who also designed the railroad terminal in Hoboken, has been converted to commercial purposes. A nearby school from the same era (Baldwin St. and Glen Ridge Ave.), with its 12-foot-high windows and all, has been converted into apartments.

The Crane House Museum* (110 Orange Rd.; 973-744-1796) was built in 1796 by Israel Crane. A direct descendant of one of Montclair's original settlers (part of today's Montclair was once called Cranetown), Crane was a highly successful businessman who engaged in a wide variety of enterprises from cider, cotton, and woolen mills to turnpikes and quarries; the writer Stephen Crane (1871–1900) was connected to this family. The house, which was altered in the mid-19th century by Israel Crane's son, is now run as a house museum by the Montclair Historical Society. A rare example of a North Jersey Federal-style mansion, with Greek Revival additions, it has been furnished to reflect the years the Cranes lived in the house, from 1796 through the 1800s. The society offers a variety of programs year-round. Guided tours Friday and Saturday 1–4, Sunday 2–5. Demonstrations of open-hearth cooking are given on most Sundays, September–May. Group tours by appointment. Also on the property is a c. 1820 house, in which you will find an exhibit of a 19th-century general store and the society's gift shop. Open Sunday 2–5. A local-history library and the society's offices are located in the Clark House, next door to the Crane house, at 108 Orange Rd. Open Monday–Friday, 9–5.

The historical society runs a second historic house museum. Evergreens, the Shultz House Museum (30 N. Mountain Ave.; 973-744-1796) was built in 1896 by Charles Shultz, president of a bank in Hoboken, who commuted to his house in Montclair. Many architectural styles, from Queen Anne to Arts and Crafts, are apparent in the 21-room house, which contains all its original fixtures, as well as many of the original furnishings and three generations worth of family collections. Guided tours 1st and 2d Sunday of the month,

April–October, 3 P.M. Admission charged (pay at the Clark House). Group tours by appointment.

The Montclair Art Museum* (3 S. Mountain Ave.; 973-746-5555), housed in a Greek Revival 1914 building, has an unusually fine permanent collection for a town the size of Montclair. The collection specializes in American painting and sculpture from the mid-18th century to the present and includes Native American art. The museum puts on changing exhibitions and sponsors classes, workshops, lectures, and other special events. Open Tuesday–Sunday, 11–5. The museum's Le Brun Library is open Tuesday–Thursday, 10–12 and 2–4.

The Van Vleck House & Gardens (21 Van Vleck St.; 973-744-4752) are also noteworthy; built in 1916, the house is now a center for nonprofit activities. The gardens include many of the varieties developed by Howard Van Vleck, a noted horticulturalist who was the last Van Vleck to live in the house, and include a striking display of rhododendron and wisteria. The gardens are open to the public mid-April–October, 10–5; classes and a variety of special events are also offered.

The fine and performing arts are stressed at Montclair State University (Normal Ave. and Valley Rd.; 973-655-4000). The university, established in 1908 on a 200-acre campus, sponsors a variety of programs in theater, music, and dance. Its student and professional programs are open to the public (call 973-655-5112 for information on theater and dance), as are its art galleries (973-655-7640). At both the University Art Gallery (Life Hall) and Gallery One (Life Hall Annex), shows focus on contemporary art and change roughly every two months; once each year there is usually an international show. Open Monday–Friday, 10–5; Saturday, 11–4. The music department offers over 100 concerts a year that are open to the public, including student and faculty recitals, campus groups, and guest performers. It is also home to the collection of unusual instruments developed by Harry Partch.

For such a densely settled area, the amount of open space is surprising. At the northwestern end of town are Mills Reservation (Reservoir Dr.; 973-268-3500) and Mountainside Park (500 Upper Mountain Ave.; 973-783-5974). The former is a 157-acre county facility with a lookout point, bridle and hiking trails, good birding, and no buildings, the latter a town facility with the world-famous Presby Memorial Iris Gardens (1927). The gardens contain 2,000 kinds of iris (totaling some 10,000 individual plants), each labeled with the year it was first recognized or hybridized; the earliest dates from the 16th century. The display usually reaches its spectacular peak mid-May through early June. At the 1870s Walther house next door, there is a wonderful Victorian garden. Educational programs for children take place at the carriage house. The office is open limited hours in the mornings; during bloom season the garden is open 10–8; tours by appointment. The park itself is open during daylight hours.

The opportunities for bird-watchers are also remarkable. In the northwestern area is the Montclair Hawk Lookout (Edgecliff Rd.;

908-766-5787; take Upper Mountain north to Bradford, turn left on Bradford, right on Edgecliff), a New Jersey Audubon Society sanctuary and a national natural landmark situated on an outcropping on the first Watchung ridge. Because of the ridge, there are updrafts, essential to hawks on their long migrations. The season runs from mid-September through November, with the peak during the first four weeks. In mid-September you can see as many as 2,000 broad-winged hawks in a few hours, and although it doesn't happen often, there have been days when 10,000 hawks have been spotted. This is the second-oldest continuous hawk watch in the country. Farther east is the town's Alonzo F. Bonzal wildlife preserve (Riverview Dr. off Alexander Ave.), 23 acres of natural area with trails.

On the eastern edge of town is Brookdale Park (Bellevue Ave.; 973-268-3500), which Montclair shares with Bloomfield. This 121-acre park is one of the many Essex County parks to have been designed by the noted Frederick Law Olmsted firm. It has a rose garden, fitness and interpretive trails, playgrounds and playing fields, and tennis courts. A concert series takes place in the park in the summer.

Moorestown Burlington 19,107

NJ 38, C 537

A Quaker town that was laid out in the 1720s, Moorestown is the home of the well-known Moorestown Friends School.* Founded in 1785, the school has grown from its original stone building to a 44-acre complex off E. Main St. in the center of town. Several buildings in the town center are of particular interest. Note the old town hall* (40 E. Main St.) and the First Baptist Church (1877; 19 W. Main St.), connected to a 19th-century brick building, once the parsonage. The Smith-Cadbury Mansion* (12 High St.; 856-235-0353), c. 1738, 1766, serves as the headquarters of the Moorestown Historical Society. The house has been furnished almost entirely by donations and reflects 18th- and 19th-century styles. Tall clocks and other items of antique furniture are on display, as are examples of Quaker clothing and other items from the society's extensive collection of period clothes, samplers, quilts, and some Moorestown memorabilia. Open Tuesday and the 2d Saturday of the month, 1–4, and by appointment. You can also pick up a walking tour of Moorestown at the mansion. Taking Main St. (C 537) west out of town takes you through a particularly lovely stretch of houses. At 436 E. Main St. (just west of Poplar Ave.) is the bondsman's house, c. 1780, which is one room wide and two rooms deep, with 12-inch-thick stone walls.

A well-known worshipper in the Friends Meeting House (1802; E. Main between Chester Ave. and Schooley St.) was Samuel Allen, inventor of the hand cultivator, a manure spreader, and the Flexible Flyer sled. The Lutheran Home (E. Main St. between Zelley Ave. and Curtis) was his house,

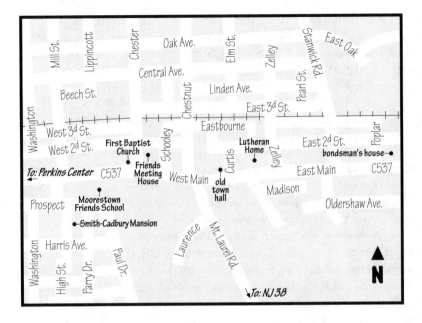

which, according to legend, the meeting considered too ostentatious for a Friend. In 1920 it was bought by Eldridge R. Johnson, founder of the Victor Talking Machine Company (later part of RCA; *see* Camden); it was bought by the Lutherans in 1946.

The Perkins Center for the Arts★ (Camden Ave. and Kings Hwy; 856-235-6488), located in a 1910 Tudor house on the site of a nursery that specialized in ornamental trees as far back as 1815, features fine arts and crafts exhibits; classical chamber music and folk, blues, and jazz concerts; special events; and a wide range of classes in the visual and performing arts. There are six shows a year, each lasting three to four weeks; they include an annual juried photography show, a members and faculty show, a works-on-paper show, and a special children's show (Young at Art). The center has a summer day camp for children from Camden and Moorestown, and the parks department puts on an outdoor summer concert series at the house. Gallery open Thursday and Friday, 10–4, weekends, 12–4. The center also sponsors programs at its new satellite in Collingswood.

Morristown Morris 18,544

I 287, US 202, NJ 24, 124, C 510, 511

The county seat of Morris County, Morristown was settled early in the 18th century and developed as an iron town and commercial center. It played an important role in the Revolution: after the victories at Trenton and Princeton in the winter of 1776–77, George Washington brought his tired troops here to spend the winter. While the troops encamped in the Loantaka Valley, Washington made his headquarters at Arnold Tavern in the center of town. He returned again in 1779–80; this time he stayed at a substantial private house in Morristown while the troops were quartered at Jockey Hollow, some six miles southwest of town. The strategic location of Morristown was such that there were always soldiers stationed here during the war, and the British army never went through Morristown. After 1838, when the Morris and Essex Railroad provided connections to Newark, the town attracted large numbers of wealthy residents, and it developed a reputation for having the densest concentration of millionaires in the state. Because of the Depression, many owners of large estates and houses could no longer maintain them, and you will come across several public buildings in Morristown that once were private homes.

Morristown is at the center of an explosive growth in corporate headquarters that took place in the '70s and '80s. Much of that growth occurred in the surrounding townships, but there are some striking signs of it in town as well, the most obvious being Headquarters Plaza. Despite these taller buildings and the enormous increase in traffic, the look of Morristown is still dominated by its large green, which was laid out in 1715 and is one of the few surviving town greens in the state. It is also interesting that Morristown has the feel of a city rather than of a town; in fact, its population is not that large and has only increased about 5 percent since 1970.

Morristown's historic district* includes Green, South, DeHart, Elm, Madison, Ann, Court, High, Hill, James, King, Doughty, Market, Morris, Oak, Prospect, Washington, and Pine sts.; Macculloch, Madison, Maple, Ford, Mt. Kemble, Speedwell, Western, Wetmore, and Colles aves.; Altamont Ct.; Catherine La.; Miller Rd.; and Blachley, Franklin, King, Lackawanna, Odgen, N. Park, Schuyler, and Farragut pls. This is primarily a 19th- and 20th-century area, but there are still some 18th-century buildings to be seen in town, among them the Condict house* (51 South St.), now the Women's City Club, and the Timothy Mills house* (27 Mills St.), c. 1740. Note also the courthouse* (Washington St. between Court St. and Western Ave.), built in 1827; the Presbyterian Church (65 Park Pl.), from 1895; and the former town hall (South St.), built just after World War I as a private home. At 100 South Street in a 1937 movie house the Community Theater (973-539-8008) features a wide variety of dance, musical, and theater events. If you happen to notice an unusual number of Seeing Eye dogs as you wander through the center of town, this is because The Seeing Eye, which trains the dogs, has its headquarters nearby. You can arrange a tour by calling 973-539-4425.

Several sites and buildings related to Washington's second time in Morristown make up the Morristown National Historical Park, the first historical park established by the federal government (in 1933). (Arnold Tavern, where Washington stayed the first time, was moved in 1886 to make way for an office building; it later burned and had to be torn down.) In addition to the Ford Mansion (30 Washington Place; 973-539-2016), where Washington had his headquarters, and the Jockey Hollow Encampment Area, where the troops were quartered, the park includes a museum (located behind the Ford house), the New Jersey Brigade Area, and the site of Fort Nonsense. Jacob Ford Jr. was a wealthy Morristown merchant and powder maker who died early in the Revolution; his widow offered Washington the use of her beautiful Georgian house, built earlier in the 1770s. The house has been furnished to look as it did when Washington was in residence (this means much of it is quite sparsely furnished, as Mrs. Ford was concerned that her belongings not be pilfered by colonial troops). Adjacent to the Ford Mansion is the Historical Museum and Library, with displays relating to the 1779–80 encampment and other artifacts and memorabilia of Washington and the Revolution. Museum open daily, 9–5. Tours of the mansion leave from the museum daily, 10–4. Admission charged. Closed New Year's Day, Thanksgiving, and Christmas. The museum will be closed for a period in 2005, but tours of the mansion will continue.

To reach the Jockey Hollow area take Western Ave. south for about six miles. On your way you will pass the entrance to the site of Fort Nonsense, an earthwork built on a 600-foot hill, fortified on Washington's orders in

1777. Nothing remains of the fortification, but there is an explanatory plaque and a view of the town that will give you a sense of why—situated as it is on a shoulder of Mt. Kemble with the Normandy Heights and the Watchung Mountains to the east, Gillespie Hill to the west, and Horse Hill to the north—Morristown was a strategically advantageous location. The fort's name is supposed to have developed because people forgot why the fort had been built and assumed it must have been created to make work. (Frank Stockton, who lived in Morristown for a while, accepted this theory, and in "The Story of Fort Nonsense" he offers it as evidence of Washington's astute understanding of the need to keep his troops feeling useful.)

Some 10,000 troops were quartered at Jockey Hollow in 1779–80 and endured a winter worse than the one at Valley Forge. Model huts, like those the soldiers built for themselves, were re-created during the 1930s by the Civilian Conservation Corps, and the various areas used by the troops have been delineated and are clearly marked. Also at Jockey Hollow is the Wick House, a mid-18th-century farmhouse and garden, which have been restored to show how a prosperous farmer would have lived. According to legend, the Wick daughter hid her horse in the house to prevent the soldiers from appropriating it. There are usually school programs in the Wick House in the morning, November–May, but you are welcome to look around in the afternoon if someone is there. Office usually open 9:30–4:30. You can pick up maps at the visitor center (973-543-4030) and take your own tour of the park, and there is usually someone around to answer questions. The New Jersey Brigade Area is two miles southwest of Jockey Hollow. This site, like Fort Nonsense, is not staffed, but there are interpretive signs. (The Cross Estate Gardens are nearby; *see* Bernardsville.) The park also has 26 miles of trails for hikers, riders, and cross-country skiers, and there are picnic facilities and a lake for swimming in the adjacent Lewis Morris Park (*see* below).

The park schedule often changes, so it is best to check before you go (this applies to the museum and mansion as well). The grounds at Jockey Hollow are open daily, dawn–dusk, and the visitor center is open 9–5 daily. Closed New Year's Day, Thanksgiving, and Christmas.

While Alexander Hamilton, who accompanied Washington to Morristown, was staying at the Ford Mansion, he courted and became betrothed to Elizabeth Schuyler, then visiting her aunt at what is now the Schuyler–Hamilton–Jabez Campfield House (5 Olyphant Pl.; 973-267-4039, 973-539-7502; Jabez Campfield was a surgeon in the Revolutionary Army and owner of the house). This colonial clapboard house (1760) has been lovingly restored with period furnishings by the D.A.R.; a re-created colonial garden is on the grounds. Open Sunday, 2–4 and by appointment. Closed holidays. Admission charged.

One of the local ironworks was Stephen Vail's Speedwell, which, in the early 19th century, built most of the machinery for the S.S. *Savannah*, the first trans-Atlantic steamship. The ironworks was converted to a cotton factory in the 1820s. The first public demonstration of the telegraph took place at Speedwell in 1838: Vail's son had worked with Samuel F. B. Morse in developing it. Much of the Vail homestead has been preserved and forms the backbone of Historic Speedwell* (333 Speedwell Ave.; 973-540-0211), a national historic site. On the site are several 18th- and 19th-century buildings, including the Vail factory, now a national historic landmark. Not all the buildings were originally part of the Vail homestead. Exhibits in various of the buildings deal with early ironworks, the development of the telegraph, farm tools, the S.S. *Savannah*, and the like. Open April–October, Wednesday–Saturday, 10–5, Sunday, 12–5; groups by appointment. Admission charge.

Another of Morristown's 19th-century residents who influenced the development of the state was George P. Macculloch, the driving force behind the construction of the Morris Canal. His house, started in 1810, lived in by his descendants until 1949, and now the Macculloch Hall Historical Museum (45 Macculloch Ave.; 973-538-2404), is furnished with period pieces. The permanent collection focuses on English and American decorative arts of the 18th and 19th centuries and incudes fine china, oriental rugs, and the largest collection in the United States of the prints, drawings, and memorabilia of Thomas Nast (*see* below), who apparently did not want his work to be "consigned to the cold tomb of a museum." Changing exhibits tend to focus on New Jersey history and art and to reflect what is in the permanent collection. The gardens have been preserved; of particular note is the wisteria, apparently the first in the country, brought from Japan by Commodore Matthew C. Perry as a house gift. Museum open Wednesday, Thursday and Sunday, 1–4; groups by appointment. Admission charged. Gardens open daily dawn–dusk.

One of Morristown's renowned citizens at the turn of the 20th century was the cartoonist Thomas Nast, remembered today for having invented the donkey and elephant as symbols of the Democratic and Republican parties and for popularizing the image of Uncle Sam in striped trousers and tall hat, and, possibly, that of Santa Claus suggested by Clement Moore's "The Night before Christmas." To his contemporaries, however, he was known for his crusade against the corruption of Boss Tweed and Tammany Hall. His house,* known as Villa Fontana (Macculloch Ave. and Miller Rd.), built in the 1860s, is a national historic landmark.

The Morris Museum (6 Normandy Heights Rd.; 973-971-3700) is a general museum with permanent and changing exhibits in the arts and sciences. Among the collections are dolls, toys, early American and Native American artifacts, costumes and textiles, and dinosaurs and fossils. Located in the former house of Peter H. B. and Adaline Frelinghuysen, the museum is also home to the Bickford Theater (973-971-3706), which puts on plays, a children's theater program, and a jazz series. The museum sponsors a variety of workshops and educational programs. Open Tuesday, Wednesday, Friday, and Saturday, 10–5; Thursday, 10–8, Sunday 1–5. Admission charge.

Acorn Hall* (68 Morris Ave.; 973-267-3465), an Italianate house built in 1853 and the headquarters of the Morris County Historical Society, is also a museum. Most of the furnishings have been in the house since it was built, and the gardens have been restored to represent a Victorian garden from the 1853–88 period. Inside the house are exhibits on Morris County history; these change twice a year. The society also sponsors a lecture series (here and at the Freylinghausen Arboretum). Gardens open daily dawn to dusk. House open Monday and Thursday, 10–4 (last tour at 3:30), Sunday, 1–4 (last tour at 3:30); groups by appointment other days. Closed major holidays. Admission charge.

On Whippany Farm, built in 1891 as a summer home for George Griswold and Sarah Ballantine Frelinghuysen, is the Frelinghuysen Arboretum (973-326-7600). The Morris County Park Commission uses the Colonial Revival house* as its administrative headquarters, but the extensive arboretum (127 acres) is open to the public. Among its attractions are a rose garden, a crabapple collection, a lilac garden, two self-guiding trails, and a braille nature trail. You can pick up maps and guides at the Joseph F. Haggerty Education Center. The center has a botany library and classrooms; in the lobby art shows are hung; these change every month. The center is attached to the stable where the better horses were kept, and you can see some of their carriages there. Tours of the arboretum are given weekends at 2, April–October. The gardens are open daily (except Thanksgiving, Christmas, and New Year's), 8:30–sunset; the buildings close at 4:30.

About a mile west of the center of town (take Washington St., NJ 24, to Kahdena Rd.; 973-326-7645) is Fosterfields Living Historical Museum. This museum is actually a working farm, used to demonstrate farming methods from 1880 to 1930. The mid-19th-century main house was built by the grandson of Paul Revere, and for a short time in the 1870s it was rented to Bret Harte. It is open for tours Thursday–Sunday at 1:30. There are several outbuildings and barns, including a restored carriage house, which has on display three carriages used by the Fosters. The first floor of the farmhouse, which dates from 1918–27 (and replaces the original 18th-century house, which burned), is open for tours. Animals on the farm include chickens, draft horses, Jersey cows, sheep, and pigs. Future plans include a transportation museum. Open April–October, Wednesday–Saturday and holidays, 10–5; Sundays, 12–5. Groups by appointment. On Labor Day weekend one of the most popular sheepdog trials in the Northeast— attracting some 2,000 spectators—takes place at Fosterfields (call 973-326-7645 for more information).

On a hill with lovely views into town is the campus of the Rabbinical College of America (226 Sussex Ave., off Speedwell Ave.), said to be the world's largest campus for Hasidic Judaic Studies (81 acres). The original buildings were once the campus for a Catholic reform school for girls.

Adjacent to Jockey Hollow is Lewis Morris County Park amd Cultural Center (also accessible from NJ 24; 973-326-7600), the oldest park in the

Morris County park system. Named for the first governor of New Jersey, the 1,100-acre park contains facilities for picnicking, swimming, boating, fishing, biking, horseback riding, and camping. There are also several miles of hiking and cross-country ski trails, a fitness trail, fields, open woods, a children's play area, and playing fields. The cultural center (300 Mendham Rd.) is used for occasional public concerts and is available for use by nonprofit groups.

South of town are the Seaton Hackney Stables (440 South St.; 973-267-1372), part of the Loantaka Brook Reservation (973-326-7600). The reservation stretches southward into Chatham Township to include trails that end in the stables and at the Green Village post office. Available in other parts of the reservation are picnic facilities, softball fields, a children's play area, a fitness cluster, and trails suitable for hikers, bicyclers, and cross-country skiers.

North of the center of town is the William G. Mennen Sports Arena (161 Hanover Ave.; 973-326-7651), a three-rink skating facility with a year-round schedule. Special events are scheduled here, including dog shows and an annual circus.

The county is also developing Patriots' Path, a network of trails and open spaces linking parks, watersheds, and historic sites in southern Morris County. Within Morristown you can pick it up at the arboretum and near Speedwell Village, among several other places. Running parallel to the New Jersey Transit lines from Morris Ave. to Convent Rd. in Convent Station is the Traction Line recreation trail. This three-mile paved path also has a fitness course.

About four miles south of Morristown (take James St. out of town to C 663) is the village of New Vernon. Its historic district* includes Lee's Hill, Village, Millbrook, and Glen Alpin roads. The Tunis-Ellicks House (16 Village Rd.; 973-292-0161), a farmhouse built in 1795, is run as a house museum by the Harding Township Historical Society. Its restored kitchen wing is used for demonstrations of open-hearth cooking, and around the house is a re-created 1800 parlor garden featuring over 100 varieties of herbs and perennials. A tramp house dating to the 1870s has been reconstructed behind the house. On display in the house are exhibits depicting 18th-century life, as well as Tunis artifacts and other artifacts and pictures related to local history. Archives and office (973-292-3661) open Thursday, 10–4; house open by appointment. Nearby is the Silver Lake Historic District,* which includes Blue Mill, Dickson's Mill, Beuren, and Red Gate rds. and James St.

North of Morristown (take Speedwell Ave.) in the borough of Morris Plains is the Morris Plains museum (77 Glenbrook Rd; 973-683-1089). Housed on the second floor of the library, the museum expects to move in 2005 to the community center on Jim Fear Dr. The museum concentrates on the history of the borough, with a collection that includes artifacts, old photographs, fossils, and tools. Call for the hours in the new location.

Mountainside Union 6,602

First settled in the late 1660s by a group of miners from Cornwall, England, who were looking for mineral deposits in the Watchung Mountains, Mountainside is primarily a residential community. A large portion of Union County's 2,000-acre wooded Watchung Reservation falls within its borders. Within the reservation is the Trailside Nature and Science Center (452 New Providence Rd.; 908-789-3670), a complex containing a visitor center (currently closed for expansion) and a natural history museum (built in 1941 and apparently the state's first nature center). The original visitor center was a Michael Graves building dating to 1974; after it reopens (by 2006), it will be twice as large and contain the museum as well, with permanent exhibits that focus on the history (both human and natural) of the reservation, pond life, and reptiles, as well as changing exhibits of artwork and photographs. The museum's current exhibits include taxidermy, birds and mammals found on the reservation, fluorescent minerals, fossils, and a butterfly garden. A bird-attraction area, and herb, wildflower, and fern gardens are on the grounds. Open daily, 1–5; groups by appointment. The center supplies information and referrals on plants and animals including injured and orphaned wildlife and offers a variety of workshops and educational programs for children and adults.

Within the reservation are over 13 miles of marked hiking trails, several nature trails, and over 25 miles of bridle trails. In winter all the trails are open for cross-country skiing. Stop at the visitor center for maps. The Watchung Riding Stable (1160 Summit La.; 908-789-3665) offers classes for adults and children and a summer camp for children, sponsors shows and a drill team, and rents horses by the hour. Open daily, 7:30–4, mid-March–November; 8–4, December–mid-March (rental hours are much more limited). You can explore the deserted village of Feltville* (*see* Berkeley Heights), a factory town dating from the 1840s; fish in Seeley's Pond and Green Brook; and fish and boat (with permission from the parks department) in Surprise Lake. The county nursery is also at the reservation.

Also partially in Mountainside is Echo Lake Park (Mountain Ave; 908-527-4900), one of the many parks in Union County designed by Frederick Law Olmsted. Its 140 acres offer opportunities for boating, fishing, sledding, snow-boarding, and ice-skating. There are athletic fields, a playground, a dog park (908-628-4900), and picnic facilities, as well as a fitness course that includes a 10-station course for people in wheelchairs.

Part of the Children's Specialized Hospital (New Providence Rd. south of 22; 908-233-3720) is in a 1750 farmhouse built by Jonathan Crane. The house was purchased in 1875 by Thomas Drew, related by marriage to the

Barrymore family of actors; according to local legend, John, Ethel, Lionel, and Maurice Barrymore all stayed here. Although the hospital, which purchased the property in 1891, has altered the house considerably, it tries to maintain the look of a late-19th-century mansion in the older section. Call for more information about visiting.

Also on New Providence Rd. (on the westbound side of 22; 908-232-9282) is the Deacon Hetfield house★ (c. 1760 with 19th-century additions), moved half a mile along 22 in 1985. This house, which retains its original plaster, beams, and mantels, was the home of the writer MacKinlay Kantor in the 1930s. The kitchen, part of the oldest section, has been restored as a colonial kitchen; the parlor is Victorian. Open 3d Sunday of the month, March–May and September–December, 1–3, and for various special events such as holiday and spring craft boutiques and Union County's annual Four Centuries in a Weekend program.

Mount Holly   Burlington   10,728

NJ 38, C 537, 541, 628, 630

Mount Holly, the Burlington County seat, was settled by Quakers in the 18th century and exhibits the characteristic brick buildings and wide streets of the early Quaker communities. A mill was established on the north branch of Rancocas Creek in the 1720s and an ironworks and clothing factory in the 1730s. (The clothing factory was set up by Josiah White, ancestor of the Josiah White who realized the importance of coal as a fuel and formed the Lehigh Coal and Navigation Company, and of Joseph C. White and Elizabeth C. White, who developed New Jersey's cranberry and blueberry industries respectively.) Also in the 1730s Benjamin Franklin published in the *Pennsylvania Gazette* an account of a Mount Holly witch trial in which two witches were accused of making the livestock sing and dance; accusers and accused had to stand trial together, and only the accused sank in the trial by water. Franklin apparently made up the tale out of whole cloth, but what motivated his choice of place is the source of much speculation.

By the late 18th century, Mount Holly was important enough to be made the county seat. The Burlington County Court House (west side of High St. at Union St.), a beautiful two-story brick Georgian building dating from 1796, may be the oldest courthouse in the United States still used for its original purpose. The two flanking buildings date from 1807.

Until its conversion into a museum in 1966, the Burlington County Prison Museum★ (128 High St.; 609-265-5476, 609-518-7667) was probably the oldest operating jail in the United States. Designed by the architect of the Washington Monument and built in 1810 according to the most modern principles of penal practice (prisoners had individual cells and could learn a trade in the prison workshop), the stone jail may have been the first fireproof building in the United States. The building is now a national historic landmark. Open Thursday–Saturday, 10–4, Sunday, 12–4.

What is probably the state's oldest surviving schoolhouse★ on its original foundations is to be found at 35 Brainerd St. (609-267-6996). The one-room brick building, dating from 1759, is run as a museum by the New Jersey chapter of the Colonial Dames of America. It is furnished as a mid-18th-century schoolroom, with a schoolmaster's desk and Bible, benches for 15–20 children, old copybooks, period maps, and quill pens. Open by appointment. And what may be the oldest volunteer fire department in the state—it dates from 1752—is to be found at 15 Pine.

John Woolman, the Quaker whom many have credited with beginning the antislavery movement in this country and whose journal remains a well-loved and much-read book (it was the second book chosen for the Harvard Classics), was born nearby and moved to Mount Holly in 1740. The house he built for his daughter (99 Branch St.; 609-267-3226) in 1771 (the "i. e. w. 1783" visible on the south elevation refers to Jabez Woolman and his wife, who bought the house that year), with two acres surrounding it, once Woolman's orchards, has been preserved as a memorial. There is a lovely garden, and in the peaceful room (used for the Mount Holly Quaker meetings January–April to save heating the big house in town) are a few mementos of Woolman and his times, among them his chair and a fragment of his handwriting. Open Friday, 10–2; groups and other times by appointment.

Woolman's grandfather Henry Burr in 1695 purchased Peachfield Plantation from the widow of John Skene, the first Freemason resident in America. Burr built a new, ironstone, house on the property in 1725; a wing was added in 1732. The property remained in the Burr family until the late 1920s, when the house was severely damaged in a fire. Rebuilt and handsomely furnished with 18th- and 19th-century pieces, Peachfield* (180 Burr Rd.; 609-267-6996) is run as a house museum by the Colonial Dames of America; the Peachfield land is still being farmed. Open by appointment. Admission charged.

John Brainerd, the famous missionary, was also active in Mount Holly, preaching here from 1767 to 1775, preaching at the Native American reservation in nearby Brotherton (now Indian Mills), and founding the Mount Holly Presbyterian Church. He sold the land on which the Friends Meeting House (1775; Garden and Buttonwood sts.) stands. The house was used by the Hessians as a slaughterhouse in December 1776 (apparently, the marks of their cleavers are still to be seen on the benches) and by the state legislature in 1779.

The Mount Holly Historic District* encompasses much of the town's center and includes 18th- and 19th-century buildings on Mill, Pine, High,

MOUNT HOLLY

Garden, White, Union, Bispham, Madison, Buttonwood, Branch, Church, and Ridgeway sts., as well as Park Dr. and Commerce Place. At 211 Mill St. is the Stephen Girard house (c. 1779). The American financier who was later to be prominent in financing the Revolution and who founded Girard College in Philadelphia lived here for a year or two. The Three Tuns Tavern (Pine and Mill sts.) dates from 1723. Off Pine St. is Mount Holly Park, situated on the holly-covered hill that gave the town its name. In the municipal parking lot is the Shinn Curtis Log House (Municipal Dr.; 609-267-8844). Discovered in the 1960s when Rancocas Rd. was being widened, this 1712 house has been moved and restored; it now serves as a visitor center and museum for the local historical society. The exhibits, which change from time to time, feature an eclectic set of artifacts, mainly relating to local and county history. Open Friday, 10–2; Groups and other times by appointment.

Two miles east of Mount Holly (C 530 or 621 to the Smithville-Jacksonville Rd.; turn left off 530, right off 621) is Smithville County Park* (609-261-5068, 609-261-3780). In the 1850s Shreveville (as Smithville was then called) was the site of a large industrial complex, where cotton was spun, woven, and printed. The enterprise failed, and between 1858 and 1865 Shreveville lay dormant. In 1865 the complex was purchased by Hezekiah Bradley Smith, a machinery manufacturer from Lowell, Massachusetts. Smith converted the various cotton factories and began producing woodworking machines; eventually, the H. B. Smith Machine Company would produce one-quarter of the country's woodworking machinery. Its Star bicycle also proved highly successful. Smith renovated the workers' houses, built new ones, and added a boardinghouse with a dining room and theater. Three hundred acres of farmland were added to the complex, supplying much of the town's food. He expanded the Shreves' mansion, adding, among other amenities, a billiard room and bowling alley. After Smith's death the company continued, and one of its most remarkable achievements was the Bicycle Railway, intended to carry employees from Mount Holly to Smithville. Workers glided along a rail on special self-propelled bicycles, reaching a maximum speed of 18 miles per hour, but since a second rail was never built, there were always delays when a rider approached from the opposite direction. Although the Smithville company was a victim of the Depression, descendants of the family continued to live in the mansion until 1962. Since 1975 it has belonged to the county, and the facilities currently include the orientation and exhibit center, the Victorian house museum, the casino annex and art gallery, and the formal gardens and grounds. You can also take a self-guided walking tour. The grounds are open 8–5, weekdays, the mansion is open for tours at 1, 2, and 3, Wednesday and Sunday, May–October; groups by appointment (609-265-5068). Admission fee.

The park itself includes land along Rancocas Creek and Smithville Lake, and provides opportunities for hiking, biking, fishing, canoeing, and picnicking. Open daily, dawn to dusk.

Northwest of Mount Holly, on the Mount Holly–Rancocas Rd. (C 626) is Rancocas State Park (609-726-1191), 1,252 acres of largely undeveloped land, suitable for fishing, hiking, bird-watching, and informal picnics. A self-guided interpretive trail goes through the natural area along the Rancocas Creek. Part of the land north of the river has been leased to the New Jersey Audubon Society. Its Rancocas Nature Center (794 Rancocas Rd.; 609-261-2495) encompasses 200 acres of fields, woodlands, and freshwater tidal marsh, with self-guiding nature trails. In a mid-19th-century farmhouse is a small hands-on nature center; here you can see nature displays and live New Jersey reptiles. The center also sponsors a large number of educational programs and field trips. Open mid-March–mid-October, Tuesday–Saturday, 9–5, Sunday, 12–5; mid-October–mid-March, Tuesday–Saturday, 9–4, Sunday, 12–4.

Just beyond Timbuctoo, off 626, is the Rancocas Indian Reservation (609-261-4747), 350 acres the Powhatan Renape Nation has leased from the state. At the Indian Heritage Museum you will find some 30 cases containing a variety of exhibits and dioramas, some showing types of settlements or the part played by animals in different Native American cultures, others containing artifacts, ranging from musical instruments to weapons. There is also an art gallery, an outdoor re-creation of a Woodland village, and nature trails that take you down to the river, which splits at this point, one branch going to Millville, the other to the Delaware. Tours also include a look at the reservation's buffalo. A juried art show and festival takes place twice each year, in May and October. Open Saturday, 10–3, March–December; Tuesday–Thursday by appointment, July and August; Tuesday and Thursday by appointment, September–June. Admission charged.

South of Mount Holly in Lumberton (take C 541) is the Lumberton Museum (602 Main St.; 609-267-3217). Housed in the Ridgeway Gaun Building, which was built in 1896 by the Junior Order of American Mechanics Lodge and served as the Lumberton town hall from 1938 to 1982, the museum features artifacts from the area, including arrowheads from the creek and turn-of-the-20th-century clothing. Talks at the monthly meetings (the 3d Tuesday of the month) are open to the public. Museum open September–June, 3d Saturday of the month, 10–12.

Mount Laurel Burlington 40,221

 NJ TNPK EXIT 4, I 295, NJ 38, 73

Composed of several old communities, the modern township of Mount Laurel has seen its population increase almost sevenfold over the last 40 years. The name of the town is familiar to many in New Jersey because of the 1975 and 1983 court decisions requiring the town to provide a certain amount of middle- and low-income housing, a decision that has had repercussions in most other growing New Jersey communities.

Mount Laurel was the home of the noted suffragist Alice Paul (1885–1977). Trained as a sociologist, Paul helped revitalize a faltering women's suffrage movement, continuing her fight for women's rights after the 20th Amendment was passed. She drafted what is believed to be the earliest version of the Equal Rights Amendment. Paulsdale,* the Greek Revival farmhouse in which she was born (118 Hooten Rd.; 609-231-1885), was built c. 1840 and is a national historic landmark. Now home to the Alice Paul Institute, which works as a leadership development center for women and girls, Paulsdale has been restored, and the institute plans to restore the garage and icehouse as well. The institute sponsors a variety of special events, including a summer camp and a women's history book club. Tours by appointment (three weeks' notice is requested).

The Evesham Friends' Meeting House* (Moorestown–Mt. Laurel Rd.) dates to 1760 and replaced the original 17th-century building. The eastern end was built, with the help of Native Americans, from sandstone quarried across the street, the western end was added in 1798. Twenty years before that the meetinghouse had served as a barracks for the British. The Thomas Smith House* (also known as the General Clinton House, 1645 Hainesport–Mt. Laurel Rd.), built in 1764 with a second section added 20 years later, served as headquarters for the British commander that same year. Note also Farmers Hall* (Hainesport–Mt. Laurel and Moorestown–Mt. Laurel rds.), built in the 1860s.

PAWS Farm Nature Center (1105 Hainesport–Mt. Laurel Rd., east of Hartford Rd.; 609-778-8795), located on an 18th-century farm, shelters wild and domestic animals. The farmhouse, smokehouse, ice house, and dairy barn are open to visitors, and there are nature displays, a butterfly garden, an archaeological trail, a self-guided nature trail, and a 20th-century welcome center with many hands-on exhibits. The farm sponsors a visiting-pet program, summer classes and field trips, educational programs, and a variety of special events. Open Wednesday–Sunday, 10–4; groups by appointment. Admission charge.

Mullica Hill Gloucester 1,658

US 322, NJ 45, 77, C 581

Mullica Hill, located in the center of one of the largest fruit-growing regions in New Jersey, was settled in the late 17th century by four Finns, the brothers Eric, John, Olaf, and William Mullica. (Because Finland was controlled by Sweden at the time, they are often identified as Swedes.) There were many Quakers among the early settlers as well, and the town is reputed to have sent an all-Quaker company to the Civil War. The Mullica Hill Historic District* includes over 100 buildings on East Ave., Woodstown Rd., and Church, High, Mill, New, and Union streets. The Friends Meeting House (c. 1806; Main St.) stands on land purchased from the first person to settle on the south side of Raccoon Creek. Many of the older buildings have been converted to crafts and antiques shops, and there are some 80 antiques and specialty shops in Mullica Hill. The Merchants Association (856-881-6800) sponsors several special events: open houses, a doll and toy show, and a tour of historic houses the first Saturday in December. Call for the precise dates. Because of the orchards, the area is particularly lovely in spring. (The peach blossoms are usually at their peak in mid-April.)

The Old Town Hall Museum (S. Main St., NJ 77, and Woodstown Rd., NJ 45; 856-478-4949) occupies the former town hall, built in 1871 by a private stock company. The museum, run by the Harrison Township Historical Society, includes a re-created country store and schoolroom and features permanent and changing exhibits. The collection includes farm implements and Native American artifacts. Exhibits usually focus on South Jersey, particularly Harrison Township; past ones, for example, have dealt with agriculture, Quakerism, and images in art of southern New Jersey. The historical society sponsors annual ghost tours and a Groundhog Day Dinner; it also offers programs for children. Open weekends April–3d weekend in May and mid-October–1st weekend in December, 1–4, and for some of the special events in town; groups and other times by appointment.

South and west of town on US 322 is Heritage Vineyards (480 Mullica Hill Rd., US 322; 856-589-4474). The vineyard is on land that has been operated as a farm by the same family since 1851, and there are also many acres of fruit trees, particularly peach trees. During growing season hayrides are available weekends, 9–5, for those picking their own fruits and vegetables; hayrides and tours for groups by appointment. It is hoped that eventually the winery can be included on the tours. Open daily Easter–December, 8–8; January–Easter, weekdays, 9–5, weekends 9–6.

National Park Gloucester 3,205

C 642, 643

The site of an important battle in the Revolutionary War, Red Bank Battlefield,* a national historic landmark, is in the borough of National Park (so named because Congress in 1870 authorized the purchase of a portion of the battlefield). Fort Mercer was hastily erected here in the apple orchard of James and Ann Whitall (he was a wealthy Quaker farmer and merchant) to protect the river approach to Philadelphia. Troops under Christopher Greene built a trick wall in the earthworks and withheld their fire until the Hessian troops, who outnumbered them more than two to one, were so close that they ended up with wadding in their chests. Most historians believe the American victory helped delay the British navy's entrance into Philadelphia and helped convince the French to enter the war. Count von Donop, the Hessian commander, was fatally wounded in the battle.

After the engagement the James and Ann Whitall house* (100 Hessian Ave.; 856-853-5120) was used as a hospital for wounded Hessians and Americans. It is said that during the fighting Ann Whitall, whose nine children had retired to Woodbury for safety, continued her spinning, and when a cannonball came through the house, she picked up her spinning wheel and resumed spinning in the basement. After the battle she nursed both Hessians and Continentals. A brick building (1748) with a stone wing, the house bears scars from the battle. It now contains a county-run museum. The rooms have period furnishings, and displays change periodically. The museum sponsors a variety of special events, including encampments, an annual flower show, and a Christmas open house. Open April–October, Saturday and Sunday, 1–4; November–March, Wednesday–Friday, 9–12 and 1–4, Saturday and Sunday, 1–4; it is recommended that you call ahead. Groups by appointment. The battle is restaged annually on a Sunday close to 22 October, the date of the actual engagement, and the event includes a show and demonstrations of site-specific crafts. You can reach the river in the 44-acre park, which also has a picnic pavilion for groups with reservations. Open daily, dawn–dusk.

Nearby (100 Grove Ave.) is the James Whitall Jr. house,* built in 1766 by one of the Whitall sons.

Neptune   Monmouth 5,218 (borough) 27,690 (township)

GARDEN STATE PKWY EXIT 100, NJ 18, 33, 35, 66

The birthplace of actor Jack Nicholson, and home of the world's largest manufacturer of practical jokes and magic tricks, Neptune is the site of Monmouth County's first county park, the 580-acre Shark River Park (Schoolhouse Rd.; 732-922-3868).

The park is hilly, and there are pitch pine and oak forests with a dense understory of sheep laurel, ferns, pepperbush, and blueberries. The Shark River goes through the park, and because of the cedar swamps and sphagnum bogs, the trails can be wet. In addition to its hiking, cross-country skiing, and nature trails, the park contains picnic facilities, a pond for fishing and skating, and shuffleboard courts. A county golf course (Old Corlies Ave.; 732-922-4141) abuts Shark River Park to the east; it is open year-round.

Although the Neptune Historical Museum has been closed, its local-history collection remains in the library and will be open to the public on a limited basis. Call 732-988-5200, ext. 230, for details.

South of Neptune, in Wall Township (across from Airplane Park), is the Allgor-Barkalow Homestead Museum* (1701 New Bedford Rd.; 732-974-1430), run by the Old Wall Historical Society. The museum is housed in an early-19th-century farmhouse, and in one room the society has re-created the country store that had been in the original farmhouse. Period furnishings date to the 1840s, and there are also exhibits that change from time to time. Also on the property is a one-room schoolhouse in use 1855–1935. The society sponsors special events each year, including antiques shows in March and October and a quilt festival in June. Open Sunday, 1–4; groups and other times by appointment.

Also in Wall is the Infoage Science and History Learning Center (2201 Marconi Rd.; 732-280-3000; take New Bedford Rd. from the museum north to Belmar Blvd.; turn left on Belmar Blvd., right on Monmouth Blvd., until you reach Marconi Rd.; turn right on Marconi). The center is located in the former Camp Evans,* where from 1912 to 1998, pathbreaking advances in optics and communications, from Marconi and worldwide telegraph communications to radar (including weather radar), to bouncing signals off the moon. The displays at the center emphasize what was done in a particular building; in the Project Diana building, for example, are exhibits concerned with space travel. The National Broadcasters Hall of Fame is also located at Camp Evans. Eventually the center hopes to house its exhibits in four buildings. Open Sunday 1–4 and by appointment.

Newark Essex 273,546

I 78, 280, 287, NJ TNPK EXIT 14, US 1, 9, 22, NJ 21

New Jersey's largest city, and one of the first to be settled by the English, Newark was founded in 1666 by a group of about 40 men, women, and children who left Connecticut to seek a place where they could live as they chose, which meant a place where the church would have ascendancy over the state. They settled near the intersection of Broad and Market sts. and were soon joined by other families from Connecticut. Toward the end of the century the settlement became known for its apple cider, which was thought to be of higher quality than that produced elsewhere in the colonies.

Eventually the religious monopoly was broken, but the community continued to grow very slowly until the end of the 18th century, when small-scale manufacturing began to appear: hat factories in the 1780s, shoe factories in the 1790s. In the 1830s the coming of the Morris Canal and the railroads connected Newark more readily to raw materials (particularly coal and iron from the west) and markets (particularly in the south). The city became a leading center for all types of leather goods, for jewelry, and for carriages. Brewing, established in Newark in the 1840s, remained one of the city's largest industries until very recently (only one brewery, its copper vats and steaming smokestacks familiar to those who use Newark Airport, is in operation today). Financial services also appeared early—the first bank in 1804, the first insurance company in 1810. Newark's development as a transportation center continued with the opening of Port Newark in 1915 and of Newark Airport in 1927. Although Newark has been losing population since World War II and has suffered most of the problems faced by older cities all over the country, it remains a center for financial services and transportation, it has become a center for education, and it is attracting a considerable number of artists. Major construction projects by large companies in the area of Penn Station and on the Passaic River (before the turn of the 20th century a popular spot for recreation) have been joined by projects initiated by Rutgers University and the New Jersey Institute of Technology in the area near Military Park. Port Newark, with Port Elizabeth, is a major facility for container ships, and the airport handles some 29 million passengers a year (to say nothing of 73,000 tons of airmail). Newark has not conquered all its problems, not the least of which is its financial situation—with all the cultural, medical, and educational facilities, not to mention federal, state, and county courts and offices, as much as 80 percent of Newark's property is off the tax rolls—but most people seem to feel the corner has been turned.

The list of famous people connected with Newark is long. One of the most remarkable is Seth Boyden, who came to Newark around 1815 and, except when he took part in the Gold Rush, spent the rest of his life in the city. Boyden invented the process for making patent leather, developed a way to make malleable iron and to refine zinc from New Jersey ores, designed a train that could go up grades, invented machines to make nails and form hats, improved the daguerreotype process, and, at the end of his life, developed a giant strawberry. He profited from none of his inventions and spent his last days in a small house purchased for him by some of the men who did (he died in 1870). Another Newark resident, Hannibal Goodwin, the pastor of the House of Prayer (407 Broad St.), invented the flexible film used by Edison in the development of motion pictures.

Among the writers Newark can claim are Stephen Crane, best known for *The Red Badge of Courage*, born here in 1871 (his birthplace on Mulberry Pl. was torn down in 1940); Mary Mapes Dodge, the author of *Hans Brinker; or The Silver Skates*, described by one Dutch bookseller as the best book ever written about Holland, although Dodge did not visit the Netherlands until many years after the book was published; Howard Garis, the author of the Uncle Wiggily tales, which first appeared in the *Newark Evening News*; the playwright Imamu Amiri Baraka (LeRoi Jones); the poet Allen Ginsberg, who later lived in Paterson, where his father taught English at the high school; the novelist and dog fancier Albert Payson Terhune (*see* Wayne); and, of course, the novelist Philip Roth.

Musicians and entertainers connected with Newark include the opera singer Maria Jeritza, who moved to Newark in the 1940s; Jerome Kern, who graduated from Newark High School in 1902; and Sarah Vaughan, Jerry Lewis, Samuel Augustus Ward (he wrote "America the Beautiful" and is buried in Mount Pleasant Cemetery; *see* below), and Dore Schary, who were all born in Newark. Moe Berg, presumably the only professional baseball player who ever served as an undercover agent (in World War II), was raised in Newark, and a more recent homegrown professional athlete, Shaquille O'Neal, has a park in the South Ward named for him.

The state's first daily newspaper, the *Daily Advertiser*, was started in Newark in 1832; the first regular radio station on the eastern seaboard, WJZ, which was the first to broadcast a world series (in 1921), was a Newark station; the first municipally supported summer school was established in Newark in 1886; the first blackout test in World War II took place in Newark.

A tour of Newark's downtown should include the late-18th-century Old First Presbyterian Church★ (820 Broad St.), the direct descendant of the church built by Newark's original settlers. From the 1760s until 1986, Old First owned the prime real estate across from it on Broad Street.

North of Old First, at Washington Park, is the Newark Museum (49 Washington St.; 973-596-6550). In the late 1980s Michael Graves designed a striking addition to its 1920s building; the museum now contains 80 galleries.

Main St.
West 7th Ave.
North 7th St.
North 6th St.
North 5th St.
North 4th St.
North 3d St.
North 2d St.
North 1st St.
Branch Brook
Ridge St.
Sacred Heart Ca
Orange St.
West Market St.
Myrtle Ave.
Roseville Ave.
Gould Ave.
South 13th St.
South 12th St.
South 11th St.
South 10th St.
9th Ave.
Central Ave.
280
280
Clifton Ave.
Mt. Prospect Ave.
Victoria Ave.
Garside
Cutler
Cra
Branch Brook Park
East 7th Ave.
8th Ave.
Orange St.
Newark St.
Nesbitt St.
Or
28
North 5th St.
North 4th St.
North 3d St.
North 2d St.
North 1st St.
Morris Ave.
Sussex Ave.
Duryea St.
Hecker St.
Hudson
Jay St.
Dickerson
James St.
South 9th St.
South 8th St.
South 7th St.
South 6th St.
11th Ave.
West Market St.
Hartford St.
New St.
Bond
Hudson
New St.
Lock St.
Central Ave.
Ru
12th Ave.
Cabinet St.
Bergen St.
Cabinet St.
Norfolk St.
Newark St.
Wisley St.
N.J.I.T.
Summit St.
Blee
13th Ave.
13th Ave.
West Market St.
Raymond Blvd.
Rutger
University
Warren St.
University of Medicine & Dentristry
Essex County College
South Orange Ave.
Richmond St.
Boston St.
Wickliff St.
county park offices
Records Ave.
Stirling St.
Essex County Courthouse
14th Ave.
Littleton Ave.
Fairmount Ave.
Camden St.
Hunterdon St.
Morris Ave.
Bruce St.
Newton
Jones St.
South Orange Ave.
Howard
Dr. Martin Luther King Jr. Blvd.
Branford
University Ave.
15th Ave.
Bedford
Springfield Ave.
Mercer St.
William St.
16th Ave.
Court St.
West Kinney
Broome
Howard
Lincoln
Pear
17th Ave.
Boyd St.
Irvine Turner Blvd.
Montgomery St.
Hill
Walnut St.
18th Ave.
Spruce St.
Livingston St.
Charlton St.
Prince St.
Barclay
Somerset
Quitman
Governor
Washington
East Kinney
Bergen St.
Jelliff
Muhammad Ali Ave.
To: Lincoln Park
To: Feigenspan Mansion
Weequahic Park
South Park churc
Br

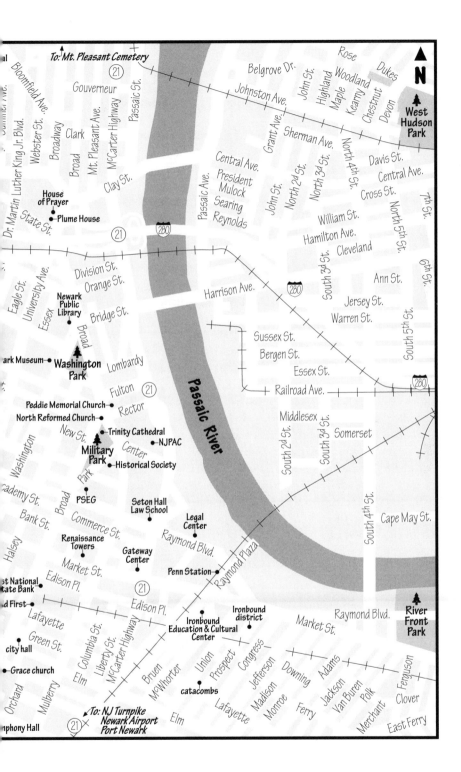

To: Mt. Pleasant Cemetery

Rose
Dukes

(21)

Belgrove Dr.

John St.
Highland
Woodland
Maple
Kearny
Chestnut
Devon

N

West Hudson Park

Bloomfield Ave.
Gouverneur
Passaic St.
Johnston Ave.
Grant Ave.
Sherman Ave.

Summit Ave.

Webster St.
Broadway
Clark
Mt. Pleasant Ave.
McCarter Highway

North 4th St.

Davis St.
Central Ave.

Broad
Clay St.

Central Ave.
President
Mulock
Searing
Reynolds

Passaic Ave.

John St.
North 2d St.
North 3d St.

Cross St.

7th St.

House of Prayer
Plume House

State St.

Dr. Martin Luther King Jr. Blvd.

(21)

(280)

William St.
Hamilton Ave.
Cleveland

North 5th St.

6th St.

Division St.
Orange St.

Ann St.

Eagle St.
University Ave.

Newark Public Library

Bridge St.

Harrison Ave.

(280)

South 3d St.

Jersey St.
Warren St.

South 5th St.

Essex

Broad

ark Museum
Washington Park

Lombardy

Sussex St.
Bergen St.
Essex St.

Railroad Ave.

(280)

Fulton

(21)

Rector

Middlesex

Somerset

South 2d St.
South 3d St.

Peddie Memorial Church
North Reformed Church

New St.

Trinity Cathedral
NJPAC

Military Park
Center
Historical Society

Washington

Park

PSEG

Seton Hall Law School

cademy St.

Broad

Commerce St.

Legal Center

Raymond Blvd.

South 4th St.

Cape May St.

Bank St.

Renaissance Towers

Gateway Center

Halsey

Market St.

Penn Station

Raymond Plaza

st National ate Bank

Edison Pl.

d First

(21)

Edison Pl.

Ironbound district

Raymond Blvd.

River Front Park

Lafayette

Green St.

city hall

Grace church

Columbia St.
Liberty St.
McCarter Highway

Ironbound Education & Cultural Center

Market St.

Elm

Bruen
McWhorter

Union
Prospect
Congress
Jefferson
Madison
Monroe
Downing
Ferry
Adams
Jackson
Van Buren
Polk
Merchant

Ferguson

Clover

Orchard

Mulberry

catacombs

Lafayette

nphony Hall

(21)

To: NJ Turnpike
Newark Airport
Port Newark

Elm

East Ferry

A pioneer in the recognition of folk art, the museum is also known for its collection of American painting and sculpture, its Tibetan art, its decorative arts, its coin collection, its classical collection, and its educational programs. In its garden is a sculpture collection that includes works by David Smith, George Segal, and Tony Smith, all, incidentally, New Jersey artists. Also in the garden are the Old Stone Schoolhouse* (1784), one of Newark's oldest buildings, which was moved to the museum grounds, and, in an old carriage house, a small fire-fighters' museum. Attached to and part of the museum is Ballantine House,* a national historic landmark built in 1885 by John Ballantine, the son of the founder of Ballantine Brewery. Built with Victorian abandon in a variety of styles and with considerable attention to detail, the building is the only mansion remaining around Washington Park (Washington and Broad sts.), once a fashionable residential district. (The park was laid out as a marketplace in 1667; note the statue of Seth Boyden.) The Ballantine House serves as the gallery for the museum's collection of decorative arts, which date from the 17th to the 20th century. The two floors of period rooms also form part of an interpretive scheme that examines the meaning of home in the late 19th century and more generally. Special Christmas holiday exhibits are held in the Ballantine house. Also part of the museum is the planetarium, which offers public programs weekends, September–June, and on an expanded schedule the rest of the year. The planetarium gallery is open when the rest of the museum is open. There is also a junior museum with many special programs and workshops; a natural science gallery (Dynamic Earth: Revealing Nature's Secrets) opened in 1999. Museum open Wednesday–Friday, 12–5, weekends, 10–5; admission charge for planetarium; group tours by appointment (973-596-6613).

Near the museum is the Newark Public Library (5 Washington St.; 973-733-7793). Its splendid early-20th-century Renaissance building houses a large collection, and the Centennial Hall, available for private use, has served as the site of a rump meeting of the state legislature, a Spike Lee preview, a concert by the New Jersey Symphony Orchestra, and corporate dinners. Exhibits in the library's galleries, which change frequently, cover a wide range and focus on showing off the library's extraordinary holdings. Often honoring the varied ethnic communities of Newark, the exhibits include annual African American and Hispanic shows but can range from an exhibit on shopping bags or travel posters to one honoring the 200th anniversary of the newspaper that is today the Star-Ledger. The library continues its long tradition of civic involvement, working with community groups and offering concerts, film and lecture series, and outreach programs. Open June–mid-September, Monday, Tuesday, Thursday, Friday, 9–5:30, Wednesday, 9–8:30, Saturday, 9:30–1:30; mid-September–May, Monday, Friday, Saturday, 9–5:30, Tuesday–Thursday, 9–8:30.

Military Park (Broad St. and Park Pl.), once a training ground for the militia, was laid out in 1667 by Newark's original settlers. In 1776 it was used by George Washington's troops as a camping area; it was during that encampment that Thomas Paine wrote "The Crisis" ("These are the times that try men's souls"). The park contains *The Wars of America*, a large bronze group done by Gutzon Borglum, the sculptor of Mount Rushmore. Also in the park is Trinity and St. Philip's Cathedral,* 1744–46, possibly the only church in New Jersey to be situated in a public park. This church is said to owe its origins to the decision of one of the stalwarts of Old First to harvest his hay on a Sunday because rain threatened; the ensuing argument with Old First led him to help found Trinity. A plane tree that was in the park when the troops were there is still to be seen.

The Essex House* (1926) in Military Park is the home of the New Jersey Historical Society (52 Park Pl.; 973-596-8500), which moved in on Friday, 13 June 1997. Founded in 1845 (in Trenton) and calling itself the oldest cultural institution in the state, the society has its headquarters here, as well as its library (used by some 7,000 people in 2003), galleries, museum, and publication and education departments. The society's collection includes a wide variety of objects, from clothing and furniture to paintings, tools, and documents, all relating to the history of the state. It sponsors a variety of exhibits (subjects have ranged from Paul Robeson to the New Jersey Turnpike to Newark's sports teams) and educational programs and estimates that over 200,000 people a year visit, either in person or on the web. The museum is open Tuesday–Saturday, 10–5, the library Tuesday–Saturday, 12–5; groups by appointment.

Across from the northwest corner of Military Park are the exhibition spaces and offices of Aljira, A Center for Contemporary Art (591 Broad St.; 973-622-1600). Aljira (pronounced with a long *i*) is the Australian aboriginal word for dreamtime, and the center is committed to showing the work of emerging and underrepresented artists. Shows change three to five times a year and include one show of middle-school student art, curated by middle-school students. The center engages in an education program, which includes seminars for emerging artists. Open Wednesday–Friday, 12–6, Saturday, 12–4.

On a 12-acre tract across Park Pl. from Military Park (and, in fact, not far from where the city's settlers landed) is the New Jersey Performing Arts Center (Theater Sq.; 973-648-8989). The building, containing two performance spaces (one of 2,750 seats, the other 500), opened in 1997 and serves as the permanent home of the New Jersey Symphony.

Walking along Broad St. (first paved in 1852) notice (at State St.) the House of Prayer Episcopal Church* and rectory* (Plume House, c. 1740), in which Goodwin invented flexible film; the 19th-century North Reformed Church* (510); the First Baptist Peddie Memorial Church* (at Fulton), from the late 1880s; the Griffith building* (605) from the 1920s; First National State Bank* (810), 1912; Old First and City Hall; and Richard Upjohn's Gothic Revival Grace Church* (at Walnut), a national historic landmark. West of Washington and Military parks, on the way to the concentration of educational institutions, is the James St. Commons historic district*

(University, Bleeker, New, Linden, James, Essex, Burnet, Washington, and Summit sts. and Central Ave.).

Among the educational institutions to be found in Newark are Rutgers University, the University of Medicine and Dentistry of New Jersey, the New Jersey Institute of Technology, Seton Hall Law School, and Essex County College. The Rutgers unit was formed in 1946, when the University of Newark, itself an amalgam of several colleges, was incorporated into Rutgers. Its Paul Robeson Center Gallery (350 Martin Luther King Jr. Blvd.; 973-648-5119, 973-648-1610) changes exhibits roughly eight times a year, with three annual exhibits of student works, including one of drawings by New Jersey Institute of Technology architecture students. Open weekdays, 11:30–5; sometimes closed in August. At the Dana Library (973-648-5222) exhibits change roughly every six weeks and cover a wide range; past exhibits have included Ella Fitzgerald, boat-making, Spanish culture, and painting and sculpture. Open when the library is open (daily, September–April; closed Sunday, May–August). Prospective students can arrange tours of the Rutgers campus by calling 973-648-5205. The New Jersey Institute of Technology, founded in 1881 as the Newark Technical School, has offices in Eberhardt Hall★ (323 Martin Luther King Blvd.), once an orphanage and now a national historic landmark. In the dental school building (110 Bergen St.; 973-982-4633) old equipment is on display. Open weekdays, 9–4:30.

Across Market St. from Essex County College is the Essex County Courthouse★ (470 High St.), a national historic landmark designed by Cass Gilbert and opened in 1907. On the steps of this impressive marble building, which replaced an earlier Egyptian-style one (1836), is a seated statue of Lincoln, also by Borglum. The informal quality of the figure and the fact that you can sit right down on the bench next to Lincoln caused something of a stir when it was dedicated in 1911. The courthouse and the statue have been recently restored.

North of the educational cluster, on one of the highest points in the city, are various offices housed in the few remaining mansions built by Newark's wealthy. The Feigenspan Mansion★ (1905; 710 Martin Luther King Blvd.), the last of the mansions to be built on what was then High Street, is used by a service agency. The Coles mansion, also on Martin Luther King Blvd., houses a drug rehabilitation agency.

Penn Station★ (Raymond Plaza W.), built in the 1930s, is a national historic landmark. The station serves New Jersey Transit, Conrail, Amtrak, and PATH trains; a monorail links the station to the airport, and it serves as a stop for the Newark subway and long-distance buses. Roughly 68,000 people pass through this art deco building every day, some third of them heading for the buses or subways. The subway runs on trolley tracks laid in the 1930s in the old Morris Canal bed; it comes up at Branch Brook Park. Outside the subway entrance note the sculpture of seven life-size figures done by Grigory Gurevich and students at the Newark School of Fine and Industrial Arts.

Near the station is Clinton Plaza (207–215 Market St.), once the Newark News building (the paper folded in 1972), now condominiums. The oldest structure in the complex dates to 1915; some of its ceilings are 12 feet high. Nearby St. Joseph Plaza* (233 Market St.) contains offices and recreational dining facilities in what was once St. Joseph's Church, built in 1880 to serve the Irish immigrant community.

Also near the station is the Gateway Center office complex, a multibuilding project that the Prudential Life Insurance Company (established in the 1870s in a Broad St. storefront and now the nation's largest insurance firm) became involved in when a company for which Prudential held the mortgage went bankrupt. The 26-story headquarters of the Public Service Enterprise Group is on Park Pl., as is the former home office building of the Fireman's Insurance Company,* which dates from the 1920s.

Also along the river is the Legal Center (1 River Front Plaza); the center has a triangular footprint and contains high-tech offices. This is an area favored by law firms; at 1 Newark Center, the office building adjoins the Seton Hall University Law School, and it too is home to many law firms. Pedestrian skywalks connect Penn Station to some of this riverfront development, which also includes offices, a hotel, shops, and a garden.

The Lincoln Park historic district* includes the park and parts of Spruce, Broad, and Washington sts. and Clinton Avenue. The Cathedral Evangelica Reformada* (27 Lincoln Park at Halsey St.) was once the First Reformed Church, dedicated in 1872. The South Park Calvary United Presbyterian Church* (1035 Broad St. at Lincoln Park) was built in 1853.

Just north of Lincoln Park is Newark Symphony Hall* (1020 Broad St.). It was built as the Salaam Temple in 1925 (at a cost of $2.5 million, a considerable sum in those days) and later became known as the Mosque Theater. Second in size on the East Coast only to Radio City Music Hall, it was extensively renovated in the mid-'80s.

East of Symphony Hall is the Ironbound section; the name derives from the train tracks that more or less define its borders. Ironbound was once an Italian enclave; today a large portion of its residents are of Portuguese descent, and the annual Portugal Day Festival in June is the largest such festival inside or outside Portugal (as many as 500,000 people have attended the festival). In the Ironbound section are what are said to be the only catacombs in the United States. Modeled on those in Rome, they are in a former church (now used by the board of education as an annex of the Lafayette St. School) and are run by the Immaculate Heart of Mary Church (212 Lafayette St.; 973-589-8249). Open Saturday, 9–2, by appointment only. Also in the Ironbound section note the Ironbound Education and Cultural Center* (178-184 Edison Pl.), built in 1848 as the Second Reformed Dutch Church (later Our Lady of Mount Carmel). Riverfront Stadium (450 Broad St.; 973-483-6900), home to Newark's minor league baseball team, opened in 1999.

Newark's Branch Brook Park* (Clifton Ave.; 973-268-3500, ext. 4), dedicated in 1895, is the first county park in the United States. Situated on a marsh once known as Old Blue Jay Swamp and used as an army training camp in the Civil War, the park was designed by the Frederick Law Olmsted firm. The Beaux Arts entrance gate (Lake St.) was a gift from Robert Ballantine, and the turn-of-the-20th-century stone lions at the concert mall once guarded the entrance to the Prudential Building. In 1910 the world's largest fountain was installed, but it had to be abandoned because it endangered the city's water supply. Branch Brook is perhaps best known for its Japanese cherry trees, first planted in 1929. In the spring, when some 2,500 of them are in bloom, the park's display surpasses that in Washington, D.C. Half a million people visit the park in April, and the park commission sponsors various special events, including the 10-kilometer Cherry Blossom Run.

East of Branch Brook is the Gothic Revival Cathedral Basilica of the Sacred Heart* (89 Ridge St.; 973-484-4600), a national historic landmark. This huge cathedral, which was started in 1899 but not completed until 1954, is modeled somewhat on that at Rheims. Among its noteworthy features are 200 stained-glass windows, woodwork of Appalachian white oak, and the angle of the wings of the facade. Tours the first Sunday of the month following the noon mass; groups by appointment. The cathedral also sponsors a Sunday concert series (973-484-2400). Near the cathedral is the Essex County Park Commission Administration Building* (115 Clifton Ave.), built in 1914.

East of the cathedral is Newark's oldest continuously operating cemetery. Mt. Pleasant Cemetery* (375 Broadway; 973-483-0288), a national historic landmark, was opened in the 1840s (the Gothic gate and adminis-tration building were erected in 1877). Some of the graves are older than the cemetery since headstones and remains uncovered in downtown building projects have been moved here. Among the people buried in Mt. Pleasant are Seth Boyden, Peter Ballantine, and John Dryden, a U.S. senator and founder of the Prudential Insurance Company, whose mausoleum is hard to miss. Note also the fire hydrants at the firemen's lot. Cemetery open daily, 8–5; office open weekdays, 8–4:30; office closed on major holidays.

South of downtown is Weequahic Park (Elizabeth Ave.; 973-268-3500). The park, also designed by the Olmsted firm, contains an 80-acre lake for boating and fishing, a rose garden, the world's longest resilient surfaced track (two miles around the lake), and a golf course. Formerly known as the Waverly Fair Grounds (the state fair was held here in the late 19th century), it had a trotting track, and President Grant is said to have ridden here. Note the field house (1907) and the Gothic comfort station (1916).

Newark Liberty International Airport is east of Weequahic Park. Opened in the late 1920s, the airport for a time was the only one serving the New York metropolitan area. For period flavor, note, at the northern end of the airport, Building No. 1,* the airport's original building and a national historic landmark, moved to its current site in 2002; Brewster hangar;* and the medical building,* all dating from the late 1920s. Operated by the Port Authority of New York and New Jersey, the airport currently serves over 30 million passengers a year and generates some $11.3 billion in economic activity. Tours of the facilities can be arranged for groups (973-961-6265), but they must provide their own transportation.

Adjacent to the airport on Newark Bay is Port Newark. It and Port Elizabeth, directly to the south, together constitute one of the busiest container ports in the world, handling 17 million tons of cargo annually. With channels dredged to 40 feet, they can accommodate the newest generation of container ships. On the 930 acres are sheds, warehouses, distribution buildings, refrigerated storage (one facility can handle 6.5 million gallons of orange juice concentrate), wharves, cranes, railroad tracks, and roadways; 165 acres are used to store automobiles. Tours of the New Jersey marine terminals can be arranged by appointment (call the facility staff assistant at 973-589-7100), but you must provide your own transportation.

Twenty-five of the 26 American cities named Newark were founded by someone from this Newark, and every two years representatives from Newark, New Jersey, take part in a Newarks of the World conference. In 2005 the library mounted a major exhibition on the Newarks of the World.

New Brunswick   Middlesex   48,573

NJ TNPK EXIT 9, US 1, NJ 18, 26, 27, 91, 171, 172, C 514

 The settlement of New Brunswick goes back to the 1680s, when a group of English colonists from Long Island, among them John Inian, purchased some 10,000 acres along the Raritan River, described at the time as "the handsomest and pleasantest country that man can behold." Inian established a ferry across the river in 1686, eventually adding an inn, docks, and a road to Trenton; in 1697 he gained exclusive rights to the crossing. The settlement, originally known as Prigmore's (or Pridmore's) Swamp, came to be called Inian's Ferry, but early in the 18th century it was again renamed, becoming New Brunswick, in honor of the English royal house (George I was also the duke of Brunswick).

New Brunswick developed as an active shipping center during the 18th century and saw considerable action during the Revolution. The Continental army retreated here after the defeat at Fort Lee, and Alexander Hamilton commanded an artillery battery that stalled the British while George Washington moved south toward the Delaware River. Between 29 November and 1 December 1776, Washington made his headquarters at Cochrane's Tavern, at the corner of Neilson and Albany streets. In all, Washington visited New Brunswick five times. The third reading of the Declaration of Independence in the colonies took place here on 6 July 1776.

Although many from New Brunswick were accused of favoring the loyalists, local merchant shippers successfully harassed British shipping.

New Brunswick continued as a transportation center during the 19th century (and hence its nickname, Hub City), but the coming of the railroads shifted the action from water to land. The city also developed industrially. Its preeminence as a pharmaceutical town dates to c. 1885, when the Johnson brothers moved their adhesive tape and gauze business (founded in 1873) to an old mill in New Brunswick. Incorporating as Johnson & Johnson in 1887, the firm recruited workers from Hungary, giving New Brunswick at the time the largest Hungarian population, proportionally, of any city in the United States. Joyce Kilmer (1886–1918), New Brunswick's best-known poet, was the son of the scientific director at Johnson & Johnson (Kilmer's birthplace is at 17 Joyce Kilmer Ave.). Other industries that have been important to New Brunswick include rubber, hosiery, and musical instruments. The New Jersey Rubber Shoe Company, later part of US Rubber, was founded here in 1839, and the National Musical String Company* (1898; 120 Georges Rd.), a manufacturer of steel strings, was the first firm in the United States to make harmonicas. Of these only the pharmaceutical industry remains as a major presence (Johnson & Johnson was later joined by E. R. Squibb, now Bristol-Myers Squibb).

Another major presence in the city is, of course, Rutgers University. The eighth college to be founded in the colonies and the only state university to have existed before the Revolution, Rutgers was chartered in 1766 as Queen's College, its mission the training of Dutch Reformed ministers. In 1771 it opened in a New Brunswick tavern, the Sign of the Red Lion, with one instructor (Frederick Frelinghuysen), one sophomore, and a handful of freshmen. In 1774 it graduated its first student, Matthew Leydt, whose clergyman father was a trustee and founder of the college. Its early years were rocky, but in 1825 it changed its name to Rutgers College in honor of Colonel Henry Rutgers, a New York philanthropist who had fought in the Revolution and been a trustee of the college. He gave the college some modest financial assistance and the bell that still hangs in the cupola of Old Queen's (it is the oldest bell in Middlesex County). Rutgers became a land-grant institution in 1864, and over the years various colleges—among them agriculture, engineering, pharmacy, Douglass College for women (the largest women's college in the United States), and education—were added. In 1924 Rutgers College became Rutgers University and in 1945 the state university. It now enrolls some 51,000 students in its 29 schools and colleges on three campuses (Camden, Newark, and New Brunswick; the university's general information number is 732-932-4636).

Now considered a major university (its library, for example, is ranked among the top 25 in the country), Rutgers is also widely known for the Rutgers tomato (developed in 1934) and streptomycin, the first broad-spectrum antibiotic (developed by Selman Waksman in 1943). The first intercollegiate football game (Princeton vs. Rutgers) was played at New Brunswick in 1869, the Princeton team arriving by train. Rutgers won, 6–4. The faculty apparently disapproved of football, but the captain of the Princeton team went on to become chief justice of the New Jersey supreme court, the captain of the Rutgers team a leader in the Dutch Reformed church. Rutgers was not to beat Princeton again until 1938 at the game dedicating the new stadium (the new stadium was replaced by a larger one in 1994).

Two other large institutions also shape New Brunswick. As the county seat, it is home to the county courthouse (1 John F. Kennedy Sq.) and a host of county agencies. It is also home to two teaching hospitals: Saint Peter's University Hospital (254 Easton Ave.) and the Robert Wood Johnson University Hospital (1 R. W. Johnson Pl.), founded in 1884 by a group of concerned laypeople. New Brunswick, incidentally, had been a leader in colonial medicine—the country's first professional medical association, the Medical Society of New Jersey, was founded here in 1766.

Like many other cities of the Northeast, New Brunswick suffered a decline after World War II, and in 1975 a coalition of business, university, community, and government leaders formed to reverse that decline. In part through their efforts downtown New Brunswick has a new look: the central business district was redesigned by I. M. Pei Associates; Johnson & Johnson built a new headquarters building; there are other new office buildings, a new hotel, and townhouses; and the city has developed a reputation for the quality of its restaurants.

The New Brunswick Cultural Center (19 Livingston Ave.; 732-247-7200) began with four existing buildings (a department store, a 1921 theater, a YMCA building, and a warehouse). The center includes two professional repertory theaters (George Street Playhouse, 732-846-2895, and Crossroads Theatre Company, 732-729-9559); the 2,000-seat State Theatre (built in 1921 and used as a vaudeville house and movie theater; 732-246-7469), presenting classical music, opera, jazz, country music, theater, entertainers, and film; and the American Repertory Ballet Company (formerly the Princeton Ballet, 732-249-1254). The center engages in a wide variety of educational programs. At 33 Livingston the Civic Square Building houses studios of the university's Mason Gross School of the Arts (732-932-7511). Seven galleries on the first floor feature biweekly exhibits of students' and guest artists' work. Open weekdays, September–May, 10–4 and by appointment.

Although NJ 18 cut off the city from the water, there have been efforts to reverse that loss. Boyd Park was restored in the late '90s, and from the park you can walk along the towpath and see the restored swing bridge and outlet lock of the Delaware and Raritan Canal,* which ended in New Brunswick at Landing Lane Bridge. Boyd Park is home to many festivals, including the Hispanic Riverfront festival in August, which celebrated its 25th anniversary in 2003.

The Hungarian Heritage Center (300 Somerset St; 732-846-5777) offers concerts and lectures; call for information. The museum at the center features changing exhibits of Hungarian fine and folk arts; at the annual Festival of Trees in December and January trees are decorated to reflect other ethnic traditions. Museum open Tuesday–Saturday, 11–4, Sunday, 1–4. A Hungarian festival is held each June; the festival generally draws some 15,000 people.

The Fire Department Museum (81 Remsen Ave; 732-745-5167) is housed in a former fire station (1886). The museum contains a variety of vintage artifacts—a water bucket dating to 1835, old helmets, a 19th-century megaphone—as well as historic photographs and written records. Open by appointment.

Despite all the rebuilding, which has involved considerable demolition, there are still a few historic buildings to be seen in New Brunswick. The old Hiram Market historic district (once listed on the state register of historic places) encompasses parts of Albany, Bayard, Church, Dennis, Hiram, Neilson, Paterson, Peace, and Richmond sts. and Memorial Parkway, but middle-income townhouses have replaced most of the older structures. In the 19th century rubber factories were located here (Daniel Webster won a patent case for one of New Brunswick's firms), and the area includes two old churches (one English, one Dutch, reflecting part of the city's history—

Dutch settlers from Albany began arriving in 1730). Middlesex County's oldest church (1812, replacing an early-18th-century stone church; the clock dates to c. 1830, the interior was rebuilt in 1847, 1862, and again in the 1970s after a fire damaged the interior), the First Reformed Church of New Brunswick* (732-545-1005), is on the west side of Neilson St., opposite Hiram Street. In the cemetery are graves going back to 1746. You can visit the church when the office is open (September–June, Tuesday–Friday, 9–1; July and August, Thursday, 9–1); guided tours by appointment.

Christ Episcopal Church* (5 Paterson St.) is also in the Hiram Market district, and it too has a pre-Revolutionary cemetery. The building dates from the 1850s (with later alterations and additions) and uses the stone from the original church built 100 years earlier.

Buccleuch Mansion* (Easton Ave. in Buccleuch Park, across the street from Saint Peter's University Hospital; 732-745-5094), is an 18th-century house (c. 1739) built by Anthony White, a cavalryman who married Lewis Morris's daughter. In 1821 the house was acquired by Colonel Joseph Warren Scott, son of the surgeon-general of the Continental army and himself a noted New Jersey lawyer, who named it after a Scottish ancestor, the duke of Buccleuch. His grandchildren gave the house to the city in 1911, and it has been operated as a museum since 1915. The house has 16 rooms, which have been furnished to show how styles have changed over its lifetime; particularly noteworthy is the hand-blocked wallpaper, with scenes of Paris and of Indian tiger hunting, dating from c. 1820. The saber and spur marks made by the Enniskillen dragoons, who were quartered in the house in 1776–77, are still visible. Open Sunday, 2–4, June–October; guided tours by appointment. Buccleuch Park itself (George St. and Easton Ave.; 732-745-5112) consists of 78 acres overlooking the Raritan River.

The Henry S. Guest house* (Livingston Ave. and Morris St.; 732-745-5108) was built c. 1760 (the front doorway and porch were added c. 1825 and the house moved to its present location 100 years later). Guest was a whaler and tanner, and among his guests were John Adams, Thomas Paine, and Lafayette. Paine, in fact, was hidden from the British in Guest's house. Collections in the handsome stone house include local Civil War artifacts from an 1888 time capsule found almost 100 years later at George St. and Livingston Ave. In another room is a display of artifacts from the Delaware and Raritan Canal. You can arrange to visit the Guest house at the public library next door (732-745-5108), but it is advisable to call ahead to make sure someone is available to help you. The library, a handsome Carnegie building dating from 1903, has on permanent display a collection of Japanese artifacts. Open weekdays, 9–4:30. Driving south on Livingston Ave. toward US 1, you will see a considerable number of substantial late-19th-, early-20th-century houses.

The university's Queen's campus* (part of the College Ave. campus) combines 18th- and 19th-century buildings, and Old Queen's itself (north side of Somerset St. between George St. and College Ave.) is a national historic landmark. A three-story brownstone built between 1808 and 1825, it was intended to serve the needs of a grammar school, a college, and a theological college of the Dutch Reformed Church, with living quarters for two professors. The architect, John McComb Jr., was also the architect of New York's City Hall, designed at about the same time. University administrative offices are here, including the president's office. One of the fireplaces has a preserved Dutch oven, and some of the windowpanes are handmade.

The College Ave. campus has an unusual sense of space for an urban campus, and many fine old houses are scattered throughout the area. West of Old Queen's is the Rutgers University Geological Museum (732-932-7243). The collection includes dinosaurs, a mastodon, a mummy, and items relating to the natural history of the state. Open Monday, 1–4; Tuesday–Friday, 9–12; Sunday, 12–4; but it is always advisable to call ahead. The Daniel S. Schanck Observatory (c. 1865–66), two octagons connected by a one-story passage, was Rutgers's first building intended exclusively for scientific purposes; it is no longer being used. South of Old Queen's is the Jane Voorhees Zimmerli Art Museum (George and Hamilton sts.; 732-932-7237), the third-largest university art museum in the country. Exhibits include both items from the permanent collection and temporary exhibits. The permanent collection includes the largest collection of Russian and former Soviet art in the West and a nationally renowned print collection particularly strong in 19th-century French prints and 20th-century American graphics. Rotating exhibits from the permanent collection of illustrations for children's literature are exhibited in the lower wing; temporary exhibits are shown in the other galleries. Open Monday, Tuesday, Thursday, Friday, 10–4:30; weekends, 12–5. Tours by appointment (732-932-7096).

At the northern end of the College Ave. campus are a statue of William of Orange (William the Silent, referred to locally as Willy), who led the Dutch to independence from Spain; and the New Brunswick Theological Seminary, founded in 1784. The Gardner A. Sage Library (21 Seminary Pl.; 732-247-5243) was built in 1875; the archives of the Reformed Dutch church (now known as the Reformed Church in America) repose there. Among the remarkable items at the library are the stained-glass windows and the materials brought back by missionaries, which are on display. Open for visits weekdays, 10–6, but you must call for a reservation before coming. Note also the Doolittle-Demarest house (southwest corner of George St. and Seminary Pl.; 1850–70), and the painted Suydam statue. The red brick former headquarters of Johnson & Johnson are visible toward the river.

At 101 Somerset St. is Alexander Johnston Hall (1830, 1870), once the home of Rutgers Preparatory School,* the oldest independent college prep school in the state and one of the oldest in the country. Joyce Kilmer's birthplace (17 Joyce Kilmer Ave.; 732-745-5117), a modest 18th- and 19th-century farmhouse, is used as an office by New Brunswick Dial-A-Ride.

(Kilmer was a student at Rutgers Prep.) The house contains some period furniture and pictures of members of the Kilmer family. Individuals may stop by the house weekdays, 9–3; group tours by appointment.

On the university's Douglass campus is the Nicholas Music Center, where public concerts are presented from September through July. Also on this campus are two theaters where plays and dance concerts are presented. (Another theater on the Cook campus also presents dance concerts.) For information on all these events, call 732-932-7511.

On the university's Cook campus is the New Jersey Museum of Agriculture (College Farm Rd. just off US 1 south; 732-249-2077), which opened in 1990, 61 years after Hiram Deats had given a plow designed by his grandfather (*see* Stockton) to the dean of the College of Agriculture in the hopes it would provide the nucleus for just such a museum. The collection, the largest in the mid-Atlantic, covers three centuries of farm implements, and the museum offers a wide variety of interactive history and science programs for children (in 2003 close to 10,000 schoolchildren were involved in museum programs; the total number of visitors was over 22,000). There are also weekend family programs and workshops and a summer camp. Past programs have ranged from quilting bees and maple-sugaring to studying bats and potatoes. Open Tuesday–Saturday, 10–5; Sunday, 12–5; closed Christmas Eve and Christmas Day, New Year's Eve and New Year's Day. Admission charge.

On the east side of US 1 are the Rutgers Gardens (off Ryders La. about 1 mile south of NJ 18; 732-932-8451). Here you will find one of the world's largest collection of American hollies, as well as large numbers of other holly varieties. Also in the gardens are collections of small trees, shade trees, rhododendrons, and azaleas, as well as a sun and shade garden, a native plant garden, and a bamboo forest. Many new and unusual annuals can be seen in the display gardens, and the gardens have been described as an outdoor teaching laboratory. A spring flower festival takes place on Mother's Day weekend, there is an open house in the summer, and there is a foliage festival in the fall. At these festivals there are tours , instructional sessions, and activities for children. Open daily, dawn–dusk.

Newton Sussex 8,244

US 206, NJ 94, C 519

Newton, the seat of Sussex County, was settled in the mid-18th century. Until recently it was the center of a bustling farming community providing the legal, financial, and medical services associated with a county seat, but it is becoming more of a bedroom community for Morris County, and even some New York City, commuters. It is said that the first beer to be sold in cans was produced in Newton.

Much of Newton retains its 19th-century air, and if you can ignore the cars, you can get a strong sense of earlier times. The Newton Town Plot historic district* includes over 50 buildings along Church, High, Main, Moran, and Spring sts. and Park Pl. and 1 Dunn Place. Try to walk around the central square and Main St., with its well-preserved line of 19th-century shops, and drive along the streets off the square. The county courthouse* (High and Spring sts.), built in 1847, replaces the first one (1765), which burned (though portions of the original building may be contained within the current one). A Greek Revival building with six Doric columns, it is strikingly sited on a steep hill. (The last hanging in New Jersey took place behind this courthouse.) George Washington stopped at the inn at Main and Spring sts. on his way to Newburgh, New York, in 1782. The First Presbyterian Church (High and Church sts.) dates from the 1860s and is listed in the state register of historic buildings.

The public gallery in the Judicial Center (43–47 High St.; 973-383-0027) features art exhibits sponsored by the Sussex County Arts and Heritage Council; the exhibits are changed quarterly. Open weekdays, 8:30–4:30. The council also has its own gallery downtown (9 Moran Ave.; 973-383-0027). The shows feature artists from the tri-state area, and change monthly (with a First Friday wine and cheese reception open to the public). Open

MERRIAM HOUSE

Wednesday and Thursday, 9–6, Friday, 9–8, weekends 12–5. Art exhibits are also featured at the fine arts building (building C) of Sussex County Community College (1 College Hill Rd.; 973-300-2144).

The Hill Memorial Building★ at the corner of Church and Main sts. houses the Sussex County Historical Society's headquarters and museum (973-383-6010). The building was built in 1916 specifically for the society; it contains a fireplace with stones taken from various buildings and sites of historic interest. Among the items on display are handwork, agricultural tools, a mastodon skeleton, and Civil War memorabilia. Displays are changed once or twice a year. Open Friday, 10–5, Saturday 8–12.

The Newton Fire Museum (150 Spring St.; 973-383-0396) is housed in the department's first station and includes old equipment, much of it from the 19th century (an 1863 hand pumper, an 1873 steamer, hand-drawn hose carts and ladder wagons), memorabilia, and photographs. Open Saturday, 10–3; groups and other times by appointment. The department, incidentally, gave up its horses in 1923.

The Merriam house* (131 Main St.) is a particularly splendid example of Queen Anne architecture. Built in the 1880s for the founder of the Merriam Shoe Company, it is now a retirement home. The factory itself (75 Sparta Ave.), which once employed some 750 people, now contains apartments and a fitness center. (Shoes made at the factory are in the museum.) About one mile south on 206 note St. Paul's Abbey. The original structure (now the right wing) dates from 1840, the rest from 1932.

Some two miles south of Newton off US 206 (head west on Fredon Rd., 618, across from the Newton Airport) is the Whittingham Wildlife Management Area. Of the area's 1,900 acres, 400 are designated a natural area, in which live beaver, otter, and many species of waterfowl. On the limestone cliffs in this northern swamp and floodplain forest you can see rare species of fern. The open places are kept open, which makes this a good spot for watching butterflies, and there are mowed paths and dirt roads to walk on. Horseback riding is allowed with a permit, and you can also hunt and fish here.

About five miles west of Newton on C 622 is Swartswood State Park (973-383-5230), over 2,250 acres with facilities for picnicking, swimming, boating, fishing, hiking, riding, biking, camping, and (in season) hunting, cross-country skiing, ice-fishing, ice-boating, and skating. The park is also a good place for bird-watching. Swartswood is New Jersey's first state park—it dates to 1914—and one of the state's most popular parks; it can see some 150,000 visitors annually. Open 8–sunset in summer (Memorial Day–Labor Day), sunrise–sunset in winter. Parking fee in summer.

About four miles south of Swartswood on C 521, in the community of Stillwater, is the Stillwater Museum (941 Stillwater Rd.; 973-383-4822). Housed in a mid-19th-century schoolhouse, the museum contains a re-created early-20th-century country store, farming and household tools, an unusual collection of 19th-century gowns, Native American artifacts, and fluorescent rocks. Ask at the museum for a brochure. Open early June–Labor Day, Sunday, 1–4; groups by appointment. There are many striking 18th- and 19th-century buildings to be seen along Main Street, including a gristmill dating from 1844, built to replace the 1764 mill lost in a fire. A group of nonprofit organizations is working to restore the mill, have it running again, and open it for tours.

If you follow Main Street east to Cedar Ridge Road, you will come to the Snowmobile Barn Museum (928 Cedar Ridge Rd.; 973-383-1708). The collection, showing the 90-year history of mechanized snow vehicles, contains a large number of one-of-a-kind and prototype vehicles and some 130 sleds, as well as thousands of not necessarily related artifacts (toys, jewelry, ornaments). Also on the property are a petting zoo, a working waterwheel, some old barns, and a mid-18th century house. Open weekends, 10–4; other times by appointment. Donations requested. The Paulinskill Trail, open for horse-back riding, mountain-biking, and cross-country skiing, goes through the farm.

West of Swartswood at Fairview Lake (off Fairview Lake Rd., C 624 at that point) is the Fairview Lake YMCA camp and conference center (973-383-9282). Trails here are open to the public for cross-country skiing.

North Bergen · Hudson · 58,092

I 495, US 1, 9, C 501

Louis XVI once had a garden here, and it is said that the country's first Lombardy poplar trees were introduced into this garden by André Michaux, the king's official botanist. At the eastern end of the township is James Braddock Park (J. F. Kennedy Blvd. E. and Bergenline Ave.), a 167-acre county park. Part of it lies on the Palisades, offering views of the Hudson River and New York City, and a scenic path goes down steps to the river valley. West of the boulevard the land is more rolling, and the park contains a lake, with fishing, boating, and skating. Other facilities include a children's playground, athletic fields, picnic areas, and tennis courts. There are also woods, rare in Hudson County.

At Flower Hill Cemetery (J. F. Kennedy Blvd. at 55th St.), there is a splendid view of the wetlands to the west, and the architecture of the gatehouse and the mausoleum with the gray stone windows is worth a look. Note also the mid-19th-century Egyptian-Revival sphinxlike creature guarding a crypt.

Wandering around in North Bergen you will come across many interesting buildings: Schuetzen Park (3167 J. F. Kennedy Blvd.), now used for banquets and weddings but once an opera house, and the Fritz Reuther Altenheim (3161 J. F. Kennedy Blvd.) tell us something of North Bergen's ethnic past. For something from the present, the firehouse on Tonnelle Ave. between 43d and 44th sts. has been designed not just as a striking backdrop to the adjacent playground but with glass to let the children using the playground see the trucks.

Nutley · Essex · 27,362

GARDEN STATE PKWY EXITS 150, 151, NJ 7, 21

Settled in the 17th century by colonists from Newark, Nutley was once known as Franklinville after William Franklin, New Jersey's last royal governor (and Benjamin Franklin's natural son; *see* Perth Amboy). The town still boasts one house dating from the beginning of the 18th century (the Vreeland house, now used by the Woman's Club of Nutley, 216 Chestnut St.; the town hall across the street was once a textile mill). After the Civil War, it attracted a colony of artists and writers, many of whom lived in the Enclosure historic

On the map: Bloomfield, Poplar Pl., Daily St., Hawthorne Ave., High, East Plaza, West Plaza, Yantacaw, Kingsland St., Kingsland Manor, Vreeland, Coeyman St., Prospect St., Brookfield Ave., High, Cleveland, Lakeside, Kingsland Lake, Raymond Ave., Hillside Ave., Dodd, Edgar, Elm, Kingsland Park, Passaic Ave., Whitford, Rutgers Pl., Oak St., Beech St., Franklin Ave., Memorial Park, Vreeland, Maple, North Rd., Mountainview, Vreeland house, Enclosure, Calico, Satterthwaite Ave., Franklin Reformed Church, Chestnut, Warren, town hall, Enclosure historic district, Whitford, Highfield La., Nutley museum, Church St., Nutley Ave., Walnut St., New St., Vincent Pl., Third River, Shepard, Evelyn Pl., Passaic Ave., Chestnut, Grant Ave., William, Park Way, N

district* (Enclosure and Calico las.). Mark Twain was a frequent visitor here (the editor of *Puck* was his host), and Frank Stockton wrote his most famous story, "The Lady or the Tiger?," at his home on Walnut Street. Annie Oakley was another famous resident. Near the Enclosure is Memorial Park, a lovely linear park along the Third River.

Tradition has it that Mussolini once owned a one-acre tract in Nutley, now the site of the Amvets Memorial Post 30 clubhouse. He was the only creditor of a local bank that tried to pay him before declaring bankruptcy, but the bank didn't wait long enough, and the draft didn't clear. Since 1929 Hoffmann–La Roche has had a presence in Nutley (340 Kingsland St.); the local facility (the North American headquarters for pharmaceutical discovery, development, manufacturing, marketing, and sales) employs some 5,000 people.

The Nutley Historical Society museum* (65 Church St.; 973-667-1528), housed in an attractive brick building, features local history, including exhibits of Annie Oakley memorabilia. Open September–June, 1st and 3d Sunday of the month, 2–4; groups and other times by appointment. Across the street is the Franklin Reformed Church, an attractive wooden building, with a cemetery dating to 1860. The Vincent Methodist Cemetery (corner of Passaic and Oakridge aves.) dates to 1800. Both cemeteries are open during daylight hours.

Kingsland Manor* (3 Kingsland St.; 973-284-4966), a large sandstone structure, most of which dates to the late 18th century (a portion was built earlier, and the structure was altered in the 19th century), has recently been restored. It served as a home for the wealthy Kingsland family between 1790 and 1909; in the 20th century it saw service as a training camp for prizefighters, a speakeasy, a club, and a convalescent home. Now a historic house museum, it has been restored and furnished to reflect the mid-18th century. One room on the second floor has a display of artifacts, primarily related to the Kingsland family. The house is open for concerts and special events throughout the year; regular hours will also be established soon. Tours and groups by appointment.

Oakland Bergen 12,466

US 202, NJ 208

Oakland is one of Bergen County's older communities, and several early stone houses remain, particularly along Ramapo Valley Dr. (US 202), to remind us of that past. One of these, the Van Allen House* (Franklin Ave. and Ramapo Valley Rd.; 201-405-7726), is maintained as a museum by the Oakland Historical Society. This 18th-century structure, which for a brief period served as George Washington's headquarters when he was traveling from Morristown to West Point and other northern spots, and for another brief period functioned as the Bergen County courthouse, has exhibits of clothing and colonial furnishings intended to convey the atmosphere of a Dutch colonial household. The society also conducts educational programs for children. Usually open the third Sunday of the month, 1–4, but it is best to call ahead. Also on the property is a stream house, built in 1902 as the office and manager's living quarters of a dairy farm; dairy products were stored in the basement over the stream, which kept them cool. The society is restoring the house, which will serve as a 19th-century museum and educational center. (A former architectural attraction, Oakland's diner, was transported to Baltimore, where it served as the principal set for the movie *Diner*.)

Northwest of Oakland (take W. Oakland Ave. to Skyline Dr.; turn right; you can park near the creek) is Ramapo Mountain State Forest (973-962-7031), a 4,200-acre preserve that includes Rotten Pond and Ramapo Lake Natural Area. The forest is open for hiking, horseback riding, mountain-biking, canoeing, bird-watching, and fishing, and, in season, hunting, sledding, ice-fishing, and cross-country skiing, but no motorized vehicles are permitted. Trail maps are available at Ringwood State Park (*see* Ringwood).

Ocean City Cape May 15,378

NJ 52, C 619, 623, 656

Founded in 1879 by three brothers, Methodist ministers looking to create a wholesome year-round family resort, Ocean City is still a dry community that has maintained its reputation as a family-oriented place. With its well-kept look, eight miles of beach, and more than two miles of boardwalk, including a late-1920s music pier (Moorlyn Terrace) on which summer concerts are given, Ocean City can find its population swelling to 150,000 during the summer months. The community sponsors many special events in the summer, including a hermit-crab beauty contest (to say nothing of a hermit crab who looks for his shadow each spring), a baseball card show, an antique car show, a sand-sculpting contest, and what is billed as the oldest baby parade in the country. In early spring the town braces itself for the summer season with a parade that features old cars, comic marchers, and in recent years as many as 575 basset hounds.

Ocean City's historic district* runs from Atlantic to Asbury aves. between 3d and 7th sts. Included within the district is the former lifesaving station (Atlantic Ave. and 4th St.; 609-525-0284). Built in 1885–86, the building passed from the Life-Saving Service to the Coast Guard in 1915 and in 1945 was decommissioned and bought by a private party. There are hopes that the building can be saved, restored to its 1915 appearance, and converted into a museum that would concentrate on the history of the Life-Saving Service. Check at the Chamber of Commerce Information Center (9th St. causeway, NJ 52; 609-399-2629) for brochures describing a self-guided tour of the historic district. Open May–Labor Day, Monday–Saturday, 9–5, Sunday, 10–2; Labor Day–April, Monday–Saturday, 10–5, Sunday, 10–2.

The Ocean City Historical Museum (1735 Simpson Ave.; 609-399-1801), housed in the Ocean City Community and Cultural Center, features artifacts, apparel, and other items related to the history and the natural history of Ocean City. Included among these are mementos of John Fulton Short, said to be America's only matador. Of particular interest is the Sindia Room, with mementos of the four-masted bark that went aground on the Ocean City beach in 1901. (Rumors of contraband still in the hull have led to periodic talk of salvage operations; one proposal included installing an amphitheater so the public—for a fee—could watch the operation.) The Sindia Pavilion (17th St. and the boardwalk) marks the location of the wreck. The museum's library contains many early deeds and other papers relating to Ocean City and Cape May County. Open May–October, Monday–Friday, 10–4, Saturday 11–2; November–April, Monday–Friday, 1–4, Saturday, 11–2; groups by appointment. The Friends of the Ocean City Historical Museum sponsor various special events, including lectures and an annual antique and craft fair.

On the second floor of the same building is the Ocean City Arts Center (609-399-7628). The center's gallery exhibits change roughly every month; the center also offers a variety of classes and other programs, including an annual fine arts boardwalk exhibit, which features up to 200 artists. Open Monday–Thursday, 9–9; Friday, 9–4; Saturday, 9–12.

Corson's Inlet State Park (Ocean Dr.; 609-861-2404) is off the southern end of Ocean City. The park's 300-odd acres offer opportunities for fishing, boating, and hiking. This is a popular park in the summer, although flies and poison ivy can be problems. The inlet is surrounded by the Cape May

Wetlands Wildlife Management Area, more than 11,000 acres, most of it salt marsh, with excellent opportunities for boating and bird-watching.

About five miles from Ocean City in Palermo (take Bay Ave. to Roosevelt Blvd. to US 9 and turn left) is the Friendship School (Ocean Ave. and Shore Rd.; 609-390-5656). A reconstruction and restoration of an 1830s school, school privy, and coat and storage shed, the complex is run by the Historical Preservation Society of Upper Township. Open April, May, October, and November, 1st Sunday of the month, 1–4; groups and other times by appointment.

Another complex run by the Historical Preservation Society of Upper Township is the J. W. Gandy Farmstead* (26 Tyler Rd.; 609-390-5656). Located in the Greenfield section of the township (from the Friendship School, go south on US 9 to the traffic light at Hope Corson Rd., turn right; at C 50 turn right again; turn right on Tyler Rd., which is C 616), the house was built around 1815 as a home for a tenant farmer. The society hopes eventually to create a farmstead museum, with various outbuildings, orchards, and a grape arbor. Open April, May, October, and November, 1st Sunday of the month, 1–4; groups and other times by appointment.

Ocean Grove Monmouth 4,256

NJ 33, 71

Founded in 1869 by Methodists as a religious summer colony, the town of Ocean Grove was for 100 years run by the Methodist Camp Meeting Association. In 1979 the state supreme court declared Ocean Grove's government unconstitutional, and Ocean Grove became part of Neptune Township. At that point most of the community's strictly enforced blue laws, which included Sunday prohibitions against driving (the gates leading into the community were closed at midnight Saturday), bicycle riding, boating, swimming, and hanging laundry outside, no longer applied. The land still belongs to the association, however, and it is still the case that no alcoholic beverages can be sold, and that the beach does not open on Sunday until noon. Many residents of the community, which roughly doubles its population in the summer (from about 3,500 in winter to about 7,500), are concerned that the local increases in property values, which far exceed the rest of the county, will force many longtime residents to leave.

Ocean Grove's historic district* (the area between Main St., the Atlantic Ocean, and Wesley and Fletcher lakes) is distinguished by its generally homogeneous Victorian look. Permanent tents (actually houses extended in the summer by tents) are clustered around the Great Auditorium; there are fine old hotels with porches on Ocean Ave.; there are still a few of the old tile street signs. The auditorium (54 Pitman Ave.; 732-775-0035), a magnificent pile built in 1894 (President Grant attended the dedication ceremonies) and now a national landmark, seats over 5,500; each summer a series of concerts ranging from classical to popular to barbershop quartets is held there.

Between the auditorium and the Camp Meeting office is the Historical Society of Ocean Grove's museum (50 Pitman Ave; 732-774-1869). The exhibits concentrate on memorabilia related to Ocean Grove's past, including furniture, portraits of people associated with that past (John Philip Sousa played at the auditorium in the early 1930s), collectibles, and antique maps. The society also has exhibits at Centennial Cottage (Central Ave. and McClintock St.), an 1870s summer home, moved to its present site in 1969, and dedicated to celebrate Ocean Grove's centennial. The cottage is furnished to reflect the time it was built, and a period garden has been created on the property. Exhibits generally change yearly. The museum is open June–August, Monday, Wednesday, Thursday, 10–4, Friday and Saturday, 10–5; September, Wednesday–Saturday, 10–4, October–December, Friday and Saturday, 10–4. Centennial Cottage is open July and August, Monday–Saturday 10:30–2:30; group tours by appointment. The society sponsors a house tour each summer; tours of the town can also be arranged.

For beach information, call 732-988-5533.

Oceanville Atlantic [Galloway Township]

US 9

About one mile east of the center of Oceanville are the headquarters of the Edwin B. Forsythe National Wildlife Refuge (Great Creek Rd.; 609-652-1665), named in honor of a conservation-minded congressman. This is the refuge's Brigantine unit, founded in 1939, primarily to protect the Atlantic Flyway. Its 46,000 acres contain a variety of habitats: marshes (salt, brackish, and fresh water), creeks, ponds, upland fields, shrubby areas, and forests. Over 200 species of birds are known to frequent this spot. Some 1,400 acres have been impounded, creating freshwater habitats. One of the high points of this popular refuge (some 200,000 people visit it each year) is an eight-mile car trail along the impoundment dikes that gives you a view of the freshwater ponds, the salt marshes, and the mud flats (not to mention an eerie view of the Atlantic City skyline across the bay). There are 14 stops along the auto trail, and many of the birds have become accustomed to the cars and go about their business (cracking clam shells on the highway, leading their young across the road) as if you weren't there. There are also two short self-guided nature trails through the fields and woods and limited hunting, fishing, and crabbing. For leaflets describing the auto trail and the two nature trails, stop at the visitor center; for information on hunting permits, go to the headquarters building across the road, which also contains some natural history exhibits. The refuge is open daily, dawn to dusk; the office,

8–4 weekdays. Group orientation programs by appointment. The trails are occasionally closed to protect the animals, so it is advisable to check before coming. Admission fee. This is the Brigantine division of the refuge; for the Barnegat division, call 609-698-1387, for the Cape May division, 609-463-0994.

Mid-March to mid-April is the peak of the northbound waterfowl migration. To see young birds, come in mid-April through May for the Canada geese and mid-June to mid-July for the ducks. (The end of May is also a good time to see a major display of dragon's mouth orchid and grass pink on Great Creek Rd., about half a mile west of the entrance to the refuge.) The first 10 days in November usually produce spectacular concentrations of ducks, geese, and brant in the pools—as many as 100,000 birds have congregated on the impoundments, but the numbers have been declining in recent years. Mid-November to mid-December is the best time to see snow geese.

The other side of Lily Lake is southern New Jersey's first art museum, the Noyes Museum (Lily Lake Rd.; 609-652-8848). Opened in 1983, this lovely building is beautifully situated. The museum features contemporary fine and folk art, with an emphasis on southern New Jersey, and presents rotating exhibits in its four galleries. The museum also sponsors several concerts a year and various other special events and is engaged in educational programs for schoolchildren. Open Tuesday–Saturday, 10–4:30, Sunday, 12–5; closed national holidays. Admission fee.

West of Oceanville is the Firefighters Museum of Southern New Jersey (333 E. Ridgewood Ave; 609-652-8895). The collection includes 15 fire engines, both hand drawn and motorized, as well as old equipment and other items related to fire fighting. Open by appointment only, but it is hoped that regular hours can be established soon.

North of Oceanville is Smithville (US 9 and Moss Mill Rd.; 609-652-4040), once touted as a reconstruction of a colonial village. Some of the buildings are genuinely old, but the emphasis now is entirely on the stores and restaurants, not history.

West of Smithville (continue on Moss Mill Rd. to Vienna Ave. and turn right) is Sylvin Farms (24 N. Vienna Ave.; 609-965-1548), a winery that grows all its own grapes. Open weekends by appointment.

Oldwick Hunterdon [Tewksbury Township]

C 517, 523

Oldwick, situated in the rolling hills of northeastern Hunterdon County, was settled by German immigrants in the mid-18th century. Originally called New Germantown, the town changed its name during the World War I days of pervasive anti-German sentiment. Strikingly untouched by the 20th century, Oldwick today is a beautiful village set in the midst of beautiful agricultural country.

In the center of the village is the Zion Lutheran Church (31 Old Turnpike Rd., C 517), said to be the state's oldest Lutheran church in continuous use. Built in 1749, but altered considerably during the course of the 19th and 20th centuries, the church housed what was apparently New Jersey's first organ. On the west side of Old Turnpike Rd., a bit farther south, is the former Oldwick Methodist Church; it dates from the mid-1860s. The community center and town library (31 Old Turnpike Rd., C 517) dates from 1807 and was given to the town by Dr. Oliver Barnet (his house, built in 1771, lies on the eastern continuation of Church St.) to serve as a classical academy and meetinghouse. It remained in the public school system until 1951 and has served as the community center since the mid-1950s.

Just north of Church St. on C 517 is the Cold Brook Preserve (Old Turnpike Rd.; 908-782-1158), formerly the Van Doren farm. The 287 acres of rolling fields, orchards, and old pastures are administered by the county park system as a natural area. Part of the land is still being farmed, and it is hoped that this unusual combination of farm area and adjoining conservation easements will help preserve some of Hunterdon County's rural heritage. You are welcome to hike, cross-country ski, and mountain-bike in the park, but you are asked to respect the farmer's fields. Open to limited hunting.

Also just north of town on C 517 are the facilities of the Somerset Hills Handicapped Riders Club (83 Old Turnpike Rd.; 908-439-9636); visitors are welcome to observe the lessons. Call for information.

Further north of the center of town is the Christie Hoffman Farm Park (108 Fairmount Rd. West; 908-439-0022, ext. 727), 150 acres of woods, fields, and wetlands. There are hiking and horseback-riding trails here, as well as hills for sledding, opportunities for bird-watching, and athletic fields. Another former farm is now Pascale Farm Park (Fairmount Rd. east; 908-439-0022, ext. 727), 140 acres with forest trails designed to minimize the impact of the trails. North and west of town is the Whittemore Wildlife Sanctuary (7 Rockaway Rd.; 908-439-0022, ext. 724), close to 200 acres, open for hiking and horseback riding. Tewksbury Township runs an active environmental education program for children here.

The headquarters and museum of the Tewksbury Township Historical Society are at the western side of the township, in Mountainville (take Potterstown Rd. west to Rockaway Rd. and turn left, or north). Housed in a former one-room schoolhouse (60 Water St.; 908-832-6734), the museum contains Dr. Barnet's desk, as well as historic maps and archives available for research. Exhibits generally change twice a year. The society plans to establish regular hours, but for now the museum is open by appointment.

Oradell Bergen 8,047

GARDEN STATE PKWY EXIT 165, C 503

One of Bergen County's many Dutch settlements, Oradell still has some of its early stone houses, particularly along Kinderkamack and Paramus rds. On Midland Rd. you can also see an example of a Stickley house. The Edward W. Vaill house* (863 Midland Rd.) was built in 1911 according to one of the plans published in the *Craftsman* and furnished completely in Arts and Crafts style. The railroad station* (400 Maple Ave.) dates to 1890. In a converted late-19th-century firehouse, the Bergen County Players (298 Kinderkamack Rd.; 201-261-4200), a community group founded in the early 1930s, presents eight shows each season, including a special show for children each December. Tours of the theater can be arranged by writing the theater.

The hometown of Walter Schirra, the astronaut who orbited around the earth six times in 1962, Oradell is also the home of the Hiram Blauvelt Art Museum (705 Kinderkamack Rd.; 201-261-0012), an unusual museum devoted to a personal collection focusing on wildlife. Housed in the former carriage house of the late-19th-century Blauvelt mansion (the dark house with turrets and towers that looks like a haunted house in a Grade B movie), the collection includes examples of animals from around the world as well as paintings and sculpture related to animal themes. Among the holdings is a rare Audubon edition. Open Wednesday–Friday, 10–4; weekends, 2–5; groups by appointment.

Before the Revolution, a mill stood on the site on which the former Hackensack Water Company built a pumping station* (1882) and other facilities (in the New Milford Ave., Elm and Grove sts. area, often referred to as van Buskirk's Island). The water company stopped using this extraordinary facility in 1990 and turned the site over to the county. Much of the machinery, of a type no longer used, has been well preserved, and the buildings present a striking picture of late-19th-century Romanesque Revival architecture. The site is to be preserved intact, and various ideas have been suggested for creative reuse of the buildings as a museum, a research center, an environmental center, or an education center. For current information check with the Water Works Conservancy (201-967-0133), an organization that successfully fought to save the buildings.

Just south of Oradell, in New Milford, is the Art Center of Northern New Jersey (250 Center St.; 201-599-2992). Housed in a former church built in the 1890s, the center sponsors exhibits in its gallery and offers classes in all media. Exhibits change several times a year. Open Monday–Friday, 9:30–5:30; Saturday, 10–2; Sunday by appointment; special hours for exhibit openings.

Oxford Warren 2,307

NJ 31, C 624, 625, 645

Situated on the slopes of Scotts Mountain, Oxford (originally known as Oxford Furnace) became an important iron town in the 1740s, producing cannonballs for the Revolutionary Army. It was the first ironworks in the United States to use the hot blast method (1834), which revolutionized iron making in this country. A variety of iron products was made here, including railroad wheels and firebacks, until the furnaces were blown out in the 1880s (another furnace, built later, did continue operations until the early 1900s). The mines continued to be worked until 1964, and ore from these mines went into munitions for both world wars. The remains of the original Oxford Furnace* can be seen on the west side of Washington Ave. (between Belvidere Ave. and Cinder St.); there are explanatory plaques at the site. Farther up the hill is the Shippen Manor* (1744; 8 Belvidere Ave.; 908-453-4381), now serving as a house museum and home to the Warren County Cultural and Heritage Commission. During one period in the mid-18th century, the Oxford ironworks were owned by the Shippen brothers from Philadelphia; their niece Peggy Shippen, who became Benedict Arnold's wife, visited Oxford frequently to take part in its active social whirl of balls and hunts. Shippen Manor is open for tours, 1–4, 1st and 2d Sunday of the month; other times and groups by appointment. Concerts are given on the lawn on Sundays in the summer, and there are other special events from spinning demonstrations to French and Indian War encampments. Oxford's industrial historic district* includes parts of NJ 31; Belvidere, Buckley, and Washington aves. and the area around them; Jonestown and Mine Hill rds.; and Academy and Church sts.

North of Oxford on the south side of US 46, a little less than three miles east of the intersection with NJ 31 (the approach is well marked), is the Pequest Trout Hatchery and Natural Resource Education Center (605 Pequest Rd.; 908-637-4125). The facility is located within the Pequest Wildlife Management Area, an area chosen for the hatchery because of the exceptionally high quality of the water in the Pequest Valley. The hatcheries produce some 600,000 brook, brown, and rainbow trout each year for stocking the roughly 200 streams and lakes open for public fishing. (Some 95,000 people fish for trout in New Jersey waters each year.) This is basically a put-and-take operation, as few New Jersey streams can support trout naturally. Visitors can look into the nursery rooms and watch the upper raceways from an observation ramp. Many of the exhibits in the handsome educational center, which relate to the management of natural resources generally, as well as to fishing, forestry, and the Jersey shore, are hands-on and interactive. The annual open house the week before trout season opens includes a living history encampment and can draw as many as 8,000 people. The center operates programs for school groups, conservation organizations, camps, and casual visitors. A popular facility, the center can become crowded except in the winter months. A 15-minute video showing the behind-the-scenes operations (how the eggs are collected, for example) runs continuously, and there is a self-guiding tour. On the grounds are also a fishing education pond, a butterfly garden, nature trails, and facilities for picnicking. Open daily, 10–4; groups by appointment. Fishing courses taught April–October. Some of the wildlife management area land is leased to local farmers who grow small grain and corn to attract game birds and deer; within designated areas you can hike, hunt, and fish.

Some three miles south of Oxford on 31 in Washington, once known as the organ capital of the world, the Washington Historical Society maintains a display of local memorabilia. The display is at the Washington Township Improvement Society (21 Belvidere Ave.; 908-689-4800). Open weekdays, 9–5.

Paramus Bergen 25,737

GARDEN STATE PKWY EXITS 163, 165, NJ 4, 17

Settled in the mid-17th century by Dutch emigrants, Paramus may have derived its name from the Indian word *permessing,* for "abundance of turkeys." Over 60 years ago the town was described by the WPA guide to New Jersey as "an old Dutch farm community . . . growing vegetables for the city markets." You can still find scattered about the town a half-dozen or so old Dutch stone houses (drive along Paramus and E. Ridgewood aves.), but any sense of being in anything as compact as a farm community is gone (and the turkeys, of course, disappeared long ago).

In fact, Paramus is noted among historians of the city for having led in the development of the post–World War II shopping mall. (It has even been described as the mecca of malls.) The Garden State Plaza (NJ 4 and 17), which opened in 1957, was an early example of the open mall that served several regional community functions (it has since been converted to a closed mall), and the Paramus Park Mall (Garden State Pkwy and NJ 17) is an early example of the newer type of enclosed mall that for many has taken over some of the functions of the city's downtown. Paramus Park Mall was once architecturally appealing: its interior used to house a waterfall and fountain.

Housed in another of Paramus's malls is the Bergen County Museum of Art and Science (Bergen Mall, NJ 4 and Forest Ave.; 201-291-8848). Because the museum moved to this location from a larger space, many of its exhibits are works in progress. The museum's science materials feature a well-known mastodon skeleton unearthed nearby, when the excavation for I 80 was underway. The science exhibits will stress geological and ecological issues. Art exhibits change roughly every eight weeks and usually consist of one-person shows by artists from northern New Jersey and metropolitan New York City. The museum also features work by students in the Bergen County schools; these exhibits change roughly every six weeks. Occasionally items from the permanent collection are on display, and the museum has an active schedule of children's educational programs and workshops. Open Monday–Saturday, 10–5;

PARAMUS PARK MALL

groups and gallery tours by appointment. Donation requested.

West of this complex, off Ridgewood Ave. on the other side of the Garden State Parkway, is the New Jersey Children's Museum (599 Valley Health Plaza; 201-262-5151). Intended for children up to eight and adults, the facility features a variety of interactive and educational exhibits and activities. Open May–October, weekdays, 9–5, weekends, 10–5; October–April, daily, 10–6. Admission charge.

Paramus's oldest extant building, the Midland School* (239 W. Midland Ave.), was built in 1876. In 1924 the one-room schoolhouse became the borough hall. It later housed the police department and the entire library. Recently restored and tastefully enlarged, it is now the Charles E. Reid branch library. Also on Midland note the Mount Saint Andrew Villa, a retirement home run by the Sisters of Saint Elizabeth in Convent Station, and across the street the Church of the Annunciation.

Next door to the Paramus Golf Course (in the former superintendent's house) is the Fritz Behnke Historical Museum (330 Paramus Rd.; 201-445-1804). The museum's goal is to give visitors a sense of what daily life was like in the early 1920s when Paramus incorporated. It is furnished with objects from the period, and on display are the tools of everyday life for farmers and housewives, toys, photographs, and a variety of memorabilia. Open Sunday, 1–5 and by appointment. The clubhouse at the golf course was originally a sandstone-foundation carriage barn dating to the late 18th century.

Van Saun Park (Forest, Continental, and Howland aves.; 201-261-7312), one of Paramus's two county parks (it shares Van Saun with River Edge), is one of the county's most popular parks; it can be crowded in the summer. Its 10-acre zoo (201-262-3771) features some 200 animals representing 65 species from North and South America. The zoo is involved in an endangered species program and has managed to use its small space so that the animals do not appear crowded. A 4,000-square-foot aviary constructed like a circus tent and covered with netting replicates the environment of the Meadowlands. A boardwalk goes through the aviary over a 9,000-gallon artificial pond, which contains native fish, turtles, and waterfowl. (The aviary is closed when it is too cold to hose down the walks.) The zoo offers a wide range of educational programs—some 10,000 children a year take part in the formal programs—as well as seasonal events like sheepshearing. An 1860s Bergen County farmyard, complete with appropriate animals, has been re-created, and during the summer months (April–October) a miniature train with a replica of an 1866 locomotive runs around the zoo and the farmyard. Zoo open daily 10–4:30; tours by appointment (201-262-3771). At Washington Spring Park (between Van Saun's areas M and L), so called because Washington's army camped near here in 1780 and according to legend took water from the natural spring, is a shade garden. There are also picnic grounds, a lake and boat basin, a bicycle-pedestrian path, sledding slopes, large age-appropriate playgrounds, and a tennis center (201-265-1028). Open May–September, 9–5; October–April, 9–4:30.

One section of Saddle River County Park is on Dunkerhoof Rd. (off Paramus Rd.; 201-444-1117); here are a wooded picnic area and one section of the five-mile trail that links several recreation areas along the Saddle River. Bergen Community College, on the site of a former golf course, is a compact campus joined by covered walks. Along the Saddle River at the southwestern corner of the borough (Red Mill Rd., just south of 4 and east of Saddle River Rd.) is the Easton tower and waterwheel, reconstructed in the 1960s to replace the original complex built in 1899 on the site of an 18th-century mill that produced blankets for the army in the Civil War.

Park Ridge Bergen 8,708

GARDEN STATE PKWY EXIT 172S

Richard Nixon's home for the last years of his life, Park Ridge is also the hometown of James Gandolfini and the singing group the Roches and, since the late 1980s, home base for the Hertz Corporation, the world's largest rental-car company. Like much of Bergen County, Park Ridge was settled by Dutch farmers, and there are old Dutch stone houses to be seen on Pascack and Rivervale roads. At 13 Pascack Rd., for example, is the Wortendyke Dutch Barn* (201-930-0124, 201-366-7268). Exhibits at this 18th-century barn focus on the history of the family whose farm it was and on farming in the northern part of Bergen County. (The Wortendykes left this land in the 19th century, but it continued to be farmed into the mid-20th century.) Open April–October, Wednesday, Saturday, and Sunday, 1–5; groups by appointment. Directly across the road (12 Pascack Rd.) is the late-18th-century Frederick Wortendyke house.*

From about 1775 until 1889 Park Ridge was the site of a wampum mint. Wampum, manufactured here by John W. Campbell and his descendants, was used by the U.S. government and by fur traders (John Jacob Astor bought wampum from the Campbells) in their dealings with Native Americans in the West. Most wampum was manufactured by hand, but the Campbells invented a machine that could drill holes in six shells at once. They are reputed to have given picnics at which one could eat all the shellfish one wanted without charge as long as the shells were not broken. Their machine, thought to be unique in the world, is on exhibit at the Pascack Historical Society Museum (19 Ridge Ave.; 201-573-0307, 201-666-0121), along with other tools from the mint and collections of old implements, cabinetmakers' tools, paperweights, textiles, wedding dresses, and many other items. The museum, housed in an 1873 Congregational church built "under the guidance of" Henry Ward Beecher, concentrates on exhibits that highlight life in the Pascack Valley. The central exhibit generally changes every year or two. The society also sponsors public lectures and slide programs. Open Sunday, 1–4; groups and other times by appointment.

Parsippany–Troy Hills Morris 50,649

I 287, I 80, US 202, NJ 10, 46, 53

Parsippany is known to have been settled since at least the early 18th century; at that time the area was considered the "most notable in the state for grazing." In the 19th century dairy products replaced hay and wood, and in the 20th truck gardening and poultry farming were dominant. The area was also popular as a resort from the 19th century into the 1920s and '30s, and some of the local lakes were created for that market. Like many other townships, Parsippany–Troy Hills is made up of smaller settlements, some of which grew in an uncontrolled way after World War II, and the remnants of their past are often hard to find among the corporate offices and superhighways. (Four superhighways—I 287, I 80, US 202, and NJ 46—slice through the township, often making it awkward to get from one part to another.) Parsippany is far and away the county's largest municipality; it also boasts over 12 million square feet of commercial space (to say nothing of the 4.8 million square feet of industrial space). Among the corporate tenants is Tiffany's, and the Vince Lombardi silver Superbowl trophy is crafted in Parsippany.

One of the township's remaining late-18th-century buildings, the Bowlsby House* (320 Baldwin Rd.; 973-263-4397), is being used as the township's historical museum. Here you can see a variety of artifacts, memorabilia, and photographs relating to the town, including, for example, the wagon and high chair belonging to John Grimes, head of the Underground Railroad in Morris County. Open weekdays, 12–4.

Old Troy Park (Reynolds Ave.; 973-326-7600), is a 96-acre county park, with playing fields, picnic facilities, horseshoe pits, a wooden train for children, and trails suitable for hiking, cross-country skiing, and snowshoeing.

In the western part of the township is Craftsman Farms* (2352 NJ 10 W. at Manor La.; 973-540-1165), a national historic landmark designed and built by Gustav Stickley (on land that had been farmed since the 18th century). From 1908 to 1911 he worked to build his home and a farm school that would further the Arts and Crafts movement, but by 1918 he was bankrupt. Eventually, the property was rescued from the jaws of a developer, and of the 650 acres Stickley had purchased, 31 remain. The main house, sometimes described as the biggest log cabin in the eastern United States, is being lovingly restored and serves as a museum of the arts and crafts movement. There are guided tours of the house, which is also used for lectures, crafts demonstrations, and other special programs. Grounds open daily; house open April–mid-November, Wednesday–Friday, 12–3, weekends, 11–4. Groups by appointment. Craftsman Farms was the first site in New Jersey to receive a National Trust for Historic Preservation National Honor Award.

In the southwestern part of the township (off NJ 53) is the community of Mount Tabor. Formed as a camp meeting in the late 1860s (by a committee that included Stephen Crane's father), it gradually evolved from a tent camp to a more permanent summer religious colony to its present condition as a distinctive section of the larger township. The Mount Tabor Golf Club is on land that was part of the colony, and the colony's past is distinguishable in the Victorian gingerbread that characterizes many of the houses. The Mount Tabor Historical Society (973-586-1693) presents concerts at the Tabernacle (973-983-8346) and holds an annual house tour in the fall.

East of the township in East Hanover Township is Troy Meadows (973-962-7031), 350 acres of marshy land created by the last glacier. This natural area is the largest remaining cattail marsh in New Jersey, one of the few places in the state where you can see bog turtles, and an excellent spot for bird-watchers.

Passaic Passaic 67,861

NJ 21

Passaic at one time was a center of the country's textile industry—it was once the country's leading manufacturer of linen and linen thread, in 1910 it was first in the state and fourth nationally in the production of worsted, and at one point over half the country's handkerchiefs were manufactured here. Botany Worsted Mills claimed to have the largest complete textile manufacturing facility in the world, and the Botany Worsted Mills Historic District* can be seen at 80–82 and 90 Dayton Ave. and 6–32 Mattimore St. The city was also an important producer of rubber, and the first pre–World War II TV sets were manufactured here by the Du Mont company. The mills began to move south after World War II, and today the remaining large industrial buildings are occupied by a mix of small companies. Over the last 20 years the decline in population has reversed, and the city has passed the numbers it had in the 1930s.

As industry developed after the Civil War, the original Dutch and Irish farmers in the area were joined by European immigrants. In the 1910 census, Passaic had the largest percentage of foreign-born residents in the state, and in the 1930s about one-third of the residents were foreign born. Poles were then the largest single group, although there were large numbers from Hungary, Italy, Russia, and elsewhere. The tradition continues: today, for example, there are so many Peruvians in Passaic and Paterson that Peru opened a consulate in the county.

In the heart of the old Hungarian district, now primarily Hispanic, you can visit a museum devoted to one of Passaic's many cultures: the American Hungarian Museum is housed on the second floor of the Reid Memorial Library (80 Third St.; 973-473-0013, 201-836-4869). The permanent exhibit has examples of folk and fine art, historical artifacts, and photographs, from the old country and from the Hungarian American community. The museum also sponsors concerts, lectures, and videos. Open October–May, by appointment during library hours; special programs Sunday, 1–5.

Paterson Passaic 149,222

I 80, NJ 4, 20

 First settled by the Dutch in the late 17th century, Paterson remained an agricultural community until late in the 18th century. It was an unusually early tourist attraction—the 77-foot-high Great Falls of the Passaic River drew visitors from as far away as New York when it took three days to get to the site. During the Revolution, George Washington, Alexander Hamilton, and the marquis de Lafayette had stopped to eat lunch at the Great Falls, and Hamilton had been struck by the power that lay in them. He believed that the success of the young country depended on its establishing its own industrial base, and 12 years after his visit to the Great Falls, as secretary of the treasury, he proposed to Congress the establishment of an industrial district. When Congress was unenthusiastic about funding the project, he arranged private support for what was in effect the country's first planned industrial city. Thus was the Society of Usefull Manufactures (S.U.M.), born in 1791. Pierre L'Enfant, later to design Washington, D.C., was hired to design the city. His scheme proved too expensive, although the raceways were laid out according to his plan, and the work was taken over by Peter Colt, a member of a family that had much to do with the S.U.M. and Paterson's development. The area surrounding the falls was named Paterson in honor of the then governor of the state and signer of the Declaration of

Independence, William Paterson. The society, which was granted many financial and legal privileges by the state, continued to operate until after World War II.

Over the course of the 19th century Paterson became a leading industrial city, known as the home of the Colt revolver ("The gun that won the West") and the submarine, as a leading producer of cotton and the home of cotton duck sails, as Silk City, as a major producer of locomotives and then airplane engines, as the scene of momentous labor struggles. It was also a major stop on the Underground Railroad. By 1900 it had become the 15th-largest city in the United States. Many famous people were Paterson natives, among them Nicholas Murray Butler, the president of Columbia University for over 40 years; Garret A. Hobart, vice-president during McKinley's first term; Albert

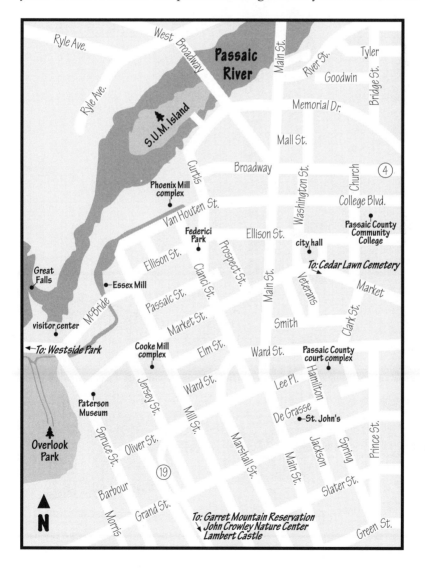

Sabin, developer of the oral polio vaccine; Larry Doby, the first African American in the American Baseball League; Allen Ginsberg, the poet; and Lou Costello, the comedian (in 1992 a statue was erected in his honor in Federici Park). Perhaps less well remembered today is Sam Patch, a cotton spinner who jumped into the falls when drunk one night. He survived and started a second career as "the Great Descender," achieving a successful jump at Niagara Falls. (He died in the Genessee Falls.) Although not a native (he came from Rutherford), the poet William Carlos Williams is forever associated with Paterson because of his long poem of that name.

PATERSON

The first factory was in operation by 1794, producing calico goods, and cotton was Paterson's first important product. In the 1830s Sam Colt began manufacturing his revolver in what came to be known as the Gun Mill (the walls of the first two stories are still to be seen at Van Houten St.). The venture was not successful, and he sold the factory. When the government decided it wanted to order the revolver (apparently because of a recommendation from the Texas Ranger Sam Walker, who had used it in 1838), Colt had no model at hand. In one version of the story, he paid an exorbitant price to buy someone else's gun; in another, he redesigned the gun. In either case, there is agreement that he made his fortune from the revolver, but this time it was manufactured in Connecticut.

At about the same time that Colt first made his revolver, Thomas Rogers manufactured the country's first steam locomotive, the Sandusky. Over the next 50 years four companies were manufacturing locomotives in Paterson and among them produced roughly 40 percent of the nation's locomotives. Paterson also produced most of the rotary snowplows used on locomotives.

The silk industry began in Paterson in the 1840s, cotton by then having moved to New England, and by the 1880s Paterson was called Silk City. Every stage of production, except growing the silkworms, took place in Paterson, and unlike the other industries mentioned, silk continued as a prominent industry into the 20th century. In fact, the famous silk workers strike of 1913 (*see* Haledon) took place when the industry was still vital to the city. Silk ceased being important to the city when synthetic fibers were developed.

A Paterson schoolteacher, John P. Holland, developed the first successful submarine in 1878 and tested it in the Passaic River. Although Holland's ideas lie behind today's atomic submarines, for years the navy did not take him seriously, even when he surprised a navy ship on a secret maneuver. When he won a contest sponsored by the navy, the navy decided to sponsor another contest.

After World War I the Wright Aeronautical Corporation, manufacturers of airplane motors, moved to an old silk factory in Paterson, where they made the engine for Charles Lindbergh's *Spirit of St. Louis*. For a time this was Paterson's dominant industry, but it moved elsewhere after World War II.

Although Paterson is no longer a leading industrial city, it has found creative ways to reuse its remaining 19th-century industrial buildings and is experiencing new vitality as a different sort of city. The S.U.M. historic district* (encompassing W. Broadway; Ryle, Wayne, and McBride aves.; Grand, Morris, Barbour, Spruce, Market, Mill, Van Houten, Curtis, River, Oliver, and Reservoir sts.; Stoney Rd.; and the Passaic River) is a national historic landmark district. The buildings here date from the 18th to the 20th century, and many of the industrial buildings have been converted to a variety of uses. In the Rogers Locomotive Mill building (16–32 Spruce St.), for example, the New Jersey Community Development Corporation runs its

Transportation Opportunity Center. And in the Rogers Locomotive Erecting Shop (1874) is the Paterson Museum (2 Market St.; 973-881-3874), dedicated to preserving the industrial, technological, and geological history of Paterson. There are both changing and permanent exhibits: among the displays are ones relating to the aircraft engine industry, locomotives, Colt guns, local rocks and minerals, and textiles, as well as two of Holland's submarines. Open Tuesday–Friday, 10–4; weekends, 12:30–4:30. Admission charge.

The Great Falls Historic District Cultural Center (65 McBride Ave. Ext.; 973-279-9587) is located in a converted 1930s gas station (itself a retrofitted mid-19th-century boardinghouse). Here you can see photographs of the falls and orientation videos and pick up a map for a self-guided tour, as well as other material. Open weekdays, 9–4:30; Saturday the hours are variable so it is advisable to call first.

Wandering through the district you will see not just old mills but workers' houses, the raceways, churches, even the bar (Cianci and Van Houten sts.) that served as I.W.W. headquarters during the silk strike. Some of the mills have been converted to living quarters: the Phoenix Mill complex (Van Houten St.), 1815–70, has been turned into cooperative apartments; the Essex Mill (Mill St.), 1807–72, which used to manufacture mosquito netting, into subsidized apartments for artists. The Cooke Mill Complex (Mill St.) has been converted to apartments and a family health center. In the mid-'80s the People's Republic of China even purchased an old paper mill to manufacture cardboard.

The falls, 77 feet high and 280 feet wide, have been declared a national natural landmark, and their energy is once again being harnessed. They are best observed from Overlook Park (McBride); from there you can also see much of Paterson's geological history in the rocks. Another attractive option is to walk on the foot trail that follows an old Native American trail (Stoney Rd.) and travels along the ridge.

A visit to downtown Paterson, which is close to the Great Falls district, is also rewarding. Note particularly the Cathedral of St. John the Baptist* (Main and Grand sts.), 1865, a national historic landmark; the Passaic County courthouse annex, originally the post office (Hamilton St.), built at the turn of the century as a copy of the medieval Haarlem Guild house (to honor the first settlers of Paterson); the late-19th-century city hall (155 Market St.), modeled on that in Lyons, France (also a silk-producing city); and the county courthouse, 1903 (Clark St.).

Another aspect of the silk industry can be seen in Lambert Castle,* also known as Bella Vista (Valley Rd.; 973-247-0085), a pretentious late-19th-century stone mansion built by one of the leaders of the industry, Catholina Lambert. The house now serves as a museum run by the Passaic County Historical Society. Although Lambert was forced to sell his art collection (it included works by Rembrandt, El Greco, Renoir, and Monet), a few pieces remain. The first floor is decorated to reflect life as someone in Lambert's social class would have lived it in Victorian times, with an attempt to have each room reflect the purpose it served when the Lamberts lived there. In some cases, Lambert's actual furnishings are available (the dining room set, for example). The second floor is devoted to local history more generally, the third floor to exhibits that change at least three times a year. The house itself is striking: note the hand-carved oak structure that places anyone descending the steps in a picture frame, and be sure to take in the view from the terrace. The grounds have also been restored to reflect the 1930s landscaping designed by the Olmsted Brothers (a noted landscaping firm run by the sons of Frederick Law Olmsted). Open Wednesday–Sunday, 1–4, except during the setting up and running of the annual holiday boutique (usually mid-October–mid-December, but it's a good idea to check the dates). Admission charge.

Lambert Castle is located in Garret Mountain Reservation, a 560-acre county park with open fields, a fishing pond, a three-mile cross-country track, an overlook, an equestrian center, and picnic areas. Garret Mountain has an unusual number and variety of rare minerals and is in fact a national natural landmark because of the volcanic activity associated with its formation. It is also good place to watch for hawks and has been described as one of the best migrant traps in the state, providing opportunities to watch (and listen) for warblers, vireos, flycatchers, and other nontropical migrants.

South of Garret Mountain, in Rifle Camp Park (Rifle Camp Rd.), is the John Crowley Nature Center (973-523-0024). The center, which includes an astronomical observatory, a seismograph, and a weather station, has changing nature and mineral displays and sponsors a variety of programs for children and adults. Public evenings at the observatory usually take place twice a month, except in January. Open Monday–Saturday, 9–5; closed holidays. Group tours by reservation. There are hiking trails, a bird blind, and a fitness course in the park; the picnic areas include one suitable for handicapped visitors. The park is open daily, dawn–dusk.

Many of Paterson's distinguished citizens, including Lambert, Rogers, Hobart, and Butler, are buried in the Cedar Lawn Cemetery (McLean Blvd., NJ 20), opened in 1867. This cemetery, which includes a Greek Revival temple for Hobart designed by Henry Bacon, who designed the Lincoln Memorial, is rich in examples of Victorian funerary architecture. North of Cedar Lawn (take McLean Blvd.), in what was Paterson's wealthy area, is Eastside Park, laid out in the 1890s. There is a splendid view here, and some of the mansions from Paterson's days of glory surround the park. At Westside Park★ (112–242 Totowa Ave.), you can see the Van Houten house (18th and 19th centuries).

At Passaic County Community College (1 College Blvd.) is a large mural depicting the history of the city from Hamilton to the visit of Martin Luther King in 1968. (King's visit took place shortly before his assassination.) Also on the campus is a life-size brass-and-copper statue of King. The poetry center sponsors readings, workshops, conferences, and contests.

The Hamilton Club Building (32 Church St.; 973-684-5448), built in the early 20th century as an exclusive gentleman's club, houses the Federici Studio Collection, an art collection that came with the building, and changing exhibits of contemporary art. Open Monday–Friday, 8–5. Changing exhibits are also to be seen at the Broadway & LRC Galleries (Broadway at Memorial Dr.; 973-684-5448). Open Monday–Friday, 9–9; Saturday, 9–5. Tours by appointment. A theater series for young people also takes place at the college. For information on all cultural events that are open to the public, call 973-684-6555.

Paulsboro   Gloucester   6,160

NJ 44

Settled in the 1680s, Paulsboro is named for one of the first families to arrive in the area. Fort Billings Park (Delaware River, Billingsport Rd. at 3d St., Clonmell Rd., N. Delaware St.), listed on the state historic register, commemorates the fort, which was built by the U.S. government in 1776 to keep the British from getting to Philadelphia. The land bought for Fort Billings represented the new government's first land purchase (the Pauls were the sellers), and the fort was designed by Tadeusz Kosciuszko, the Polish patriot. The Gill Memorial Library (Broad and Commerce sts.) is in a stone house built c. 1810 by John Clark and named in honor of Matthew Gill, a prominent 19th-century Paulsboro man who, among other charitable activities, in the 1870s gave the land on which the Episcopal Church stands. (The current church building dates to 1910; the original one burned.) The Samuel Philip Paul house (212 E. Broad St.), like the library, dates to 1810, although the back portion may be much older. The Exxon-Mobil refinery just south of the park (known as the Paulsboro plant, it is actually in Gibbstown) opened in 1917; the refinery on the Paulsboro side, completed in the early 1990s, is said to be the country's largest producer of lubricating oil.

Southwest of Paulsboro, in Gibbstown, is the C. A. Nothnagle log house* (406 Swedesboro Rd.; 609-423-0916), a mid-17th-century structure that may well be the oldest log cabin in the country. Originally constructed without nails, the 16-by-22-foot house is still in its original location. It has a unique corner fireplace and dovetail construction. Inside are an 18th-century cabinet and various artifacts. Open by appointment.

Also in Gibbstown is Greenwich Lake Park (Tomlin Station Rd; 856-468-0100). The 40-acre spring-fed lake is stocked with trout, and you can fish year-round. The boat launch is open weekends from the start of the trout season to Memorial Day and daily Memorial Day–Labor Day; the lake is open for swimming June–Labor Day. Picnic tables are also available, and a variety of wildlife is to be seen in the wetlands surrounding the lake. Open April–November, sunrise–sunset.

North of Paulsboro, in an athletic field in Billingsport, is the Tinicum Rear Range Lighthouse (Mantua Ave. and 2d St.; 856-423-1505). This light has been continuosuly active since 1880. You can visit the 80-foot steel tower the third weekend of the month, April–October, Saturday, 10–3, Sunday, 12–4.

Peapack-Gladstone   Somerset 2,433

US 202, 206, C 512

Situated in an area of rolling hills and large estates, Peapack and Gladstone (together they form a single borough) are both attractive villages. Many of the estates have been converted to other uses—the former Blair mansion, for example, a French château built in 1903 that overlooks Ravine Lake, was for many years Saint Joseph's Villa, a religious retreat. Thirty-eight acres from that estate and some of the other buildings—the stables, the carriage barn, and three brick houses employees of the estate had lived in—became the nucleus for the current campus of the Matheny School, an institution that has pioneered in the effort to provide severely learning disabled children and young adults with an education that will enable them to live independently.

The former Ladd estate, built in the early 20th century, and converted to a convalescent home for "deserving gentlewomen" was bought by King Hassan II of Morocco in 1983 in what was then the largest domestic real estate transaction in the state's history ($7.5 million). In the almost 20 years he owned the estate, the king apparently only visited a few times and never spent the night. The estate now belongs to the county, which plans to lease the mansion (designed by the architect who designed the Boston Museum of Fine Arts) and 80-some acres for commercial use as a spa; the remaining 400 acres will be added to the county's open-space inventory. For information call 908-722-1200.

A small portion of Hamilton Farms, a former 5,000-acre estate with stables that were characterized when they were built in 1916 as "the most lavish" in the country, now serves as the headquarters of the United States Equestrian Team (USET) Foundation (Pottersville Rd.; 512, just west of US 206; 908-234-1251). The team no longer trains here, but master classes and competitions are held. Open to the public weekdays, 8:30–4:30, and for special events. You are free to wander the grounds any time. From May to October, there are generally one or two special events or competitions each month, usually including the Festival of Champions in June; admission may be charged on these occasions.

A little north of Gladstone are two Morris County facilities, both on former, albeit more modest, estates—Willowwood Arboretum and Bamboo Brook Outdoor Education Center (continue on 512 past Hamilton Farms to Union Grove Rd., right on Union Grove, left on Longview; about a half-mile to your left is the driveway leading to Willowwood; another half-mile to your left the driveway to Bamboo Brook; 973-326-7600). On 130 acres of rolling farmland in the Hacklebarney Hills, Willowwood contains some 3,500 kinds of plants, both native and exotic, as well as one section of undisturbed forest. There are impressive collections of lilacs, ferns, magnolias, and hollies, and a hillside of pink lady slippers. Near the house, which dates from 1792, are two small formal gardens, but most of the paths meander through open areas and woodland.

Bamboo Brook, formerly Merchiston Farm, was for many years the home of Martha Brookes Hutcheson, one of the first women in the United States to be trained as a landscape architect. On the center's 100 acres are fields, forest, and a five-acre formal garden designed by Hutcheson. The earliest section of the house dates from the 1720s; the lecture hall is a music room added in the 1920s. The house is now used by the New Jersey Conservation Foundation. The gardens include a cedar arbor, pool garden, and ha-ha. As in the Willowwood Arboretum, trails here wind through the fields and along the brook. Classes, tours, and workshops are held at both facilities. The grounds in both parks are open dawn–dusk; tours by appointment.

Because the two facilities are in different geological sections—Willowwood is in the Piedmont and much of Bamboo Brook in the Highlands—the contrast between the two adjacent sites is of interest. The wooded area between them contains examples of Roxbury pudding stone.

Near Peapack-Gladstone on US 206 the pharmaceutical company Pfizer occupies a facility that, seen from the highway, looks something like an Italian hill village. Occupying 30 acres of an 850-acre tract, the buildings are linked by arcades, there are formal gardens and landscaped courts, and dominating all is the 88-foot campanile.

Pemberton Burlington 1,210

C 530

This small Pinelands community, just a few miles west of Fort Dix and McGuire Air Force Base, was settled by Quakers in the late 17th century and named in the 19th century for James Pemberton, a Philadelphia merchant. An early-19th-century house and mill* can still be seen where Rancocas Creek crosses Hanover St. An 18th-century Quaker meetinghouse* still stands in Arneys Mount, north of Pemberton.

Also on Hanover Street is the North Pemberton railroad station,* now the home of Pemberton's Station Museum (3 Fort Dix Rd., C 616; 609-894-0546). The station, which replaced one from the 1860s that was lost in a fire, dates to 1892. Outside the station is a collection of railroad equipment, including locomotives and cars from the first half of the 20th century; eventually the complex will look as it did 100 years ago, with

5,000 feet of track. Inside the museum is a variety of objects, including a collection of New Jersey minerals and crystals, old lamps, tools, tickets, and old railroad maps. The museum is also involved in various special events, including a lantern show, a train show, and a December hayride. Open Wednesday, Friday, Saturday, and Sunday, 10–4; groups and other times by appointment.

Burlington County College is south of the borough on the Pemberton–Browns Mills Rd. (C 530; 609-894-9311, ext. 7289). Exhibits in the Creation Gallery in the Lewis Parker College Center are devoted to works by students and local artists and change monthly; the permanent collection is in the academic center. Most of the pieces in the sculpture gallery change annually. The exhibits are open to the public during normal college hours; call for information. The Foundation Theatre (609-894-2138), a professional company, performs at the college.

If you continue on C 530 and turn right on New Lisbon Rd. (C 646), after about four miles you will enter Brendan T. Byrne State Forest (609-726-1191). The state began acquiring this forest, formerly known as Lebanon State Forest, early in the 20th century; it now covers almost 35,000 acres and contains 400 miles of road and more than 25 miles of marked trails. Two units of the Civilian Conservation Corps, one all African American, were active here in the 1930s, developing 60 miles of road; building shelters and cabins, three of which are still in use; creating Pakim Pond out of a former cranberry reservoir (the pond is near the site of the Lebanon Glass Works, active for a few years in the 1860s, which gave the forest its former name); and planting more than 3 million seedlings. In the past, trees from that planting were occasionally harvested and taken to Batsto (*see* Hammonton) to be sawn into lumber to use in the forest for repairs and signs.

Among the many attractions of this Pinelands tract is the Cedar Swamp Natural Area, an Atlantic white cedar swamp surrounded by a pitch pine forest, in which can be found many of the unusual plants that thrive in the Pinelands. This is the northern limit of commercially useful Atlantic white cedar. Hikers can find many miles of unmarked sand roads as well as marked trails and a section of the 50-mile Batona Trail, which begins in the forest at Ong's Hat and ends in Bass River State Forest (*see* Tuckerton). Horseback riders will also enjoy the sand roads. The forest is open for picnicking, camping, fishing, and hunting. Nature programs are offered in conjunction with the Pinelands Institute for Natural and Environmental Studies (609-893-1765; *see* below). For information and trail maps, stop at the office (the entrance is off NJ 72, 1 mi. south of the NJ 70–72 intersection).

If you continue on C 530, past New Lisbon Rd. (at Browns Mills, 530 turns right and becomes Lakehurst Rd.), about 4½ miles east of Browns Mills, you will reach Whitesbog Road. Turning left here takes you to the community of Whitesbog,* developed in the 1860s by Joseph J. White, a cranberry cultivator who discovered the value of flooding cranberry bogs and became known as the cranberry king. His eldest daughter, Elizabeth C. White, was responsible for developing the commercial blueberry from native huckleberries. In 1916, five years after she began working with a U.S. Department of Agriculture scientist, she marketed her first commercial crop. White maintained her interest in the development of the blueberry all her life and donated land for further work. (She also maintained a lifelong interest in and concern for those who tended the plants.) New Jersey now leads the nation in the production of blueberries for consumption fresh (40 million pounds in 2003) and is second in overall production (41 million pounds in 2003) and acreage (7,800 acres in 2003), and blueberries are now the official state fruit. (The acidic soil of the Pinelands, combined with the blueberry's low fertility requirements, make this the ideal place to grow them.) At one time the White plantation employed 80 full-time and 600 migrant workers. Although cranberries and blueberries are still grown commercially around Whitesbog (some of the land is leased to the White company, which has been modernizing some of the bogs), many of the buildings suffered from neglect. The Whitesbog Preservation Trust (609-893-4646) has been working on the remaining buildings, including the packing house, the old general store, the barrel house, the workers' cottages, and a Sears catalogue house.* The trust sponsors an annual blueberry festival and offers frequent moonlight walks, nature walks, and other educational programs. Call for the schedule. General store open weekends, 10–4, early February–mid-December. Village open daily, dawn–dusk; tours by appointment.

The Pineland Institute for Natural and Environmental Studies (referred to as Pines; 609-893-1765) has been located in Whitesbog since 1968. Run by Burlington County College, the institute, which operates out of the old general store, sponsors educational environmental programs. Attended by some 8,000 people a year, the programs focus on the natural resources of the Pinelands and the environmental impact of human activity. This is a wonderful area to walk in, but as in all hikes on unmarked Pinelands roads, it is easy to get lost unless you take care to watch for distinguishing landmarks.

Pennington   Mercer 2,596

NJ 31

First settled late in the 17th century, Pennington was named Queenstown in honor of Queen Anne, but came to be called Penny Town, possibly because it was so small (less than one square mile). By the mid-18th century, the name had solidified as Pennington. In 1776 the town was occupied by British and Hessian troops, who apparently used it as a base for raids on Trenton. Lord Cornwallis had his headquarters here for a time, and members of the British cavalry are said to have jumped their horses over the wall in front of the

First Presbyterian Church. (The present building on Main St. dates to 1875; the earlier building burned.)

Pennington today is much admired for its well-preserved look. The Pennington School (112 W. Delaware Ave.), founded in 1838, is the oldest Methodist secondary school in the United States. Established as a Methodist Episcopal male seminary, in 1854 it became coeducational. Reverting to a boys' school in 1910, it went coed again in 1972. Among Pennington's many attractive buildings note the 18th-century John Welling house* (52 E. Curlis Ave.), with its fish-scale shingles, and the railroad station* at the corner of Green St. and Franklin Ave. (c. 1882).

East of the center of town is the Stony Brook–Millstone Watershed Association (31 Titus Mill Rd.; 609-737-3735), a conservation organization that operates out of a farmhouse on over 800 acres. Also on the property are the Buttinger Nature Center, an organic farm, a pond house, a butterfly house (open spring to fall), and 12 miles of trails suitable for hiking and cross-country skiing. Maps are available for self-guided tours. The nature center (609-737-7592) has two discovery rooms, hands-on exhibits, a library, a puppet theater, and a children's reading nook. The farm (260 Wargo Rd.; 609-737-8899), with one of the largest community-supported organic agriculture programs in the country, is used as an experimental and demonstration farm. The association is involved in an active educational program for children and adults; it also sponsors a day camp in the summer and frequent special events. The nature center is open Tuesday–Saturday, 10–5; the reserve daily, dawn–dusk; and the office weekdays, 9–5.

About two miles east of the center of town (take E. Delaware Ave. to Federal City Rd.) is Rosedale Park (609-989-6530), a 472-acre county facility. The lake is stocked with trout, and you can boat (no gasoline engines) and canoe; there are family and group picnic areas (the latter by reservation only; call 609-989-6536). Environmental tours of the park for groups by reservation (609-989-6532). Open daily until dusk.

Nearby is the county's equestrian facility (431B Federal City Rd.; 609-730-9059), which operates out of a renovated cow barn. It offers both regular and therapeutic riding lessons, as well as educational programs and a summer camp. The trails are open to private horses as well. Open weekdays, 8–7, weekends, 8–5, except in December, when the stable closes to the public at 6.

Just north of Pennington (take N. Main St.) is the Baldwin Lake Wildlife Management Area, a small (47 acres) protected area with a popular 18-acre fishing lake, notable for bass and sunfish.

Pennsauken Camden 35,737

US 130, NJ 90, C 543

The township of Pennsauken lies on the Delaware River (it is in fact bisected by the approach to the Betsy Ross Bridge) and is bounded on the north by Pennsauken Creek. The area was inhabited by Native Americans, and this is the only town in Camden County with a Native American name (Pennsauken means "place where tobacco was traded"). It is also the site of the first recorded English settlement in West Jersey: in the 1630s a group of English colonists built a fort here, which they named after a Native American chief. The fort was abandoned after four years, but the Griffith Morgan House* (Griffith Morgan La. off River Rd., C 543, by the Aluminum Shakes plant; 609-665-1948), built c. 1693, is still standing. This stone house, the oldest house in Camden County, was damaged by a fire set by vandals. Enough remained standing so that it could be rebuilt to look the way it had, and plans currently call for adding on another section that had been in the original. The house is furnished with pieces dating primarily from the early 1700s to around 1820; on the top floor is a museum that concentrates on life in the area. A variety of memorabilia and artifacts, including fossils from southern New Jersey, as well as the work of local artists, is featured. Open houses are held several times a year, and groups can arrange for tours by appointment. A video tour of the house is available on the first floor for those who do not want to deal with the steps.

The Burrough-Dover House* (9201 Burrough-Dover La.; 856-662-3002), an early-18th-century stone house (c. 1710) with a late-18th-century addition (1793), serves as headquarters of the Pennsauken Historical Society. Many of the furnishings are of historic interest, and in the basement is a collection of old toys and tools. The society opens the house four times a year and gives tours by appointment.

The Aluminum Shakes company apparently constructed the largest aluminum scaffolding ever built; it was used in the repair of the Statue of Liberty.

Pennsville Salem 13,195

NJ 49

The first area in Salem County to be settled, Pennsville was founded by Swedes and Finns around 1640. It later became a center for shad (and some sturgeon) fishing and the terminal for ferry service to Delaware. (At the foot of Church Landing Rd. is a marker showing where the early Scandinavian settlers crossed the river to Wilmington, Delaware, to worship on Sunday.) Today the

Delaware Memorial Bridge crosses at Pennsville, and many from the township use it to commute to Delaware or even Philadelphia. A large township, Pennsville still retains a few pre-Revolutionary homes.

St. George's Episcopal Church (NJ 49 and Church Landing Rd.) was founded by the Church of Sweden in 1714. When the Swedish missionaries left, the log-cabin church became Episcopal. It was replaced in 1802 by the present structure (now minus its second story, which was removed in 1860 because it was too heavy). In the parish house are various artifacts from the Swedish settlers. Tours for groups can be arranged by calling 856-678-5411.

Toward the end of Church Landing Rd. is the Church Landing Farmhouse Museum (86 Church Landing Rd.; 856-678-4453). This Gothic Revival farmhouse (c. 1860), restored by the Pennsville Township Historical Society, is furnished to show what life would have been like in a mid-19th-century farmhouse. Also on the site is a small maritime museum; among its displays are items relating to fishing, once an important occupation in town, and shad. Another building houses changing displays of the museum's collection of artifacts. A third building is devoted to items from an amusement park that once flourished on the site of Riverview Beach Park, a municipal park at Broadway between Lakeview Ave. and Pittsfield St.; it closed in 1967. The society also sponsors a day-at-the-farm fair in June. Open Sunday and Wednesday, 1–3; other times and groups by appointment. Closed February.

If you continue south on Broadway from Riverside Park, turning right at Fort Mott Rd., you will see to your left the Finns Point Rear Range Light* (197 Lighthouse Rd.; 609-935-1487), a 115-foot lighthouse with a Greek doorway, built in 1876, a rare surviving example of a wrought-iron lighthouse. The view from the lighthouse, which was decommissioned in 1950, is spectacular. Open April–October, 3d Sunday of the month, 12–4, and on New Jersey Lighthouse Day.

The lighthouse is part of the Supawna Meadows National Wildlife Refuge (856-935-1487), and an interpretive display at the site has information about the light on one side and the refuge on the other. The refuge, close to 3,000 acres, is of interest to naturalists because it is less saline than the ocean and a good spot for glossy ibis, cattle and snowy egrets, bald eagles, northern harriers, and red-winged blackbirds. The refuge has two walking and one boat trail, and you can fish and hunt at designated times in designated places. Call the refuge for information on guided nature walks as well as on trail maps and regulations.

Continuing south on Fort Mott Rd. will bring you to Fort Mott* State Park (856-935-3218), a 104-acre waterfront park with buildings and concrete gun embattlements dating to the Spanish-American War. Acquired by the state in 1947, the park, which is a stop on the New Jersey Coastal Heritage Trail, has a splendid view of the Delaware, facilities for picnicking and fishing, playing fields, and a nature trail that leads to Finn's Point National Cemetery. At the welcome center, housed in a former ordnance building, there is an exhibit that interprets the history and fortifications of Fort Mott, as well as exhibits on maritime life and history, and changing exhibits related to historic aspects of the fort. At the center you can pick up a walking-tour brochure that will explain the fortifications. The welcome center is open year-round (except Thanksgiving, Christmas, and New Year's Day), 9–4; the park is open 8–4 during the winter (Labor Day–Memorial Day) and 8–7:30 in the summer (Memorial Day–Labor Day).

On the same spit of land is Finn's Point National Cemetery* (609-877-5460), where many Confederate soldiers (and several German World War II prisoners) are buried. The lodge dates to the late 19th century, as does the marble monument to the Union dead (the cupola was added in 1936); the Confederate obelisk dates to 1910. Civil War buffs generally hold memorial services at the cemetery around Memorial Day. Open daily, 8–5.

The roads around Fort Mott traverse salt marshes and wild rice marshes, but it is often difficult to see the marshes because of the tall phragmites that line the roads. Also in this area is the Killcohook Coordination Area. This is where army engineers, engaged in a never-ending battle to keep the Delaware River open to navigation, dump the sludge from their dredging. Sixty years of dumping have produced hills that are 30–40 feet high. If you drive around the perimeter of this desolate area, you will pass into the state of Delaware, even though you will still be on the east side of the Delaware River. This is because the original deed for Wilmington included the land within a 12-mile radius of a particular point, and since this was all swamp at the time, no one paid the anomaly much mind.

Perth Amboy Middlesex 47,303

NJ 35, 440

Perth Amboy, situated at the mouth of the Raritan River, was established in 1683 by William Penn and 11 other men, the Proprietors of East New Jersey, who had purchased the East Jersey tract from the estate of Sir George Carteret, the original grantee, in 1682. Their aim was to set up East Jersey's principal town on what was described as "a sweet, wholesome, and delightful place," and the town plan they developed, with its central green, survives more or less intact today. The town was actually settled by a group of Scottish proprietors, but their attempt to name the settlement New Perth, in honor of the earl of Perth, was unsuccessful, and eventually their choice merged with the community's original name, Ambo Point, to form today's Perth Amboy.

The community did indeed serve as the capital of East Jersey from 1686 to 1702 and then as one of the twin capitals of New Jersey; in 1718 it became the first incorporated municipality in the colony. Because of its strategic position at the mouth of the Raritan River, Perth Amboy suffered in the

Revolution—it was occupied by the armies of both sides—and in 1790 the capital was moved to Trenton. Three years later the county seat was moved to New Brunswick, and for a while the city stagnated.

In the early 19th century, Perth Amboy became a fashionable resort and began to develop an oyster industry. The arrival of the railroad in the 1830s encouraged increased industrial activity; the town's rich clay deposits led to a flourishing brick, ceramic, and terra cotta industry. It was also a leading center of copper and silver refining, and at one point had the second largest copper refinery in the world. The Raritan Copper Works building (Elm and Market sts.) is listed in the state register of historic places, but the building is occupied by another company, and the giant American Smelting and Refining Company plant is gone.

RARITAN BAY

The increased pace of industrialization after the Civil War resulted in a wave of immigration; by the 1930s close to three-quarters of the inhabitants of Perth Amboy were foreign-born. Slavs predominated, followed by Danes, Italians, and Poles; now a large portion of the residents are from Puerto Rican, other Hispanic, and Caribbean backgrounds. In the mid-1980s, for example, there were more Anguillans living in Perth Amboy than lived on the island of Anguilla; today almost three-quarters of the population speaks a language other than English at home.

The heterogeneity of Perth Amboy's population is reflected in the town square (intersection of Market and High sts.). In this spacious square the weekly markets were held; from the 1740s to the 1840s the market house, a large brick shed, stood in the middle of the square. Now the square has been converted to a park; the statue of George Washington, by Nils Alling, a local sculptor, was given to the town in 1896 by the local Scandinavian community. Scattered about the park are plaques commemorating trees planted in honor of George Washington in 1932 (the town's 250th birthday) by Perth Amboy's various ethnic associations, including those of Italians, Poles, Germans, Scandinavians, Hungarians, Ukrainians, and Greeks.

At 260 High St. are the city hall*—the oldest public building in continuous use in the United States—and the surveyor general's office.* Begun in 1713, the city hall, which is painted white to hide the scars of numerous fires and alterations, served as the county courthouse until the county seat moved to New Brunswick; it also housed the state assembly until 1790. It was in this building that New Jersey became the first state to ratify the Bill of Rights and Thomas Mundy Peterson the first African American to vote under the auspices of the 15th Amendment. The surveyor general's office, built in 1860, houses the records of the Board of Proprietors of Eastern New Jersey, the oldest active corporation in the state.

The houses around the square generally date to the 18th and 19th centuries; in the one at 83–85 Market St. (1730) William Dunlap (1766–1839), sometimes called the father of American drama, who was also a painter (he studied with Benjamin West) and a historian of the theater and design, received his early education. The Gothic Revival First Presbyterian Church (1902) was built on the site of an 1802 church; its manse (1887) is at 236 High Street.

The Proprietary House* (149 Kearny Ave.; 732-826-5527) is the country's only remaining official royal governor's house. Built in the 1760s, this imposing brick Georgian mansion originally sat on 11 acres. Occupied first by Chief Justice Frederick Smyth, it was Governor William Franklin's home from 1774 until his arrest for supporting the English cause in 1776. (His father, Benjamin Franklin, visited him here in an unsuccessful attempt to persuade him to change his allegiance.) In 1809 it was converted to a resort hotel, the Brighton, and the third floor and south wing were added. (The wing involved the first use of structural cast iron in the United States.) It has also served as a retirement home for Presbyterian clergymen, a hotel, a private residence, and a rooming house. There were once even rumors that Joseph Bonaparte would live here (see Bordentown). The property was subdivided in 1904, and the house began a long decline. The state bought the house in 1911 and used it primarily as a rooming house until 1967. The Proprietary House Association, formed in 1966, has been working on restoring the house for many years. The upper floors have been rented out, but the association runs a museum on the ground floor and basement. The drawing room reflects in its furnishings and decorative matter the time of William Franklin, the dining room the early 19th century. The head housekeeper's room, which serves as the gift shop, is one of the least-altered rooms and still has its 18th-century decorative molding. Open Wednesday, Friday, 10–4, Sunday, 1–3, and by appointment. The small candlelit tearoom is open Wednesday 1–4. Admission charged. The association also sponsors a variety of special events, including an annual reenactment of William Franklin's arrest in June.

The Kearny Cottage* (63 Catalpa St.; 732-826-1826) dates from the 1780s and was the home of Elizabeth Lawrence Kearny—the poet Madame Scribblerus and half-sister of Captain James Lawrence of "Don't give up the ship" fame (see Burlington)—and her husband, Michael Kearny. Their son, Lawrence Kearny (1789–1868), who was born in the house and lived there all his life, was a naval officer who was in large part responsible for the open-door policy in China. Operated as a house museum by the Kearny Cottage Historical Society, the cottage's four rooms contain displays reflecting the nautical background of the house's owners and the history of Perth Amboy; the colonial garden has plant specimens that go back to the first half of the 19th century. Open Monday, Thursday, and the last Sunday of the month, 2–4; other times by appointment.

At the foot of Smith St. is the Perth Amboy ferry slip (973-672-0100). Service between Perth Amboy and Staten Island began in 1684 and continued until 1963. The present structure, a shed* containing a wooden lift mechanism, was built in 1904 by the Staten Island Railroad. For a while there was talk of restoring the Staten Island service, but those plans seem to be on hold.

At the intersection of Rector and Gordon sts. is Saint Peter's Episcopal Church,* the oldest Episcopal parish in the state (first service 1685, organized 1698). The present Gothic Revival building, on the site of one begun in 1719, dates from 1849, the cemetery from 1722. William Dunlap and Thomas Mundy Peterson are both buried here. The rectory (222 Rector St.) is a Tudor Revival building built in 1914. From Water St. there are fine views of the harbor and many interesting houses, most from the 19th century, but including Perth Amboy's oldest house (228 Water St.) from the early 18th century. At 160 Water St. the striking house (c. 1875), now occupied by the Raritan Yacht Club (the second-oldest yacht club in the country), has its original double doors. At 222 Water St. is the old rectory of Saint Peter's (1815).

Along the waterfront, at the corner of Front and Gordon sts., is the old United States Naval Armory. Built in 1929, this large brick building has been converted to commercial space. There are plans to build a new city marina, but for now you can fish off the two new fishing piers at the southern end of the waterfront, and enjoy the harbor walk running from the old ferry slip to the park abutting Sadowski Parkway to S. 2d Street.

Also along the waterfront is the Perth Amboy Center for the Arts (211 Front St.; 732-826-8083). Exhibits are primarily of painting or sculpture and change monthly. Open Tuesday–Sunday, 1–6.

Outerbridge Crossing is a cantilevered structure that crosses Arthur Kill to reach Staten Island. Opened in 1928, it was named not for its location but for Eugenius H. Outerbridge, the first chairman of the Port Authority of New York and New Jersey. It carries over 30 million vehicles each year.

Phillipsburg Warren 15,166

I 78, US 22, NJ 57, C 519, 621, 646

The site of a Native American village known as Chintewink, Phillipsburg was settled by farmers early in the 18th century and, thanks to its location, became a transportation hub in the 19th. The town is situated at the Delaware River just across from the point the Lehigh River joins it. The western end of the Morris Canal was in Phillipsburg, and a network of railroads reached it as well, making it convenient to both markets and raw materials for a variety of products. Early in the 20th century it became an industrial center—in 1904 Ingersoll-Rand opened a compressed air and hydraulic machinery plant that at one time employed 6,000 workers—and although much of the manufacturing activity is gone, Phillipsburg retains the feel of a city. There are still Victorian homes to be seen up on the hill that rises from the Delaware, there is a river walk to the south of the city, and in 2004, the Belvidere Delaware River Railroad began running excursion trains on the surviving tracks of the old Belvidere and Delaware railroad. The trains, pulled during the summer by steam locomotives, run south from Lehigh Junction station (Market St.; 908-797-7300) to Carpentersville and back; plans are afoot to extend the trip further south. Weekends, May–October, though it is best to check because the season can be extended, and special trains may run during the holiday season.

More about historic trains can be seen at the Friends of the New Jersey Transportation Heritage Center (178 S. Main St.; 908-689-0472), housed in the former New Jersey–Lackawanna railroad station (1914). The exhibit includes historic photographs, station models, dioramas, artifacts connected with transportation, lithographs, and a display of paintings of the Morris Canal. The Transportation Heritage Center's long-range plans include opening near its current building a second, larger facility that will enable it to display its sizable collection of rolling stock, which includes several vintage buses, coaches, antique trucks, and a trolley car. In the current exhibit is an 8-by-12-foot model of a possible future home, which shows the building and the tracks. Open on the days that excursions run.

Northeast of Phillipsburg, in Harmony Township (take 57 to Montana Rd. and turn left), is the Merrill Creek Environmental Resource Center (34 Merrill Creek Rd.; 908-454-1213), a 290-acre environmental preserve with 2,000 additional acres of woods and fields, all surrounding a 650-acre reservoir that a group of utilities built to store water when the Delaware River is low. The preserve is open for passive recreation: you can fish and boat (electric motors only) in the reservoir and hike and cross-country ski on the trails. There are two wildlife observation blinds, and one of the trails is barrier free. Along the way you may notice the stabilized remains of late-18th-, early-19th-century houses. At the nature center, which offers a variety of educational programs for children and adults, there are exhibits dealing with the history of the area, its flora and fauna, and the operation of the reservoir, as well as interactive exhibits for children and a demonstration butterfly and hummingbird garden. You can pick up a trail map here. The outdoor areas are open every day during daylight hours; the visitor center is open daily, 8:30–4:30, except New Year's Day, Easter, Thanksgiving, Christmas Eve, and Christmas; the boat ramp's hours are more limited.

A weekend sheep and fiber festival takes place in September at the Warren County fairgrounds in Harmony (C 519 at Strykers Rd.; 908-730-7189). You can watch dog-herding, sheepshearing, and other contests; see demonstrations of a variety of Old World crafts, and wander among goats, sheep, rabbits, llamas, and alpacas, some of them rare examples. A six-day farmers' fair, run by an organization with roots in the 19th century (it was incorporated in 1859 as the Warren County Farmers', Mechanics', and Manufacturers' Association) takes place at the grounds in midsummer. The fair includes demonstrations of traditional crafts, a midway, truck and tractor pulls, a demolition derby, horse shows, and hot air balloons. Call 908-859-6563 for details.

Piscataway Middlesex 50,482

I 287, NJ 18, C 514 SPUR, 529

According to one version of Piscataway's history, the community was settled in 1666 by people from the Piscataqua River valley in New Hampshire, which accounts for its name. In other versions, the name derives from various Native American words—the possibilities include "it is getting dark," "place of dark night," "great deer river," and "division of the river." Whichever version is correct, it is apparently undisputed that there was a settlement here on the east bank of the Raritan River in the 17th century, that there was for a time a flourishing shipping trade at the community known as Raritan Landing, and that the competitive advantages of the Delaware and Raritan Canal* and the greater depth of the river at New Brunswick put an end to Raritan Landing's days as a shipping center. Not that Piscataway has remained stagnant—the population has more than doubled since 1960.

Three of the buildings that date from Raritan Landing's more prosperous days do remain, however, among them the Cornelius Low House* (1225 River Rd.; 732-745-4177), also known as Ivy Hall. Built in 1740–41 for Low, a prominent merchant, surveyor, and attorney, the sandstone Georgian manor house now serves as the Middlesex County Museum. The museum focuses on state and local history and offers hands-on educational workshops, lectures, and outreach programs; exhibits usually change once a year. The museum closed for extensive renovations in 1993 and while it was closed offered workshops on the restoration process and a variety of traveling programs; it reopened in the spring of 1997. Open Tuesday–Friday and Sunday, 1–4; groups and other times by appointment. (The museum parking lot is on Sutphen La. on the Rutgers University Busch campus.)

The Metlar–Bodine House Museum* (1281 River Rd.; 732-463-8363) is another of the three remaining sites from Raritan Landing (the third is Buccleuch Mansion; *see* New Brunswick). Its earliest section dates to 1728, and it is now a museum devoted to showing how transportation has affected the development of the area. The museum has a permanent collection of Piscataway memorabilia, rotating exhibits, programs of historical interest, and special tours for children. The house was seriously damaged by fire in 2003, but is being restored; it is hoped it will reopen in 2006.

Rutgers University's Busch campus and most of the Livingston campus fall within Piscataway, as does the football stadium. The University of

Medicine and Dentistry of New Jersey–Robert Wood Johnson Medical School and the Center for Advanced Biotechnology and Medicine are two of the facilities on the Busch campus.

Stretching along the banks of the Raritan for about two miles, with a view of New Brunswick across the river, is Johnson Park (732-745-3900), one of Middlesex County's most popular parks. Established on land donated by the family of Johnson & Johnson, the 470-acre park contains a small zoo and animal shelter and a wildflower sanctuary, as well as picnic areas, a trail, lakes, playgrounds, and athletic facilities. There are summer concerts at the park, an annual fishing derby, and, in the fall, an old-car show. One of the Piscataway area's many prehistoric sites is located in Johnson Park.

Also within the park is East Jersey Olde Towne Village (River Rd. and Old Hoes La.; 732-745-3030), a 12-acre site on which colonial and Revolutionary War buildings have been re-created or moved from other central New Jersey locations, and arranged as they might have been in a real 18th-century village. The buildings include houses, barns, a school, a barracks, a wheelwright's shop, a blacksmith's shop, a church, and a reconstruction of the mid-18th-century Indian Queen Tavern (visited by John Adams and other founding fathers) that contains much of the tavern's original materials. Brochures are available explaining the history of each building. The village offers a wide range of programs, focusing on the history of the Raritan Valley. Open Tuesday–Friday, 8:30–4:15, Sunday, 1–4, guided tours 1:30 except when events are scheduled.

At the township municipal building (455 Hoes La.; 732-562-2301), art shows are hung in the council chamber in the central part of the building. These shows, sponsored by the town's Cultural Arts Advisory Commission, change roughly once a month and include one juried show each year. Open weekdays, 8:30–4:30; closed holidays. The commission also sponsors performances and concerts in a variety of venues. Call 732-562-2301 for the schedule. You can also often find art shows at the J. F. Kennedy Library (500 Hoes La.; 732-463-1633).

Northwest of the municipal building is Ambrose & Doty's Brooks Park (South Randolphville Rd.; 732-745-3900), a 225-acre undeveloped county park with natural areas and informal trails along the brooks.

Pitman Gloucester 9,331

NJ 47, C 553

Pitman was founded in 1871 as a summer religious camp and named Pitman Grove Camp Meeting in honor of the Reverend Charles Pitman, a powerful camp-meeting preacher. The community was laid out in the shape of a wheel, with an auditorium at the hub, 160 small frame cottages on spokes radiating from the center, and a circular road marking the perimeter. (The

Pitman Grove historic area* includes East, West, North, South, Webb, S. Oak, Wesley, Embury, and 1st–12th aves.) Popular in the 1880s and 1890s, the meetings attracted thousands of visitors—12,000 one day in 1880. Gradually the year-round population began to increase and the cottages were winterized and enlarged; in 1905 the borough of Pitman was incorporated, and in 1910 the Episcopalians built a splendid stone church. Pitman's residents today tend to commute to Camden, Philadelphia, and nearby Rowan University.

Alcyon Lake (Holly and Cedar aves.), once the site of a Native American village, was known from the 1870s until 1945 as a park and recreation site. Closed for a time when chemicals from a nearby toxic dump polluted the water and made it one of the most severely polluted sites in the United States (according to the town, "the nation's number one Superfund site"), the lake has since reopened for boating and fishing. Note also the buildings on Broadway and Pitman Ave., including the mid-1920s Broadway Theater (now threatened with demolition), the two 1920s bank buildings, and the Hotel Pitman (1917).

Plainfield Union 47,829

NJ 28, C 531

Plainfield was settled in the 1680s by Scottish families from Perth Amboy who called it Blondyn Plains. After a gristmill was built on the Green Brook in 1760, the town became known as Milltown, and in 1800 it received its current name. During the Revolution, there was a militia post on the east bank of the Green Brook, and George Washington was in Plainfield often during and after the battle for the Watchungs. In the early 19th century, Plainfield was known for the many hatteries operating along the Green Brook. Rail service to Elizabeth began in the 1830s, and after direct service to New York City (including a ferry at Jersey City) was established in 1869, Plainfield developed as one of the first bedroom communities. It was also one of the wealthier railroad suburbs, as can be seen today from the scale of the houses. (Over 100 millionaires are supposed to have lived in the Van Wyck Brooks historic district* alone.) Some industry had arrived by the 1880s, but the city, though distinctly urban, is still primarily residential. (In the days of the Jack Benny radio show, Plainfield achieved considerable, probably unwanted, publicity in jokes about Mary Livingston's mother.) Its symphony orchestra, founded in 1919, claims to be the oldest in the state, and John Philip Sousa gave his first concert as leader of his own band in Plainfield in 1892, an event celebrated in 1992 with a gathering of bands. Although Plainfield has experienced some of the problems of urban decline, it has held its own, and many of its large late-19th- and early-20th-century houses have been restored or converted to apartments. There are realtors who specialize in publicizing the attractions of Plainfield houses in New York City newspapers.

In Plainfield's historic districts you will find a large variety of buildings, most from the late 19th and early 20th centuries, which reflect many of the building styles popular over those years. Four of these districts are Crescent* (including Crescent Ave.; 1st, 2d, and 3d pls.; Park Ave. between Crescent and 9th St.; 9th St. between Park Ave. and Watchung Ave.; Watchung Ave. between 7th and 9th sts.; 7th St. between Watchung Ave., 9th St., and Franklin Pl.); Hillside Ave.* (Hillside Ave. from Watchung to Martine Ave.); the North Ave. commercial district* (parts of Park, North, and Watchung aves.); and the Van Wyck Brooks* area (parts of W. 8th and 9th sts., Arlington, Madison, Central, Stelle, and Field aves.), named for the author who lived in the area for a time.

One of Plainfield's earliest structures is the Friends' Meetinghouse (Watchung Ave. and E. 3d St.; 908-757-5736), which has been in continuous use since 1788. This was the first house of worship in Plainfield, and there are Native Americans buried in the graveyard. The Nathaniel Drake House* (602 W. Front St.; 908-755-5831) was built in 1746 and served as Washington's headquarters in June 1777. In the 1860s, the Drake family sold the house to John Harberger, president of the New York bank that was to become Chase

Manhattan. At that time the house was enlarged and altered (the towers were a still later addition). Now operated as a museum, the house has period rooms reflecting both the Drake and the Harberger eras, from the 1740s kitchen to the 1880s library. Upstairs, exhibits change roughly every two months and are usually related to Plainfield history. Open weekdays, 3–4:30, Saturday, 10–1, Sunday, 2–4; groups and other times by appointment.

Among the many eye-catching buildings, note the Masonic building (525 Park Ave.), which now houses stores; the Netherwood railroad station⋆ (Netherwood and South aves.), 1894; the public library (Park Ave. and 8th St.; 908-757-1111), where there are changing exhibits in the front lobby; the Orville Taylor Waring house⋆ (900 Park Ave.), 1881, now a commercial building; the old Elks building (116 Watchung Ave.); Grace Church (200 Cleveland Ave., near E. 7th St.), 1891, 1904; and the 7th Day Baptist Church⋆ (501 Central Ave.), built in the 1890s. Note also the bronze lampposts (1915) in front of the main post office (201 Watchung Ave.); they were stolen in 1995 but found and returned within a month. Two large Bierstadt paintings hang in the municipal courthouse (325 Watchung Ave.). These can be seen during normal court hours.

Cedar Brook Park (Park, Randolph, and Pemberton aves.; 908-527-4900) is an 85-acre county park built on a former garbage dump and swamp. It has a pond where you can fish and skate, playgrounds, a fitness trail, tennis courts, and picnic facilities. The Shakespeare Garden includes plants mentioned by Shakespeare and common in his day. Green Brook Park (West End, Myrtle, and Clinton aves.), 95 acres along a stretch of the river, has picnic facilities, basketball courts, athletic fields, and playgrounds.

Point Pleasant Ocean 19,306

NJ 35, 88

Known as a meeting place for the Lenape in the 16th century, Point Pleasant was first settled by Europeans in the mid-17th century. It flourished as a logging and boat-building community and has been popular as a summer resort. The Point Pleasant Canal, which goes through town, is the northernmost leg of the Inland Waterway.

Housed in one of the local boat works is the New Jersey Museum of Boating (732-859-4767). The museum has exhibits on the history of boat building in the area and in the rest of the state, and on lifesaving, as well as a collection of small boats and artifacts, including some from the *Morro Castle* (*see* Asbury Park). The exhibits are changed throughout the year. Eco-cruises of Barnegat Bay are offered (by appointment) Wednesday during July and August. The museum hosts maritime art and photography shows, which change four or five times a year. Special programs include an annual antique and classic boat show in September. Open daily, 10–4.

The Point Pleasant Historical Society's museum (416 New Jersey Ave.; 732-892-3091) is housed in the Point Pleasant Beach Borough Hall. The museum focuses on photographs and memorabilia relating to local history, including, for example, World War II scrapbooks compiled by the editor of the local paper. Open the 2d Thursday of the month, 1–4, and by appointment.

Pomona   Atlantic 4,019

GARDEN STATE PKWY EXIT 44, US 30, C 575

Pomona is the home of the Richard Stockton College of New Jersey (Jim Leeds Rd.), opened in 1971 on 1,600 forested acres (this includes land leased to two hospitals), 400 of which have been set aside as an ecological reserve. The campus is remarkable for its prizewinning architecture (it was recently cited as one of New Jersey's architectural treasures); most activities take place in a series of buildings that are linked by an interior street, and leading architects have been responsible for much of the campus. The college also boasts one of the world's largest closed-loop geothermal heating and cooling systems, by means of which it can air-condition and heat its buildings with significant savings in the consumption of electricity and natural gas and probably in cost as well. The Performing Arts Center (609-652-9000) sponsors guest productions in dance; popular, folk, and classical music; and theater, including children's theater, that are open to the public.

The Federal Aviation Administration's William J. Hughes Technical Center (which includes the Atlantic City International Airport) is also at Pomona. Built by the federal government during World War II, the airport was bought by the Federal Aviation Administration in 1958 as a test center. The FAA now runs this large research-and-development center (5,000-plus acres, 1,600-plus employees), which studies problems of air traffic control, aircraft safety, and communication and navigation, while Atlantic City uses 80 acres for its airport. The airport also houses what has been described as "the world's most elaborately equipped test heliport." Limited tours by appointment (609-485-4482).

Princeton   Mercer 14,203 (borough) 16,027 (township)

US 206, NJ 27, C 526, 571, 583

Once known primarily as a university town of quiet, tree-lined streets, Princeton is showing the effects of the post–World War II growth in the township (referred to locally as the doughnut surrounding the hole of Princeton Borough—the township's population is almost three times what it was in 1950; the

To: Community Park North
To: Herrontown Woods
To: Woodfield Reservation
To: US 1 Plasma Physics Lab
To: Drumthwacket
To: Princeton Battlefield State Park
Thomas P. Clarke house
Friends meetinghouse
Updike Farm
To: Institute for Advanced Study

Wilson
Wescott
Cleveland La.
Hodge
Cleveland house
Stanworth
John St.
Lytle
Witherspoon
Green
Robeson Pl.
Spring
Vandeventer
Park
Wiggins
Hamilton
Jefferson
Moore
Spruce
Maple
Linden
Chestnut
Moran
Nassau St.
Olden St.
Charlton
William
Murray Pl.
Library Pl.
Hodge
Boudinot
Bayard La.
Bank
Hulfish
Palmer Square
Bainbridge house
Firestone Library
Nassau Hall
Prospect St.
Morven
Aquinas Institute
Stockton St.
Maclean house
Princeton University
University Pl.
Ivy La.
Western Way
site of Palmer Stadium
Theological Seminary
Einstein house
Marquand Park
Mercer St.
College Rd.
Alexander St.
Dinky station
Elm Dr.
Washington Rd.
Faculty Rd.
Elm Rd.
Lovers La.
Springdale
Lake Carnegie
D&R Canal
Princeton cemetery

N

borough's has risen by about 16 percent). Settled at the end of the 17th century, principally by Quakers, Princeton was known as Stony Brook until 1724. It grew along the site of an old Native American trail, now Nassau St., which was to prove an important thoroughfare in the Revolution. The town played a significant role in that war, and many historians consider the battles of Trenton and Princeton as turning points in the struggle for independence. For a brief time in 1783, while the Continental Congress sat in the university's Nassau Hall,* Princeton was the capital of the country. Midway between New York and Philadelphia, it prospered in the 19th century as a stagecoach stop.

The university, founded by Presbyterians as the College of New Jersey in 1746 in Elizabeth, moved from there to Newark, and settled in its present location in 1756. (The association of the town with the university has been long remarked: according to a late-18th-century visitor from Poland, "Princeton is notable only for its college, which is a building erected before the Revolution and rather large.") Other educational institutions followed, among them the Princeton Theological Seminary, founded in the early 19th century by a group of dissident Presbyterians who felt the university had become too lax. The Institute for Advanced Study was founded over 70 years ago; Abraham Flexner was its first director, Albert Einstein one of its first professors. Also in town are the American Boychoir School and the

Westminster Choir College (now part of Rider University; *see* Lawrenceville). The Gallup Poll has been a Princeton institution since 1935, and Educational Testing Service, although it is actually in Lawrence Township, has a Princeton address.

Corporate research laboratories moving into the area, among them RCA and Cyanamid, changed the character of the town after World War II. More recently, many large corporations have been moving their headquarters or other offices to the so-called Princeton Corridor (US 1 between Trenton and New Brunswick) or other parts of what is now referred to as Greater Princeton, and even those actually located in neighboring communities often list their addresses as Princeton. The focus of the town is thus increasingly toward the outside. With the resultant increases in population, the town is busier and the buildings in the center are taller, but you can still find a pre-Revolutionary building on Nassau St., and it is still lined with trees.

Many famous names have been associated with Princeton. Aaron Burr and Grover Cleveland are both buried in the Princeton cemetery (Witherspoon and Wiggins sts.; 609-924-1369), as are most Princeton University presidents and Paul Tulane, the founder of Tulane University. At 112 Mercer St. you can see the 1870s house* (now a national historic landmark) where Einstein lived. T. S. Eliot, a visitor at the Institute for Advanced Study in 1948, wrote much of *The Cocktail Party* at 14 Alexander Street. Thomas Mann lived in the house now owned by the Aquinas Institute at the corner of Stockton St. and Library Pl.; Woodrow Wilson lived at 72 and 82 Library Pl. and at 25 Cleveland La., Grover Cleveland at 15 Hodge Rd.* (Cleveland's house, built in the 1850s, is a national historic landmark.) Other literary names associated with either the university or the town include, of course, F. Scott Fitzgerald and John O'Hara and, of more recent vintage, John McPhee, Toni Morrison, Paul Muldoon, Joyce Carol Oates, and C. K. Williams.

Although a considerable variety of architectural styles is represented on the Princeton University campus, the tone is set by Collegiate Gothic. As you stroll through the arches and courtyards, keep an eye out for gargoyles. (Notice, too, the black squirrels, descendants of specimen squirrels released from a private estate, although they may have been native to the area earlier.) Setting off the Gothic atmosphere is a large collection of 20th-century outdoor sculpture by distinguished artists. The Henry Moore, located in the courtyard formed by Stanhope, West College, Alexander Hall, and Nassau Hall, is a special favorite of children; before a controversial cleaning in the early 1990s, the highly polished lower portion attested to that popularity. There are also works by Picasso, Lipchitz, and Nevelson. George Segal's Kent State memorial, rejected by Kent State University, is in the courtyard below the chapel and Firestone Library.

Nassau Hall,* built in 1756 but several times remodeled, is reputed to have been at one time the largest building in the colonies. A national historic landmark, it once housed the entire college and has also served as barracks, hospital, and home of the Continental Congress. It is now used for higher administrative offices and faculty meetings. The Faculty Room contains portraits of past university presidents and a Charles Wilson Peale of George Washington. Note how worn the interior steps are.

Of the fieldstone buildings planned to harmonize with Nassau Hall, Stanhope and West College remain. Stanhope, an early-19th-century building, has a lovely staircase and stairwell and contains public toilets.

Although the stacks of Firestone Library are no longer open to the public, the exhibits there sponsored by the Department of Rare Books and Special Collecitons (609-258-3184) are worth a visit, and children (and their parents) will enjoy the displays and special programs at the Cotsen Children's Library (609-258-1510). Both venues open weekdays, 9–5; weekends, 12–5; Rare Books exhibits also open Wednesday evening, 5–8. In summer the hours are earlier; call for details. (The university library system as a whole contains over 6 million printed works and manuscripts and grows at the rate of about 10,000 volumes a month.) The chapel, considered an outstanding example of Collegiate Gothic, is one of the largest university chapels in the United States. The art museum (609-258-3788), housed in McCormick Hall, features changing exhibits; the permanent collection is particularly strong in early Mediterranean, Oriental, and pre-Columbian art, but do keep an eye

PRINCETON

out for Pliny's two left feet in Angelica Kauffmann's 1785 *Pliny the Younger and His Mother*. During the spring and fall semesters there are public gallery talks (Friday at 12:30, Sunday at 3:30) and talks for children aged five to nine (Saturday at 11). Open Tuesday–Saturday, 10–5, Sunday, 1–5. Tours by appointment (609-258-3043).

Chancellor Green Library and Alexander Hall are examples of later 19th-century Ruskinesque and Richardsonian architecture. The exuberance of Alexander Hall, which now contains the Richardson concert hall, has won it many ardent devotees. Concerts at Richardson (609-258-4239) are open to the public and feature a wide range of performers, from students to the internationally famous. The Institute for Advanced Study (609-734-8228) also runs a concert series that is open to the public. And McCarter Theatre (609-258-2787), built 75 years ago for the university's Triangle Club productions, and for a time popular with Broadway-bound producers as a tryout venue, presents a full season of theater (including its own and touring productions), music, and dance.

Prospect House,* from 1879 until 1969 the home of the university's presidents and now a faculty club (and a national historic landmark), is one of several examples of John Notman's Italianate buildings to be found in Princeton. Its formal gardens are open to the public, and the splendid trees around the building, like many other trees on the campus, carry identification plaques.

Modern university buildings include Robert Venturi's Lewis Thomas Laboratory (Washington Rd.), the recent reworking of the Woolworth Music Building by Juan Navarro Baldeweg, and the Woodrow Wilson School (Washington Rd.), designed by Minoru Yamasaki (the decorative pool in its courtyard was for a time so popular in the summers that it became a public-health problem). The mansions on Prospect St. just east of Washington Rd. belong to the eating clubs; these social clubs at which many students eat their meals were once encouraged as an alternative to fraternities (some of the clubs no longer exist, and their buildings have been converted to serve more academic purposes). The university's Orange Key Guide Service, located in the Frist Campus Center, offers walking tours of the campus Monday–Saturday, 10, 11, 1:30, and 3:30; Sunday, 1:30 and 3:30. These last about one hour; they visit Nassau Hall and the chapel and usually go through Prospect gardens, the exact itinerary varying with the size of the group and the weather.

The town also has its outdoor sculpture, much of it the work of Seward Johnson (*see* Hamilton Township). Note the man reading the *New York Times* in front of Borough Hall, the man reading a book near the kiosk in Palmer Sq., and the fishermen in Community Park North.

Princeton's historic district* includes 18th- to 20th-century buildings on Nassau, Mercer, Prospect, William, Stockton, Wiggins, Alexander, and Olden sts.; Springdale and College rds., Lovers La., and Library Pl., but older houses remain in almost all areas of central Princeton. Bainbridge House

(158 Nassau St.; 609-921-6748) is a pre-Revolutionary building, the birthplace of William Bainbridge, commander of the frigate *Constitution* (better known as *Old Ironsides*). Run as a museum by the Historical Society of Princeton, Bainbridge features thematic exhibits (for example, the Italian American community in Princeton, the Delaware and Raritan Canal,* relocated buildings in Princeton, the history of the local African American community) that usually change twice a year. Among the society's holdings is Einstein's furniture. The society offers a guided walking tour of historic Princeton every Sunday at 2 and arranges guided tours for other times; you can also pick up a brochure for a self-guided walking tour at Bainbridge House. Open Tuesday–Sunday, 12–4; archives and library open Tuesday and Saturday, 1–4.

Morven* (55 Stockton St.; 609-924-8144), built c. 1754 for Richard Stockton, a signer of the Declaration of Independence, was for many years the governor's mansion. The national historic landmark is now a museum, which focuses on the history of the building in the West Wing and exhibits of fine, folk, and decorative arts in its six galleries. The gardens include heirloom annuals and the recreation of a Colonial Revival style garden that had flourished early in the 20th century. Open Wednesday–Friday, 11–3; weekends, 12–4; groups by appointment (609-824-8144, ext. 106). Closed major holidays; admission charge. Gardens open dawn–dusk.

Today Drumthwacket* (354 Stockton St.; 609-683-0057) serves as the governor's mansion. Built in the 1830s by Charles Smith Olden and considerably enlarged in the 1890s by Moses Taylor Pyne (he is responsible for the black squirrels mentioned above), Drumthwacket was restored in the 1980s and furnished with 19th-century pieces. Tours most Wednesdays, September–November and January–July, 10–11:30; groups by appointment (609-683-0591). In December you are welcome to tour on your own most Wednesdays and one Sunday, 11–2; call for details. Also on the property is the Olden house,* built in the mid-18th century, which houses the offices of the Drumthwacket Foundation and a gift shop, and features a period herb garden. Open when Drumthwacket is open for tours.

The Friends meetinghouse (Quakerbridge Rd. and Mercer St.), 1760, is thought to resemble closely the original building (1724), destroyed by fire. Further south on Quakerbridge Rd. is the Updike Farm, since 2004 a property of the Historical Society of Princeton. The farm dates to the 18th century, and when the buildings, which include a Federal farmhouse, barns, sheds, chicken coops, and a corncrib, have been stabilized and restored, the society will be able to move its offices and archives here, freeing the second floor of Bainbridge House for exhibits. The society also plans to use the farm for special events.

Two particularly attractive concentrations of houses from a single period are the row of white frame houses on upper Alexander St. built by Charles Steadman in the 1830s and 1840s and the 18th-century group at the crossroads known as Queenston or Jugtown (Nassau and Harrison sts.; this is part of the Jugtown historic district,* which also includes Evelyn Pl.).

Princeton Battlefield State Park* (Mercer Rd.; 609-921-0074), the site of the Battle of Princeton and a national historic landmark, is about 1½ miles west of the center of town. At the southwest end of the battlefield, its back to the field, is the Thomas P. Clarke house (500 Mercer Rd.; 609-921-0074), a pre-Revolutionary farmhouse that has been converted to a museum of 18th-century life. The oldest part of the house is furnished as it would have been during the Revolutionary era; the 1840s wing contains maps, paintings, and weapons having to do with the Revolutionary War. Future plans include establishing a working farm on the property, planting gardens, and adding a visitor center. Open Wednesday–Saturday, 10–12 and 1–4; Sunday, 1–4. Special events are scheduled at various times throughout the year, often including 4 July and the December holidays. The columns across the road in the northern portion of the field are not related to the battle; they come from a stately home that was torn down in the 20th century.

If you follow the trails southeast from the park, you will enter the Institute Woods, a 250-acre portion of the more than 550 acres of woodlands, wetlands, and farmlands owned by the Institute for Advanced Study (Olden Ave.; 609-734-8000; you can also park on Olden La. and enter from behind the central building of the institute). These woods connect to the Charles Rogers Wildlife Refuge to the east, and the entire area is beloved of bird-watchers—close to 200 species have been observed here, close to 100 nest here, and the spring warbler migration is particularly impressive. The woods also contain an unusual diversity of tree species and have been described as "a virtual laboratory for studies of forest succession." A swaying suspension bridge, according to legend built by visiting scholars, is a favorite of children.

Across US 1 from town, on the university's Forrestal campus, is the Princeton Plasma Physics Laboratory, where scientists working to produce energy by fusion (which unlike fission does not leave radioactive waste products,) have already produced enough electricity to light a small city or two, albeit only for extremely short periods. (Commercial production of energy by fusion isn't expected for another 50 years or so.) Tours by appointment (609-243-2757).

Also across US 1 from town is the David Sarnoff Library (201 Washington Rd.; 609-734-2636). Housed in a building constructed by RCA to celebrate Sarnoff's accomplishments, the library contains a museum devoted to the history of radio, television, recording, radar, electron microscopes, and many many more technologies connected with Sarnoff and RCA. Exhibits include photographs, documents, and artifacts; future plans include adding interactive exhibits and regular hours. For now the museum is open by appointment.

North of the center of town is the Herrontown Woods Arboretum (Snowden La. and Herrontown Rd.; 609-989-6532). This 142-acre woodland was donated to the county by Oswald Veblen, a professor at the Institute for Advanced Study (and a nephew of the economist Thorstein Veblen). The arboretum contains a range of habitats that provide a clear illustration of succession; its 3½ miles of trails are well marked. Open daily until dusk. Tours by appointment.

Community Park North (US 206 north of the center) has hiking trails, a fitness course, and a pond. Concerts and plays are given in the amphitheater in the summer. Directly to its west is Mountain Lake Nature Preserve (609-921-2772; the park and the preserve share a parking lot off Mountain Ave.). There are trails through its 90 acres, and in February and March, lectures are given on Sunday afternoon. Woodfield Reservation (take Elm Rd. north to the Great Rd. W.) also has trails that go through hilly woods. Access to the Delaware and Raritan Canal State Park (*see* Kingston) is possible at Basin Park (Alexander St.), Washington Rd., and Harrison Street.

Rahway Union 26,500

NJ 27, 35

Possibly named for the Native American chief Rahwack, Rahway is one of the oldest settlements in New Jersey. The first houses date from the mid-17th century and the first sawmills from the 1680s. Rahway was a transportation center, first as a stop on the stagecoach line between New York and Philadelphia; then, after the Revolution, as a port; and, after 1835, as a stop on the railroad. In later years the town became an industrial center: Three-in-One oil was developed in Rahway in the late 19th century, and a few years later the Merck company, one of the world's largest producers of prescription drugs, bought land in Rahway (in 1993 Merck moved its headquarters to Whitehouse Station, but there are still some 4,300 employees here, occupying 125 buildings on over 200 acres and working in the company's research and development headquarters as well as in manufacturing). Rahway possessed what was reputed to be the nation's first solar-heated city hall (Main St. and E. Milton); although the panels are no longer operative, they add to the look of the building. Among Rahway's best-known native sons are the sculptor John Frazee (*see* South River), the economist Milton Friedman, the former senator Clifford Case, and the scientist and author Carl Sagan. Abraham Clark, a signer of the Declaration of Independence, is buried in the Rahway cemetery (St. Georges Ave. near Westfield Ave.).

The Merchants and Drovers Tavern* (St. Georges and Westfield aves.; 732-381-0441), owned and operated by the Merchant and Drovers Tavern Museum Association, dates from the late 18th century. (The township of Rahway was created in this tavern in 1804.) The four-story frame building (it was enlarged early in the 19th century) continued in use as a tavern until the mid-1930s. Transformed into a museum focusing on early tavern life and stagecoach transportation, it features permanent exhibits that tell the story of this particular tavern, of taverns in central New Jersey, of the role played by taverns generally, and of the role of stagecoaches in transportation across the state. On the property is another tavern (Rahway once boasted seven), the much smaller Terrill Tavern (c. 1763), now at its third location. George Washington was a guest in this building on one of his trips through the area. A museum shop is in the Terrill Tavern. The society holds educational programs for schoolchildren and sponsors a variety of special events. The museum association has sponsored archaeological digs in the tavern yard and is working to set up exhibits that will illuminate that history. The museum is open Thursday, Friday, the 1st and 3d Saturday of the month, and the 2d and 4th Sunday, 10–4. Also open by appointment Tuesday, 10–4.

At the junction of Central Ave. and Main and Irving sts. is the Union County Arts Center* (732-499-8226), housed in a 1,300-seat theater built as a vaudeville house in 1927–28. The gold-leaf decor has been restored, and the original Wurlitzer organ is in place. The center sponsors a variety of events, among them classical, jazz, country, and pop concerts; plays; films (including silent films accompanied by the organ); and dance.

One block east of the arts center on Irving St. at Seminary Ave. is the Arts Guild of Rahway (1670 Irving St., 732-381-7511). Its striking building was one of the first in the state to be built specifically for a town library; the front section dates from 1869, the back section from 1891. The public exhibits focus on New Jersey artists, both established and emerging, and change roughly once a month September–June. Concerts are also given in the gallery, and the guild offers occasional seminars and lectures. Gallery open September–June, Wednesday, Friday, Saturday, 1–4, Thursday 1–3, 5–7; groups by appointment. As you walk around this part of town, keep an eye out for Victorian-era houses and striking commercial buildings.

The Rahway River Parkway, designed by the Olmsted firm, strings together many small parks, such as the Rahway River Park (St. Georges Ave. and River Rd.), and Milton Lake Park (W. Lake and Madison aves.), both county facilities. Along the river off Lawrence Ave. is the Riverfront Park Conservation Area, a small park created when the county incinerator opened nearby. The area is rich in wildlife, and you can walk along the river, much of the time on a floating boardwalk.

Ramsey Bergen 14,351

NJ 17, C 507

Now primarily a commuters' town, Ramsey was originally settled by the Dutch. In one of their early stone houses (c. 1745) is the Old Stone House Museum* (538 Island Rd.; 201-327-2655). Three rooms on the main floor are furnished to show how a pre-Revolutionary Dutch household would have looked. A junior museum with toys and other items from the turn of the century is upstairs. There are also changing exhibits. The house is only scheduled to be open a few Sundays of the year, so it is best to call for the exact schedule. Groups and other times by appointment.

Other 18th- and early-19th-century stone houses can be found at 171 Lake St., 245 Shadyside Rd., and 37 W. Crescent Ave.* Part of Darlington County Park (*see* Mahwah) extends into Ramsey.

Red Bank Monmouth 11,844

NJ 35, C 34, 520

Situated at the mouth of the Navesink River, Red Bank began as a transportation center, deriving its prosperity from trade with New York City. By the late 1820s, 13 sloops and schooners were in regular service between Red Bank and New York City, taking vegetables, wood, and oysters to New York and coming back with manufactured goods. Regular steamship service began in the 1830s and continued until the 1920s, after which Red Bank's career as a port was over. The once-prized local oysters have also disappeared, casualties of polluted water. One of Red Bank's water-related activities, ice-boating, has continued. Farm sled races, presumably the ancestors of ice-boat races, were recorded here as early as 1879, the same year the Monmouth Boat Club* (31 Union St.) was founded. The club is still active; among its other activities is frostbite racing. Also still active is the North Shrewsbury Iceboat and Yacht Company, founded in 1880. Some members of both clubs have taken up renovating and occasionally racing late-19th- and early-20th-century boats.

Red Bank (the name can be found in a 1734 log and presumably derives from the clay in the riverbanks) can boast at least two famous native sons: Edmund Wilson, the author and critic, was born here in 1895; Count Basie, the jazz musician, was born here in 1904 and began his career playing piano to accompany films at the Palace Theater. The musical tradition continues: Red Bank today is home to the East Coast's largest bagpipe band.

The town has a distinctly late-19th-century appearance, partly the result of a fire that led to the complete rebuilding of Broad St. in the late 19th century. But red brick and other 19th-century features are found on other streets as well: note, for example, the borough hall* (1892; 51 Monmouth St.), once the Shrewsbury Town Hall; the railroad station* (1878; Bridge Ave. and Monmouth St.); the Navesink Hook & Ladder Company No. 1 (1872; Mechanic St.); the library (84 Front St.), once the Red Bank Seminary and for a time at the turn of the 20th century the home of bandmaster and composer John Philip Sousa; the lumber company that was once the St. James School (1879; 9 Wall St.); St. James Church (1894; Broad St. at Peters Pl.).

The largest uniform-manufacturing company in the world was started in Red Bank by Sigmund Eisner in 1885. Specializing in military and Boy Scout uniforms, the company stopped manufacturing in the late 1940s. Its five buildings on Bridge Ave. and W. Front St. have been converted into a commercial complex with offices, shops, restaurants, and art galleries. The clock tower was added in 1986.

At 99–101 Monmouth St. is the Count Basie Theatre (732-842-9000). Built as a vaudeville theater (it opened in 1926), it was later converted to a movie house. In 1973 it was purchased by the Monmouth County Arts Council, making the council the only one in the state to own and operate a performing arts center. The arts council bowed out in 1999, and the theater is now run by an independent nonprofit group. The house is being thoroughly renovated; new seats were installed in 2004 (replacing the seats from the old Carnegie Hall that had been installed in the mid-'80s). Programs at the 1,575-seat theater include dance, drama, jazz, classical and folk music, and a family entertainment series; performers range from members of the Monmouth County Arts Council to international stars. Call for the schedule.

In 2005 the Two River Theater Company opened its new theater as part of the Red Bank arts corridor (21 Bridge Ave.; 732-345-1400). The house, designed by Hardy, Holzman, and Pfeiffer, will be home to the company's own productions and educational programs, as well as offering space to other groups.

Up the Swimming River, a mile or two from Red Bank, is the Swimming River Natural Area (732-938-2371). Located at the confluence of the Swimming River and Pine Brook, these 100-plus acres contain a variety of habitats. There are wetlands and uplands (there was once a farm here), forests, and steep slopes, and the area is a good one in which to hike and look for birds and other animals.

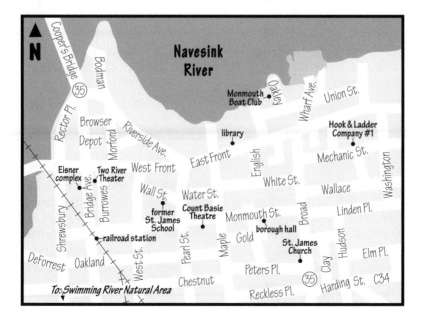

Ridgewood   Bergen   24,936

Because the Dutch Reformed Church in Ridgewood, built in 1735, was situated at a strategic crossroads, it was used steadily for military purposes during the Revolution and fell into disrepair. Although it may have served as George Washington's headquarters for a few days, and had witnessed Aaron Burr's marriage and part of Charles Lee's court-martial (Lee's court-martial was held in several places to avoid taking army officers away from their wartime duties; *see* Freehold), the congregation decided to replace it and in 1800 built the Old Paramus Reformed Church* (660 E. Glen Ave.). The bell ordered from London for the 1800 church, made by the same firm that made the Liberty Bell, is still in use.

On the church grounds, in an 1873 schoolhouse, is the Schoolhouse Museum (650 E. Glen Ave.; 201-670-0886), run by the Paramus Historical & Preservation Society and devoted to local history. Among the exhibits are a Dutch room containing a 1690 Dutch Bible and other items from the Netherlands that the Dutch settlers, preponderant in this area, might have brought with them; a Victorian schoolroom containing old school equipment; an early-18th-century kitchen; and a church exhibit containing items from both the 1735 and 1800 churches. Each year there is a thematic exhibit, changed to coordinate with the society's annual heritage show in February. Open May–October, Sunday, 2:30–4:30; other times and tours of the church by appointment.

In the center of Ridgewood, in Van Neste Sq., is a World War I memorial column designed by Henry Bacon, the architect of the Lincoln Memorial. There are in Ridgewood several examples of early Dutch stone houses. Note, for example, the David Ackerman house* (415 E. Saddle River Rd.); most of it was built in the 1720s and 1730s, but the earliest portion may be late 17th century. Other old houses are to be seen on E. Glen, Lincoln, Doremus, N. Maple, and E. Ridgewood aves., Grove and Prospect sts., and E. Saddle River Rd. The town is known for having one of the oldest and biggest 4 July parades in New Jersey, and for the consistently high test scores achieved by its school population.

At the Stable (259 N. Maple Ave.; 201-670-5560), the headquarters of the Ridgewood Parks and Recreation Department, you can see a small collection of 19th-century farm equipment. The late-19th-century building was once a stable, and after a fire destroyed the house on the farm it was part of, it was rescued by a citizens' group. There are also art exhibits in the Stable; they change each month. Open weekdays, 8:30–4:30. Helen Nearing, who with her husband, Scott Nearing, was an influential social activist and proponent of a return to the land, was a native of Ridgewood and a graduate of the high school.

Ringoes Hunterdon [East Amwell Township]

US 202, NJ 31, 179, C 579

The log hut that John Ringo built at the intersection of two Native American trails in 1720 was the nucleus around which today's attractive town of Ringoes developed. The hut became not just Ringo's house but a tavern as well, and the tavern prospered after 1769, when it became a stop for the Swift-Sure Stagecoach line. According to one legend, Ringo made a fortune, but fearing robbery, he buried it and died without revealing its location.

The Amwell Academy (NJ 179, the Old York Rd.), now an inn, was built as a school in 1811 and bought by Dr. C. W. Larison in 1868. Well known as an educator in the 19th century, Larison believed strongly in phonetic spelling and in 1885 published *Geografy: A Text Buk in Fonic Orthografy*. On the other side of the road, about a half-mile closer to town, is the Landis house, possibly the oldest house in Hunterdon County. The marquis de Lafayette is supposed to have recuperated from an illness here. The Ringoes historic district* includes portions of Old York, John Ringo, Wertsville, and Boss Rds. and Larison La.

The Black River & Western Railroad (C 579; 908-782-6622), which runs an old-fashioned steam train between Ringoes and Flemington, has its yards and depot in Ringoes. The station dates to the 1870s, and the engine house and yard started life as a creamery. From April through mid-December, there are several round trips to Flemington on weekends; in July and August, trips also run Thursday and Friday. Jack Frost specials to Three Bridges and back run January–March. The railroad also hosts several special railroad events, such as a Santa Claus special, a Great Train Robbery, a treasure hunt, and a circus train. It also offers hot-air balloon rides by appointment. Fee charged.

There are two wineries in Ringoes, both with lovely views out over the Amwell valley. Unionville Vineyards (9 Rocktown Rd.; 908-788-0400) occupies a mid-19th-century farm that began with a peach orchard, switched to apples when the peach blight hit, became a dairy farm, and then grew grain. Operating out of a restored mid-19th-century dairy barn, the winery grows grapes on 34 of its 90 acres. The winery is home to festivals and special events throughout the year. Open for winery tours and tasting, Thursday–Sunday, 11–4. Amwell Valley Vineyard (80 Old York Rd.; 908-788-5852) was one of the first wineries to be established when New Jersey laws changed to allow an increase in the number of wineries, provided they grew their own grapes. Tours and tasting weekends, 1–5; other times by appointment.

The Hunterdon County 4H and Agricultural Fair takes place in August at South County Park (NJ 179 just off US 202; 908-782-6809, 908-788-1341), once the site of the county's first and only drive-in theater. The fair, formerly known as the Flemington Agricultural Fair, traces its roots back to 1745.

Ringwood Passaic 12,396

C 511

Located near the New York border, the borough of Ringwood developed first as an iron-mining town and then as a summer resort (there are many lakes in the area). Between 1950 and 1980, it was a rapidly growing commuter town; since 1980 that growth seems to have slowed. Almost two-thirds of Ringwood's land is open space, including much of the Ringwood Manor,* Skylands Manor,* and Shepherd Lake sections of Ringwood State Park. The Ringwood Manor section can be reached from Sloatsburg Rd. (off C 511); the other two sections are to the east; the park as a whole occupies over 5,000 acres.

Ringwood Manor* (973-962-7031), a national historic landmark, is a rambling mansion of 50-odd rooms, with 24 fireplaces and 250 windows, situated on spacious grounds. It too owes its existence to the iron industry. The Ringwood Company was active in this area from the 1740s to the early 1930s, and during the American Revolution the ironworks were important suppliers to the Continental troops. At that time the works were run by Robert Erskine, general surveyor to the Continental army and known for the accuracy of the maps he drew for George Washington (a frequent visitor to Ringwood). Although ironmasters first lived on this site in the mid-18th century, the earliest part of the present mansion dates to the first decades of the 19th century, when Martin Ryerson was the ironmaster. In the mid-19th century, the works and house were owned by Peter Cooper, a versatile inventor, entrepreneur, and philanthropist, perhaps best known as the founder of Cooper Union in New York City. His daughter and son-in-law, the Abram S. Hewitts, decided to make Ringwood their permanent summer home, and most of the present house was built by them between the 1850s and the 1870s. Among the noteworthy features are the wood-paneled great hall and dining room and the Delft tile fireplace in the library. The furnishings, 95 percent of which belonged to the former owners or are original to the period, reflect the occupants' lives over the 120 years from 1810 to 1930 and include many fine pieces. Various mementos of the iron industry lie about the grounds, including links from a chain similar in type to the one stretched across the Hudson during the Revolution as a barrier to British ships. The columns in the garden come from the New York Life Insurance building in New York City. Within this section of the park there are picnic tables, fishing ponds, and hiking trails. The area is also suitable for cross-country skiing. Manor house open Wednesday–Sunday, 10–4; park open sunrise to sunset; office open daily, 10–4. Parking charge Memorial Day weekend–Labor Day weekend (weekends only at Ringwood and Skylands manors).

At the Skylands Manor section of the park (973-962-7031) is New Jersey's first official botanic garden (973-962-7527). Originally designed in the 1920s for Clarence McKenzie Lewis, an investment banker who was also a trustee of the New York Botanical Garden, the 300 acres of gardens were neglected for many years and only saved with the help of volunteers. There is almost always something blooming here amid the variety of formal and less formal layouts, which include a crab apple vista, a magnolia garden (unusual this far north), a bog garden, and a winter garden. The 40-room mansion* was built by Lewis in the 1920s (of stone quarried on the estate). The Skylands Association (973-962-7527) gives tours of the house the first Sunday of the month, March–November. Concerts are given in the garden many Friday evenings in summer. The gardens are open daily from sunrise to sunset. Tours of the garden are given Sunday at 2, May–October. There are also hiking trails and hunting in season.

The Shepherd Lake section (973-962-6526) is north of Skylands Manor and centers around the lake where you can swim, fish, boat, and picnic. Some of the trails can be used by horseback riders, cyclists, mountain bikers, and cross-country skiers.

At the southwestern corner of the borough, adjacent to the Norvin Green State Forest (973-962-7031), is the Weis Ecology Center (150 Snake Den Rd.; 973-835-2160), founded in the 1970s and since 1995 a New Jersey Audubon Society sanctuary. The center building, originally part of a 1930s working-class rural getaway, contains displays, and the center sponsors a variety of programs for children and adults, from autumn hawk watches to maple-sugaring to cross-country skiing instruction. The visitor center is open Wednesday–Sunday, 8:30–4:30. The close to 4,000 acres of state forest have one of the most extensive trail systems in the state and, with elevations up to 1,300 feet, splendid views of the area and the New York City skyline. The birding is good, and you can fish here and in season hunt, cross-country ski, and sled. Trail maps are available at the Weis Center.

Some three miles west of Ringwood Manor (take Margaret King Ave., which becomes Greenwood Lake Tnpk), along the Wanaque River, are the remains of the 18th- and 19th-century Long Pond Ironworks.* These works, which were run by the same ironmasters who were active at Ringwood, were last operated in the 1880s; they take their name from the former name of nearby Greenwood Lake. The site, now part of the Long Pond Ironworks State Park (973-962-7031), includes remains of the ironworking complex and its surrounding village. This is said to be the only site in the United States where you can still see three generations of technology. The Friends of Long Pond Ironworks (973-657-1688) offers tours of the historic area, the second full weekend of the month, April–November. The Long Pond Ironworks Museum, housed in the restored country store, is open 1–4 weekends, April–November; other times by appointment. Living History weekends take place in the spring (the Civil War) and fall (the Revolutionary War), and the Friends also sponsors a variety of other special events, including ironworking demonstrations, lantern tours, and Shakespeare in the State Park. Call for the schedule. Within the park's 2,500 acres, which include the Monksville Reservoir, are trails for hiking, horseback riding, and mountain biking, and facilities for boating, fishing, ice-fishing, cross-country skiing, and sledding.

Also to the west of Ringwood is Tranquility Ridge (off C 511; 973-881-4832), over 2,100 acres of woodland. (The park name was chosen by a contest.) Originally part of the Sterling Forest tract that was slated for development, these unspoiled woods provide excellent hiking oportunities. Fishing and hunting are also possible here.

River Edge Bergen 10,946

NJ 4, C 503

River Edge played a crucial part in the Revolution when George Washington, in November 1776, led his army over the Hackensack New Bridge after the surprise attack by the British at Fort Lee. At that spot is Steuben House* (1209 Main St., just north of NJ 4; 201-487-1739), a state historic site that houses the museum of the Bergen County Historical Society. The oldest portion of the sandstone house was probably built in 1713, making this the oldest extant house in the county, but there had been a gristmill on the site for several years before that. During the Revolution the house was owned by Jan Zabriskie, a leading merchant and a Tory. It was confiscated and offered to Major General Baron von Steuben in gratitude for his work in training the American troops. The house had suffered considerable abuse during the war: because of its strategic location at the bridge it was used for various military purposes, including serving as a fort, throughout the Revolution. According to one legend, Steuben declined the offer because he didn't want to displace the Zabriskies; according to another, its condition made it undesirable. Actually, Steuben did live in the house for a time and, according to an advertisement for its sale, repaired the damage. At one point he rented the house to the Zabriskies, who entertained him there and charged the costs of the entertainment to the general's account. Eventually Steuben sold the house to Zabriskie's son for a handsome sum.

Most of the items on display in the Steuben House, including, for example, the furniture and pottery, were manufactured or used in the area. A Native American dugout canoe found in Hackensack in the mid-19th century is also to be seen. Various special events take place at the Steuben House, including an annual Christmas exhibit that traces the evolution of the holiday from ancient to modern times. Open Wednesday–Saturday, 10–12 and 1–5; Sunday, 2–5; groups by appointment.

The Steuben House has an idyllic setting, known as New Bridge Landing Historic Park.* There are other buildings in the park, including the Campbell Christie House* (1201 Main St.; 201-343-9492), a colonial sandstone house moved from New Milford, and restored as a tavern by the Bergen County Historical Society. Usually open 2d Sunday of the month, 2–5, and for special events. To arrange individual and group tours, call the Steuben

House (201-487-1739). The Demarest House* (Main St. between the Steuben House and the Campbell Christie House; 201-261-0012), an early stone house, was also moved here from New Milford. Once thought to have been built in the late 1670s by the Huguenot settler David des Marest, it is more likely a late-18th-century successor on that site. Its two rooms are furnished with period pieces. Usually open Sunday, 2–5. A late-19th-century barn and an 1880s iron-truss swing bridge,* probably the oldest extant highway swing bridge in the state, and an authentic out-kitchen built by the historical society, are also in the park. The houses and the barn are often open for visits during special events at the park.

Riverton Burlington 2,759

C 543

Situated on the Delaware River and founded in 1851 as a resort by a group of wealthy businessmen from Philadelphia, Riverton has lovely views of the river along Bank Avenue. Several of the mansions built by the founders remain, as does the Riverton Yacht Club (Bank Ave. at the foot of Main St.), built in 1880 at the end of an 1869 iron pier. The club, founded in 1865, is the oldest on the Delaware, and claims to be the ninth oldest in the country. A walk or drive along Bank Ave., Main St. (note the public library), Lippincott St., and Carriage House La. (where many of the Victorian carriage houses have been converted to residences) is a pleasant way to see what kind of a community its founders must have intended. Over 350 buildings are included in Riverton's historic district,* which is bounded by the Delaware River, Park and Thomas aves., and Fulton St.

There were farms in this area in the 18th century, and some of the early farmhouses are reputed to have been stops on the Underground Railroad. The Taylor Wildlife Refuge (Taylors La. off 130; 856-786-0809) is a 90-acre preserve that is part of an organic farm that has been in the same family since the early 18th century and is now the only working farm along this stretch of the river; the two houses date to the 1830s and the 1880s. The preserve contains swamp, woodlands, and open pasture and is particularly attractive to birders. There are marked trails. Open dawn to dusk.

Rockaway Morris 5,473 (borough) 22,930 (township)

I 80 EXIT 37, US 46, NJ 15, C 513

Rockaway Borough (incorporated in 1894) and Township (incorporated in 1844) lie in the heart of a region that once supported a flourishing iron industry. Four-fifths of the iron mined in New Jersey came from a narrow strip running through this area southwest to northeast. The Mount Hope mine, the largest in the state, has been in almost continuous operation since 1710. Although the iron mine did shut down in 1959 (it had a brief revival in the '70s), road-building material is being excavated at the site (this is a large operation; in 1990 there were 2,000 truck trips a day at Mount Hope).

The former Colonel Joseph Jackson house* (82 E. Main St.; 973-627-5709) is now home to the borough's Foster Memorial Library. The early 19th-century house still has its original clapboard as well as some of the original glass panes and a beehive oven. In one room of the library is a museum that contains artifacts and archives, primarily connected to local history, and including, for example, some materials from the Jackson family. Open the 1st Saturday of the month, 11–1 and for special events. Other times by appointment.

The Ford-Faesch house* (Mt. Hope Rd., a little over a mile north of interchange 35 on I 80; 973-366-6730) was built in 1768 by Jacob Ford Jr., who went on to build himself a mansion in Morristown, used by Washington as his headquarters in 1779–80 (see Morristown). The Faesch in question is John Jacob Faesch, a Swiss who came to this country in 1764 to run the Ringwood mine (see Ringwood). In 1770 he moved to Rockaway Township to supervise the Mount Hope mines and eventually bought the business and the house. The house, a national historic landmark, is being stabilized and restored by the Historical Society of the Rockaways, which is planning to reconstruct the west wing that was torn off some years back when a bay window was added. For now the society sponsors a 4 July and an early-December Christmas event at the house.

The whole area is rich in history: these mines supplied raw material for weapons crucial to the Revolutionary War. Mount Hope Historical Park (Teabo Rd.; 973-829-8666), which opened in 1997, includes three formerly independent properties: the Richard, Allen, and Teabo mines. Trails here are open for hikers, and as you hike through these beautiful woods, you will see the effect of 200 years of mining on the landscape. It will also be obvious why park regulations forbid leaving the marked trails: the deep subsidence pits are a clear danger. You can pick up brochures for self-guided tours in the parking lot. Trails open daily, 9–dusk. The Mount Hope Conservancy, in cooperation with the Morris County Park Commission, offers guided tours of the area throughout the year. (For information on other mine tours, see Ringwood.)

If you take exit 37 from I 80 and go north on C 513 toward Hibernia, another of the iron towns within Rockaway Township, you will pass through the Wildcat Ridge Wildlife Management Area. Here are 3,000 acres in which you can hike (the mines in this area are all secured, some by a developer who had hoped to build houses and a golf course on top of the ridge), watch for birds, and fish. There are spectacular views from the top of the ridge, and this area is home to New Jersey's largest collection of bats, some of them endangered, which took over some of the caves that resulted when the mines were abandoned. At the moment, there is more concern to protect the bats from the people than vice versa. At the top of the ridge is an official Hawk Migration Association of North America hawkwatch. During migration season you can see from its platform large numbers of hawks; there are also spectacular views of the Highlands and on clear days the New York City skyline. Volunteers are at the platform August 15–November 15 and February 15–May 15. You can pick up a trail map at the kiosk in the parking lot.

Farther north is Farney State Park (Durham Rd.; 973-962-7031), more than 3,900 noncontiguous acres. This is an undeveloped park with woodlands, streams, ponds, and a reservoir, with facilities for hiking (there are trails and an old logging road), fishing, ice-fishing, bird-watching, and cross-country skiing.

Rocky Hill Somerset 662

C 518, jUSt EaSt of US 206

This small town (less than a square mile in area) served as George Washington's headquarters in the fall of 1783 while the Continental Congress was meeting in Princeton. Here Washington entertained, among others, Alexander Hamilton, John Witherspoon, Thomas Jefferson, Thomas Paine, and James Madison, and here he wrote the address that has come to be known as "Washington's Farewell to the Troops" (he could not have delivered a farewell to the troops here because there weren't many around). Washington's house, Rockingham★ (take C 518 east to C 603 and turn right; Rockingham is the first house on the right; 609-683-7132), is now a state-run historic-house museum. The house was moved from its original site in the late 1890s, moved again in the 1960s because it was threatened by blasting from the nearby Traprock Industries quarry, and moved once more in 2001 to a larger site in Kingston, close to the Millstone River and near where the house originally sat. The house is furnished with pieces from 1783 or earlier and includes reconstructed outbuildings and a colonial kitchen garden. Annual events include a candlelight tour in December and a celebration of Washington's birthday. Open Wednesday–Saturday, 10–12 and 1–4; Sunday, 1–4; closed New Year's Day, Thanksgiving, and Christmas. Groups by appointment. Restoration of an 1890s stone building to function as a visitor center and a restored washhouse to serve as a hands-on museum for young children is expected to be complete by the end of 2005.

Rocky Hill is a well-preserved and attractive village. Its historic district★ includes 19th- and 20th-century buildings on Washington St. and Montgomery, Crescent, and Princeton avenues. The pre-Revolutionary mill at 200 Washington St., now a potter's studio and gallery, was once owned by John Hart, one of New Jersey's five signers of the Declaration of Independence.

The Millstone River and the Delaware and Raritan Canal* flow through Rocky Hill, and you can walk (or bicycle or horseback ride) along the towpath here (*see* Kingston). The remains of a well-known terra cotta plant, now a private house, are visible from the towpath. The firm supplied the tiles for the Woolworth Building in New York City, and you can also see examples of the terra cotta work in the Rocky Hill firehouse, 156 Washington Street.

North of Rocky Hill, in Montgomery Township (take Montgomery Ave. until it becomes Montgomery Rd. or pick up Montgomery Rd. from US 206 north), is the 1860 House (124 Montgomery Rd.; 609-921-3272), the home of the Montgomery Cultural Center for the Arts. Connected to the mid-19th-century house by a glass breezeway is an early-20th-century wood-paneled library, moved from a northern New Jersey house by a member of the Ballantine brewery family. The center sponsors concerts, lectures, classes, and a summer arts camp. Exhibits in the house change roughly every six weeks. Open Tuesday–Friday, 10–3; Sunday, 1–4.

Behind the cultural center is the Van Harlingen Historical Society of Montgomery Township's barn museum (908-359-8404, 908-359-3498). Inside the 19th-century barn are mementos of the days when the township was an agricultural community, including agricultural implements and a sleigh. Open by appointment.

The Van Harlingen Historical Society also maintains the Dirck Gulick house* (C 601, the Belle Mead–Blawenburg Rd., at the point C 604, the Dutchtown-Harlingen Rd., intersects it from the east; 908-359-8404, 908-359-3498), a stone Dutch house dating to 1752, as its headquarters and library. Open the last Saturday of the month, 10–12 and by appointment. Another of the society's projects is the Bedensville Schoolhouse (Burnt Hill Rd., behind the elementary school; 908-359-8404; 908-359-3498), a one-room schoolhouse built in 1853 and moved to this site after it closed. Open by appointment and for the township's Independence Day celebration.

If you continue north on 601 and turn left on E. Mountain Rd., you will come to the Sourland Mountain Preserve (908-722-1200), a Somerset County preserve of over 2,800 acres. This is rocky and hilly terrain with a wide range of habitats and consequently of birds and wildflowers. Open for passive recreation daily, dawn–dusk.

If you go west on C 518 until you get to C 501 (Great Rd.), you will come to the Blawenburg historic district,* which includes C 588 and Mountain View Rd., an attractive collection of primarily 19th-century buildings, including the Reformed Dutch Church of Blawenburg* (424 C 518). The Blawenburg Band, said to be one of the oldest community bands in the state, was founded in 1890 and has been continuously active except during the two world wars. It gives more than 30 performances each year.

Roebling Burlington [Florence Township]

(DELAWARE RIVER BETWEEN BORDENTOWN
AND BURLINGTON, JUST WEST OF US 130)

Roebling was founded as a company town early in the 20th century, when the Roebling Company, famous for making the wire rope and cables used in suspension bridges, decided to make for itself the steel that went into those products. The plant was built on the site of a 115-acre peach and potato farm that bordered the Delaware River; it turned out a variety of products, including the cable used in the George Washington and Golden Gate bridges. The town itself was designed by Charles G. Roebling, the third son of the famous John A. Roebling, who had invented steel cable, had created the Roebling company, had built his first cable suspension bridge in Pittsburgh in 1846, and had designed and begun construction of the Brooklyn Bridge. (The Brooklyn Bridge was completed by another son, Washington A. Roebling.)

Charles Roebling envisioned a model community for the workers in the new plant. He laid out the village on a rectangular grid, with Main St. a boulevard that expanded into a circle at the intersection with 5th Ave., and provided a park, an auditorium, and a general store that "sold everything from pork chops to pianos." Those higher up in the company lived in the larger houses along Riverside Ave., but the workers' brick row houses were solidly built, the rent was half that of the neighboring towns, maintenance and lawn care were provided, and the view of the river from the park is lovely. In the 1950s the company was sold, and the plant shut down in the '80s. The town is now part of Florence Township, many of the original structures are gone, and the buildings are privately owned, but the distinctive quality of the community is still apparent. The Roebling historic district* includes 2d–8th, Alden, Norman, and Amboy avenues. St. Nicholas Byzantine Catholic Church (191 Norman Ave.) has a picnic grove at the end of the street where an annual ethnic festival sponsored by the church takes place.

The Roebling Historical Society (609-499-7632) is working on plans to establish a museum in the former Main Gate building (2d Ave.), which is expected to open by 2006. Exhibits will focus on the history of the company; the processes it used; the products it made; and the people, including the Roebling family and those who worked at the factory, who made it happen. The grounds will contain a sculpture garden with items like a forklift and a 26-foot-diameter flywheel on display.

Roosevelt Monmouth 933

C 571

Conceived as a utopian community that would be a self-sufficient agricultural and industrial unit, Roosevelt,* founded in the 1930s and known as Jersey Homesteads until the death of President Franklin Delano Roosevelt, was actually owned by the federal government. The early community, a project of the Federal Resettlement Administration, contained a cooperative factory (the Workers Aim Cooperative Factory, 34 N. Valley Rd., dedicated in 1936, now housing a packaging manufacturer and art studios) and a cooperative store. Communal farms were also part of the original conception.

Although 151 of the original structures remain, the farms have been sold, the cooperatives are long since gone, and the government sold the town to the residents in the late 1940s. But underneath the extensive architectural alterations, you can usually still see the boxlike houses and rational layout of the original Bauhaus-inspired scheme, the work of Alfred Kastner (his assistant was Louis Kahn).

Most of the residents are now commuters, but the town has long been a haven for artists and writers, of whom Ben Shahn is probably the best known. His large mural, depicting incidents and people involved in the history of labor, immigration into the United States, and the founding of Roosevelt, is to be found in the elementary school (School La., just west of C 571; 609-448-2798). Visitors are welcome to come see the mural during school hours (8–3:30), as well as the photography exhibit showing scenes from the time when Roosevelt was still Jersey Homesteads (on permanent loan from the state museum), but you are asked to stop by at the front office first.

Shahn is buried in the community cemetery (Eleanor La.); the memorial he designed himself. The cemetery is still free to residents. In the park with the amphitheater on the west side of C 571 (N. Rochdale Ave.) is a monumental bust of Roosevelt, modeled by Shahn's son Jon.

Other Roosevelt residents have included Jacob Landau and Gregorio Prestopino. Landau's former studio (30 Lake Dr.), a geodesic dome, still holds some of his work. Tours of the studio can be arranged by appointment (215-368-2536).

The Roosevelt Arts Project (609-448-4616) presents a variety of cultural events, including poetry readings, concerts, and art exhibits. Most events take place at the Roosevelt Municipal Building (341 N. Rochdale Ave.), but there is an annual show at the Landau studio, and an occasional show in the factory.

At the corner of N. Valley Rd. and Homestead La. is Britton House, one of the farmhouses predating the foundation of Jersey Homesteads. And at the foot of Farm La. is a prizewinning project from the 1980s, Roosevelt

Solar Village, a low-income solar housing project for the elderly, modeled on an English village.

To the south and west of Roosevelt, off C 571 (and also accessible from C 524, C 539, and many lesser roads) is the Assunpink Wildlife Management Area, 6,000 acres containing three lakes, open fields, marsh, lowland forest, upland woods, and hedgerows. Some of the land is leased to farmers. The area is reputed to be one of the best spots for bird-watching in central New Jersey, with over 250 species having been seen here. Fishing is possible along most of the shore of all three lakes, one can hike, and there is limited hunting.

The Horse Park at Stone Tavern (609-259-0170) occupies 147 acres within the wildlife management area and, with five rings, over 250 stalls, and a covered grandstand, has facilities for international equestrian events of all kinds. Shows, festivals, and other events take place here almost every weekend, March–November.

For an inside look at the world of harness racing you can visit nearby Showplace Farms (505 NJ 33; 732-446-3100; from the Horse Park take 571 north to Perrineville Rd. and turn right; turn left on Prodelin Way and right on 33). This large (more than 20 barns stabling more than 400 horses), well-groomed training facility welcomes visitors, but you are asked to call first. Groups by appointment.

ROOSEVELT

Roseland Essex 5,298

I 280, C 527

What is apparently the oldest (founded in 1847) and largest flag maker in the world, Annin & Co., has had its headquarters in Roseland since the 1980s. The 60-by-90-foot American flag that flies from the George Washington Bridge on patriotic holidays (and weighs 500 pounds) was made by Annin, as are flags of all the other countries of the world, to say nothing of American states, Swiss cantons, and innumerable organizations.

The Harrison House* (126 Eagle Rock Ave.; 973-228-0742), a white clapboard house with its original beehive oven and walk-in fireplace, dates to the 1820s and serves as the headquarters for the Roseland Historical Society. The society holds several open houses during the year, and the house is open other times by appointment. You are welcome to visit the attractive garden any time. The society also owns a portion of the former Becker Dairy Farm (35 Livingston Ave.) and hopes eventually to develop space there to exhibit its collection of dairy and farm tools, its milk sleigh, and the like. For the moment, its museum, which is primarily devoted to farm tools and implements, is in the Becker Center (which once housed the dairy's delivery wagons and later its trucks). Open Saturday, 10–3, May–October.

Roselle Union 21,274

NJ 27

The first city in the world to be lit by incandescent bulbs (and the first in the United States to be lit by electricity), Roselle was settled in the late 1670s by Abraham Clark, who migrated here from Long Island and was the great-grandfather of the Abraham Clark who signed the Declaration of Independence. The town remained basically rural for almost 200 years until John C. Rose, after whom it is named, began buying up farms and developing the area. Today Roselle has an attractive, lived-in look and many interesting buildings, including, for example, the oldest building in town, the Federal-style Cavalier Jouet house (238 E. 2d Ave.).

A replica of the Abraham Clark house, which burned in the early years of the twentieth century, has been built at 9th Ave. and Chestnut St. (908-245-1777). The house, not that distinguishable from its neighbors, sits a few hundred feet from the site of the original house on land that once belonged to Clark. The museum wing features a small collection of items primarily related to the history of the Clark family and the history of Roselle, including for example, some early light bulbs. Open by appointment only.

The First Presbyterian Church (5th Ave. and Chestnut St.) dates from the

1890s and was the first church in the United States to be lit by incandescent light. The original Electrolier, still in use, is a brass chandelier with milk-glass reflectors that was designed and installed by Edison; damaged by fire, it was restored in the 1960s. (A plaque marks the site of Edison's laboratory at Locust St. and 1st Ave.) The Second Baptist Church (2d Ave. and Locust St.) also dates from the 1890s.

In the southeastern corner of the borough (Thompson and St. Georges Ave.) is Warinanco Park, best known for its indoor skating rink (908-298-7850). The 210-acre park, one of Union County's many Olmsted-designed parks, was named for one of the three chiefs of the Lenape. In the spring its Chatfield Garden has a sensational display of tulips. The park has facilities for boating (908-289-7845), fishing, outdoor ice-skating, and picnicking, as well as bicycle paths, a fitness trail, tennis courts (201-245-2288), a playground, and athletic fields. The skating rink is open Tuesday–Sunday from the first weekend in October to the first weekend in April.

North of Roselle, in Roselle Park, is the Roselle Park Museum (9 W. Grant Ave.; 908-245-1776). Housed in an apartment building said to date from the 1890s, the museum has a collection of photographs and other memorabilia relating to the history of the borough, which celebrated its centennial in 2001. Open Monday, 7–9 P.M.; Wednesday, 10–2. On the same block is the Robert Gordon school, the first public building to use Thomas Edison–designed cement. Roselle Park's high school has a prizewinning band, featured in the 1990s in a Disney TV show.

South of Roselle, in Linden, is a large private collection of Hank Williams memorabilia (910 Wheatsheaf Rd.; 908-486-7761). Included are photographs, magazines, posters, records, personal items, and a bronze bust. Open weekends, 10–4; weekdays by appointment.

Rutherford Bergen 18,110

NJ 3, 17

Once a settlement known as Boiling Springs (there is a Boiling Springs Ave. just over the border in East Rutherford), Rutherford was developed in 1862 on land that had belonged to John Rutherford, a patriot and friend of George Washington. There are still early-18th-century houses to be seen in Rutherford: the oldest portion of the Nathaniel Kingsland house (245 Union Ave.), where Washington rested on his journey from Newburgh to Princeton, dates from 1670, making it one of the oldest houses in the state. (The adjoining Richard Outwater house dates from 1821.) Washington also visited the Kip Homestead* (12 Meadow Rd.). Another old Dutch stone house, the Yereance-Berry house,* contains the Meadowlands Museum (91 Crane Ave.; 201-935-1175), which specializes in area history. Permanent exhibits include New Jersey minerals, antique toys and dolls, early to mid-19th-century household items, and pre-electric kitchens; there are also changing exhibits and a variety of programs and workshops for children and adults. Open January–June and September–December, Monday, Wednesday, and Saturday, 1–4, Sunday, 2–4, July and August, Monday–Thursday, 1–4; Sunday, 2–4; group tours by appointment.

Rutherford is the birthplace of the poet William Carlos Williams, and until 1996 his house* (9 Ridge Rd. at Park Ave.) remained in the hands of his family. One block from his house is the William Carlos Williams Center (Park Ave. between Glen Rd. and Spring Dell; 201-939-6969), built around the Rivoli, a 1922 vaudeville theater that was converted into a movie house but burned in 1977. Claiming to be one of the few arts centers in the United States to be named after a poet, the Williams Center is currently undergoing renovation.

Until the main theater is fully restored the center is concentrating on its children's theater series, its film series, and its arts and education series.

The Felician College of New Jersey campus was the original home of Fairleigh Dickinson (*see* Madison, Teaneck). Iviswold Castle (Passaic and Montrose aves.), the building Fairleigh Dickinson purchased when it first opened in 1942, was built as a summer home in the 1880s and was inspired by the French châteaux of Chaumont and Amboise. Felician College of New Jersey took over the campus in 1997 and is restoring Iviswold.

Salem Salem 5,857

NJ 45, 49

In 1675 a group of Quakers led by John Fenwick settled on the banks of the Delaware River and named their community Salem, from *shalom*, the Hebrew word for "peace." Immigrants from other countries had preceded them—the Swedes and Finns, for example, had established a settlement at Fort Elfsborg (also known as Fort Myggenborgh because of the mosquitos, located near today's Point Elsinboro) in 1643, and there had also been Dutch and Puritans from New Haven in the area—but their communities did not last (Fort Elfsborg was abandoned in 1653), and Salem became the first permanent English settlement in West Jersey.

Salem thrived as a shipping center (it was designated an official port in 1682) until the Revolution, when shipping activity moved to Camden and Philadelphia. The port fell into disuse, but in 1982, some 300 years after its founding, it was officially reopened, and a load of grain was shipped out of the harbor for the first time in 100 years. The port has prospered, and in 1995 almost 38,000 tons, largely containerized shipping and used vehicles, left Salem, much of it heading for the Caribbean.

Improvident farming practices depleted the soil around Salem, and in the early 1800s many of its citizens headed west, among them Zadock Street, who left in 1802 and founded the towns of Salem, Ohio, and Salem, Indiana. His son Aaron Street was responsible for Salem, Iowa, and Salem, Oregon.

The discovery of marl nearby made it possible to replenish the soil, and agriculture prospered again. Salem, in fact, has a footnote in agricultural history. Robert Gibbon Johnson, a wealthy local landowner, is credited with importing the first tomato plants from South America. On 15 September 1820, he is supposed to have stood on the courthouse steps and eaten a tomato, which most people believed to be poisonous. Tomatoes are now, of course, an important crop in New Jersey, and many of them are grown in Salem County.

Johnson was also one of the founders of the New Jersey Historical Society (1845) and its first vice-president. His elegant house (90 Market St.), built in 1806 with additions dating from 1850, now serves as a county

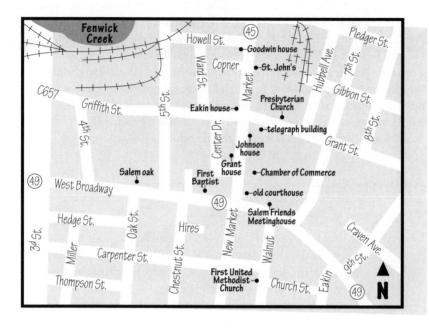

building and is one of the many brick buildings that, with the wide streets, help give Salem its distinctly West Jersey look.

At Market St. and Broadway is the old Salem County Courthouse. Portions date from 1735, but the courthouse was almost completely rebuilt in 1817 and extensively remodeled again in 1908. The outside now dates basically from 1817, the inside from 1908. To visit the courthouse, stop in at the Chamber of Commerce (104 Market St.; 856-299-6699). Open weekdays 9–3, weekends 9–4.

Next to the Johnson house is the mid-19th-century Presbyterian Church, which has a Tiffany window over the pulpit in the sanctuary. Farther along Market St. (north of Grant) is St. John's Episcopal Church, originally Church of England. The present building dates from 1836.

At 79–83 Market St., in the Alexander Grant house, part of which dates from 1721, are the headquarters, museum, and library of the Salem County Historical Society (856-935-5004). Furnished to show how the occupants of such a house would have lived, the museum exhibits antiques that reflect the county's heritage, as well as various special collections, including glass from Wistarburg, the first glassworks in the colonies (1739); Native American relics; and dolls. Behind the Grant house, on the historical society's property, is the John Jones law office, a tiny octagonal brick building, c. 1735, believed to be the oldest surviving law office in the country. There is also a re-creation of a South Jersey stone barn built in 1957 that contains some of the larger items owned by the society as well as some of the specialized collections. A mid-18th-century log cabin, dismantled and moved here from another site, was restored and erected on the grounds. It is used as an education center and schoolroom for visiting school groups, with slates and "McGuffy's

Readers" and the like. Open Tuesday–Saturday, 12–4. Admission charged. The society is also restoring the nearby Alfonso L. Eakin house (89 Market St.), a late-18th-century house that was remodeled in 1841.

On the north side of E. Broadway, at Walnut St., is the Salem Friends Meetinghouse. Dating from 1772, it has the longest record of continuous service of any religious building in New Jersey. Built of brick in a Flemish-bond pattern, its walls are 16–18 inches thick, much of its glass may be from Wistarburg, and its fences are made of New Jersey bog iron.

On W. Broadway, opposite Oak St., is the Friends burial ground. Here you will find the famous Salem Oak, a massive white oak tree believed to be over 400 years old. According to local legend, in October 1675 John Fenwick signed a treaty with the Native Americans under this tree. When a limb falls, people line up to take pieces home as souvenirs. The tree has been heavily braced, and there is hope that it will be around for some time.

If possible, walk up and down Market St. and along Broadway: a large section of Market St. and E. Broadway is in the Market St. historic district,★ and many buildings have identifying plaques. The house at 47 Market St. served as a stop on the Underground Railroad when Elizabeth and Abigail Goodwin lived there. Many of the houses in the area were derelict or had been vandalized, and the renovation efforts have been heroic. The Greek Revival house at 28 Market St. (c. 1800) is one of those renovated. It stands taller than its neighbors because it was built by a tailor who had his shop in the basement (the basement windows and doorway have been removed). See also the small frame saltboxes at 18 Market. The First United Methodist Church (Walnut St., opposite Church St.) dates from 1888, the First Baptist Church (130 W. Broadway) from 1846. At 185 Grant St. is the former telegraph building; built in 1856 and used by Western Union from 1917 to 1955, it is being restored by Preservation Salem to serve as an office and resource center.

Scotch Plains Union 22,732

US 22, NJ 28, C 509

Scotch Plains was settled in 1684 by Scottish Dissenters from Perth Amboy who were soon followed by Quakers. By the 1740s there were more Baptists than Quakers or Scottish Dissenters. An agricultural community, Scotch Plains grew slowly (by refusing to let the railroad come through the town, it stayed rural longer), but after World War II it doubled in size and became a commuter town. James Manning, the founder of Brown University, came from Scotch Plains, and Arthur Brisbane, the journalist and editor, was a resident.

Scotch Plains's first substantial building, the Stage House Inn★ (Front St. and Park Ave.; 908-322-4224), built c. 1737, and from roughly 1769 to 1829 a stagecoach stop on the Swift-Sure Stagecoach line, is now the cornerstone for Stage House Village, in which various older buildings, some from other sites, have been converted to shops and restaurants. Nearby is the Osborn Cannonball House (1840 Front St.; 908-232-1199), c. 1720, so named because it was hit by a cannonball (fired by a Continental soldier) during the Revolution. Maintained as a museum by the Scotch Plains and Fanwood Historical Society, the house has its original kitchen, complete with a beehive oven. One parlor is furnished with colonial pieces, the other with Victorian ones. There is also a colonial bedroom. The society's collection includes antique clothing; exhibits change frequently and tend to be thematic (historic bridal gowns in June, for example). Open the 1st Sunday of the month, 2–4. Tours by appointment.

The Ruskinesque-Gothic Baptist Church (311 Park Ave.) dates from the 1870s, but the parsonage★ (Park Ave. and Grand St.) is almost 100 years older (1786, with a later addition). Built of boulders from the Green Brook, supposedly because the new parson was from Pennsylvania and accustomed to stone, it was the first stone parsonage in the area. The Second Baptist Church (Grand and Union), now the YMCA, dates from c. 1817. Note also the Romanesque All Saints' Episcopal Church (559 Park Ave.), 1882.

The Ephraim Tucker farmhouse (Jerusalem Rd. near Plainfield Ave.), c. 1740, enlarged in the 19th century and considerably altered in the 20th, served for many years as the clubhouse for the Scotch Hills Country Club (908-232-9748). Founded as the Westfield Golf Club in the 1890s, the club became the Shady Rest Country Club in the 1920s (apparently the first African American country club in the state). Purchased by the township in the 1960s, it is now one of the few municipally owned clubs in New Jersey. John Shippen, the first African American pro in the PGA and the first American-born golf professional to compete in a U.S. Open, was the pro at Shady Rest for over 40 years. His portrait hangs in the lobby (note the fireplace), and each year the John Shippen Memorial Tournament raises money for student scholarships. The farmhouse is now used for special events. Tours by appointment (908-322-6700, ext. 221).

East of Raritan Rd. are the Ash Brook Reservation and the Ash Brook golf course (*see* Clark). Part of the Watchung Reservation also falls within Scotch Plains (*see* Mountainside).

Seaside Park   Ocean 2,263

NJ 35

The tiny beach community of Seaside Park is nestled between Seaside Heights to the north—with its boardwalk and night life, reputed to have more people per square inch in the summer than any other community—and Island Beach State Park (732-793-0506) to the south—10 miles of one of the last completely unspoiled beaches in New Jersey and one of the largest section of undeveloped barrier island along the North Atlantic. Because there are no jetties or groins on Island Beach, the natural forces shaping the beach are unimpeded. Actually, Island Beach is no longer an island, its name dating to the time it was, from the mid-18th to the early 19th century.

Owned in the 1920s by Henry Phipps, a partner of Andrew Carnegie, who planned to convert the area into a luxurious seaside resort, Island Beach was purchased by the state and turned into a park in the 1950s. One of the Phipps houses saved by the state now serves as the governor's summer home. The former boat-storage building (and later municipal garage) has been converted to the Forked River Interpretive Center (732-793-1285). There is a short self-guided tour here, and you can pick up trail maps. The lifesaving station* dates from the 1890s.

With the ocean on one side and Barnegat Bay on the other, the park offers visitors a wide variety of activities. Over half the acreage consists of natural areas, but there are recreation areas as well. There is only one road into the park, and when the parking lots are full (in high season as many as 15,000 may visit daily), no more cars are let in. (There is also a limit on the number of four-wheel-drive vehicles driven by those planning to fish.)

At the nature center (732-793-1698), displays focus on barrier islands—their history and bird life, and the environment of barrier beaches—and include a diorama that transects a barrier island. You can take a self-guided tour behind the nature center. Kayak tours and a wide range of nature programs are offered in the summer months. Educational programs for groups can be arranged; call for details on all the programs. The nature center is open daily Memorial Day weekend–Labor Day, 9–4, weekends only the rest of the year.

The bay side is generally closed, but tours can be arranged. The park naturalists conduct tours through the northern natural area, and you are free to walk in the southern natural area, which has a bird blind and launching areas for canoes and kayaks. The north bathhouse has a 180-gallon saltwater tank display. From the third week in June to Labor Day some areas of the beaches are protected by lifeguards, and it is also possible to fish, scuba dive, and surf in designated areas. The bird-watching is excellent, and although there are no tables or fireplaces, you are welcome to picnic on the beach; you can build a fire (except in the bathing areas) as long as you keep your fire at least 50 feet east of the dunes. Even at the height of the summer season, you can find empty stretches of beach to walk along if you leave the guarded areas. From October through April you can bring a horse onto the beach (advance reservations are necessary). Parking fees year-round.

Secaucus Hudson 15,931

NJ TNPK EXITS 16E, 17, NJ 3

Secaucus, which must once have had one of the worst reputations of any city in the state, was settled in the early 1680s by a few hardy souls willing to cross the damp meadowland to reach high ground. The name comes from a Native American word meaning "where the snake hides," and the Native Americans are said to have avoided the area. Laurel Hill, the nearly leveled mineral-rich rock formation familiar to those who travel by train, bus, or car to or from New York City, was once known as Snake Hill and is said to have been used by George Washington's troops as a lookout during the Revolution. When the county opened Laurel Hill Park in the mid-1990s, it was its first new park in over 80 years. The park stretches about a quarter-mile along the river, with a waterfront walk and a boat launch; there are also multi-use playing fields and a playground. The Hackensack Riverkeeper (201-968-0808) has a canoe and kayak livery at the park (open weekends, April–October) and also offers (by reservation) eco-cruises on a pontoon boat. Other Riverkeeper programs include eco-walks to the Mill Creek wetlands, guided tours, and community cleanups. In 2004 more than 6,000 people took part in the Hackensack Riverkeeper's programs.

To the west of the Mill Creek wetlands is a new city park, Mill Creek Point Park (Mill Ridge Rd.). These seven acres provide access to the river with a boat launch for canoes and kayaks. There are wildlife viewing areas and interpretive signs; eventually the park will serve as the northern end of the Secaucus Greenway, a 15-mile walking trail that will run parallel to the river down to Laurel Hill Park.

Part of Secaucus's bad reputation came from its pig farms—until about 40 years ago, there were some 50 of them—and slaughterhouses. When the New Jersey Turnpike was built, several of the farms were destroyed, and the town forbade the establishment of new ones. One pig farmer, Henry Krajewski, ran for president as an Independent Populist in 1952 and 1960.

Known also as an area of warehouses and freight yards, Secaucus may have suffered from the idea, accepted until fairly recently, that marshland was waste land, good only for pig farms and freight yards. In recent years, however, Secaucus has attracted so much industrial, commercial, and residential development that there is considerable concern about overbuilding on the marshland. Among the projects from the 1980s are the immense Harmon Cove and Harmon Meadow developments, which contain housing, marinas, office and hotel space, child-care facilities, shops and restaurants, a cinema and a health club.

One of the newest projects is the Frank R. Lautenberg Secaucus Rail Station at Allied Junction, a transfer station, which connects 10 of the state's 11 rail lines. The station was conceived as a way of cutting travel time to

New York City as well as encouraging more people to use the trains. A light-rail line to the Meadowlands Sports Complex (*see* East Rutherford) is part of the project. The building is striking, with murals of the marshes and the Pulaski Skyway, and an eight-sided light-filled rotunda.

Other striking buildings in Secaucus include Lincoln Towers (County Ave. near Dorigo La.), a barrier-free housing project for the elderly and handicapped, the last subsidized project to be approved by HUD before funds were cut in 1981. Note also the dramatic municipal building (1203 Paterson Plank Rd.). When the studios of WOR-TV (9 Broadcast Plaza) opened in the mid-'80s, they were in one of the few buildings in the country built specifically as a television facility.

Secaucus today is a popular stop for shoppers because of the abundance of factory outlets. What is interesting about these outlets is that they are located among working warehouses, so that to go from one store to another shoppers must negotiate around 18-wheelers, driving down streets with names like Enterprise Ave. and Venture Way. Among the companies to be found in Secaucus is the 80-year-old Goya Foods, said to be the largest Hispanic-owned company in the country.

Sergeantsville Hunterdon [Delaware Township]

C 523, 604

First settled around 1700, Sergeantsville (pronounced *sir'-gents-ville*) is named for Charles Sergeant, a Revolutionary War soldier. (Before the 1830s it was known as Skunktown.) This tiny village at the intersection of county routes 523 and 604 (the Stockton-Flemington Rd. and the Rosemont-Ringoes Rd.) lies in as yet largely undeveloped, rolling land characteristic of Hunterdon County. From Sergeantsville came Dr. George Larison, the founder of Hunterdon County's peach industry. He first planted his orchards in the 1850s; by 1890 there were 2 million peach trees in Hunterdon County, yielding some million bushels of peaches a year. An infestation of San Jose scale in the 1890s resulted in the destruction of most of the trees.

Roughly a mile southwest of the crossroads on the Rosemont-Ringoes Rd. as it crosses the Wickecheoke Creek, is Green Sergeant's Covered Bridge,* the last of New Jersey's 75 pre-20th-century covered bridges (one was built in the 1950s in Cherry Hill, almost a century after the state's last wooden covered bridge). Built in 1872 on the site of one dating to 1750, the bridge was threatened with a modern replacement in the 1950s. Saved by concerned citizens, it was rebuilt on a steel frame, retaining over half of the original trusses and members.

There are many 18th- and 19th-century buildings in Sergeantsville. The inn was actually built as a private house in the 18th century and greatly enlarged in 1835. The fieldstone and stucco house on the southeast side of

C 604 at the creek dates from around 1740. At the intersection of C 604 and Headquarters Rd. is the mid-18th-century Headquarters Farm, so named because George Washington is believed to have camped here on his way to Trenton. Included on the property are a stone mansion, a tenant house, slave quarters, and a four-story gristmill. Well into the 20th century there was a community here with a store and post office. Since 1973 Sergeantsville has held a house tour the first weekend in November (609-397-3571, 908-996-4677); it is possible then to see some of the many remaining 18th- and 19th-century houses and farms. On 4 July you can take part in the town's Great Crate Race, in which children and adults race in homemade coaster cars.

Another annual event is the Covered Bridge Artisans holiday studio tour (609-397-1535, 908-996-6152). Each year five venues, which could include pottery workshops, or glass workshops, or an herb farm, are open to the public Thanksgiving weekend.

About three miles north of the bridge on the Locktown-Sergeantsville Rd. (at the intersection of the Locktown Rd. with the Locktown School Rd.) you will come to the Locktown Stone Church* (1819), also known as the Old School Baptist Meeting House. The community is supposed to have gotten its name during a dispute among the Baptists. One of the factions put a lock on the door to keep the other out, but the other added a lock of its own, thereby keeping everyone out. (Another version has the name deriving from the Lockatong Creek.) The Friends of the Locktown Stone Church sponsor a fall concert series in the church (609-397-4047); to visit the handsome stone church at other times, call 908-996-2254.

Shrewsbury Monmouth 3,590 (borough) 1,098 (township)

NJ 35, C 13A

Shrewsbury is one of New Jersey's oldest settlements (the first buildings date to 1664; the township was incorporated in 1667), and over 40 of its buildings are at least 100 years old, but because its historic center is at the intersection of two broad, heavily traveled highways, much of the feeling of the past is obscured by the noise of the traffic. (Much of the traffic is generated by Fort Monmouth; see Eatontown.) Part of the Monmouth Patent of 1665, Shrewsbury was settled by Quakers, Anglicans, and Scotch Presbyterians, many of whom came to the area by way of Rhode Island and Long Island. The spot put its settlers to mind of Shrewsbury in England, and they named it accordingly. (During World War II, Monmouth County's Shrewsbury raised a considerable amount of money to help England's Shrewsbury, and the contact continued; in the mid-'80s, the vicar of the abbey in Shrewsbury, England, preached in Christ Church in Shrewsbury, New Jersey, while Christ Church's vicar was visiting in Shrewsbury, England.)

Sycamore Ave., one of Shrewsbury's two main crossroads (Broad St. is the other), follows the Burlington Trail, an old Native American path that ran from Freehold to the sea; Broad St. was once the Kings Highway; together they define Shrewsbury's historic district.* At their intersection are an old house, a meetinghouse, a church, and an old estate. On the northwest corner is the Allen House* (732-462-1466), built in 1667; at various times it has served as a private residence, a tavern, a tea room, and an antiques shop. Since 1968 the Allen House has belonged to the Monmouth County Historical Association, which now operates it as a museum. Restoring the house to look as it had in the 1750s and 1770s, when it was said to be "the most noted tavern in Shrewsbury," the historical association gathered and arranged the furnishings to show what a tavern would have been like in the mid-18th century. Outside is a colonial herb garden. Open May–September, Thursday–Saturday, 1–4; groups by appointment.

At the northeast corner is the Friends Meeting House (1816). Shrewsbury's first Quaker meetinghouse was built in 1672; it was the town's first public building. In 1727 bricks were imported from Holland to build another meetinghouse, and some of those bricks were used again in the present building.

At the southeast corner stands Christ Church (732-741-2220), erected in 1769 with funds raised largely by a lottery. (In 1879 President Ulysses S. Grant attended the church's centennial celebration.) Among the curiosities of the church are its crown (rare, because most churches wanted to remove this tie to the monarchy), its Bible, and the canopied pew for the colonial governor (apparently the only original canopies left in the country). The crown sits atop the tower (added in 1874) above a gilt ball and the weather vane. The gilt ball is a replacement for the original orb; during the Revolution soldiers tried to destroy this symbol of the English monarchy, and the scars from their shots are still to be seen on the ball (visitors can see the old ball in the church's archives). The Bible is a Vinegar Bible (a Bible printed at Oxford in 1717, full of typographical errors, including the substitution of "vinegar" for "vineyard" in the heading of Matthew 20). Tours by appointment (732-741-2220).

On the fourth corner, on the grounds of an estate that can be traced to the 1600s, are the Shrewsbury Historical Society's (732-530-7974) museum and library, Borough Hall, and the 18th-century Wardell House,* used by the Monmouth County Library. The historical society's building is on the site of the estate's carriage house, which burned. Of particular interest at the historical society are scale models of Shrewsbury's churches, which enable you to see what the interiors of the churches look like even when it is not possible to enter them. There are also memorabilia from the Broadmeadow family (James Broadmeadow began canning tomatoes in a factory on Sycamore St. in 1863). Usually open Tuesday 1–4 and the first Saturday of the month, 10–4, but it is advisable to call first.

The Presbyterian Church (1821) stands east of Christ Church on Sycamore Ave. and replaces an early-18th-century building. On Broad St. near

Sycamore is Paddington Farms, a housing development built on the former 86-acre Chalmar horse farm, an early-19th-century estate that once served as a summer retreat for Louis V. Bell. (Bell was a wealthy New Yorker who, contrary to legend, was probably not related to Alexander Graham Bell.) The estate later became the home of David H. Marx, president of the Louis Marx Toy Company, at one time the world's largest toy manufacturer; Dwight Eisenhower visited the estate when Marx owned it. The 22-room Georgian mansion (1910) has been preserved, as has the 19th-century farmhouse.

North of the four corners is the gallery of the Guild of Creative Art (620 Broad St.; 732-741-1441). Exhibits change monthly and are primarily of paintings and drawings, though they do include some sculpture and photography. The guild also sponsors public classes. Gallery open Monday–Saturday, 12–4:30.

Somers Point Atlantic 11,614

GARDEN STATE PKWY EXITS 29, 30, US 9, NJ 52, C 559

This rapidly growing community is the oldest settlement in today's Atlantic County. Formerly known as Somerset Plantation, it was founded in 1693 by seven men (four of English, two of Dutch, and one of Swedish extraction), most of whom came from Long Island. Once a stagecoach stop, the port of entry for Great Egg Harbor (1791–1913), and the site of the county's first post office (1806), Somers Point was an active shipbuilding center in the 19th century. By the mid-19th century it was known as a resort. Today it is a popular spot for fishing and boating. It is also the home of the Gateway Playhouse (738 Bay Ave.; 609-653-0553), which offers six or seven productions a year. Because developers must now provide a public-access boardwalk around any new development or marina, you can walk along the shore here, despite all the new condominiums.

The Richard Somers Mansion* (Shore Rd. at Somers Pt. Circle; 609-927-2212), built in the 1720s, is Atlantic County's oldest surviving building. Made of brick in a Flemish-bond pattern with an unusual roof (thought to have been built by a shipwright, it looks like an inverted hull), the house was built for Richard Somers, the harbor master. Somers was a descendant of one of the town's original settlers and the grandfather of Somers Point's most illustrious native son, Richard Somers, commander of the *Intrepid*, blown up in Tripoli in 1804. The Somers family continued to live in the house until 1937. Partially restored by the Works Progress Administration (WPA) in the late 1930s, the house is now owned by the state. It is furnished in part to look much as it would have when the Somers family lived there in the 18th century, but there are some 19th-century furnishings as well. Open Friday and Saturday, 10–12, 1–4, Sunday, 1–4. Groups and other times by appointment.

Just north of the Somers Mansion is the Atlantic County Historical Society library and museum (907 Shore Rd.; 609-927-5218). The museum contains artifacts dating from precolonial days to the early 20th century as well as material relating to Richard Somers and to Somers Point's nautical role. Of particular interest are the explorer dolls, a local WPA project. Open Wednesday–Saturday, 10–3:30 and 1st Thursday of the month, 6–9 P.M. Closed legal holidays.

North of Somers Point (take C 585), in the town of Linwood, are two museums, the Leedsville School Museum* (16 Poplar Ave; 609-927-8293) and the Jim Kirk Maritime Museum (Linwood Library, Davis Ave.; 609-927-8293). The school museum building dates to 1873 and served also as the city hall and the library. Displays relate to local history. Open January–Thanksgiving, Tuesday, 10–1. Linwood was formerly a shipbuilding town, and the maritime museum is "dedicated to preserving the history of the city's economic, ecological, and genealogical connections to the sea." Almost the entire nautical tool collection comes from local families; the museum also features rare photographs and scale models. Open Monday and Wednesday, 10–8, Tuesday and Thursday, 12–8, Friday, 10–5, Saturday, 10–4; other hours and guided tours by appointment. The Linwood historical district* includes over 140 buildings on Maple and Poplar aves. and Shore Rd.

North of Linwood is Northfield,* like Linwood once a shipbuilding town. Here you will find the Risley Homestead* (8 Virginia Ave.; 609-641-8976, 609-927-5218), a late-18th-century house that was home to many generations of oyster fishers. The Atlantic County Historical Society takes guided tours through the house weekends, April–November, except on holidays.

West of the Risley Homestead, on the site of a former brick factory, is Birch Grove Park (Burton Ave. between Mill and Tilton rds.; 609-641-3778). On its 270 acres are 21 small lakes (made by the brickworkers excavating clay) where you can fish (the lakes are stocked with trout), campgrounds, a playground and picnic area, nature trails, a miniature-golf course, and a children's nature center. The park sponsors a variety of special events, including a fishing tournament, a haunted hayride, and a turkey run. Open daily, 9–7, Memorial Day week–mid-September; 9–5, the rest of the year.

Also on the park grounds are the Casto House and Northfield Museum (609-383-1505). The Casto House may date to the mid-18th century, the museum is housed in a 1915 office building. Exhibits include the history of the brick industry in Birch Grove Park, the history of the Casto family, and an old school room, all with memorabilia, old photographs, and artifacts. Open Sunday, Monday, and Wednesday, 1–3; groups and other times by appointment. Behind the museum is the town's bicentennial bandstand, where concerts are given in the summer.

Southwest of Northfield (take the Northfield–English Creek Rd., which becomes Zion Rd., and turn right on Asbury Rd.) is the Atlantic Riding Center for the Handicapped (214 Asbury Rd.; 609-926-2233). The public is welcome to watch the regular program; call for the schedule.

West of Northfield, in Cardiff (Egg Harbor Township), is Storybook Land (6415 Black Horse Pike; 609-641-7847; 609-646-0103, ext. 5), a 50-year-old theme park based on children's stories, with live animals, a picnic area, and festive lighting for the winter holiday season. Open mid-March–December; call for the schedule.

Continuing west on Black Horse Pike will take you to the Jersey Shore Children's Museum (6725 Black Horse Pike in the Shore Mall; 609-645-7741). Children ages one to ten can find costumes to put on and roles to play in the country store or the dental office or the TV newsroom. Open Monday–Saturday, 10–5, Sunday 12–5; groups by appointment. Admission charge.

West of the Children's Museum (take Black Horse Pike west to English Creek Ave. and turn left) is the Cygnus Creative Arts Centre (3056 English Creek Ave.; 609-272-1199). Housed in a 1926 former schoolhouse, the center offers programs in dance, visual arts, music, voice, and karate. Call for details on performances and exhibits that are open to the public.

Also in Egg Harbor Township at the Howard Haneman Environmental Park is the county's prize-winning recycling center (6700 Delilah Rd.; 609-272-6950). When it opened in 1991, it was the largest in the country (58,000 square feet), capable of receiving over 300 tons of recyclable material a day. Tours by appointment (609-272-6960) and during the Atlantic County Utility Authority's Earth Day celebration, which takes place the Sunday after Earth Day and attracts as many as 5,000 people.

Somerville Somerset 12,423

US 202, 206, NJ 22, 28, C 567

The seat of rapidly growing Somerset County, Somerville is changing from the center of an agricultural region to a city supporting professional and commercial services. Somerville is the birthplace of the opera singer Frederica von Stade and the home of a Memorial Day bicycle race, the oldest continuously run bicycle race in the country (some 30,000–40,000 people watch about 650 contestants each year). A bicycle under glass at West End and Mountain aves. is a memorial to two young men who won the race in its first years and died in World War II. The U.S. Bicycling Hall of Fame, ordinarily in Somerville, is temporarily closed, and exhibits have been moved to the Van Horne* house in Bridgewater (941 E. Main St.; 732-356-7016). At the hall of fame the inductees' plaques line the walls, but also on display are bicycle memorabilia, including historic bicycles, the first Stars-and-Stripes jersey made for an American rider, officials' ribbons, and the like. The hall of fame is expected to move back to Somerville, at 145 W. Main St., by 2007.

The Somerset Courthouse Green,* Main St. between Grove and N. Bridge sts., reflects the late 19th and early 20th centuries. The white

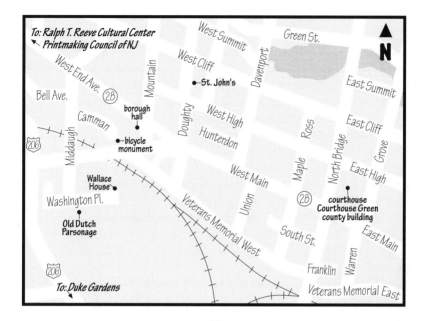

To: Ralph T. Reeve Cultural Center
↖ Printmaking Council of NJ

West Summit
Green St.
West End Ave. (28)
West Cliff
Davenport
Mountain
●—St. John's
East Summit
Bell Ave.
Camman
borough hall
Doughty
West High
Ross
East Cliff
Middaugh
(206)
●—bicycle monument
Hunterdon
Maple
North Bridge
Grove
West Main
East High
Wallace House ●
Union
(28)
courthouse
Courthouse Green
county building
East High
Washington Pl. ●
Veterans Memorial West
South St.
East Main
Old Dutch Parsonage
(206)
To: Duke Gardens
Franklin
Warren
Veterans Memorial East

marble Palladian courthouse, built in 1908 and restored in the 1990s, is famous as the site of the Hall-Mills murder trial (1922), in which Mrs. Hall and her brothers were acquitted of the charge of murdering her minister-husband and one of his married choristers. On the first floor of the county administration building (20 Grove St.) the County Cultural and Heritage Commission (908-231-7110) hangs exhibits that tend to focus on artists from the county; these change roughly every six weeks. On the third floor are changing exhibits of three-dimensional works in various media, such as ceramics, handmade books, and basketry. Exhibits are open to the public weekdays, 8:30–4:30. At the old administration building (40 N. Bridge St.) is the commission's Student Gallery @ 40 North Bridge. Here you can see a variety of shows, many of them juried, of works done by students from grade school through high school. Open weekdays, 8:30–4:30. Around the courthouse and the railroad station, the signs of new downtown growth are obvious (a second courthouse and the new administration building, among others).

Two of Somerville's historic buildings are, however, of particular interest. The Old Dutch Parsonage* (71 Somerset St.; 908-725-1015), built in 1751 by the congregation of the First Reformed Dutch Church, is a state-run historic-house museum. The country's first Dutch Reformed Theological Seminary was established here in the 1750s by John Frelinghuysen; eventually it was to become Queen's College, which in turn became Rutgers University. Frelinghuysen died three years after coming to Somerville. His widow married one of his students, Jacob Hardenbergh, who in time became the first president of Queen's. The house has been furnished to show what the building would have been like when the Hardenberghs lived in it. Farther along and across the street is the Wallace House* (71 Somerset St.; 908-725-1015), also a state historic-house museum. The house, a national historic landmark, belonged to John Wallace, a Philadelphia merchant, and was used by George Washington as his headquarters in the winter of 1779 while his troops were encamped at Middlebrook. It is furnished to reflect what a house would have looked like at the time of Wallace's ownership. Both houses sponsor special events, including Middlebrook Day in the spring, a holiday diversion in the winter, and concerts of 18th-century music. Both are open Wednesday–Saturday, 10–12 and 1–4; Sunday, 1–4. Closed holidays. Groups by appointment.

Somerville has many attractive buildings. Note the public library (35 West End Ave.) across Mountain Ave. from the bicycle monument and the mid-19th-century Speer Van Arsdale funeral home (10 West End Ave.). In one of the city's handsome older residential districts is St. John's* (W. High St. and Doughty Ave.), an 1890s stone church with a stone rectory.

An attractive Victorian garden can be seen at New Cemetery (192 S. Bridge; 908-725-1871). The cemetery, which was founded in 1871, also contains interesting stonework. Tours by appointment. The cemetery on the other side of South Bridge dates to the late 17th century.

In front of borough hall (Somerset and Main sts.) a memorial to Somerville's firemen, created by a Lambertville sculptor, shows a fireman carrying a child who is carrying a bunny. Nearby in the late-19th-century West End Hose Company No. 3 building* (15 Doughty Ave.; 908-526-7098) is the future home of the Somerville Exempt Firemen's Museum.

If you take US 206 south of town until just past the Raritan River, on your left (to the west) you will find Duke Farms (908-722-3700). Seven hundred acres of what is left of the Duke estate are open to the public for tours, as are the Duke Gardens, 11 display gardens representing various geographical and historical gardening styles, from 18th-century French and 19th-century Italian to 18th-century Japanese, from a succulent garden to a rain forest. The manor house was opened to the public in 2005 and will remain open for about two years. There is also a 1.25-mile self-guided trail. The estate itself, built by the founder of the American Tobacco Company and the benefactor of Duke University in Durham, and until the mid-'90s lived in much of the year by his daughter, Doris, was created out of flat farmland by building hills and importing trees. You can get some sense of its former extent simply by following the stone wall, supposedly built of stone from Schooley's Mountain, on the western side of 206. The farm is working on a variety of environmental programs, including, for example, seeing if native vegetation can be restored in areas that have been deer-proofed. Admission by reservation only. Duke Farms is also sponsoring a variety of cultural events. Tours of the farm Wednesday–Sunday, mid-April–mid November, 11, 2, and 3:30; greenhouse tours Wednesday–Sunday, September–May, 10:40–3:15; walking tours Wednesday–Sunday, mid-

April–mid-November, 9:30–4:30; manor house tours Wednesday–Sunday year-round, 11–3:15. Fee charged.

North of Somerville (adjacent to Station and River rds. in North Branch Station; take NJ 28 north to US 22 west, or US 202 west) is the Ralph T. Reeve Cultural Center, 35 acres of county land dedicated to promoting the arts, and the home since the 1970s of the Printmaking Council of New Jersey (440 River Rd.; 908-725-2110). The building houses studios, a library, and two galleries; the council offers classes and workshops here and has an active educational outreach program, taking portable presses into the community so that people can learn how prints are actually made. Exhibits at the galleries are open to the public Tuesday–Friday, 11–4; Saturday, 1–4. For a look at a stone house built in 1725 and in 1995 still in the hands of a descendant of the builder, continue north (take Station Rd. to the end, turn right on NJ 28 and left on Vanderveer Ave.), where you will see on your right the Jacob Ten Eyck house.

South Brunswick   Middlesex 37,734

US 1, 130, C 522

George Segal, the noted sculptor, for over 50 years made his home in the township of South Brunswick. Over those years the population grew at a rapid rate (it more than tripled in the last 40 years, more than doubled in the last 20). A township with large industrial parks and a significant number of warehouses, South Brunswick also has some undeveloped areas, among them the county's Davidson's Mill Pond Park (Riva Ave.; 732-745-3900), 480 acres with a pond where you can fish and a small-boat launching area (the waterfall where the mill was is particularly attractive). Pigeon Swamp State Park (Fresh Ponds and Rhode Hall rds.; 609-984-0370) is a large (more than 1,000 acres) undeveloped area; the name may come from Ann Pigeon, who owned this land in the 18th century, although it was also a nesting site for passenger pigeons. Hiking and hunting are possible here.

South River   Middlesex 15,322

C 527, 535

First settled in the early 18th century by Samuel Willett, South River for many years was an active port, serving the clay and fruit industries located nearby. The South River Historical Society has a local-history museum in the former Old School Baptist Church* (64–66 Main St.; 732-613-3078), built in 1785. The building has also housed a library and the borough clerk. The church's foundation was made from rocks used as ballast by cargo ships: local cedar trees were used for the walls. The columns on the portico originally contained large tree trunks; these were replaced by steel in the early 1990s. The museum concentrates on artifacts relating to local history; among the items on display are samples of the work produced by the embroidery factories that used to be active in town. Open 1st Sunday of the month, 1:30–3:30.

Among the stones in the cemetery behind the building is an urn by John Frazee in memory of his wife, who died in the 1832 cholera epidemic. (The urn is inscribed "to the wife of my youth.") Frazee was the first sculptor in the United States to receive patronage from the federal government: in 1831 he was commissioned by Congress to do a bust of John Jay for the Supreme Court chambers. For a visit to the cemetery, call the museum.

South River is known for its ethnic variety. The fact that some 40 percent of South River's population is of Polish descent is one reflection of that variety; another can be seen in the recently restored Saints Peter and Paul Russian Orthodox Church (Whitehead Ave.), built in 1916.

Across the South River from South River, in Sayreville, is the Sayreville Historical Society museum (425 Main St.; 732-390-7048). Its building, originally School No. 1, dates to 1885. Sayreville takes its name from James Sayer, a founder of Sayer & Fisher Company, the largest brickyard in the world. The company, founded in 1650, closed in 1970; the Sayer & Fisher Reading room* (Main St. and River Rd.; 1883) was built with a variety of bricks to show off the company's products. The museum contains many items relating to the town's industrial past: Sunshine biscuits were manufactured in Sayreville until the late 1990s; DuPont, Hercules, and National Lead (which closed in the 1960s) all had presences here. The museum also contains a replica of an early schoolroom, a printshop with a 19th-century printing press, and an entertainment room with an early Edison phonograph and mementos from the town's first movie theater. Among the items on display are arrowheads, pottery, and amber unearthed in Sayreville's clay pits. Open Sunday, 1:30–4.

Sparta Sussex 18,080

NJ 15, 181, C 517, 605, 613

Sparta was first settled in the late 18th century, and by the mid-19th was known as a resort area. Now on the shores of Lake Mohawk, which was created by developers in the mid-1920s, Sparta boasts an unusual commercial area built to serve the wealthy visitors to the town. The historic White Deer Plaza and Boardwalk district* (1926–35) includes the boardwalk, West Shore Trail, and Winona Parkway. Other parts of the downtown in this fast-growing community date from the same period. The First Presbyterian Church

(32 Main St.), listed on the state register of historic buildings, was started in the 1780s.

North of town (C 517 and Glen Rd.) are the Sparta Mountain Wildlife Sanctuary (908-204-8998), managed by the New Jersey Audubon Society, and the Sparta Mountain Wildlife Management Area (908-637-4125). Together they make up a 3,000-acre tract, with trails, lakes, and wetlands, known as Edison Bog. This is the area in which Thomas Alva Edison attempted to establish an ironworks (he switched to processing cement when the discovery of the Mesabi range made his ironworks unprofitable). You can still see some of the stonework from his facilities. There are several miles of hiking trails in the sanctuary; hunting and fishing are allowed in the wildlife management area.

Springfield Union 14,429

I 78, US 22, NJ 24, I 24, C 509 SPUR

Located at the head of the Rahway River and named for its springs, Springfield was first settled in the early 18th century by colonists from Hackensack. Only four colonial buildings remain, however, since the British burned the town in 1780 after losing the Battle of Springfield. It was during this battle that the Reverend James Caldwell, minister at Elizabethtown (the fighting parson to the Americans, the high priest of the Revolution to the British), broke into the church, grabbed the Watts hymnals, and took them to the troops, who were running out of wadding for their cannon. "Give 'em Watts, boys, give 'em Watts!" he is supposed to have cried, and just two weeks after his wife had been murdered by the British (*see* Union), he rallied the troops and helped spur their victory in the last major engagement on New Jersey soil. A monument to the battle is at Washington Ave. and the river.

The Cannon Ball House★ (126 Morris Ave.; 973-376-4784), one of the buildings that survived the fire, derives its name from the cannonball that lodged in its northwest gable during the battle. General Jonathan Dayton, from the family that founded Dayton, Ohio (James Caldwell was chaplain to his unit), lived here after the war. The house is now a historic-house museum run by the Springfield Historical Society. Open by appointment.

The new First Presbyterian Church★ (210 Morris Ave.) was built in 1791. The present parsonage (41 Church Mall) was built in the 1840s on the foundations of the earlier building, which had served as George Washington's headquarters for a time in June 1780.

Spring Lake Monmouth 3,567

NJ 71, C 524

Developed as a seaside resort for the wealthy in the 1870s (note the stone gate at the northern entrance on Ocean Ave.), Spring Lake* is named for a serene lake in the center of town. A family resort that once had the reputation of being the gathering place for wealthy Irish (well over half the residents are of Irish

SPRING LAKE

descent), Spring Lake is increasingly becoming a year-round town. Although many of its buildings are being converted to other uses—some of the older houses, for example, have become bed-and-breakfasts—the structures themselves are well preserved and the town has an old-fashioned, prosperous look. It is not surprising that for many years croquet tournaments were held in Spring Lake.

One of Spring Lake's splendid hotels, the Essex-Sussex beach hotel, built in 1914 and designed by Philadelphia architect Guy King, was used as a set for the movie *Ragtime*. The hotel closed in the 1980s, and after a long period of uncertainty, the building was saved and converted into age-restricted condominiums.

The park by the lake is attractive, and along Tuttle, Jersey, Mercer, Sussex, Monmouth, Atlantic, and Union aves., among others, you can see some of the buildings from the golden era of the late 19th century, to say nothing of the lawns in front of many of them. Note also the railroad station and the statue in front of St. Catharine's. On the top floor of the municipal building is the historical society's museum (5th Ave. and Warren St.; 732-449-0772), devoted to local history. Open Thursday, 11–12:30; Sunday, 1:30–3; groups and other times by appointment; closed holidays. The society also sponsors an annual house tour.

Spring Lake has two miles of ocean beach and a commerce-free boardwalk as well. Forced to replace the boardwalk after the nor'easter of December 1992, Spring Lake became one of the first communities to try a plastic and wood compound that won't rot, be eaten by insects, or (best of all) splinter. The town's five-mile run, held in the spring, became so popular that the sponsors have had to limit participation to 8,000 runners. For information on beach fees, call 732-449-8005.

Stanhope Sussex 3,584

US 206, NJ 183, C 601, 602

Like the other iron towns in New Jersey, Stanhope, the site of the country's first anthracite furnace (c. 1841), stopped growing when the iron industry shifted westward. The borough did, however, see its population double between 1960 and 1980.

Southwest of Stanhope is another mid-18th-century iron town, Waterloo Village* (west on C 604 off US 206; this is well marked; 973-347-0900). Once known as a deserted village, and threatened with destruction by a developer, it was restored and has been open to the public since 1964. Situated on the Musconetcong River, Waterloo (before 1815 and Napoleon's defeat in Belgium, it was known as Andover Forge) lies within Allamuchy Mountain Park (*see* Hackettstown). In 1760 it could boast a gristmill, sawmill, forge, and mansions for the ironmaster and forgeman (the furnace was north of the village). Their owners being loyalists, the ironworks were seized by the Revolutionary government, and Andover Forge supplied cannonballs for the Revolutionary Army. When the Morris Canal opened in 1831, the village became a canal port and entered its period of greatest prosperity. A general store was built that year and continued in business for over a century. By the mid-19th century, the railroad had also come to Waterloo, and over the years various members of the Smith family, important as landholders in Waterloo since late in the 18th century, built mansions for themselves. Competition from the railroads put the canal out of business, and when the iron industry moved west, Waterloo lost its economic raison d'être.

As a restored village, Waterloo draws tens of thousands of visitors a year, many for school tours. All but one of the buildings were on the site originally; some of the buildings are house museums, others are used by working crafters. Exhibits include a historically accurate re-created Lenape village on Waterloo Lake (Native Americans once lived in this area) and an early 19th-century subsistence farm. There is a working gristmill, a canal house, the Canal Society of New Jersey's museum, a general store, an inn, and the mid-19th-century Methodist Church, which still holds services. Plans call for eventually restoring the locks and inclined planes. Open July and August, Wednesday–Friday, 11–4, weekends 11–5; mid-May–June, September, and October, weekends 11–5; call for the weekday hours (which are worked around school groups). Admission charge. On many weekends from April to December, the village hosts a wide variety of concerts, ethnic festivals, and other special events, from Canal Day to Fall Foliage Day to wine festivals to scarecrow contests.

Just east of Stanhope off 206 is Wild West City (Lackawanna Dr., C 607; 973-347-0900), a reproduction of an 1880s frontier town, with picnic grounds, a petting zoo, museums, and shops. Open 10:30–6, daily, mid-June–Labor Day; weekends, May–mid June and Labor Day–Columbus Day. Groups by appointment. Admission charged.

Just beyond Wild West City, off 607 in the Byram Municipal Complex, is the Roseville School (Mansfield Dr.; 973-347-4585). Built in 1850, the school closed in 1925 and from 1933 to 1965 functioned as an Episcopal church. It has been restored to its original appearance and decorated to show how a mid-19th-century school would have looked. The collection also includes memorabilia relating to local history. Tours by appointment.

Stockton Hunterdon 560

NJ 29, C 523

Stockton, located on the Delaware River roughly three miles north of Lambertville, started as a ferry town in the early 18th century. Colonel John Reading, believed to be the first settler of Hunterdon County and a major force in laying out the Old York Road, ran the ferry until his death in 1717. Because the main road from New York to Philadelphia ran through Lambertville, attempts to revive the ferry were not successful. A bridge was built early in the 19th century; it lasted until the 1920s and its replacement, the bridge you see today, was built on the piers and abutments of the earlier one.

Stockton was the home of John Deats, who in the mid-18th century invented the Deats plow and corn sheller. His son Hiram set up a factory in 1852 that made threshers, reapers, mowers, and corn shellers. Another Stockton man, Joseph Wilson, was involved in Hunterdon County's famous egg industry; Wilson was the first man to ship day-old chicks.

Stockton may be best known today as the site of the Stockton Inn (formerly Colligan's) made famous by Lorenz Hart and Richard Rodgers's song, which contains the lines "There's a small hotel, with a wishing well." Built around 1710 as a private home, the building may have been converted to a hotel in the 1830s; the wishing well is still there, and the murals were painted during the Depression. The Woolverton Inn, also first intended as a private home, was built in the late 18th century by John Prall; from 1957 to 1972, it was owned by St. John Terrell, producer of the now-defunct Music Circus in Lambertville.

The Prallsville industrial district* (NJ 29; 609-397-3586) is a complex of buildings that includes Prallsville Mills (sometimes referred to as Smith's Mills, after the last owner) and a few houses across the road. The district is now part of the Delaware and Raritan Canal* State Park (*see* Kingston). The first mill was built at this beautiful spot in the early 1700s; John Prall, for whom the area was named, bought the property in 1794. The mill area includes a gristmill (1877), used for special events like craft shows and folk concerts; an attached granary (1890); a stone linseed-oil mill (1794), the venue for art exhibits; a sawmill (1850); and a wagon house (1850), which houses the canal commission offices. (If you happen to have business in the canal commission offices, do notice the photographs of the canal park.) The buildings are generally open for tours weekends, Memorial Day–Labor Day, 1–4; they are also open when there are special events, and by appointment. The Delaware River Mill Society's plans including converting the salt-pork house to a visitor center and working on the Prall House across NJ 29. The society sponsors a brown-bag lunch and talk the fourth Wednesday of the month, and at least one public event each weekend. Office open weekdays, 9–5; tours by appointment. From the mill you can hike or bicycle on the towpath past Bull's Island to north of Frenchtown or go south to Trenton.

Stone Harbor Cape May 1,128

C 619, 629

Situated on a barrier-beach island (which it shares with Avalon), Stone Harbor is the only municipality in the United States to run a heronry. Registered as a national landmark, the Stone Harbor Bird Sanctuary occupies over 20 acres between 111th and 117th sts. and 2d and 3d avenues. The birds are attracted by thickets of cedar, holly, sassafras, and bayberry and feed on the adjacent marshes. They return from their wintering grounds around mid-March, and nesting is usually well under way by early April. The number of birds occupying the sanctuary has varied considerably over the years—some years as many as 10,000 birds occupied the sanctuary at the height of the nesting season. The flights are most spectacular at dawn as the day feeders leave and the night feeders return home, and again at dusk when the pattern is reversed. At the parking area on the 3d Ave. side, you will find a good view of the birds.

The Wetlands Institute (1075 Stone Harbor Blvd.; 609-368-1211), founded in 1969, occupies 6,000 acres of protected salt marsh interspersed with tidal creeks. Dedicated to education and research, the institute contains saltwater aquariums; changing exhibits on, for example, ospreys or other raptors; and wonderful views of the surrounding marsh from the observation tower and lecture room. Outside is a habitat garden, filled with native plants that attract birds and butterflies. The hiking trail through the marsh includes a boardwalk that goes by a tidal pool, and a pier that goes over a tidal creek (you can pick up a brochure and audio-guide for a self-guided tour). Among the interactive exhibits are Wetlandia (aimed at preschoolers) and Secrets of the Salt Marsh (for ten to twelve year olds). The research programs include a permanent camera that records the nesting behavior of a pair of ospreys; inside the center you can watch what the camera is recording as it happens. Over 40,000 people a year visit the institute and participate in its programs, which include field trips, nature classes, kayak trips, workshops, and lectures, as well as the annual mid-September Wings 'n' Water Festival. Guided group tours by appointment. Open Tuesday–Saturday, 9:30–4:30, mid-October–mid May; Monday–Saturday, 9:30–4:30, Sunday, 10–4, mid-May–mid-October. Admission charge.

In a 1920s cottage is the Stone Harbor Museum (235 93d St.; 609-358-7500). The museum focuses on local history and environmental aspects of the area. Not surprisingly, storms and shipwrecks figure prominently, but the museum also has on display a 1910 working model of the train that served the town. You can also pick up walking and hiking tour brochures. Open Tuesday, Thursday, and Sunday, 1–5, Wednesday, 7–9 P.M., mid-June–mid-September; weekends 1–4, mid-May–mid-June; Saturday, 1–4, mid-September–mid-October.

Beach tags, good for Avalon's beaches too, may be purchased during off-season at Borough Hall (95th St. and 2d Ave) during the week (10–4) and at the beach at 95th St. on weekends (10–4); during high season they are available daily at the beach. At 95th St. and 3d Ave. note St. Mary's (1911; formerly known as St. Mary's by the Sea). For beach information, call 609-368-5102.

This is generally a good area for bird-watchers, and both Stone Harbor Point (follow 2d or 3d Ave. to the end) and Nummy Island (take 3d Ave. to Ocean Dr. and cross the bridge) are favored spots. Stone Harbor Point is one of the last nesting sites in the state for the least tern and piping plover.

North of Stone Harbor and Avalon (take 619 or exit 17 of the Garden State Pkwy) is Sea Isle City, a town laid out by Charles K. Landis (see Vineland). Housed in an early-20th-century house, the Sea Isle City Historical Museum (4208 Landis Ave.; 609-263-2992) features a variety of artifacts and memorabilia and an extensive collection of 19th- and 20th-century photographs. Open July and August, Monday, Wednesday, and

Friday, 10–3, Tuesday, Thursday, and Saturday, 10–1; September–Christmas and early April–June, open Saturday 10–1. Other times and groups by appointment. The Environmental Commission sponsors guided beachcomber walks June–August; for information, call 609-263-8687.

Summit Union 21,131

NJ 24, 124, C 512, 527

Known before the Revolution as Turkey Hill, Summit began to change into a suburb when the Morris and Essex Railroad was put through the town in the 1830s. It was popular as a resort in midcentury, and in the 1880s many of the wealthy visitors became permanent residents and commuters. Meryl Streep, who has had more Oscar nominations than anyone else, was born in Summit.

What is probably the oldest building in Summit is the Carter House (90 Butler Pkwy; 908-277-1747), now a house museum and the headquarters of the Summit Historical Society. Originally located on River Rd., the house was moved to its present location in 1986. The oldest part dates to the mid-18th century. Enlarged over the years, the house still retains many of its 18th-century features. Furnished with pieces appropriate to its period, the house also contains artifacts and memorabilia relating to the history of Summit. Open Tuesday, 9:30–12; Wednesday, 1:30–4; the 1st Sunday of the month, 2–4; and by appointment. The society also sponsors four public lectures each year.

Summit has long had a reputation as a culturally active town. The Summit Chorale developed from a singing group founded in 1909; the Summit Playhouse has occupied the old Summit library (10 New England Ave.; 908-273-2192), a Romanesque Revival structure from the 1890s, since 1918. The New Jersey Center for Visual Arts (68 Elm St.; 908-273-9121), founded in 1933 and housed in an interesting new building (1973), specializes in contemporary American painting and sculpture. There are three galleries, and new exhibits open every six to eight weeks. The center has an extensive program of art classes, teaching everything from drawing and painting to ceramics, papermaking, and Chinese brush painting. Special events, including concerts, are scheduled frequently. Galleries open weekdays, 12–4; weekends, 2–4. The office and gift shop are open daily, 9–5. Group tours by appointment. The center has recently undergone a major expansion but expects the new galleries to be open by 2006.

In the northern part of Summit is the Reeves Reed Arboretum* (165 Hobart Ave., near NJ 24; 908-273-8787), 12½ acres that were once part of a Revolutionary War–era farm. The arboretum, a wildlife habitat, includes a natural hardwood forest, native and imported trees, open fields, a native meadow, lawns, formal gardens, a rose garden, an alpine rock garden, a bog garden, and an herb garden. Trails go through the woods. On the property are several kettles from the Wisconsin glacier; in one large kettle in the front, thousands of daffodils are planted, forming a carpet in spring (the daffodils usually peak sometime in April). Educational programs for children and adults are offered, and the Elephant Tree Day Camp (named for a huge gray beech much beloved of children) is offered for children in the summer. In the Colonial Revival house, which dates from the late 1880s, are the arboretum's administrative offices and the horticultural library; the house is also used for art exhibits, which change every six weeks; lectures; meetings; and occasional concerts. You can pick up a brochure for a self-guided tour there or at the kiosk by the greenhouse. Most educational activities, particularly those with a hands-on component, take place in the former carriage house. Grounds open dawn–dusk daily, year-round; office open Monday–Friday, 9–3; garden shop (908-277-1190) open Monday–Saturday, 10–4.

Briant Park (Springfield Ave. and Briant La.; 908-527-4900) has facilities for fishing and ice-skating, a fitness course, and a picnic area. You can also fish and picnic at the Passaic River Park (Passaic Ave.; 908-527-4900), which has a nature trail as well. Part of the Watchung Reservation (*see* Mountainside) falls at the southern edge of Summit.

Sussex Sussex 2,145

NJ 23, 284, C 639

Sussex, in the heart of the county's dairy country, used to be known as Deckertown, in honor of Peter Decker, who built a cabin here in the 1730s. About one mile southwest of Sussex on C 565 (head south out of Sussex on Loomis Ave., C 639) is Sussex Airport, site of an annual air show (973-875-0783). Held the last weekend in August, the show features stunt flying, model airplanes, parachute-jumping, wing-walking, flyovers by modern and World War II military planes, a race between a jet truck and a plane, and the like. The airport also has two shows a year for those who build their own planes.

About four miles west of Sussex, on NJ 23 in Wantage Township, is the Elias Van Bunschooten Museum* (1097 NJ 23; 973-875-4058), run by the local chapter of the DAR in a late-18th-century house built by the local Dutch Reformed minister. The house, which stayed in the same family until the late 1920s, contains both 18th- and 19th-century furnishings, some dating back to the original owner, some donated by descendants. Also on the property is a wagon house* containing antique farm equipment and carriages, a Greek Revival privy,* and an ice house with a milk room.* Open mid-May–mid-October, Thursday and Saturday, 1–4. Admission charge.

Another four miles north and west on C 23 (and picking up C 519) will bring you to the entrance to High Point State Park* (1480 NJ 23; 973-875-4800), over 15,000 acres in the Kittatinny Mountains. Given to the state in 1923 by Colonel and Mrs. Anthony R. Kuser, the park encompasses the highest point in New Jersey (1,803 feet above sea level). At this point, accessible by car or foot, is a recently restored monument from which there are spectacular views out over New Jersey, New York, and Pennsylvania.

The Kusers had used this area as their summer home, converting the High Point Inn (1888) into their summer mansion. The building was allowed to deteriorate and is now gone; the Gatehouse (1912), however, is occupied by a member of the park staff.

Within the park is the state's first natural area, the John Dryden Kuser Natural Area (in honor of the former senator and noted conservationist, the son of Anthony Kuser), dedicated in 1965 and now containing some 800 acres. The area's 200-acre cedar swamp is an excellent example of a mature bog, with a stand of Atlantic white cedar unusual at 1,500 feet. The Cedar Swamp Trail loops around the bog, which contains a wide variety of plants and animals, including insectivorous plants.

The extensive trail system, which includes a stretch of the Appalachian Trail, offers a wide range of possibilities, from Sunday strolls to strenuous up-and-down hikes. Many of the trails were developed by the Civilian Conservation Corps (CCC), which also constructed shelters and dams. Lake Marcia is a spring-fed glacial lake. No hunting is allowed in the park, but you can fish, swim, camp, boat, picnic, participate in an annual snowshoeing event, and cross-country ski (973-702-1222; snow is made when necessary, and the trails are groomed). Trails lead directly to Stokes State Forest (*see* Branchville). The park is open year-round, though weather conditions in winter sometimes make it impossible to get in. Open daily, 8–8 in summer

(Memorial Day weekend–Labor Day), 8–4:30 the rest of the year; admission charged in summer.

Swedesboro Gloucester 2,055

 C 538, 551, 605

Swedish farmers settled along Raccoon Creek in the mid-17th century, and Swedesboro, first known as Raccoon, was for many years the Swedish center of the area. It later became a transportation center for the surrounding agricultural region.

Trinity Episcopal Old Swedes Church* (Church and Main sts.), familiarly known as Old Swedes, is the oldest deeded church property in Gloucester County and was the first Lutheran congregation in the state (it became Episcopal in 1786 when the Swedes stopped sending ministers to the colonies). Among its ministers was Peter Kalm, the noted Swedish naturalist whose journal is a mine of information about 18th-century New Jersey. Today's Flemish-bond brick building, which dates from the 1780s, replaced a log-cabin church that burned in the Revolution; the tower and steeple were added in the 1830s. The congregation still uses, on special occasions, a beaten silver communion service dating to 1730. Many Revolutionary War heroes are buried in the churchyard, among them Colonel Bodo Otto. Some of the history is explained in interpretive signs; tours may be arranged by calling 856-467-1227.

On the church grounds, known as New Sweden Park, is the early-18th-century Schorn log cabin (also known as the Vanleer cabin or the Mortonson-Schorn cabin). Moved from the banks of the Raccoon Creek west of Swedesboro, it may well be one of the oldest original cabins of Swedish-Finnish design. It was probably used as a granary and is reputed to have served as a stop on the Underground Railroad.

The Hatton house (1935 Kings Hwy) is a mid-18th-century house that belonged to John Hatton, a customs collector who tried to enforce the Stamp Act. He fled to England during the Revolution, and the house was confiscated by the county. The original lion's-head door knocker, a symbol of the British crown, remains on the front door. Records indicate that what is today called the Old Swedes Inn (1301 Kings Hwy) was operating as a tavern in the 1770s. There are also interesting 19th-century buildings in Swedesboro, for example, the John C. Rulon house* (1428 Kings Hwy), and at the intersection of the Kings Hwy and Lake Ave. note the early-20th-century borough hall.

Just north of Raccoon Creek on the Kings Highway is Stratton Hall,* built in the 1790s. Charles C. Stratton, governor of the state from 1845 to 1848, was born in the brick house in 1796 (he died there in 1858). Stratton was the first governor from Gloucester County and the first elected by popular vote rather than by the legislature.

North of Swedesboro (take Locke Ave. out of town to the Swedesboro-Bridgeport Rd. and continue on Oak Grove Rd., C 671) is Adams Methodist Episcopal Church* (Oak Grove and Stone Meeting House rds.), the oldest Methodist church building in the county. Note how the regular stones are in front, the irregular ones on the side.

Three miles south of Swedesboro, on Sharptown Rd. (take 605 to the fork and bear right) at Oliphant's Mill, is the Moravian Church,* built in the 1780s of brick in a Flemish-bond pattern. For more information about the church, call the Gloucester County Historical Society (856-845-4771).

Teaneck   Bergen 39,260

I 95 EXIT 70, NJ 4

Bergen County's second-most populous community, Teaneck was settled by the Dutch in the 17th century. Some stone houses remain, particularly on Teaneck and Riverneck roads. The 18th-century Brinkerhoff-Demarest house* (493 Teaneck Rd.) is a national historic landmark. The source of the town's name is obscure: perhaps from *Tekene,* a Native American word for "the woods"; perhaps from the Dutch *Tee Neck,* referring to a curved piece of land alongside a stream. In 1949 the town was chosen by the Army Corps of Engineers as a model American community, and material on Teaneck was used as part of the army's program to explain American democracy to the Japanese. The town has since developed a reputation as a multi-ethnic community. It was the first in the country in which a white majority voted for school integration; the mosque on Fabry Ct. was the first in the county; the Bahai Center (130 Evergreen Pl.) was visited by the grandson of the religion's founder in the early 20th century; and in 1992 Teaneck elected the country's first Indian-born mayor.

At the northwest corner of Overpeck Park (*see* Fort Lee) is the Puffin Cultural Forum (20 E. Oakdene Ave.; 201-836-8923), which specializes in grants to individuals and groups who might otherwise not be heard. The forum offers a variety of programs and special events, including performances and workshops in theater, music, dance, and the visual arts. On the grounds is the Puffin Sculpture Garden, and from the garden you can walk into the Teaneck Creek Conservancy, where eventually 1½ miles of walking trails will be open to the public. Gardens open daylight hours. Gallery usually open weekdays, 1–5. Weekends, other times, and groups by appointment. You can also walk for 3½ miles along the river on the Hackensack River Greenway. The Teaneck Greenway Friends (201-836-8623) lead guided walks on the greenway, usually one a month between March and November. Call for the schedule.

At Fairleigh Dickinson's Teaneck-Hackensack campus (the Hackensack River flows through the campus, putting it in both communities), the

Garage Theatre (Becton Theatre, 908 River Rd.; 201-569-7710), the county's only professional theater, presents four plays a year and offers a variety of classes. Art exhibits at the Edward Williams Gallery (150 Kotte Pl., Hackensack; 201-692-2449) change roughly eight times a year. Open weekdays 8:30 A.M.–8:30 P.M., Saturday 9:30–2:30. There are also art exhibits, frequently of student works, on the Teaneck side of the river at the University College Art Gallery (1000 River Rd.; 201-692-2801). Open weekdays, 9:30–4:30, but it is advisable to call ahead.

Tenafly Bergen 13,806

US 9W, C 501

One of Bergen County's Dutch settlements, whose name may be derived from the Dutch words for "garden valley" (or perhaps "willow marsh") Tenafly developed in the 1870s when the railroad reached the town. Service ended in the 1960s, but the sandstone station* (1872–74; Hillside Ave.) with its Venetian Gothic details, thought by some to have been designed by Cleveland Cady, has been converted to retail purposes. (In the mid-'90s the town won a state preservation award for its work on the station's exterior.) The feminist Elizabeth Cady Stanton came from Tenafly, and her house* (135 Highwood Ave.) is a national historic landmark.

The Tenafly Public Library (100 Riveredge Rd.; 201-568-8680) presents both permanent and changing art exhibits; many of the permanent exhibits feature works by artists with local connections. One room is devoted to exhibits that change roughly six times a year. The library also sponsors concerts, lectures, and book discussion groups that are open to the public. Piano recitals use the library's Steinway grand, once the property of Chico Marx. Open Monday, Tuesday, Thursday, 10–9, Wednesday, 10–6, Friday and Saturday, 10–4, Sunday 12–4, September–June. Closed Sunday July and August.

At 23 Bliss Ave. is the S.M.A. Fathers African Art Museum (off Engle St. [501] at the southern edge of Tenafly; 201-567-0450). Founded in France in the mid-19th century, the S.M.A. (Society of African Missions) Fathers collected and preserved West African artifacts. The exhibits, which change every few months, include pieces in wood, ivory, brass, bronze, and other metals. The museum also sponsors a variety of educational programs, including crafts, lectures, and concerts, and an annual S.M.A. African festival. Open weekdays, 9–5; tours and other hours by appointment.

The Tenafly Nature Center (313 Hudson Ave.; 201-568-6093) is an environmental education center that abuts the Lost Brook Preserve. The two parcels together contain 380 acres of woodlands, including one of the few remaining stands of northeastern deciduous woodland near the New York metropolitan area. There are six miles of trails here, a pond rich in ducks and herons, heavy spring and fall songbird migrations, and some hawks. You can pick up a booklet for a self-guided tour of the trail at the visitors' center in the John A. Redfield Building. Inside the building is a small natural history museum with live animals and a variety of other exhibits. Outside the building is a small demonstration backyard habitat and an open-air education pavilion, with picnic tables made of recycled wood. Cross-country skiing and ice-skating are also possible here. The center offers a wide range of programs and workshops and attracts some 15,000 visitors a year. Trails open dawn–dusk. Center open Tuesday–Sunday, 9–5; closed major holidays.

Greenbrook Sanctuary (US 9W; 201-768-1360; 201-784-0484), run by the Palisades Nature Association, is a 165-acre nature preserve on top of the Palisades. The sanctuary contains a 5-acre pond and adjoining bog, the 250-foot Greenbrook Falls, and 6½ miles of marked trails. Since 1946 the association has been conducting research and field studies; it offers weekend field trips and programs about flora, fauna, geology, and ecology. The sanctuary also has a small natural history museum. Trails open to members; programs and tours by appointment only. Each year the sanctuary hosts a visitors' day and opens the sanctuary to the public.

Teterboro Bergen 18

I 80, US 46, NJ 17

New Jersey's smallest municipality, Teterboro is home to New Jersey's third busiest airport. Owned and operated by the Port Authority of New York and New Jersey, Teterboro Airport does not serve scheduled aircraft, and the planes that use it are subject to weight limits; nevertheless, it remains one of the busiest in the country for private craft (in 2003, over 200,000 takeoffs and landings were logged; each day more than $15 billion in canceled checks moves through this airport). The oldest operating airport in the metropolitan area, it has been in more or less constant use since 1920, and many of the nation's leading pilots, among them Floyd Bennett, Admiral Richard E. Byrd, Amelia Earhart, and Charles A. Lindbergh, trained at Teterboro. The astronauts Buzz Aldrin and Walter Shirra got their first flying experience at this airport. Gates's Flying Circus operated out of Teterboro, and Anthony Fokker (who designed the Red Baron's plane) manufactured aircraft here. Most of the borough is taken up by the airport and plants belonging to some 90 companies; housing consists of 21 units (nine older houses on Huyler St. and 12 newer condominium units on Vincent Pl.).

Located at the airport is the Aviation Hall of Fame & Museum of New Jersey (201-288-6344), dedicated to "preserving the history of aviation in New Jersey and honoring those who made it." Located on the east side of the field near the control tower, the museum features memorabilia from the early days of flying in New Jersey, and from Arthur Godfrey's aviation collection, as well as historic engines and wooden propellers, a model plane collection, the world's first hovercraft, helicopters, airplanes, flight simulators, an ejection seat, and a hot air balloon basket. There are displays on space flight, lighter-than-air flight, and women in aviation, all with an emphasis on the state. The museum shows films on the history of aviation in New Jersey, old-time stunt flyers, the destruction of the *Hindenburg*, and the history of the airport. There are two aircraft that children can board. Private parties can be arranged; there is also a picnic area. Open Tuesday–Sunday, 10–4. Admission charged. Large groups by appointment.

Titusville Mercer [Hopewell Township]

NJ 29

This tiny Delaware River community lies near the spot where George Washington crossed the ice-choked river on 25 December 1776 to begin the famous Battle of Trenton, generally believed to be a turning point in the Revolutionary War. Volunteers have reenacted the event almost every Christmas afternoon for over 50 years.

Titusville's 19th-century historic district* lies along River Drive. West of the historic district is Washington Crossing State Park (bounded by NJ 29, Church Rd., C 546, and C 579; 609-737-0623). The 2,000-plus-acre park is a national historic landmark, and its visitor center (off 546; 609-737-9304) concentrates on the events that occurred in the crucial 10 days between 24 December 1776 and 3 January 1777. A memorable collection of Revolutionary War artifacts is on display at the center, and there are changing exhibits as well. Open Wednesday–Sunday, 9–4:30. Much of the collection at the center comes from the Swan Foundation. (The foundation hopes to open a National Museum of the American Revolution elsewhere, but will leave items on display here.)

Also at the park is the restored Johnson Ferry House (609-737-2515). Built in 1740, the house served briefly as Washington's headquarters during the crossing. The house is furnished as it might have looked when the Johnson family lived there (1740–70), and special living-history programs are regularly scheduled. Open Wednesday–Saturday, 10–4; Sunday, 1–4; groups by appointment.

The park's nature–interpretive center is housed in a building constructed specifically as a nature house, with exhibit, classroom, and workshop spaces and a wildlife observation area; the center offers regularly scheduled educational programs. Open Wednesday–Saturday, 9–4; Sunday, 12–4:30. Tours and special programs by appointment (609-737-0609).

Formerly the site of the state tree nursery (*see* Cassville), the park boasts over 80 species of trees and shrubs. It also includes the George Washington Memorial Arboretum; a 140-acre natural area; picnic areas; campsites; some 15 miles of trails for hiking, skiing, and snowshoeing; and an open-air theater. Fishing is also possible. Park open daily. Admission charge summer weekends and holidays. Visitor center open daily, 9–5, Memorial Day–Labor Day; Wednesday–Sunday, 9–4:30, the rest of the year.

The park was also formerly the site of a dairy farm whose owner developed the automatic egg candler and sorter, establishing his first factory in a converted cannery in Titusville. Egomatic continued to produce egg-sorting machines for a worldwide market until the 1980s.

About three miles north of Titusville, on NJ 29 between Valley and Pleasant Valley rds., is the Mercer County Wildlife Center (609-883-6606), where injured and orphaned wild animals are treated and rehabilitated. The center also engages in off-site educational programs, and once its new hospital is completed, plans to build cages for its educational animals so that the public can be invited to observe the animals used in the educational programs (the animals being rehabilitated are protected from too much exposure to humans so that they can be more successfully returned to the wild). The center, which has a release rate of 65 percent, in 2003 treated close to 2,000 animals. Messages about animals needing help can be left 24 hours a day.

Farther east on Valley Rd. is the 19-acre Valley Rd. group picnic area (609-989-6536), with playing fields as well as picnic facilities. Open April–October, 10–dusk, by reservation only.

Still farther east (turn left on Woodens La.) is the Howell Living History Farm (609-737-3299), a county park located on what was once the 18th-century Phillips Farm.* This is a working farm dedicated to farming as it was done c. 1900–1910. Saturday programs include demonstrations of various aspects of horse-drawn farming, such as haying, sowing, harvesting, and cultivating. There are also demonstrations of blacksmithing, sheep-shearing, ice-harvesting, and maple-sugaring, as well as hayrides for children, nature walks, and a variety of workshops. The farm's corn maze (609-397-2555) is open weekends, September–November. The farm is open to the public Tuesday–Saturday, 10–4, February–1st week in December, Sunday, 12–4, April–November. Food raised or cooked on the farm is sold Saturday, year-round. Groups by appointment.

Some of the area around Howell Farm—along Woodens La. and Hunter, Pleasant Valley, and Valley rds.—forms the Pleasant Valley Historic District.* Here you can still see some of the outbuildings, barns, farmhouses, and fencing that characterized a Delaware Valley agricultural community at the turn of the 20th century.

Toms River Ocean 86,327

Situated on the northern bank of the river from which it takes its name, Toms River has been a fishing and boatbuilding community; a yachting center (the Toms River Cup is said to be the oldest continually raced-for trophy in yachting); the site during the Revolution of an important saltworks; and, since the county was founded in 1850, the Ocean County seat. (It also boasts a Halloween parade that began in 1919 and is now the second largest in the world.) The central portion of the courthouse* (Hooper Ave.), built in 1850, was planned as a more modest imitation of Hudson County's (the wings date from 1950). Although the city may no longer be as financially dependent on water-related activities as it once was, much of its interest for visitors still lies along the river.

The town's connection with the water is celebrated in the Toms River Seaport Society Maritime Museum (Hooper Ave. and E. Water St.; 732-349-9209). The museum is located in the carriage house (1868) from Joseph Francis's estate (Francis invented the Lifecar, an early maritime rescue boat). On display inside are artifacts relating to local marine history, historic boats and models, a library, and a restoration workshop. Outside you will find some of the many boats owned by the society, with an emphasis on those particularly tied to the Barnegat Bay area. The society sponsors a variety of programs and events, including an annual wooden-boat festival and classes in decoy-carving and boat- and model-building. Open Tuesday, Thursday, and Saturday, 10–2, or by appointment. In the fall of 2004 the society opened a second facility at the Hankins Boatyard in Lavalette (504 Grand Central Ave.). Here the society displays its collection of Hankins boats and its A cat, *Spy*.

The Ocean County Historical Society Museum (26 Hadley Ave.; 732-341-1880), located in a Victorian house, features a variety of displays, including a Victorian kitchen, a music room, a child's room with old dolls and toys, Victorian crafts, lighter-than-air aviation (*see* Lakehurst), early local industries, and Native American artifacts. There are also rotating exhibits. Open for guided tours only Tuesday and Thursday, 1–4; Saturday, 10–4; last tour leaves at 3. Groups by appointment.

The Charles Waterhouse Historical Museum (17 Washington St.; 732-818-9040) has on display over 400 of Waterhouse's paintings, sculpture, drawings, and prints, which tell the story of New Jersey and American history. Waterhouse is the only artist to have been named artist in residence by the Marine Corps, but the works are not all military. Open Thursday–Saturday, 1–4, groups by appointment other times.

West of the Seaport Society Museum is the first museum in New Jersey devoted solely to bugs. The Insectorium (1761 Lakewood Rd.; 732-349-0559) is scheduled to open in 2005. Admission charged.

The Robert J. Novins Planetarium at Ocean County College (College Dr., off Hooper Ave.; 732-255-0343, 732-255-0342) has programs for the general public (the main features are not suitable for children under six). These are usually scheduled for Friday and Saturday evening at 8 and Saturday and Sunday at 2:30 P.M., although in the summer there are daytime shows Tuesday–Friday as well. A seasonal-sky program takes place at 1 P.M. Tuesday–Sunday in the summer and weekends the rest of the year. (The planetarium is closed for cleaning in June.) Groups by appointment. Admission charged.

The art gallery at the college (College Dr.; 732-255-0340) is also open to the public. Shows change roughly every six weeks and include an annual Senior Citizens of Ocean County exhibit. When the college is in session, the gallery is open 8 A.M.–10 P.M.; for vacation time it is best to call first.

Cattus Island Park (1170 Cattus Island Blvd., off C 571, north of the center of town; 732-270-6960) is a 500-acre county park with a variety of habitats, including salt marshes, maple-gum lowland, pine-oak upland forest, a white cedar swamp, and a mature pitch-pine stand. The park is named for John V. A. Cattus, who, in 1895, built a mansion on Cattus Island as a hunting and fishing lodge. (The mansion was destroyed by an arsonist in the 1970s.) The park has some 10 miles of hiking trails, including a boardwalk path through the swamp; open playing fields; and facilities for picnics. At Cattus Island Park is the Cooper Environmental Center, named for Betty and A. Morton Cooper, who helped preserve this section of the shore. Among the innovations at the center is a porous parking lot, which allows water to drain. Inside the building are nature displays featuring species native to Ocean County, including live reptiles, turtles, and fish; the exhibits change from time to time. This popular center (18,000 people made use of it in 2003) sponsors a variety of programs for children and adults, including nature walks, birding workshops, and nature and birding boat tours. The Cattus Island Nature Center Festival takes place the first Sunday in October. Open daily (except New Year's Day, Easter, Thanksgiving, and Christmas), 8–4:30. The park grounds are open dawn to dusk. Groups by appointment.

Sightseeing cruises on a reproduction of a paddle-wheel riverboat are available Tuesday, Thursday, and Saturday, May–September. For information, call 732-349-8664.

A few miles toward the ocean, on the south bank of the river, is the Ocean Gate Historical Society's museum (Cape May and Asbury aves.; 732-269-8040; 732-269-3468). Housed in a 1909 railroad station, the museum has a railroad ambience, with a ticket window and a 1909 hose cart that was formerly owned by the Pennsylvania Railroad. The exhibits also include area artifacts and a hand-pumper fire engine. Open Wednesday, 6:30–8, and Saturday, 10–12, June–September; groups, other times, and off season by appointment.

There are hopes that a shortwave radio transmitting station at Ocean Gate, which stopped service in 1999, can be converted into a radio-telephone museum. The road to Ocean Gate passes through Pine Beach, once the home of the Admiral Farragut Academy (Riverside Dr.), the country's first naval preparatory school, founded in 1933. When the school closed in 1994, the contents of its memorable marine museum were sold at auction.

Trenton Mercer 85,403

US 1, 206, NJ 29, 31, 33, 129, C 579, 583

Located at the navigable head of the Delaware River, New Jersey's capital was almost the nation's: the Continental Congress, meeting in Trenton in 1784, voted money for the construction of federal buildings in Trenton, but for various reasons (including, apparently, George Washington's opposition) it never came to pass. A thriving community with about a hundred houses, several churches, and considerable economic activity at the time of the Revolution, Trenton became a major manufacturing center in the 19th century. The city was known the world over for steel (the Roebling Company that made the cables that support suspension bridges was located here; *see* Roebling); pottery, both fine (Lenox, the first American company to make china for the White House, was founded in 1889; Greenwood Pottery, the first to make china for restaurant use, in the mid-19th century) and sanitary (the oversize bathtub ordered by President William Howard Taft for the White House—because he kept getting wedged in the one that was there—was made by Motts in Trenton); and rubber goods. Like other industrial cities, Trenton suffered after World War II, but unlike some, the decline was largely downtown, and many neighborhoods survived almost intact. In addition, extensive construction of various state offices and facilities has injected a considerable amount of money into the city's economy, and many people who were relocated into the area because of the corporate boom along US 1 discovered Trenton as a city with housing bargains. These factors have made optimistic statements about Trenton's renaissance seem believable.

In 1679 Mahlon Stacy, Trenton's first white settler, built a house and gristmill near the falls of the river, and in 1714 his son sold some 800 acres of his land along the Assunpink Creek to William Trent, a Philadelphia merchant and later New Jersey's first chief justice. Trent subdivided the parcel for sale in 1721 and established Trent's Town. The town prospered: it became a shipping center for communities up the Delaware, and regular ferry service across the Delaware was inaugurated in 1727, simplifying travel between New York City and Philadelphia. Two important Revolutionary War battles were fought in Trenton, the first on 26 December 1776, after George Washington had crossed the Delaware some eight miles upstream (*see* Titusville). Although the Hessians may not have been in the post-Christmas drunken stupor commonly ascribed to them, the Americans did surprise

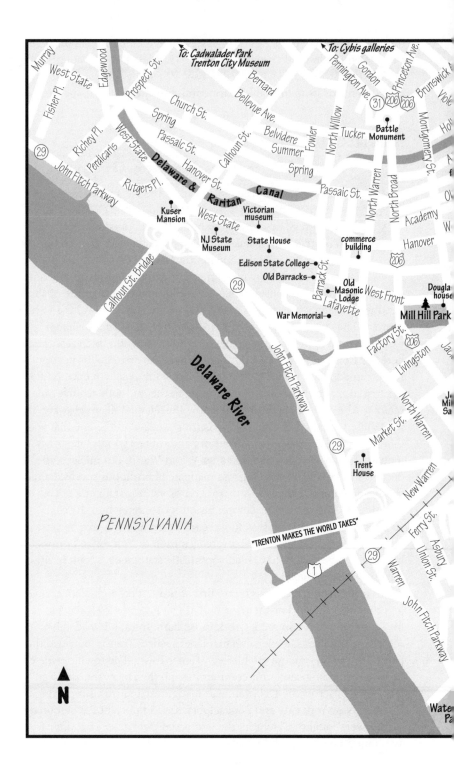

To: Cadwalader Park
Trenton City Museum

To: Cybis galleries

Murray
West State
Edgewood
Prospect St.
Bernard
Pennington Ave.
Gordon
Princeton Ave.
Brunswick A
Viole
Fisher Pl.
Church St.
Bellevue Ave.
31
206
206
Montgomery St.
Hot
Richey Pl.
Spring
Calhoun St.
Belvidere
Fowler
North Willow
Tucker
Battle
Monument
A
f
29
West State
Passaic St.
Summer
Perdicaris
Hanover St.
Spring
North Warren
North Broad
Academy
Ol
John Fitch Parkway
Rutgers Pl.
Delaware &
Passaic St.
W
Kuser
Mansion
Raritan
Canal
Victorian
museum
Hanover
West State
NJ State
Museum
State House
commerce
building
206
Calhoun St. Bridge
29
Edison State College
Old Barracks
Barrack St.
Old
Masonic
Lodge
West Front
Dougla
house
War Memorial
Lafayette
Mill Hill Park
Factory St.
206
Delaware River
John Fitch Parkway
Livingston
Jac
North Warren
Market St.
J
Mi
Sa
29
Trent
House
New Warren
PENNSYLVANIA
"TRENTON MAKES THE WORLD TAKES"
Ferry St.
Asbury
Union St.
29
1
Warren
John Fitch Parkway
N
Wate
Pa

358   Trenton

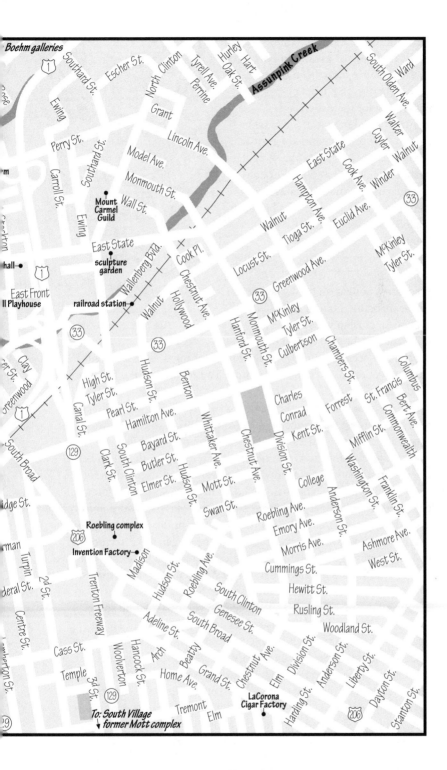

Boehm galleries

Assunpink Creek

Southard St.
Escher St.
North Clinton
Hurley
Hart
Oak St.
Tyrell Ave.
Perrine
South Olden Ave.
Ward

Ewing
Grant
Lincoln Ave.
Walker
Cuyler
Walnut

Perry St.
Southard St.
Model Ave.
Monmouth St.
East State
Cook Ave.
Winder

Carroll St.
Wall St.
Hampton Ave.
Euclid Ave.
(33)

Mount
Carmel
Guild
Walnut
Tioga St.
McKinley
Tyler St.

Ewing
East State
sculpture
garden
Cook Pl.
Locust St.
Greenwood Ave.

hall
East Front
Il Playhouse
railroad station
Wallenberg Blvd.
Chestnut Ave.
Walnut
Hollywood
(33)
McKinley
Tyler St.
Culbertson

(33)
(33)
Monmouth St.
Hanford St.
Chambers St.
Columbus

Clay
Greenwood
(1)
High St.
Tyler St.
Canal St.
Hudson St.
Benton
Charles
Conrad
Kent St.
Forrest
St. Francis
Bert Ave.
Commonwealth

South Broad
Pearl St.
Hamilton Ave.
Whittaker Ave.
Chestnut Ave.
Division St.
Mifflin St.
Washington St.
Franklin St.

(129)
Bayard St.
Butler St.
South Clinton
Clark St.
Elmer St.
Hudson St.
Mott St.
College
Anderson St.

idge St.
Swan St.
Roebling Ave.
Emory Ave.

rman
Roebling complex
(206)
Invention Factory
Madison
Morris Ave.
Ashmore Ave.
West St.

Turpin
2d St.
Trenton Freeway
Hudson St.
Roebling Ave.
Cummings St.
Hewitt St.

deral St.
South Clinton
Genesee St.
Rusling St.
Woodland St.

Centre St.
Cass St.
Temple
3d St.
Woolverton
Adeline St.
South Broad
Arch
Beatty
Grand St.
Hancock St.
Home Ave.
Chestnut Ave.
Elm
Division St.
Harding St.
Anderson St.
Liberty St.
Dayton St.
Stanton St.

(129)
Tremont
Elm
LaCorona
Cigar Factory
(206)

To: South Village
former Mott complex

them and did win the battle, taking close to 1,000 prisoners and, of greater importance, taking the initiative away from the British. The second battle, on 2 January 1777, was again a victory for the Americans.

Trenton became the state's capital in 1790, and by 1792 construction of the State House had begun. It is today the second oldest state capitol still in use, although little of the current building dates from the 18th century, and much that does has been remodeled and looks Victorian.

Trenton's importance as a transportation center was encouraged by the work of John Fitch, who had a steam-powered boat running on the Delaware in 1786, 20 years before Fulton. By 1789 there was regular steamship service on the Delaware, but Fitch, who during the Revolution had been expelled from his church for repairing Continental guns on Sunday, did not remain in Trenton. The road along the Delaware behind the State House honors him.

THE STATE HOUSE

In 1806 the first permanent bridge across the Delaware was built, and today Trenton's most famous bridge—the one at Bridge St. with the "Trenton Makes, the World Takes" sign—rests on those original piers and abutments. The sign resulted from a contest sponsored by the Chamber of Commerce in 1910, and the slogan won out over almost 1,500 other entries. The bridge is now owned and maintained by the Delaware River Joint Toll Bridge Commission, no easy task, for heavy winds and the vibration from traffic can knock out letters. The sign was restored in the 1980s and again in 2005 (some controversy arose about retaining the slogan since Trenton had lost its manufacturing base). The oldest bridge across the Delaware still used for vehicular traffic is the Calhoun St. bridge;* the current (1884) span was placed on the original (1861) piers and abutments.

Despite all the massive new state buildings, you can still find some survivors from Trenton's colonial past. The 1719 William Trent House Museum* (15 Market St.; 609-989-3027), in the oldest standing building in the city, is owned and operated by the city. This elegant brick house, conceived as a summer estate on the Delaware, is a national historic landmark. It has been restored to its colonial appearance and furnished to reflect the inventory made shortly after Trent's death. On the grounds is a colonial kitchen garden, and the museum sponsors a variety of children's educational programs and special events for children and adults. Open daily, 12:30–4; closed municipal holidays; groups and tours by appointment. Admission charged.

Another 18th-century national historic landmark is the Old Barracks* (Barrack St.; 609-396-1776), built c. 1758. It is the only barracks remaining of the five built in New Jersey to house soldiers fighting in the French and Indian wars, and the only example of this type of freestanding barracks in the country. Many of the Hessians captured in the first Battle of Trenton were quartered here; at various times it also housed British troops, Continental troops, and prisoners of war, and served as a military hospital. After independence, it was sold; considerably altered, it was put to a variety of uses. It has now been restored to its colonial appearance and is set up as a museum. The north wing is devoted to period rooms and the south to a "history lab," with exhibits, some interactive, dealing with the field of history and the restoration of the Barracks. This is one of the state's most popular sites with students—over 20,000 schoolchildren visit each year—and the Barracks also runs a day camp for children in the summer and sponsors youth camp-ins and a youth fife and drum corps. One gallery features changing exhibits; past ones have included celebrating the Barrack's 100 years as a museum and the finds from the archaeological dig when the tunnel was built. The collection includes firearms, prints, mementos of Washington, and an 18th-century medical room. Interpreters wear period clothing. Special events take place throughout the year, and there are special holiday exhibits. Open daily, 10–5; groups by appointment. Admission charge.

Close by the Old Barracks is the Old Masonic Lodge (Barrack St. and W. Lafayette), built in 1793 with a mid-19th-century brick addition. In the 1830s the state's first free school opened in this building. The lodge was replaced by a new one in the mid-1860s, but this building was returned to Masonic control, restored, and moved to this site c. 1915. The lodge is now occupied by the Trenton Convention & Visitors Bureau (609-777-1770), but in the upstairs room the ceiling designs have been restored, and you can also see what is believed to be some of the lodge's original furniture. At the visitor center you can pick up information on places of interest not just in Trenton but throughout the state. Open daily, 10–4. Walking tours of the city arranged through Walk This Way (609-396-9419) leave from the center April–October, Sunday at 1; other days by appointment.

The successful stand against the British in the second Battle of Trenton took place in what is now the Mill Hill historic district* (E. Front, Mercer, Jackson, Market, Livingston, Clay, and Broad sts. and Greenwood Ave.). After the battle Washington met with his advisers in the Douglass house,* which dates from 1766, and planned the next day's Battle of Princeton. The Douglass house (Front and Montgomery sts., moved from S. Broad; 609-394-1965; 609-396-4478) serves as the headquarters for the Trenton Historic Society. The society sponsors monthly programs open to the public; the house is open other times by appointment only. The Mill Hill Playhouse (Front and Montgomery sts.) was once a Lutheran church. Each December since the mid-1960s the Old Mill Hill Society (609-989-8977) has sponsored a house tour; in June the society sponsors a garden tour.

Marking the spot where the Continental artillery pounded the British garrison is the Battle Monument* (Broad and Warren sts., Brunswick, Pennington, and Princeton aves.; 609-737-0623). Built in 1891, the tower is over 150 feet high. At its base are copies of bronze plaques by Thomas Eakins depicting scenes from the battle (the originals are on display in the New Jersey State Museum). An elevator takes you to the observation platform. Open Memorial Day–Labor Day, Thursday, 11–3, Friday and Saturday, 9–4, Sunday, 1–4; hours more restricted the rest of the year. Tours by appointment.

In 1996 the Station Plaza sculpture garden (S. Clinton Ave.) opened next to the Trenton railroad station. Here over 15 works, some created for the spot, are displayed in a carefully landscaped project.

Among the large complex of state buildings is the New Jersey State Museum (205 W. State St.; 609-292-6308), devoted to both the arts and the sciences. The main building houses exhibits of fine arts, decorative arts (with emphasis on local porcelain and other household items), natural science, and archaeology and ethnology (which includes artifacts of Native American and other world groups). The adjacent 150-seat planetarium (609-292-6333) ordinarily has shows for the general public on weekends (some of the shows have age requirements for children), and the auditorium is used by the museum for a variety of programs, including films, concerts, lecture-demonstrations, and plays. However, the museum closed for renovation in 2004. Until it reopens it will present shows in the galleries at the Department of State building (225 W. State St.), which is open weekdays, 9–5.

The State House historic district* includes W. State and Willow streets. Tours of the State House (125 W. State St.; 609-633-2709) take place on the hour Tuesday, Wednesday, and Friday, 10–3, Saturday, 12–3. Note the Edison chandelier in the Assembly Room. The State House Annex, built in the early 1930s, has also been renovated and boasts a new stained-glass skylight made at Wheaton Village (see Millville) that depicts important historical figures and geographical features of the state. Another building of interest is the Contemporary Victorian Museum (176 W. State St.; 609-392-9727), an Italianate townhouse from the 1840s now owned by the Contemporary Club, with high ceilings, detailed woodwork, etched glass, a handsome square piano, and a Victorian grand piano. Open 3d Sunday of the month, 2–4, and by appointment. One day in spring the club runs four tours of the city, each focusing on a specific area or historical theme.

Thomas Edison State College (101 W. State St.; 609-984-1100) occupies the Kelsey building.* Kelsey, a local banker and philanthropist, commissioned the building as a memorial to his wife and donated it to the Trenton School of Industrial Arts. Built in 1911, it was modeled on the Palazzo Strozzi in Florence and designed by Cass Gilbert. The Prudence Townsend Kelsey Memorial Room houses Mrs. Kelsey's collection of ceramics. Open by appointment (call 609-984-1191). The college also occupies the five adjacent historic brownstones and the Kuser Mansion (one block west on W. State St.). Chartered in 1972, Edison State, which caters to older students and is known for its off-campus degree possibilities, offers both undergraduate and graduate programs.

In the 200 block of W. State St. note the seven brick buildings, dating from the 1870s, known as the Pride of Lions because of the reliefs of lions on the facades. Note also the detail on the facade of the Kuser Mansion* (315 W. State St.), from 1910. George Segal's 23-foot-high sculpture of construction workers among interlocking steel I-beams and other paraphernalia of a building site stands in front of the new commerce building (W. State and Warren sts.). Farther east is the Old City Hall* (309 E. State), built in 1907.

Trenton's War Memorial* (between the State House and the river; 609-984-8484), finished in 1932, was extensively renovated in the late 1990s. It is used for conferences, concerts (including a regular series by the New Jersey Symphony Orchestra), and opera performances. Two of Trenton's most famous musical citizens, the tenor Richard Crooks and the composer George Antheil, were classmates at Trenton High School.

West of the state buildings, in Cadwalader Park (Parkside and Stuyvesant aves.), is Ellarslie,* the Trenton City Museum (609-989-3632). Housed in a mansion built in the 1840s for Henry McCall, a Philadelphia industrialist, the museum displays on its upper floor items from its permanent collection, which focuses on the city's porcelain and ceramic art industries, the Roeblings, and home furnishings with Trenton associations. On the first floor are changing exhibits of contemporary art. Open Tuesday–Saturday, 11–3; Sunday, 1–4. The park itself was laid out by the Frederick Law Olmsted firm in the 1890s; among its other attractions is its deer park. It honors Dr. Thomas Cadwalader, a pioneer in smallpox inoculation and the donor of the state's first public library. The Cadwalader Heights residential area (Parkside Ave. between Bellevue and Stuyvesant aves.) was developed from 1910 to 1930 and was also designed by the Olmsted firm.

South of Cadwalader Park is the Berkeley Square historic district* (Parkside, Riverside, and Overbrook aves. and W. State St.), an area built up c. 1890–1910, notable for its solid houses with stained-glass windows, chestnut and oak woodwork, marble fireplaces, and the like. West of the park is the Trenton Psychiatric Hospital, founded in the 1840s under the influence of Dorothea Dix, who lived her last years in an apartment at the hospital.

North of the state buildings in the headquarters of the fire department is the Meredith Havens Fire Museum (244 Perry St.; 609-989-4038). The collection includes equipment and other items related to the history of fire fighting, with special emphasis on Trenton's fire departments. The museum also has a collection of Civil War material. Open daily, 8 A.M.–10 P.M.

Many of Trenton's industrial buildings are being put to other uses. The headquarters of the Mount Carmel Guild (73 N. Clinton Ave.), for example, was once the home of the head of Greenwood Pottery. The turn-of-the-century Stokely–Van Camp cannery complex* (Lalor St. at Stokely Ave.) has become part of South Village I and II, a public housing development and senior citizen residence; the Millhouse Residential Center (325 Jersey St., off Lalor St.) was once part of the J. L. Mott complex, where sanitary porcelain products were manufactured; the Spanish-looking 1930s La Corona Cigar Factory* (507 Grand St.) has been converted to apartments. Unfortunately, the ambitious project planned for the 45-acre historic Roebling complex has not proceeded as hoped. The complex includes 40 buildings dating from the 1850s through the 1950s that belonged to the Roebling Company and the Trenton Iron Company. (The Trenton Iron Company, founded by Peter Cooper [see Ringwood] in 1850, eventually became a subsidiary of U.S. Steel and continued operating until 1987.) The headquarters for the New Jersey Housing Mortgage Finance Agency are in the former Physical Testing House and South Rope Shop from the late 1920s; next door is a large retail complex; a county administration building is in the same block; the former mill yard has been converted to a small urban park. (The Invention Factory Science Center is no longer open.) Other projects under construction, on the drawing board, or as visions in many people's minds are a senior citizen housing complex, a performing arts center, a hotel and convention center, and a sports arena. Along the river (south of the US 1 bridge) is a new executive park as well as Waterfront Park Stadium, where the Trenton Thunder (1 Thunder Rd.; 609-394-8236), the city's popular minor league baseball team, plays.

Also along the river (actually on top of the NJ 29 tunnel) is the six-acre South River Walk park, with a bicycle and pedestrian path, playgrounds, and pavilions. A time tunnel provides a history of the city.

Although sanitary pottery may no longer be as important to the city as it once was, the production of art porcelain continues; Boehm, Cybis, and Ispanky are all currently active. The Boehm galleries (25 Fairfacts St.; 609-392-2207) are open weekdays, 9–4:30; groups by appointment. Among the pieces on display at the Cybis galleries (65 Norman Ave.; 609-392-6074) are replicas of items sent to heads of state on various historic occasions. Tours by appointment.

The first weekend in June Trenton celebrates its past with Heritage Day on the State House block. Other annual events include a professional bicycle race in early summer and the reenactment of the Battle of Trenton the first Saturday after Christmas.

Tuckerton   Ocean 3,157

Settled in the late 1690s, Tuckerton was an important port in colonial days, later serving as the shopping center for the surrounding region. In 1912 the country's tallest radio tower was built just south of Tuckerton in what is now Mystic Island (take Radio Rd. south out of town); at the time this was the only transmitter that could broadcast to Europe without a relay. The transmitter was built in Germany for a French company and assembled here under the supervision of a German engineer, and although it was taken over by the government during both world wars, rumors swirled around its German connection. Today Tuckerton is the western terminus of the world's first fiber-optic trans-Atlantic cable (located in an underground building on Cable Rd.), completed in 1988 and able to carry some 40,000 simultaneous telephone conversations.

The Tuckerton Seaport (120 W. Main St.; 609-296-8868) is a re-created working village illustrating some of the port-related activities that occupied Tuckerton's residents in the 18th and 19th centuries. (According to local legend, Tuckerton in 1791 was the colonies' third port of entry, after New York and Philadelphia.) The facility includes a mix of historic buildings and replicas and features demonstrations of such crafts as clamming, decoy carving, and boatbuilding. The visitor center is in a replica of the mid-19th-century Tucker's Island lighthouse. Among the authentically old buildings are the Sea Captain's house (1769), which houses the seaport offices and a Victorian parlor, and the Sunny Brae Salt Box House (early 1700s). On the upper level of the Tuckerton Yacht Club is the Jacques Cousteau National Estuarine Research Reserve Visitor Center, which features exhibits on the biology and ecology of estuarine habitats. The seaport is open daily, April–October, 10–5; it is open limited hours November and December and closed January–March. The office is open year-round.

West of Tuckerton, just south of US 9, is the Giffordtown Schoolhouse (Wisteria La. and Leitz Blvd.; 609-294-1547, 609-296-2584), an 1880s school building run as a museum by the Tuckerton Historical Society. Its two rooms contain artifacts connected to various aspects of local history, including wireless transmission, the Tuckerton railroad, and the early Quakers. Exhibits change roughly twice a year. The society also sponsors a variety of programs throughout the year; the Saturday after Labor Day, for example, the society runs the Clamtown antique flea market (Tuckerton used to be known as Clamtown). Museum open Wednesday, 10–4, mid-January–mid-December. Tours by appointment.

South of Tuckerton is the Great Bay Boulevard Wildlife Management Area (Great Bay angles south off US 9 just west of the intersection with Green St.), one of the largest (over 5,000 acres) and least-disturbed stretches of marshland in the state. The area is heavily used by waterfowl and nesting shorebirds and is much favored by bird-watchers. It is also favored by those who like fishing, boating, clamming, and crabbing, although the insects can be fierce in summer. Parking and a small-boat launching ramp are available off Great Bay Blvd.

About five miles northwest of the US 9–Green St. intersection is Bass River State Forest (609-296-1114), more than 26,000 acres with facilities for picnicking, swimming, boating (electric motors only), camping, cross-country skiing, horseback riding, hiking, and hunting. A short nature trail in the Lake Absegami region gives a vivid depiction of the Pinelands as it moves through various types of forest to a cedar bog and back. The forest has five easy self-guided walking tours; the Batona Trail also goes through the forest. The area known as the Pygmy Forest in the West Pine Plains Natural Area is the largest forest of this type of stunted trees (pine and oak) in the world. Office open 9–4 in winter, extended hours in summer.

Union Union 54,405

 I 78, US 22, GARDEN STATE PKWY EXITS I 39, I 40, NJ 82, I 24

Settled in 1667 by several families from Connecticut, Union (known at first as Connecticut Farms) claims to have what was once the tallest water sphere in the world—familiar to many motorists on the Garden State Parkway. (Although the water sphere is probably still the tallest in the county, taller ones have since been built elsewhere.)

Union's Connecticut Farms Presbyterian Church* (Stuyvesant Ave. at Chestnut St.) was the first building in New Jersey to be placed on the national register of historic places. The church was built in 1788 to replace the 1730 church burned by the British during the Revolution. The Reverend James Caldwell, the fighting parson (*see* Springfield), then minister at Elizabethtown, had moved his family here, apparently believing they would be safer. Versions of what happened differ, but his wife was killed by British snipers as she sat in the parsonage in June 1780. A later parsonage, built c. 1783 on the foundations of the earlier one, is now the Union Township Historical Society Museum* (909 Caldwell Ave.; 908-687-7977). It is decorated to show what life might have been like in a 19th-century parsonage; many of the objects came from Connecticut Farms' original settlers. On the walls are three large paintings of the Battle of Connecticut Farms. Also on the property is the early-19th-century carriage house; here the society stores its large collection of farm tools. Tours by appointment. The society's meetings, generally held the 3d Sunday of the month, are open to the public; call for the schedule.

On Morris Ave., just north of North Ave., is Liberty Hall* (1085 Morris Ave.; 908-737-5950), also known as the Livingston-Kean house, a national historic landmark built in 1772 by William Livingston, New Jersey's first elected and very popular governor (he served until 1790). George and Martha Washington both stayed in Liberty Hall, as did Alexander Hamilton, and Livingston's daughter Sarah married John Jay in the house (before he became the first Supreme Court chief justice). John Kean, a member of the Second Continental Congress, married Livingston's niece Susan, and Liberty Hall remained in the Kean family until 1995. Now open as a museum, the main house features 14 rooms furnished with pieces dating from the Revolution to the 1940s. Almost all the contents of the museum either belonged to or were purchased by the seven generations of Keans and Livingstons who lived in the house. Liberty Hall sits on 23 acres, and on the grounds are a handsome garden and a carriage house with a few restored carriages and sleighs. Plans call for adding a fire museum in the near future. The museum sponsors a variety of special events, such as holiday candlelight tours, a pumpkin-patch watch, a gingerbread workshop, Wednesday tea, and a summer children's program. Open for tours April–December, Wednesday–Saturday, 10–4, Sunday, 12–4. Admission charge.

Across Morris Ave. from Liberty Hall is Kean University (908-737-5326), founded in 1855 as Newark State College and now the third largest public university in the state. In 1958 the university moved onto 120 acres that were also once part of the Kean estate. A complex of French Norman–style buildings, once part of the Kean family farm and later known as Kean Library, was remodeled into a single building in 2002. Now known as Kean Hall, it houses the undergraduate admissions office and a variety of student

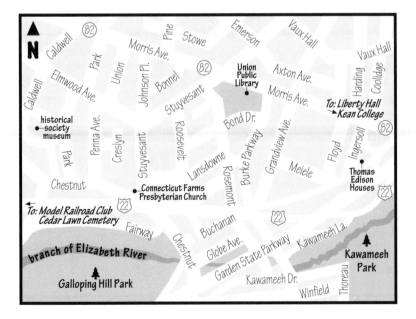

services and administrative offices. The 1790 James Townley house* is used by the first aid squad. Most of the campus buildings, however, are new. Exhibits in the James Howe Gallery, which is located in the striking Vaughn Eames Building, are open to the public Monday–Thursday, 10–2 and 5–7; Friday, 10–12. The students' art gallery in the Campus Center is open when the college is open. At the theater (908-737-4350) you can see college productions as well as a variety of professional theatrical, musical, and dance events. The college's Holocaust Resource Center (908-737-4660) is also open to the public weekdays, 8–5, but it is recommended that you call ahead. Guided tours of the campus start from Kean Hall Friday at 10; advance reservations recommended. Just east of the campus, in Hillside, on the old grounds of the Pingry School (one of the nation's oldest country day schools), is Kean College's east campus (take North Ave., NJ 439).

At Ingersoll Terrace (south off Morris Ave. just west of the Garden State Pkwy) are the Thomas Edison Houses, poured concrete houses made by a process invented by Edison in 1908. Edison's plan to build a much larger project never materialized, but you can still see close to a dozen of the unusually shaped "varmint-free" houses, some bricked over, some with stucco added, some covered with aluminum siding.

At the A. Paul Mallery Model Railroad Center (295 Jefferson Ave., off US 22 just east of the Cedar Lawn Cemetery; 908-964-8808, 908-964-9724), the Model Railroad Club (said to be the oldest such club in the country) maintains HO-, N-, and G-scale layouts. Built primarily by members of the club, but belonging to the county, the building houses one of the largest exhibit spaces for model trains in the world. The larger HO is roughly 40 by 40 feet with a heavy-duty main line, a 1920s-style interurban trolley line, and a short line. The smaller N layout, as well as a second HO layout, runs along three walls of another room. A larger outdoor display, known as G-gauge, was installed in 2001. The club is working on an HO layout that will eventually be 80 by 50 feet (the basic 40 by 40 layout took 27 years to complete). Open Saturday, 1–4 (club members are usually working on the trains at this time, although some equipment is running) and some Sundays. A holiday show is held on the first three weekends following Thanksgiving, at which time the trains are run as an exhibit. Visitors can watch from a viewing balcony as theatrical lighting illuminates the trains and a tape describes what is happening. The club also offers a series of hands-on educational classes on various Saturdays. Admission charged.

The Les Malamut Gallery in the Union Public Library (Morris Ave. next to the municipal building; 908-851-5450) features fine art exhibits in many media. Exhibits change every six to seven weeks. Open Monday–Thursday, 10–9; Friday and Saturday 9–5 (Saturday 9–12, Memorial Day–Labor Day).

Union City Hledon 67,088

I 495

Once a major center for the lace and embroidery industry—
many factories were established by German and Swiss
immigrants in the 1870s—Union City now has a reputation for
being one of the nation's most densely settled communities.
Although it is often said that it is the most densely settled town,
according to the census nearby Guttenberg is denser. (There is some feeling
in Union City that Guttenberg consists of one large apartment building,
which shouldn't count.) Union City is also known for the size of its Hispanic
community, which makes up some 75 percent of the population. Because so
many Cubans arrived in the 1960s, Union City has the second largest (or,
according to some sources, the largest) Cuban community in the United
States.

The Park Performing Arts Center (560 32d St.; 201-865-6980, ext. 15),
makes its home in a 1,400-seat theater built in 1931 by the German members
of a Catholic order for their cultural and educational programs. Continuing
that tradition, the center presents a wide range of professional and
community theater, music (classical, folk, jazz), and dance. PPAC also
offers a wide variety of classes in dance, art, and music. The center has a
long-running exhibit on the history of the embroidery industry, as well as
changing exhibits of contemporary art. Open by appointment. The center is
also home to the nation's longest-running Passion Play, which was first
performed in the spring of 1915.

Union City has recently been hit by gentrification, but you can still see
large neighborhoods of modest workers' housing, as well as a stunning city
hall (3715 Palisades Ave.), half of which was a late-19th-century schoolhouse,
and the mid-19th-century Saint Michael's Church* (West St. and Monastery
Pl.), now home to the North Hudson Korean Presbyterians.

Vernon Township Sussex 24,686

NJ 94, C 515, 517, 565

Vernon Township's location in the mountains of the
Highlands has determined the character of its two largest
industries: satellite telecommunications (microwave
transmission is least disturbed in mountains) and recreational
skiing. With the country's highest concentration of microwave
transmitters, the residents of this large (68 sq. mi.) and rapidly growing
township (the population increased almost tenfold between 1960 and
1990) are concerned about the effects of these transmitters on their
health.

Vernon's mountains apparently served as a source of rock for Native Americans 6,000 years ago—what looks like the remains of two mines have been found—and Native American artifacts turn up frequently. Matilda, a mastodon skeleton unearthed here in the 1950s, is on display at the State Museum in Trenton.

Among the historic buildings still standing in the township is the Price's Switch School (Price's Switch, C 515, and Meadowburn rds.), built c. 1840, moved and enlarged in the late 1800s, and finally closed in 1958, the last one-room schoolhouse in the county. Tours by appointment through the Vernon Township Historical Society (973-764-8554). The Barrett House museum (173 Barrett Rd.; 973-764-8554) is run by the society and features a variety of programs. The society's library and archives are in the Vernon Township municipal building (973-764-4055, ext. 278). Also on Meadowburn Rd. is Meadowburn Farm.* Started c. 1760 by William Willet DeKay, one of Vernon's earliest settlers, it maintains the gardens designed by Helena Rutherfurd Ely, a well-known writer on gardening, who lived in the house from 1880 to 1920. Also in the township is High Breeze Farm, a working mid-19th-century farm that was relatively untouched by the 20th century (*see* Highland Lakes).

Within the township is the Hamburg Mountain Wildlife Management Area (NJ 23, C 517), 2,400 acres of mountainous, heavily forested land. Access to the area is limited, but it is open for hiking, skiing, fishing, and hunting. Adjacent to the management area is the Mountain Creek ski facility (973-827-2000), which is popular with snowboarders and free-style skiers and has the largest snowmaking equipment in the East. Downhill mountain-biking is available in the fall, and Mountain Creek water park (973-827-4528) operates in the area when the ski facility is closed. Call for hours and rates.

North of the Hamburg Mountain area is the Hidden Valley ski area (973-764-4200). Open weekdays, 9 A.M.–9 P.M.; weekends and holidays, 8:30 A.M.–9 P.M. In addition to trails for skiing and snowboarding, Hidden Valley has facilities for snow-tubing and, in summer, swimming, tennis, and a day camp.

The Wallkill River National Wildlife Refuge (973-702-7266), opened in 1992, lies partially in Vernon Township (it is also in Wantage and Hardyston townships). This is the first river-floodplain refuge in the state, and hopes are that in the future it will encompass some 8,000 acres. The refuge supports an unusually high number of species, some of them on the state's endangered list. You can fish, hike, bird-watch, canoe, and kayak at the refuge, which has three nature trails. Open sunrise to sunset. Headquarters for the refuge are in a late-19th-century farmhouse at 1547 C 565 (about 1½ miles northeast of NJ 23). Photographs and other exhibits are on display at the headquarters. Open 8–4:30 weekdays.

On a farm whose original deed predates the formation of the state is the Bobolink Dairy (42 Meadow Burn Rd.; 973-764-4888). Cows, some from old strains, graze on the dairy's 200 acres, and cheese is made from their milk.

The buildings probably date to the 19th century, but the adze-cut beams in the barn probably supported a colonial barn. Classes in cheese- and bread-making are offered. Open Wednesday–Friday, 12–6, weekends 9–5.

Vineland Cumberland 56,271

NJ 47, 55, C 540, 552, 555

Physically New Jersey's largest city, Vineland is also one of New Jersey's first planned cities. It was founded in 1861 by Charles K. Landis, a 28-year-old, who envisioned businessmen and industrialists living in the center of his city, while artisans with farms and orchards surrounded the core. To prevent speculation he stipulated that anyone who bought land had to build a house and till the soil. Each homeowner also had to plant shade and fruit trees and follow Landis's sanitary codes. Recruiting Italians to come as farmers, he encouraged workers to buy property, offering them long-term loans to build houses on their own land. Within 20 years the population had reached 6,000.

Landis had hoped the community would prosper by growing grapes (hence the name), but in the 1880s a blight destroyed the vines. Agriculture did flourish, however, and Vineland is now the dandelion capital of the world (though production has declined over the years, over $200,000 worth of dandelions still passes through the produce auction); an annual dandelion dinner is held in March (609-691-7400). Vineland is also a major center for eggplant and asparagus seed (New Jersey is among the top five states in both eggplant and asparagus; in 2003 eggplant contributed over $4.5 million and asparagus some $3 million to the state's economy). It was once a major egg center, but, like the rest of the New Jersey egg industry, Vineland's is declining in importance. Vineland's produce auction (N. Main Rd.) is one of the largest in the country and the largest of its kind on the East Coast. Almost all the produce sold at the 75-year-old auction is for consumption fresh, not for processing, and most of it is being picked while the auction is going on (sample cases are brought in for the auction). Open daily, late April–November.

Welch's grape juice was a 19th-century Vineland creation. T. B. Welch, a Vineland dentist and staunch Methodist, objected to the use of fermented grape juice in the church. He introduced unfermented juice, and by the time he moved his company from Vineland in the 1890s, it was on the way to becoming a major firm. Because of the sandy soil, many cities in Cumberland County are centers of glass manufacturing, and this is one of Vineland's primary industries. (John Mason patented his lid for the Mason jar, familiar to home canners, in 1858.) Other local industries include textile manufacturing, food processing, water-purification systems (one of the world's largest manufacturer of these systems has been in Vineland since the mid-1990s), construction, and truck-related operations.

The Vineland Training School (1667 E. Landis Ave., C 540, between Main and Spring rds.) was founded in 1888 to serve the mentally retarded. The institution was the first in the country to use the Binet intelligence scales; it also drafted the first army IQ tests. Its research and therapy programs have won it an international reputation.

You can still see some of the logic of Landis's plan as you drive through town. The streets are straight, the intersections at right angles. The railroad, which runs through the center of town (and ran through the center of Landis's property when he bought it), has been integrated into a boulevard. Notice also the rows of brick houses, some with interlaced color at the corners, on Chestnut St., east of the railroad. And for a splendid example of another era, note the white marble building built for the Vineland Trust Company in 1913, with its stained glass, ceramic tiles, brass, and mahogany.

An example of yet another era is the Landis Theater* (834 E. Landis Ave.; 856-794-6021), a 1937 art deco movie palace threatened with demolition but saved by concerned citizens. The man who built the Landis broke the moviemakers' monopoly on the showing of first-run movies (he also managed to build the Garden State Park Racetrack in 1942; *see* Cherry Hill). The Landis Theater Redevelopment Association is working to restore the theater. For now the space is used for a variety of events from car shows to concerts, most of them outdoors, and most in the summer. Tours are given during the events, and if people happen to be working on the theater as you pass it, you may be welcomed inside and offered a tour.

The Vineland Historical and Antiquarian Society (108 S. 7th St.; 856-691-1111) is one of the oldest historical societies in the state. Founded in 1864, it is housed in a building specially built for it in 1910. The collection focuses on local history and includes Lenape artifacts, local glass (some connected to Welch's grape juice), paintings of local interest, a fire department display, and furnishings from Landis's house. Changing exhibits also focus on items of local historical interest. Open Saturday, 1–4 (the office is open for research Tuesday–Saturday, 1–4); groups by appointment.

Five miles northwest of Vineland is Parvin State Park (Centerton-Norma Rd., C 540; 856-358-8616). Within its 1,300 acres is a variety of terrain—including woodland, swamps, lakes, and streams—and of species—including those from the Pinelands, the Piedmont, and the Inner Coastal Plain. Much of Parvin, which dates from 1933, was developed by the Civilian Conservation Corps, which had a camp there. The CCC dug mud out of the lakes and replaced it with sand, cleared trails, built roads, built bridges over swamps, and dug a new lake, all without power equipment. It constructed buildings out of bricks salvaged from structures that were being torn down in Philadelphia. Its barracks (now gone) were used during World War II to house German POWs, Japanese-Americans from the West Coast, and Kalmuks exiled from the Soviet Union. The park, open all year, includes 15 miles of hiking and biking trails, a 4-mile blacktop trail for bicycles, a 465-acre natural area, picnic tables, and facilities for boating, swimming, fishing, camping, and cross-country skiing. The park sponsors a variety of special programs, including nature walks, nature crafts, and migratory-bird walks. The nature walks take place daily Memorial Day–Labor Day, weekends the rest of the year. The protected swimming area is staffed from Memorial Day to Labor Day. Admission charged Memorial Day–Labor Day. Guided hikes by reservation.

The road from Vineland to Parvin passes through Norma, one end of the 19th-century Jewish settlement of Alliance. The other end (turn right on Gershel Ave.) is at Brotmanville (named for Abraham Brotman, who established a factory here). Very little is left of the settlement, but at the Alliance Cemetery (Gershel Ave. less than a mile from C 540) is a brick chapel that contains artifacts, old documents, and photographs showing what life was like in these settlements in the 1880s. A synagogue, open annually for the High Holidays, is across the street, and an old house or two can be seen. The cemetery is open except on Saturdays; for information on visiting the chapel, call the Cumberland County Jewish Federation (856-696-4445).

Just north of Vineland, in Newfield, is the Matchbox Road Museum (Pearl St.; 856-697-2800, 800-976-7623), featuring a collection of some 30,000 Matchbox items. Open by appointment.

Also north of Vineland is the Unexpected Wildlife Refuge (110 Unexpected Rd.; 856-697-3541), 540 acres dedicated to the preservation of native wildlife through preservation of the environment. Except for the bluebird habitat (which is mowed), a blueberry patch, some trails, a poplar garden (used to supply branches to the beavers), and many birdhouses, the wetlands, lakes, and forests are left undisturbed. There have been as many as seven active beaver lodges and as many as six pairs of nesting bluebirds on the reserve, which is home to a large variety of birds. Visits may be arranged by appointment. Guided tours available for groups of five.

Northeast of Vineland, in Landisville, is Bellview Winery (150 Atlantic St.; 856-697-7172), which grows all its own grapes on land that has been in the family since early in the 20th century. Open January–mid-April, Friday–Sunday, 11–5; mid-April–Thanksgiving, Wednesday–Sunday, 11–5; Thanksgiving–Christmas, daily, 11–6. Tours by appointment.

Walpack Township Sussex 41

C 615

A township with a population density of 1.7 people per square mile (the lowest in the state), Walpack is located within the Delaware Water Gap National Recreation Area (*see* below), where you can find some of the state's most spectacular mountain scenery. It is an area that is also rich in history, although how much of the physical evidence of that history will be around for people to look at depends on what the National Park Service decides should be the future of the recreation area.

For now, you can still visit the mid-19th-century Walpack Center historic district* and explore the remaining old houses along the Old Mine (*see* Blairstown) and other roads. The Old Mine Road Historic District* extends into the townships of Montague, Sandyston, and Hardwick (which in 1997 absorbed Pahaquarry). The Walpack Historical Society has a small museum in the First Rosenkrans House (Main St., next to the post office; 973-948-6671) with local and Victorian artifacts. Open May–October, 3d Sunday of the month, 1–5.

Southwest of Walpack Center, the 19th-century village of Millbrook (908-496-4458) has been restored; it contains a blacksmith's, a weaver's, and a shoemaker's shop, a store, a church, and a school. Long-range goals include restoring the mill, a project complicated by the fact that its waterpower came from what is now a protected trout stream. The buildings are open mid-May–mid-October, Friday–Sunday, 9–5; occasionally volunteers demonstrate crafts. You are free to wander around other times, and you will find in the brochure box a pamphlet with a self-guided tour.

The Isaac Van Campen Inn (Old Mine Rd., about 2½ miles north of the intersection with Pompey Rd.; 973-948-6671) was built in the mid-18th century as a farmhouse. The solid stone structure served as a fortress during times of trouble with Native Americans, and because it was frequented by travelers, has come to be known as an inn. John Adams was among its visitors, George Washington mentioned it by name in correspondence, and Count Pulaski used the house as his headquarters for three months during the Revolution. Although much altered over the years, the house retains many of its original features (doors, hinges, stair structure, paneling). Open Sunday, 1–5, May–October, and for various annual special events, which can include reenactors; groups by appointment. The stretch of the Old Mine Road north of Pompey Rd. runs along the river; it is beautiful, but it is not maintained, and to save your car you may prefer to approach from the other direction (take Kuhn Rd. west out of Peters Valley [*see* Bevans] and turn left on the Old Mine Rd., driving south for about 2½ miles). Near the inn in an old cemetery is the grave of Anna Symmes, mother-in-law of William Henry Harrison (she died in 1777).

About five miles southwest of Walpack Center is the Walpack Wildlife Management Area. It is one of the earliest such areas (begun in 1932) and is located on over 350 acres of woodlands and fields. The Big Flatbrook, which goes through the tract, is one of the state's best-known trout streams, and the area is also open for hiking, bird-watching, and hunting. The office is on C 521 at Bevans in the Flatbrook-Roy Wildlife Management Area.

The Delaware Water Gap, where the river has carved out a channel through the Kittatinny Mountains some 1,300 feet deep (the river itself is only 900 feet wide at this point), is a breathtaking site, long an attraction to tourists and painters. In pursuit of its plan to build a huge dam and recreation area at Tocks Island, the federal government came to own some 70,000 acres on both sides of the river, most of it north of the gap. To the relief of many, the project has been at least temporarily stalled, and the government has converted the area into the Delaware Water Gap National Recreation Area. Although the army engineers destroyed many of the old buildings, they are not all gone, and some of the villages, like Walpack Center and Millbrook (*see also* Bevans), have been converted to tourist attractions or are being used for environmental education programs. Recreational opportunities in the park abound: you can hike (there are more than 100 miles of trails), fish, rock-climb, canoe, swim, horseback ride, hunt, and bicycle. In winter, designated sections are open for ice-fishing, ice-skating, cross-country skiing, and snowmobiling. Information and trail maps are available at the Kittatinny Point Visitor Center (off I 80; 908-496-4458). The center is usually open 9–5 daily in high season and on weekends the rest of the year, but the hours can vary widely, so it is best to call the general information number first (570-588-2451). Interpretive programs and tours for groups can often be arranged (908-496-4458).

Wayne Passaic 54,069

US 202, NJ 23, C 502, 504

Even when it was incorporated in the 1840s (and named in honor of Mad Anthony Wayne), the township of Wayne did not have a single center but was made up of a collection of settlements. Now, as the population increases (almost 85 percent since 1960), the spaces between the communities are shrinking.

Wayne was the home of Albert Payson Terhune (1872–1942), best known for his tales of the collies he raised at Sunnybank. His house was destroyed, but the land (on the Terhune Dr. section of US 202 at the northern end of the township) now forms Terhune Memorial Park (sometimes referred to as Sunnybank Park), with gardens and a picnic ground. Terhune's great-grandfather can be seen in Emanuel Leutze's famous painting of George Washington crossing the Delaware (he's the near bow oarsman). Cecil B. De Mille's childhood home was near Sunnybank Park.

In Preakness Valley Park is the Dey Mansion (199 Totowa Rd.; 973-696-1776). Built c. 1740–50, this beautiful Georgian house was the home of Theunis Dey, a Revolutionary patriot, and served as Washington's headquarters in July, October, and November of 1780. Here he heard the news of Rochambeau's arrival, and here he came after Benedict Arnold's treachery. The county has restored the house to its 18th-century appearance and furnished it with pieces appropriate to the first three-quarters of the 18th century. Displays in the attic change every year or two; past ones have included Revolutionary War muskets and textiles. On the grounds near the house are replicas of various outbuildings, as well as a forge used by the blacksmith for special events, a Williamsburg-style garden, and a picnic grove. Open Wednesday–Friday, 1–4; weekends, 10–12; closed major holidays. Admission charged. Groups by appointment. Special events are scheduled at the house, including lectures, demonstrations of colonial crafts on many Sunday afternoons, a Revolutionary War encampment in the fall, and an annual Christmas holiday exhibit. Also in Preakness Valley Park (973-742-6373), one of Passaic County's most heavily used parks, are a golf course, shag field, and tennis courts.

The Wayne Museum (533 Berdan Ave.; 973-694-7192) is in the Van Riper–Hopper house,* built in 1786 by descendants of 17th-century Dutch settlers; their descendants were active as farmers until 1920. The house is furnished with period pieces and reflects the agricultural history of the area; there is also a permanent exhibit of Terhune memorabilia. A variety of programs and special events takes place at the house, including, for example, historic-skills classes and an annual paint-a-pumpkin festival. The view across the grounds to the Point View Reservoir is lovely, and on the grounds are the early-18th-century Mead–Van Duyne house museum,* an archaeological laboratory, and an herb garden. The Mead–Van Duyne house, threatened by highway construction, was moved to this spot in 1975; the laboratory is filled with artifacts excavated at the house's former site. The Mead–Van Duyne house has been restored and can be visited. It and the Van Riper–Hopper house are open by appointment. Still to be restored is the George Washington Colfax Barn Museum, which will also be on the property. Saved from demolition and moved to the property, this barn (c. 1790) was the last standing timber-frame New World Dutch barn in Passaic County. After it is restored and reassembled, it is expected to serve as a community center as well as a museum.

The oldest house in Wayne is the Schuyler-Colfax house museum,* c. 1696 (2343 Paterson-Hamburg Tnpk), which remained in the same family until quite recently. George and Martha Washington visited the house, and the father of Ulysses S. Grant's vice-president was raised here. The house is being restored and is expected to open in 2005. Other historic houses in Wayne include the Van Saun house* (23 Laauwe Ave.), an 18th-century house that may have been Lafayette's headquarters in 1780, and the Demarest house (378 Fairfield Rd.), built in 1760 and, some say, dismantled and rebuilt in 1850 to rid it of ghosts.

On a wooded hilltop in the northeast corner of the township, with views over the surrounding metropolitan area, is William Paterson University. (Access to parking lots is from Pompton Rd., C 504.) Most of the buildings on the 325-acre campus are new, but the president's office is in Hobart Manor,* a neo-Tudor mansion erected in the 1870s by John McCollough, a Scottish immigrant who had made a fortune in wool, and expanded to 40 rooms in 1915 by the Hobart family. A national historic site, Hobart Manor has four rooms restored and furnished to reflect its early-20th-century appearance. The Shea Center for the Performing Arts (973-720-2371) is used for a variety of musical events, including a jazz series, a new music series, lunch concerts, and concerts by the High Mountain Symphony (formerly the Wayne Chamber Orchestra). This is also home base for the internationally renowned New Jersey Percussion Ensemble. The Ben Shahn Galleries (973-720-2654) contain three exhibition spaces and mount some 12 shows a year, with the focus on contemporary art of all kinds. There are also an annual faculty show and an annual students show. During the school year, exhibits are open to the public weekdays, 10–5; other times by appointment. As you walk about the campus, note the outdoor sculpture.

North of the college (off the Paterson-Hamburg Tnpk between Valley Rd. and Duncan La.) is High Mountain Wilderness Park, the largest remaining tract of forest land in this part of the state. In it are many rare and endangered plant and animal species. As yet undeveloped, it is open for walking and bird-watching.

Weehawken Hudson 13,501

I 495, C 505

From about 1799 to 1835 Weehawken, situated on the bluffs overlooking the Hudson, was notorious for its "infamous dueling ground," a grassy shelf some 20 feet above tidewater. The most famous duel to take place there was, of course, that between Alexander Hamilton and Aaron Burr. (In 2004 the town celebrated the 200th anniversary of the occasion.) A monument to Hamilton can be found in Weehawken, but not at the actual site. (An earlier monument on the site was destroyed in the 1820s by citizens outraged by the practice of dueling; the grassy shelf itself was later swallowed by the railroads.) Today's monument is on Hamilton Ave. (off Blvd. East as it makes a right-angle turn). A bust of Hamilton rests atop a stone on which, according to the inscription, "rested the head of Alexander Hamilton." The inscription replaces a bronze plaque, several times stolen; the four holes that secured the plaque are sometimes seen as bullet holes. The semicircular stone wall is supposed to have been built by a friend to keep Washington Irving, who used to fall asleep while viewing the Hudson, from falling over the edge.

Just north of the monument, on Blvd. East, is Hamilton Plaza, a popular scenic overlook maintained by the town of Weehawken. Stop here for a spectacular view of Manhattan and the river. Awareness of Weehawken as a viewing spot goes back to the 18th century, and the town was once a resort town, the bluffs occupied by estates, beer gardens, and large Adirondack-style wooden hotels. Ferry service ran from New York City, and elevators carried the visitors up to the buildings on the cliff.

The New Jersey entrance to the Lincoln Tunnel, once the world's only three-tube tunnel (there is now a four-tube tunnel in Germany), is in

Weehawken. The first tube opened in 1937; today's three tubes carry over 21 million vehicles a year from Weehawken to Manhattan.

Many drivers entering and leaving the tunnel are aware of the Richardsonian gray stone Weehawken Public Library. There are other splendid late-19th-century stone buildings to be seen on the bluffs; for a coherent Victorian neighborhood, walk through the Kingswood section near the Hamilton monument. (Walk along Hamilton and King aves., Bonn Pl., Bellevue St., and Kingswood Rd.; much of this area was built by a single developer around 1900.) Blvd. East Promenade connects Hamilton Plaza, Hamilton Monument, Soldiers and Sailors Monument, and Old Glory Park; eventually it will be one of the alternative routes for the river walk running from the George Washington Bridge to the Bayonne Bridge.

The Hackensack Water Company's brick tower* (4100 Park Ave.), dating from 1883, is all that remains of a large complex where the Tower Plaza Mall now sits. Modeled on the Palazzo Vecchio in Florence, the 175-foot tower formerly held the water company's offices in its base and a 150,000-gallon water tank at its top; it is listed in the navigation guides for river boats and blimps.

Marinas, condominiums, office buildings, hotels, an all-weather driving range, and restaurants have sprouted on the former freight yards and no-longer-active piers (when one of the first restaurants opened in May 1985, the International Longshoremen's Association picketed on the grounds that it had the right to control the waterfront). Ferry service to New York City was restored in 1986, and some 30,000 riders a day now take the ferry from Weehawken, Hoboken, or Jersey City. Several kinds of harbor cruises are available; not all of them run year-round (call 800-533-3779 for information).

Westfield Union 28,644

NJ 28, C 509

Westfield was founded in the 17th century—West Fields meant the western fields of Elizabethtown (now Elizabeth)—and remained primarily a farm community until the railroad came through in the 1860s. The Revolution intruded in 1777 when the British camped in and plundered Westfield, and again in the 1780s when James Morgan, an American sentry, killed the Reverend James Caldwell (also known as the fighting parson; see Elizabeth; Springfield). The circumstances of the murder are unclear, but Morgan was tried and condemned in the Presbyterian Church on Mountain Avenue. (The church now standing on the site dates from the 1860s.) He was hanged a few blocks from the church on Gallows Hill Road. The cemetery contains a substantial number of 18th-century tombstones (the date and nature of many of the graves have been color coded by the DAR).

At 614 Mountain Ave. is the Miller-Cory House* (908-232-1776), a living museum of early American farm life. With the help of an early-19th-century inventory, the house has been decorated to reflect life at the time it was built (c. 1740). On the grounds are a colonial herb garden, a kitchen garden, and a dye garden. Among the crafts demonstrated at the museum are open-hearth cooking, sheepshearing, candlemaking, and maple-sugaring; the museum is also involved in extensive educational programs. Open mid-September–mid-June, Sunday, 2–5 (in January and February the hours are 2–4), except on major holiday weekends. Groups by appointment other times. Admission charged. The Westfield Historical Society maintains a museum and archives on the second floor of the Westfield Town Hall (425 E. Broad St.; 908-789-4047). Open Tuesday and Wednesday, 10–12; other times by appointment.

Cartoonist Charles Addams was born here (at 522 Elm St.), and there is some feeling that the house at 314 Elm St. may have been the model for the Addams Family mansion. The Stoneleigh Park Historic District* includes buildings from 1904 to 1929, but there are also an unusual number of Revolutionary-era buildings. Westfield is a prosperous community with an attractive downtown. Among the interesting buildings downtown, note in particular the Spanish Revival fire headquarters* (405 North Ave.), and the railroad stations. Among the events that take place at the Westfield Armory (500 Rahway Ave.; 732-815-4875) is an annual juried exhibition of arts and crafts (800-834-9437). Westfield is also known for its professional symphony orchestra (908-232-9400), which performs a regular series at the Presbyterian Church.

Part of Echo Lake Park (*see* Mountainside) is in Westfield. Mindowaskin Park (E. Broad next to the municipal building) has ice-skating in the winter and concerts in the summer. Brightwood Park (Prospect St.) has nature trails and a pond.

West Long Branch Monmouth 8,258

NJ 71, C 32

Monmouth University (Cedar and Norwood aves.; 732-571-3400) in West Long Branch was founded in 1933 as Monmouth Junior College, one of six Depression-era colleges created in New Jersey with funds from the Federal Emergency Relief Administration. Today the university is situated on two former estates, and much of its 138-acre campus retains the formal landscaping of another era. Woodrow Wilson Hall* (1929), formerly Shadow Lawn, is a 128-room limestone mansion modeled on Versailles. This national historic landmark was built on the site of Woodrow Wilson's 1916 Summer White House, which burned; among the many features of this extraordinary building (Daddy Warbucks's mansion in the movie version of *Annie*) are a three-story great hall and a Venetian stained-glass skylight, believed to be the largest of its kind in the world. You are welcome to walk around the campus weekdays, 9–5; walking-tour brochures are available at the admissions office in Wilson Hall. The art galleries (the 800 Gallery in a former barn, the Rotary Icehouse Gallery in a former icehouse; 732-571-3428) feature some six to eight exhibits during the academic year; when exhibits are in place, they are open to the public, Monday–Thursday, 2:30–4. Performing arts series, featuring programs of music, theater, and dance, are presented at the Lauren K. Woods Theatre (732-571-3483), housed in the former carriage house of the Murry Guggenheim estate, and in the larger Pollak Theatre (732-571-3483). Garret A. Hobart, the only vice-president to come from New Jersey (*see* Paterson), once lived where the Guggenheims built their estate. Across Cedar Ave. from Wilson Hall and the theater is the Murry and Leonie Guggenheim Mansion* (1903), which contains the school's library.

The public library (95 Poplar Ave.; 732-222-5993) sponsors monthly art exhibits concentrating on living local artists and work of local interest. Open Monday–Thursday, 9:30–8:30, Friday, 9:30–5, Saturday, 9–1.

Directly south of West Long Branch (take Monmouth Ave., NJ 15) in the community of Oakhurst is the Township of Ocean Historical Museum (163 Monmouth Rd.; 732-531-2136). Housed in a room at the old Oakhurst school (1900), which now functions as the administration building for the Board of Education, the museum specializes in memorabilia related to the area, including vintage clothing, old toys, and photographs. The museum runs educational programs for children and sponsors centenary plaques for local houses. Open Tuesday, 1–4. Future plans include moving the museum to its own site, in an 18th-century building that had been owned and occupied by the same family for over 225 years.

West Orange Essex 44,943

I 280, NJ 10, C 508, 577

In 1887 Thomas Alva Edison settled in West Orange, buying a house in Llewellyn Park* and setting up his laboratory*—an invention factory, he called it—on Main Street. From 1887 until his death in 1931 Edison developed a steady stream of inventions; his years in West Orange yielded over half the 1,093 patents he received in his lifetime (more than any other individual). New ideas or improvements stemming from the West Orange years involved the phonograph, motion pictures, storage batteries, poured concrete, the fluoroscope, and the extraction of latex from goldenrod. The laboratory itself was an invention, the prototype of today's industrial research lab, where large groups work simultaneously on assigned projects. The laboratory complex included a physics laboratory, a chemistry laboratory, and a metallurgical laboratory, and since Edison built his own machines to run his experiments, a machine shop and a pattern shop. The labs were surrounded by factory buildings; at one time T. A. Edison Incorporated employed some 6,000–7,000 people in manufacturing operations here, in nearby Bloomfield, and in Warren and Sussex counties. Although only one of the factory buildings still stands (the reinforcement of these concrete structures was so much stronger than government regulations require that dynamite was used to demolish them), most of the laboratory buildings remain and are now a national historic landmark (Main St. between Alden St. and Lakeside Ave.; 973-736-0550). The labs, which attracted some 50,000 visitors a year, closed in 2003 for extensive restoration and are expected to reopen late in 2005.

The visitor center, also temporarily closed, was in the former powerhouse, and had on display samples of most of Edison's major inventions. As late as 1984, there was a tour guide who had worked in the labs when Edison was alive, but even without such a direct human link, the physical arrangement of the labs conveys a strong sense of what this organization, so influential in shaping American life today, was like in its heyday.

Llewellyn Park (1857), where Edison bought his home, was one of the country's earliest planned residential developments and the site of the first large-scale naturalization of crocus, narcissus, and jonquils. When Edison moved there, the houses were all large, as was their acreage (Edison's house has 22 rooms and was then on 11 acres). Only those who lived there or their authorized visitors could enter Llewellyn Park, and that is still true today. Edison, who apparently did not like fussing about such things, bought Glenmont (Park Way and Glen Ave., less than half a mile west of Main St.) completely furnished and ready to move into from an executive who had embezzled money to pay for the house. Glenmont is also temporarily closed for renovation.

Part of the South Mountain Reservation (973-268-3500), a 2,000-acre county park designed by the Olmsted firm, which West Orange shares with South Orange, Maplewood, and Millburn, is at the southwestern edge of West Orange (take Main St. south to Northfield and head west on Northfield). At this end of the park is Turtle Back Zoo (560 Northfield Ave.; 973-731-5800), which has some 300 animals representing 100 species. The zoo, which has recently completed extensive renovations and added exhibits, engages in outreach and other educational programs and has been involved in a program to reintroduce endangered species to the wild; it also features a petting zoo and arranges birthday parties for children. Popular attractions at the zoo include pony rides and rides on a miniature antique train (these are not offered in bad weather). Open daily, 10–4, in summer; winter hours are usually more limited; call for the schedule. Also at this end of the park is the South Mountain Arena (973-731-3828), two ice-skating rinks that together provide 12 time slots open to the public each week from Labor Day to mid-June. Mid-June to mid-August, the arena is open Tuesday and Thursday; call for the schedule.

South Mountain Reservation is on a ridge that protected Washington's army when it was quartered at Morristown in the winter of 1779–80, for from the ridge the soldiers could keep an eye on the British troops on Staten Island. The reservation contains many miles of carriage roads and paths suitable for jogging, walking, hiking, horseback riding, and cross-country skiing. Picnicking and fishing (with a permit) are also possible.

At the northern end of West Orange is another county park, Eagle Rock Reservation (Eagle Rock Ave.; take Prospect, C 577, north out of West Orange; 973-268-3500), also designed by the Olmsted firm, which West Orange shares with Verona and Montclair. Its overlook is considered one of the state's most spectacular spots for viewing the New York City skyline. Casino in the Park, an early-20th-century Italian Renaissance structure next to the overlook, has been converted into a restaurant. Eagle Rock also has picnic tables and fireplaces, bridle and foot trails, and a wildlife reservation.

The Francis A. Byrne golf course (Pleasant Valley Way and Mount Pleasant Ave.; 973-736-2306) is also a county facility.

South of Eagle Rock is the Oskar Schindler Performing Arts Center (4 Boland Dr. between I 280 and Eagle Rock Ave.; 973-669-7385), an amphitheater on land donated to the town by a New Jersey developer whose life was saved by Schindler and who named a street after Schindler in every development he built. From June through September the center presents concerts in a variety of genres, films, and plays and is actively involved in promoting the arts, particularly for young people.

At Seton Hall University in South Orange (400 S. Orange Ave.; 800-843-4255), the state's third largest university and the first diocesan college in the United States (founded in 1856, it moved here in 1860), exhibits at the Walsh Library Gallery (973-275-2033) are open to the public weekdays, 10–4:30, and by appointment. For information on theater programs, call 973-761-9098; for information on public lectures, 973-761-9739. Seton Hall's preparatory school, whose original campus is now the site of St. Elizabeth's in Convent Station (*see* Madison), is housed in the former West Orange high school (Northfield Ave.). The university's art and music center is in the former Eugene Kelley carriage house* (1887). There are many striking houses and public buildings in this hilly town, said to be the first in the country to issue its own credit card. Note the late-19th-century South Orange Village Hall* (S. Orange Ave. and Scotland Rd.), the Mountain railroad station* from 1915 (449 Vose Ave.), and the South Orange station* built a year later (19 Sloan St.).

West Windsor Township   Mercer 21,907

US 1, C 526, 533, 535, 571

Like many other New Jersey townships, West Windsor is made up of several small communities that were formerly separated by farmland. Parts of West Windsor were settled in the 18th century (it celebrated the bicentennial of its incorporation in 1997), and it remained an agricultural community until fairly recently. Between the 1980 and 2000 censuses, however, its population more than doubled. Nevertheless, some 38 percent of the land remains undeveloped, including a 3,000-acre protective greenbelt, and the township has won awards for its zeal in planting trees and for its planning—linking development to highway construction. The growth in commercial activity has been equally striking; US 1 between New Brunswick and Trenton has seen a rapid expansion of corporate centers, corporate headquarters, other forms of office space, and shopping malls, and a fair amount of this expansion falls within West Windsor. At one of these office parks, 2½ acres are devoted to sweet corn, harvested each summer by those who work there.

The earliest mill in the area was at Grovers Mill, a community made famous in 1938 by Orson Welles's radio adaptation of H. G. Wells's *War of the Worlds*, in which Martians landed on Grovers Mill Pond (Clarksville and Cranbury rds.), now part of Van Nest Park. The broadcast was so realistic that telephone switchboards all over the country were jammed by frightened callers. Other older communities that retain some coherence and charm include Dutch Neck and Edinburg. Another older community, Penns Neck, at least retains its Baptist Church★ (US 1 and Washington Rd.), built in 1812 and altered in the 1870s, although noise, vibrations, and CB radios from the truck traffic can intrude on the services and may threaten the structure.

The West Windsor Historical Society is restoring the Zaitz-Schenck property on Southfield Rd. (between C 571 and Village Rd. across from the golf course; 609-452-8598), with its farmhouse (c. 1790, c. 1830), barn, and one-room schoolhouse. The house, which serves as the society's headquarters, also contains the historical society's library and a museum of local history. Open the 2d Sunday of the month, January–June and September–November, 1–4, and by appointment.

Mercer County Park (access from Hughes Dr. and Edinburg and S. Post rds.; 609-989-6530) occupies 2,500 acres in the southwestern corner of the township. One hundred of these acres are devoted to playing fields, but the park also has a 300-acre boating lake (swimming and gasoline motors are not permitted), a five-mile bicycle path, two picnic groves, an ice-skating rink (609-371-1669), and tennis courts (609-448-8007). There are unpaved trails, and you are welcome to walk north of the lake and Assunpink Creek, although here you must be careful to respect the private homes. The brick house on the hill near the marina is the mid-18th-century John Rogers House* (S. Post Rd.), a rare example of a Flemish-bond house of the type seen more frequently in South Jersey, which is unfortunately being left to deteriorate. The park is open year-round, the marina (609-448-4004, off-season 609-989-6538) May–September (weather permitting), the tennis courts April–October, and the ice-skating rink mid-November–mid-March. Tours with the naturalist by appointment (609-989-6532).

The Trenton Kennel Club (609-448-6247) holds its annual show in the park on the 18th Sunday of the year. Running almost every year since 1926 (the club itself was first formed in 1911), the show is probably the biggest one on the East Coast—close to 4,000 dogs are entered each year—and one of the most important for competitors. When their dogs are not being judged, handlers and owners are usually happy to answer spectators' questions.

Adjacent to the park is Mercer County Community College. Art exhibits can be seen at the gallery on the second floor of the Communications Center (609-586-4800, ext. 3589). Open Monday, 10 A.M.–12:40 P.M., Tuesday, 11–5:30, Wednesday, 11–3, Thursday, 11–5:30 and 7–9 P.M., Friday, 11–1, and Saturday, 1–3. To see a really striking building, drive east on C 571 to the former PA Consulting Services headquarters (just east of the intersection with C 535, in East Windsor Township). This architectural tour de force has an exposed structure, a roof suspended from cables with the heating and ventilating equipment hung from its center, and translucent walls that glow at night like a lantern.

North of Grovers Mill (take Millstone Rd., which becomes Grovers Mill Rd., jog right, take the first left, and continue on Edgemere Rd. to Plainsboro Rd.), in Middlesex County, is the township of Plainsboro. Plainsboro was once part of both South Brunswick and Cranbury, but dissatisfaction with the schools led it to break away and become an independent township in 1919. One of its first acts was to build a school. At one time the dairy company Walker-Gordon was the largest employer in town, and the Rotolactor, its rotating milking machine that could milk 1,400 cows in less than six hours, was a popular tourist attraction. Elsie the Cow was also a Plainsboro resident.

In the Wicoff House (641 Plainsboro Rd.; 609-799-9049), which dates from the 1880s, the Plainsboro Historical Society has installed a museum of local history. Included are exhibits featuring artifacts and memorabilia from Native Americans, local farms and families, Walker-Gordon (including Elsie), and the Princeton University Forrestal campus (see Princeton). Some of the exhibits change frequently, as do the contents of the permanent exhibits. Open 1st and 3d Sundays, 2–4:30. Groups and other times by appointment. While in town, note also Bethel Cemetery (Plainsboro Rd. just west of the train tracks), owned by the historical society. The cemetery sits on land donated to the church in 1812. The building was demolished in the 1930s, but the society has erected a memorial marker showing what the church looked like.

Some 1,000 acres rescued from threats of development now form the New Jersey Audubon Society's Plainsboro Preserve (80 Scotts Corner Rd.; 609-897-9400). The preserve's environmental education center contains many interactive and hands-on displays, and the society runs a variety of natural history programs and workshops, including day camps and guided hikes. The preserve has 5 miles of hiking trails, many with interpretive signs, and the 50-acre McCormack Lake, a remnant from a quarry operation. The preserve is home to more than 150 species of birds and more than 10 species of rare or endangered plants. Building open Tuesday–Saturday, 9–5, Sunday, 12–5; trails open daily as posted (usually sunrise to sunset).

Whippany Morris [Hanover Township]

NJ 10, C 511

Once known as a center of paper manufacturing, Whippany is also the site where the concept of the cellular car phone was developed (in the Bell Systems laboratory here in the 1940s). In the depot yard of the old Morristown & Erie Railway is the Whippany Railway Museum (1 Railroad Plaza, at the intersection of NJ 10 W. and Whippany Rd.; 973-887-8177). On display are rolling stock and locomotives, including Steam Locomotive No. 4039,* the Official Steam Locomotive of Morris County. In the former freight house (c. 1904) are toy trains, scale models, and railroad memorabilia. Open April–October, Sunday, 12–4. Admission fee. The museum also offers special holiday excursions to Morristown or Roseland and back on a train pulled by one of the Morristown & Erie diesels.

Among the buildings of interest on Whippany Rd. note particularly Our Lady of Mercy Chapel* (1853; 100 Whippany Rd.) and the green Queen Anne part of the Crestwood Nursing Home (Whippany Rd. and Eden La.). There are interesting buildings on NJ 10 as well, but the traffic moves so quickly it is hard to see them.

The Wildwoods Cape May 5,436 (Wildwood)
4,935 (North Wildwood) 3,980 (Wildwood Crest)

NJ 47, C 621

The Wildwoods—Wildwood, North Wildwood, and Wildwood Crest—share some five miles of Atlantic beach. These areas were frequented by Native Americans in the summer and, before they were developed as resorts, were used by mainland farmers to graze their animals, creating a problem with feral animals that continued into the 20th century. Fishermen settled here in the 1870s, about the time the lighthouse was built (*see* below), and commercial fisherman are still at work in the region. Known both as family resorts and for their nightlife, the communities today are basically summer resorts. (The population of the three soars from its wintertime total of about 14,350 to as high as 125,000 on a summer weekday, to say nothing of 250,000 on the weekends, and in North Wildwood the tops of the parking meters are removed from the municipal lot in the fall.) In Wildwood there are several amusement piers (the tallest roller coaster at the shore is on one of them; Wildwood also boasts the largest Ferris wheel at the shore) and some 10,000 hotel and motel rooms.

The George Boyer Historical Museum (3907 Pacific Ave.; 609-523-0277), run by the Wildwood Historical Society, features local history and memorabilia, and includes the National Marbles Hall of Fame. Open May–October, Monday–Saturday, 9:30–2, November–April, Thursday–Saturday, 9:30–2; groups by appointment. The national marbles tournament, which dates to 1923 and claims to be the oldest regularly occurring tournament for children, has been held in Wildwood for over 40 years. Other annual events include water-slide and kite-flying championships and a Labor Day Craft Show. For information on special events, call 800-992-9732 or 609-729-9000.

In North Wildwood, originally a fishing village known as Anglesea, the Hereford Inlet Lighthouse* (1st St. and Central Ave.; 609-522-4520) has been undergoing a careful restoration. Built in 1874 and designed by the architect who designed the Library of Congress, the lighthouse, unusual in that it looks more like a house than a tower, continued in use until 1964. A light was reinstalled in the 1980s, and the lighthouse again functions as a navigation aid. In the house, which is designed as a living-history museum, you can see a fourth-order Fresnel lens like the one that was originally used. The lighthouse's prize-winning gardens were established in the 1980s. Various special events, such as arts and crafts shows in the summer and an annual tree lighting ceremony in December, take place at the house. Plans are afoot to combine the lighthouse with the adjoining former Coast Guard property and establish the Anglesea Historic Maritime Village. Open for tours daily, mid-May–mid-October, 9–5; Wednesday–Sunday, mid-October–mid-May, 10–4; groups by appointment. Admission charged.

The Wildwood information center (609-522-1407) is on the boardwalk at Shellinger Ave., the North Wildwood center (609-729-8686) at 22d St. and the boardwalk, and the Wildwood Crest center (609-522-0221) at Rambler Rd. and the beach. All three centers are open daily during the summer. North Wildwood has a second center at 5th St. and New Jersey Ave. (609-522-7722) that is open limited hours in the winter.

The Wildwood Crest welcome center is also the new home of the Doo Wop Preservation League (609-729-4000), an organization that has been working to save the 1950s and 1960s Doo Wop architecture for which the

Wildwoods have become known. (There are hopes that a Doo Wop Historic District, running roughly from Farragut Rd. to Cresse Ave. and Atlantic Ave. to the beach will be recognized in 2005.) The welcome center's Doo Wop roof comes from the former Surfside Restaurant (a 1960s establishment demolished in 2002), and the museum has on display neon signs, lamps, and furniture designed by Herman Miller and Ray and Charles Eames. You can pick up brochures for self-guided tours here, and the league, in conjunction with the Mid-Atlantic Center for the Arts, offers Doo Wop trolley tours in the summer. Call for the hours.

West of Wildwood (in Erma, at the Cape May County Airport) is the Naval Air Station Wildwood (500 Forrestal Rd.; 609-886-8787). Established in the 1940s, it was originally known as Naval Air Station Rio Grande (the airport property extends to the town of Rio Grande) but troubles with mail and cable delivery (apparently this Rio Grande was confused with the better-known one to the south) led to the change of name. Here in Hangar No. 1* you can see an impressive collection of aircraft, aircraft engines, and various military memorabilia, as well as a Vietnam exhibit. Open 9–5 daily July and August; 9–4 daily March–June, September–December; weekdays only 9–4, January–February. Group tours by appointment. Admission charge.

North of Wildwood, in Whitesboro (Middle Township) is the Whitesboro Historical Foundation museum (2215 US 9 S.; 609-465-3960). Whitesboro was founded at the turn of the 20th century by Reconstruction-era congressman George White as a haven for free blacks. Installed in one of the oldest houses in the town (1903) the museum features artifacts, archives, and memorabilia from local families. The museum also engages in a variety of outreach programs. Open by appointment, although the hope is that regular hours may eventually be established.

Winfield Union 1,514

GARDEN STATE PKWY EXIT 136

Union County's smallest municipality in both population and size (0.2 sq. mi.), Winfield began as Winfield Park, a community built by the federal government in 1941 to house shipyard defense workers and their families. Enclosed within a bend of the Rahway River, Winfield, which was named for General Winfield Scott, purchased itself from the government after the war and paid off its mortgage in 1984. Somewhat similar to a cooperative apartment, the town is actually a mutual housing corporation, with the residents as shareholders. The street names—Gulfstream, Seafoam, Wavecrest—reflect its nautical origins, and the houses, despite the additions of gabled roofs, decks, porches, and extra rooms, still betray their barrackslike origins as defense workers' housing.

Woodbine Cape May 2,716

C 550, 557

The largest of South Jersey's 15 pathbreaking 19th-century Jewish settlements, Woodbine dates from the 1890s, when several hundred Russian refugees established over 50 30-acre farms here. With 2,500 residents by the turn of the century, Woodbine incorporated in 1903 and was the first community in the country in which Jews filled all the official posts. The Baron De Hirsch Agricultural School, which opened in Woodbine in 1894, is said to be the country's first agricultural technical high school. Although little of Woodbine's past remains, one of the early buildings, the former Woodbine Brotherhood Synagogue* (610 Washington Ave.), built in 1896, now houses the Sam Azeez Museum of Woodbine Heritage (609-861-5355). Included in the museum's displays are documents, artifacts, and photographs, going back to the founding of Woodbine and continuing to the present. Open June–September, Wednesday–Friday and Sunday, 10–4; October–May, Wednesday and Sunday, 10–4. Groups and other times by appointment.

North of Woodbine, on Webster Ave. (C 550), is the largest segment of Belleplain State Forest (609-861-2404), over 22,000 noncontiguous acres of swamp hardwood forest. The Civilian Conservation Corps was active here from 1937 to 1941, and in addition to doing a great deal of tree work, the corps built roads, bridges, maintenance buildings, dams, and the nature center, mostly by hand. It also created (by hand) Lake Nummy (named for the last Native American chief to rule in this part of the state) out of an abandoned cranberry bog. There are lifeguards at the lake in the summer, a self-guided nature trail, and a fitness trail. The forest is also open for hikers, campers (including tent and trailer sites, group sites, lean-tos, and a cabin), horseback riders, cross-country skiers, and hunters. Trail maps are available from the park warden. At the interpretive center (609-861-1354), housed in the former CCC office, you can find information and displays relating to the Pinelands, native plants and animals (including a few live animals), and maritime activities. Open daily, 8:30–4, Memorial Day–Labor Day, Thursday–Monday the rest of the year.

West of Woodbine (and another section of Belleplain) is the Dennis Creek Wildlife Management Area, 6,100 acres of salt marsh open for hiking, boating, bird-watching, fishing, crabbing, and hunting. Shingles made from Dennis Creek cedar windfalls (healthy trees knocked over by the wind) are apparently extremely durable, and shingles from Dennis Creek cedars were used on the roof of Independence Hall in Philadelphia. Although some people are still mining cedar from the swamps in this area, the industry is no longer as important as it once was. This is also a good place to see eagles in winter, and sometimes otters in spring, but it can be ferociously buggy in summer. It is also a good spot to observe migrating shorebirds.

South of Woodbine in Dennisville is the Dennis Township Museum and History Center (Petersburg Rd. and Hall Ave; 609-861-1899, 609-861-2413). Housed in a school built in 1874 (the second floor was destroyed in a fire), the museum contains artifacts, memorabilia, and oral histories relating to the area's past, including items having to do with the cedar-mining and shipbuilding industries. Also on display are carved ducks, songbirds, and shorebirds (serving as guides for hunters was another local industry). Open Saturday, 10–2; open as well when there are special events in the area, and by appointment.

Woodbridge Middlesex 97,203

I 95, US 1, 9, NJ TNPK EXIT 11, NJ 27, 35, C 514

The oldest original township in the state (settled in 1664, chartered in 1669), Woodbridge remained relatively small until the Garden State Parkway was built in the 1950s (its population doubled between 1950 and 1960). The colony's first gristmill was erected in 1670 by Jonathan Dunham, and his house, built in 1670 from bricks brought from Holland as ballast, is now the rectory of Trinity Church (*see* below).

Woodbridge was settled largely by New Englanders, most of them from Newbury, Massachusetts (among them Captain John Pike, an ancestor of Zebulon Pike). According to one theory, the town was named for the assistant pastor of the Newbury church, one John Woodbridge, but he spent very little time in Woodbridge; others say it was named for a town in Suffolk, England. The settlers built their first sawmill in 1682 and their first tavern in 1683. In 1730, they drank the first cup of tea in the colonies. In 1751, the first permanent printing press and publishing house in New Jersey were established by James Parker (1714–70). Parker, who had served as an apprentice to Benjamin Franklin and William Bradford and was the official printer for New Jersey until his death, in 1758 printed the first magazine in today's meaning of the word: the *New American Magazine* contained articles on current events and history, essays, and short stories. (An earlier attempt at a periodical, the *Independent Reflector*, printed in 1752, was unsuccessful.) Joseph Bloomfield is the only Woodbridge-born citizen to become governor of New Jersey. Much later, in 1877, at a graduation ceremony at the Union Town school, Thomas Alva Edison demonstrated the telephone. And, later still, in 1928, Woodbridge became the first community in the United States to have a cloverleaf highway intersection (at US 1 and NJ 35).

Although the first Episcopal service in Woodbridge took place in 1698 and the first building dates from 1713, today's Trinity Church★ (650 Rahway Ave.) dates from 1861. Contrary to popular belief, Richard Upjohn did not design the building, although he did draw up some plans for it and the church possesses one of his renderings. The church owns many 18th-century artifacts, including its royal charter, a silver chalice, and a first edition of the American Book of Common Prayer. The cemetery dates from 1714, although the earliest existing stone is from 1750. The rectory, Woodbridge's oldest remaining documented building, was considerably altered some 300 years after Dunham built it, but you can still see its original Flemish-bond brickwork, and the adze-hewn beams remain.

In Barron Library* (1877) Woodbridge had one of the first free public libraries in the state. This small but wonderfully detailed Romanesque Revival stone structure, designed by J. Cleveland Cady (who designed the old Metropolitan Opera House), now houses the Barron Arts Center (582 Rahway Ave.; 732-634-0413). The building has a massive clock tower,

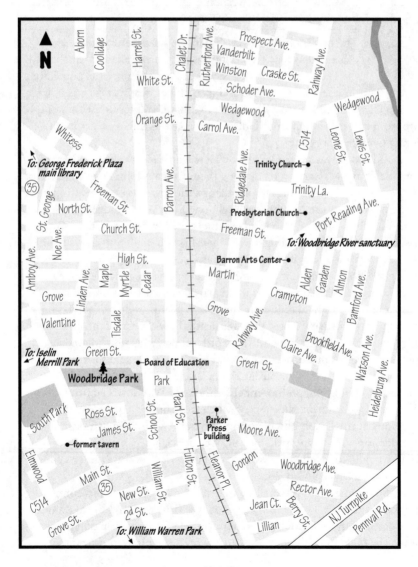

ornamented cornices, a Delft-tiled fireplace, and an elaborately foliated foyer. The center's exhibits range from the fine arts to local history to theater design and change roughly once a month. The center also presents monthly poetry readings, a train show during the winter holiday season, and occasional concerts and lectures. Open weekdays, 11–4; Sunday 2–4; large groups by appointment.

The Parker Press building (Rahway Ave. and Parker Press Park; 732-596-4048) is a reconstruction of Parker's shop, which was burned by the British in 1777. Inside are two old iron-frame letterpresses and some type. There are still hopes that these can be restored to working condition and the building made available for tours. Parker Press Park is the site of a variety of special town events, from Easter egg hunts to Civil War encampments to Halloween hayrides.

Although there is little left of Woodbridge's earliest history, you will still feel a sense of community in the center of town, and Woodbridge has several times been designated an all-American or typical American city. Other buildings you might want to look at include the tavern George Washington slept in the night before he was sworn in as president. Originally located where the Knights of Columbus building now stands (Amboy Ave. and Main St.), it has been moved back to 142 James Street. Converted to apartments (during a recent reenactment "Washington" had tea with the residents), the building may also have served as a post office (Woodbridge was one of the country's original 10 post office sites). The First Presbyterian Church (600 Rahway Ave.; 732-634-1024), known locally as the White Church, has been remodeled and covered with white brick so that you would be hard pressed to guess its age (it was built in 1803). The interior, however, did not suffer the same fate, and in the cemetery is a stone dating to 1692. Tours by appointment. Note also the main library (George Frederick Plaza; 732-634-4450), which has a display case with changing exhibits near the children's section, and the Board of Education adminis-tration building (School St.), an 1876 school.

West on Green St. into Iselin will take you to Merrill Park (Middlesex-Essex Tnpk; 732-745-3900), a 179-acre county park with walking and nature trails, playing fields, tennis courts, fishing and picnic areas, and a small zoo that features farm animals. At the library in Iselin is the Garden for the Blind and Physically Handicapped (1081 Green St.; 732-283-1200). The garden is open daily, dawn–dusk, with the peak bloom in spring and summer.

South of the center of town (take NJ 35) is William Warren Park (Florida Grove Rd.; 732-745-3900). Much of this 126-acre county park, which has athletic fields, picnic groves, woods with foot trails, and summer concerts, is built on reclaimed clay pits. In the 19th century, clay mining and brick manufacturing were Woodbridge's principal industries; the clay from these pits was used to make firebricks.

Northeast of William Warren Park is the township's 40-acre Woodbridge River sanctuary (north side of Port Reading Rd. and east of Rahway Ave.).

Woodbridge won an award for cleaning up this wetlands area, which now provides a home for wildlife. Open for hiking and bird-watching.

Woodbury   Gloucester   10,397

NJ 45, C 534, 551, 553

Founded in 1683 by Henry Wood, a Quaker from Bury in England, Woodbury has been the seat of Gloucester County since 1785. Located near the confluence of the Delaware River and Woodbury Creek (originally called Pescozackasing, a Lenape word possibly meaning "place of black burrs"), it was once something of a manufacturing center, with lively traffic in patent medicines, glass, and other products. Today's residents tend to work in county offices, the hospital, at the nearby ExxonMobil facility, and in Philadelphia and Camden. Broad St., the major north-south thoroughfare and once part of the old Kings Highway from Burlington to Cape May, is, as so often happens in South Jersey, appropriately named. There is an interesting mix of buildings in Woodbury, many preserved in their original 18th- and 19th-century form, others adapted, often gracefully, to contemporary uses, and large portions of the town have been placed on the state register of historic places.

Among the early buildings is the Friends Meeting House* (120 N. Broad St.), the west side of which dates from 1715 and the east from 1785. The building was used as a barracks and hospital for British troops after the nearby Battle of Red Bank in 1777 (*see* National Park). Furthermore, in Woodbury the Hicksite–Orthodox split did not produce two meetinghouses, as happened in so many other Quaker communities; instead, the two groups continued to use the same meetinghouse, simply dividing it with movable partitions. From 1827 to 1927 they shared the building, and in 1954 the two groups rejoined. Another Quaker building from the 18th century now forms the easternmost part of the city hall (33 Delaware St.); this is the Deptford Free School building, dating from 1744 (the second story was added in 1820).

In 1793, the country's first airborne trip ended in Woodbury, when Jean-Pierre Blanchard, who had taken off in Philadelphia, landed his hot-air balloon in a farmer's field a few miles northwest of town (near Clements Bridge off NJ 42 near the Deptford Mall). In that same year the Gloucester County Abolition Society was formed, one of the first in the nation.

The county courthouse (Delaware and Broad sts.) is a splendid stone building, completed in 1887. Its white-columned neighbor dates from 1926, as does the Masonic Temple across the street.

At 58 N. Broad St. is the Hunter-Lawrence-Jessup House* (c. 1765; 856-848-8531). The *Hunter* refers to Reverend Andrew Hunter, a chaplain in the Revolutionary army and a participant in the Greenwich tea party (*see* Greenwich), who was head of the town's distinguished Woodbury

Academy (founded 1791); the *Lawrence* to John Lawrence, older brother of James Lawrence, the naval hero (*see* Burlington), who lived with his brother while attending the Woodbury Academy; and the *Jessup* to John S. Jessup, a late-19th-century judge and civic leader. The house is maintained as a museum by the Gloucester County Historical Society, which bought it in 1924. The society's collections include period furniture, guns, toys, and other artifacts. Among the society's holdings are a walnut desk and bookcase that had belonged to Elizabeth Haddon (*see* Haddonfield) and an audience chair (No. 425) that was in Ford's Theater the night Lincoln was shot. The society has reconstructed in its basement the fireplace from Hugg's Tavern near Gloucester where Betsy Griscom, known as the designer of the American flag, and John Ross were married. A copy of their license hangs over the mantel (the original is in the society's library). The society has preserved one wall from the Cooper house, used by Cornwallis as his headquarters (bayonet marks made by British soldiers trying to force a door are still visible). Exhibits change four times a year. Open Monday, Wednesday, and Friday, 1–4; the last Saturday and Sunday of the month, 2–5; groups by appointment. Admission fee. Around the corner from the museum is the historical society's library (17 Hunter St.; 856-845-4771). Open weekdays, 1–4; Tuesday and Friday evening, 6–9:30; first Saturday of the month, 1–4, last Sunday of the month, 2–5. Donation requested.

Opposite the meetinghouse is the former Bull's Head Inn (111 N. Broad St.), possibly built c. 1720 (the earliest records date to 1737), supposedly from bricks left over from the construction of the meetinghouse. This building has functioned continuously as a tavern and restaurant for over 250 years.

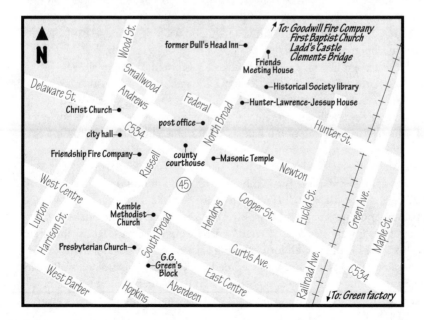

At the corner of S. Broad and W. Centre sts. is the Presbyterian Church (1833). The congregation was founded in 1721, and this building replaces an earlier one, supposedly abandoned because it had been used by British troops in 1777 and was thought to be haunted. This odd-shaped building does not look its age. In 1906 the church was connected to its stone chapel (1895), and the entire structure was faced in stone. Then, in 1965, the stone was removed, new bricks were used, and the front was extended. At that time a cupola was built to house the church's 12th-century bell, cast in Bordeaux and brought to Woodbury in the late 18th century from Santo Domingo, when the French Revolution caused upheaval on the islands.

Next door to the city hall is the Friendship Fire Company museum (29 Delaware St.; 856-845-0066), a one-room museum attached to a working firehouse. The company was founded in 1793, though its present building dates from 1898. The museum's collection of artifacts tracks the company's history from its founding to the present and includes the company's original 1799 hand pumper and its 1911 steam fire engine. Open weekdays 7 A.M.–9 P.M.; weekends by appointment. Groups are encouraged to call ahead.

Another fire company, the Goodwill Fire Company (N. Broad St.), operates out of a firehouse (1889) with a round window and cupola. Other buildings of interest include the post office (1928), the First Baptist Church (1857), and the Kemble Methodist Church (1888), all on Broad Street. Also on Broad St., between Centre and Hopkins sts., are the remains of the splendid red brick G. G. Green's Block* (1880); there are plans afoot to convert it into some form of entertainment center. Green was perhaps Woodbury's most successful entrepreneur, making a fortune from patent medicines and associated businesses. His former factory (122 Green Ave.), now known as Woodbury Mews, has been converted into a senior citizen complex. On the north side of Delaware is Christ Episcopal Church (1856), with two hitching posts still in place. Brochures for a self-guided walking tour are available in city hall (open weekdays, 9–4).

About one mile north of town (take NJ 45 north to Colonial Ave. and turn left, or west) is Ladd's Castle (1337 Lafayette Ave.), also known as Candor Hall. Built in 1688 by John Ladd, who is said to have surveyed Philadelphia for William Penn and to have been thrown out of the Society of Friends for marrying non-Quaker couples, it is now a private home.

A few miles southwest of Woodbury in Blackwood Terrace (Deptford Township) is the Old Pine Farm Natural Lands Trust (Rankin Ave.; 856-227-5723). Here along Big Timber Creek you will find trails going through 30 acres of varied terrain, including grassland savanna, hardwoods uplands, and thick maple swamp. Birds are abundant, and the tidal creek is home to many species of fish. A trail goes through the trust lands, and there is also a dock on the creek for launching a canoe or kayak. The trust generally arranges one or two scheduled walks a year, and guided walks can be arranged for groups by appointment. Timber Creek Park, a township park, lies to the east of the trust lands and features an undeveloped nature trail that goes to the tidal estuary of the creek. This is also a good spot for bird-watchers. The trust and park lands are open dawn–dusk.

Woodstown   Salem 3,136

US 40, NJ 45

A Quaker settlement dating back to the early 1700s, Woodstown retains many of its old buildings, and a string of 18th-century structures can be found along Main and Marlton streets. There are also many striking Victorian buildings, both domestic and commercial. Among the earlier buildings is the Joseph Shinn house* (68 N. Main St.); its central section was built in 1742, and its southern section may have been a 17th-century Native American trading post moved from another location. The Woodstown Friends meetinghouse is also on N. Main, as is the Samuel Dickeson house (42 N. Main; 856-769-4588), the home of the Pilesgrove-Woodstown Historical Society. The house dates to 1749; in it the society runs a museum that concentrates on genealogy and items of local history, such as marl equipment and grandfather clocks manufactured in the area. Open Saturday, 10–1. Behind the museum is the Eldridges Hill School, a one-room schoolhouse dating to 1840 that was moved in from Pilesgrove Township. The schoolhouse is furnished as a mid-19th-century schoolhouse would have been. Tours by appointment. The society also sponsors a house tour the first Friday in December.

Roughly two miles west of Woodstown, just west of Sharptown (a stop on the Underground Railroad) is the Cowtown Rodeo (US 40; 856-769-3200), which has been in existence since 1929 and run continuously since the mid-1950s. An outgrowth of the local livestock auctions, it is the oldest weekly rodeo in the United States and is run by a family that has lived within a few miles of Sharptown for 11 generations. It is sanctioned by the Professional Cowboys Association and draws riders from all over the country. Open Memorial Day–September, Saturday, 7:30 P.M. Admission charged. The auctions, which take place Tuesday at noon, are also open to the public, as is the year-round farmers' market, Tuesday and Saturday, 8–4.

South of Woodstown (take S. Main south to Eastlake Rd. and turn right) is Joy Farm (87 Eastlake Rd.; 856-769-1526). In the early 20th century there was a chicken farm on this property (its owner patented a chicken waterer). It is now a fiber farm dedicated to preserving the Jacob sheep, an unimproved breed that is thought to descend from the sheep mentioned in Genesis. Spinning lessons are offered at the farm, which also raises white and colored angora goats. A sheep and yarn festival takes place at the Salem County Fairgrounds (US 40 across the road and just west of the rodeo) the fourth weekend in September. Call Joy Farm for information.

Roughly two miles northeast of Woodstown in Pilesgrove Township (take Main St., the Old Kings Hwy, to the intersection with Woodstown-

Auburn Rd.) is the Seven Stars Tavern,* now a private home. The earliest portion dates to 1762, and the tavern may well be one of the oldest drive-ins in the country: a window off the taproom was set up so that riders could have their drinks without dismounting. In the 19th century the building was used as a farmhouse.

Wyckoff Bergen 16,508

NJ 208, C 502

Bergen County's James A. McFaul Wildlife Center (Crescent Ave. south of C 502; 201-891-5571) is in Wyckoff. This 81-acre wildlife sanctuary has outdoor displays of native mammals and birds, a self-guided nature trail, an ornamental grass garden, an herb garden, a butterfly and hummingbird garden, and an old-fashioned-roses garden. Inside the exhibit hall are live native animals, natural history displays (including a demonstration beehive with a glass viewing panel), an observatory overlooking the pond, and a changing art exhibit. The center sponsors nature education programs for schools and other groups. The building is open weekdays, 8–4:45; weekends and holidays (except Thanksgiving, Christmas, and New Year's Day), 1–4:45. The park is open dawn–dusk. Groups by appointment.

Wyckoff was originally a Dutch settlement, and some of the early Dutch stone houses remain (try Wyckoff and Franklin aves.). One of these, the Van Voorhees–Quackenbush–Zabriskie House* (421 Franklin Ave.; 201-445-9188), is now a house museum. Started in the mid-18th century (the larger section dates from 1824), the house was occupied almost entirely by direct descendants of the original builder until 1973, when it was given to the township. Its furnishings, which reflect the Dutch colonial heritage, are period pieces collected by the last inhabitant. Open Friday, 9–3, when the schools are in session, and for an annual December open house. The hours can change, so it is best to call ahead; groups and other times by appointment. Admission charge for the open house. Note also the Wyckoff Reformed Church* (580 Wyckoff Ave.), which dates from 1806.

The Gardens of Wyckoff (Crescent Ave. near Wyckoff Ave.), a 13-acre passive park that includes flower gardens, a pond, a brook, and markers that identify the plants, is open dawn–dusk spring–fall.

The New Jersey Turnpike Tour

Opened in November 1951, the New Jersey Turnpike is the most heavily traveled toll road in the United States in terms of number of vehicles per roadway mile. In 2003 an average of over 16 million vehicles per roadway mile traveled on the turnpike. The average trip length per vehicle was around 23 miles; on holiday periods and on weekends, that number is higher. On holiday weekends, traffic can reach over 700,000 cars a day. Traditionally, the Wednesday before Thanksgiving has been the heaviest single day, but in 2003, that distinction went to 28 August, when 805,767 paying vehicles traveled on the turnpike.

The turnpike is also one of the nation's safest highways. Its 1,200-foot acceleration and deceleration lanes, median dividers capable of stopping an 18-wheeler doing 55 miles per hour (and still effective even at today's speed limits), and full shoulder lanes on all bridges help contribute to its safety record. (Such features also contribute to its cost—the 8-mile Newark Bay–Hudson County extension, opened in 1956, was one of the most expensive stretches of toll road in the United States.) Other safety features include computerized traffic control: electronic detectors that monitor traffic have been placed under the roadbed; these relay information to the administration building in New Brunswick. (The hope that these sensors could provoke automatic adjustments to the message signs and thereby change posted speed limits or divert traffic from one part of the road to another proved premature; the information they pick up is digested by the human beings in the control room at the headquarters in New Brunswick.) A highway advisory telephone and a highway advisory radio are also in use, and the turnpike's reputation as a well-run road attracts highway administrators from all over the world.

All 148 miles are limited-access highway, ranging in width from 4 to 14 lanes (the Turnpike Authority refers to the 12- and 14-lane portions as the dual-dual). They consist of a 122-mile mainline; the Hudson County and Pennsylvania Turnpike extensions, which together total 14 miles; and a westerly alignment that adds 12 miles. (The eastern and western alignments rejoin as express and local lanes.) Tolls provide over 90 percent of the turnpike's revenue (it uses no municipal, state, or federal tax funds), and the cards provide a good deal of information, though with the popularity of E-ZPass, they are no longer ubiquitous. Received opinion has it that the turnpike is simply an efficient means of connecting Philadelphia and New York City, but some studies have suggested that over half the trips begin and end within the state. Nevertheless, for many people the turnpike has created a negative impression of the state as a whole. Presumably this is because those entering from the north at the Lincoln Tunnel immediately pass into an industrial area, which most people find unattractive and which at times does smell (usually of mercaptan, a harmless by-product of various chemical processes). For many years, though, pig farms were numerous at the northern end, and they smelled all the time. And many people remember when the landfills smoldered, producing, with the pig farms, a pungent combination. There are no more pig farms and the landfills no longer smolder (some have been converted to parks, others will soon host golf courses), but the unfortunate reputation lingers. The southern end has its industrial stretches too, but land is cheaper at that end, and more of it has been used for plantings that screen the factories.

The Turnpike Authority hopes that its plan for widening the highway, which has not been without controversy, will make the road able to handle traffic easily to the year 2050. The mileage of the dual-duals has increased; some sections now have 14 lanes, in some cases with an HOV (high-occupancy vehicle) lane during rush hour; and some of the toll plazas have been realigned or expanded. In addition, a flyover bridge has been built to improve conditions at the "southern mixing bowl" (between interchanges 14 and 15E), once highly congested and the most dangerous section of the road. The most recent project is to convert the stretch south of interchange 8A into a dual-dual.

The authority has also engaged in projects intended to improve the appearance of the turnpike (although it is also increasing the number of billboards). Planting trees along the roadway is not an easy task: roadside conditions are not ideal for a young tree, maintenance workers mowing the grass sometimes decapitate the young trees, and in some areas construction plans forestall planting. The authority claims a high success rate for its plantings, and the amount of screening has increased dramatically. Some of the screening today, though, is done by sound barriers, which unfortunately are neither as attractive as trees nor as diverting as observing what's off the roadway. To prevent the theft of evergreen trees during the holiday season, the Turnpike Authority coats likely victims with a compound that releases a disagreeable odor when it hits room temperature, an odor that lasts well beyond the Christmas season.

This tour is meant for those who are going to be using the turnpike anyway and assumes that if you know what you are looking at as you speed by, you will find it more interesting. The tour may not convince the doubters that the turnpike is attractive, but it may make the time pass more quickly. The Turnpike Authority's mileage markers (the numbers on the small green stakes along the edges of the roadway) are used to help you identify sites. The numbers start in the south and increase as you go north, so if you are traveling south, you will have to begin at the end of the tour. Each entry begins with a mileage number. The letter following that number tells you which side of the road is being talked about: **N** means the right side when you are traveling north (toward New York City), **S** the right side when you are traveling south (toward Philadelphia and Delaware). Mainline mileage is given without a prefix; the western alignment is prefixed by a **W**, the Hudson extension by an **H**. Thus, W 115 S tells you to look to the right when you are traveling south on the western alignment (away from the George Washington Bridge), to the left when you are traveling north on that stretch.

Unfortunately, the mileage indicators cannot tell you exactly when to look. The particular mileage marker at which you see something depends on how fast you are traveling, which part of the dual-dual you are in (the all-car or the car-truck-and-bus section), how much traffic there is, which lane you are using, and what kind of vehicle you are traveling in. If traffic is heavy, you may be able to see very little to your left, particularly if you are in the right half of the dual-dual. This tour, unlike other entries in this guide, recognizes that you cannot stop the car and turn around to get a second look, or park and get out for a closer one. Most of the items described in the tour, however, are large enough that you will not miss them if you don't look at precisely the right moment unless you are traveling way over the speed limit.

A further problem is that the sound barriers, while serving an obviously desirable function, often make it hard to see what is being pointed out. By the spring of 2004 the Turnpike Authority had installed 24 miles of barriers, so by the time you take this tour, there is likely to be even more mentioned here that can no longer be easily seen.

The entries come thicker and faster for the northern, more industrial parts of the tour; the southern stretch is more like other high-speed roads— in fact, people even complain to the Turnpike Authority that the southern stretch is boring. Although southern New Jersey is developing rapidly, large areas are still rural, and, as mentioned before, it is often harder to see what borders the highway in the south because of the screening (this is true for farms and stables, not just the industrial parts). Because many of the trees are deciduous, the southern stretch is particularly attractive in the fall (and you can see more in the winter).

The tour starts near Deepwater in Salem County. In the first 20 miles you will find many farms that raise Holsteins, vegetables, and grain, yet much of the state's chemical industry is along the Delaware River just north of the Delaware Memorial Bridge.

I N, S—Interchange 1 to the Delaware Memorial Bridge. The toll booths here date from 2004 (they were built a little north of the original 1952 booths and finished before the original booths were removed; it proved necessary to post signs on the old booths telling people not to stop there). The curved building enables the supervisor to look in both directions, and the tower's resemblance to a lighthouse is intentional; the architect wanted a welcoming symbol at the first interchange. The new facility also enables toll takers to reach their booths by crossing over the highway, rather than on it or under it. The highway here crosses Game Creek. The concrete guardrails often prevent you from seeing the many rivers crossed by the turnpike. You may notice Game Creek again at 3 S.

2–4 N, S—There are farms and stables on both sides of the highway here, though most of them are obscured by trees. At 3 N, S the road crosses Penny Run.

5 N, S—John Fenwick (N) and Clara Barton (S) service areas. All the turnpike's service areas are named for individuals with ties to the state, generally with ties that are geographically close to the service area. Barton and Fenwick are both associated with southern New Jersey (for Fenwick, *see* Salem; for Barton, Bordentown).

7 N, S—The road crosses Oldman's Creek, which divides Salem and Gloucester counties. There are farms visible for the next two miles.

11 N, S—The road crosses Narraticon Run. Lake Narraticon (S) and the old community of Swedesboro (S) are nearby; you can see a church steeple in Swedesboro.

12 N, S—Interchange 2. One of the turnpike's smallest interchanges (4 toll booths), 2 is the one you should take to visit Swedesboro or to get to US 322, which goes west to the Commodore Barry Bridge over the Delaware and east to Glassboro. The road crosses Raccoon Creek, which flows along the northern edge of Swedesboro, itself first known as Raccoon.

13–18 N, S—You can see the radio tower at one of the turnpike's maintenance yards (N). Each year litter crews pick up over 5,600 bags from the roadway alone (if you add in litter from the service areas, the number of bags increases dramatically, but at least the total is decreasing). The road crosses Still Run, Edwards Run, and Mantua creeks. Mantua Creek is particularly lovely. At 18 N you can see the Martin Luther King Memorial Gardens. Note the rumble strips in the shoulder; they were introduced in 1993 to cut down accidents caused by vehicles running off the road. By 2002, with the rumble strips in place, this kind of accident had decreased 55 percent.

19–21 N, S—The turnpike passes through Woodbury Heights, crossing Woodbury Creek.

23–25 N, S—The turnpike crosses first a tributary of and then Big Timber Creek itself, the boundary between Gloucester and Camden counties. Walt Whitman used to spend his summers near here (*see* Laurel Springs). In Camden County the road also crosses Beaver Branch and goes through Runnemede and Bellmawr. Massive amounts of housing are visible at 23 S.

26 N, S—Interchange 3. This is where you get off for Woodbury, South Camden, and NJ 168. The road continues through Barrington and Lawnside.

27 N—The next few miles are an industrial area. A large Pegasus sign is visible.

29 N, S—The highway crosses the rusty tracks of the Lindenwold high-speed line.

29 N—The Hussman Corporation's water tower is clearly visible. This company, which began manufacturing supermarket equipment at this spot in the late 1950s, was the first major industry in the area.

29 S—In this mile are a truck-rental maintenance depot and the Melitta Filter company, which makes coffee makers and filters.

30 S—The Walt Whitman Service Area. Whitman lived his last years in Camden. The mushroom-shaped Cherry Hill water tower is 133 feet tall and holds 2 million gallons of water.

33 N, S—The road crosses Pennsauken Creek, which divides Camden and Burlington counties, and goes through an area of small industrial establishments and housing developments.

34 N, S—Interchange 4. This exit takes you to Camden and to NJ 73 (to the Tacony-Palmyra Bridge, a drawbridge notorious for its effect on rush-hour traffic). On both sides of the turnpike there are hotels serving the Camden area.

35 N—The tanks of the Colonial Pipeline Company are visible.

35 S—The large industrial buildings here include a Martin Marietta facility (*see* 38 S).

38 S—What appears to be a landlocked ship belongs to Martin Marietta's Missile and Surface Radar division; since 1977 the "cruiser in the cornfield" has been the center for land-based testing and training for the U.S. Navy's Aegis combat weapons system, designed to protect ships from missile threats. Seen from a little closer, the cruiser looks less like a warship and more like what it is: a 122-foot superstructure, bristling with radar antennas, perched on the roof of a three-story building. The radio tower is also visible. In the fall a "Beat Army" banner often hangs from the superstructure. I 295 can be seen running parallel to the turnpike.

39 N, S—The turnpike crosses Parkers Creek; those heading north will find the James Fenimore Cooper Service Area. Cooper was born in Burlington.

41 N, S—The turnpike crosses Rancocas Creek. A boardwalk goes into a nature area (N), but if you want to walk here, approach it from off the turnpike. For Rancocas State Park, *see* Mount Holly. A large warehousing facility is here (N).

43 N, S—The road crosses Mill Creek. This is an area of large dairy farms.

44 N, S—Interchange 5: use this exit for Burlington and Mount Holly.

47–49 N, S—Farms, stables, fields, and woods continue. The road crosses Assiscunk Creek.

51 N, S—Interchange 6 takes you to the Pennsylvania Turnpike spur, interchange 6A to Florence. Trees screen the highway for most of the spur's 6 miles; in some cases the woods are reclaimed pastures.

54 N, S—Interchange 7, for Bordentown, Trenton, and US 206. For a while a beaver who took up residence at the wetlands mitigation pond here was threatening the authority's trees. The highway crosses the Old York Road and Blacks Creek.

56 N, S—The highway crosses Crosswicks Creek, which divides Burlington from Mercer County and flows into the Delaware at Bordentown.

56 S—The road skirts the New Jersey State Prison Farm. A turnpike maintenance "igloo" is visible.

58 N, S—Here are the Woodrow Wilson (N) and Richard Stockton (S) service areas. Both these men are associated with Princeton. Farms are still visible on both sides of the highway. The turnpike's first variable (as opposed to changeable) traffic sign is here; these signs (there are 10 of them now) permit the authority to post messages by radio rather than satellite.

60 N, S—Interchange 7A: here you can get to I 195, taking you north to Trenton and Hamilton Township and south to the shore.

61–63 N, S—There are farms on both sides of the road. The highway crosses Assunpink Creek and goes through a portion of the Assunpink Wildlife Management Area (*see* Roosevelt). At 62 S, a billboard, partially obscured, welcomes you to Mercer County.

66 N, S—Cedar Brook is crossed.

66 S—A sign lets you know that the Peddie School golf course lies beyond the woods (*see* Hightstown).

67 N, S—Interchange 8, taking you to Hightstown, Freehold, and NJ 33. Between here and interchange 8A are many chemical companies. The highway crosses Rocky Brook.

67 S—At the Turnpike Authority's large maintenance depot here, you can sometimes see the green roadway signs being worked on. The road passes Local 827 of the AFL-CIO International Brotherhood of Electrical Workers building.

68 N, S—The highway crosses the Millstone River, which divides Mercer from Middlesex County.

69 N, S—The highway crosses a tributary of the Millstone River and Conrail tracks. Over the next 10 miles, much of the land adjoining the turnpike is owned by housing developments.

70 N, S—Cranbury Brook is on both sides of the highway.

70 S—The Jamesway Distribution Center abuts the highway here.

71 N—Carter Wallace, a large manufacturer of pharmaceuticals, diagnostic kits, and over-the-counter products, has a facility here.

71 S—The Molly Pitcher Service Area. Molly Pitcher is associated with the Battle of Monmouth (*see* Freehold). This is the busiest service area on the turnpike, serving close to 200,000 travelers each month. A sprinkling of historical material relating to Molly Pitcher is on exhibit in the lobby of the food-services building.

72 N—Rhone-Poulenc warehouses dominate here.

73 N, S—Interchange 8A takes you to Jamesburg and Cranbury. The increase in warehousing facilities has led to a large increase in truck traffic in this area, and the Turnpike Authority hopes to add more lanes.

73 N—The turnpike's neighbors here are Forsgate Country Club and Rossmoor (*see* Jamesburg). A Shop-Rite warehouse, said to be equipped with over a mile of computer-controlled conveyor belts, is visible across the field.

73 S—The Monroe Township municipal water facility is here; the tower is clearly visible. This is a growing industrial area.

74 N, S—The highway crosses the former Jamesburg branch of the Pennsylvania Railroad.

75 N—A Canon warehouse is visible in this mile.

75 S—A large BASF facility that once manufactured Styrofoam products sits largely empty, most of it for rent. There are several empty warehouses in this general area.

76 S—The heavy equipment belongs to Local 825 of the International Union of Operating Engineers (AFL-CIO), which runs a training school here. Each year more than 1,000 carefully screened union members (including many who have already spent years in the construction industry) come to this school to learn to operate more than a dozen kinds of equipment: bulldozers, front-end loaders, pans, graders, combination backhoes, cranes. The center works with the Occupational Safety and Health Administration (OSHA) and the state's Department of Environmental Protection, offering, for example, a course in hazardous-waste removal. The center serves all of New Jersey and part of New York State. The pond belongs to the Dallenbach Sand Company and gets deeper and lighter in color as more sand is removed.

77 N, S—The turnpike crosses Ireland Brook. Middlesex County plans to add hiking trails to the undeveloped park along the brook. Both warehouses and woods are visible here.

78 N—The Joyce Kilmer Service Area. Kilmer was born in New Brunswick. This is the second busiest service area, serving over 130,000 customers a month.

78 S—Much of the land in this mile belongs to the Tamarack Golf Club.

8O N, S—Crossing the road here is a turnpike service road. The Milltown Water Tower is visible to the east, as are some box stores.

8I N, S—The turnpike crosses the Saw Mill Brook and the (freight only) Raritan River railroad.

83 N, S—Interchange 9 for New Brunswick, NJ 18, and the shore. The highway crosses Lawrence Brook.

83 S—Tower Center, visible for many miles along the turnpike, consists of two 16-story towers with offices (said to be the tallest in central New Jersey), a 360-room hotel, and parking for 4,200 cars. The turnpike's administration building can be seen above the road.

84 N, S—In this mile the highway crosses the Raritan River and the old Lehigh Valley railroad tracks.

84 N—The ferryboat in the Raritan River is the *Mary Murray*, christened in 1938, and active on the Staten Island run until 1975. Its current owner had apparently hoped to convert it to a restaurant. Slowly deteriorating, the boat evidently frequently inspires passers-by to call and either let the Turnpike Authority know it is there or ask why it is. (A story about it in the *Star-Ledger* apparently reduced the volume of calls.) Public Service Electric and Gas Company has a generating station here.

84 S—Raritan Center is one of the largest industrial parks in the East. As many as 10,000 people have worked on its 2,350 acres, once part of the Raritan Arsenal, an army supply depot. Middlesex County College and Thomas A. Edison Park (*see* Edison) are also on the site. At this point the river is deep enough to accommodate medium-sized oceangoing ships.

85 N—This is an area of warehouses, industrial parks, and garden apartments, although in summer trees screen much of the view from the road. The United States Army Reserve's 78th Division armory is visible.

86–87 N, S—The road crosses Bridge-Mill Brook and the old Bonhampton branch of the Pennsylvania Railroad and passes through an area of warehouses and garden apartments.

87 N—Here you can see the *New York Times*'s state-of-the-art color printing plant and distribution facility, opened in 1992. In a space big enough to hold 22 football fields (1.3 million sq. ft.), stands an army of high-speed presses (70,000 impressions an hour) that can turn out well over 1 million copies of the Sunday paper, several hundred thousand of the daily.

88 N, S—Interchange 10, taking you to I 287, Metuchen, and Perth Amboy. The highway goes under I 287 and crosses Conrail's Perth Amboy branch.

89 S—There are Tudor-style condominiums and a municipal playground on this side.

89 N—A water tower is visible here.

90 N, S—The road going over the turnpike is the Garden State Parkway, and interchange 11 will take you to it, as well as to Woodbridge and the Amboys. This is the busiest interchange on the turnpike (processing in 2003 over 22.2 million exiting vehicles and 21.5 million entering vehicles), and, with 26 toll booths, the second-largest single interchange. Between this exit and interchange 12 you will notice many oil-storage terminals.

90 S—The New Jersey National Guard and a racquet club are visible here.

91 N—The clay pits here once provided the material used to produce millions of bricks; Middlesex County has reclaimed much of this land as part of William Warren Park (*see* Woodbridge). The Turnpike Authority stores salt at the maintenance facility. In 1994, a particularly snowy winter, it used over 61,000 tons of rock salt (18,000 tons is more usual, but in 1995 only 7,400 were needed). The igloos you see from time to time along the turnpike are used for storing salt. The building with the cupola is Saint Joseph's Convent, in Woodbridge, the American headquarters for an order of nuns founded in Poland (most of the sisters are Polish). The house was built in 1856 by a brick magnate as a wedding present for his daughter; it was later used as an orphanage. The house has beautiful woodwork and other fine details, but earlier plans to open it for tours have apparently not materialized. Because of the sound barriers, it is harder to see Saint Joseph's after you've passed the crest of the hill.

91 S—The Hess Oil office building, over 10 stories high, was the first high-rise building in Woodbridge. Its luxurious interior has solid teak walls and Italian and Vermont marble floors.

92 N—The Grover Cleveland Service Area is named for the only president of the United States to serve two nonconsecutive terms (*see* Caldwell). The road crosses the Woodbridge River.

92 S—The Thomas Edison Service Area (*see* Edison; West Orange).

93 N—You can see the Hess storage tanks and refinery. The red and white stacks in the distance belong to the Chevron refinery on the Arthur Kill. There's a good view of the New York City skyline.

94 N—The Hess Wetlands, so named because of the Hess sign nearby, are part of a wetlands mitigation project. (When the turnpike was widened between interchanges 11 and 15, some wetlands were filled in.) The sticks are there to protect the planted wetlands vegetation from predators until it is established. You can often see waterfowl, including some threatened species, on the two ponds.

94 S—The Colonial Pipeline Company stores heating oil and liquid petroleum products here.

95 N, S—Interchange 12 to Carteret and Rahway.

95 N—There are garden apartments here and small companies.

95 S—Several businesses are here, including Wiz warehouses. The Public Service high-tension lattice tower is visible.

96 N, S—The highway crosses the Rahway River, which divides Middlesex from Union County.

96 N—Conrail tracks are to the side of the road.

96 S—The white Colonial Pipeline Company's tanks are visible here. Joseph Medwick Memorial Park, a Middlesex County park honoring a member of the Baseball Hall of Fame who grew up in Carteret, is along the river.

97 N—The Allied Chemical plant here dates from World War I. The company's first plant, it was one of the state's first chemical factories. Now part of GAF, it makes a wide range of products, at one time including fluorocarbons. From here you can see the Northville storage tanks, Mobil tanks, and Staten Island. During the gasoline shortages in the 1970s, most of the oil companies along the turnpike painted out their identification signs.

98 N—Public Service Electric and Gas Company's Linden generating station, with its three steam turbines and six gas turbines, has half the capacity of the generators at Hoover Dam. In 1974 a natural-gas plant was added to the site; it is turned on during periods of peak demand in the winter.

98 S—Cogen Technologies and the Linden cogenerating plant across the turnpike occupy the site once occupied by the Exxon Bayway refinery, formerly the world's largest catalytic cracking plant and the country's third-largest refinery.

99 N, S—Interchange 13, taking you to I 278, Elizabeth, and the Elizabeth seaport.

99 N—The Goethals Bridge over the Arthur Kill to Staten Island provides a direct connection between the turnpike and the Staten Island Expressway. Opened in 1928, this cantilevered structure has a center span of more than 650 feet. Its four lanes carry over 14 million eastbound cars a year. The road crosses the Elizabeth River. You can sometimes see ships on the Arthur Kill.

100 N, S—The highway passes through the eastern part of Elizabeth, the state's fourth-largest city (see Elizabeth).

100 N—More good views of the New York City skyline come in this mile. The Conrail tracks once belonged to the Central Railroad Company, and you can still see the Elizabeth Gas Company's production plant. Several interesting buildings are visible. The black triangular steeple belongs to Greystone Presbyterian church, built in 1893 from stones blasted from the

bottom of New York's East River. The gold Byzantine dome belongs to Sts. Peter and Paul's Greek Catholic Church, built in 1919. The church with the green copper roof and the clock tower is St. Adalbert's Roman Catholic Church, built in 1905. Its congregation, once largely Polish, is now becoming Hispanic. The twin Gothic spires belong to St. Patrick's. Built in 1887, apparently by Irish Catholics weary of walking to Newark, St. Patrick's is modeled on various French cathedrals and is so big it's hard to heat. The sound barriers can be a problem here.

100 S—For part of this mile the houses are extremely close to the turnpike. From the street it is clear that the highway has sliced right through a neighborhood, and the elevated roadway casts a shadow over the remaining houses.

101 N, S—Interchange 13A takes you to Newark Liberty International Airport, Elizabeth, and Elizabeth seaport. In 2004 the city of Elizabeth began an advertising campaign promoting the interchange; the exit has its own website.

101 N—Until 1994, this was the site of the William F. Halsey Service Area. Admiral Halsey, commander of Allied naval forces in the Pacific during World War II, was born in Elizabeth. (The inn at the site of his birthplace is also gone.) Note the igloos in the turnpike maintenance yard.

101 S—A Vintage warehouse is visible here.

102 N—Ikea's busiest American store is here, as are many box stores. A large enclosed outlet mall is to the north.

102–103 S—This is Newark Liberty International Airport, the metropolitan area's only airport until just before World War II, when LaGuardia Airport opened. Legend has it that Fiorello La Guardia, at the time mayor of New York City, refused to get off a plane when it arrived at Newark Airport, saying he had bought a ticket to New York and this was not New York, and thus was born LaGuardia Airport. As it happens, the future LaGuardia Airport was by then already under construction and reporters had been tipped off in advance. This very busy airport belongs to the city of Newark and is run by the Port Authority of New York and New Jersey. (For more information on Newark Airport, see Newark.) The dividing line between Union and Essex counties runs through the airport and into the Elizabeth Channel.

103 N, S—Here you can see four modes of transportation cheek by jowl. Starting from the east, you have ports Elizabeth and Newark, Conrail yards, the turnpike, and Newark Airport. The two ports make up one of the world's largest facilities for container shipping, Port Elizabeth having been built in 1958 specifically as a container port. (Port Newark dates to 1915.) Together the ports occupy over 2,100 acres and have roughly 5 million square

feet of warehousing and distribution space. With their combined 36,000 linear feet of berth space, they handle not just containers but break-bulk cargo. The buildings include a facility for storing and blending orange juice concentrate and a high-tech plant that produces copper rod. Bananas and cars are two of the major imports. Keeping the channels deep enough to accommodate modern cargo ships requires considerable dredging, and disposing of the silt has environmental and political ramifications.

IO3 N—Shipping lines and associated industries dominate this mile; the most obvious landmarks are the Sea-Land warehouse, Cargill, and the giant Maersk cranes.

IO4 N, S—Interchange 14, taking you to I 78, US 1 and 9, Newark Airport, and the Hudson County extension. (For the Hudson County extension, *see* H 1–8 at the end of the tour.) This interchange, with 27 toll booths, is the largest.

IO4 N—A deepwater inlet and the Port Authority's Port Newark administration building are here.

IO4 S—The DHL plane you almost always see here stays in this spot precisely so that people will notice it. At this point the highway begins to split, the eastern branch going to the Lincoln Tunnel and the western to the George Washington Bridge.

IO5 N, S—This is an area of container storage, auto wreckers, small plants, trucking companies, and warehouses.

IO5 N—The Passaic Valley Sewer Commission has a pumping station here.

IO5 S—An Englehard facility occupies much of this mile.

IO6 N, S—Interchange 15E to Newark, Jersey City, and US 1 and 9. Oak trees were planted at this interchange in the 1980s as part of the governor's beautification program. This mile contains more warehouses, chemical companies, container storage, car dumps, and a good view of the Newark skyline.

IO6 N—The Newark police have a car pound and pistol range here.

IO6 S—The multiplex theater here replaced one of the last of the state's drive-in theaters.

IO7 N, S—The Pulaski Skyway crosses the turnpike. Built in the 1920s and named for the Polish general who fought with the Continental army, it soars 145 feet over the Passaic and Hackensack rivers. A daring design for its day, it cut the travel time between New Jersey's two biggest cities, Newark and Jersey City, from 25 minutes to 5. It now carries US 1 and 9 over the Passaic River. The turnpike crosses the Passaic River.

I08 N, S—The road crosses the Hackensack River.

I08 N—The hill you see here is a former landfill, closed in accordance with the latest environmental principles. A plan to create a work of art on the site had to be put on hold until the dump finishes settling, although some of the plantings are already in place. In the meantime, methane is being pumped from the fill, processed, and sold to Public Service. At night you can see the illuminated Cathedral of the Sacred Heart (*see* Newark).

I08 S—At this point you can cross over to Exit 15W.

I09 N—This is Public Service Electric and Gas Company's Essex generating station. AM radio towers are visible here (*see* W 111–114), as are the western extension of the turnpike and the Hackensack Meadowland Development Commission's Environment Center (*see* Lyndhurst).

I09 S—The remains of a fallen AM tower could once be seen in the marsh.

II0 S—The dark rock, sometimes decorated with graffiti, is Snake Hill, a volcanic mass that the County of Hudson used to lease to mining interests. (For a while there were rumors that the hill would be completely mined away; that didn't happen—the turnpike, it seems, is structurally dependent on Snake Hill.) A lookout point for Continental soldiers during the Revolution, it has also been the site of a poorhouse, insane asylum, sanitorium, and communicable diseases hospital. In the late 19th century, it served as the inspiration for the Prudential Insurance Company's Rock of Gibraltar advertising slogan: an advertising executive on his way home from a meeting with the Prudential company struck on the idea as his train passed the hill. Cedar trees once grew in the Hackensack Meadowlands, but salt water entered the area, killing them off. Hudson County now has a park in this area, with a boat launch and nature trails (*see* Secaucus).

III N—The Frank R. Lautenberg Secaucus Rail Station, a transfer station, is here (*see* Secaucus).

III S—The Alexander Hamilton Service Area. Hamilton met his future wife in New Jersey (*see* Morristown), he was responsible for founding the city of Paterson (*see* Paterson), and he met his death in New Jersey (*see* Weehawken).

II2 N, S—Here are interchanges 16E to the Lincoln Tunnel, Secaucus, and NJ 3, and 18E to the George Washington Bridge, I 80, I 95, and US 46.

II2 S—Interchange 17 is a limited-access interchange. If you are coming from the north you can exit here and head for the Lincoln Tunnel. You can also enter at 17, but only if you want to head north. In this mile are a state motor vehicle inspection station, a Public Service transformer, Meadowview Hospital, a UPS facility, and an industrial park.

I I 3 N—A large Meadowlands Development project is here (*see* East Rutherford).

I I 4–I I 5 N—This is an area of warehouses.

I I 5 S—Note the Phragmites, a tall, aggressive reed grass that is relatively tolerant of pollution. Phragmites have taken over large portions of New Jersey's wetlands, but, unfortunately, they are not as nourishing for birds and animals as some of the vegetation they have driven out. Four AM radio towers, arranged in a rectangle, can be seen, as can the bridge from the turnpike's western alignment, which looks particularly graceful.

I I 6 N, S—The Vince Lombardi Service Area. Early in his career Lombardi coached at an Englewood high school. There used to be a display of Lombardi memorabilia at the food-service building, but his widow removed the collection after a drug bust at the service area. This is the turnpike's third busiest service area (96,000 customers a month). Wildlife preserves border this service area (created by the turnpike to compensate for areas destroyed in construction).

I I 7 N, S—The western alignment joins the main branch, and the turnpike ends shortly thereafter.

I I 7 S—This is Public Service's Bergen generating plant. The western alignment was built in 1966. It took almost a year to dredge and fill the Hackensack Meadowlands so that the road could be built. Attitudes toward building on wetlands were different then, and the Turnpike Authority was praised for its leadership in the development of engineering methods for building on swamps.

W I 07 N, S—The turnpike goes under the Pulaski Skyway (*see* 107 N, S) and crosses the Passaic River.

W I 07 N—Note the vertical-draw railroad bridge. In the next few miles there are several drawbridges.

W I 07 S—Here you can cross over to exit 15E.

W I 08 N, S—Interchange 15W to Newark, the Oranges, and I 280. There are plantings of native trees and shrubs in this area.

W I 09 N, S—The highway crosses the main Amtrak line.

W I 09 S—In this mile there's a good view of the Newark skyline and a landfill mesa.

W I 10 S—The environmental and visitor center of the Richard W. DeKorte Park (*see* Lyndhurst), named after a state assemblyman, is visible here. The sanitary landfill that was also once visible here is now part of the park. The center, which concentrates on environmental concerns, is well worth a visit.

W III–II4 N, S—In this stretch you will see a good many radio transmitters, often in groups of three or four. Salt marsh provides an efficient medium for AM radio waves, which is why so many of New York City's AM stations have their towers here.

W III N—Harmon Cove, Harmon Plaza, Meadowlands Hilton, and the Tiger Racquet Club are along this stretch. This is a Hartz Mountain development (the company used to be known for its pet products; it is now also a major real estate developer). Included in this 800-acre development, which began in the late 1960s, are townhouses, condominiums, research facilities, offices, warehouses, retail stores, a hospital, hotels, movie theaters, marinas, and industrial space.

W II2 N, S—Interchange 16W takes you to Secaucus, Rutherford, the New Jersey Sports Complex, and NJ 3.

W II2 S—This is the Meadowlands Sports Complex. What is now called the Continental Airlines Arena is the building closest to the highway, but the complex also includes a racetrack and a stadium (*see* East Rutherford).

W II3 N, S—Interchange 18W to the George Washington Bridge, I 80, I 95, and US 46. More money is taken in here than at any other interchange (over $52 million in 2003). The highway also crosses Cedar Creek.

W II4 N, S—The road crosses Moonachie Creek. Note the poplars.

W II5 N, S—Another entrance to the Vince Lombardi Service Area (*see* 116 N, S). The road crosses the Hackensack River.

W II7 S—Public Service's Bergen station is here. The turnpike's western alignment joins the mainline, and the turnpike formally ends in Ridgefield Park, although the 4½ miles to the George Washington Bridge are now owned by the Turnpike Authority. The authority in 1992 bought the 4½ miles from the state for more than it had cost to build the first stretch of the road 40 years earlier.

Even when the Hudson County extension is not actually going north or south, the suffix **N** means what is to the right as you are driving toward New York City, the suffix **S** what is to the right as you are driving toward Philadelphia.

H I–2 N, S—The turnpike crosses Newark Bay. Bayonne is visible to your right as you head toward New York City, Jersey City to your left.

H I N—There are usually an impressive number of new cars unloaded on the dock here, awaiting shipment elsewhere. Oil tanks are also visible.

H I S—At the Newark Industrial Center you can see the Toys-R-Us warehouse.

H 2 N—A city park is along the water.

H 2 S—The Society Hill development (on totally flat land) sits on the site of the old Roosevelt Stadium (*see* Jersey City).

H 3 N, S—Interchange 14A to Bayonne.

H 3 N—The tracks belong to Conrail's Greenville Yards. From here on there are often good views of the New York City skyline.

H 3 S—According to one story, in one of Jersey City's dirtier election campaigns, someone jammed the elevators in this public housing project to keep its residents from voting.

H 4 N—Caven Point is a recognized birding area and a popular fishing spot. There are good views of the Statue of Liberty.

H 4 S—Auto wreckers are prevalent in this section.

H 5 N, S—Interchange 14B takes you to Jersey City and Liberty State Park; interchange 14C, about a half-mile north of 14B, to the Holland Tunnel and eventually to a park-and-ride facility. As you come down to street level and the entrance to the tunnel, you can see Jersey City to your right (as you head toward New York City) and Hoboken to your left.

H 5 N—Liberty State Park (*see* Jersey City) and the Statue of Liberty are visible now. The Morris Canal basin is at the northern end of the park.

H 6–8, N, S—As the road goes through Jersey City, you may see some of the new riverside office towers and various municipal parks and other facilities. The building with the stepped side next to the three tall buildings at 7 S was part of the Jersey City Medical Center* before it built its new quarters. The very large yellow-and-white building with classical elements on the hill at 7 S is Dickinson High School.

Index

The index is divided into the following categories:

Art exhibition spaces

Aljira, A Center for
  Contemporary Art:
  Newark
Art Center of Northern
  New Jersey: Oradell
Artspace: Jersey City
Atlantic City Art Center:
  Atlantic City
Atlantic Community
  College: Mays Landing
Barron Arts Center:
  Woodbridge
Bayonne Public Library:
  Bayonne
Ben Shahn Galleries:
  Wayne
Berrie Center for
  Performing and Visual
  Arts: Mahwah
Boehm galleries: Trenton
Bristol-Myers Squibb:
  Lawrenceville
Camden County College:
  Blackwood
Cape May County Art
  League: Cape May
College Center and
  Presidential Galleries:
  Edison Township
Conant Hall: Lawrenceville
Courtney Gallery: Jersey
  City
Cybis galleries: Trenton
Dana Library: Newark
Educational Testing
  Service: Lawrenceville
Extension Gallery:
  Hamilton Township
Ferry Gallery:
  Hackettstown
Firestone Library: Princeton
Fort Lee Library: Fort Lee

Gallery One: Montclair
Gardner A. Sage Library:
  New Brunswick
Grounds for Sculpture:
  Hamilton Township
Guild of Creative Art:
  Shrewsbury
Henry T. Chauncy
  Conference Center:
  Lawrenceville
Holman Hall Art Gallery:
  Ewing Township
Hunterdon Arts Center:
  Clinton
James Howe Gallery: Union
Jane Voorhees Zimmerli
  Art Museum: New
  Brunswick
Johnson Atelier: Hamilton
  Township
Judicial Center: Newton
Kean University: Union
Korn Gallery: Madison
Les Malamut Gallery:
  Union
Lewis Parker College
  Center: Pemberton
LRC Gallery: Paterson
Main Gallery: Montclair
Mariboe Art Gallery:
  Hightstown
Mason Gross School of the
  Arts: New Brunswick
Masters Octave: Keyport
Mercer County
  Community College:
  West Windsor Township
Michael Gilligan Student
  Union Building Gallery:
  Jersey City
Monmouth University:
  West Long Branch

Montclair State University:
  Montclair
Montgomery Cultural
  Center: Rocky Hill
Myhelan Cultural Arts
  Alliance: Long Valley
Newark Public Library:
  Newark
New Jersey Center for
  Visual Arts: Summit
Ocean City Arts Center:
  Ocean City
Ocean County College:
  Toms River
Paper Mill Playhouse:
  Millburn
Paul Robeson Center
  Gallery: Newark
Performing Arts Center of
  Middle Township: Cape
  May Court House
Piscataway municipal
  building: Piscataway
Polish Cultural Foundation:
  Clark
Potter Library: Mahwah
Prallsville industrial district:
  Stockton
Princeton University art
  museum: Princeton
Quietude Sculpture
  Garden: East Brunswick
Ralph T. Reeve Cultural
  Center: Somerville
Rider University Student
  Center: Lawrenceville
Sage Library: New
  Brunswick
Selden Rodman Gallery of
  Popular Arts: Mahwah
S.M.A. Fathers African Art
  Museum: Tenafly

Historic-house and school museums

United States Golf Association museum: Far Hills
University of Medicine and Dentistry: Newark
Van Allen House: Oakland
Van Bunschooten Museum: Sussex
Van Campen Inn: Walpack Township
Van Riper–Hopper House: Wayne
Van Voorhees–Quackenbush–Zabriskie House: Wyckoff
Vincentown Schoolhouse museum: Medford
Vincentown–Tabernacle Telephone Museum: Medford
Vincentown two-cell lockup: Medford
Vineland Historical and Antiquarian Society museum: Vineland
Volendam Windmill Museum: Milford
Wallace House: Somerville
Warren County Historical and Genealogical Society Museum: Belvidere
Washington Township Historical Society museum: Long Valley
Waterloo Village: Stanhope
Wayne Museum: Wayne
Westfield Historical Society museum: Westfield
Wetlands Institute and Museum: Stone Harbor
Wheaton Village: Millville
Whippany Railway Museum: Whippany
Whitall House: National Park
Whitebriar Farmhouse: Burlington
Whitesboro Historical Foundation Museum: The Wildwoods
White Township Museum: Belvidere
Whitman House and Library: Camden
Whitman-Stafford Farmhouse: Laurel Springs
Wicoff House: West Windsor Township

William Trent's House: Trenton
Woodruff House: Hillside
Woolman Memorial: Mount Holly
Wortendyke Dutch Barn: Park Ridge
Zimmerli Art Museum: New Brunswick

Natural and wildlife-management areas
Absecon Wildlife Management Area: Absecon
Absegami Trail Natural Area: Tuckerton
Assunpink Wildlife Management Area: Roosevelt
Baldwin Lake Wildlife Management Area: Pennington
Batsto Natural Area: Hammonton
Bearfort Mountain Natural Area: Highland Lakes
Bear Swamp Wildlife Management Area: Branchville
Beaver Swamp Wildlife Management Area: Cape May Court House
Bennett Bogs Preserve: Cape May
Bevan Wildlife Management Area: Millville
Black River Wildlife Management Area: Chester
Butterfly Bogs Wildlife Management Area: Cassville
Buttermilk Falls: Mendham
Cape May National Wildlife Refuge: Cape May Court House
Cape May Wetlands Wildlife Management Area: Ocean City
Capoolong Creek Wildlife Management Area: Clinton
Cedar Ridge Trail: Hopewell
Cedar Swamp Natural Area: Pemberton
Cheesequake Natural Area: Matawan
Clarks Pond Wildlife Management Area: Bridgeton

Clinton Wildlife Management Area: Clinton
Cold Brook Preserve: Oldwick
Colliers Mills Wildlife Management Area: Cassville
Cook Natural Area: Kingston
Dennis Creek Wildlife Management Area: Woodbine
Dismal-Harmony Natural Area: Mendham
Dismal Swamp: Metuchen
Dix Wildlife Management Area: Bridgeton
Dryden Kuser Natural Area: Sussex
Edward G. Bevan Wildlife Management Area: Millville
Edwin B. Forsythe National Wildlife Refuge: Oceanville
Fairview Farms: Far Hills
Fairview Lake YMCA camp: Newton
Fisherman's Cove Conservation Area: Manasquan
Flatbrook-Roy Wildlife Management Area: Bevans
Glassboro Wildlife Management Area: Glassboro
Great Bay Boulevard Wildlife Management Area: Tuckerton
Great Swamp National Wildlife Refuge: Basking Ridge
Greenbrook Sanctuary: Tenafly
Greenwood Forest and Pasadena Wildlife Management Area: Forked River
Hainesville Wildlife Management Area: Branchville, Montague
Hamburg Mountain Wildlife Management Area: Vernon Township
Higbee Beach Wildlife Management Area: Cape May Point
Jockey Hollow Environmental Studies Center: Mendham
John Dryden Kuser Natural Area: Sussex

Poricy Park Nature Center: Middletown
Raccoon Ridge: Blairstown
Rancocas Nature Center: Mount Holly
Raptor Trust: Basking Ridge
Ridge and Valley Conservancy: Blairstown
St. Hubert's: Madison
Scherman-Hoffman Sanctuaries: Bernardsville
Stone Harbor Bird Sanctuary: Stone Harbor
Stony Brook–Millstone Watershed Association: Pennington
Tenafly Nature Center: Tenafly
Trailside Nature and Science Center: Mountainside
Washington Crossing State Park nature center: Titusville
Weis Ecology Center: Ringwood
Wells Mills Nature Center: Barnegat
Wetlands Institute: Stone Harbor
Wharton Forest Nature Center: Hammonton
Woodford Cedar Run Wildlife Refuge: Medford

Parks, gardens, and forests
Abram S. Hewitt State Forest: Highland Lakes
Allaire State Park: Farmingdale
Allamuchy Mountain Park: Hackettstown, Stanhope
Alonzo F. Bonzal wildlife preserve: Montclair
Ambrose & Doty's Brooks Park: Piscataway
A. Paul King County Park: Manahawkin
Ash Brook Reservation: Clark, Scotch Plains
Bamboo Brook Outdoor Education Center: Peapack-Gladstone
Barnegat Lighthouse State Park: Barnegat Light
Bass River State Forest: Tuckerton
Bayonne Park: Bayonne
Baysholm Conservation Area: Freehold

Belleplain State Forest: Woodbine
Birch Grove Park: Somers Point
Bonzal wildlife preserve: Montclair
Boyd Park: New Brunswick
Branch Brook Park: Newark
Brendan T. Byrne State Forest: Pemberton
Briant Park: Summit
Brookdale Park: Bloomfield, Montclair
Buccleuch Park: New Brunswick
Buck Hill Park: Mendham
Bull's Island: Kingston, Stockton
Cadwalader Park: Trenton
Campgaw Mountain County Reservation: Mahwah
Cape May County Park: Cape May Court House
Cape May Migratory Bird Refuge: Cape May Point
Cape May Point State Park: Cape May Point
Cattus Island Park: Toms River
Cedar Brook Park: Plainfield
Charles Rogers Wildlife Sanctuary: Princeton
Cheesequake State Park: Matawan
Christie Hoffman Farm Park: Oldwick
City of Bridgeton Park: Bridgeton
Colonial Park: Millstone
Community Park North: Princeton
Cora Hartshorn Arboretum and Bird Sanctuary: Millburn
Corson's Inlet State Park: Ocean City
Cross Estate Gardens: Bernardsville
Crosswicks Creek Park: Allentown
Darlington County Park: Mahwah, Ramsey
Davidson's Mill Pond Park: South Brunswick
Deep Cut Park: Middletown
Deer Path Park: Clinton
DeKorte State Park: Lyndhurst

Delaware and Raritan Canal State Park: Griggstown, Kingston, Lambertville, Princeton, Rocky Hill, Stockton
Delaware Water Gap National Recreation Area: Bevans, Blairstown, Walpack Township
Dr. Ulysses S. Wiggins Waterfront Park: Camden
Dorbrook Recreation Area: Colts Neck
Double Trouble State Park: Forked River
Duke Gardens: Somerville
Duke Island Park: Bridgewater
Durand Conservation Area: Freehold
Eagle Rock Reservation: West Orange
East Brunswick Community Park: East Brunswick
East Freehold Park: Freehold
Eastside Park: Paterson
Echo Lake Park: Mountainside
Edwin B. Forsythe National Wildlife Refuge, Brigantine Division: Oceanville
Estell Manor Park: Mays Landing
Etra Lake Park: Hightstown
Farney State Park: Rockaway
Flat Rock Brook Center: Englewood
Forsythe National Wildlife Refuge, Brigantine Division: Oceanville
Fort Billings Park: Paulsboro
Fort Lee Historic Park: Fort Lee
Fort Mott State Park: Pennsville
Frelinghuysen Arboretum: Morristown
Garden for the Blind and Physically Handicapped: Woodbridge
Garret Mountain Reservation: Paterson
Gaskill Park: Mays Landing
Gateway National Recreation Area: Highlands
Gilder Field: Bordentown

Wildwood Crest: The
Wildwoods
Willingboro: Burlington

Wineries
Alba Vineyard: Milford
Amalthea Cellars:
Blackwood
Amwell Valley Vineyard:
Ringoes
Balić Winery: Mays
Landing
Bellview Winery:
Vineland
Cape May Winery: Cape
May
Cream Ridge Winery:
Allentown
DiMatteo Winery:
Hammonton

4 JG's Orchards &
Vineyards: Colts Neck
Four Sisters Winery: Hope
Heritage Vineyard of
Richwood: Mullica Hill
Hopewell Valley Vineyards:
Hopewell
Renault Winery: Egg
Harbor City
Silver Decoy Winery:
Hightstown
Sylvin Farms: Oceanville
Tomasello Winery:
Hammonton
Turdo Vineyards: Cape May
Unionville Vineyards:
Ringoes
Valenzano Winery:
Medford
Westfall Winery: Montague

Zoos
Cape May County Park:
Cape May Court House
Cohanzick Zoo: Bridgeton
Johnson Park: Piscataway
Merrill Park: Woodbridge
Popcorn Park Zoo: Forked
River
Schaefer Farm: Flemington
Snowmobile Barn Museum:
Newton
Space Farms Zoo and
Museum: Beemerville
Thompson Park:
Jamesburg
Turtle Back Zoo: West
Orange
Van Saun Park Zoo:
Paramus, River Edge
Wild West City: Stanhope

To the Users of This Book

No matter how careful one tries to be, errors are bound to creep into a guidebook of this kind. If you do come across mistakes, I hope you will send them to me at 40 Pine Street, Princeton, NJ 08542 (or at bwestergaard@aol.com). I would also welcome suggestions for additions and other improvements for possible future editions. Thank you.

Barbara Westergaard